AMERICAN GOVERNMENT

and Politics Today

THE ESSENTIALS

2017–2018 Edition

Barbara A. Bardes
University of Cincinnati

Mack C. Shelley II
Iowa State University

Steffen W. Schmidt
Iowa State University

 CENGAGE

Australia • Brazil • Mexico • Singapore • United Kingdom • United States

American Government
and Politics Today,
The Essentials
2017—2018 Edition
Bardes, Shelley, Schmidt

SVP for Social Science and Qualitative
    Business: Erin Joyner
Product Director: Paul R. Banks
Product Manager: Bradley J. Potthoff
Content Developer: Alison Duncan
Content Development Manager:
    Jessica Badiner
Content Team Assistant: Cazzie Reyes
Product Assistant: Staci Eckenroth
Sr. Marketing Manager: Valerie Hartman
Production Director: Lauren MacLachlan
Sr. Content Project Manager: Ann Borman
Sr. Digital Content Specialist:
    Jacklyn Hermesmeyer
Manufacturing Planner: Fola Orekoya
Inventory Analyst: Jessica Sayers
Inventory Manager: Erika Downey
Sr. IP Director: Julie Geagan-Chavez
IP Analyst: Alexandra Ricciardi
IP Project Manager: Reba Frederics
Art Director: Sarah Cole
Interior design: Ke Design

**Design elements: Which Side Are You
On?** Oculo, iStock photo; **Elections 2016:**
albertc111, iStock illustration; **Beyond Our
Borders:** Sonya illustration, Shutterstock;
Consider the Source: mattjeacock, iStock
photo; **How You Can Make a Difference:**
albertc111, iStock illustration.

For product information and technology assistance, contact us at
Cengage Customer & Sales Support, 1-800-354-9706

For permission to use material from this text or product,
submit all requests online at **www.cengage.com/permissions**
Further permissions questions can be emailed to
permissionrequest@cengage.com

Library of Congress Control Number: 2016956306

Student Edition ISBN: 978-1-337-09121-3
Looseleaf Edition ISBN: 978-1-337-09123-7

Cengage
20 Channel Center Street
Boston, MA 02210
USA

Cengage is a leading provider of customized learning solutions
with employees residing in nearly 40 different countries and sales in more
than 125 countries around the world. Find your local representative at
www.cengage.com.

Cengage products are represented in Canada by
Nelson Education, Ltd.

To learn more about Cengage platforms and services, register or access
your online learning solution, or purchase materials for your course, visit
www.cengage.com.

Printed at CLDPC, USA, 09-18

BRIEF CONTENTS

DETAILED CONTENTS

Part 1
The American System

Chapter 1
THE DEMOCRATIC REPUBLIC   *1*

Chapter 2
THE CONSTITUTION   *29*

Chapter 3
FEDERALISM   *59*

Part 2
Civil Rights and Liberties

Chapter 4
CIVIL LIBERTIES *85*

Chapter 5
CIVIL RIGHTS *115*

Chapter 10
THE MEDIA   265

Part 4
Political Institutions

Chapter 11
THE CONGRESS   287

Chapter 12
THE PRESIDENT   319

Chapter 16
FOREIGN POLICY *435*

Appendices

A Letter to INSTRUCTORS

The fundamental theme of *American Government and Politics Today: The Essentials, 2017–2018 Edition* continues to be the importance of participating in active citizenship, emphasizing critical thinking about political issues, and encouraging students to take action and become involved in the political process. Whether the topic is immigration, trade deals, Supreme Court rulings, or taxation, we constantly strive to involve students in the analysis. Our goal is to make sure that politics is not just an abstract process, but a very human enterprise. We emphasize how different outcomes can affect students' civil rights and liberties, employment opportunities, and economic welfare. To make sure students understand the link between themselves and the subject matter they are reading, new ***Why Should You Care about...?*** features grab students' attention while they are reading the materials. We further encourage interaction with the political system by ending each chapter with a feature titled ***How You Can Make a Difference,*** which shows students how to become politically involved and why it is important that they do so. ***Which Side Are You On?*** features challenge students to find the connection between a current controversy and their personal positions. And to help students think critically about the world around them and spark discussion in your classroom, we pose questions for critical analysis with almost every boxed feature, table, chart, exhibit, and photo.

New to This Edition

We have made numerous changes to this volume for the 2017–2018 Edition. We have rewritten the text as necessary, added many new features, and updated the book to reflect the events of the past two years. For a detailed list of changes, please contact your Cengage learning consultant.

- Because we know that students respond to up-to-date information about political events, we incorporate compelling, thought-provoking current examples throughout. We also include the results of the November 2016 elections and analyze how the rise of Donald Trump will change the way we look at American politics. In each **new *Election 2016*** feature, we place the election results in the context of the chapter's subject matter.

- The 2017–2018 Edition includes a **separate Chapter 10 on The Media.** Because the new media have become so important, we felt it necessary to devote an entire chapter to this topic. We look at content providers and aggregators. We look at the importance of media in campaigns. Net neutrality is an important topic in this chapter. Finally, we examine the issue of media bias and talk radio.

- **More demographics material** is included throughout, particularly in Chapter 1, which presents material on positive and negative trends, such as unemployment and inequality, and falling crime and teen pregnancy rates, and rising mortality rates among members of the rural white working class.

- **Major updates to the content** have been made in the areas of public opinion, interest groups, modern political parties, social media in politics, and the Obama legacy. The chapters on Domestic and Economic Policy and Foreign Policy have been completely updated and modernized. The text reflects the current events that most interest you and your students, including recent Supreme Court rulings and state legislation on same-sex marriage, marijuana, privacy and recent NSA revelation coverage, current civil rights issues including the role of the police, foreign policy coverage of Syria and Ukraine, and more!

MindTap

MindTap is here to simplify your workload as an instructor, organize and immediately grade your students' assignments, and allow you to customize your course as you see fit. Through deep-seated integration with your Learning Management System (LMS), grades are easily exported and analytics are pulled with just the click of a button. MindTap provides you with a platform to easily add in current events videos and RSS feeds from national or local news sources. Looking to incorporate more recent and late-breaking news into the course? Add in our KnowNow American Government Blog link for weekly updated news coverage and pedagogy.

Barbara A. Bardes, Mack C. Shelley II, Steffen W. Schmidt

A Letter to STUDENTS

The 2016 presidential elections proved to be the most consequential in years. If Democrat Hillary Clinton had been elected, the nation would have carried on much as it had under the last six years of the Barack Obama administration. We would have a Democratic president constrained by a Republican House of Representatives. That is not what happened, however. Republican Donald Trump is now president of the United States of America. Republicans control both chambers of Congress. Furthermore, Trump is not a conventional Republican. Would he really impose major restrictions on imports? Deport millions of unauthorized immigrants? Snuggle up to Russia's Vladimir Putin? Above all, how can he meet the expectations of his millions of energized supporters? What will happen to the economy? How far will Congress go in unraveling the Obama legacy? Whatever Trump and the Republicans do, the effect is likely to be felt by every citizen.

You'll learn about all of these developments and more in the *2017–2018 Edition of American Government and Politics Today: The Essentials.*

Our hope is that this book inspires you to join the exciting process of being an active, informed citizen. Your American Government course and the material you'll read here will give you the knowledge you'll need to understand our political system and develop well-informed opinions on the current issues and controversies you'll encounter in your daily life. We strive to highlight how American government and politics directly affect you in every chapter. We also suggest easy ways that you can take action in your community and become involved in the political process.

Special Features

- *Take Action: A Guide to Political Participation* is filled with resources and suggestions to help students stay informed and get involved in the political process.

- Thought-provoking *What If . . . ?, Beyond Our Borders,* and *Consider the Source* features help you understand key concepts and current events as well as develop a more informed and global perspective.

- *Why You Should Care about . . . ?* marginal features demonstrate why the topic at hand directly affects you and matters in your life.

- *Which Side Are You On?* sections challenge you to take a stand on controversial issues.

- *How You Can Make a Difference* features conclude each chapter with ways in which you can become actively involved in American politics.

- *Election 2016* features highlight the important impact of the 2016 elections and include an analysis of the campaigns and election results.

- **Critical-thinking questions** now accompany almost all boxed features, figures, tables, and photo captions, helping you apply and analyze the information presented.

- **Learning Outcomes** appear in each chapter opener, correlate to each major section to help you target your reading, and are revisited in each Chapter Summary and end-of-chapter Quiz to help you assess your comprehension and master the book's key concepts. Every chapter also concludes with key terms and a list of additional print and media resources. And the book is now seamlessly integrated with MindTap, directing you to a variety of online interactive activities that will help you test yourself on the book's Learning Outcomes.

The Benefits of Using MindTap

For you as a student, the benefits of using **MindTap** with this book are endless. With automatically graded practice quizzes and activities, an easily navigated learning path, and an interactive eBook, you will be able to test yourself inside and outside of the classroom with ease. The accessibility of current events coupled with interactive media makes the content fun and engaging. On your computer, phone, or tablet, MindTap is there when you need it, giving you easy access to flashcards, quizzes, readings, and assignments.

Barbara A. Bardes, Mack C. Shelley II, Steffen W. Schmidt

RESOURCES

Students

Access your *American Government and Politics Today: The Essentials* resources by visiting www.cengagebrain.com/shop/isbn/9781337091213

If you purchased MindTap access with your book, enter your access code and click "**REGISTER.**" You can also purchase the book's resources here separately through the "**RESOURCES**" tab, or access the free content through the "**FREE MATERIALS**" tab.

Instructors

Access your *American Government and Politics Today: The Essentials* resources via www.cengage.com/login.

Log in using your Cengage Learning single sign-on username and password, or create a new instructor account by clicking on "**NEW FACULTY USER**" and following the instructions.

MindTap for *American Government and Politics Today: The Essentials, 2017–2018 Edition*

Instant Access Code: 9781337091244

MindTap for American Government is a fully online, personalized learning experience built upon Cengage Learning content and correlating to a core set of learning outcomes. MindTap guides students through the course curriculum via an innovative Learning Path Navigator where they will complete reading assignments, challenge themselves with focus activities, and engage with interactive quizzes. Through a variety of gradable activities, MindTap provides students with ample opportunities to check themselves for understanding, while also allowing faculty to measure and assess student progress. Integration with programs like YouTube, Evernote, and Google Drive allows instructors to add and remove content of their choosing with ease, keeping their course current while tracking local and global events through RSS feeds. The product can be used fully online with its interactive eBook for *American Government and Politics Today: The Essentials,* or in conjunction with the printed text.

Instructor Companion Web Site for *American Government and Politics Today: The Essentials, 2017–2018 Edition*

ISBN: 9781337091381

This Instructor Companion Web site is an all-in-one multimedia online resource for class preparation, presentation, and testing. Accessible through cengage.com/login with your faculty account, you will find available for download: book-specific Microsoft® PowerPoint® presentations; a Test Bank compatible with multiple learning management systems; an Instructor's Manual; Microsoft® PowerPoint® Image Slides; and a JPEG Image Library.

The Test Bank, offered in Blackboard, Moodle, Desire2Learn, Canvas, and Angel formats, contains Learning Objective–specific multiple-choice, critical thinking short answer questions, and essay questions for each chapter. Import the test bank into your Learning Management System to edit and manage questions and to create tests.

The Instructor's Manual contains chapter-specific learning objectives, an outline, key terms with definitions, and a chapter summary. Additionally, the Instructor's Manual features a critical thinking question, lecture-launching suggestion, and an in-class activity for each learning objective.

The Microsoft® PowerPoint® presentations are ready-to-use, visual outlines of each chapter. These presentations are easily customized for your lectures and are offered along with chapter-specific Microsoft® PowerPoint® Image Slides and JPEG Image Libraries. Access the Instructor Companion Web site at **www.cengage.com/login.**

Cognero for *American Government and Politics Today: The Essentials, 2017–2018 Edition*

ISBN: 9781337091374

Cengage Learning Testing Powered by Cognero is a flexible, online system that allows you to author, edit, and manage test bank content from multiple Cengage Learning solutions, create multiple test versions in an instant, and deliver tests from your LMS, your classroom, or wherever you want. The test bank for *American Government and Politics Today: The Essentials* contains Learning Objective–specific multiple-choice and essay questions for each chapter.

CourseReader for American Government

CourseReader for MindTap is available through the MindTap Instructor's Resource Center. This new feature provides access to Gale's authoritative library reference content to aid in the development of important supplemental readers for political science courses. Every Political Science MindTap provides Faculty access to a CourseReader database of readings, images, and videos from the resource center, all of which can be immediately added to MindTap with the click of a button. This capability can replace a separate reader and conveniently keeps all course materials in one place within a single MindTap. The selections within CourseReader are curated by experts and designed specifically for introductory courses.

ACKNOWLEDGMENTS

In preparing this 2017–2018 edition of *American Government and Politics Today: The Essentials,* we were the beneficiaries of the expert guidance of a skilled and dedicated team of publishers and editors. We have benefited greatly from the supervision and encouragement given by our Product Manager Bradley Potthoff. Alison Duncan, our Content Developer, deserves our thanks for her efforts in coordinating reviews and in many other aspects of project development. We are especially appreciative of the photo research that she and Content Team Assistant Cazzie Reyes undertook for us. We are grateful to our Senior Content Project Manager Ann Borman for her ability to make this project as smooth running and as perfect as is humanly possible.

Our gratitude goes to all of those who worked on the various supplements offered with this text, especially the test bank author, Scott Wallace from Indiana University-Purdue University Indianapolis, and the Instructor's Manual author, Tamra Ortgies-Young from Georgia Perimeter College. We would also like to thank Senior Marketing Manager Valerie Hartman for her tremendous efforts in marketing the text and Product Assistant Staci Eckenroth for her contributions to this project. We are indebted to Lachina Publishing Services for the accurate and timely composition of this text. Their ability to generate the pages for this text quickly and accurately made it possible for us to meet our ambitious printing schedule.

Many other people helped during the research and editorial stages of this edition. Gregory Scott provided excellent editorial and research assistance from the outset of the project to the end. Kristi Wiswell's copyediting and Beverly Peavler's proofreading skills contributed greatly to the book. Roxie Lee served as a coordinator for the flow of manuscript and pages with all of their corrections. We thank her profusely. We also thank Sue Jasin of K&M Consulting for her contributions to the smooth running of the project.

Any errors remain our own. We welcome comments from instructors and students alike. Suggestions that we have received in the past have helped us to improve this text and to adapt it to the changing needs of instructors and students.

REVIEWERS

We would also like to thank the instructors who have contributed their valuable feedback through reviews of this text:

Pat Andrews, *West Valley College*
Marcos Arandia, *North Lake College*
Sara C. Benesh, *University of Wisconsin, Milwaukee*
Sherman Brewer, Jr., *Rutgers University, Newark*
Martyn de Bruyn, *Northeastern Illinois University*
Gary Castaneda, *Miracosta College*
Ann Clemmer, *University of Arkansas at Little Rock*
Beatriz Cuartas, *El Paso Community College*
Jodi Empol, *Montgomery County Community College*
Crystal Garrett, *Georgia Perimeter College, Dunwoody*
Joseph Georges, *El Camino College*
Jack Goodyear, *Dallas Baptist University*
Willie Hamilton, *Mt. San Jacinto College*
Matthew Hansel, *McHenry County College*
Joanne Hopkins-Lucia, *Baker College of Clinton Township*
Frank Ibe, *Wayne County Community College*
Mark S. Jendrysik, *University of North Dakota*
Roger Jordan, *Baker College of Flint*
Jon Kelly, *West Valley College*
Thomas R. Kemp, *University of Arkansas at Little Rock*
Kevin Kniess, *Lakeland College*
Linda Lien, *Westwood College, Los Angeles*
William Madlock, *University of Memphis*
Jan McCauley, *Tyler Junior College*
James Mitchell, *California State University, Northridge*
Dr. Michael Mitchell, *Georgia Perimeter College*
Eric Nobles, *Atlanta Metropolitan College*
Tamra Ortgies-Young, *Georgia Perimeter College*
Lisa Perez-Nichols, *Austin Community College*
William Parent, *San Jacinto College, Central Campus*
Travis N. Ridout, *Washington State University*
Ron Robinson, *Schoolcraft College*
Steven R. Rolnick, *Western Connecticut State University*
Margaret E. Scranton, *University of Arkansas at Little Rock*
Shyam Sriram, *Georgia Perimeter College*
Arlene Story Sanders, *Delta State University*
Judy Tobler, *NorthWest Arkansas Community College*
June Trudel, *California State University, San Marcos*
Scott Wallace, *Indiana University-Purdue University, Indianapolis*
Robert Whitaker, *Hudson Valley Community College*
Dr. Adam M. Williams, *Kennesaw State University*

About the AUTHORS

Barbara A. Bardes

Barbara A. Bardes is professor emerita of political science and former dean of Raymond Walters College at the University of Cincinnati. She received her B.A. and M.A. from Kent State University. After completing her Ph.D. at the University of Cincinnati, she held faculty positions at Mississippi State University and Loyola University in Chicago. She returned to Cincinnati, her hometown, as a college administrator. She has also worked as a political consultant and directed polling for a research center.

Bardes has written articles on public opinion and foreign policy and on women and politics. She has authored *Thinking about Public Policy; Declarations of Independence: Women and Political Power in Nineteenth-Century American Fiction;* and *Public Opinion: Measuring the American Mind* (with Robert W. Oldendick).

Bardes's home is located in a very small hamlet in Kentucky called Rabbit Hash, famous for its 150-year-old general store. Her hobbies include traveling, gardening, needlework, and antique collecting.

Mack C. Shelley II

Mack C. Shelley II is professor of political science and statistics at Iowa State University. After receiving his bachelor's degree from American University in Washington, D.C., he completed graduate studies at the University of Wisconsin–Madison, where he received a master's degree in economics and a Ph.D. in political science. He taught for two years at Mississippi State University before arriving at Iowa State in 1979.

Shelley has published numerous articles, books, and monographs on public policy. From 1993 to 2002, he served as elected co-editor of the *Policy Studies Journal.* His published books include *The Permanent Majority: The Conservative Coalition in the United States Congress; Biotechnology and the Research Enterprise* (with William F. Woodman and Brian J. Reichel); *American Public Policy: The Contemporary Agenda* (with Steven G. Koven and Bert E. Swanson); *Redefining Family Policy: Implications for the 21st Century* (with Joyce M. Mercier and Steven Garasky); and *Quality Research in Literacy and Science Education: International Perspectives and Gold Standards* (with Larry Yore and Brian Hand).

His leisure time includes traveling, working with students, and playing with the family dog and cats.

Steffen W. Schmidt

Steffen W. Schmidt is professor of political science at Iowa State University. He grew up in Colombia, South America, and studied in Colombia, Switzerland, and France. He obtained his Ph.D. in public law and government from Columbia University in New York.

Schmidt has published 14 books and more than 130 journal articles. He is also the recipient of numerous prestigious teaching prizes, including the Amoco Award for Lifetime Career Achievement in Teaching and the Teacher of the Year award. He is a pioneer in the design, production, and delivery of Internet courses and a founding member of the American Political Science Association's section on Computers and Multimedia. He is known as "Dr. Politics" for his extensive commentary on U.S. politics in U.S. and international media. He is a weekly blogger for Gannett and comments on CNN en Español and Univision. He is the chief political and international correspondent of the Internet magazine Insideriowa.com.

Schmidt likes to snow ski, ride hunter jumper horses, race sailboats, and scuba dive.

CAREER OPPORTUNITIES:
Political Science

Introduction

It is no secret that college graduates are facing one of the toughest job markets in the past fifty years. Despite this challenge, those with a college degree have done much better than those without since the 2008 recession. One of the most important decisions a student has to make is the choice of a major. Many consider future job possibilities when making that call. A political science degree is useful for a successful career in many different fields, from lawyer to policy advocate, pollster to humanitarian worker. Employer surveys reveal that the skills that most employers value in successful employees—critical thinking, analytical reasoning, and clarity of verbal and written communication—are precisely the tools that political science courses should be helping you develop. This brief guide is intended to help spark ideas for what kinds of careers you might pursue with a political science degree and the types of activities you can engage in now to help you secure one of those positions after graduation.

Careers in Political Science

Law and Criminal Justice

Do you find that your favorite parts of your political science classes are those that deal with the Constitution, the legal system, and the courts? Then a career in law and criminal justice might be right for you. Traditional jobs in the field range from lawyer or judge to police or parole officer. Since 9/11, there has also been tremendous growth in the area of homeland security, which includes jobs in mission support, immigration, and travel security, as well as prevention and response.

Public Administration

The many offices of the federal government combined represent one of the largest employers in the United States. Flip to the bureaucracy chapter of this textbook and consider that each federal department, agency, and bureau you see looks to political science majors for future employees. A partial list of such agencies would include the Department of Education, the Department of Health and Human Services, and the Federal Trade Commission. There are also thousands of staffers who work for members of Congress or the Congressional Budget Office, many of whom were political science majors in college. This does not even begin to account for the multitude of similar jobs in state and local governments that you might consider as well.

Campaigns, Elections, and Polling

Are campaigns and elections the most exciting part of political science for you? Then you might consider a career in the growing industry based around political campaigns. From volunteering and interning to consulting, marketing, and fundraising, there are many opportunities for those who enjoy the competitive and high-stakes electoral arena. For those looking for careers that combine political knowledge with statistical skills, there are careers in public opinion polling. Pollsters work for independent national organizations such as Gallup and YouGov, or as part of news operations and campaigns. For those who are interested in survey methodology there are also a wide variety of non-political career opportunities in marketing and survey design.

Interest Groups, International and Nongovernmental Organizations

Is there a cause that you are especially passionate about? If so, there is a good chance that there are interest groups out there that are working hard to see some progress made on similar issues. Many of the positions that one might find in for-profit companies also exist in their non-profit interest group and nongovernmental organization counterparts, including lobbying and high-level strategizing. Do not forget that there are also quite a few major international organizations—such as the United Nations, the World Health Organization, and the International Monetary Fund—where a degree in political science could be put to good use. While competition for those jobs tends to be fierce, your interest and knowledge about politics and policy will give you an advantage.

Foreign Service

Does a career in diplomacy and foreign affairs, complete with the opportunity to live and work abroad, sound exciting for you? Tens of thousands of people work for the State Department, both in Washington, D.C., and in consulates throughout the world. They represent the diplomatic interests of the United States abroad. Entrance into the Foreign Service follows a very specific process, starting with the

Foreign Service Officers Test—an exam given three times a year that includes sections on American government, history, economics, and world affairs. Being a political science major is a significant help in taking the FSOT.

Graduate School

While not a career, graduate school may be the appropriate next step for you after completing your undergraduate degree. Following the academic route, being awarded a Ph.D. or Master's degree in political science could open additional doors to a career in academia, as well as many of the professions mentioned earlier. If a career as a researcher in political science interests you, you should speak with your advisors about continuing your education.

Preparing While Still on Campus

Internships

One of the most useful steps you can take while still on campus is to visit your college's career center to discuss an internship in your field of interest. Not only does it give you a chance to experience life in the political science realm, it can lead to job opportunities later down the road and add experience to your resume.

Skills

In addition to your political science classes, there are a few skills any number of which will prove useful as a complement to your degree:

> **Writing:** Like anything else, writing improves with practice. Writing is one of those skills that is applicable regardless of where your career might take you. Virtually every occupation relies on an ability to write cleanly, concisely, and persuasively.

> **Public Speaking:** An oft-quoted 1977 survey showed that public speaking was the most commonly cited fear among respondents. And yet oral communication is a vital tool in the modern economy. You can practice this skill in a formal class setting or through extracurricular activities that get you in front of a group.

> **Quantitative Analysis:** As the Internet aids in the collection of massive amounts of information, the nation is facing a drastic shortage of people with basic statistical skills to interpret and use this data. A political science degree can go hand-in-hand with courses in introductory statistics.

> **Foreign Language:** One skill that often helps a student or future employee stand out in a crowded job market is the ability to communicate in a language other than English. Solidify or set the foundation for your verbal and written foreign language communication skills while in school.

Student Leadership

One attribute that many employers look for is "leadership potential," which can be quite tricky to indicate on a resume or cover letter. What can help is a demonstrated record of involvement in clubs and organizations, preferably in a leadership role. While many people think immediately of student government, most student clubs allow you the opportunity to demonstrate your leadership skills.

Conclusion

We hope that reading this has sparked some ideas on potential future careers. As a next step, visit your college's career placement office, which is a great place to further explore what you have read here. You might also visit your college's alumni office to connect with graduates who are working in your field of interest. Political science opens the door to a lot of exciting careers; have fun exploring the possibilities!

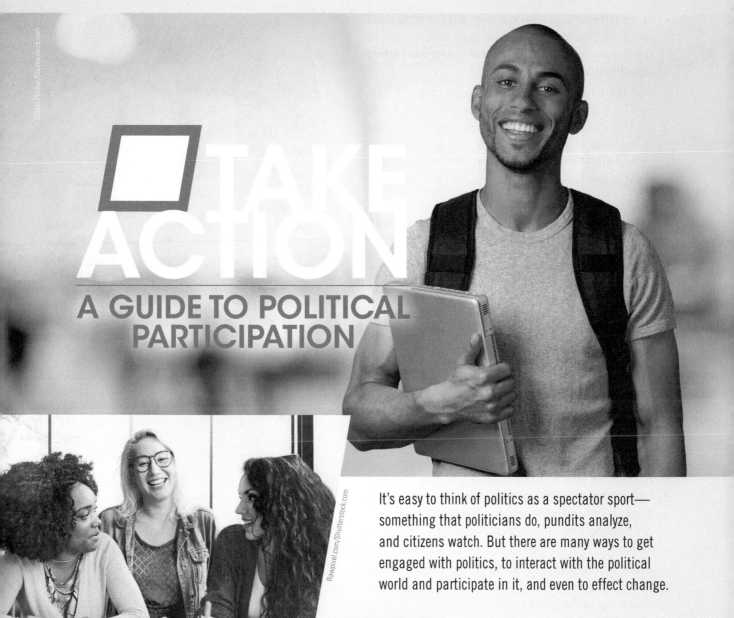

TAKE ACTION
A GUIDE TO POLITICAL PARTICIPATION

It's easy to think of politics as a spectator sport—something that politicians do, pundits analyze, and citizens watch. But there are many ways to get engaged with politics, to interact with the political world and participate in it, and even to effect change.

GET INFORMED.

Find Out Where You Fit and What You Know

- You already have some opinions about a variety of political issues. Do you have a sense of where your views place you on the political map? Get a feel for your ideological leanings by taking The World's Smallest Political Quiz: **www.theadvocates.org/quiz/**.

- Which Founding Founder Are You? The National Constitutional Center can help you with that. Go to **constitutioncenter.org/foundersquiz/** to discover which Founding Father's personality most resembles your own.

- The U.S. Constitution is an important part of the context in which American politics takes place. Do you know what the Constitution says? Take the Constitution I.Q. Quiz: **www.constitutionfacts.com/**. Was your score higher than the national average?

- At the National Constitution Center you can explore the interactive Constitution and learn more about provisions in that document: **constitutioncenter.org/interactive -constitution**.

- Find out what those who want to become U.S. citizens have to do—and what they have to know. Go to the U.S. Citizenship and Immigration Services website at **www.uscis.gov/**. What is involved in applying for citizenship? Take the Naturalization Self-Test at **https:// myuscis.gov/preptest/civics**. How did you do?

Think about How Your Political Views Have Been Shaped

- Giving some thought to how agents of political socialization—your family, your schools, your peers, for example—have contributed to your political beliefs and attitudes may help you understand why others might not share your views on politics. Then have conversations with people in your classes or in your residence hall about the people, institutions, and experiences that influenced the way they view the political world.

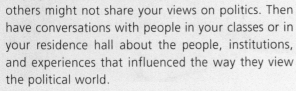

- Explore how your views on political issues compare with those of a majority of Americans. There are a number of good polling sites that report public opinion on a range of topics.

  □ The Pew Research Center for the People & the Press conducts regular polls on politics and policy issues: **www.people-press.org/**.

  □ Public Agenda reports poll data and material on major issues: **publicagenda.org/**.

  □ The results of recent polls and an archive of past polls can be found at Gallup: **www.gallup.com/**.

  □ The Roper Center for Public Opinion Research is a leading archive of data from surveys of public opinion: **ropercenter.cornell.edu/**.

  □ PollingReport organizes public opinion data from various sources by keyword: **pollingreport.com/**.

- Keep up with news—print, broadcast, and online. Remember that different news organizations (or media brands) will report the same information in

different ways. Don't avoid certain news sources because you think you might not agree with the way they report the news. It's just as important to know how people are talking about issues as it is to know about the issues themselves.

  □ One of the best ways to get to the source of the news is to get your information from the same place that journalists do. Often they take their cues or are alerted to news events by news agencies like the nonprofit cooperative, Associated Press: **ap.org/**.

  □ Installing a few key apps on your phone or tablet can make all the difference in being informed. Try downloading the Associated Press (AP) app for short updates from news around the world, as they happen. There are tons of other great political apps, some of which are fairly polarized, others that are neutral, and still others that are just plain silly.

Blogs

The blogosphere affords views of politics that may be presented differently than the way the mainstream media does it. In the last several decades, blogs have surged in popularity as a source for political news and opinion.

Social Media

Staying connected can be as simple as following local, national, or international politics on social media. U.S. House Majority Whip Kevin McCarthy, President Barack Obama, Senator Elizabeth Warren, House Speaker Paul Ryan, and even the White House have Instagram accounts worth following. Numerous politicians and political outlets are also on Twitter and Facebook.

Check the Data

- It's not always easy to figure out whether a news report or public statement is accurate. PolitiFact, a project of the *Tampa Bay Times,* is a good place to go to get the facts: **www.politifact.com/**. Check out the Truth-O-Meter, and get it on your smartphone or tablet.

- A project of the Annenberg Public Policy Center, **www.factcheck.org/** is a nonpartisan, nonprofit "consumer advocate" for voters that monitors the factual accuracy of what political players are saying in TV ads, speeches, and interviews.

Keep Up During Election Season

- Project Vote Smart offers information on elections and candidates: **votesmart.org/**

- Nate Silver's FiveThirtyEight features election analysis, in addition to covering sports and economics: **www.fivethirtyeight.com/**

- Stay connected to the horse-race aspect of electoral politics by tracking election polls. There are many good sources:

  □ For a comprehensive collection of election polls, go to the RealClearPolitics website: **realclearpolitics.com/polls/**. RealClearPolitics is a good source for other political news and opinions as well.

□ Polls for U.S. federal elections, including state-by-state polls, can be found at **electoral-vote.com/**.

□ HuffPost Pollster publishes pre-election poll results combined into interactive charts: **elections.huffington post.com/pollster/**. During presidential elections, additional maps and electoral vote counts can be found at HuffPost Politics Election Dashboard.

Monitor Money and Influence in Politics

The Center for Responsive Politics website is an excellent source for information about who's contributing what amounts to which candidates: **www.opensecrets.org/**. You can also use the lobbying database to identify the top lobbying firms, the agencies most frequently lobbied, and the industries that spend the most on lobbying activities. Explore the site's information on the revolving door, which identifies the lobbying firms, agencies, and industries that have the highest numbers of people who have moved between government and interest group positions.

Connect with Congress

You can, of course, learn a lot about what's going on in Congress from the websites of the House of Representatives and the Senate: **www.house.gov/** and **www.senate.gov/**. But check out GovTrack to find out where your representative and senators fall on the leadership and ideology charts, as well as their most recently sponsored bills and votes on legislation: **www.govtrack.us/**.

Dragon Images/Shutterstock.com

bikeriderlondon/Shutterstock.com

GET INVOLVED.

Take an Interest in Your Community—Offer to Help

Every community—large or small—can use energetic people willing to help where there is a need. Local nonprofit agencies serving the homeless, battered women, or troubled teens often welcome volunteers who are willing to pitch in. You can learn a lot about the public policies that focus on social services while doing some good for others.

The Internet also has abundant resources about nonprofits and charities and how you can get involved:

- **Idealist.org** is a great place to find organizations and events that are looking for employees, interns, and volunteers. Filter by type and area of focus (women, disaster relief, animals, etc.) to find a cause that fits you.

- **Tinyspark.org** is a watchdog for nonprofits and charity organizations. It highlights individuals and groups that are doing good things in communities and around the globe and checks on those who may not be doing as much good as you'd think. Tinyspark also has a podcast.

- **Charitynavigator.org** is another tool for checking on charities. It reports on charities in terms of how much of their donations go to the cause, which charities are in the red, which are worth promoting, and so on—it's kind of like opensecrets.org for charities.

Design Your Own Ways to Take Action

- Start a network to match those who need assistance and those who want to help. For example, there may be people on your campus who, because of a disability or recent injury, need someone to help carry belongings, open doors, or push wheelchairs.

- Do you want to raise awareness about an issue? Is there a cause that you think needs attention? Talk with friends. Find out if they share your concerns. Turn your discussions into a blog. Create videos of events you think are newsworthy and share them online.

Join a Group on Campus

You probably see fliers promoting groups and recruiting members posted all over campus—in the student center, in the residence halls, in classroom buildings. Chances are, there's a group organized around something you're interested in or care about. Maybe it's an organization that works to bring clean water to remote parts of the world. Perhaps it's an organization that works to foster tolerance on campus. The American Civil Liberties Union may have a chapter on your campus. The American Red Cross may be there, too. You'll find College Republicans, College Democrats, groups organized around race or culture, groups that go on alternative spring break trips to give direct service to communities in need, service organizations of all kinds; groups that serve to create community among culturally underrepresented students, and groups that care about the environment. The list goes on and on.

If you have an interest that isn't represented by the groups on your campus, start your own. Your college or university should have an office of campus life (or something similar) that can help you navigate the process for establishing a student organization.

Remember, too, that there are hundreds of political interest groups with national reach. Check out their Web sites to see if you want to join.

Vote (But Don't Forget to Register First)

- Voting is one of the most widely shared acts of participation in American democracy. You can learn about the laws governing voting in your state—and all of the others—by going to the Web site of the National Conference of State Legislatures and its link to Voter Identification Requirements: **www.ncsl.org/research/elections-and-campaigns/voter-id/**

- Register: Enter "register to vote in [your state]" in a search engine. The office in your state that administers voting and elections (in some states it's the office of the Secretary of State, in others it might be the State Board of Elections) will have a website that outlines the steps you will need to follow. If you need to vote absentee, you'll find out how to do that here, too.

- If you want to view a sample ballot to familiarize yourself with what you'll be looking at when you go to the polls, you will probably be able to view one online. Just enter "sample ballot" in a search engine. Your local election board, the League of Women Voters, or your district library often post a sample ballot online.

- Vote: Make sure you know the location and hours for your polling place.

Work for a Campaign

Candidates welcome energetic volunteers. So do groups that are supporting (or opposing) ballot measures. While sometimes tiring and frustrating, working in campaign politics can also be exhilarating and very rewarding. Find the contact information for a campaign you're interested in on their website and inquire about volunteer opportunities.

Be Part of Campus Media

Do you have a nose for news and do you write well? Try reporting for the university newspaper. Work your way up to an editor's position. If broadcast media is your thing, get involved with your college radio station or go on air on campus TV.

Try Your Hand at Governing

Get involved with student government. Serve on committees. Run for office.

Engage with Political Institutions, Government Agencies, and Public Policymakers— at Home and Abroad

- Remember that your U.S. Representative has district offices—one may be in the town in which you live. Your U.S. Senators also have offices in various locations around the state. Check to see if internships are available or if there are opportunities for volunteering. If you plan to be in Washington, D.C. and want to visit Capitol Hill, you can book a tour in advance through your senators' or representative's offices. That's where you get gallery passes, too.

- Spend some time in Washington. Many colleges and universities have established internship programs with government agencies and institutions. Some have semester-long programs that will bring you into contact with policymakers in Congress and in the bureaucracy, with journalists, and with a variety of other prominent newsmakers. Politics and government come alive, and the contacts you make while participating in such programs can often lead to jobs after graduation.

- If you're interested in the Supreme Court and you're planning a trip to Washington, try to watch oral argument. Go to the Court's website to access the link for oral arguments: **www.supremecourt.gov/**. You'll find the argument calendar and a visitor's guide. (The secret is to get in line early.)

☑ GET INFORMED.
☑ GET CONNECTED.
☑ GET INVOLVED.

- If you can't make it to Washington, D.C. for a semester-long program or even a few days, become a virtual tourist. Take the U.S. Capitol Virtual Tour: **www.aoc.gov/virtual-tours/capitolbldg/tourfiles/**.

- You can take a virtual tour of the Supreme Court at the Web site of the Oyez Project at IIT Chicago-Kent College of Law: **www.oyez.org/tour/**. And you can listen to Supreme Court oral arguments wherever you are. Go to the Oyez site and check ISCOTUSnow (**blogs.kentlaw.iit.edu/iscotus/**).

- Studying abroad, of course, is a great way to expand your horizons and to get a feel for different cultures and the global nature of politics and the economy. There are programs that will take you virtually anywhere in the world. Check with the Study Abroad Office at your college or university to find out more.

- You can gain some insight into dealing with global issues even if you stay stateside. Participate in the Model UN Club on your campus (or start a Model UN Club if there isn't one). By participating in Model UN, you will become aware of international issues and conflicts and recognize the role that the United Nations can play in forging collective responses to global concerns. Model UN conferences are simulations of a session of the United Nations; your work as part of a country's UN delegation will give you hands-on experience in diplomacy.

THE DEMOCRATIC REPUBLIC

A voter-registration drive on a university campus. *What do we call a system in which we elect the people who govern us?*
Blend Images/Alamy

These five **LEARNING OUTCOMES** *below are designed to help improve your understanding of this chapter:*

1: Define the terms *politics, government, order, liberty, authority,* and *legitimacy.*

2: Distinguish the major features of direct democracy and representative democracy, and describe majoritarianism, elite theory, and pluralism.

3: Summarize the conflicts that can occur between the values of liberty and order, and between those of liberty and equality.

4: Discuss conservatism, liberalism, and other popular American ideological positions.

5: Explain how a changing American population and other social trends may affect the future of our nation.

What if... We Had No Bill of Rights?

Background

You know that you have the right to speak freely about the government without fear of being arrested for what you say. You have probably heard of the right to bear arms. These rights come from the Bill of Rights, the first ten amendments to the U.S. Constitution. Because of these amendments, the government may not pass laws that limit freedom of speech, religion, and many other freedoms. You will learn more about the civil liberties guaranteed by the Bill of Rights in Chapter 4.

The Bill of Rights is built into the founding document that guides our government. As a result, it commands a certain reverence. Merely by its existence, it can dissuade citizens and government leaders from impairing the civil liberties of fellow Americans.

What If We Had No Bill of Rights?

Because the Bill of Rights protects our fundamental liberties, some people jump to the conclusion that, without it, we would have no rights. Consider, though, that almost all state constitutions enumerate many of the same rights. It is true that if the rights of the people were not written into state and national constitutions, these rights would be entirely dependent on the political process—on elections and on laws passed by the U.S. Congress and state legislatures. Popular rights would still be safe. Unpopular ones would be in danger.

The Right To Bear Arms

Take as an example the Second Amendment, which guarantees to citizens the right to bear arms. If the Bill of Rights did not exist, would it mean that individuals would be unable to keep firearms in their homes? Probably not. Few localities in the United States have tried to ban handguns completely. Almost all states have gun laws that are far more permissive than they have to be under the Constitution. Indeed, it was not until 2008 and 2010 that the highest court in the land, the Supreme Court, even addressed this issue. The Court ruled that complete bans on possessing handguns are unconstitutional.

The Rights of Criminal Defendants

According to the Sixth Amendment, accused individuals have the right to a speedy and public trial. Also, according to the Fifth Amendment, no accused "shall be compelled in any criminal case to be a witness against himself, nor be deprived of life, liberty, or property, without due process of law." These rules protect people who are accused of crimes. Certainly, without the Bill of Rights, we could imagine many more restrictions on the rights of criminal defendants. Why? Because those accused of crimes are not a popular group of people. Many of the protections now given to criminal defendants would probably not exist if there were no Bill of Rights.

Free Speech

Without the Bill of Rights, we would probably see many more laws restricting political contributions and advertising. We could expect laws against violent video games and pornography on the Internet. In contrast, given current popular attitudes, it is unlikely that "subversive" speech would be greatly restricted. Most Americans and their elected representatives support the right to denounce the government.

For Critical Analysis

▶ **The Fifth Amendment guarantees that no one can lose her or his liberty or property without due process. Yet, during World War II, we imprisoned tens of thousands of Japanese American citizens, based solely upon their race. Could that happen today to some other group of citizens, such as Muslim Americans? Why or why not?**

▶ **Which of the rights mentioned in this feature do you think are the most important? Why?**

Image 1–1 A conservative protester holds up a copy of the Bill of Rights. *Which of the rights mentioned here might be especially popular with conservatives?*

Tom Carter/Alamy

Politics, for many people, is the "great game"—better than soccer, better than chess. Scores may be tallied only every two years, at elections, but the play continues at all times. The game, furthermore, is played for high stakes. Politics can affect what you spend. It can determine what you can legally do in your spare time. (The *What If . . .* feature that opened this chapter examined some of the ways in which your freedoms might be restricted if the Bill of Rights did not exist.) In worst-case circumstances, politics can even threaten your life.

Few topics are so entertaining as politics—and so important. How did the great game turn out in the elections held on November 8, 2016? We address that question in this chapter's *Election 2016* feature.

In our democratic republic, citizens play an important role by voting. Although voting is extremely important, it is only one of the ways that citizens can exercise their political influence. Americans can also join a political organization or interest group, stage a protest, or donate funds to a political campaign or cause. There are countless ways to become involved. Informed participation begins with knowledge, however, and this text aims to provide you with a strong foundation in American government and politics.

Politics and Government

Learning Outcome **1:**

Define the terms *politics, government, order, liberty, authority,* and *legitimacy.*

What is politics? **Politics** can be understood as the process of resolving conflicts and deciding, as political scientist Harold Lasswell put it in his classic definition, "who gets what, when, and how."[1] More specifically, politics is the struggle over power or influence within organizations or informal groups that can grant benefits or privileges.

We can identify many such groups and organizations. In every community that makes decisions through formal or informal rules, politics exists. For example, when a church decides to construct a new building or hire a new minister, the decision is made politically. Politics can be found in schools, social groups, and any other organized collection of individuals. Of all the organizations that are controlled by political activity, however, the most important is the government.

What is the government? Certainly, it is an **institution**—that is, an ongoing organization that performs certain functions for society. An institution has a life separate from the lives of the individuals who are part of it at any given moment in time. The **government** can be defined as an institution within which decisions are made that resolve conflicts and allocate benefits and privileges. The government is also the preeminent institution within society because it has the ultimate authority for making these decisions.

Government Is Everywhere

The government is even more important than politics. Many people largely ignore politics, but it is impossible to ignore government. It is everywhere, like the water you drink and the air you breathe. Both air and water, by the way, are subject to government pollution standards. The food you eat comes from an agricultural industry that is heavily regulated and subsidized by the government. Step outside your residence, and almost immediately you will walk down a government-owned street or drive on a government-owned highway.

From Your Birth. The county government records your birth. Your toys, crib, and baby food must meet government safety standards. After a few years, you'll start school, and 86 percent of all children attend public—which is to say, government—schools. Some children attend private schools or are home schooled, but their education must also meet government

politics
The struggle over power or influence within organizations or informal groups that can grant benefits or privileges.

institution
An ongoing organization that performs certain functions for society.

government
The institution that has the ultimate authority for making decisions that resolve conflicts and allocate benefits and privileges within a society.

---

1. Harold Lasswell, *Politics: Who Gets What, When, and How* (Gloucester, Mass.: Peter Smith Publisher, 1990; originally published in 1936).

standards. Public school students spend many hours in an environment designed and managed by teachers and other government employees. If you get into trouble, you'll meet government employees you'd rather not see: the police, court employees, or even jail staff.

Throughout Your Life. Most young people eagerly look forward to receiving their government-issued driver's license. Many join the military on graduating from high school, and for those who do, every minute of the next several years will be 100 percent government issue. (That's why we call soldiers "GIs.") A majority of young adults attend college at some point, and if you are reading this textbook, you are probably one of them. Many private colleges and universities exist, but 73 percent of all college students attend public institutions. Even most private universities are heavily dependent on government support.

In nearly all states, you began paying sales taxes from the moment you had your own funds to spend. Some of those funds are made up of currency issued by the government. When you enter the workforce, you'll begin paying payroll and income taxes to the government. If, like most people, you are an employee, government regulations will set many of your working conditions. You might even work for the government itself—16 percent of employees do. If you are unfortunate enough to lose a job or fall into poverty, government programs will lend you a hand.

To the Very End. Later in life, you may have health problems. Even before President Barack Obama's health-care plan went into effect on January 1, 2014, the federal government was already providing half of all the nation's health-care funding. Much of that spending came, and continues to come, from the federal Medicare program, which funds health care for almost everyone over the age of sixty-five. At that point in your life, you'll probably receive Social Security, the national government's pension plan that

Election 2016

The Outcome of the Elections

Republican Donald Trump's victory in the 2016 presidential elections came as a surprise to many. Most public opinion polls taken immediately before the elections showed Democratic candidate Hillary Clinton with a 3 to 4 percentage point advantage. The polls were wrong. Trump and Clinton wound up effectively tied in the popular vote—the count right after the elections had Clinton ahead by 0.2 percent. U.S. presidential elections are decided by the electoral college, however, not the popular vote. There, Trump's breakthrough in the Midwest propelled him to a decisive majority. Voter turnout was key. More Trump supporters voted than expected, and fewer Democrats turned out. The Rocky Mountain and the Pacific Coast states were relatively immune to Trump's nationalist appeal.

Trump's victory dragged down some Democratic senatorial hopefuls, although the Democrats did add two Senate seats. The total was now 52 Republican senators versus 48 Democrats. The Democrats also picked up a net gain of eight seats in the House of Representatives, but the Republicans retained their majority. Following runoff elections in Louisiana, the House margin was expected to be 241 to 192. With Republicans in control of the presidency and both chambers of Congress, a blizzard of Republican legislation seemed certain. Possibilities included the repeal of the Affordable Care Act (Obamacare), a reversal of Obama's environmental measures, and tax cuts aimed primarily at those with large incomes. The actual outcome depended on negotiations between Trump's team and the Republicans in Congress—the two groups did not entirely share the same goals.

covers most employees. Eventually, the county government will record your death, and a government judge will oversee the distribution of your assets to your heirs.

Why Is Government Necessary?

Perhaps the best way to assess the need for government is to examine circumstances in which government, as we normally understand it, does not exist. What happens when multiple groups compete violently with one another for power within a society? There are places around the world where such circumstances exist. A current example is the Middle Eastern nation of Syria, run by the dictator Bashar al-Assad. In 2011, peaceful protesters were killed, which led to an armed rebellion. The government lost control of much of the country, and its forces repeatedly massacred civilians in contested areas. Some rebels, such as the so-called Islamic State, were extreme Islamists. Others were more moderate. By 2013, rebels were fighting each other as well as the government. In much of Syria, law and order had broken down completely. By 2016, as many as 400,000 people had been killed, and almost half of the country's people had been driven from their homes.

Image 1–2 Syrians in a government-held district gather at the scene of a suicide bombing. Members of the group known as ISIS blew themselves up during the morning rush hour. *How would we describe what is happening in Syria?*

As the example of Syria shows, one of the original purposes of government is the maintenance of security, or **order**. By keeping the peace, a government protects its people from violence at the hands of private or foreign armies and criminals. If order is not present, it is not possible for the government to provide any of the other benefits that people expect from it. Order is a political value to which we will return later in this chapter.

Limiting Government Power

A complete collapse of order and security, as seen in Syria, is actually an uncommon event. Much more common is the reverse—too much government control. In 2016, the human rights organization Freedom House judged that fifty of the world's countries were "not free." These nations contain 36 percent of the world's population. Such countries may be controlled by individual kings or dictators. Saudi Arabia's king Abdullah bin Abdulaziz and North Korea's dictator Kim Jong-un are obvious examples. Alternatively, a political party, such as the Communist Party of China, may monopolize all the levers of power. The military may rule, as in Thailand since 2014.

In all of these examples, the individual or group running the country cannot be removed by legal means. Freedom of speech and the right to a fair trial are typically absent. Dictatorial governments often torture or execute their opponents. Such regimes may also suppress freedom of religion. Revolution, whether violent or nonviolent, is often the only way to change the government.

In short, protection from the violence of domestic criminals or foreign armies is not enough. Citizens also need protection from abuses of power by their own government. To protect the liberties of the people, it is necessary to limit the powers of the government.

Liberty—the greatest freedom of the individual consistent with the freedom of other individuals—is a second major political value, along with order. We discuss this value in more detail later in this chapter.

order
A state of peace and security. Maintaining order by protecting members of society from violence and criminal activity is one of the oldest purposes of government.

liberty
The greatest freedom of the individual that is consistent with the freedom of other individuals in the society.

Authority and Legitimacy

Every government must have **authority**—that is, the right and power to enforce its decisions. Ultimately, the government's authority rests on its control of the armed forces and the police. Few people in the United States, however, base their day-to-day activities on fear of the government's enforcement powers. Most people, most of the time, obey the law because this is what they have always done. Also, if they did not obey the law, they would face the disapproval of friends and family. Consider an example: Do you avoid injuring your friends or stealing their possessions because you are afraid of the police—or because if you undertook these actions, you no longer would have friends?

Under normal circumstances, the government's authority has broad popular support. People accept the government's right to establish rules and laws. When authority is broadly accepted, we say that it has **legitimacy**. Authority without legitimacy is a recipe for trouble.

Events in several Arab nations since 2011 serve as an example. The dictators who ruled Egypt, Libya, and Tunisia had been in power for decades. All three dictators had some popular support when they first gained power. None of these nations had a tradition of democracy, and so it was possible for undemocratic rulers to enjoy a degree of legitimacy. After years of oppressive behavior, these regimes slowly lost that legitimacy. The rulers survived only because they were willing to employ violence against any opposition. In Egypt and Tunisia, the end came when soldiers refused to use force against massive demonstrations. Having lost all legitimacy, the rulers of these two countries lost their authority as well. In Libya, the downfall and death of the dictator Muammar Gaddafi came only after a seven-month civil war. (Egypt's shaky new democracy collapsed in 2013 when the army seized power.)

Democracy and Other Forms of Government

Distinguish the major features of direct democracy and representative democracy, and describe majoritarianism, elite theory, and pluralism.

authority
The right and power of a government or other entity to enforce its decisions.

legitimacy
Popular acceptance of the right and power of a government or other entity to exercise authority.

totalitarian regime
A form of government that controls all aspects of the political, social, and economic life of a nation.

authoritarianism
A type of regime in which only the government itself is fully controlled by the ruler. Social and economic institutions exist that are not under the government's control.

The different types of government can be classified according to which person or group of people controls society through the government.

Types of Government

At one extreme is a society governed by a **totalitarian regime**. In such a political system, a small group of leaders or a single individual—a dictator—makes all decisions for the society. Every aspect of political, social, and economic life is controlled by the government. The power of the ruler is total (thus, the term *totalitarianism*). Examples of such regimes include Germany under Adolph Hitler and the former Soviet Union under Joseph Stalin.

A second type of system is authoritarian government. **Authoritarianism** differs from totalitarianism in that only the government itself is fully controlled by the ruler. Social and economic institutions, such as churches, businesses, and labor unions, exist that are not under the government's control.

Many of our terms for describing the distribution of political power are derived from the ancient Greeks, who were the first Western people to study politics systematically. One form of rule was known as *aristocracy*, literally meaning "rule by the best." In practice, this meant rule by wealthy members of ancient families. Another term from the Greeks is *theocracy*, which literally means "rule by God" (or the gods). In practice, theocracy means rule by self-appointed religious leaders. Iran is a rare example of a country in which supreme power is in the hands of a religious leader, the Grand Ayatollah Ali Khamenei. One of the most straightforward Greek terms is *oligarchy*, which simply means "rule by a few."

Anarchy is a term derived from a Greek word meaning the absence of government. Advocates of anarchy envision a world in which each individual makes his or her own rules for behavior. In reality, the absence of government typically results in rule by competing armed factions, many of which are indistinguishable from gangsters. This is the state of affairs in Syria, which we described earlier.

Finally, the Greek term for rule by the people was **democracy**. Within the limits of their culture, some of the Greek city-states operated as democracies. Today, in much of the world, the people will not grant legitimacy to a government unless it is based on democracy.

Direct Democracy as a Model

The Athenian system of government in ancient Greece is usually considered the purest model for **direct democracy** because the citizens of that community debated and voted directly on all laws, even those put forward by the ruling council of the city. The most important feature of Athenian democracy was that the **legislature** was composed of all of the citizens. (Women, resident foreigners, and slaves, however, were excluded because they were not citizens.) This form of government required a high level of participation from every citizen. That participation was seen as benefiting the individual and the city-state. The Athenians believed that although a high level of participation might lead to instability in government, citizens, if informed about the issues, could be trusted to make wise decisions.

Direct democracy also has been practiced at the local level in Switzerland and, in the United States, in New England town meetings. At these town meetings, important decisions—such as levying taxes, hiring city officials, and deciding local ordinances—are made by majority vote. (In recent years, however, turnout for such meetings has declined.) Some states provide a modern adaptation of direct democracy for their citizens. In these states, representative democracy is supplemented by the **initiative** or the **referendum**. Both processes enable the people to vote directly on laws or constitutional amendments. The **recall** process, which is available in many states, allows the people to vote to remove an official from state office before his or her term has expired.

The Dangers of Direct Democracy

Although they were aware of the Athenian model, the framers of the U.S. Constitution were opposed to such a system. Democracy was considered to be dangerous and a source of instability. But in the 1700s and 1800s, the idea of government based on the *consent of the people* gained increasing popularity. Such a government was the main aspiration of the American Revolution in 1775, the French Revolution in 1789, and many subsequent revolutions. At the time of the American Revolution, however, the masses were still considered to be too uneducated to govern themselves. The masses were too prone to the influence of demagogues (political leaders who manipulate popular prejudices), and too likely to subordinate minority rights to the tyranny of the majority.

democracy
A system of government in which political authority is vested in the people. The term is derived from the Greek words *demos* ("the people") and *kratos* ("authority").

direct democracy
A system of government in which political decisions are made by the people directly, rather than by their elected representatives; probably attained most easily in small political communities.

legislature
A governmental body primarily responsible for the making of laws.

initiative
A procedure by which voters can petition to vote on a law or a constitutional amendment.

referendum
An electoral device whereby legislative or constitutional measures are referred by the legislature to the voters for approval or disapproval.

recall
A procedure allowing the people to vote to dismiss an elected official from state office before his or her term has expired.

AP Images/Toby Talbot

Image 1–3 These Woodbury, Vermont, residents cast their ballots after a town meeting. They voted on the school budget and sales taxes. *What type of political system does the town meeting best represent?*

James Madison, while defending the new scheme of government set forth in the U.S. Constitution, warned of the problems inherent in a "pure democracy":

> *A common passion or interest will, in almost every case, be felt by a majority of the whole . . . and there is nothing to check the inducements to sacrifice the weaker party or an obnoxious individual. Hence it is that such democracies have ever been spectacles of turbulence and contention, and have ever been found incompatible with personal security or the rights of property; and have in general been as short in their lives as they have been violent in their deaths.*[2]

Like other politicians of his time, Madison feared that pure, or direct, democracy would deteriorate into mob rule. What would keep the majority of the people, if given direct decision-making power, from abusing the rights of those in the minority?

A Democratic Republic

The framers of the U.S. Constitution chose to craft a **republic**, meaning a government in which sovereign power rests with the people, rather than with a king or a monarch. A republic is based on **popular sovereignty**. To Americans of the 1700s, the idea of a republic also meant a government based on common beliefs and virtues that would be fostered within small communities.

The U.S. Constitution created a form of republican government that we now call a **democratic republic**. The people hold the ultimate power over the government through the election process, but all national policy decisions are made by elected officials. For the founders, even this distance between the people and the government was not sufficient. The Constitution made sure that the Senate and the president would not be elected by a direct vote of the people. Senators were chosen by state legislatures, although a later constitutional amendment allowed for the direct election of senators. The founders also established an *electoral college* to choose the president, in the hope—soon frustrated—that such a body would prevent voters from ultimately making the choice.

Despite its limits, the new American system was unique in the amount of power it granted to the ordinary citizen. Over the course of the following two centuries, democratic values became more and more popular, at first in Western nations and then throughout the rest of the world. The spread of democratic principles gave rise to another name for our system of government—**representative democracy**. The term *representative democracy* has almost the same meaning as *democratic republic,* with one exception. Recall that in a republic, not only are the people sovereign, but there is no king. What if a nation develops into a democracy but preserves the monarchy as a largely ceremonial institution? That is exactly what happened in Britain. The British, who have long cherished their kings and queens, found the term *democratic republic* unacceptable. A republic, after all, meant there could be no monarch. The British therefore described their system as a representative democracy instead.

Principles of Democratic Government. All representative democracies rest on the rule of the people as expressed through the election of government officials. In the 1790s in the United States, only free white males were able to vote, and in some states they had to be property owners as well. Women in many states did not receive the right to vote in national elections until 1920, and the right to vote was not secured in all states by African Americans until the 1960s. Today, **universal suffrage** is the rule.

republic
A form of government in which sovereign power rests with the people, rather than with a king or a monarch.

popular sovereignty
The concept that ultimate political authority is based on the will of the people.

democratic republic
A republic in which representatives elected by the people make and enforce laws and policies.

representative democracy
A form of government in which representatives elected by the people make and enforce laws and policies; may retain the monarchy in a ceremonial role.

universal suffrage
The right of all adults to vote for their government representatives.

---

2. James Madison, in Alexander Hamilton, James Madison, and John Jay, *The Federalist Papers,* No. 10 (New York: Signet, 2003), p. 71. See Appendix C of this textbook.

Because everyone's vote counts equally, the only way to make fair decisions is by some form of *majority* will. But to ensure that **majority rule** does not become oppressive, modern democracies also provide guarantees of minority rights. If political minorities were not protected, the majority might violate the fundamental rights of members of certain groups—especially groups that are unpopular or dissimilar to the majority population, such as racial minorities.

To guarantee the continued existence of a representative democracy, there must be free, competitive elections. Thus, the opposition always has the opportunity to win elective office. For such elections to be totally open, freedom of the press and speech must be preserved so that opposition candidates can present their criticisms of the government to the people.

Constitutional Democracy. Another key feature of Western representative democracy is that it is based on the principle of **limited government**. Not only is the government dependent on popular sovereignty, but the powers of the government are also clearly limited, either through a written document or through widely shared beliefs. The U.S. Constitution sets down the fundamental structure of the government and the limits to its activities. Such limits are intended to prevent political decisions based on the whims or ambitions of individuals in government rather than on constitutional principles.

Image 1–4 The actor Wilmer Valderrama promotes National Voter Registration Day at Miami Dade College in Florida. *Why is voting so important for democracy?*

What Kind of Democracy Do We Have?

Political scientists have developed a number of theories about American democracy, including *majoritarianism, elite theory,* and *pluralism*. Advocates of these theories use them to describe American democracy either as it actually is or as they believe it should be.

Some scholars argue that none of these three theories, which we discuss next, fully describes the workings of American democracy. These experts say that each theory captures a part of the true reality but that we need all three theories to gain a full understanding of American politics.

Democracy for Everyone. Many people believe that, in a democracy, the government ought to do what the majority of the people want. This simple proposition is the heart of majoritarian theory. As a theory of what democracy should be like, **majoritarianism** is popular among both political scientists and ordinary citizens. Many scholars, however, consider majoritarianism to provide a surprisingly poor description of how U.S. democracy actually works. They point to the low level of turnout for elections. Polling data have shown that many Americans are neither particularly interested in politics nor well informed. Few are able to name the persons running for Congress in their districts, and even fewer can discuss the candidates' positions.

Democracy for the Few. If ordinary citizens are not really making policy decisions with their votes, who is? One theory suggests that elites really govern the United States. **Elite theory** holds that society is ruled by a small number of people who

majority rule

A basic principle of democracy asserting that the greatest number of citizens in any political unit should select officials and determine policies.

limited government

A government with powers that are limited either through a written document or through widely shared beliefs.

majoritarianism

A political theory holding that, in a democracy, the government ought to do what the majority of the people want.

elite theory

A perspective holding that society is ruled by a small number of people who hold the ultimate power to further their self-interests.

exercise power to further their self-interests. American democracy, in other words, is a sham democracy. Few people today believe it is a good idea for the country to be run by a privileged minority. In the past, however, many people believed that it was appropriate for the country to be governed by an elite. Consider the words of Alexander Hamilton, one of the framers of the Constitution:

All communities divide themselves into the few and the many. The first are the rich and the wellborn, the other the mass of the people. . . . The people are turbulent and changing; they seldom judge or determine right. Give therefore to the first class a distinct, permanent share in the government. They will check the unsteadiness of the second, and as they cannot receive any advantage by a change, they therefore will ever maintain good government.[3]

Some versions of elite theory posit a small, cohesive elite class that makes almost all the important decisions for the nation,[4] whereas others suggest that voters choose among competing elites. Popular movements of varying political persuasions often advocate simple versions of elite theory.

Why should you care about THE CONSTITUTION?

We assume that our leaders will protect our democratic institutions, but the experience of other nations shows that this does not always happen. In any democracy, citizens must remain vigilant. How do you stay vigilant? One way is to stay informed about what's going on in government. Staying informed is a lot easier today than it was, say, a hundred years ago. Newspapers and news magazines are everywhere. Perhaps more importantly, the Internet allows you to stay in constant touch with what your government is doing. There are blogs galore of all political stripes that you can check out.

Democracy for Groups. A different school of thought holds that our form of democracy is based on group interests. Even if the average citizen cannot keep up with political issues or cast a deciding vote in any election, the individual's interests will be protected by groups that represent her or him.

Theorists who subscribe to **pluralism** see politics as a struggle among groups to gain benefits for their members. Given the structure of the American political system, group conflicts tend to be settled by compromise and accommodation. Because there are a multitude of interests, no one group can dominate the political process. Furthermore, because most individuals have more than one interest, conflict among groups need not divide the nation into hostile camps.

Many political scientists believe that pluralism works very well as a descriptive theory. As a theory of how democracy *should* function, however, pluralism has problems. Poor citizens are rarely members of interest groups. At the same time, rich citizens are often overrepresented. As political scientist E. E. Schattschneider once observed, "The flaw in the pluralist heaven is that the heavenly chorus sings with a strong upper-class accent."[5] Still, the unorganized poor do receive useful representation from religious and liberal groups.

There are also serious doubts as to whether group decision making always reflects the best interests of the nation. Indeed, critics see a danger that groups may grow so powerful that all policies become compromises crafted to satisfy the interests of the largest groups. The interests of the public as a whole, then, are not considered. Critics of pluralism have suggested that a democratic system can be almost paralyzed by the struggle among interest groups. We will discuss interest groups at greater length in Chapter 7.

pluralism
A theory that views politics as a conflict among interest groups. Political decision making is characterized by compromise and accommodation.

3. Alexander Hamilton, "Speech in the Constitutional Convention on a Plan of Government," in Joanne B. Freeman, ed., *Writings* (New York: Library of America, 2001).

4. Michael Parenti, *Democracy for the Few*, 9th ed. (Belmont, Calif.: Wadsworth Publishing, 2010).

5. E. E. Schattschneider, *The Semi-Sovereign People* (Hinsdale, Ill.: The Dryden Press, 1975; originally published in 1960).

Fundamental Values

Learning Outcome **3:**

Summarize the conflicts that can occur between the values of liberty and order, and between those of liberty and equality.

The writers of the U.S. Constitution believed that the structures they had created would provide for both popular sovereignty and a stable political system. They also believed that the nation would be sustained by its **political culture**—the patterned set of ideas, values, and ways of thinking about government and politics that characterized its people.

Even today, there is considerable consensus among American citizens about certain concepts—including the rights to liberty, equality, and property—that are deemed to be basic to the U.S. political system. Given that the vast majority of Americans are descendants of immigrants having diverse cultural and political backgrounds, how can we account for this consensus? Primarily, it is the result of **political socialization**—the process by which political beliefs and values are transmitted to new immigrants and to our children. The two most important sources of political socialization are the family and the educational system. (See Chapter 6 for a more detailed discussion of the political socialization process.)

The most fundamental concepts of the American political culture are those of the dominant culture. The term *dominant culture* refers to the values, customs, and language established by the groups that traditionally have controlled politics and government in a society. The dominant culture in the United States has its roots in Western European civilization. From that civilization, American politics inherited a bias toward individualism, private property, and Judeo-Christian ethics.

Liberty versus Order

In the United States, our **civil liberties** include religious freedom—both the right to practice whatever religion we choose and the right to be free from any state-imposed religion. Our civil liberties also include freedom of speech—the right to express our opinions freely on all matters, including government actions. Freedom of speech is perhaps one of our most prized liberties, because a democracy could not endure without it. These and many other basic guarantees of liberty are found in the **Bill of Rights**, the first ten amendments to the Constitution, which we described in the *What If . . .* feature at the beginning of this chapter. Americans are often more protective of their civil liberties than are citizens of other democratic countries, a point that we discuss in this chapter's *Beyond Our Borders* feature.

Liberty, however, is not the only value widely held by Americans. A substantial portion of the American electorate believes that certain kinds of liberty threaten the traditional social order. The right to privacy is a particularly controversial liberty. The United States Supreme Court has held that the right to privacy can be derived from other rights that are explicitly stated in the Bill of Rights. The Supreme Court has also held that under the right to privacy, the government cannot ban either abortion[6] or private homosexual behavior by consenting adults.[7] Some Americans believe that such rights threaten the sanctity of the family and the general cultural commitment to moral behavior. Of course, others disagree with this point of view.

Security is another issue that follows from the principle of order. When Americans have felt particularly fearful or vulnerable, the government has emphasized national security over civil liberties. Such was the case after the Japanese attack on Pearl Harbor in 1941, which plunged the United States into World War II. Thousands of Japanese Americans were arrested and held in internment camps, based on the assumption that their loyalty to this country was in question. More recently, the terrorist attacks on the World

political culture

A patterned set of ideas, values, and ways of thinking about government and politics that characterize a people.

political socialization

The process by which political beliefs and values are transmitted to new immigrants and to our children. The family and the educational system are the most important sources of the political socialization process.

civil liberties

Those personal freedoms, including freedom of religion and freedom of speech, that are protected for all individuals. Civil liberties restrain the government from taking certain actions against individuals.

Bill of Rights

The first ten amendments to the U.S. Constitution.

---

6. *Roe v. Wade*, 410 U.S. 113 (1973).
7. *Lawrence v. Texas*, 539 U.S. 558 (2003).

Beyond our borders
Civil Liberties in Germany and Japan

Americans tend to value civil freedoms more than the people of most other democratic countries do. Americans, in particular, prize freedom of speech. Not all democratic countries value it so highly.

Free Speech in Germany

In Germany, for example, it is illegal to display the swastika, the emblem adopted by the Nazis. Swastikas cannot be affixed to plastic models of World War II–era aircraft. It is even a crime to give a Nazi-style straight-arm salute. Recently, a German sculptor got into serious trouble by crafting a satirical statue of a garden gnome giving such a salute. The German constitution gives the government the power to ban organizations that threaten the democratic order.

Germany has tried to restrict access to Hitler's autobiography and political statement, *Mein Kampf* (*My Struggle*). Until 2015, the German state of Bavaria owned the rights to the book and refused to allow new copies to be printed. (You could still buy used copies or get it from another country via the Internet.) In 2015, however, the copyright expired, and Bavaria released a highly annotated edition of the work.

Rights of the Accused in Japan

Most Americans are concerned about crime. Many Americans, however, would be even more concerned about possible injustices if they learned that 99.8 percent of all criminal prosecutions resulted in a conviction. Yet that is exactly what happens in democratic Japan. In that country, suspects can be held for up to twenty-three days before they are charged. The high conviction rate in Japan stems from a high confession rate. Those who are detained have no access to defense lawyers and no idea how long interrogation sessions will last. The Japanese constitution guarantees detainees the right to remain silent, but few Japanese citizens who are arrested are able to take advantage of that right. In several recent cases, innocent people have been browbeaten into making false confessions that are almost impossible to retract.

For Critical Analysis

▷ Why would Germany continue to criminalize Nazi symbols more than seventy years after the end of World War II?

Trade Center and the Pentagon on September 11, 2001, renewed calls for greater security at the expense of some civil liberties.

Equality versus Liberty

The Declaration of Independence states, "All men are created equal." The proper meaning of *equality,* however, has been disputed by Americans since the Revolution.[8] Much of American history—and, indeed, world history—is the story of how the value of **equality**—the idea that all people are of equal worth—has been extended and elaborated.

First, the right to vote was granted to all adult white males, regardless of whether they owned property. The Civil War (1861–1865) resulted in the end of slavery and established that, in principle at least, all citizens were equal before the law. The civil rights movement of the 1950s and 1960s sought to make that promise of equality a reality for African Americans. Other movements have sought equality for additional racial and ethnic groups, for women, for persons with disabilities, and for gay men and lesbians. We discuss many of these movements in Chapter 5.

Although many people believe that we have a way yet to go in obtaining full equality for all of these groups, we clearly have come a long way already. No American in the

equality

As a political value, the idea that all people are of equal worth.

8. Gary B. Nash, *The Unknown American Revolution: The Unruly Birth of Democracy and the Struggle to Create America* (New York: Viking, 2005).

Everett Collection Inc/Alamy

Image 1–5 One of the most fundamental rights Americans have is the right to vote. Here, African Americans in Alabama vote for the first time after passage of the 1965 Voting Rights Act. *How are elected officials likely to respond when faced with a large group of new voters?*

nineteenth century could have imagined that the 2008 Democratic presidential primary elections would be closely fought contests between an African American man (Illinois senator Barack Obama) and a white woman (New York senator Hillary Rodham Clinton). The idea that same-sex marriage could even be open to debate would have been mind-boggling as well.

Promoting equality often requires limiting the right to treat people unequally. In this sense, equality and liberty can be conflicting values. Today, the right to deny equal treatment to members of a particular race has very few defenders. Yet as recently as sixty years ago, this right was a cultural norm. It can also be argued that liberty and equality are complementary. For example, people or groups cannot really enjoy liberty if they do not have equal rights under the law.

Economic Equality. Equal treatment regardless of race, religion, gender, or other characteristics is a popular value today. Equal opportunity for individuals to develop their talents and skills is also a value with substantial support. Equality of economic status, however, is a controversial value.

For much of history, the idea that the government could do anything about the division of society between rich and poor was not something about which people even thought. Most people assumed that such an effort was either impossible or undesirable. This assumption began to lose its force in the 1800s. As a result of the growing wealth of the Western world and a visible increase in the ability of government to take on large projects, some people began to advocate the value of universal equality, or egalitarianism. Some radicals dreamed of a revolutionary transformation of society that would establish an egalitarian system—that is, a system in which wealth and power were redistributed more equally.

Image 1–6 These women were married by a judge at the Fulton County Government Center in Atlanta, Georgia, on June 26, 2015. The ceremony took place hours after the United States Supreme Court ruled that gay marriage is a constitutional right. *What, if anything, does the Bill of Rights say about this topic?*

Many others rejected this vision but still came to endorse the values of eliminating poverty and at least reducing the degree of economic inequality in society. Antipoverty advocates believed then and believe now that such a program could prevent much suffering. In addition, they believed that reducing economic inequality would promote fairness and enhance the moral tone of society generally.

Property Rights and Capitalism. The value of reducing economic inequality is in conflict with the right to **property**. This is because reducing economic inequality typically involves the transfer of property (usually in the form of tax dollars) from some people to others. For many people, liberty and property are closely entwined. Our capitalist system is based on private property rights. Under **capitalism**, property consists not only of personal possessions but also of wealth-creating assets such as farms and factories. The investor-owned corporation is in many ways the preeminent capitalist institution. The funds invested by the owners of a corporation are known as *capital*—hence, the very name of the system. Capitalism is also typically characterized by considerable freedom to make binding contracts and by relatively unconstrained markets for goods, services, and investments.

Property—especially wealth-creating property—can be seen as giving its owner political power and the liberty to do whatever he or she wants. At the same time, the ownership of property immediately creates inequality in society. The desire to own property, however, is so widespread among all classes of Americans that radical egalitarian movements have had a difficult time securing a wide following in this country. We discuss whether our tax system promotes excessive inequality in this chapter's *Which Side Are You On?* feature.

The Proper Size of Government

Opposition to "big government" has been a constant theme in American politics. Indeed, the belief that government is overreaching dates back to the years before the American Revolution. Tensions over the size and scope of government have plagued Americans ever since. Citizens often express contradictory opinions on the size of government and the role that it should play in their lives. Those who complain about the amount of taxes that they pay each year may also worry about the lack of funds for teachers in the local schools.

Americans tend to oppose "big government" in principle even as they endorse its benefits. Indeed, American politics in the twenty-first century can be described largely in terms of ambivalence about big government.

Big Government and the Great Recession. In September 2008, a financial meltdown threatened the entire world economy. The impact of the Great Recession was so strong that even by 2016, the share of Americans with jobs was not yet back to the 2007 level. (You can see employment statistics in Figure 1–5 later in this chapter.) Voters demanded government action to save the economy, yet most programs aimed at accomplishing that goal were unpopular. A $700 billion bailout of financial institutions angered Republicans and Democrats alike.

property

Anything that is or may be subject to ownership. As conceived by the political philosopher John Locke, the right to property is a natural right superior to human law (laws made by government).

capitalism

An economic system characterized by the private ownership of wealth-creating assets, free markets, and freedom of contract.

Which side are you on?

Does Our Tax System Promote Excessive Inequality?

Without question, the rich have gotten richer. Since 1983, the top 1 percent of households has seen an 82 percent increase in net wealth. The bottom 60 percent has seen a net 14 percent decrease.

Don't Kill the Geese that Lay the Golden Eggs

It is true that top income earners now receive more of the national income than in the recent past. Yet since 1980, the share of federal income taxes paid by the top 1 percent of earners has increased from 18 percent to 38 percent—more than one-third of all income taxes.

Many Americans pay no federal income tax at all, although they do pay Social Security, Medicare, and other taxes. Some receive more through the income tax system than they pay. The Earned Income Tax Credit substantially reduces the Social Security and Medicare taxes of working families with children and incomes below about $50,000.

Usually, those with really large incomes have earned them. Today, we live in a global society. Globalization increases the rewards earned by the very best, whether in entertainment or in business. People all over the world are willing to pay J. K. Rowling so they can read about Harry Potter. They vastly outnumber those who were once willing to pay, say, Charles Dickens.

If we use taxes to "soak the rich," we will tax the most productive individuals in the country. High marginal tax rates discourage effort. The higher the rate, the greater the discouragement, and this will reduce the rate of economic growth. More income will be redistributed, but is that the ultimate goal of our society? The American way is to celebrate the best.

Yes, the Rich Should Pay More in Taxes

If, in the future, we don't slash Social Security, Medicare, and similar programs, eventually we will need to raise taxes. It seems appropriate that those who have benefited the most from America's economic system should pay more. They can afford it—and that's where the money is.

Consider also that our economic system may naturally generate inequality. Economist Thomas Piketty, in his best seller *Capital in the Twenty-First Century,* argues that wealth earns new wealth faster than labor can earn it. True, inequality fell in much of the twentieth century because wars and depressions destroyed vast amounts of wealth. After World War II, inequality did not rise again because top marginal federal income tax rates exceeded 90 percent. That didn't stop the economy from growing. Today, these rates are about 40 percent, and inequality is soaring. The children of today's top earners are on their way to becoming a new aristocracy that gets its wealth from inheritance, not striving.

When the U.S. income tax was introduced in the early twentieth century, its sponsors didn't see it merely as a way to fund the government. They also saw it as a way to protect the republic by curbing the growth of vast fortunes. Once, Americans knew that there is a point at which inequality becomes incompatible with democracy. We need to relearn that.

For Critical Analysis

▶ Is it possible that higher taxes—and a lower after-tax income—could actually make some people work more?

In November 2008, the voters handed Democrat Barack Obama a solid victory in the presidential elections, and Democrats increased their margins in the House and Senate. Obama took major actions in an attempt to combat the recession, including an $800 billion stimulus package in 2009 and the rescue of the automobile companies General Motors and Chrysler.

Conservatives quickly grew alarmed at the new government activism. One result was the Tea Party, an uncompromising grassroots conservative movement organized in 2009. In 2010, Congress and President Obama approved a major health-care initiative that had no direct connection to fighting the recession. For many, this act completed the picture of big government out of control. In November 2010, voters swung heavily to the Republicans, granting them control of the House.

Image 1–7 These members of the Tea Party movement in Florida assembled to voice their opposition to "big government." *What are some of the things paid for by our taxes?*

Cheryl Casey/Shutterstock.com

The Partisan Tug of War. From 2011 on, Republicans sought to use their control of the House to obtain leverage over the federal government as a whole. Given that Democrats still held the Senate and the presidency, very little new legislation was adopted. House Republicans also threatened to block the normal functioning of government in an attempt to force cuts in spending. By 2012, for many voters, fears that Republicans would cut valued social programs may have balanced concern over Democratic affection for government. President Obama was reelected in November 2012, but the Democrats were unable to retake the House.

The 2014 elections again favored the Republicans, who gained control of the Senate. One cause was low voter turnout by Democrats. Compared with the average Democrat, the typical Republican was older, wealthier, and more likely to vote. Democrats were encouraged by the changing ethnic makeup of the country, which we discuss later in this chapter. In 2014, however, increased white support for the Republicans counterbalanced the growing number of Democratic Latinos and Asian Americans.

Who Benefits from Big Government? The 2015–2016 election cycle provided new information on popular attitudes toward the size of government. Businessman Donald Trump quickly established himself as the front-runner in the Republican primaries. It soon became clear that neither Trump nor his followers were particularly enamored of traditional small-government conservatism. Trump's supporters had no problems with programs such as Medicare and Social Security that benefited older voters, most of whom were white. They did oppose programs such as Obama's health-care plan that were seen as primarily benefiting poorer Americans in general and minority group members in particular.

The question, in other words, was not so much the size of government but who benefits from big government. The "who benefits" viewpoint had been common among ordinary Tea Party supporters, but that fact was obscured because traditional small-government conservatives soon took control of national Tea Party organizations.[9] The rise of this attitude among Republican voters threatened to create serious complications for small-government conservatives.

Learning Outcome **4:**

Political Ideologies

Discuss conservatism, liberalism, and other popular American ideological positions.

A political **ideology** is a closely linked set of beliefs about politics. The concept of *ideology* is often misunderstood. Many people think that only individuals whose beliefs lie well out on one or the other end of the political spectrum have an ideology. Actually, almost everyone who has political opinions can be said to have an ideology. Some people may have difficulty in explaining the principles that underlie their opinions, but the principles are there nonetheless.

ideology

A comprehensive set of beliefs about the nature of people and about the role of an institution or government.

9. See Theda Skocpol and Vanessa Williamson, *The Tea Party and the Remaking of Republican Conservatism* (New York: Oxford University Press, 2012).

Political ideologies offer people well-organized theories that propose goals for society and the means by which those goals can be achieved. At the core of every political ideology is a set of guiding values. The two ideologies most commonly referred to in discussions of American politics are *conservatism* and *liberalism*.

Conservatism

Over the years, those who favored the ideology of **conservatism** have sought to conserve traditional practices and institutions. In that sense, conservatism is as old as politics itself. In America, limited government is a key tradition. For much of our history, limited government has included major restrictions on government's ability to interfere with business. In the past, enterprises were largely free to act as they pleased in the marketplace and in managing their employees. Government regulation of business increased greatly in the 1930s, as Democratic president Franklin D. Roosevelt (1933–1945) initiated a series of massive interventions in the economy in an attempt to counter the effects of the Great Depression. Many conservatives consider the Roosevelt administration to be a time when America took a wrong turn.

Modern Conservatism. It was in the 1950s, however, that American conservatism took its modern shape. The **conservative movement** that arose in that decade provided the age-old conservative impulse with a fully worked-out ideology. The new movement first demonstrated its strength in 1964, when Senator Barry Goldwater of Arizona was nominated as the Republican presidential candidate. Goldwater lost badly to Democrat Lyndon B. Johnson, but from that time forward *movement conservatives* have occupied a crucial position in the Republican Party.

Conservative Values. American conservatives generally place a high value on the principle of order. This includes support for patriotism and traditional ideals. As a result, conservatives typically oppose such social innovations as same-sex marriage. Conservatives strongly endorse liberty, but they generally define it as freedom from government support of nontraditional ideals such as gay rights or as freedom from government interference in business. Conservatives believe that the private sector probably can outperform the government in almost any activity. Therefore, they usually oppose initiatives that would increase the role of the government in the economy, such as President Obama's health-care reforms. Conservatives place a relatively low value on equality. Believing that individuals and families are primarily responsible for their own well-being, they typically oppose high levels of antipoverty spending and government expenditures to stimulate the economy, favoring tax-rate cuts instead. Trump supporters, with their anti-immigrant, nationalist views, emphasized different aspects of the conservative tradition than those championed by the conservative movement. Still, Trump's followers were clearly conservative in a broad sense.

Liberalism

The term **liberalism** stems from the word *liberty* and originally meant "free from prejudice in favor of traditional opinions and established institutions." Liberals have always been skeptical of the influence of religion in politics, but in the nineteenth century they were skeptical of government as well. From the time of Democratic presidents Woodrow Wilson (1913–1921) and Franklin D. Roosevelt, however, American liberals increasingly

Why should you care about **THE CONSTITUTION?**

To learn more about how government works, consider local legislative bodies. They can have a direct impact on your life. Consider that city councils typically oversee the police department, and the behavior of the police is a matter of interest, even if you live on campus. If you live off campus, local authorities are responsible for an even greater number of issues that affect you directly. For example, are there items that your local sanitation department refuses to pick up? You might be able to change its policies by talking with your councilperson.

conservatism
A set of beliefs that includes a limited role for the national government in helping individuals, support for traditional ideals and life choices, and a cautious response to change.

conservative movement
An American movement in the 1950s that provided a comprehensive ideological framework for conservative politics.

liberalism
A set of beliefs that includes the advocacy of positive government action to improve the welfare of individuals, support for civil rights, and tolerance for political and social change.

Image 1–8 Hillary Clinton campaigns for the Democratic presidential nomination in Bowling Green, Kentucky. *What is her ideology?*

John Sommers II/Getty Images

sought to use the power of government for nontraditional ends. Their goals included support for organized labor and for the poor. New programs instituted by the Roosevelt administration included Social Security and unemployment insurance.

Modern Liberalism. American liberalism took its modern form in the 1960s. Liberals rallied to the civil rights movement, which sought to obtain equal rights for African Americans. As the feminist movement grew in importance, liberals supported it as well. Liberals won new federal health-care programs such as Medicare and Medicaid, and the promotion of such programs became a key component of liberal politics. Finally, liberals reacted more negatively to U.S. participation in the Vietnam War (1965–1975) than did other Americans, and for years thereafter liberalism was associated with skepticism about the use of U.S. military forces abroad.

Liberal Values. Those who favor liberalism place a high value on social and economic equality. As we have seen, liberals champion the rights of minority group members and favor substantial antipoverty spending. In the recent health-care policy debates, liberals strongly endorsed the principle that all citizens should have greater access to insurance. In contrast to conservatives, liberals often support government intervention in the economy. They believe that capitalism works best when the government curbs capitalism's excesses through regulation. Like conservatives, liberals place a high value on liberty, but they tend to view it as the freedom to live one's life according to one's own values. Liberals, therefore, usually support gay rights, often including the right to same-sex marriage. Liberals are an influential force within the Democratic Party.

The Traditional Political Spectrum

A traditional method of comparing political ideologies is to arrange them on a continuum from left to right, based primarily on how much power the government should exercise to promote economic equality. Table 1–1 shows how ideologies can be arrayed on a traditional political spectrum. In addition to liberalism and conservatism, this example includes the ideologies of socialism and libertarianism.

Socialism falls on the left side of the spectrum.[10] Socialists play a minor role in the American political arena, although socialist parties and movements have been important in other countries around the world. In the past, socialists typically advocated replacing investor ownership of major businesses with either government ownership or ownership by employee cooperatives. Socialists believed that such steps would break the power of the very rich and lead to an egalitarian society. In more recent times, socialists in Western Europe have advocated more limited programs that redistribute income.

On the right side of the spectrum is **libertarianism**, a philosophy of skepticism toward most government activities. Libertarians strongly support property rights and typically oppose regulation of the economy and redistribution of income. Libertarians support

socialism

A political ideology based on strong support for economic and social equality. Socialists traditionally envisioned a society in which major businesses were taken over by the government or by employee cooperatives.

libertarianism

A political ideology based on skepticism or opposition toward most government activities.

10. The terms *left* and *right* in the traditional political spectrum originated during the French Revolution, when revolutionary deputies to the Legislative Assembly sat to the left of the assembly president and conservative deputies sat to the right.

Table 1–1 The Traditional Political Spectrum

Which of these platforms are likely to be popular? Why?

	Socialism	Liberalism	Conservatism	Libertarianism
How much power should the government have over the economy?	Active government control over major economic sectors.	Positive government action in the economy.	Positive government action to support capitalism.	Almost no regulation over the economy.
What should the government promote?	Economic equality, community.	Economic security, equal opportunity, social liberty.	Economic liberty, morality, social order.	Total economic and social liberty.

laissez-faire capitalism. (*Laissez faire* is French for "let it be.") Libertarians also tend to oppose government attempts to regulate personal behavior and promote moral values. We might expect, therefore, that a consistent libertarian would support same-sex marriage. Many libertarians are also skeptical about U.S. military interventions abroad.

Problems with the Traditional Political Spectrum

Many political scientists believe that the traditional left-to-right spectrum is not sufficiently complete. Take the example of libertarians. In Table 1–1, libertarians are placed to the right of conservatives. If the only question is how much power the government should have over the economy, this is where they belong. Libertarians, however, strongly advocate freedom in social matters. They oppose government action to promote traditional moral values, although such action is often favored by other groups on the political right. Their strong support for cultural freedoms seems to align them more closely with modern liberals than with conservatives.

Liberalism is often described as an ideology that supports "big government." If the objective is to promote equality, the description has some validity. In the moral sphere, however, conservatives tend to support more government regulation of social values and moral decisions than do liberals. Thus, conservatives tend to oppose gay rights legislation and propose stronger curbs on pornography. Liberals usually show greater tolerance for alternative life choices and oppose government attempts to regulate personal behavior and morals.

A Four-Cornered Ideological Grid

For a more sophisticated breakdown of recent American popular ideologies, many scholars use a four-cornered grid, as shown in Figure 1–1. The grid includes four possible ideologies. Each quadrant contains a substantial portion of the American electorate. Individual voters may fall anywhere on the grid, depending on the strength of their beliefs about economic and cultural issues.

Economic Liberals, Cultural Conservatives. Note that there is no generally accepted term for persons in the lower-left position, which we have labeled "economic liberals, cultural conservatives." Some scholars have used terms such as *populist* to

Figure 1–1 A Four-Cornered Ideological Grid

In this grid, the colored squares represent four different political ideologies. The vertical choices range from cultural order to cultural liberty. The horizontal choices range from economic equality to economic liberty. *Why, in your opinion, have conservatives been so successful in making liberal an unpopular label?*

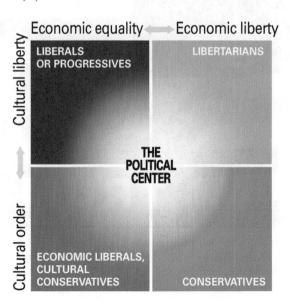

progressive

A popular alternative to the term *liberal.*

describe this point of view, but these terms can be misleading. *Populism* more accurately refers to a hostility toward political, economic, or cultural elites, and it can be combined with a variety of political positions. In the 2016 presidential primary elections, both Donald Trump and Senator Bernie Sanders (D., Vt.) made appeals that could be called populist, though their positions on the issues were radically different.

Individuals who are economic liberals and cultural conservatives tend to support government action both to promote the values of economic equality and fairness and to defend traditional values, such as the family and marriage. These individuals may describe themselves as conservative or moderate. They may vote for a Republican candidate, based on their conservative values. Alternatively, they may be Democrats due to their support for economic liberalism. Many of these Democrats are African Americans or members of other minority groups.

Libertarians. As a position on the four-cornered grid, *libertarians* does not represent the small Libertarian Party, which has only a minor role in the American political arena. Rather, libertarians more typically support the Republican Party. Economically successful individuals are more likely than members of other groups to hold libertarian opinions.

Liberal versus Progressive. Even though all four ideologies are popular, the various labels we have used in the four-cornered grid are not equally favored. Voters are much more likely to describe themselves as conservative than as liberal. In the political battles of the last several decades, the conservative movement has consistently made *liberal* a term of abuse, and they have succeeded in devaluing the term among much of the public. Indeed, few politicians today willingly describe themselves as liberal, and many liberals prefer to describe themselves as **progressive** instead. This term dates back to the years before World War I (1914–1918), when it referred to advocates of reform in both of the major political parties. Public opinion polls suggest that *progressive* is a relatively popular label.

One Nation, Divided

In the past, the ideology of conservatism did not dominate the Republican Party in the way that it does today. Likewise, liberalism was much less tightly linked to the Democrats. Forty years ago, the Republican Party contained a liberal faction that was especially numerous in the northeastern states. Thirty years ago, some of the most ardent conservatives in Congress were Democrats, many of them from the South. Much history lay behind these factions—they represented allegiances dating back to the U.S. Civil War.

In recent decades, however, liberal Republicans have all but vanished. A number of Americans continue to describe themselves as conservative Democrats, but almost none of them serve in Washington, D.C. By 2008, the most conservative Democrats in Congress had voting records that were more liberal than the records of the most moderate Republicans. The major parties no longer exhibited any ideological overlap—progressives and conservatives had sorted themselves completely into opposing political parties.

Image 1–9 Republican presidential candidate Donald Trump speaks in Mesa, Arizona. *Why was he a controversial choice for the Republican nomination?*

Ralph Freso/Getty Images

Partisanship and Polarization. The result has been political polarization. In Congress, the two major political parties have never been more disciplined. Republicans and Democrats have become used to voting as monolithic blocks. Neither progressives nor conservatives trust the intentions of the other camp. In bookstores, among political bloggers on the Internet, and on radio and television, political rhetoric is more intense and furious than it has been in a long time. The other side is not just wrong. It is evil.

Political polarization has resulted in the almost complete inability of Republicans and Democrats in Congress to agree on legislation. Most of the major Democratic initiatives in 2009 and 2010 passed with no Republican votes at all. After the 2010 elections, when the Republicans took the House, the inability of the parties to agree meant political gridlock. In 2011 and 2012, Congress passed 283 bills, the least amount of legislation in the sixty-five years since records were first kept. In 2013 and 2014, the number was 296. Most of this legislation has been trivial. One result of gridlock has been unpopularity. A recent Gallup poll showed that only 7 percent of respondents had confidence in Congress.

Toward the Future. The Republican Party faced some special problems in the 2016 elections. Senators serve for six years, and 2016 fell six years after the election of 2010, which had been unusually favorable to the Republicans. Those Republican senators who won election in Democrat-leaning states in 2010 were now up for reelection, and some were sure to lose. Also, 2016 was a presidential year when young citizens were more likely to vote. Finally, while Democratic presidential candidate Hillary Clinton was not very popular, her likely Republican opponents were less popular still.

In the long run, Democrats hoped to benefit from growing numbers of Latino and Asian American voters. It's also worth noting that younger voters were trending toward the Democrats. In particular, Bernie Sanders, a self-identified socialist, was wildly popular among young Democrats—a promising sign for the liberal cause. For the near future, however, such support was counterbalanced by growing support for Republicans, especially among what has been called the white **working class**. Traditionally, the phrase *working class* was defined by what its members did for a living. In recent years, however, political scientists have begun defining it in terms of education. Thus, persons with no more than a high school diploma are considered to be working class.[11] Since the onset of the Great Depression, many in this group have suffered great economic and social stress. Some have responded by moving to the right, especially toward the nationalist version of conservatism championed by Donald Trump. (Of course, this was not true of the large share of the working class that is African American or Latino.)

The Changing Face of America

Learning Outcome **5:**

Explain how a changing American population and other social trends may affect the future of our nation.

The face of America is changing as its citizens age and become more diverse. Like other economically advanced countries, the United States has in recent decades experienced falling birthrates and an increase in the number of older citizens. The "aging of America" is a modest phenomenon when compared with what is happening in many other countries, however. Today, 14 percent of the U.S. population is age 65 or older. By 2050, this percentage is expected to rise to 22. In Europe, Japan, and China, the share of the elderly is expected to be much greater than that.

working class
Traditionally, individuals or families in which the head of household was employed in manual or unskilled labor. Currently, often defined as those with no more than a high school diploma.

11. Another definition is whether people consider themselves to be working class. In recent public opinion polls, just under half of respondents identify themselves as working class if that is an option in the survey.

total fertility rate

A statistic that measures the average number of children that women in a given group are expected to have over the course of a lifetime.

The End of the Population Explosion

In recent decades, population growth rates have been falling throughout the world. The great population explosion of the late twentieth century is reaching its end—the world's population, currently just over 7 billion, is expected to stabilize at perhaps 10 billion in the later part of the twenty-first century. Population growth rates remain high in many African and Muslim nations, but many economically advanced nations will have smaller populations in 2050 than they do today. The United States, however, will continue to grow during these years.

The number of babies born helps determine future population levels. We can measure this effect by looking at the **total fertility rate** of a population. The total fertility rate measures the average number of children that a group of women are expected to have over the course of a lifetime. In 2007, shortly before the onset of the Great Recession, the United States had a total fertility rate of about 2.1 children per woman. By 2015, the rate had fallen to 1.9. The Census Bureau expects that the rate will go back up again as economic conditions improve, however.

As it happens, a fertility rate of 2.1 is called the "long-term replacement rate." In other words, if a nation maintains a fertility rate of 2.1 over a long period of time, the population of that nation will eventually stabilize—it will neither grow nor shrink. The fact that the U.S. fertility rate has been about 2.1 does not mean that the population of the United States is likely to stabilize any time soon, however. Immigration allows us to grow faster than the fertility rate would suggest. Also, because of past growth, our population is younger than it would otherwise be. This means that there are more potential mothers and fathers. Only after its residents age can the population of a country stabilize.

Ethnic Change in America

From the very beginning, America has been a country of multiple racial and ethnic groups. For much of our history, the most important distinction between groups was between Americans from Europe and Americans from Africa. How to deal with the institution of African slavery—abolished following the American Civil War—was perhaps the most important issue the nation has ever faced.

African Americans. Figure 1–2 shows the distribution of the African American population today. Beginning in the 1920s, many African Americans moved north to seek

Figure 1–2 The African American Population in the United States

What effect might the share of African Americans in a state's population have on its politics?

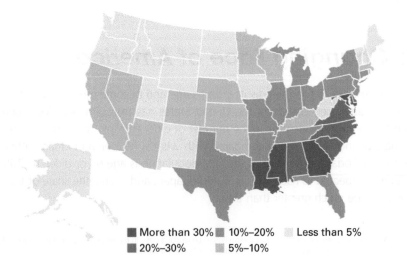

■ More than 30%　■ 10%–20%　　Less than 5%
■ 20%–30%　　■ 5%–10%

economic opportunity and better conditions. Even today, however, a majority of African Americans live in the southern states where slavery was once legal.

The Rise of the Latinos. In recent decades, the number of Latino—or Hispanic—Americans has grown substantially, to the point where they are now the largest minority group in the nation. Many new immigrants are Latino, and this also serves to increase the Latino population.

A word on terminology: the U.S. Bureau of the Census defines a **Hispanic** as someone who can claim a heritage from a Spanish-speaking country. Hispanics can be of any race. Because the federal government uses *Hispanic*, we take note of it. An alternative term, **Latino** (*Latina* in the feminine), is widely used by social scientists. Public opinion polls, however, indicate that both words are about equally popular among Hispanics/Latinos. Therefore, we use both in this text.

Of the four largest groups of Latinos, Mexican Americans are the largest at 64.1 percent of all Latinos. Puerto Ricans, all of whom are U.S. citizens, are 9.5 percent of the total. Salvadorans make up 3.7 percent, and Cuban Americans 3.7 percent. Coming from so many countries, Latino Americans are a highly diverse population. Most prefer a name that identifies their heritage specifically—Mexican Americans would often rather be called that than Latino or Hispanic.

Figure 1–3 shows the current distribution of the Latino population. The black line on the map is the northern border of Mexico before 1836, when Texas declared its independence from Mexico. Latinos in eastern states such as New Jersey and Florida are often from Puerto Rico or Cuba.

The Demographic Impact. As a result of differences in fertility rates and immigration, the ethnic character of the United States is changing. In 2007, non-Hispanic white Americans had a fertility rate of 1.9. African Americans had a fertility rate of 2.1. Latinos had a rate of 2.8. By 2014, these rates had fallen—non-Hispanic white Americans to 1.8, African Americans to 2.0, and Latinos to 2.4. As we noted earlier, the Census Bureau assumes that the low current rates will be temporary. Figure 1–4 shows the projected changes in the U.S. ethnic distribution in future years based on Census Bureau predictions.

Hispanic

A term used by the federal government to describe someone who can claim a heritage from a Spanish-speaking country.

Latino

An alternate word for *Hispanic*. The feminine is *Latina*.

Figure 1–3 The Latino Population in the United States

Non-Hispanic whites are expected to be a minority in Texas years before they become a minority in the nation as a whole. The black line shows the northern border of Mexico before 1836. *What might be the consequences of such a development?*

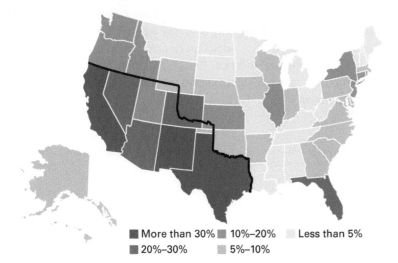

■ More than 30% ■ 10%–20% ☐ Less than 5%
■ 20%–30% ☐ 5%–10%

Figure 1–4 Projected Changes in U.S. Ethnic Distribution

What political changes could result when non-Hispanic whites are no longer a majority of the U.S. population?

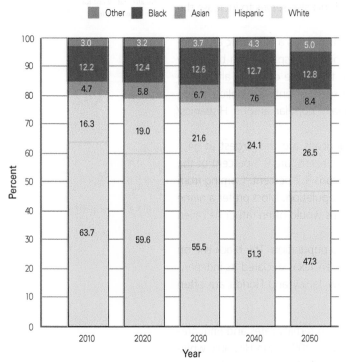

Data for 2010 are from the 2010 census. Data for 2020 through 2050 are Census Bureau projections.

Hispanics (Latinos) may be of any race. The chart categories *White, Black, Asian,* and *Other* are limited to non-Hispanics. *Other* consists of the following non-Hispanic groups: *American Indian, Native Alaskan, Native Hawaiian, Other Pacific Islander,* and *Two or more races.*

Sources: U.S. Bureau of the Census and author's calculations.

Are We Better Off?

Are we better off today than we were in the recent past? That question is not easy to answer. Certainly, the nation as a whole is richer today than it ever has been. Not everyone has benefited from this increased wealth, however. From 1979 to 2015, weekly earnings, corrected for inflation, rose only 3 percent for the median worker. In contrast, economist Emmanuel Saez estimates that between 2009 and 2014, the top 1 percent of earners captured 58 percent of total income growth.[12] Levels of employment have not recovered from the blow they took during the Great Recession, as shown in this chapter's *Consider the Source* feature.

Social Indicators. Statistics suggest that many trends are moving in a positive direction—although some are not. First, the good news. The murder rate per 100,000 persons, which peaked at 10.2 in 1980, was down to 4.5 in 2014, almost an all-time low. Acts of sexual violence committed against women were 5.0 per 1,000 females in 1995, but 2.2 in 2014. Divorces peaked in 1981 at 5.3 per 1,000 people, but were down to 3.2 by 2014. Births to teen-aged mothers were 62 per thousand female teens in 1991, but 24 in 2014. Automobile accident deaths, use of tobacco, high school graduation rates—these and more are headed in a positive direction. Despite concerns about inequality, unemployment, and high levels of debt, it appears that American youth in particular are much better behaved than in earlier generations.

Other statistics, however, suggest that many Americans are in trouble. All over the world, death rates are falling. In the United States, death rates have fallen among African Americans and Latinos. From 1990 to 2014, however, the death rate for white women age 35 to 39 living in rural areas has risen by 48 percent. Other white female age groups have also posted startling rises. Death rates among rural white men are up as well. This catastrophe does not appear to affect whites who have college degrees or who live in large urban areas. The increased mortality is largely driven by excessive drug and alcohol consumption and by suicide. In fact, addiction to prescription opioids and to heroin has grown dramatically in white rural America. This crisis suggests that an epidemic of cultural despair is afflicting the rural white working class. U.S. politicians have not even begun to grapple with this problem.

12. Emmanuel Saez, "Striking It Richer: The Evolution of Top Incomes in the United States," updated with 2014 preliminary estimates, eml.berkeley.edu/~saez/saez-UStopincomes-2014.pdf.

Consider the source

How Many Americans Have Jobs?

One of the most important ways in which people are integrated into society and gain a sense of self-worth is to have a job. Women have entered the labor force in ever-larger numbers in recent decades. As a result, the share of prime-age (age 25 to 55) Americans with jobs was greater in 2000 than ever before in our nation's history. Since then, the employment picture has not been so bright. Figure 1–5 shows employment trends in recent decades.

The Source: Federal Reserve Economic Data (FRED)

The *Federal Reserve,* often simply called the "Fed," is the government agency that, among other things, is responsible for the nation's money supply. Fed staff members also engage in economic research. As a service to researchers everywhere, the Federal Reserve Bank of St. Louis, Missouri, has created an economic database called FRED.

You can find this service through an Internet search engine such as Google. Simply enter "fred," and FRED should appear at the top of the resulting page. Click on FRED, and you'll discover that it lets you graph and download any of 385,000 U.S. and world data sets. These include information not only about employment, but also about the cost of living, the size of the economy, the government's debt, interest rates, and much more. FRED collected the data in Figure 1–5 from the Organization for Economic Cooperation and Development (OECD).

For Critical Analysis

▶ Why do you think that the employment rate for males is always greater than that for females, as shown in Figure 1–5?

Figure 1–5 Employment Rate for Prime-Age Americans, 1990 to 2013

What might people do when they have been unemployed for a long time?

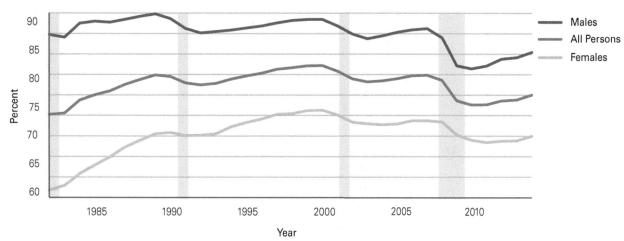

Shaded areas indicate U.S. recessions.

Source: Federal Reserve Economic Data (FRED); Organisation for Economic Cooperation and Development.

How you can make a difference

If you want to affect our democracy, you have to learn firsthand how a democratic government works. The easiest way is to attend a session of a local legislative body.

- To do so, call the clerk of your local city council or county commission. Find out when the next city council or county board meeting is.

- If you live in a state capital, such as Baton Rouge, Louisiana, or Santa Fe, New Mexico, you can view a meeting of the state legislature instead.

- In many communities, city council meetings and county board meetings can be seen on public-access TV channels.

- When attending a business session of the local council or commission, keep in mind the theory of representative democracy. The commissioners or council members are elected to represent their constituents. Observe how often the members refer to their constituents or to the special needs of their communities.

- Listen for sources of conflict. If, for example, there is a debate over a zoning proposal that involves the issue of land use, try to figure out why some members oppose the proposal.

- If you want to follow up on your visit, try to get a brief interview with one of the members of the council or board. In general, legislators are very willing to talk to students, particularly students who also are voters.

- Ask the member how he or she sees the job of representative. How can the wishes of constituents be identified? How does the representative balance the needs of the particular ward or district that she or he represents with the good of the entire community?

KEY TERMS

CHAPTER SUMMARY

Learning Outcome 1 Politics is the process by which people decide which members of society receive certain benefits or privileges and which members do not. It is the struggle over power or influence within institutions or organizations that can grant benefits or privileges. Government is an institution within which decisions are made that resolve conflicts and allocate benefits and privileges. It is the predominant institution within society because it has the ultimate decision-making authority.

Two fundamental political values are order, which includes security against violence, and liberty, the greatest freedom of the individual consistent with the freedom of other individuals. To be effective, government authority must be backed by legitimacy.

Learning Outcome 2 Many of our terms for describing forms of government came from the ancient Greeks. In a direct democracy, such as in ancient Athens, the people themselves make the important political decisions. The United States is a democratic republic, also called a representative democracy, in which the people elect representatives to make the decisions. Theories of American democracy include majoritarianism, in which the government does what the majority wants; elite theory, in which the real power lies with one or more elite groups; and pluralism, in which organized interest groups contend for power.

Learning Outcome 3 Fundamental American values include liberty, order, equality, and property. Not all of these values are fully compatible. The value of order often competes with civil liberties, and economic equality competes with property rights.

Learning Outcome 4 Popular political ideologies can be arrayed from left (liberal) to right (conservative). We can also analyze economic liberalism and conservatism separately from cultural liberalism and conservatism.

Learning Outcome 5 Population growth in the United States is slowing. By 2050, it is estimated that non-Latino whites will be a minority of the total population. Despite concerns about inequality and unemployment, many social indicators, such as crime rates, have improved in recent years. An increase in death rates among rural whites, however, is a cause for concern.

ADDITIONAL RESOURCES

The Pew Research Center asks, "Are you a Solid Liberal? A Steadfast Conservative? Or somewhere in between?" You may have a good sense of your personal political ideology. Then again, you may not. Pew has a "Political Typology Quiz" that you can locate by searching for that term in your browser. Take the quiz to find out how Pew classifies your politics. Alternatively, your instructor can set it up so that your entire class can take the quiz together (see "help political typology quiz"). If your class takes the test, responses of individual students are anonymous.

Online Resources

The Internet has become a vehicle to improve your understanding of any academic subject. A word of caution about political sites: not all of them care about accuracy. Many are interested only in providing ammunition for use in debates, regardless of whether the statements are true or not. You will need to use judgment when surfing the Internet for political resources.

- To find out more about conservative politics in the United States, try **www.facebook.com/nationalreview**. You'll see posts by the staff of *National Review*, a conservative magazine.

- To learn more about liberal politics, visit **twitter.com/thenation**. You'll see tweets by the staff of *The Nation*, a liberal publication.

- The Internet is a good place to learn about political science as a profession. Try visiting the site of the American Political Science Association at **www.apsanet.org**.

Books

Fukuyama, Francis. *Political Order and Political Decay: From the Industrial Revolution to the Globalization of Democracy.* New York: Farrar, Straus and Giroux, 2015. Fukuyama, a well-known political theorist, analyzes what makes modern governments successful—and how they can fail.

Judis, John B. *The Populist Explosion: How the Great Recession Transformed American and European Politics.* New York: Columbia Global Reports, 2016. Judis, a seasoned political journalist, argues that economic stresses have led to a worldwide growth in conservative nationalism, represented in the United States by Donald Trump.

Tierney, John J., Jr. *Conceived in Liberty: The American Worldview in Theory and Practice.* Piscataway, New Jersey: Transaction Publishers, 2016. Tierney, a professor at the Institute of World Politics in Washington, D.C., contends that liberty is the foundational American value, from which other values flow.

Video

American Feud: A History of Conservatives and Liberals—Directed by Richard Hall, this 2008 documentary explores popular American ideologies through interviews with leading political commentators.

The Other Side of Immigration—This highly acclaimed 2010 documentary seeks to understand why so many Mexicans wish to come to the United States by interviewing both immigrants and those who are left behind in Mexico.

Quiz

Multiple Choice and Fill-Ins

Learning Outcome 1 Define the terms *politics, government, order, liberty, authority,* and *legitimacy.*

1. When citizens of a nation do not enjoy liberty, the government frequently will:
   a. abolish the right to a fair trial.
   b. provide government funds to churches.
   c. hold regular elections.

2. When authority is broadly accepted, we say that it has _____.

Learning Outcome 2 Distinguish the major features of direct democracy and representative democracy, and describe majoritarianism, elite theory, and pluralism.

3. A democratic republic is based on all of the following principles except:
   a. popular sovereignty.
   b. majority rule.
   c. unlimited government.

4. _____ theory describes our democratic system in terms of competition among groups.

Learning Outcome 3 Summarize the conflicts that can occur between the principles of liberty and order, and between those of liberty and equality.

5. A major theme of American politics during the twenty-first century has been:
   a. arguments over whether all citizens should have the right to vote.
   b. controversies over the proper size of government.
   c. disputes as to whether the government should assume the ownership of major banks.

6. Under _____, property consists not only of personal possessions but also of wealth-creating assets.

Learning Outcome 4 Discuss conservatism, liberalism, and other popular American ideological positions.

7. Popular American ideologies include:
   a. conservatism, liberalism, and libertarianism.
   b. conservatism, liberalism, and socialism.
   c. communism, liberalism, and libertarianism.

8. A common term that has come to replace liberalism in current American politics is _____.

Learning Outcome 5 Explain how a changing American population and other social trends may affect the future of our nation.

9. Most immigrants who are now in this country come from:
   a. Europe.
   b. Africa.
   c. Latin America (especially Mexico) and Asia.

10. In terms of race, Latinos _____ .

Essay Questions

1. In Australia and Belgium, citizens are legally required to vote in elections. Would such a requirement be a good idea in the United States? What changes might take place if such a rule were in effect?

2. In your own life, what factors have contributed to your political socialization? To what extent were your political values shaped by your family, by school experiences, by friends, and by the media?

THE CONSTITUTION

The façade of the National Constitution Center in Philadelphia on September 13, 2012. On that day, the world-renowned boxer and civil rights leader Muhammad Ali was presented with the Liberty Medal. Ali died in June 2016. *Why was he so widely loved?*
Mark Makela/Getty Images

These five **LEARNING OUTCOMES** *below are designed to help improve your understanding of this chapter:*

1: Explain how the colonial experience prepared Americans for independence, the restrictions that Britain placed on the colonies, and the American response.

2: Describe the significance of the Declaration of Independence and the Articles of Confederation, as well as the weaknesses of the Articles.

3: Discuss the most important compromises reached at the Constitutional Convention and the basic structure of the resulting government.

4: Summarize the arguments in favor of and the arguments against adopting the Constitution, and explain why the Bill of Rights was adopted.

5: Describe the process of amending the Constitution and the informal ways in which Constitutional interpretation has changed over time.

What if...

The Founders Adopted a Parliamentary System?

Background

In Chapter 1, in the section "A Democratic Republic," we observed that the authors of the U.S. Constitution sought to keep the people from choosing the president through an *electoral college.* The various states choose *electors,* and then the electors choose the president. In short order, however, most would-be electors were publicly pledged to specific presidential hopefuls. The scheme to keep the public from picking the president therefore failed.

A second goal of the electoral college was a success, however—it kept the choice of the chief executive out of the hands of Congress. This arrangement was a major part of James Madison's plan to divide the powers of government among multiple branches. Today, most Americans would consider it an infringement of their rights if Congress, not the voters, chose the chief executive. In many democratic countries, however, the legislature does exactly that. Such nations have parliamentary systems. Almost all European nations have such a system. What would the American government have been like if the founders had adopted a parliamentary system?

What If the Founders Adopted a Parliamentary System?

If the founders had based the Constitution on one of the initial proposals at the Constitutional Convention, such as the Virginia Plan, the United States might have ended up with a parliamentary system. These initial proposals called for an executive elected by Congress.

In a *parliamentary system*, the people in each district elect one or more members of parliament. Often, voters can choose among candidates from several parties. Following the election, the largest party or coalition of parties names an executive team—the cabinet—led by a prime minister, premier, or chancellor. The cabinet takes office when it wins a vote in the lower house of parliament. If at any point the prime minister and cabinet lose the support of the lower house, they are out. If an alternative coalition cannot be formed, an election is called on short notice.

In other words, the executive serves at the pleasure of the lower house. If a majority of

house members become dissatisfied with the executive, that majority can vote the executive out of office on short notice. If an alternative executive team cannot be formed, a new election may be necessary.

Effective versus Limited Government

One obvious consequence of a parliamentary system is that the executive and the majority of the lower house must be of the same party or coalition of parties. True, many parliamentary systems have an upper house or senate, which can complicate matters. In most countries, however, the powers of the upper house are limited. As a result, the executive has little difficulty in passing its programs. The executive has few restraints on what it can do—a state of affairs known as *effective government.*

Our system, in contrast, promotes *limited government.* Various powers within the government have the ability to prevent action. A law can be blocked in the Senate or the House of Representatives. If it passes, it can be vetoed by the president or ruled unconstitutional by the United States Supreme Court. In short, the political gridlock that marks our politics today is no accident. The founders deliberately sought to make it more likely.

One feature of a parliamentary system can make gridlock possible. As noted, a parliamentary system encourages multiple political parties. For example, the British House of Commons contains four major parties and a few small ones. What if no party or coalition has a majority? After a recent election, the Chamber of Representatives in Belgium contained eleven parties. It took 589 days to settle on a permanent executive—a world record.

For Critical Analysis

◗ How might your vote for the U.S. House of Representatives change if you knew that you were simultaneously voting for a national executive leader?

◗ If the House always chose the executive, what effect would that have on the role of the U.S. Senate?

Image 2–1 James Madison (1751–1836) has been called the "master builder of the Constitution." *Why did Madison want to keep Congress from choosing the president?*

We the People of the United States, in Order to form a more perfect Union, establish Justice, insure domestic Tranquility, provide for the common defence, promote the general Welfare, and secure the Blessings of Liberty to ourselves and our Posterity, do ordain and establish this Constitution for the United States of America.

Every schoolchild in America has at one time or another been exposed to these famous words from the Preamble to the U.S. Constitution. The document itself is remarkable. The U.S. Constitution, compared with others in the fifty states and in the world, is relatively short. Because amending it is difficult, it also has relatively few amendments. The Constitution has remained largely intact for more than two hundred years. To a great extent, this is because the principles set forth in the Constitution are sufficiently broad that they can be adapted to meet the needs of a changing society.

How and why the U.S. Constitution was created is a story that has been told and retold. It is worth repeating, because knowing the historical and political context in which this country's governmental machinery was formed is essential to understanding American government and politics today. The Constitution did not result just from creative thinking. Many of its provisions were grounded in the political philosophy of the time.

The delegates to the Constitutional Convention in 1787 brought with them two important sets of influences: their political culture and their political experience. In the years between the first settlements in the New World and the writing of the Constitution, Americans had developed a political philosophy about how people should be governed and had tried out several forms of government. These experiences gave the founders the tools with which they constructed the Constitution—a document that was unique in the world both then and now, as you can see from this chapter's opening *What If . . .* feature.

The Colonial Background

In 1607, a company chartered by the English government sent a group of settlers to establish a trading post, Jamestown, in what is now Virginia. Jamestown was the first permanent English colony in the Americas. The king of England gave the backers of this colony a charter granting them "full power and authority" to make laws "for the good and welfare" of the settlement. The colonists at Jamestown instituted a **representative assembly,** a legislature composed of individuals who represented the population, thus setting a precedent in government that was to be observed in later colonial adventures.

Separatists, the *Mayflower*, and the Compact

The first New England colony was established in 1620. A group made up in large part of Separatists, who wished to break with the Church of England, came over on the ship *Mayflower* to the New World, landing at Plymouth (Massachusetts). Before going onshore, the adult males—women were not considered to have any political status—drew up the Mayflower Compact, which was signed by forty-one of the forty-four men aboard the ship on November 11, 1620.

The reason for the compact was obvious. This group was outside the jurisdiction of the Virginia Company of London, which had chartered its settlement. The Separatist leaders feared that some of the *Mayflower* passengers might conclude that they were no longer under any obligations of civil obedience. Therefore, some form of public authority was imperative. As William Bradford (one of the Separatist leaders) recalled in his accounts,

Learning Outcome 1:

Explain how the colonial experience prepared Americans for independence, the restrictions that Britain placed on the colonies, and the American response.

representative assembly
A legislature composed of individuals who represent the population.

The Granger Collection, NYC

Image 2–2 In 1620, the Mayflower Compact was signed by almost all of the men aboard the *Mayflower* just before they disembarked at Plymouth, Massachusetts. *Was it a constitution? Why or why not?*

there were "discontented and mutinous speeches that some of the strangers [non-Separatists] amongst them had let fall from them in the ship; That when they came ashore they would use their own liberty; for none had power to command them."[1]

The Significance of the Compact. The compact was not a constitution. It was a political statement in which the signers agreed to create and submit to the authority of a government, pending the receipt of a royal charter. The Mayflower Compact's historical and political significance is twofold: it depended on the consent of the affected individuals (and thus served as an example of popular sovereignty), and it served as a prototype for similar compacts in American history.

By the time of the American Revolution, the compact was well on its way toward achieving mythic status. In 1802, John Quincy Adams, son of the second American president, spoke these words at a founders' day celebration in Plymouth: "This is perhaps the only instance in human history of that positive, original social compact, which speculative philosophers have imagined as the only legitimate source of government."[2]

Pilgrim Beliefs. Although the Plymouth settlers committed themselves to self-government, in other ways their political ideas were not those that are prevalent today. The new community was a religious colony. Separation of church and state and most of our modern civil liberties were alien to the settlers' thinking. By the time the U.S. Constitution was written, the nation's leaders had a very different vision of the relationship between religion and government. We look at some of the founders' beliefs in this chapter's *Which Side Are You On?* feature.

More Colonies, More Government

Another outpost in New England was set up by the Massachusetts Bay Colony in 1630. Then followed Rhode Island, Connecticut, New Hampshire, and others. By 1732, the last of the thirteen colonies, Georgia, was established. During the colonial period, Americans developed a concept of limited government, which followed from the establishment of the first colonies under Crown charters. Theoretically, London governed the colonies. In practice, owing partly to the colonies' distance from London, the colonists exercised a large measure of self-government.

The colonists were able to make their own laws—for example, the Fundamental Orders of Connecticut in 1639. The Massachusetts Body of Liberties in 1641 supported the protection of individual rights. In 1682, the Frame of Government of Pennsylvania was passed. Along with the Pennsylvania Charter of Privileges of 1701, it foreshadowed our modern Constitution and Bill of Rights. All of this legislation enabled the colonists to acquire crucial political experience. After independence was declared in 1776, the states quickly set up their own new constitutions.

1. Nathaniel Philbrick, *Mayflower: A Story of Courage, Community, and War* (New York: Penguin, 2007), p. 37.

2. Ibid., p. 352. Today, the Mayflower Separatists are frequently referred to as the Pilgrims, but that name did not come into common use until two centuries after the colony was founded.

Which side are you on?

Should the United States Be a Christian Nation?

Christianity utterly permeated the world of the first English settlers in America. Founded as religious settlements, the New England colonies had theocratic tendencies. North and South, church attendance was often mandatory. Nine colonies had churches that were established by law.

The Declaration of Independence, however, makes no reference to Christ. The word *God* does not appear in the Constitution. By 1790, officially established churches were found only in Connecticut and Massachusetts, and the Congregational Church in Massachusetts had drifted so far from its Puritan origins that many of its members no longer accepted the divinity of Jesus. That is, they belonged to *Unitarian* congregations. One result of this development was that in the national elections of 1796 and 1800, neither major party fielded a presidential candidate who was, by modern definition, a Christian. John Adams, Unitarian, squared off against Thomas Jefferson, freethinker.

These facts raise the question: Just how Christian were the founders? More to the point, did the founders intend the United States to be a "Christian nation"? Scholars and school boards often differ on these issues.

One Nation, Under God

Christian conservatives point out that numerous American leaders throughout history have characterized the country as a Christian nation. The revolutionaries of 1776 often viewed the struggle in religious terms. Quite a few believed that God had a special plan for America to serve as an example to the world. The overwhelming majority of the colonists considered themselves Christians. Today, 71 percent of Americans identify themselves as such. If the term *Christian nation* merely identifies the beliefs of the majority, it is undeniably an accurate label.

To Christian conservatives who would like to change what is taught in the schools, however, the term means much more. They contend that American law is based on the laws of Moses as set down in the Bible. They also believe that America's divine mission is not just an opinion held by many people—it should be taught as literal truth. Finally, this group argues that "freedom *of* religion does not mean freedom *from* religion." The language of the First Amendment means only that the national government should not prefer one church over another.

Church and Government Must Not Mix

Mainstream scholars disagree with the previous arguments, often vehemently. For example, researchers have been unable to find American court cases that reference the laws of Moses. Ultimately, these people say, to argue that the founders were not serious about the separation of church and state is to ignore the plain language of the Constitution. True, most of the authors of the Constitution were Christians, but the founders were also steeped in *Enlightenment rationalism*. Enlightenment figures such as England's John Locke (1632–1704), France's Voltaire (1694–1778), and Scotland's Adam Smith (1723–1790) emphasized reason and individualism rather than tradition. Enlightenment thinking also rejected "enthusiasm" in religion. *Enthusiasm* referred to the spirit that allowed Protestant and Catholic Europeans to kill one another in the name of God over a period of two centuries. For the founders, mixing church and government was a recipe for trouble.

For Critical Analysis

◗ Today, candidates for president clearly benefit when they use religious language and when they are comfortable discussing their faith. Is this at all troubling? Why or why not?

British Restrictions and Colonial Reactions

The conflict between Britain and the American colonies, which ultimately led to the Revolutionary War, began in the 1760s when the British government decided to raise revenues by imposing taxes on the American colonies. Policy advisers to Britain's King George III, who ascended to the throne in 1760, decided that it was only logical to require the

Image 2–3 The minutemen were members of a colonial militia that was ready to fight the British at a moment's notice. *In what ways might a local militia be less effective than an actual army in combating the British?*

American colonists to help pay the costs of Britain's defending them during the French and Indian War (1754–1763). The colonists, who had grown accustomed to a large degree of self-government and independence from the British Crown, viewed the matter differently.

In 1764, the British Parliament passed the Sugar Act, which imposed a tax that many colonists were unwilling to pay. Further legislation was to come. In 1765, Parliament passed the Stamp Act, providing for internal taxation of legal documents and even newspapers. The colonists' Stamp Act Congress, assembled in 1765, called this act "taxation without representation." The colonists boycotted the purchase of English commodities in response.

The success of the boycott (the Stamp Act was repealed a year later) generated a feeling of unity within the colonies. The British, however, continued to try to raise revenues from the colonies. When Parliament passed duties on glass, lead, paint, and other items in 1767, the colonists again boycotted British goods. The colonists' fury over taxation climaxed in the Boston Tea Party: colonists dressed as Mohawk Indians dumped almost 350 chests of British tea into Boston Harbor as a gesture of tax protest. In retaliation, Parliament passed the Coercive Acts (the "Intolerable Acts") in 1774, which closed Boston Harbor and placed the government of Massachusetts under direct British control. The colonists were outraged—and they responded.

The First Continental Congress

New York, Pennsylvania, and Rhode Island proposed a colonial gathering, or congress. The Massachusetts House of Representatives requested that all colonies hold conventions to select delegates to be sent to Philadelphia for such a congress.

The First Continental Congress was held at Carpenters' Hall in Philadelphia on September 5, 1774. It was a gathering of delegates from twelve of the thirteen colonies (delegates from Georgia did not attend until 1775). At that meeting, there was little talk of independence. The congress passed a resolution requesting that the colonies send a petition to King George III expressing their grievances. Resolutions were also passed requiring that the colonies raise their own colonial militias and boycott British trade. The British government condemned the congress's actions, treating them as open acts of rebellion.

The Second Continental Congress

By the time the Second Continental Congress met in May 1775 (all of the colonies were represented this time), fighting already had broken out between the British and the colonists. One of the main actions of the Second Continental Congress was to establish an army. It did this by declaring the militia that had gathered around Boston an army and naming George Washington as commander in chief. Congressional participants still attempted to reach a peaceful settlement with the British Parliament. One declaration of the congress stated explicitly that "we have not raised armies with ambitious designs of separating from Great Britain, and establishing independent states." But by the beginning of 1776, military encounters had become increasingly frequent.

Public debate was acrimonious. Then Thomas Paine's *Common Sense* appeared in Philadelphia bookstores. The pamphlet was a colonial best seller. (To do relatively as well today, a book would have to sell between 9 million and 11 million copies in its first year of publication.) Many agreed that Paine did make common sense when he argued that

> *a government of our own is our natural right: and when a man seriously reflects on the precariousness* [instability, unpredictability] *of human affairs, he will become convinced, that it is infinitely wiser and safer, to form a constitution of our own in a cool and deliberate manner, while we have it in our power, than to trust such an interesting event to time and chance.*[3]

Paine further argued that "nothing can settle our affairs so expeditiously as an open and determined declaration for Independence."[4]

Students of Paine's pamphlet point out that his arguments were not new—they were common in tavern debates throughout the land. Rather, it was the near poetry of his words—which were at the same time as plain as the alphabet—that struck his readers.

An Independent Confederation

On April 6, 1776, the Second Continental Congress voted for free trade at all American ports with all countries except Britain. This act could be interpreted as an implicit declaration of independence. The next month, the congress suggested that each of the colonies establish state governments unconnected to Britain. Finally, in July, the colonists declared their independence from Britain.

The Resolution for Independence

On July 2, the Resolution for Independence was adopted by the Second Continental Congress:

> *RESOLVED, That these United Colonies are, and of right ought to be, free and independent States, that they are absolved from allegiance to the British Crown, and that all political connection between them and the state of Great Britain is, and ought to be, totally dissolved.*

In June 1776, Thomas Jefferson already was writing drafts of the Declaration of Independence. When the Resolution for Independence was adopted on July 2, Jefferson argued that a declaration clearly putting forth the causes that compelled the colonies to separate from Britain was necessary. The Second Continental Congress assigned the task to him.

July 4, 1776—The Declaration of Independence

Jefferson's version of the Declaration was amended to gain unanimous acceptance (for example, his condemnation of the slave trade was eliminated to satisfy Georgia and North Carolina), but the bulk of it was passed intact on July 4, 1776. On July 19, the modified draft became "the unanimous declaration of the thirteen United States of America." On August 2, it was signed by the members of the Second Continental Congress.

---

3. *The Political Writings of Thomas Paine*, Vol. 1 (Boston: J. P. Mendum Investigator Office, 1870), p. 46.
4. *Ibid.*, p. 54.

Milestones in Early U.S. Political History

1607	Jamestown established; Virginia Company lands settlers.
1620	Mayflower Compact signed.
1630	Massachusetts Bay Colony set up.
1639	Fundamental Orders of Connecticut adopted.
1641	Massachusetts Body of Liberties adopted.
1682	Pennsylvania Frame of Government passed.
1701	Pennsylvania Charter of Privileges written.
1732	Last of the thirteen colonies (Georgia) established.
1754	French and Indian War begins.
1765	Stamp Act; Stamp Act Congress meets.
1774	First Continental Congress.
1775	Second Continental Congress; Revolutionary War begins.
1776	Declaration of Independence signed.
1777	Articles of Confederation drafted.
1781	Last state (Maryland) signs Articles of Confederation.
1783	"Critical period" in U.S. history begins; weak national government until 1789.
1786	Shays' Rebellion.
1787	Constitutional Convention.
1788	Ratification of Constitution.
1791	Ratification of Bill of Rights.

Describe the significance of the Declaration of Independence and the Articles of Confederation, as well as the weaknesses of the Articles.

Universal Truths. The Declaration of Independence has become one of the world's most famous and significant documents. The words opening the second paragraph of the Declaration indicate why this is so:

> *We hold these Truths to be self-evident, that all Men are created equal, that they are endowed by their Creator with certain unalienable Rights, that among these are Life, Liberty, and the Pursuit of Happiness—That to secure these Rights, Governments are instituted among Men, deriving their just Powers from the Consent of the Governed, that whenever any Form of Government becomes destructive of these Ends, it is the Right of the People to alter or abolish it, and to institute new Government.*

Natural Rights and Social Contracts. The statement that "all Men are created equal" and have **natural rights** ("unalienable Rights"), including the rights to "Life, Liberty, and the Pursuit of Happiness," was revolutionary at that time. Its use by Jefferson reveals the influence of the English philosopher John Locke (1632–1704), whose writings were familiar to educated American colonists, including Jefferson. In his *Two Treatises of Government,* published in 1690, Locke had argued that all people possess certain natural rights, including the rights to life, liberty, and property. This claim was not inconsistent with English legal traditions.

Locke went on to argue, however, that the primary purpose of government was to protect these rights. Furthermore, government was established by the people through a **social contract**—an agreement among the people to form a government and abide by its rules. As you read earlier, such contracts, or compacts, were not new to Americans. The Mayflower Compact was the first of several documents that established governments or governing rules based on the consent of the governed.

After setting forth these basic principles of government, the Declaration of Independence goes on to justify the colonists' revolt against Britain. Much of the remainder of the document is a list of what "He" (King George III) had done to deprive the colonists of their rights. (See Appendix A at the end of this book for the complete text of the Declaration of Independence.)

natural rights

Rights held to be inherent in natural law, not dependent on governments. John Locke stated that natural law, being superior to human law, specifies certain rights of "life, liberty, and property."

social contract

A voluntary agreement among individuals to secure their rights and welfare by creating a government and abiding by its rules.

The Significance of the Declaration. The concepts of equality, natural rights, and government established through a social contract were to have a lasting impact on American life. The Declaration of Independence set forth ideals that have since become a fundamental part of our national identity. The Declaration also became a model for use by other nations around the world.

Certainly, most Americans are familiar with the beginning words of the Declaration. Yet few Americans ponder the obvious question: What did these assertions in the Declaration have to do with independence? Clearly, independence could have been declared without these words. Even as late as 1857, Abraham Lincoln admitted, "The

Image 2–4 Benjamin Franklin (left) sits with John Adams while Thomas Jefferson looks on during a meeting outside the Second Continental Congress. *What important document came out of that congress?*

The Granger Collection, NYC

assertion that 'all men are created equal' was of no practical use in effecting our separation from Great Britain; and it was placed in the Declaration, not for that, but for future use."[5]

Essentially, the immediate significance of the Declaration of Independence, in 1776, was that it established the legitimacy of the new nation in the eyes of the colonists themselves. In addition, the Declaration made it possible for foreign governments to recognize the United States as an independent nation. What the new nation needed most were supplies for its armies and a commitment of foreign military aid. Unless it appeared to the world as a political entity separate and independent from Britain, no foreign government would enter into an agreement with its leaders. In fact, foreign support was crucial to the success of the revolution.

The Rise of Republicanism

Although the colonists had formally declared independence from Britain, the fight to gain actual independence continued for five more years, until the British general Charles Cornwallis surrendered at Yorktown in 1781. In 1783, after Britain formally recognized the independent status of the United States in the Treaty of Paris, Washington disbanded the army. During these years of military struggles, the states faced the additional challenge of creating a system of self-government for an independent United States.

Some colonists had demanded that independence be preceded by the formation of a strong central government. But others, who called themselves Republicans (not to be confused with today's Republican Party), were against a strong central government. They opposed monarchy, executive authority, and almost any form of restraint on the power of local groups.

These Republicans, although not organized as a political party, were still a major political force from 1776 to 1780. Indeed, they almost prevented victory over the British by their unwillingness to cooperate with any central authority.

During this time, all of the states adopted written constitutions. Eleven of the constitutions were completely new. Two of them—those of Connecticut and Rhode Island—were old royal charters with minor modifications. In most states, republican sentiment led to increased power for the state legislatures. In Georgia and Pennsylvania, **unicameral** (one-body) **legislatures** were unchecked by executive or judicial authority. In almost all states, the legislature was predominant.

The Articles of Confederation: Our First Form of Government

The fear of a powerful central government led to the passage of the Articles of Confederation, which created a weak central government. The term **confederation** is important. It means a voluntary association of independent **states,** in which the member states agree to only limited restraints on their freedom of action. As a result, confederations seldom have an effective executive authority.

In June 1776, the Second Continental Congress began the process of composing what would become the Articles of Confederation. The final draft of the Articles was completed by November 15, 1777. It was not until March 1, 1781, however, that the last state, Maryland, agreed to ratify the Articles. Well before the final ratification of the Articles, however, many of them were implemented: the Continental Congress and the thirteen states conducted American military, economic, and political affairs according to the standards and the form specified by the Articles.[6]

unicameral legislature

A legislature with only one legislative chamber, as opposed to a bicameral (two-chamber) legislature, such as the U.S. Congress. Today, Nebraska is the only state in the Union with a unicameral legislature.

confederation

A political system in which states or regional governments retain ultimate authority except for those powers they expressly delegate to a central government; a voluntary association of independent states, in which the member states agree to limited restraints on their freedom of action.

state

A group of people occupying a specific area and organized under one government. It may either be a nation or a subunit of a nation.

---

5. David Armitage, *The Declaration of Independence: A Global History* (Cambridge, Mass.: Harvard University Press, 2007), p. 26.

6. Keith L. Dougherty, *Collective Action under the Articles of Confederation* (New York: Cambridge University Press, 2006).

Figure 2–1
The Confederal
Government Structure
under the Articles
of Confederation

*Why would a state send multiple
ambassadors if it only had one vote?*

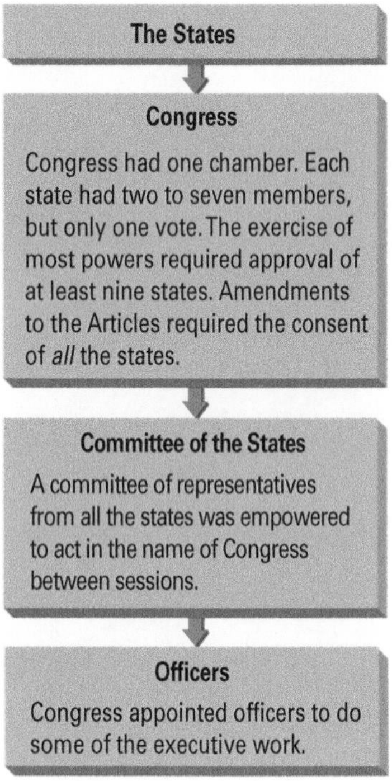

The Articles Establish a Government.

Under the Articles, the thirteen original colonies, now states, established on March 1, 1781, a government of the states—the Congress of the Confederation. The congress was a unicameral assembly of so-called ambassadors from each state, with each state possessing a single vote. Each year, the congress would choose one of its members as the president of the congress (that is, the presiding officer), but the Articles did not provide for a president of the United States.

The congress was authorized in Article X to appoint an executive committee of the states "to execute in the recess of Congress, such of the powers of Congress as the United States, in Congress assembled, by the consent of nine [of the thirteen] states, shall from time to time think expedient to vest with them." The congress was also allowed to appoint other committees and civil officers necessary for managing the general affairs of the United States. In addition, the congress could regulate foreign affairs and establish coinage and weights and measures. But it lacked an independent, direct source of revenue and the necessary executive machinery to enforce its decisions throughout the land. Article II of the Articles of Confederation guaranteed that each state would retain its sovereignty. Figure 2–1 illustrates the structure of the government under the Articles of Confederation. Table 2–1 summarizes the powers—and the lack of powers—of congress under the Articles of Confederation.

Accomplishments under the Articles.

The new government had some accomplishments during its eight years of existence under the Articles of Confederation. Certain states' claims to western lands were settled. Maryland had objected to the western land claims of the Carolinas, Connecticut, Georgia, Massachusetts, New York, and Virginia. It was only after these states consented to give up their land claims to the United States as a whole that Maryland signed the Articles of Confederation. Another accomplishment under the Articles was the passage of the Northwest Ordinance of 1787, which established a basic pattern of government for new territories north of the Ohio River. All in all, the Articles represented the first real pooling of resources by the American states.

Figure 2–1
The Confederal
Government Structure
under the Articles
of Confederation

*Why would a state send multiple
ambassadors if it only had one vote?*

The States

Congress

Congress had one chamber. Each state had two to seven members, but only one vote. The exercise of most powers required approval of at least nine states. Amendments to the Articles required the consent of *all* the states.

Committee of the States

A committee of representatives from all the states was empowered to act in the name of Congress between sessions.

Officers

Congress appointed officers to do some of the executive work.

Table 2–1 The Continental Congress—Powers and Limits

Why would states be reluctant to forward taxes to the Confederation?

Congress Had Power to	Congress Lacked Power to
• Declare war and make peace.	• Provide for effective treaty-making power and control foreign relations—it could not compel states to respect treaties.
• Enter into treaties and alliances.	
• Establish and control armed forces.	
• Request soldiers and revenues from states.	• Compel states to meet military quotas—it could not draft soldiers.
• Regulate coinage.	
• Borrow funds and issue bills of credit.	• Regulate interstate and foreign commerce—it left each state free to tax imports from other states.
• Fix uniform standards of weight and measurement.	
• Create admiralty courts.	• Collect taxes directly from the people—it had to rely on states to collect and forward taxes.
• Create a postal system.	
• Regulate Indian affairs.	• Compel states to pay their share of government costs.
• Guarantee citizens of each state the rights and privileges of citizens in the several states when in another state.	• Provide and maintain a sound monetary system or issue paper money—this was left up to the states, and the paper currencies in circulation differed tremendously in value.
• Adjudicate disputes between states on state petition.	

Weaknesses of the Articles. In spite of these accomplishments, the Articles of Confederation had many defects. Although congress had the legal right to declare war and to conduct foreign policy, it did not have the right to demand revenues from the states. It could only ask for them. Additionally, the actions of congress required the consent of nine states. Any amendments to the Articles required the unanimous consent of the congress and confirmation by every state legislature. Furthermore, the Articles did not create a national system of courts.

Basically, the functioning of the government under the Articles depended on the goodwill of the states. Article III simply established a "league of friendship" among the states—no national government was intended.

Probably the most fundamental weakness of the Articles, and the most basic cause of their eventual replacement by the Constitution, was the lack of power to raise funds for the armed forces. The Articles contained no language giving congress coercive power to raise revenue (by levying taxes) to provide adequate support for the military forces controlled by congress. Due to a lack of resources, the Continental Congress was forced to disband the army after the Revolutionary War, even in the face of serious Spanish and British military threats.

Image 2–5 Alexander Hamilton was among those who wanted a monarchy.

Shays' Rebellion and the Need to Revise the Articles. Because of the weaknesses of the Articles of Confederation, the central government could do little to maintain peace and order in the new nation. The states bickered among themselves and increasingly taxed each other's goods. By 1784, the country faced a serious economic depression. Banks were calling in old loans and refusing to make new ones. People who could not pay their debts were often thrown into prison.

In August 1786, musket-bearing farmers led by former revolutionary captain Daniel Shays seized county courthouses and disrupted the trials of debtors in Springfield, Massachusetts. Shays and his men then launched an attack on the federal arsenal at Springfield, but they were repulsed. Shays' Rebellion demonstrated that the central government could not protect the citizenry from armed rebellion or provide adequately for the public welfare. The rebellion spurred the nation's political leaders to action.

The Constitutional Convention

Learning Outcome **3:**

The Virginia legislature called for a meeting of all the states to be held at Annapolis, Maryland, on September 11, 1786—ostensibly to discuss commercial problems only. It was evident to those in attendance (including Alexander Hamilton of New York and James Madison of Virginia) that the national government had serious weaknesses that had to be addressed if it was to survive. Among the important problems to be solved were the relationship between the states and the central government, the powers of the national legislature, the need for executive leadership, and the establishment of policies for economic stability.

The result of this meeting was a petition to the Continental Congress for a general convention to meet in Philadelphia in May 1787 "to consider the exigencies of the union." The Continental Congress approved the convention in February 1787. When those who favored a weak central government realized that the Philadelphia meeting would in fact take place, they endorsed the convention. They made sure, however, that the convention would be summoned "for the sole and express purpose of revising the Articles of Confederation." Those in favor of a stronger national government had different ideas.

The designated date for the opening of the convention at Philadelphia, now known as the Constitutional Convention, was May 14, 1787. Few of the delegates had actually arrived in Philadelphia by that time, however, so the opening was delayed. The Convention

Discuss the most important compromises reached at the Constitutional Convention and the basic structure of the resulting government.

formally began in the East Room of the Pennsylvania State House on May 25.[7] Fifty-five of the seventy-four delegates chosen for the convention actually attended. (Of those fifty-five, only about forty played active roles at the convention.) Rhode Island was the only state that refused to send delegates.

Who Were the Delegates?

Who were the fifty-five delegates to the Constitutional Convention? They certainly did not represent a cross section of American society in the 1700s. Indeed, most were members of the upper class. Consider the following facts:

1. Thirty-three were members of the legal profession.
2. Three were physicians.
3. Almost 50 percent were college graduates.
4. Seven were former chief executives of their respective states.
5. Six were owners of large plantations.
6. Eight were important businesspersons.

They were also relatively young by today's standards: James Madison was thirty-six, Alexander Hamilton was only thirty-two, and Jonathan Dayton of New Jersey was twenty-six. The venerable Benjamin Franklin, however, was eighty-one and had to be carried in on a portable chair borne by four prisoners from a local jail. Not counting Franklin, the average age was just over forty-two.

The Working Environment

The conditions under which the delegates worked for 115 days were far from ideal and were made even worse by the necessity of maintaining total secrecy. The framers of the Constitution believed that if public debate took place on particular positions, delegates would have a more difficult time compromising or backing down to reach agreement. Consequently, the windows were usually shut in the East Room of the State House. Summer quickly arrived, and the air became humid and hot by noon of each day. The delegates did, however, have a nearby tavern and inn to which they retired each evening—the Indian Queen. It became the informal headquarters of the delegates.

Factions among the Delegates

We know much about the proceedings at the convention because James Madison kept a daily, detailed personal journal. A majority of the delegates were strong nationalists—they wanted a central government with real power, unlike the central government under the Articles of Confederation. George Washington and Benjamin Franklin were among those who sought a stronger government.

Among the nationalists, some—including Alexander Hamilton—went so far as to support monarchy. Another important group of nationalists was of a more republican stripe. Led by James Madison of Virginia and James Wilson of Pennsylvania, these republican nationalists wanted a central government founded on popular support.

Many of the other delegates from Connecticut, Delaware, Maryland, New Hampshire, and New Jersey were concerned about only one thing—claims to western lands. As long as those lands became the common property of all of the states, these delegates were willing to support a central government.

---

7. The State House was later named Independence Hall. This was the same room in which the Declaration of Independence had been signed eleven years earlier.

Finally, there was a group of delegates who were totally against a national authority. Two of the three delegates from New York quit the convention when they saw the nationalist direction of its proceedings.

Politicking and Compromises

The debates at the convention started on the first day. James Madison had spent months reviewing European political theory. When his Virginia delegation arrived ahead of most of the others, it got to work immediately. By the time George Washington opened the convention, Governor Edmund Randolph of Virginia was prepared to present fifteen resolutions proposing fundamental changes to the nation's government. In retrospect, this was a masterful stroke on the part of the Virginia delegation. It set the agenda for the remainder of the convention—even though, in principle, the delegates had been sent to Philadelphia for the sole purpose of amending the Articles of Confederation.

The Virginia Plan. Randolph's fifteen resolutions proposed an entirely new national government under a constitution. Basically, it called for the following:

1. A **bicameral** (two-chamber) **legislature,** with the lower chamber chosen by the people and the smaller upper chamber chosen by the lower chamber from nominees selected by state legislatures. The number of representatives would be proportional to a state's population, thus favoring the large states. The legislature could void any state laws.
2. The creation of an unspecified national executive, elected by the legislature.
3. The creation of a national judiciary, appointed by the legislature.

It did not take long for the smaller states to realize they would fare poorly under the Virginia Plan, which would enable Massachusetts, Pennsylvania, and Virginia to form a majority in the national legislature. The debate on the plan dragged on for a number of weeks. It was time for the small states to come up with their own plan.

bicameral legislature

A legislature made up of two parts, called chambers. The U.S. Congress, composed of the House of Representatives and the Senate, is a bicameral legislature.

Image 2–6 George Washington presided over the Constitutional Convention of 1787. *Why might he have been chosen for this position?*

North Wind Picture Archives/Alamy

The New Jersey Plan. On June 15, William Paterson of New Jersey offered an alternative plan. He proposed the following:

1. The fundamental principle of the Articles of Confederation—one state, one vote— would be retained.
2. Congress would be able to regulate trade and impose taxes.
3. All acts of Congress would be the supreme law of the land.
4. Several people would be elected by Congress to form an executive office.
5. The executive office would appoint a Supreme Court.

Basically, the New Jersey Plan was simply an amendment of the Articles of Confederation. Its only notable feature was its reference to the **supremacy doctrine,** which was later included in the Constitution.

The "Great Compromise." The delegates were at an impasse. Most wanted a strong national government and were unwilling even to consider the New Jersey Plan. But when the Virginia Plan was brought up again, the small states threatened to leave. It was not until July 16 that a compromise was achieved. Roger Sherman of Connecticut proposed the following:

1. A bicameral legislature in which the lower chamber, the House of Representatives, would be apportioned according to the number of free inhabitants in each state, plus three-fifths of the slaves.
2. An upper chamber, the Senate, which would have two members from each state elected by the state legislatures.

This plan, known as the **Great Compromise** (it is also called the Connecticut Compromise because of the role of the Connecticut delegates in the proposal), broke the deadlock. It did exact a political price, however, because it permitted each state to have equal representation in the Senate. Having two senators represent each state diluted the voting power of citizens living in more heavily populated states and gave the smaller states disproportionate political power. Nonetheless, the Connecticut Compromise resolved the controversy between small and large states. In addition, the Senate would act as a check on the House, which many feared would be dominated by the masses and excessively responsive to them.

The Three-Fifths Compromise. The Great Compromise also settled another major issue—how to deal with slaves in the representational scheme. Slavery was still legal in several northern states, but it was concentrated in the South. Many delegates were opposed to slavery and wanted it banned entirely in the United States. Charles Pinckney of South Carolina led strong southern opposition to a ban on slavery. Furthermore, the South wanted slaves to be counted along with free persons in determining representation in Congress. Delegates from the northern states objected. Sherman's three-fifths proposal was a compromise between northerners who did not want the slaves counted at all and southerners who wanted them counted in the same way as free whites. Actually, Sherman's Connecticut Plan spoke of three-fifths of "all other persons" (and that is the language of the Constitution itself). It is not hard to figure out, though, who those other persons were.

The three-fifths rule meant that the House of Representatives and the electoral college would be apportioned in part on the basis of *property*—specifically, property in

Why should you care about **THE CONSTITUTION?**

The laws of the nation have a direct impact on your life, and none more so than the Constitution—the supreme law of the land. The most important issues in society are often settled by the Constitution. For example, for the first seventy-five years of the republic, the Constitution implicitly protected the institution of slavery. If the Constitution had never been changed by an amendment, the process of abolishing slavery would have been much different and might have involved extra-constitutional measures.

slaves. Modern commentators have referred to the three-fifths rule as valuing African Americans only three-fifths as much as whites. Actually, the additional southern representatives elected because of the three-fifths rule did not represent the slaves at all. Rather, these extra representatives were a gift to the slave owners—the additional representatives enhanced the power of the South in Congress.

The Slave Trade and the Future of Slavery. The three-fifths compromise did not completely settle the slavery issue. There was also the question of the slave trade. Eventually, the delegates agreed that Congress could not ban the importation of slaves until after 1808.

The compromise meant that the matter of slavery itself was never addressed directly. The South won twenty years of unrestricted slave trade and a requirement that escaped slaves in free states be returned to their owners in slave states.

Clearly, many delegates, including slave owners such as George Washington and James Madison, had serious objections to slavery. Why, then, did they allow slavery to continue? Historians have long maintained that the framers had no choice—that without a slavery compromise, the delegates from the South would have abandoned the convention. Indeed, this was the fear of a number of antislavery delegates to the convention. Madison, for example, said, "Great as the evil is, a dismemberment of the Union would be even worse."[8]

A number of historians have made an additional point. Many American leaders believed that slavery would die out naturally. These leaders assumed that in the long run, slave labor could not compete with the labor of free citizens. This assumption turned out to be incorrect.

Other Issues. The South also worried that the northern majority in Congress would pass legislation unfavorable to its economic interests. Because the South depended on agricultural exports, it feared the imposition of export taxes. In return for acceding to the northern demand that Congress be able to regulate commerce among the states and with other nations, the South obtained a promise that export taxes would not be imposed. As a result, the United States is among the few countries that do not tax their exports.

There were other disagreements. The delegates could not decide whether to establish only a Supreme Court or to create lower courts as well. They deferred the issue by mandating a Supreme Court and allowing Congress to establish lower courts. They also disagreed over whether the president or the Senate would choose the Supreme Court justices. A compromise was reached under which the president would nominate the justices and the Senate would confirm the nominations.

These compromises, as well as others, resulted from the recognition that if one group of states refused to ratify the Constitution, it was doomed.

Working toward Final Agreement

The Connecticut Compromise was reached by mid-July. The makeup of the executive branch and the judiciary, however, was left unsettled. The remaining work of the convention was turned over to a five-man Committee of Detail, which presented a rough draft of the Constitution on August 6. It made the executive and judicial branches subordinate to the legislative branch.

The Madisonian Model—Separation of Powers. The major issue of **separation of powers** had not yet been resolved. The delegates were concerned with structuring the government to prevent the imposition of tyranny, either by the majority or by a minority. It was Madison who proposed a governmental scheme—sometimes

separation of powers
The principle of dividing governmental powers among different branches of government.

---

8. Speech before the Virginia ratifying convention on June 17, 1788, as cited in Bruno Leone, ed., *The Creation of the Constitution* (San Diego: Greenhaven Press, 1995), p. 159.

Madisonian model

A structure of government proposed by James Madison in which the powers of the government are separated into three branches: executive, legislative, and judicial.

checks and balances

A major principle of the American system of government whereby each branch of the government can check the actions of the others.

called the **Madisonian model**—to achieve this: the executive, legislative, and judicial powers of government were to be separated so that no one branch had enough power to dominate the others. The separation of powers was by function, as well as by personnel, with Congress passing laws, the president enforcing and administering laws, and the courts interpreting laws in individual circumstances.

Each of the three branches of government would be independent of the others, but they would have to cooperate to govern. According to Madison, in *Federalist Paper* No. 51 (see Appendix C), "the great security against a gradual concentration of the several powers in the same department consists in giving to those who administer each department the necessary constitutional means and personal motives to resist encroachments of the others."

The Madisonian Model—Checks and Balances. The "constitutional means" Madison referred to is a system of **checks and balances** through which each branch of the government can check the actions of the others. For example, Congress can enact laws, but the president has veto power over congressional acts. The Supreme Court has the power to declare acts of Congress and of the executive branch unconstitutional, but the president appoints the justices of the Supreme Court, with the advice and consent of the Senate. (The Supreme Court's power to declare acts unconstitutional was not mentioned in the Constitution, although arguably the framers assumed that the Court would have this power—see the discussion of *judicial review* later in this chapter.) Figure 2–2 outlines these checks and balances.

Figure 2–2 Checks and Balances

The major checks and balances among the three branches are illustrated here. The U.S. Constitution does not mention some of these checks, such as the president's ability to refuse to enforce judicial decisions or congressional legislation. Checks and balances can be thought of as a confrontation of powers or responsibilities. Two branches in conflict can result in a balance or stalemate, requiring one branch to give in or both to reach a compromise. *Which result is more likely?*

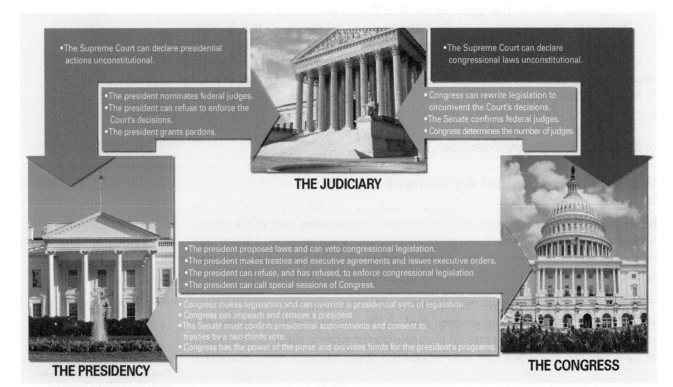

- The Supreme Court can declare presidential actions unconstitutional.
- The president nominates federal judges.
- The president can refuse to enforce the Court's decisions.
- The president grants pardons.

- The Supreme Court can declare congressional laws unconstitutional.
- Congress can rewrite legislation to circumvent the Court's decisions.
- The Senate confirms federal judges.
- Congress determines the number of judges.

THE JUDICIARY

- The president proposes laws and can veto congressional legislation.
- The president makes treaties and executive agreements and issues executive orders.
- The president can refuse, and has refused, to enforce congressional legislation.
- The president can call special sessions of Congress.

- Congress makes legislation and can override a presidential veto of legislation.
- Congress can impeach and remove a president.
- The Senate must confirm presidential appointments and consent to treaties by a two-thirds vote.
- Congress has the power of the purse and provides funds for the president's programs.

THE PRESIDENCY

THE CONGRESS

Photo Credits: left: Orhan Cam/Shutterstock.com, center top: Orhan Cam/Shutterstock.com, right: Mesut Dogan/Shutterstock.com

The Development of the Madisonian Model.

In the years since the Constitution was ratified, the checks and balances built into it have evolved into a sometimes complex give-and-take among the branches of government. Generally, for nearly every check that one branch has over another, the branch that has been checked has found a way of getting around it. For example, suppose that the president checks Congress by vetoing a bill. Congress can override the presidential veto by a two-thirds vote. Additionally, Congress holds the "power of the purse." If it disagrees with a program endorsed by the executive branch, it can simply refuse to appropriate the funds necessary to operate that program.

Similarly, the president can impose a countercheck on Congress if the Senate refuses to confirm a presidential appointment, such as a judicial appointment. The president can simply wait until Congress is in recess and then make what is called a "recess appointment," which does not require the Senate's immediate approval.

The Executive.

Some delegates favored a plural executive made up of a committee. This idea was abandoned in favor of a single chief executive. Some argued that Congress should choose the executive. To make the presidency completely independent of the proposed Congress, however, an **electoral college** was adopted. As we explained in this chapter's opening *What If . . .* feature, the voters of the various states choose electors, and then the electors actually choose the president. The number of electors in each state is equal to the number of each state's U.S. representatives and senators added together. In addition, the Twenty-third Amendment to the Constitution now gives the District of Columbia the same number of electors as the least populous state.

The founders hoped that through this system, the president would be elected by prominent citizens, not ordinary voters. In fact, for some years after the Constitution was adopted, electors in about half the states were chosen by the state legislature, not directly by the voters. Even in those states, however, the organization of political parties from 1796 on gave ordinary voters some input into choosing the president. A vote for a party's state legislative candidate, after all, was also a way to support that party's presidential candidate. By 1832, the South Carolina legislature was the only one still choosing electors.

The Final Document

On September 17, 1787, the Constitution was approved by thirty-nine delegates. Of the fifty-five who had attended originally, only forty-two remained. Three delegates refused to sign the Constitution. Others disapproved of at least parts of it but signed anyway to begin the ratification debate.

The Constitution that was to be ratified established the following fundamental principles:

1. Popular sovereignty, or control by the people.
2. A republican government in which the people choose representatives to make decisions for them.
3. Limited government with written laws, in contrast to the powerful British government against which the colonists had rebelled.
4. Separation of powers, with checks and balances among branches to prevent any one branch from gaining too much power.
5. A federal system that allows for states' rights, because the states feared too much centralized control.

A Federal System.

You will read about federalism in detail in Chapter 3. Suffice it to say here that in the **federal system** established by the founders, sovereign powers—ruling powers—were divided between the states and the national government. The Constitution expressly granted certain powers to the national government. For example, the national

electoral college

A group of persons called electors selected by the voters in each state and the District of Columbia (D.C.). This group officially elects the president and vice president of the United States.

federal system

A system of government in which power is divided between a central government and regional, or subdivisional, governments. Each level must have some domain in which its policies are dominant and some genuine political or constitutional guarantee of its authority.

government was given the power to regulate commerce among the states. The Constitution also declared that the president is the nation's chief executive and the commander in chief of the armed forces. Additionally, the Constitution made it clear that laws passed by the national government take priority over conflicting state laws. At the same time, the Constitution provided for extensive states' rights, including the right to control commerce within state borders and to exercise those governing powers that were not delegated to the national government. We look at some important clauses of the Constitution in this chapter's *Consider the Source* feature.

A Novel Form of Government. The federal system created by the founders was a novel form of government at that time—no other country in the world had such a system. It was invented by the founders as a compromise solution to the controversy over whether the states or the central government should have ultimate sovereignty. As you will read in Chapter 3, the debate over where the line should be drawn between states' rights and the powers of the national government has characterized American politics ever since. The founders did not go into detail about where this line should be drawn, thus leaving it up to elected officials and judges to divine the correct constitutional balance.

Learning Outcome **4:**

Summarize the arguments in favor of and the arguments against adopting the Constitution, and explain why the Bill of Rights was adopted.

The Difficult Road to Ratification

The founders knew that **ratification** of the Constitution was far from certain. Indeed, because it was almost guaranteed that many state legislatures would not ratify it, the delegates agreed that each state should hold a special convention. Elected delegates to these conventions would discuss and vote on the Constitution. Further departing from the Articles of Confederation, the delegates agreed that as soon as nine states (rather than all thirteen) approved the Constitution, it would take effect, and Congress could begin to organize the new government.

The Federalists Push for Ratification

The two opposing forces in the battle over ratification were the Federalists and the Anti-Federalists. The **Federalists**—those in favor of a strong central government and the new Constitution—had an advantage over their opponents, called the **Anti-Federalists,** who wanted to prevent the Constitution as drafted from being ratified. In the first place, the Federalists had assumed a positive name, leaving their opposition the negative label of *Anti*-Federalist.[9] More important, the Federalists had attended the Constitutional Convention and knew of all the deliberations that had taken place. Their opponents had no such knowledge, because those deliberations had not been open to the public.

Thus, the Anti-Federalists were at a disadvantage in terms of information about the document. The Federalists also had time, power, and wealth on their side. Communications were slow. Those who had access to the best communications were Federalists— mostly wealthy bankers, lawyers, plantation owners, and merchants living in urban areas, where communications were better. The Federalist campaign was organized relatively quickly and effectively to elect Federalists as delegates to the state ratifying conventions.

The Anti-Federalists, however, had at least one strong point in their favor: they stood for the status quo. In general, the greater burden is always placed on those advocating change.

ratification
Formal approval.

Federalist
The name given to one who was in favor of the adoption of the U.S. Constitution and the creation of a federal union with a strong central government.

Anti-Federalist
An individual who opposed the ratification of the new Constitution in 1787. The anti-federalists were opposed to a strong central government.

---

9. There is some irony here. At the Constitutional Convention, those opposed to a strong central government pushed for a federal system because such a system would allow the states to retain some of their sovereign rights (see Chapter 3). The label *Anti-Federalists* thus contradicted their essential views.

Consider the source

The Powers of Congress

One of the most important parts of the Constitution is Section 8, which lays out the powers of Congress. More than any other section, it describes what the new government is meant to do. The opening clauses of the section deal with financial matters:

Clause 1: Taxing. The Congress shall have Power to lay and collect Taxes, Duties, Imposts and Excises, to pay the Debts and provide for the common Defense and general Welfare of the United States; but all Duties, Imposts and Excises shall be uniform throughout the United States;

Clause 2: Borrowing. To borrow Money on the credit of the United States;

Clause 3: Regulation of Commerce. To regulate Commerce with foreign Nations, and among the several States, and with the Indian Tribes;

Clause 4: Naturalization and Bankruptcy. To establish an uniform Rule of Naturalization, and uniform Laws on the subject of Bankruptcies throughout the United States;

Clause 5: Money and Standards. To coin Money, regulate the Value thereof, and of foreign Coin, and fix the Standard of Weights and Measures;

Subsequent clauses of Section 8 address the postal system, the federal courts, the military, and other topics. The section ends with one of the most important clauses in the Constitution:

Clause 18: The Elastic Clause. To make all Laws which shall be necessary and proper for carrying into Execution the foregoing Powers, and all other Powers vested by this Constitution in the Government of the United States, or in any Department or Officer thereof.

Section 9, which follows, lists the powers that are denied to Congress. You can find a full copy of the Constitution, with amendments and annotations, in Appendix B.

The Source: Article I, Section 8

Entire books have been written about each of these clauses. It is easy to see why. Some clauses are quite sweeping. Clause 1 gives Congress the power to provide for "the general Welfare of the United States." That could mean almost anything. Clause 2 places no limit on the power to borrow. Clause 3, the commerce clause, does not say what commerce is, or how it should be regulated.

Let's take a quick look at one example of constitutional interpretation. Clause 1 on taxes seems broad enough. It is limited, however, by Section 9, Clause 4: "No Capitation, or other direct, Tax shall be laid, unless in Proportion to the Census or Enumeration herein before directed to be taken." A "direct" tax was understood to be a tax on persons or property.

Section 9, Clause 4 would appear to rule out national real estate or income taxes, which is why the Constitution was amended in 1913 to authorize a national income tax. Why would the founders have sought to ban taxes on persons or property? It was because they had one type of property in mind—slaves, who were both persons and property. Without a limit on direct taxes, Congress could effectively abolish slavery by taxing it out of existence.

For Critical Analysis

❯ If the ban on direct taxes did not exist, and the national government sought to tax property in slaves, what might have happened?

The *Federalist Papers*. In New York, opponents of the Constitution were quick to attack it. Alexander Hamilton answered their attacks under a pseudonym in newspaper columns and secured two collaborators—John Jay and James Madison. In a very short time, those three political figures wrote a series of eighty-five essays in defense of the Constitution and of a republican form of government.

These widely read essays, called the *Federalist Papers,* appeared in New York newspapers from October 1787 to August 1788 and were reprinted in the newspapers of

Hulton Archive/Getty Images

Image 2–7 Patrick Henry (1736–1799). A revolutionary-era leader, Henry was a member of the Continental Congress and twice governor of Virginia. He and other Anti-Federalists opposed the new Constitution. *What kinds of arguments did the Anti-Federalists make?*

other states. Although we do not know for certain who wrote every one, it is apparent that Hamilton was responsible for about two-thirds of the essays. These included the most important ones interpreting the Constitution, explaining the various powers of the three branches, and presenting the theory of judicial review. Madison's *Federalist Paper* No. 10 (see Appendix C), however, is considered a classic in political theory. It deals with the nature of groups—or factions, as he called them. We discuss the ways in which groups influence our government in Chapter 7. In spite of the rapidity with which the *Federalist Papers* were written, they are considered by many to be perhaps the best example of political theorizing ever produced in the United States.[10]

The Anti-Federalist Response. Many Anti-Federalist attacks on the Constitution were also brilliant. The Anti-Federalists claimed that the Constitution was written by aristocrats and would lead to aristocratic tyranny. More important, the Anti-Federalists believed that the Constitution would create an overbearing central government hostile to personal liberty. (The Constitution said nothing about freedom of the press, freedom of religion, or any other individual liberty.) They wanted to include a list of guaranteed liberties, or a bill of rights. Finally, the Anti-Federalists decried the weakened power of the states.[11]

The Anti-Federalists cannot be dismissed as unpatriotic extremists. They included such patriots as Patrick Henry and Samuel Adams. They were arguing what had been the most prevalent view in that era. This view derived from the French political philosopher Montesquieu, an influential political theorist. Montesquieu believed that a republic was possible only in a relatively small society governed by direct democracy or by a large legislature with small districts. The Madisonian view favoring a large republic, particularly as expressed in *Federalist Papers* No. 10 and No. 51, was actually an exceptional view in those years. Indeed, some researchers believe it was mainly the bitter experiences with the Articles of Confederation, rather than Madison's arguments, that persuaded the state conventions to ratify the Constitution.

The March to the Finish

The struggle for ratification continued. Strong majorities were procured in Connecticut, Delaware, Georgia, New Jersey, and Pennsylvania. After a bitter struggle in Massachusetts, that state ratified the Constitution by a narrow margin on February 6, 1788. By the spring, Maryland and South Carolina had ratified by sizable majorities. Then on June 21 of that year, New Hampshire became the ninth state to ratify the Constitution. Although the Constitution was formally in effect, this meant little without Virginia and New York. Virginia ratified it a few days later, but New York did not join in for another month (see Table 2–2).

---

10. Some scholars believe that the *Federalist Papers* played only a minor role in securing ratification of the Constitution. Even if this is true, they still have lasting value as an authoritative explanation of the Constitution.

11. Herbert J. Storing edited seven volumes of Anti-Federalist writings and released them in 1981 as *The Anti-Federalist*. Political science professor Murray Dry has prepared a more manageable, one-volume version of this collection: Herbert J. Storing, ed., *The Anti-Federalist: An Abridgment of the Complete Anti-Federalist* (Chicago: University of Chicago Press, 2006).

Table 2-2 Ratification of the Constitution

What might have happened if Rhode Island had never joined the Union?

State	Date	Vote For–Against
Delaware	Dec. 7, 1787	30–0
Pennsylvania	Dec. 12, 1787	43–23
New Jersey	Dec. 18, 1787	38–0
Georgia	Jan. 2, 1788	26–0
Connecticut	Jan. 9, 1788	128–40
Massachusetts	Feb. 6, 1788	187–168
Maryland	Apr. 28, 1788	63–11
South Carolina	May 23, 1788	149–73
New Hampshire	June 21, 1788	57–46
Virginia	June 25, 1788	89–79
New York	July 26, 1788	30–27
North Carolina	Nov. 21, 1789*	194–77
Rhode Island	May 29, 1790	34–32

*Ratification was initially defeated on August 4, 1788, by a vote of 84–184.

Did the Majority of Americans Support the Constitution?

In 1913, historian Charles Beard published *An Economic Interpretation of the Constitution of the United States.*[12] This book launched a debate that has continued ever since—the debate over whether the Constitution was supported by a majority of Americans.

Beard's Thesis. Beard argued that the Constitution had been produced primarily by wealthy property owners who desired a stronger government able to protect their property rights. Beard also claimed that the Constitution had been imposed by undemocratic methods. He pointed out that there was never any popular vote on whether to hold a constitutional convention in the first place. Furthermore, even if such a vote had been taken, state laws generally restricted voting rights to property-owning white males.

State Ratifying Conventions. The delegates to the various state ratifying conventions had been selected by only 150,000 of the nation's approximately 4 million total inhabitants. That does not seem very democratic—at least not by today's standards. Some historians have suggested that if a public opinion poll could have been taken at that time, the Anti-Federalists would probably have outnumbered the Federalists. Much has also been made of the various machinations used by the Federalists to ensure the Constitution's ratification, including the purchase of at least one printing press to prevent the publication of Anti-Federalist sentiments.

---

12. Charles A. Beard, *An Economic Interpretation of the Constitution of the United States* (New York: Macmillan, 1913; New York: Free Press, 1986).

J.B. Handelsman The New Yorker Collection/The Cartoon Bank

Image 2–8 *"Hey, the Constitution isn't engraved in stone."*

Support Was Probably Widespread. Many small farmers feared that the Constitution would result in oppressive domination by a wealthy elite. Still, the perception that a strong central government was necessary to keep order and protect the public welfare appears to have been widespread among all classes, rich and poor alike. No doubt an effective national government would benefit the wealthy, as Beard argued. Yet it could help workers and small farmers as well. After all, the economic and political crisis that the nation faced in the 1780s fell even harder on the poor than on the rich.

Further, although the need for strong government was a major argument in favor of adopting the Constitution, even the Federalists sought to craft a limited government. Compared with constitutions adopted by other nations in later years, the U.S. Constitution, through its checks and balances, favors limited government over "energetic" government to a marked degree.

The Bill of Rights

The U.S. Constitution would not have been ratified in several important states if the Federalists had not assured the states that amendments to the Constitution would be passed to protect individual liberties against incursions by the national government. Many of the recommendations of the state ratifying conventions included specific rights that were considered later by James Madison as he labored to draft what became the Bill of Rights. (We introduced the Bill of Rights in the *What If . . .* feature that opened Chapter 1.)

A "Bill of Limits." Although called the Bill of Rights, the first ten amendments to the Constitution essentially were a "bill of limits," because the amendments limited the powers of the national government over the rights and liberties of individuals.

Ironically, a year earlier Madison had told Jefferson, "I have never thought the omission [of the Bill of Rights] a material defect" of the Constitution. Jefferson's enthusiasm for a bill of rights apparently influenced Madison, however.

Was a Bill of Rights Necessary? Many framers thought that it was dangerous to enumerate specific civil liberties in a bill of rights. Future governments might assume that rights that were not listed did not exist. (This concern was addressed in the Bill of Rights itself by the Ninth Amendment.)

Also, the Constitution already listed certain rights. The original document prohibits *bills of attainder*—laws that impose punishment on named individuals without trial. The original Constitution also bars *ex post facto* laws, which make an act illegal only after it has already happened. A trial by jury is required in federal criminal cases. Finally, individuals may not be jailed without due process of law. A judge can demand to know why a particular person is in custody (the demand is called a *writ of habeas corpus*). If no proper explanation is given, the judge can order the individual's release.

Madison Drafts the Bill. Madison had to cull through more than two hundred state recommendations. It was no small task, and in retrospect he chose remarkably well. One of the rights appropriate for constitutional protection that he left out was equal protection under the laws—but that was not commonly regarded as a basic right at that time. Not until 1868 was the Constitution amended to guarantee that no state shall deny equal protection to any person.

The final number of amendments that Madison and a specially appointed committee came up with was seventeen. Congress tightened the language somewhat and eliminated five of the amendments. Of the remaining twelve, two—dealing with the apportionment of representatives and the compensation of the members of Congress—were not ratified immediately by the states. Eventually, Supreme Court decisions led to reform of the apportionment process. The amendment on the compensation of members of Congress was ratified 203 years later—in 1992![13]

Adoption of the Bill of Rights. On December 15, 1791, the national Bill of Rights was adopted when Virginia agreed to ratify the ten amendments. On ratification, the Bill of Rights became part of the U.S. Constitution. The basic structure of American government had already been established. Now the fundamental rights and liberties of individuals were protected, at least in theory, at the national level. The proposed amendment that Madison characterized as "the most valuable amendment in the whole lot"—which would have prohibited the states from infringing on the freedoms of conscience, press, and jury trial—had been eliminated by the Senate. Thus, the Bill of Rights as adopted did not limit state power, and individual citizens had to rely on the guarantees contained in a particular state constitution or state bill of rights. The country had to wait until the violence of the Civil War before significant limitations on state power in the form of the Fourteenth Amendment became part of the national Constitution.

Altering the Constitution

Learning Outcome **5:**

Describe the process of amending the Constitution and the informal ways in which Constitutional interpretation has changed over time.

As amended, the U.S. Constitution consists of about seven thousand words. It is shorter than any state constitution except that of Vermont. The federal Constitution is short because the founders intended it to be only a framework for the new government, to be interpreted by succeeding generations. One of the reasons it has remained short is that the formal amending procedure does not allow for changes to be made easily. Article V of the Constitution outlines the ways in which amendments may be proposed and ratified (see Figure 2–3).

The Formal Amendment Process

Two formal methods of proposing an amendment to the Constitution are available: (1) a two-thirds vote in each chamber of Congress or (2) a national convention that is called by Congress at the request of two-thirds of the state legislatures. This second method has never been used.

Ratification can occur by one of two methods: (1) by a positive vote in three-fourths of the legislatures of the various states or (2) by special conventions called in the states and a positive vote in three-fourths of them. The second method has been used only once, to repeal Prohibition (the ban on the production and sale of alcoholic beverages). That situation was exceptional—it involved an amendment (the Twenty-first) to repeal another amendment (the Eighteenth, which had created Prohibition). State conventions were necessary for repeal of the Eighteenth Amendment because prohibitionist forces were in control of the legislatures in many states where a majority of the population actually

---

13. For perspectives on these events, see Richard E. Labunski, *James Madison and the Struggle for the Bill of Rights* (New York: Oxford University Press, 2008); and Steven Waldman, *Founding Faith: How Our Founding Fathers Forged a Radical New Approach to Religious Liberty* (New York: Random House Trade Paperbacks, 2009).

supported repeal. (Note that Congress determines the method of ratification to be used by all states for each proposed constitutional amendment.)

Many Amendments Proposed, Few Accepted. Congress has considered more than eleven thousand amendments to the Constitution. Only thirty-three amendments have been submitted to the states after having been approved by the required two-thirds vote in each chamber of Congress, and only twenty-seven have been ratified—see Table 2–3. (The full, annotated text of the U.S. Constitution, including its amendments, is presented in Appendix B.) It should be clear that the amendment process is much more difficult than a graphic depiction such as Figure 2–3 can indicate. Because of competing social and economic interests, the requirement that two-thirds of both the House and the Senate approve the amendments is hard to achieve.

Table 2–3 Amendments to the Constitution

Why have so few amendments been adopted in the course of the nation's history?

Amendment	Subject	Year Adopted	Time Required for Ratification
1st–10th	The Bill of Rights	1791	2 years, 2 months, 20 days
11th	Immunity of states from certain suits	1795	11 months, 3 days
12th	Changes in electoral college procedure	1804	6 months, 3 days
13th	Prohibition of slavery	1865	10 months, 3 days
14th	Citizenship, due process, and equal protection	1868	2 years, 26 days
15th	No denial of vote because of race, color, or previous condition of servitude	1870	11 months, 8 days
16th	Power of Congress to tax income	1913	3 years, 6 months, 22 days
17th	Direct election of U.S. senators	1913	10 months, 26 days
18th	National (liquor) prohibition	1919	1 year, 29 days
19th	Women's right to vote	1920	1 year, 2 months, 14 days
20th	Change of dates for congressional and presidential terms	1933	10 months, 21 days
21st	Repeal of the Eighteenth Amendment	1933	9 months, 15 days
22d	Limit on presidential tenure	1951	3 years, 11 months, 3 days
23d	District of Columbia electoral vote	1961	9 months, 13 days
24th	Prohibition of tax payment as a qualification to vote in federal elections	1964	1 year, 4 months, 9 days
25th	Procedures for determining presidential disability and presidential succession and for filling a vice-presidential vacancy	1967	1 year, 7 months, 4 days
26th	Prohibition of setting the minimum voting age above eighteen in any election	1971	3 months, 7 days
27th	Prohibition of Congress's voting itself a raise or cut in pay that takes effect before the next election	1992	203 years

Figure 2–3 The Formal Constitutional Amending Procedure

There are two ways of proposing amendments to the U.S. Constitution and two ways of ratifying proposed amendments. Among the four possibilities, the usual route has been proposal by Congress and ratification by state legislatures. *What could happen if Congress were to call a convention?*

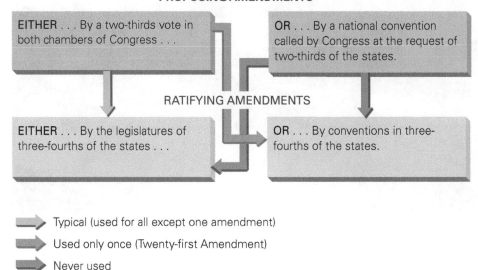

PROPOSING AMENDMENTS

EITHER . . . By a two-thirds vote in both chambers of Congress . . .

OR . . . By a national convention called by Congress at the request of two-thirds of the states.

RATIFYING AMENDMENTS

EITHER . . . By the legislatures of three-fourths of the states . . .

OR . . . By conventions in three-fourths of the states.

Typical (used for all except one amendment)

Used only once (Twenty-first Amendment)

Never used

After an amendment has been approved by Congress, the process becomes even more arduous. Three-fourths of the state legislatures must approve the amendment. Only those amendments that have wide popular support across parties and in all regions of the country are likely to be approved.

Why was the amendment process made so difficult? The framers feared that a simple amendment process could lead to a tyranny of the majority, which could pass amendments to oppress disfavored individuals and groups. The cumbersome amendment process does not seem to stem the number of amendments that are proposed in Congress, however, particularly in recent years. Proposing an amendment that will never pass is an effective way for a legislator to engage in "grandstanding," that is, showing off.

Time Limits on Ratification. The framers of the Constitution specified no time limit on the ratification process. The Supreme Court has held that Congress can specify a time for ratification as long as it is "reasonable." Since 1919, most proposed amendments have included a requirement that ratification be obtained within seven years. This was the case with the proposed Equal Rights Amendment, which sought to guarantee equal rights for women. When three-fourths of the states had not ratified it in the allotted seven years, however, Congress extended the limit by an additional three years and three months. That extension expired on June 30, 1982, and the amendment still had not been ratified.

The National Convention Provision. The Constitution provides that a national convention requested by the legislatures of two-thirds of the states can propose a constitutional amendment. Congress has received approximately 400 convention applications since the Constitution was ratified—every state has applied at least once. Fewer than 20 applications were submitted during the Constitution's first hundred years, but more than

Image 2–9 Students visit the Assembly Room in Independence Hall, Philadelphia. This is the room in which the Declaration of Independence and the Constitution were signed. At the time of the Revolution, Philadelphia was our largest city. *For what other reasons might Philadelphia have been our first capital?*

150 have been filed in the past two decades. No national convention has been held since 1787, and many national political and judicial leaders are uneasy about the prospect of convening a body that conceivably could do what the Constitutional Convention did—create a new form of government.

Informal Methods of Constitutional Change

Looking at the sparse number of formal constitutional amendments gives us an incomplete view of constitutional change. The brevity and ambiguity of the original document have permitted great alterations in the Constitution by way of varying interpretations over time. As the United States grew, both in population and in territory, new social and political realities emerged. Congress, presidents, and the courts found it necessary to interpret the Constitution's provisions in light of these new realities. The Constitution has proved to be a remarkably flexible document, adapting itself time and again to new events and concerns.

Congressional Legislation. The Constitution gives Congress broad powers to carry out its duties as the nation's legislative body. For example, Article I, Section 8, of the Constitution gives Congress the power to regulate foreign and interstate commerce. Although there is no clear definition of foreign commerce or interstate commerce in the Constitution, Congress has cited the *commerce clause* as the basis for passing thousands of laws.

In addition, Congress has frequently delegated to federal agencies the legislative power to write regulations. These regulations become law unless challenged in the court system. Nowhere does the Constitution outline this delegation of legislative authority.

Presidential Actions. Even though the Constitution does not expressly authorize the president to propose bills or even budgets to Congress,[14] presidents since the time of Woodrow Wilson (1913–1921) have proposed hundreds of bills to Congress each year that are introduced by the president's supporters in Congress. Presidents have also relied on their Article II authority as commander in chief of the nation's armed forces to send American troops abroad into combat, although the Constitution provides that Congress has the power to declare war.

Presidents have also conducted foreign affairs by the use of *executive agreements,* which are legally binding understandings reached between the president and a foreign head of state. The Constitution does not mention such agreements.

Judicial Review. Another way that the Constitution adapts to new developments is through judicial review. **Judicial review** refers to the power of U.S. courts to examine the constitutionality of actions undertaken by the legislative and executive branches of government. A state court, for example, may rule that a statute enacted by the state legislature violates the state constitution. Federal courts (and ultimately, the United States Supreme Court) may rule unconstitutional not only acts of Congress and decisions of the national executive branch, but also state statutes, state executive actions, and even provisions of state constitutions.

The Constitution does not specifically mention the power of judicial review. Those in attendance at the Constitutional Convention, however, probably expected that the courts would have some authority to review the legality of acts by the executive and legislative branches, because, under the common law tradition inherited from England, courts exercised this authority. Indeed, Alexander Hamilton, in *Federalist Paper* No. 78 (see Appendix C), explicitly outlined the concept of judicial review. In 1803, the Supreme Court claimed this power for itself in *Marbury v. Madison,*[15] in which the Court ruled that a particular provision of an act of Congress was unconstitutional.

Through the process of judicial review, the Supreme Court adapts the Constitution to modern situations and changing values. For example, it ruled in 1896 that "separate-but-equal" public facilities for African Americans were constitutional. By 1954, however, the times had changed, and the Court reversed that decision.[16] Woodrow Wilson summarized the Court's work when he described it as "a constitutional convention in continuous session." Basically, the law is what the Supreme Court says it is at any point in time.

Interpretation, Custom, and Usage. Changes in ways of doing political business have also led to the reinterpretation of the Constitution. For example, the Constitution does not mention political parties, yet these "extraconstitutional" organizations make the nominations for offices, run the campaigns, organize the members of Congress, and in fact change the election system from time to time.

In many ways, the Constitution has been adapted from a document serving the needs of a small, rural republic to one that provides a framework of government for an industrial giant with vast geographic, natural, and human resources.

Collection of the Supreme Court of the United States. Photographer: Steve Petteway

Image 2–10 Supreme Court Justice Antonin Scalia, who died in February 2016. Scalia was a leader of the Court's conservative wing. Naming a replacement for him was so politically charged that his seat remained open until after the 2016 elections. *How much of a problem is it if the Supreme Court has only eight members and can therefore deadlock 4–4?*

---

14. Note, though, that the Constitution, in Article II, Section 3, does state that the president "shall from time to time . . . recommend to [Congress's] Consideration such Measures as he shall judge necessary and expedient." Some scholars interpret this phrase to mean that the president has the constitutional authority to propose bills and budgets to Congress for consideration.

15. 5 U.S. 137 (1803). See Chapter 14 for a further discussion of the *Marbury v. Madison* case.

16. *Brown v. Board of Education of Topeka,* 347 U.S. 483 (1954).

judicial review

The power of the Supreme Court and other courts to examine and possibly declare unconstitutional federal or state laws and other acts of government.

How you can make a difference

If you want to affect our democracy, you have to learn firsthand how a democratic government works. The easiest way is to attend a session of a local legislative body.

- Various groups support or oppose a number of constitutional amendments. One proposal would create a constitutional requirement to balance the federal budget.

  If such an amendment sounds like a good idea to you, there are a variety of organizations you might investigate. These include the Balanced Budget Amendment Task Force.

- Other Americans have different concerns. In 2010, the Supreme Court struck down a wide range of campaign finance laws in *Citizens United v. Federal Election Commission*.[17] One result of this ruling was the "super PACs" that flooded television networks with attack advertisements during recent elections.

  A proposed constitutional amendment would overturn the *Citizens United* ruling. If getting the money out of politics is of interest to you, you can check out Move to Amend or Free Speech for People.

---

17. 558 U.S. 310 (2010).

KEY TERMS

Anti-Federalist 46	Federalist 46	natural rights 36	state 37
bicameral legislature 41	federal system 45	ratification 46	supremacy doctrine 42
checks and balances 44	Great Compromise 42	representative assembly 31	unicameral legislature 37
confederation 37	judicial review 55	separation of powers 43	
electoral college 45	Madisonian model 44	social contract 36	

CHAPTER SUMMARY

Learning Outcome 1 The first permanent English colonies were established at Jamestown in 1607 and Plymouth in 1620. The Mayflower Compact created the first formal government in New England.

In the 1760s, the British began to impose a series of taxes and legislative acts on their increasingly independent-minded colonies. The colonists responded with protests and boycotts of British products. Representatives of the colonies formed the First Continental Congress in 1774. The Second Continental Congress established an army in 1775 to defend the colonists against attacks by British soldiers.

Learning Outcome 2 On July 4, 1776, the Second Continental Congress approved the Declaration of Independence. Perhaps the most revolutionary aspects of the Declaration were its statements that people have natural rights to life, liberty, and the pursuit of happiness; that governments derive their power from the consent of the governed; and that people have a right to overthrow oppressive governments.

During the Revolutionary War, the states signed the Articles of Confederation, creating a weak central government with few powers. The Articles proved to be unworkable because the national government had no way to ensure compliance by the states with such measures as securing tax revenues.

Learning Outcome 3 Dissatisfaction with the Articles of Confederation prompted the call for a convention at Philadelphia in 1787. Delegates focused on creating a constitution for a new form of government. The Virginia Plan, which favored the larger states, and the New Jersey Plan, which favored smaller ones, did not garner sufficient support. The Great Compromise offered by Connecticut provided for a bicameral legislature and thus resolved the large-state/small-state controversy. The final version of the Constitution provided for the separation of powers, checks and balances, and a federal form of government.

Learning Outcome 4 The Anti-Federalists argued against adopting the Constitution, but supporters of the document won in the end. Fears of a strong central government prompted the addition of the Bill of Rights to the Constitution. The Bill of Rights, which includes the freedoms of religion, speech, and assembly, was initially applied only to the federal government, but amendments to the Constitution following the Civil War were interpreted to ensure that the Bill of Rights would apply to the states as well.

Learning Outcome 5 An amendment to the Constitution may be proposed either by a two-thirds vote in each chamber of Congress or by a national convention called by Congress at the request of two-thirds of the state legislatures. Ratification can occur either by the approval of three-fourths of the legislatures of the states or by special conventions called in the states for the purpose of ratifying the amendment and approval by three-fourths of these conventions. Informal methods of constitutional change include reinterpretation through congressional legislation, presidential actions, and judicial review.

ADDITIONAL RESOURCES

Today, you can find many important documents from the founding period online, including descriptions of events leading up to the American Revolution, the Articles of Confederation, notes on the Constitutional Convention, the Federalists' writings, and the Anti-Federalists' responses.

Online Resources

- The National Constitution Center, at **constitutioncenter.org**, provides a variety of information on the document in an entertaining format.

- Project Gutenberg offers a vast, free online collection of works that are no longer under copyright protection. For a copy of *The Federalist Papers* in any of several formats, go to **www.gutenberg.org/ebooks/1404**. For a collection of Anti-Federalist papers, see **www.thefederalistpapers.org/anti-federalist-papers**.

- You can get a free annotated copy of the Constitution and related documents as an app for your Android smart phone at **play.google.com/store/apps?hl=en**. The site offers *The Federalist Papers* for free as well. If you have an iPhone, you can find similar apps at Apple's App Store, but you'll probably have to pay ninety-nine cents for *The Federalist Papers*.

Books

Beck, Derek. *Igniting the American Revolution: 1773–1775.* New York: Sourcebooks, 2016. A dramatic retelling of the revolutionary crisis from both the American and British viewpoints. Beck is a retired Air Force officer and freelance historian.

Keyssar, Alexander. *Why Do We Still Have the Electoral College?* Cambridge, Mass.: Harvard University Press, 2016. Keyssar, a history professor at Harvard, details how the founders came to create the electoral college and why it has never been abolished.

Maier, Pauline. *Ratification: The People Debate the Constitution, 1787–1788.* New York: Simon & Schuster, 2011. Maier, a professor at M.I.T., charts the Constitution's uncertain course toward ratification.

Video

John Adams—A widely admired 2008 HBO miniseries on John Adams and his wife, Abigail Adams, and other prominent Americans of the revolutionary period. The series is largely based on David McCullough's book, *John Adams.*

Thomas Jefferson—A 1996 documentary by acclaimed director Ken Burns. The film covers Jefferson's entire life, including his writing of the Declaration of Independence, his presidency, and his later years in Virginia. Historians and writers interviewed include Daniel Boorstin, Garry Wills, Gore Vidal, and John Hope Franklin.

Quiz

Multiple Choice and Fill-Ins

Learning Outcome 1 Explain how the colonial experience prepared Americans for independence, the restrictions that Britain placed on the colonies, and the American response.

1. When the First Continental Congress convened in 1774, the British government:
   a. took no notice of it.
   b. agreed to allow the colonies to form a unified government.
   c. treated the meeting as an act of rebellion.

2. In 1620, the members of New England's first colony signed the _____ _____ at Plymouth (Massachusetts).

Learning Outcome 2 Describe the significance of the Declaration of Independence and the Articles of Confederation, as well as the weaknesses of the Articles.

3. A major defect in the Articles of Confederation was:
   a. the lack of power to raise funds for military forces.
   b. the lack of treaty-making power.
   c. the inability to easily communicate with citizens.

4. The Declaration of Independence established as unalienable rights those of life, _____, and the pursuit of happiness.

Learning Outcome 3 Discuss the most important compromises reached at the Constitutional Convention and the basic structure of the resulting government.

5. Which of the following fundamental principles was not established by the Constitution of 1787?
   a. popular sovereignty, or control by the people.
   b. limited government with written laws.
   c. a requirement that state governments uphold the liberties listed in the Bill of Rights.

6. When no branch of government—executive, legislative, or judicial—is able to dominate the others, we call this the _____ of powers.

Learning Outcome 4 Summarize the arguments in favor of and the arguments against adopting the Constitution, and explain why the Bill of Rights was adopted.

7. The major drafter of the Bill of Rights was:
   a. Washington.
   b. Jefferson.
   c. Madison.

8. Those who opposed the ratification of the Constitution were called _____.

Learning Outcome 5 Describe the process of amending the Constitution and the informal ways in which Constitutional interpretation has changed over time.

9. The reason the U.S. Constitution has so few amendments is that:
   a. the formal amendment process is exceedingly difficult.
   b. the Constitution was written so well that it hasn't needed to be amended.
   c. Congress doesn't have time to consider new amendments.

10. When an amendment to the Constitution is proposed by a two-thirds vote in both the Senate and the House and is sent to the state legislatures, then _____ of the states must approve it if it is to be adopted.

Essay Questions

1. Consider what might have happened if Georgia and the Carolinas had stayed out of the Union because of a desire to protect slavery. What would subsequent American history have been like? Would the eventual freedom of the slaves have been delayed—or advanced?

2. A result of the Great Compromise is that representation in the Senate dramatically departs from the one-person, one-vote rule. The 38 million people who live in California elect two senators, as do the half-million people living in Wyoming. What political results might occur when the citizens of small states are much better represented than the citizens of large ones?

FEDERALISM

Wind turbines in a corn field in Illinois. The national government has subsidized wind power, and many states subsidize it as well. Provision of subsidies by both the national and state governments is an example of a concurrent power, described in this chapter. *Why would the government want to subsidize this source of energy?*
Bloomberg/Getty Images

These five **LEARNING OUTCOMES** *below are designed to help improve your understanding of this chapter:*

1: Explain some of the benefits of the federal system for the United States.

2: Describe how the various provisions of the U.S. Constitution provide a framework for federalism.

3: Discuss how, in the early years of the republic, the United States Supreme Court confirmed the authority of the national government, and how that authority was ratified by the Civil War.

4: Define the terms *dual federalism, cooperative federalism, categorical grants, block grants*, and *fiscal federalism*.

5: Detail recent political developments and Supreme Court rulings that affect the distribution of power between the national government and the states.

What if...

Recreational Marijuana Were Legal in Every State?

Marijuana has been around for a long time. The earliest record we have of its use as a drug dates from the third millennium BCE. The drug was not banned in the United States until the twentieth century, however, beginning with restrictions in the District of Columbia in 1906. The Marijuana Tax Act of 1937 effectively made the drug illegal nationwide. Today, the federal government classifies marijuana as a substance with a high potential for abuse and no medical uses.

Yet nineteen states have passed decriminalization laws, beginning with Oregon in 1973. By 2016, twenty-three states allowed the sale and use of marijuana for medical purposes. In 2012, Colorado and Washington voters approved the sale and possession of marijuana for recreational use. Alaska, Oregon, and the District of Columbia joined them in 2014. As of 2016, a majority of respondents in national public opinion polls favored legalizing recreational marijuana. In that year, measures to legalize recreational marijuana passed in California, Massachusetts, and Nevada. What would happen if all states followed in the footsteps of Colorado and Washington—and the federal government changed its laws as well?

What If Recreational Marijuana Were Legal in Every State?

We have an easy way to determine the effects of legal marijuana. We merely need to look at what has happened in states such as Colorado, Oregon, and Washington. The first and most obvious conclusion is that the sky has not fallen. Life is not greatly different in any of these states. To be sure, advertisements for marijuana pop up here and there. Sharp observers may spot the new marijuana shops, which identify themselves with a green cross symbol. Driving a car while under the influence of weed is as dangerous as driving while drunk—but there has been no noticeable increase in automobile accidents. Hospitalization for excessive marijuana consumption is up, but no one ever dies simply from a marijuana overdose. Alcohol poisoning, in contrast, kills about 2,250 Americans every year.

Legalization has been a boon to state governments. Taxes on weed have brought in more than $40 million per year in Oregon and $70 million in Colorado and Washington. Experts in Washington predict the annual tax take to reach $250 million in the next few years.

Because marijuana remains tightly regulated in these states, arrests for violating various laws are still possible. Arrests, however, are way down. About 40 million Americans currently break the law by smoking pot at least once a year, so the decline in arrests is welcome to many. Past laws have been enforced more harshly against African Americans, who are jailed in large numbers. Ironically, a racial bias in arrests continues in the states that have legalized pot—but the overall drop in arrests has benefited thousands of minority group members.

Not All the News Is Good

One reason that marijuana tax revenues have been high is that consumption has gone up. In states that have adopted legalization, more people are consuming cannabis, and some are using much more of it. For many—an estimated 4.3 million people—marijuana use is an addiction. The American Medical Association claims that heavy marijuana use in adolescents causes impairments in neurocognitive performance and IQ. As one pundit put it, "The reason potheads appear stupid is because in fact they are becoming stupider." High school students who use marijuana tend to have lower grades and are less likely to get into college than nonsmokers. Of course, state laws in Colorado, Oregon, and Washington ban the possession and use of weed by minors. Still, legalizing the substance for use by adults can only mean that young people will access it more easily.

For Critical Analysis

▶ **What problems can arise when a state legalizes recreational marijuana—but the federal government continues to view it as illegal?**

▶ **When marijuana is legal, to what extent will it replace alcohol—and to what extent are users likely to consume both?**

Image 3–1 A cultivator in Colorado harvests marijuana plants. Alaska, Colorado, the District of Columbia, Oregon, and Washington have voted to legalize the recreational use of marijuana, but the drug remains illegal under federal law. *What do you think will happen?*

Kathryn Scott Osler/Getty Images

In the United States, rights and powers are reserved to the states by the Tenth Amendment. In recent years, however, it may appear that the federal government, sometimes called the national or central government, predominates. That might be an exaggerated perception, for there are 89,056 separate governmental units in this nation, as you can see in Table 3–1.

Visitors from countries such as France and Spain are often awestruck by the complexity of our system of government. Consider that a criminal action can be defined by state law, by national law, or by both. Thus, a criminal suspect can be prosecuted in the state court system or in the federal court system (or both). Often, economic regulation covering exactly the same issues exists at the local level, the state level, and the national level—generating multiple forms to be completed, multiple procedures to be followed, and multiple laws to be obeyed. Many programs are funded by the national government but administered by state and local governments.

Relations between central governments and local units can be structured in various ways. *Federalism* is one of these ways. Understanding federalism and how it differs from other forms of government is important in understanding the American political system. Indeed, many political issues today would not arise if we did not have a federal form of government in which governmental authority is divided between the central government and various subunits. States, for example, might find it impossible to set their own marijuana policies, as we discussed in this chapter's opening *What If . . .* feature.

Federalism and Its Alternatives

There are almost two hundred independent nations in the world today. Each of these nations has its own system of government. Generally, though, we can describe how nations structure relations between central governments and local units in terms of three models: (1) the unitary system, (2) the confederal system, and (3) the federal system. The most popular, both historically and today, is the unitary system.

A Unitary System

A **unitary system** of government is the easiest to define. Unitary systems place ultimate governmental authority in the hands of the national, or central, government. Consider a typical unitary system—France. The regions, departments, municipalities, and communes in France have elected and appointed officials.

So far, the French system appears to be very similar to the U.S. system, but the similarity is only superficial. Under the unitary French system, the decisions of the lower levels of government can be overruled by the national government. The national government also can cut off the funding for local government activities. Moreover, in a unitary system such as that in France, all questions of education, police, the use of land, and welfare are handled by the national government. Britain, Egypt, Ghana, Israel, Japan, the Philippines, and Sweden—in fact, a majority of all nations—have unitary systems of government.[1]

A Confederal System

You were introduced to the elements of a **confederal system** of government in Chapter 2, when we examined the Articles of Confederation. A *confederation* is the opposite of a unitary governing system. It is a league of independent states, in which a central government or administration handles only those matters of common concern expressly

---

Table 3–1
Governmental Units in the United States

The number of school districts has decreased over time, but the number of special districts created for single purposes, such as flood control, has increased from about 8,000 during World War II to more than 37,000 today. Why so many?

Federal government	**1**
State governments and District of Columbia	**51**
Local governments	
Counties	3,031
Municipalities (mainly cities or towns)	19,522
Townships (less extensive powers)	16,364
Special districts (water, sewer, and the like)	37,203
School districts	12,884
TOTAL	**89,056**

Source: U.S. Census Bureau.

unitary system
A centralized governmental system in which ultimate governmental authority rests in the hands of the national, or central, government.

confederal system
A system consisting of a league of independent states, in which the central government created by the league has only limited powers over the states.

---

1. Recent legislation has altered somewhat the unitary character of the French political system. In Britain, the unitary nature of the government has been modified by the creation of the Scottish Parliament.

Image 3–2 The National Guard distributes bottled water in Flint, Michigan, in January 2016. The city's water supply was contaminated with high levels of lead following an attempt by the Michigan state government to save money. The disaster is under investigation by both state and federal authorities. *Why can both levels of government investigate this kind of issue?*

delegated to it by the member states. The central government has no ability to make laws directly applicable to member states unless the members explicitly support such laws. The United States under the Articles of Confederation was a confederal system.

Few, if any, confederations of this kind exist. One possible exception is the European Union (EU), a league of countries that has developed a large body of Europe-wide laws that all members must observe. Many members even share a common currency, the euro.

A Federal System

The federal system lies between the unitary and confederal forms of government. As mentioned in Chapter 2, in a *federal system,* authority is divided, usually by a written constitution, between a central government and regional, or subdivisional, governments (often called *constituent governments*). The central government and the constituent governments both act directly on the people through laws and through the actions of elected and appointed governmental officials. Within each government's sphere of authority, each is supreme, in theory. Thus, a federal system

Learning Outcome 1:

Explain some of the benefits of the federal system for the United States.

differs from a unitary one, in which the central government is supreme and the constituent governments derive their authority from it. In addition to the United States, Australia, Brazil, Canada, Germany, India, and Mexico are examples of nations with federal systems. See Figure 3–1 for a comparison of the three systems. We take a quick look at how federalism works in Canada in this chapter's *Beyond Our Borders* feature.

Figure 3–1 The Flow of Power in Three Systems of Government

In a unitary system, power flows from the central government to the local and state governments. In a confederal system, power flows in the opposite direction—from the state governments to the central government. In a federal system, the flow of power, in principle, goes both ways. *Why do you think confederal systems are rare?*

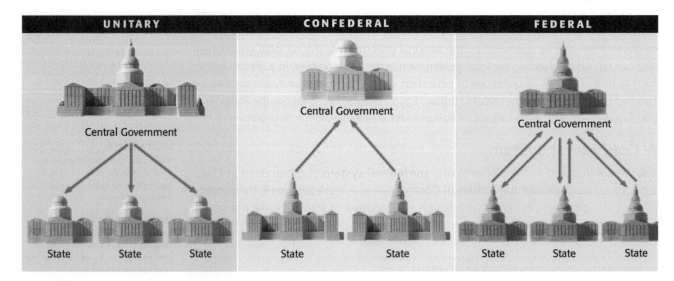

Beyond our borders
Canadian Federalism

Culturally and historically, Canada and the United States have much in common. One point of similarity is that both nations have federal constitutions. Canadian federalism is not quite like ours, however.

A Foreign Country

A key point is that Canada really is a foreign country and not a piece of America that happens to be under a separate government. Canada has a parliamentary system and close historical ties to Britain. Some may ask why Canada did not join the thirteen colonies in seeking independence. The answer is that at the time of the American Revolution, Canada was even more radically different from America than it is today. At that time, the name *Canada* meant only today's province of Québec. Most Canadians spoke French and were Roman Catholic. Americans were mainly English-speaking Protestants.

Britain recognized that it had a problem in ensuring the loyalty of its Canadian subjects, given that they were different in religion and language. Parliament therefore treated Canada more carefully than it did the thirteen colonies, and Canadians had little reason to rebel. After the American Revolution, a substantial body of Americans who were loyal to Britain emigrated to Canada, settling in what is now Ontario. These United Empire Loyalists were no more interested in becoming Americans than were the French-speaking *Canadiens*.

The Founding of Federal Canada

With the British North America Act of 1867, Canada emerged as a self-governing dominion. Its huge territory and two chief languages were strong arguments in favor of federalism. At that point, though, the United States had just concluded the Civil War. Canada's founders attributed the war in part to the looseness of America's federal system and sought to establish a tighter union. This is reflected in the very word *province*, applied to what Americans call *states*. Unlike states, provinces are never sovereign. Initial Canadian law limited the powers of the provinces, not—as in the U.S. Constitution—the national government. The central government could veto any provincial legislation.

Over time, the powers of the U.S. national government grew at the expense of the powers of the states. The opposite happened in Canada. By 1900, the government of Canada no longer sought to veto provincial legislation. In the United States, the Great Depression of the 1930s strengthened the national government. In Canada, the provinces grew stronger as they sought to deal with the consequences of this disaster.

Two Canadas?

Of Canada's ten provinces, nine are predominantly English-speaking. Québec remains loyal to French. That creates a fissure within the nation that could potentially break it apart. In fact, Québec has a major political party, the *Parti Québécois*, that advocates independence. It has never managed to persuade the people of Québec that separation would be a good idea, however. The Canadian federal government has allowed Québec an ample degree of freedom, which has blunted nationalist aspirations in *la belle province*.

For Critical Analysis

◉ **Why might Québec particularism be more broadly acceptable than states' rights in the United States?**

Why Federalism?

Why did the United States develop in a federal direction? As you saw in Chapter 2, the historical basis of our federal system was established in Philadelphia at the Constitutional Convention, where advocates of a strong national government opposed states' rights advocates. This conflict continued through to the ratifying conventions in the several states. The resulting federal system was a compromise. The supporters of the new Constitution were political pragmatists—they realized that without a federal arrangement, the new Constitution would not be ratified. The appeal of federalism was that it retained

AP Images/J. Pat Carter

Image 3–3 A teacher high-fives an elementary school student in Miami. This teacher is funded by Teach for America, a nonprofit organization that places recent high-achieving college graduates in low-income community schools. The program receives federal grants. *Should the national government have a role in educational policy?*

state traditions and local power while establishing a strong national government capable of handling common problems.

Even if the founders had agreed on the desirability of a unitary system, size and regional isolation would have made such a system difficult operationally. At the time of the Constitutional Convention, the thirteen states taken together were much larger geographically than England or France. Slow travel and communication, combined with geographic spread, contributed to the isolation of many regions within the states. It could take several weeks for all of the states to be informed about a particular political decision.

Other Arguments for Federalism

Even with modern transportation and communications systems, the large area or population of some nations makes it impractical to locate all political authority in one place. Federalism brings government closer to the people. It allows more direct access to, and influence on, government agencies and policies, rather than leaving the population restive and dissatisfied with a remote, faceless, all-powerful central authority.

Benefits for the United States. In the United States, federalism historically has yielded additional benefits. State governments long have been a training ground for future national leaders. Many presidents made their political mark as state governors. The states themselves have been testing grounds for new government initiatives. As United States Supreme Court justice Louis Brandeis once observed:

> *It is one of the happy incidents of the federal system that a single courageous state may, if its citizens choose, serve as a laboratory and try novel social and economic experiments without risk to the rest of the country.*[2]

Examples of programs pioneered at the state level include unemployment compensation, which began in Wisconsin, and air-pollution control, which was initiated in California. Same-sex marriage was first adopted in one state—Massachusetts. Recently, states have also tried new ways to manage marijuana. We took a closer look at these developments in this chapter's opening *What If . . .* feature.

Allowance for Many Political Subcultures. The American way of life always has been characterized by a number of political subcultures, which divide along the lines of race and ethnic origin, region, wealth, education, and, more recently, degree of religious commitment and sexual preference. The existence of diverse political subcultures would appear to be incompatible with a political authority concentrated solely in a central government. Had the United States developed into a unitary system, various political subcultures certainly would have been less able to influence government behavior than they have been, and continue to be, in our federal system.

Arguments against Federalism

Not everyone thinks federalism is such a good idea. Some see it as a way for powerful state and local interests to block progress and impede national plans. Smaller political

---

2. *New State Ice Co. v. Liebmann,* 285 U.S. 262 (1932).

units are more likely to be dominated by a single political group. (This was essentially the argument that James Madison put forth in *Federalist Paper* No. 10, which you can read in Appendix C of this text.) In fact, the dominant groups in some cities and states have resisted implementing equal rights for minority groups. Some argue, however, that the dominant factions in other states have been more progressive than the national government in many areas, such as environmental protection.

Critics of federalism also argue that too many Americans suffer as a result of the inequalities across the states. Individual states differ markedly in educational spending and achievement, crime and crime prevention, and even the safety of their buildings. Not surprisingly, these critics argue for increased federal legislation and oversight. This might involve creating national standards for education and building codes, national expenditure minimums for crime control, and similar measures.

Others see dangers in the expansion of national powers at the expense of the states. President Ronald Reagan (1981–1989) said, "The Founding Fathers saw the federalist system as constructed something like a masonry wall. The States are the bricks, the national government is the mortar. . . . Unfortunately, over the years, many people have increasingly come to believe that Washington is the whole wall."[3]

The Constitutional Basis for American Federalism

Learning Outcome **2:**

Describe how the various provisions of the U.S. Constitution provide a framework for federalism.

The term *federal system* cannot be found in the U.S. Constitution. Nor is it possible to find a systematic division of governmental authority between the national and state governments in that document. Rather, the Constitution sets out different types of powers. These powers can be classified as (1) the powers of the national government, (2) the powers of the states, and (3) prohibited powers. The Constitution also makes it clear that if a state or local law conflicts with a national law, the national law will prevail.

Powers of the National Government

The powers delegated to the national government include both expressed and implied powers, as well as the special category of inherent powers.

Enumerated Powers. Most of the powers expressly delegated to the national government are found in the first seventeen clauses of Article I, Section 8, of the Constitution. (We examined portions of this clause in the *Consider the Source* feature in Chapter 2.) These **enumerated powers,** also called *expressed powers,* include coining money, setting standards for weights and measures, making uniform naturalization laws, admitting new states, establishing post offices and post roads, and declaring war. Another important enumerated power is the power to regulate commerce among the states—a topic we deal with later in this chapter.

The Necessary and Proper Clause. The implied powers of the national government are also based on Article I, Section 8, which states that the Congress shall have the power

> to make all Laws which shall be necessary and proper for carrying into Execution the foregoing Powers, and all other Powers vested by this Constitution in the Government of the United States, or in any Department or Officer thereof.

enumerated powers

Powers specifically granted to the national government by the Constitution. The first seventeen clauses of Article I, Section 8, specify most of the enumerated powers of the national government.

---

3. As quoted in Edward Millican, *One United People: The Federalist Papers and the National Idea* (Lexington: The University Press of Kentucky, 1990).

This clause is sometimes called the **elastic clause,** or the **necessary and proper clause,** because it provides flexibility to our constitutional system. It gives Congress the power to do whatever is necessary to execute its specifically delegated powers. The clause was first used in the Supreme Court decision of *McCulloch v. Maryland*[4] (discussed later in this chapter) to develop the concept of implied powers. Through this concept, the national government has succeeded in strengthening the scope of its authority to meet the many problems that the framers of the Constitution did not, and could not, anticipate.

Inherent Powers. A special category of national powers that is not always implied by the necessary and proper clause consists of what have been labeled the *inherent powers* of the national government. These powers derive from the fact that the United States is a sovereign power among nations, and so its national government must be the only government that deals with other nations. Under international law, it is assumed that all nation-states, regardless of their size or power, have an inherent right to ensure their own survival. To do this, each nation must have the ability to act in its own interest among and with the community of nations—by, for instance, making treaties, waging war, seeking trade, and acquiring territory.

Note that no specific clause in the Constitution says anything about the acquisition of additional land. Nonetheless, the federal government's inherent powers allowed it to make the Louisiana Purchase in 1803 and then go on to acquire Florida, Oregon, Texas, California, Alaska, Hawaii, and other lands.

Some constitutional scholars categorize inherent powers as a third type of power, completely distinct from the delegated powers (both expressed and implied) of the national government. Others point out that some—but not all—inherent powers are also spelled out in the Constitution. Article 1, Section 8, for example, gives Congress the power to declare war, to raise and support armies, and to maintain a navy.

Powers of the State Governments

The Tenth Amendment states that the powers not delegated to the United States by the Constitution, nor prohibited by it to the states, are reserved to the states, or to the people. These are the *reserved powers* that the national government cannot deny to the states. Because these powers are not expressly listed, there is sometimes a question as to whether a certain power is delegated to the national government or reserved to the states.

State powers have been held to include each state's right to regulate commerce within its borders and to provide for a state militia. States also have the reserved power to make laws on all matters not prohibited to the states by the U.S. Constitution or state constitutions and not expressly, or by implication, delegated to the national government. Furthermore, the states have **police power**—the authority to legislate for the protection of the health, morals, safety, and welfare of the people. Their police power enables states to pass laws governing such activities as crime, marriage, contracts, education, intrastate transportation, and land use.

It is also worth noting that while the United States as a whole uses a federal system of government, each state has a unitary system. Hence, it is said that county, municipal, and other local governments are "creatures of the state." In principle, a state can alter or abolish a local government (though in some instances that might require an amendment to the state constitution). An example of a state exercising such power was the March 2013 takeover of the city of Detroit by the state of Michigan. At that point, Detroit was effectively bankrupt.

elastic clause, or necessary and proper clause

The clause in Article I, Section 8, that grants Congress the power to do whatever is necessary to execute its specifically delegated powers.

police power

The authority to legislate for the protection of the health, morals, safety, and welfare of the people. In the United States, most police power is reserved to the states.

4. 17 U.S. 316 (1819).

The ambiguity of the Tenth Amendment has allowed the reserved powers of the states to be defined differently at different times in our history. When there is widespread support for increased regulation by the national government, the Tenth Amendment tends to recede into the background. When the tide turns the other way (in favor of states' rights), the Tenth Amendment is resurrected to justify arguments supporting the states.

Prohibited Powers

The Constitution prohibits, or denies, a number of powers to the national government. For example, the national government has expressly been denied the power to impose taxes on goods sold to other countries (exports). Moreover, any power not granted expressly or implicitly to the federal government by the Constitution is prohibited to it.

Image 3–4 *"They have very strict anti-pollution laws in this state."*

For example, many legal experts believe that the national government could not create a national divorce law system without a constitutional amendment. The states are also denied certain powers. For example, no state is allowed to enter into a treaty on its own with another country.

Concurrent Powers

In certain areas, the states share **concurrent powers** with the national government. Most concurrent powers are not specifically listed in the Constitution—they are only implied. An example of a concurrent power is the power to tax. The types of taxation are divided between the levels of government. For example, states may not levy a tariff (a set of taxes on imported goods). Only the national government may do this. Neither government may tax the facilities of the other. If the state governments did not have the power to tax, they would not be able to function independently of the national government.

Additional concurrent powers include the power to borrow funds, to establish courts, and to charter banks and corporations. To a limited extent, the national government exercises police power, and to the extent that it does, police power is also a concurrent power. Concurrent powers exercised by the states are normally limited to the geographic area of each state and to those functions not granted by the Constitution exclusively to the national government.

One concurrent power that has been the subject of much recent controversy is the power to establish a minimum wage. Many states have recently raised their minimum wages. We examine the effect of these laws in this chapter's *Which Side Are You On?* feature.

The Supremacy Clause

The supremacy of the national constitution over subnational laws and actions is established in the **supremacy clause** of the Constitution. The supremacy clause (Article VI, Clause 2) states the following:

> *This Constitution, and the Laws of the United States which shall be made in Pursuance thereof; and all Treaties made . . . under the Authority of the United States, shall be the supreme Law of the Land; and the Judges in every State shall*

concurrent powers
Powers held jointly by the national and state governments.

supremacy clause
The constitutional provision that makes the Constitution and federal laws superior to all conflicting state and local laws.

be bound thereby, any Thing in the Constitution or Laws of any State to the Contrary notwithstanding.

In other words, states cannot use their reserved or concurrent powers to thwart national policies. All national and state officers, including judges, must be bound by oath to support the Constitution. Hence, any legitimate exercise of national governmental

Which side are you on?

Should States Raise the Minimum Wage?

A minimum wage is the lowest wage rate that an employer can legally pay. The national minimum wage is set by Congress. Currently, it is $7.25 per hour. Australia has the world's highest such wage—$15.58 in U.S. dollars.

Twenty-nine states now have a minimum wage higher than the national rate. The Maine and New Mexico rates are only 25 cents more than the national minimum. As of January 2017, Massachusetts had the highest state minimum wage at $11.00 per hour. A national movement has grown up around raising the minimum wage to $15.00 per hour, and a number of state and local governments have backed this effort. California, New York, metro Portland in Oregon, and the city of Seattle are phasing in a $15.00 minimum wage over a period of years.

Minimum wage laws are generally popular with voters. In a recent poll, 90 percent of Democrats and 53 percent of Republicans supported a higher minimum wage. Proposals to raise the minimum wage were on the ballot in half a dozen states in 2016. Economists, however, are much less likely to favor such laws than are average voters.

Higher Minimum Wages Kill Jobs

Most conservative politicians—and many economists who aren't necessarily that conservative—oppose minimum wage laws. Obviously, hiking the minimum wage raises the pay of the lowest-paid workers. These workers become more expensive to hire. It is basic economics that in normal circumstances, if something costs more, people will buy less of it. A higher minimum wage should therefore reduce the number of low-wage jobs.

Many minimum-wage workers are employed by fast-food restaurants and retail stores that cater to the poor. If minimum wages continue to rise, these businesses may need to raise their prices to recoup lost profits. The result: more expensive food and clothing for other low-income

workers. Ultimately, no businessperson will consistently pay a worker a wage rate that exceeds the value of that worker's output. Teenagers—especially minorities—who cannot find a minimum-wage job would lose out on the opportunity to learn basic work skills that could help them find better jobs later.

Higher Minimum Wages Are Good Policy

Advocates of raising minimum wages accept that they would reduce employment if they were set very high. Advocates also argue, however, that the modest increases in the minimum wage seen in many states do not in fact have such a result—the employment effect of these wage increases is so small we can't reliably measure it. For example, at the Idaho-Washington border, there appears to be no tendency to shift fast-food employment to the Idaho side, even though Idaho has no state minimum wage and the Washington rate is relatively high.

Higher minimum wages can lift many of the working poor out of poverty. Another likely outcome of higher minimum wages is less income inequality. We can also predict that with a higher minimum wage, there would be less turnover—workers would stay longer in low-wage jobs. Finally, it's worth noting that the stereotype of a minimum-wage worker as a teenager is not accurate. The average age of minimum-wage workers is thirty-five, and 88 percent are at least twenty years old. Paying workers a living wage is only fair.

For Critical Analysis

❯ If a San Francisco bookstore closes because it can't afford to pay its clerks the California minimum wage, would you blame the minimum-wage law—or Amazon?

power supersedes any conflicting state action. Of course, deciding whether a conflict actually exists is a judicial matter, as you will soon learn when we discuss the case of *McCulloch v. Maryland.*

The National Guard can serve as an example of how federal power supersedes that of the states. Normally, the National Guard functions as a state militia under the command of the governor. It is frequently called out to assist with recovery efforts after natural disasters such as hurricanes, floods, and earthquakes. The president, however, can assume command of any National Guard unit at any time. Presidents George W. Bush and Barack Obama repeatedly "federalized" such units for deployment in Afghanistan and Iraq. In the conflicts in these countries, National Guard members and reservists made up a larger percentage of the forces on combat duty than during any previous war in U.S. history.

National government legislation in a concurrent area is said to *preempt* (take precedence over) conflicting state or local laws or regulations in that area. One of the ways in which the national government has extended its powers, particularly during the twentieth century, is through the preemption of state and local laws by national legislation. In the first decade of the twentieth century, fewer than twenty national laws preempted laws and regulations issued by state and local governments. By the beginning of the twenty-first century, the number had grown into the hundreds.

Interstate Relations

So far, we have examined only the relationship between central and state governmental units. The states, however, have constant commercial, social, and other dealings among themselves. The national Constitution imposes certain "rules of the road" on interstate relations. These rules have had the effect of preventing any one state from setting itself apart from the other states. The three most important clauses governing interstate relations in the Constitution, all taken from the Articles of Confederation, require each state to do the following:

- Give full faith and credit to every other state's public acts, records, and judicial proceedings (Article IV, Section 1).
- Extend to every other state's citizens the privileges and immunities of its own citizens (Article IV, Section 2).
- Agree to return persons who are fleeing from justice in another state back to their home state when requested to do so (Article IV, Section 2).

Additionally, states may enter into agreements with one another called **interstate compacts**. Congressional consent is necessary if such a compact increases the power of the contracting states relative to other states (or to the national government). An example of an interstate compact is the Port Authority of New York and New Jersey, established by an agreement between those two states in 1921.

interstate compact

An agreement between two or more states. Agreements on minor matters are made without congressional consent, but any compact that tends to increase the power of the contracting states relative to other states or relative to the national government generally requires the consent of Congress.

Image 3–5 One World Trade Center and the 9/11 memorial site in New York City. The tower is the tallest building in the Western Hemisphere. It was erected by the Port Authority of New York and New Jersey, an interstate compact. *Which rules govern what an interstate compact can do?*

IndustryAndTravel/Shutterstock.com

Defining Constitutional Powers—the Early Years

Learning Outcome **3:**

Discuss how, in the early years of the republic, the United States Supreme Court confirmed the authority of the national government, and how that authority was ratified by the Civil War.

Although political bodies at all levels of government play important roles in the process of settling disputes over the nature of our federal system, ultimately it is the United States Supreme Court that casts the final vote. As might be expected, the character of the referee will have an impact on the ultimate outcome of any dispute. From 1801 to 1835, the Supreme Court was headed by Chief Justice John Marshall, a Federalist who advocated a strong central government. We look here at two cases decided by the Marshall Court: *McCulloch v. Maryland*[5] and *Gibbons v. Ogden*.[6] Both cases are considered milestones in the movement toward national government supremacy.

McCulloch v. Maryland (1819)

The U.S. Constitution says nothing about establishing a national bank. Nonetheless, at different times Congress chartered two banks—the First and Second Banks of the United States—and provided part of their initial capital. Thus, they were national banks. The government of Maryland imposed a tax on the Second Bank's Baltimore branch in an attempt to put that branch out of business. The branch's cashier, James William McCulloch, refused to pay the Maryland tax. When Maryland took McCulloch to its state court, the state of Maryland won. The national government appealed the case to the Supreme Court.

One of the issues before the Court was whether the national government had the implied power, under the necessary and proper clause, to charter a bank and contribute capital to it. The other important question before the Court was the following: If the bank was constitutional, could a state tax it? In other words, was a state action that conflicted with a national government action invalid under the supremacy clause?

Chief Justice Marshall held that if establishing a national bank aided the national government in the exercise of its designated powers, then the authority to set up such a bank could be implied. Having established this doctrine of implied powers, Marshall then answered the other question before the Court and established the doctrine of national supremacy. Marshall ruled that no state could use its taxing power to tax a part of the national government. If it could, "the declaration that the Constitution . . . shall be the supreme law of the land, is [an] empty and unmeaning [statement]."

Marshall's decision enabled the national government to grow and to meet problems that the Constitution's framers were unable to foresee. Today, practically every expressed power of the national government has been expanded in one way or another by use of the necessary and proper clause.

Gibbons v. Ogden (1824)

One of the most important parts of the Constitution included in Article I, Section 8, is the **commerce clause,** in which Congress is given the power "to regulate Commerce with foreign Nations, and among the several States, and with the Indian Tribes." The meaning of this clause was at issue in *Gibbons v. Ogden*.

The Background of the Case. Robert Fulton and Robert Livingston secured a monopoly on steam navigation on the waters in New York State from the New York legislature in 1803. They licensed Aaron Ogden to operate steam-powered ferryboats between New York and New Jersey. Thomas Gibbons, who had obtained a license from the U.S. government to operate boats in interstate waters, decided to compete with Ogden, but he did so without

commerce clause

The section of the Constitution in which Congress is given the power to regulate trade among the states and with foreign countries.

---

5. 17 U.S. 316 (1819).
6. 22 U.S. 1 (1824).

New York's permission. Ogden sued Gibbons. New York's state courts prohibited Gibbons from operating in New York waters. Gibbons appealed to the Supreme Court.

There were actually several issues before the Court in this case. The first issue was how the term *commerce* should be defined. New York's highest court had defined the term narrowly to mean only the shipment of goods or the interchange of commodities, *not* navigation or the transport of people. The second issue was whether the national government's power to regulate interstate commerce extended to commerce within a state (*intrastate* commerce) or was limited strictly to commerce among the states (*interstate* commerce). The third issue was whether the power to regulate interstate commerce was a concurrent power (as the New York court had concluded) or an exclusive national power.

Marshall's Ruling. Marshall defined *commerce* as all commercial interactions—all business dealings—including navigation and the transport of people. Marshall also held that the commerce power of the national government could be exercised in state jurisdictions, even though it could not reach *solely* intrastate commerce. Finally, Marshall emphasized that the power to regulate interstate commerce was an *exclusive* national power. Marshall held that because Gibbons was duly authorized by the national government to navigate in interstate waters, he could not be prohibited from doing so by a state court.

Marshall's expansive interpretation of the commerce clause in *Gibbons v. Ogden* allowed the national government to exercise increasing authority over economic affairs throughout the land. Congress did not immediately exploit this broad grant of power. In the 1930s and subsequent decades, however, the commerce clause became the primary constitutional basis for national government regulation—as you will read later in this chapter.

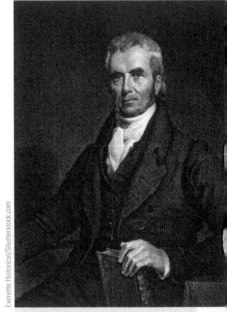

Image 3–6 When John Marshall was chief justice of the United States Supreme Court (1801–1835), he championed the power of the federal government. *What are the most famous cases that the Marshall Court decided?*

States' Rights and the Resort to Civil War

The controversy over slavery that led to the Civil War took the form of a dispute over national government supremacy versus the rights of the separate states. Essentially, the Civil War brought to an ultimate and violent climax the ideological debate begun by the Federalists and Anti-Federalists even before the Constitution was ratified.

The Shift Back to States' Rights. As we have seen, while John Marshall was chief justice of the Supreme Court, he did much to increase the power of the national government and to reduce that of the states. During the administration of President Andrew Jackson (1829–1837), however, a shift back to states' rights began. The question of the regulation of commerce became one of the major issues in federal–state relations. When Congress passed a tariff in 1828, the state of South Carolina unsuccessfully attempted to nullify the tariff (render it void), claiming that in cases of conflict between a state and the national government, the state should have the ultimate authority over its citizens.

During the next three decades, the North and the South became even more sharply divided, especially over the slavery issue. On December 20, 1860, South Carolina formally repealed its ratification of the Constitution and withdrew from the Union. On February 4, 1861, representatives from six southern states met at Montgomery, Alabama, to form a new government called the Confederate States of America.

War and the Growth of the National Government. The ultimate defeat of the South in 1865 permanently ended the idea that a state could successfully claim the right to secede, or withdraw, from the Union. Ironically, the Civil War—brought about in large part because of the South's desire for increased states' rights—resulted in the opposite: an increase in the political power of the national government.

Thousands of new employees were hired to run the Union war effort and to deal with the social and economic problems that had to be handled in the aftermath of the war. A billion-dollar ($1.3 billion, which is about $20 billion in today's dollars) national government

dual federalism

A model of federalism in which the states and the national government each remain supreme within their own spheres. The doctrine looks on nation and state as co-equal sovereign powers. Neither the state government nor the national government should interfere in the other's sphere.

budget was passed for the first time in 1865 to cover the increased government expenditures. The first (temporary) income tax was imposed on citizens to help pay for the war.

The Civil War Amendments. The expansion of the national government's authority during the Civil War was also reflected in the passage of the Civil War amendments to the Constitution. Before the war, it was a bedrock constitutional principle that the national government should not interfere with slavery in the states. The Thirteenth Amendment, ratified in 1865, did more than interfere with slavery—it abolished the institution altogether.

The Fourteenth Amendment, ratified in 1868, defined who was a citizen of each state. It sought to guarantee equal rights under state law, stating that

> [no] State [shall] deprive any person of life, liberty, or property, without due process of law; nor deny to any person within its jurisdiction the equal protection of the laws.

In time, the courts interpreted these words to mean that the national Bill of Rights applied to state governments, a development that we will examine in Chapter 4. Finally, the Fifteenth Amendment (1870) gave African Americans the right to vote in all elections, including state elections—although a century would pass before that right was enforced in all states.

The Continuing Dispute over the Division of Power

Learning Outcome **4:**

Define the terms *dual federalism*, *cooperative federalism*, *categorical grants*, *block grants*, and *fiscal federalism*.

Although the outcome of the Civil War firmly established the supremacy of the national government and put to rest the idea that a state could secede from the Union, the war by no means ended the debate over the division of powers between the national government and the states.

Image 3–7 John Brown (1800–1859), an advocate of abolishing slavery, led an ill-fated raid on a federal arsenal at Harper's Ferry, Virginia. Brown had hoped to set off a slave uprising. He was executed on charges of treason and murder. Today, we would doubtless call him a terrorist. *Why do some people nevertheless consider him a hero?*

National Archives

Dual Federalism

During the decades following the Civil War, the prevailing model of federalism was what political scientists have called **dual federalism**—a doctrine that emphasizes a distinction between national and state spheres of government authority. This doctrine looks on nation and state as co-equal sovereign powers. Neither the state government nor the national government should interfere in the other's sphere.

Various images have been used to describe different configurations of federalism over time. Dual federalism is commonly depicted as a layer cake, because the state governments and the national government are viewed as separate entities, like separate layers of a cake. The two layers are physically separate; they do not mix. For the most part, advocates of dual federalism believed that the state and national governments should not exercise authority in the same areas.

The doctrine of dual federalism represented a revival of states' rights following the expansion of national authority during the Civil War. Dual federalism, after all, was a fairly accurate model of the prewar consensus on federal–state relations. For many people, it therefore represented a return to normal.

The Civil War crisis drastically reduced the influence of the United States Supreme Court. In the prewar *Dred Scott* decision,[7] the Court had attempted to abolish the power of the national government to restrict slavery in the territories, and it also declared that African Americans could never be citizens, even if free.[8] In so doing, the Court placed itself on the losing side of the impending conflict. After the war, Congress took the unprecedented step of exempting the entire process of Southern reconstruction from judicial review. The Court had little choice but to acquiesce.

In time, the Supreme Court reestablished itself as the legitimate constitutional umpire. Its decisions tended to support dual federalism, defend states' rights, and limit the powers of the national government. The Court generally limited the exercise of police power to the states. For example, in 1918, the Court ruled that a 1916 national law banning child labor was unconstitutional because it attempted to regulate a local problem.[9] In effect, the Court placed severe limits on the ability of Congress to legislate under the commerce clause of the Constitution.

The New Deal and Cooperative Federalism

The doctrine of dual federalism receded into the background in the 1930s as the nation attempted to deal with the Great Depression. Franklin D. Roosevelt was inaugurated as president on March 4, 1933. In the previous year, nearly 1,500 banks had failed (and 4,000 more would fail in 1933). Thirty-two thousand businesses had closed down, and almost one-fourth of the labor force was unemployed. The public expected the national government to do something about the disastrous state of the economy.

The "New Deal." President Herbert Hoover (1929–1933), however, clung to the doctrine of dual federalism and insisted that unemployment and poverty were local issues. The states, not the national government, had the sole responsibility for combating the effects of unemployment and providing relief to the poor. Roosevelt did not feel bound by this doctrine, and his new Democratic administration energetically intervened in the economy. Roosevelt's "New Deal" included large-scale emergency antipoverty programs. In addition, the New Deal introduced major new laws regulating economic activity, such as the National Industrial Recovery Act of 1933, which established the National Recovery Administration (NRA).

The End of Dual Federalism. Roosevelt's expansion of national authority was challenged by the Supreme Court, which continued to adhere to the doctrine of dual federalism. In 1935, the Court ruled that the NRA program was unconstitutional.[10] The NRA had turned out to be largely unworkable and was unpopular. The Court, however, rejected the program on the ground that it regulated intrastate, not interstate, commerce. This position appeared to rule out any alternative recovery plans that might be better designed.

In 1937, Roosevelt proposed legislation that would allow him to add up to six new justices to the Supreme Court. Presumably, the new justices would be more friendly to the exercise of national power than the existing members were. Congressional Democrats refused

AP Images

Image 3–8 Child labor was still common in the early 1900s. *Why didn't the federal government simply ban it then?*

7. *Dred Scott v. Sandford*, 60 U.S. 393 (1856).

8. While Southerners often defended slavery by appealing to states' rights, *Dred Scott* was an *anti-states' rights* decision—it tried to deny Northern states the right to grant citizenship to African Americans.

9. *Hammer v. Dagenhart*, 247 U.S. 251 (1918). This decision was overruled in *United States v. Darby*, 312 U.S. 100 (1940).

10. *Schechter Poultry Corp. v. United States*, 295 U.S. 495 (1935).

Image 3–9 President Franklin Delano Roosevelt (1933–1945). Roosevelt's national approach to addressing the effects of the Great Depression was overwhelmingly popular, although many of his specific initiatives were controversial. *How did the Great Depression change the political beliefs of many ordinary Americans?*

to support the measure, and it failed. Still, changes to the membership of the Court from 1937 on proved as effective as the failed "court-packing scheme." After 1937 the Court ceased its attempts to limit the national government's powers under the commerce clause.

Cooperative Federalism. Some political scientists have described the era since 1937 as characterized by **cooperative federalism,** in which the states and the national government cooperate in solving complex common problems. Roosevelt's New Deal programs, for example, often involved joint action between the national government and the states. The pattern of federal–state relationships during these years gave rise to a new metaphor for federalism—that of a marble cake. Unlike a layer cake, in a marble cake the two types of cake are intermingled, and any bite contains cake of both flavors.

As an example of how national and state governments work together under the cooperative federalism model, consider Temporary Assistance for Needy Families (TANF). Created in 1997 to replace an earlier welfare program, TANF provides limited cash assistance to families with children who are living in severe poverty. Under the TANF program, the national government provides most of the funding, but state governments establish benefit levels and eligibility requirements for recipients. Local welfare offices are staffed by state, not national, employees. In return for national funding, the states must conform to a series of regulations on how the program is carried out. The states, however, have more discretion on how to distribute funds than under earlier welfare programs.

Methods of Implementing Cooperative Federalism

Even before the Constitution was adopted, the national government gave grants to the states in the form of land to finance education. The national government also provided land grants for canals, railroads, and roads. In the twentieth century, federal grants increased significantly, especially during Roosevelt's administration throughout the Great Depression and again in the 1960s, when the dollar amount of grants quadrupled. These funds were used for improvements in education, pollution control, recreation, and highways. With this increase in grants, however, came a bewildering number of restrictions and regulations.

Categorical Grants. In the 1980s, **categorical grants** were spread out across four hundred separate programs, but the five largest accounted for more than 50 percent of the revenues spent. These five programs were Medicaid (health care for the poor), highway construction, unemployment benefits, housing assistance, and welfare programs to assist mothers with dependent children and people with disabilities. For fiscal year 2017, the national government gave about $694 billion to the states. The shift toward a greater role for the central government in the United States can be seen in Figure 3–2, which shows the increase in central government spending as a percentage of total government spending.

Before the 1960s, most categorical grants by the national government were *formula grants*. These grants take their name from the method used to allocate funds. They fund state programs using a formula based on such variables as the state's needs, population,

cooperative federalism

A model of federalism in which the states and the national government cooperate in solving problems.

categorical grant

A federal grant to a state or local government for a specific program or project.

Figure 3–2 The Shift toward Central Government Spending

In the years before the Great Depression, local governments accounted for close to three-fifths of all government spending, and the federal government accounted for only about 30 percent. After Franklin D. Roosevelt's New Deal, national spending began to rival state and local spending combined. The national share is still about 46 percent today, not counting transfers to state and local governments. The size of the pies reflects total spending. *Note that the United States entered World War II in 1941. What effect might the national security crisis leading up to the war have had on federal spending?*

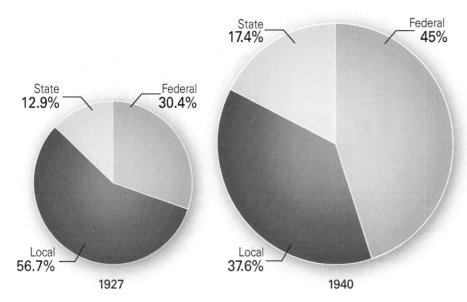

Sources: *Historical Statistics of the United States,* Bureau of the Census, and authors' calculations.

or willingness to come up with matching funds. Beginning in the 1960s, the national government began increasingly to offer *program grants*. This funding requires states to apply for grants for specific programs. The applications are evaluated by the national government, and the applications may compete with one another. Program grants give the national government a much greater degree of control over state activities than do formula grants.

Over the decades, federal grants to the states have increased significantly, as shown in Figure 3–3. One reason for this increase is that Congress has decided to offload some programs to the states and provide a major part of the funding for them. Also, Congress continues to use grants to persuade states and cities to operate programs devised by the federal government. Finally, states often are happy to apply for grants because they are relatively "free," requiring only that the state match a small portion of each grant. States can still face criticism for accepting the grants, because their matching funds may be diverted from other state projects.

Block Grants. Block grants lessen the restrictions on federal grants given to state and local governments by grouping a number of categorical grants under one broad heading. Governors and mayors generally prefer block grants because such grants give the states more flexibility in how the funds are spent. Block grants, however, make up less than 10 percent of the funds transferred to the states by the federal government.

An example of a block grant program is the Surface Transportation Program, sponsored by the Federal Highway Administration. This program provides state and local authorities with considerable flexibility. Funds can be used to repair highways and bridges,

block grant

A federal grant that provides funds to a state or local government for a general functional area, such as criminal justice or mental-health programs.

Figure 3–3 The Rise in Federal Transfers to State and Local Governments

The chart shows the percentage of the nation's state and local revenues supplied by the federal government. The national government has gained leverage over state and local governments by supplying an increasing share of their revenues. The drop in federal transfers from 1980 to 1990 took place during the presidency of Ronald Reagan, as we explain in "The 'New Federalism'" section later in this chapter. *What might the national government try to do with the leverage it holds over the states?*

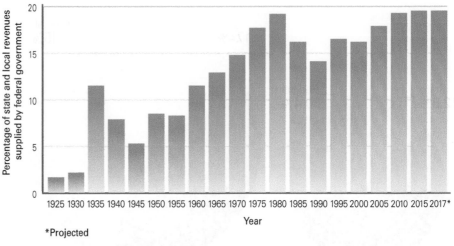

*Projected

Sources: *Historical Statistics of the United States; Statistical Abstract of the United States, 2008;* and www.usgovernmentspending.com.

or to support pedestrian, bicycle, or bus projects. Still, the program only amounts to about 16 percent of all federal transportation grants.

Fiscal Federalism and State Budgets

In discussions of government policy, you may have heard the word *fiscal*. This word simply means "having to do with government revenues and expenditures." **Fiscal** policy, therefore, is policy concerning taxing or borrowing—and then spending the revenues. When the federal government makes grants to state and local governments, funds raised through taxation or borrowing by one level of government (the national government) are spent by another level (state and local governments). We can speak of this process as **fiscal federalism.** With up to 20 percent of state and local revenues supplied by the federal government, fiscal federalism clearly has a major impact on the finances of the states.

The Great Recession in the first decade of the 2000s had a devastating impact on state budgets, and in response the federal government substantially increased the amount of funding available to the states. The funds did not fully compensate the states for lost revenue, however, and from 2011 on they were no longer available at all. State governments cut spending and employment substantially—so much so that total government spending as a share of the economy actually fell from 2010 through 2015.

Beginning in 2011, new conservative governors in many states argued that excessively generous pension benefits for state workers were a major part of state budget problems. Many of them sponsored new laws to reduce pension benefits. Several governors also campaigned against state employee labor unions, a step that led to controversy in states such as Ohio and Wisconsin.

fiscal

Having to do with government revenues and expenditures.

fiscal federalism

A process by which funds raised through taxation or borrowing by one level of government (usually the national government) are spent by another level (typically state or local governments).

Feeling the Pressure—the Strings Attached to Federal Grants. No dollars sent to the states are completely free of "strings." All funds come with requirements that must be met by the states. Often, through the use of grants, the national government has been able to exercise substantial control over matters that traditionally have been under the purview of state governments. When the federal government gives federal funds for highway improvements, for example, it may condition the funds on the state's cooperation with a federal policy. This is exactly what the federal government did in the 1980s and 1990s to force the states to raise their minimum alcoholic beverage drinking age to twenty-one.

Why should you care about **THE FEDERAL SYSTEM?**
In this chapter, we mention a variety of issues arising from our federal system that may concern you directly. For example, though the national government provides aid to educational programs, education is still primarily a state and local responsibility. The total amount of money spent on education is determined by state and local governments. Therefore, you can address the question of how much should be spent on education at the state or local level.

In 2012, for the first time, the United States Supreme Court placed limits on the ability of the national government to use federal grants to coerce state governments. In its ruling on the Affordable Care Act (Obamacare), the Court found that the penalties the act imposed on the states to compel them to expand the Medicaid program were excessive and unconstitutional. Under the health-care reform legislation, a state that refused to expand Medicaid would lose *all* Medicaid funding. Presumably, Congress could continue to coerce the states if it used less drastic penalties.[11]

Federal Mandates. For years, the federal government has passed legislation requiring that states improve environmental conditions or the civil rights of various groups. Since the 1970s, the national government has enacted hundreds of **federal mandates** requiring the states to take some action in areas ranging from voter registration, to ocean-dumping restrictions, to the education of people with disabilities. The Unfunded Mandates Reform Act of 1995 requires the Congressional Budget Office to identify mandates that cost state and local governments more than $50 million to implement. Nonetheless, the federal government routinely continues to pass mandates for state and local governments that cost more than that to put into place. For example, the National Conference of State Legislatures has identified federal mandates to the states in transportation, health care, education, environment, homeland security, election laws, and other areas with a total cost of $29 billion per year. Water-quality mandates appear to be particularly expensive.

One way in which the national government has moderated the burden of federal mandates is by granting *waivers,* which allow individual states to try out innovative approaches to carrying out the mandates. For example, governors of several conservative states agreed to expand Medicaid as part of the Obamacare program if they received waivers. The waivers allowed them to channel the new funds through private insurance companies rather than through the state government.

Competitive Federalism. When state governments have authority in a particular field, there may be great variations from state to state in how they exercise that authority. Such differentials can lead to a competition among the states, which has been called *competitive federalism.* For example, it is widely believed that major corporations are more likely to establish new operations in states with a "favorable business climate." Such a climate could result from state spending on roads and other infrastructure, a well-educated workforce, and other amenities. More often, a favorable business climate means low taxes on businesses and on the executives who run those businesses.

federal mandate
A requirement in federal legislation that forces states and municipalities to comply with certain rules.

---

11. *National Federation of Independent Business v. Sebelius,* 132 S.Ct. 2566 (2012).

Learning Outcome **5:**

The Politics of Federalism

Detail recent political developments and Supreme Court rulings that affect the distribution of power between the national government and the states.

As we have observed, the allocation of powers between the national and state governments continues to be a major issue. We look here at some further aspects of the ongoing conflict between national authority and states' rights in our federal system.

What Has National Authority Accomplished?

Why is it that conservatives have so often favored the states and liberals have favored the national government? One answer is that throughout American history, the expansion of national authority typically has been an engine of social change. Far more than the states, the national government has been willing to alter the status quo. The expansion of national authority during the Civil War freed the slaves—a major social revolution. During the New Deal, the expansion of national authority meant unprecedented levels of government intervention in the economy. In both the Civil War and the New Deal eras, support for states' rights was a method of opposing these changes and supporting the status quo.

Another example of the use of national power to change society occurred during the presidency of Lyndon B. Johnson (1963–1969). Johnson oversaw the greatest expansion of national authority since the New Deal. Under Johnson, a series of civil rights acts forced the states to grant African Americans equal treatment under the law. Crucially, these acts included the abolition of all measures designed to prevent African Americans from voting. Johnson's Great Society and War on Poverty programs resulted in major increases in spending by the national government. As before, states' rights were invoked to support the status quo—states' rights meant no action on civil rights and no increase in antipoverty spending.

The "New Federalism"

In the years after 1968, the **devolution** of power from the national government to the states became a major ideological theme for the Republican Party. Republican president Richard Nixon (1969–1974) advocated what he called a "New Federalism" that would devolve authority from the national government to the states. In part, the New Federalism involved the conversion of categorical grants into block grants, thereby giving state governments greater flexibility in spending. A second part of Nixon's New Federalism was *revenue sharing.* Under the revenue-sharing plan, the national government provided direct, unconditional financial support to state and local governments.

Nixon was able to obtain only a limited number of block grants from Congress. The block grants he did obtain, plus revenue sharing, substantially increased financial support to state governments. Republican president Ronald Reagan (1981–1989) was also a strong advocate of federalism, but some of his policies withdrew certain financial support from the states. Reagan was more successful than Nixon in obtaining block grants, but Reagan's block grants, unlike Nixon's, were less generous to the states than the categorical grants they replaced. Under Reagan, revenue sharing was eliminated. You can see the results of these actions in Figure 3–3.

Why should you care about **THE FEDERAL SYSTEM?**

Do you enjoy gambling—or do you believe that the effects of gambling make it a social disaster? State law usually determines the availability of gambling. The Constitution, however, assigns American Indian affairs exclusively to the national government. As a result of this provision, federal law requires state governments to negotiate with native tribes that want to set up gambling operations.

devolution

The transfer of powers from a national or central government to a state or local government.

The Politics of Federalism Today

In recent years, it has not been clear whether competing theories of federalism divide the Republicans from the Democrats at all, at least in practice. Consider that the passage of welfare reform legislation in 1996, which involved transferring significant control over welfare programs to the states, took place under Democratic president Bill Clinton (1993–2001). In contrast, under Republican president George W. Bush, Congress enacted the No Child Left Behind Act of 2001, which was signed into law in 2002. This act increased federal control over education and educational funding, which had traditionally been under the purview of state governments.

Beginning in 2009, however, conservative activists, especially Tea Party members, began to rediscover states' rights. One reason may be that in that year the Democrats added the presidency to their control of the U.S. House and Senate. Republicans were shut out at the national level. The ambitious program of the Obama administration also alarmed conservatives. Obama's initiatives generally involved greater federal control of the private sector, not of state and local governments. Still, many conservatives hoped that the states could be a counterweight to the newly active national government. In fact, Republicans enjoyed considerable success in winning power at the state level in the midterm elections of 2010 and 2014. As a result of these victories, Republicans had many opportunities to implement conservative legislation at the state level.

Image 3–10 A waiter takes an order in a fast food restaurant. Staff members in fast food restaurants are rarely tipped, unlike workers in traditional restaurants. *To what extent—if at all—does that strengthen the argument in favor of a $15 minimum wage?*

Paul Vasarhelyi/Shutterstock.com

Federalism and the Supreme Court

The United States Supreme Court, which normally has the final say on constitutional issues, plays a major role in determining where the line is drawn between federal and state powers. Consider the decisions rendered by Chief Justice John Marshall in the cases discussed earlier in this chapter. Since the 1930s, Marshall's broad interpretation of the commerce clause has made it possible for the national government to justify its regulation of almost any activity, even when the activity appears to be completely local in character. In the 1990s and 2000s, however, the Court has evidenced a willingness to impose some limits on the national government's authority under the commerce clause and other constitutional provisions. As a result, it is difficult to predict how today's Court might rule on a particular case involving federalism.

A Trend toward States' Rights. Since the mid-1990s, the Supreme Court has tended to give greater weight to states' rights than it did during previous decades. In a widely publicized 1995 case, *United States v. Lopez,*[12] the Supreme Court held that Congress had exceeded its constitutional authority under the commerce clause when it passed the Gun-Free School Zones Act in 1990. The Court stated that the act, which banned the possession of guns within one thousand feet of any school, was unconstitutional because

---

12. 514 U.S. 549 (1995).

it attempted to regulate an area that had "nothing to do with commerce, or any sort of economic enterprise." This marked the first time in sixty years that the Supreme Court had placed a limit on the national government's authority under the commerce clause.

The Court Sends Mixed Messages. Although the Court has tended to favor states' rights in some decisions, in other decisions it has backed the federal government's position. In 2005, the Court held that the federal government's power to declare various substances to be illegal drugs superseded California's law legalizing the use of marijuana for medical treatment.[13] Yet less than a year later, the Court favored states' rights when it upheld Oregon's controversial "death with dignity" law, which allows patients with terminal illnesses to choose to end their lives early and thus alleviate suffering.[14]

Recent Supreme Court Rulings

As noted, since President Obama took office, conservatives have taken a greater interest in states' rights. A growing number of such cases have been brought before the Supreme Court. In its rulings, the Court has shown a degree of sympathy for states' rights. Yet it has rejected arguments that would transform the relationship between the states and the federal government.

Immigration. In one important opinion, the Court found that Arizona had gone too far in its attempt to subject unauthorized immigration to state authority. Under the ruling, Arizona cannot make it a crime when illegal immigrants fail to carry identification papers or when they attempt to find work. Arizona police cannot arrest individuals solely on suspicion of illegal status.[15]

Health-Care Reform. It was the Court's opinion on the Affordable Care Act (Obamacare) that was expected to be the most important states' rights ruling in decades. In the end, the Court's 2012 verdict was somewhat anticlimactic. It did not find that the individual mandate—a penalty imposed on those who do not buy health-care insurance—violated the police powers of the states. (The Court found that while the mandate could not be justified under the commerce clause, it was legitimate under the national government's power to tax.) Chief Justice John Roberts's ruling on Medicaid expansion did hearten states' rights advocates, however. By making Medicaid expansion optional for the states, the Court for the first time put limits on the ability of the federal government to coerce states by withholding grants.[16]

Same-Sex Marriage. A 2013 ruling on same-sex marriage also tended to enhance the authority of the states. In *United States v. Windsor,* the Court found that the federal government must recognize state-approved same-sex marriages. This was a victory for states' rights, as well as for same-sex couples in the affected states.[17]

Throughout 2014, federal district and appeals courts used arguments contained in the *Windsor* decision as justification for overturning bans on same-sex marriage in more than a dozen states. The Sixth Circuit Court of Appeals then broke ranks with the other courts by upholding bans on same-sex marriage. With different appeals courts handing down contradictory rulings, the Supreme Court was forced to act. In June 2015, in

13. *Gonzales v. Raich,* 545 U.S. 1 (2005).

14. *Gonzales v. Oregon,* 546 U.S. 243 (2006).

15. *Arizona v. United States,* 132 S.Ct. 2492 (2012).

16. *National Federation of Independent Business v. Sebelius,* 132 S.Ct. 2566 (2012).

17. 133 S.Ct. 2675 (2013).

Image 3–11 An advisor with an insurance company (right) helps a Miami resident sign up for a health plan under the Affordable Care Act, also known as Obamacare. *What decisions has the Supreme Court made about the Affordable Care Act?*

Obergefell v. Hodges, the Court effectively legalized same-sex marriage throughout the entire United States.[18] Earlier states' rights rulings were therefore capped by a decision that enhanced national authority.

The Voting Rights Act. Finally, the Court's ruling on the Voting Rights Act was a striking triumph for states' rights. The 1965 act imposed certain requirements on states and localities—mostly in the South—with a history of violating the voting rights of minority group members. Such areas had to obtain preclearance from the federal government to make changes in voting procedures or districts. In June 2013, the Court effectively destroyed the preclearance system, when it ruled that the existing list of affected states and localities was based on obsolete data.[19]

In principle, Congress could update the method of identifying jurisdictions that need preclearance, but the chances of today's polarized Congress passing such a law are zero. Still, the Department of Justice continues to have the right to sue states and localities *after* they have changed their voting procedures or districts. Such suits, however, are likely to be much less effective than the preclearance system.

In 2014, the Court provided an additional victory for states' rights when it ruled that Michigan was allowed to ban affirmative action in public university admissions.[20] Affirmative action programs attempt to assist victims of past discrimination—minority group members or women—by giving them limited privileges in college admissions or in employment. Several states ban such programs, and the number of states that do so is likely to grow.

---

18. 135 S.Ct. 2584 (2015).
19. *Shelby County v. Holder,* 570 U.S. ___ (2013).
20. *Schuette v. Coalition to Defend Affirmative Action,* 572 U.S. ___ (2014).

How you can make a difference

In our modern era, the number of ways in which you can communicate your opinion is vast.

You can post a response on any of thousands of blogs. You could develop your own mini-video and post it on YouTube. If you want to effect policy change at the state or local level, however, the local newspaper, in both its paper and its online formats, continues to be essential. Blogs, YouTube, and other online venues tend to be nationally oriented. But most newspapers are resolutely local and are the natural hub for discussions of local issues. Papers often allow responses and comments on their websites, and you can make a point by contributing in that fashion. Yet nothing will win you a wider audience than an old-fashioned letter to the editor. Use the following rules to compose an effective communication:

- Use a computer, and double-space the lines. Use a spelling checker and grammar checker.

- Include a lead topic sentence that is short, to the point, and powerful.

- Keep your thoughts on target—choose only one topic. Make sure it is newsworthy and timely.

- Make sure your communication is concise. Never let it exceed a page in length (double-spaced).

- If you know that facts were misstated or left out in current news stories about your topic, supply the facts. The public wants to know.

- Don't be afraid to express moral judgments. You can go a long way by appealing to the reader's sense of justice.

- Personalize the communication by bringing in your own experiences, if possible.

- If you are writing a letter, sign it and give your address (including your e-mail address) and your telephone number. Blogs and other communications may have their own rules for identifying yourself in posted comments. Follow these rules.

- If writing a letter, send or e-mail it to the editorial office of the newspaper of your choice. Their websites usually give information on where you can send mail.

KEY TERMS

block grant **75**

categorical grant **74**

commerce clause **70**

concurrent powers **67**

confederal system **61**

cooperative federalism **74**

devolution **78**

dual federalism **72**

elastic clause, or necessary and proper clause **66**

enumerated powers **65**

federal mandate **77**

fiscal **76**

fiscal federalism **76**

interstate compact **69**

police power **66**

supremacy clause **67**

unitary system **61**

CHAPTER SUMMARY

Learning Outcome 1 There are three basic models for ordering relations between central and local governments: (a) a unitary system (in which ultimate power is held by the national government), (b) a confederal system (in which ultimate power is retained by the states), and (c) a federal system (in which governmental powers are divided between the national government and the states).

Learning Outcome 2 The Constitution expressly grants certain powers to the national government in Article I, Section 8. In addition to these enumerated powers, the national government has implied and inherent powers. Implied powers are those that are reasonably necessary to carry out the powers expressly given to the national government. Inherent powers are those held by the national government by virtue of its being a sovereign state with the right to preserve itself.

The Tenth Amendment to the Constitution states that powers not delegated to the United States by the Constitution, nor prohibited by it to the states, are reserved to the states, or to the people. In certain areas, the Constitution provides for concurrent powers (such as the power to tax), which are powers that are held jointly by the national and state governments.

The supremacy clause of the Constitution states that the Constitution, congressional laws, and national treaties are the supreme law of the land. States cannot use their reserved or concurrent powers to override national policies.

Learning Outcome 3 Chief Justice John Marshall's expansive interpretation of the necessary and proper clause of the Constitution in *McCulloch v. Maryland* (1819), along with his affirmation of the supremacy clause, enhanced the power of the national government. Marshall's broad interpretation of the commerce clause in *Gibbons v. Ogden* (1824) further extended the powers of the national government.

The controversy over slavery that led to the Civil War took the form of a fight over national government supremacy versus the rights of the separate states.

Learning Outcome 4 Since the Civil War, federalism has evolved from dual federalism to cooperative federalism. In dual federalism, each of the states and the federal government remain supreme within their own spheres. The era since the Great Depression has been labeled one of cooperative federalism, in which states and the national government cooperate in solving complex problems.

Categorical grants from the federal government to state governments help finance specific projects. By attaching conditions to federal grants, the national government can effect policy changes in areas typically governed by the states. Block grants cover general functional areas and give state and local governments more flexibility. Federal mandates—laws requiring states to implement certain policies—have generated controversy.

Learning Outcome 5 Traditionally, conservatives have favored states' rights, and liberals have favored national authority. In part, this is because the national government has historically been an engine of change. In recent years, rulings by the United States Supreme Court have tended to emphasize the rights of the states as compared to the powers of the federal government.

ADDITIONAL RESOURCES

This book refers to court cases, often decided by the United States Supreme Court. A good way to find out more about the American political system is to learn about key cases. Standard formats exist for citing cases. Consider *New State Ice Co. v. Liebmann* in footnote 2. The mysterious "285 U.S. 262" gives the location of this case in an official publication. Usually, you can just use the name of the case to search online for the ruling and articles that describe it. Sometimes, however, the name of the case is not enough. What if it is *United States v. Johnson*? There are at least twelve important cases by that name. To find this case, search for the full citation—for example, "*United States v. Johnson*, 457 U.S. 537 (1982)."

Online Resources

- The *New York Times* sponsors a series on the United States Civil War that uses contemporary accounts, diaries, and images. To follow it on Twitter, go to **twitter.com/NYTcivilwar**.

- The Reality Based Community is a good website for thoughtful discussions of drug policies, including the pros and cons of marijuana legalization. See it at **www.samefacts.com**.

Books

Caulkins, Jonathan P., Beau Kilmer, and Mark A.R. Kleiman. *Marijuana Legalization: What Everyone Needs to Know* (2d ed.). New York: Oxford University Press, 2016. A balanced and comprehensive introduction by some of the foremost authorities on U.S. drug policy.

Doonan, Michael. *American Federalism in Practice: The Formulation and Implementation of Contemporary Health Policy.* Washington: Brookings Institution Press, 2013. Doonan, a professor at Brandeis University, explains how federal–state relations have shaped American health-care policies.

Schragger, Richard C. *City Power: Urban Governance in a Global Age.* New York: Oxford University Press, 2016. Schragger, a law professor at the University of Virginia, argues that city governments have the power to improve the lives of their citizens.

Video

The Civil War—The PBS documentary series that made director Ken Burns famous. *The Civil War*, first shown in 1990, marked a revolution in documentary technique. Photographs, letters, eyewitness memoirs, and music are used to bring the war to life. The DVD version was released in 2002.

Waiting to Inhale: Marijuana, Medicine and the Law—A 2010 documentary on the controversy over legalizing marijuana in the United States for medical purposes. The film portrays patients and activists on both sides of this battle.

Quiz

Multiple Choice and Fill-Ins

Learning Outcome 1 Explain some of the benefits of the federal system for the United States.

1. Reasons why the founders chose a federal system include all except:
   a. no other type of system would have been politically acceptable.
   b. the United States was large geographically, and it would have been difficult to govern just from the national capital.
   c. the thirteen states were geographically compact, so a federal system was appropriate.

2. The system of government in the United States that existed before the adoption of the Constitution was called a _____ _____.

Learning Outcome 2 Describe how the various provisions of the U.S. Constitution provide a framework for federalism.

3. When both the national government and the state governments share certain powers, we call them:
   a. prevailing powers.
   b. concurrent powers.
   c. constitutional powers.

4. Each state must give full _____ ___ _____ to other states' public acts, records, and judicial proceedings.

Learning Outcome 3 Discuss how, in the early years of the republic, the United States Supreme Court confirmed the authority of the national government, and how that authority was ratified by the Civil War.

5. In the Supreme Court case of *McCulloch v. Maryland* (1819), the Court clearly established:
   a. that the Constitution is the supreme law of the land.
   b. that state governments can tax the national government.
   c. that the national government can tax the state governments.

6. The Supreme Court case of *Gibbons v. Ogden* (1824) involved regulation of _____ commerce.

Learning Outcome 4 Define the terms *dual federalism, cooperative federalism, categorical grants, block grants,* and *fiscal federalism.*

7. When the federal (national) government sends dollars to state governments, those funds:
   a. are given without any restrictions.
   b. are to be returned to the federal government at a later date.
   c. come with many "strings" attached.

8. When funds raised by the national government are then spent by the state governments, this is an example of

   _____ _____.

Learning Outcome 5 Detail recent political developments and Supreme Court rulings that affect the distribution of power between the national government and the states.

9. When ruling on the Affordable Care Act (Obamacare) in 2012, the Supreme Court:
   a. found the act to be entirely constitutional.
   b. found the act to be entirely unconstitutional.
   c. found the act to be mostly constitutional.

10. The transfer of powers from a central or national government to a state or local one is called _____.

Essay Questions

1. Traditionally, conservatives have favored states' rights and liberals have favored national authority. Can you think of modern-day issues in which these long-standing preferences might be reversed, with conservatives favoring national authority and liberals favoring states' rights? Explain.

2. Some members of the Tea Party movement want to repeal the Seventeenth Amendment, which provides for electing U.S. senators by popular vote. If the amendment were repealed, state legislatures would choose each state's senators. Advocates of repeal argue that it would strengthen the power of the states within the federal system. Are they right—and would such a change have good or bad consequences? Explain.

CIVIL LIBERTIES

Protestors demonstrate outside the Federal Bureau of Investigation (FBI) headquarters in support of Apple Inc. The agency was attempting to force Apple to write software that would break the security system on an iPhone. *How would you weigh the right to privacy against the need to gain information about terrorists?*
Chip Somodevilla/Getty Images

These six **LEARNING OUTCOMES** *below are designed to help improve your understanding of this chapter:*

1: Identify the rights listed in the original Constitution, describe the Bill of Rights, and discuss how it came to be applied to state governments as well as the national government.

2: Explain how the First Amendment's establishment clause and free exercise clause guarantee our freedom of religion.

3: Specify the limited circumstances in which the national and state governments may override the principles of free speech and freedom of the press.

4: Provide the constitutional basis of the right to privacy, and explain how the principle has been applied to the abortion and right-to-die controversies.

5: Cite examples of how recent security concerns have affected our civil liberties.

6: Identify the constitutional rights of those who are accused of a crime, explain the *Miranda* and exclusionary rules, and describe the current status of the death penalty.

What if... Roe v. Wade *Were Overturned?*

Background

The Bill of Rights and other provisions of the U.S. Constitution are the ultimate protections of our civil rights and liberties. But how do these rights work in practice? How do we determine what our rights are in any given situation? One way is through *judicial review*, the power of the United States Supreme Court or other courts to declare laws and other acts of government unconstitutional.

Supreme Court cases are often hotly contested, and the decision in the 1973 case *Roe v. Wade* is one of the most contentious ever handed down. In the *Roe v. Wade* case, the Court declared that a woman's constitutionally protected right to privacy includes the right to have an abortion.[a] The Court concluded that the states cannot restrict a woman's right to an abortion during the first three months of pregnancy. Forty years later, however, the debate over the legality of abortion still rages in the United States.

What If *Roe v. Wade* Were Overturned?

If the Supreme Court overturned *Roe v. Wade*, the authority to regulate abortion would fall again to the states. Before the *Roe v. Wade* case, each state decided whether abortion would be legal within its borders.

Simply overturning *Roe v. Wade* would not make abortion in the United States illegal overnight. In many states, abortion rights are very popular, and the legislatures in those states would not consider measures to ban abortion or to further restrict access to abortion. Some states have laws that would protect abortion rights even if *Roe v. Wade* were overturned. Access to abortions would likely continue in the West Coast states and in much of the Northeast. In most of the South and parts of the Midwest, however, abortion could be seriously restricted or even banned.

Already, twenty-seven states require a waiting period between when a woman receives counseling and when the procedure is performed. Seventeen states require counseling that includes information generally considered to be incorrect by the medical profession, such as the proposition that abortions can cause breast cancer. Some states have "trigger laws" that would immediately outlaw abortion if *Roe v. Wade* were overturned.

Recent Developments

After the 2010 elections, in which conservative, right-to-life candidates won victories in many state legislative elections, the volume of anti-abortion legislation exploded. In the following three years, thirty states passed more than two hundred laws. In 2015 alone, state lawmakers proposed nearly four hundred bills restricting abortion, and forty-seven of those bills were enacted.

Twenty states have banned abortions after twenty or twenty-four weeks of pregnancy. In Texas, restrictive laws in 2013 closed about one-third of the state's abortion clinics. However, on June 27, 2016, the Supreme Court struck down this Texas law. It was a victory for pro-choice advocates, who argued it would have unduly limited women's access to abortion providers. The five-to-three ruling is one of the most important Court decisions on abortion in twenty years.

It is also probable that if states could outlaw abortion, most existing state laws restricting the procedure would become irrelevant. The states that have passed such laws are generally the same states that would make abortion illegal.

For Critical Analysis

◗ Why do you think that abortion has remained a contentious topic for the forty-plus years since the *Roe v. Wade* decision? Should that decision be revisited? Why or why not?

◗ What political consequences could result from overturning *Roe v. Wade*? How might people's opinions change about abortion? About the Supreme Court?

Tom Williams//Getty Images

Image 4–1 Cecile Richards, the national head of Planned Parenthood, testifies before a House committee on whether Planned Parenthood should receive federal funds. In 2015, an antiabortion group released a secretly recorded video allegedly showing unethical behavior by a Planned Parenthood staff member. *Under what circumstances is it appropriate to withhold federal funding from an organization?*

---

a. *Roe v. Wade*, 410 U.S. 113 (1973).

"The land of the free." When asked what makes the United States distinctive, Americans will commonly say that it is a free country. Americans have long believed that limits on the power of government are an essential part of what makes this country free. Recall from Chapter 1 that restraints on the actions of government against individuals are generally referred to as *civil liberties.* The first ten amendments to the U.S. Constitution—the Bill of Rights—place such restraints on the national government. Of these amendments, none is more famous than the First Amendment, which guarantees freedom of religion, speech, and the press, as well as other rights.

Most other democratic nations have laws to protect these and other civil liberties, but none of the laws is quite like the First Amendment. Take the issue of "hate speech." What if someone makes statements that stir up hatred toward a particular race or other group of people? In Germany, where memories of Nazi anti-Semitism remain alive, such speech is unquestionably illegal. In the United States, the issue is not so clear. The courts have often extended constitutional protection to this kind of speech.

In this chapter, we describe the civil liberties provided by the Bill of Rights and some of the controversies that surround them. We especially look at the First Amendment. Finally, we discuss the right to privacy, which is at the heart of the abortion issue introduced in the *What If . . .* feature that opened this chapter. We also examine the rights of defendants in criminal cases.

The Constitutional Bases of Our Liberties

Learning Outcome **1:**

Identify the rights listed in the original Constitution, describe the Bill of Rights, and discuss how it came to be applied to state governments as well as the national government.

As you read through this chapter, bear in mind that both the original Constitution and the Bill of Rights are relatively brief. The framers set forth broad guidelines, leaving it up to the courts to interpret these constitutional mandates and apply them to specific situations. Thus, judicial interpretations shape the true nature of the civil liberties and rights that we possess. Because judicial interpretations change over time, so do our liberties and rights. As you will read in the following pages, there have been many conflicts over the meaning of such simple phrases as *freedom of religion* and *freedom of the press.* To understand what freedoms we actually have, we need to examine how the courts—and particularly the United States Supreme Court—have resolved some of those conflicts.

Protections Listed in the Original Constitution

While Americans typically think of our civil liberties as guaranteed by the Bill of Rights, three important protections were written into the main body of the Constitution. In Article I, Section 9, we find this statement: "The privilege of the Writ of Habeas Corpus shall not be suspended, unless when in Cases of Rebellion or Invasion the public Safety may require it." The section goes on to state, "No Bill of Attainder or ex post facto Law shall be passed." What is meant by all this rather obscure legal language?

A **writ of *habeas corpus*** is a court order issued to any agency that is holding a prisoner. The writ requires the jailer to bring the prisoner before the court and explain why that person is being held. If the judge finds the imprisonment to be unlawful, he or she will order the jailer to rectify the situation. The prisoner may be brought to trial—or freed. It is *habeas corpus* that prevents the government from arbitrarily and indefinitely detaining political opponents or unpopular individuals. Following the terrorist attacks of September 11, 2001, the question of whether suspected terrorists had a right to *habeas corpus* became a major political and judicial issue.

During the early years of the republic, federal courts offered *habeas corpus* rights only to federal prisoners. Following the U.S. Civil War, however, federal courts began issuing writs on behalf of prisoners held by the states.

writ of *habeas corpus*

Habeas corpus means, literally, "you have the body." A writ of *habeas corpus* is an order that requires jailers to bring a prisoner before a court or judge and explain why the person is being held.

A **bill of attainder** is a law that inflicts punishment without a trial. An ***ex post facto law*** inflicts punishment for an act that was not illegal at the time it was committed. In Article I, Section 10, of the Constitution, the prohibition of both of these types of law is explicitly extended to the states. In contrast, the Bill of Rights had a very different legal history.

Extending the Bill of Rights to State Governments

Many citizens do not realize that, as originally intended, the Bill of Rights limited only the powers of the national government. At the time the Bill of Rights was ratified, there was little concern over the potential of state governments to curb civil liberties. For one thing, state governments were closer to home and easier to control. For another, most state constitutions already had bills of rights. Rather, the fear was of the potential tyranny of the national government. The Bill of Rights begins with the words, "Congress shall make no law . . . ." It says nothing about states making laws that might abridge citizens' civil liberties. In 1833, the United States Supreme Court held that the Bill of Rights did not apply to state laws.[1]

We mentioned that most states had bills of rights. These bills of rights were similar to the national one, but there were some differences. Furthermore, each state's judicial system interpreted the rights differently. Citizens in different states, therefore, effectively had different sets of civil liberties. It was not until the Fourteenth Amendment was ratified in 1868 that civil liberties guaranteed by the national Constitution began to be applied to the states. Section 1 of that amendment provides, in part, as follows:

> *No State shall . . . deprive any person of life, liberty, or property, without due process of law. . . .*

Incorporation under the Fourteenth Amendment

There was no question that the Fourteenth Amendment applied to state governments. For decades, however, the courts were reluctant to define the liberties spelled out in the national Bill of Rights as constituting "due process of law," which was protected under the Fourteenth Amendment. Not until 1925, in *Gitlow v. New York,*[2] did the United States Supreme Court hold that the Fourteenth Amendment protected the freedom of speech guaranteed by the First Amendment to the Constitution from state infringement.

Only gradually did the Supreme Court accept **incorporation theory**—the view that the protections of the Bill of Rights are incorporated into the Fourteenth Amendment's protection against state government actions. In the years following the *Gitlow* decision, the Supreme Court incorporated into the Fourteenth Amendment the other basic freedoms (of the press, assembly, the right to petition, and religion) guaranteed by the First Amendment.

It took time for the Supreme Court to require the states to accept other liberties. Only in 2010 did the Court rule that the states were obligated to recognize an individual's right to bear arms.[3] Even with that ruling, the national and state governments retain the power to regulate the ownership of firearms. The Third Amendment bars the government from quartering soldiers in private houses during peacetime, but the Court has never imposed this obligation on the states. The reason appears to be that the Court has never heard a case in which a state allegedly violated this right. In 1982, however, a U.S. appeals court ruled to incorporate the Third Amendment.[4] You can find an annotated version of the

bill of attainder

A law that inflicts punishment without a trial.

***ex post facto* law**

A law that inflicts punishment for an act that was not illegal at the time it was committed.

incorporation theory

The view that the protections of the Bill of Rights apply to state governments through the Fourteenth Amendment's due process clause.

---

1. *Barron v. Baltimore,* 32 U.S. 243 (1833).
2. 268 U.S. 652 (1925).
3. *McDonald v. Chicago,* 561 U.S. 3025 (2010).
4. *Engblom v. Carey,* 677 F.2d 957 (2d Cir. 1982).

Consider the source

The Second Amendment

The Second Amendment is hugely popular. It is also one of the most oddly worded parts of the Bill of Rights:

> **Amendment II.** A well regulated Militia, being necessary to the security of a free State, the right of the people to keep and bear Arms, shall not be infringed.

The Amendment begins by speaking of "A well regulated Militia." For more than two hundred years, U.S. courts interpreted the "right of the people to keep and bear arms" in the context of establishing a militia. In other words, persons not part of a state militia had no constitutional right to bear arms.

Such a limited right did make sense in the context of the 1790s. The militia was seen as all adult male citizens capable of fighting. Indeed, one early law required male citizens who did not already own a musket to purchase one. It did not take many decades, however, to discover that a militia of all citizens was distinctly inferior to a professional army as a fighting force. The idea of a universal militia fell by the wayside, and with it, the generalized right of citizens to bear arms.

Gun rights enthusiasts have always argued that the right to bear arms should be independent of the need for a militia. In this view, the opening clauses of the amendment are simply excess verbiage. In 2008, a conservative majority on the Supreme Court endorsed that position.[a] In 2010, it imposed the right on the states. Unless there are specific reasons why citizens should not be allowed access to firearms, they may possess them for personal protection.

For Critical Analysis

❯ Should Americans have the right to bear arms of any type, at all times, in any location? Why or why not?

a. *District of Columbia v. Heller,* 554 U.S. 570 (2008).

Bill of Rights in Appendix B, where it follows the main body of the Constitution. In this chapter's *Consider the Source* feature, we discuss the Second Amendment—which covers the right to bear arms—as an example of constitutional interpretation.

Freedom of Religion

Learning Outcome 2:

Explain how the First Amendment's establishment clause and free exercise clause guarantee our freedom of religion.

In the United States, freedom of religion consists of two main principles that are presented in the First Amendment. The **establishment clause** prohibits the establishment of a church that is officially supported by the national government, thus guaranteeing a division between church and state. The **free exercise clause** constrains the national government from prohibiting individuals from practicing the religion of their choice.

The Separation of Church and State—The Establishment Clause

The First Amendment to the Constitution states, in part, that "Congress shall make no law respecting an establishment of religion." In the words of Thomas Jefferson, the *establishment clause* was designed to create a "wall of separation between Church and State." As interpreted by the United States Supreme Court, the establishment clause in the First Amendment means at least the following:

> *Neither a state nor the federal government can set up a church. Neither can pass laws which aid one religion, aid all religions, or prefer one religion over*

establishment clause

The part of the First Amendment prohibiting the establishment of a church officially supported by the national government. It determines the legality of giving state and local government aid to religious organizations and schools, allowing or requiring school prayers, and teaching evolution versus creationism.

free exercise clause

The provision of the First Amendment guaranteeing the free exercise of religion. The provision constrains the national government from prohibiting individuals from practicing the religion of their choice.

Image 4–2 Two Kentucky men who seek to marry speak with Kim Davis, Rowan County Clerk of Courts, in 2015. Citing religious beliefs, Davis refused to issue marriage licenses to same-sex couples in defiance of a Supreme Court ruling. A lower court later forced Davis to allow other staff members in her office to issue licenses. *Are there any circumstances under which individuals should have the right to refuse service to gays and lesbians? If so, what are they? If not, why not?*

another. Neither can force nor influence a person to go to or to remain away from church against his will or force him to profess a belief or disbelief in any religion. No person can be punished for entertaining or professing religious beliefs or disbeliefs, for church attendance or nonattendance. No tax in any amount, large or small, can be levied to support any religious activities or institutions, whatever they may be called, or whatever form they may adopt to teach or practice religion. Neither a state nor the federal government can, openly or secretly, participate in the affairs of any religious organizations or groups and vice versa.[5]

The establishment clause covers all conflicts about such matters as the legality of giving state and local government aid to religious organizations and schools, allowing or requiring school prayers, teaching evolution versus creationist theories that reject evolution, placing religious displays in schools or public places, and discriminating against religious groups in publicly operated institutions.

Aid to Church-Related Schools. In the United States, almost 11 percent of school-age children attend private schools, of which about 80 percent have religious affiliations. The United States Supreme Court has tried to draw a fine line between permissible public aid to students in church-related schools and impermissible public aid to religion.

---

5. *Everson v. Board of Education,* 330 U.S. 1 (1947).

Ty Wright/Getty Images

In 1971, in *Lemon v. Kurtzman*,[6] the Court ruled that direct state aid could not be used to subsidize religious instruction. The Court in the *Lemon* case gave its most general pronouncement on the constitutionality of government aid to religious schools, stating that (1) the aid had to be secular (nonreligious) in aim, (2) it could not have the primary effect of advancing or inhibiting religion, and (3) the government must avoid "an excessive government entanglement with religion." All laws that raise issues under the establishment clause are now subject to the three-part *Lemon* test. How the test is applied, however, has varied over the years.

In a number of cases, the Supreme Court has held that state programs helping church-related schools are unconstitutional. In other cases, however, the Supreme Court has allowed states to use tax funds for lunches, textbooks, diagnostic services for speech and hearing problems, standardized tests, computers, and special educational services for disadvantaged students attending religious schools.

School Vouchers.

An ongoing controversy concerning the establishment clause has to do with school vouchers. Some people believe that the public schools are failing to educate our children adequately. One proposed solution to the problem has been for state and local governments to issue school vouchers. These vouchers represent state-issued funds that can be used to purchase education at any school, public or private. At issue is whether voucher programs violate the establishment clause.

In 2002, the United States Supreme Court held that a voucher program in Cleveland, Ohio, did not violate the establishment clause. The Court concluded that because the vouchers could be used for public as well as private schools, the program did not unconstitutionally entangle church and state.[7] The Court's 2002 decision was encouraging to those who support school choice, whether it takes the form of school vouchers or tuition tax credits to offset educational expenses in private schools. Today, a variety of states allow public funds to be used for private school expenses. Some

Charles Barsotti/The New Yorker Collection/The Cartoon Bank

Image 4–3 *"I'm taking my voucher and going to circus school."*

have small-scale voucher or scholarship programs for a limited number of students, frequently special-needs students. A growing number of states provide tax deductions for private school expenses.

The Issue of School Prayer—*Engel v. Vitale*.

Do the states have the right to promote religion in general, without making any attempt to establish a particular religion? That is the question raised by school prayer and was the precise issue presented in 1962 in *Engel v. Vitale*,[8] the so-called Regents' Prayer case in New York. The State Board of Regents of New York had suggested that a prayer be spoken aloud in the public schools

---

6. 403 U.S. 602 (1971).

7. *Zelman v. Simmons-Harris*, 536 U.S. 639 (2002).

8. 370 U.S. 421 (1962).

Image 4–4 Larycia Hawkins, a political science professor and a Christian, wearing a hijab in solidarity with Muslims. Hawkins stated that Christians and Muslims worship the same God. As a result, in 2016 Hawkins was forced out of her job at Wheaton College, a Christian school in Illinois. She was then hired by the University of Virginia. *Why can private colleges enforce religious rules that public universities cannot?*

at the beginning of each day. The recommended prayer was as follows:

> Almighty God, we acknowledge our
>   dependence upon Thee,
> And we beg Thy blessings upon us, our
>   parents, our teachers, and our Country.

Such a prayer was implemented in many New York public schools.

The parents of a number of students challenged the action of the regents, maintaining that it violated the establishment clause of the First Amendment. At trial, the parents lost. On appeal, however, the Supreme Court ruled that the regents' action was unconstitutional because "the constitutional prohibition against laws respecting an establishment of a religion must mean at least that in this country it is no part of the business of government to compose official prayers for any group of the American people to recite as part of a religious program carried on by any government."

Forbidding the Teaching of Evolution. For many decades, certain religious groups have opposed the teaching of evolution in the schools. To these groups, evolutionary theory directly counters their religious belief that human beings did not evolve but were created fully formed, as described in the biblical story of the creation. State and local attempts to forbid the teaching of evolution, however, have not passed constitutional muster in the eyes of the United States Supreme Court. For example, in 1968 the Supreme Court held that an Arkansas law prohibiting the teaching of evolution violated the establishment clause because it imposed religious beliefs on students.[9]

Nonetheless, state and local groups around the country continue their efforts against the teaching of evolution. Some school districts have considered teaching the creationist theory of "intelligent design" as an alternative explanation of the origin of life. Proponents of intelligent design contend that evolutionary theory has "gaps" that can be explained only by the existence of an intelligent creative force (God).

The federal courts took up the issue of intelligent design in 2005. The previous year, the Dover Area Board of Education in Pennsylvania had voted to require the presentation of intelligent design as an explanation of the origin of life. In December 2005, a U.S. district court ruled that the Dover mandate was unconstitutional.[10] All of the school board members who endorsed intelligent design were voted out of office.

Since 2005, advocates of intelligent design have made continued attempts to introduce their doctrine into the public schools. Intelligent design advocates have adopted the slogan "teach the controversy" as a way of introducing creationism alongside evolution. Opponents argue, however, that there *is* no controversy among biologists. Rather, the controversy is political and religious, and if it is taught at all it should be covered in social science or politics classes.

---

9. *Epperson v. Arkansas,* 393 U.S. 97 (1968).

10. *Kitzmiller v. Dover Area School District,* 400 F.Supp.2d 707 (M.D.Pa. 2005).

Religious Displays on Public Property.

On a regular basis, the courts are asked to determine whether religious symbols placed on public property violate the establishment clause. A frequent source of controversy is the placement of a crèche, or nativity scene, on public property during the Christmas season. The Supreme Court has allowed some displays but prohibited others. In general, a nativity scene is acceptable if it is part of a broader display that contains secular objects such as lights, Christmas trees, Santa Claus figures, and reindeer. A stand-alone crèche is not acceptable.[11]

The Free Exercise Clause

The First Amendment constrains Congress from prohibiting the free exercise of religion. Does this *free exercise clause* mean that no type of religious practice can be prohibited or restricted by government? Certainly, a person can hold any religious belief that he or she wants, or a person can have no religious belief. When, however, religious *practices* work against public policy and the public welfare, the government can act.

For example, regardless of a child's or parent's religious beliefs, the government can require vaccinations. Many states, such as Texas, allow philosophical exemption from vaccination requirements—but a few others, such as California, allow documented medical exemptions only. Can government rules prevent the faithful from wearing certain articles of clothing? We examine that question in this chapter's *Which Side Are You On?* feature.

Churches and other religious organizations are tax-exempt bodies, and as a result they are not allowed to endorse candidates for office or make contributions to candidates' campaigns. Churches are allowed to take positions on ballot proposals, however, and may contribute to referendum campaigns. For example, both the Latter-Day Saints (the Mormons) and the Roman Catholic Church were able to fund the campaign for California's 2008 Proposition 8, a measure to ban same-sex marriage.

Image 4–5 This nativity scene in front of the United States Supreme Court was part of a campaign to display nativity scenes on public property. *What rules govern such displays?*

The Internal Revenue Service (IRS) rarely bothers to threaten the tax-exempt status of a church based on simple candidate endorsements, however. In October 2012, about 1,400 ministers collectively endorsed Republican presidential candidate Mitt Romney in a deliberate challenge to the 1954 law that prohibits such endorsements. The IRS did not respond. In 1995, however, the IRS did revoke the tax-exempt status of Branch Ministries, Inc., and in 2000 a federal district court supported the revocation.[12] Branch Ministries went far beyond simply endorsing a candidate from the pulpit. The church had used tax-exempt income to buy newspaper advertisements denouncing Democratic presidential candidate Bill Clinton.

---

11. *Lynch v. Donnelly*, 465 U.S. 668 (1984).
12. *Branch Ministries v. Rossetti*, 211 F.3d 137 (D.C.Cir. 2000).

Which side are you on?

When Can Wearing Religious Garb Be Restricted?

Does the free exercise clause of the First Amendment guarantee that any manifestation of religious belief is legal? If your religious beliefs dictate that you must wear a veil, can you wear it everywhere, at any time? If religion dictates that you must always wear a turban, can you join the U.S. Army and continue to wear it? Consider another situation: A man is serving a prison sentence. His religion tells him that he must wear a beard. Do prison authorities, nonetheless, have the right to make him shave it off? The United States Supreme Court recently ruled unanimously in favor of such a prisoner.[a]

Issues concerning the physical expression of one's religious beliefs are not new. As a Quaker, William Penn, founder of Pennsylvania, refused to remove his hat during an English trial in 1670. He was found in contempt of court.

Your Religious Behavior Can Be Restricted

It clearly makes sense for the Army to prevent Sikhs from wearing turbans while on active duty. After all, such turbans prevent the wearing of traditional army helmets—a safety necessity, particularly during combat duty. For airport screening, Transportation Security Administration (TSA) personnel must have the right to physically pat down turbans. Otherwise, other passengers' safety could be in danger.

Some countries have banned the use of headscarves in public schools, courtrooms, or other public places (France and Turkey are examples). In the United States and France, the government cannot sponsor any religion, so banning religiously motivated headscarves in public schools seems appropriate. All citizens should be seen as equal, and deliberately identifying one's religion interferes with this goal. Church and state must remain separate.

Freedom of Religion Means Just That

Others argue that any attempt by the government to ban religious garb violates not only the right to freely exercise one's religion, but also the right to free speech. For many Muslim women, wearing a headscarf is both a religious obligation and an expression of belief. Wearing a headscarf does no harm and does not violate the rights of anyone else. The attempt in France to ban Muslim headscarves, Jewish yarmulkes (caps), Sikh turbans, and Christian cross necklaces benefits no one. Unlike the French, we Americans celebrate our diversity. We must not stigmatize religious minorities by banning religious garb.

Even the ban on turbans in the military is misguided. True, the traditional Sikh turban will not fit under a helmet. Sikhs have developed a special close-fitting turban, however, which can easily be worn with a helmet. It is even made of the same cloth as the soldier's uniform.

For Critical Analysis

○ Many states require that driver's license photos be taken without turbans, veils, or headscarves. Why?

---

a.   *Holt v. Hobbs,* 135 S.Ct. 853 (2015).

Freedom of Expression

Perhaps the most frequently invoked freedom that Americans have is the right to free speech and a free press. For the most part, Americans can criticize public officials and their actions without fear of reprisal by any branch of our government.

No Prior Restraint

prior restraint
Restraining an activity before it has actually occurred. When expression is involved, this means censorship.

Restraining an activity before it has actually occurred is called **prior restraint.** When expression is involved, prior restraint means censorship, as opposed to subsequent punishment. Prior restraint of expression would require, for example, that a permit be obtained before a speech could be made, a newspaper published, or a movie or TV show exhibited. Most, if not all, Supreme Court justices have been very critical of any governmental action that imposes prior restraint on expression.

One of the most famous cases concerning prior restraint was *New York Times v. United States,*[13] the so-called Pentagon Papers case. In 1971, the *Times* and the *Washington Post* were about to publish the Pentagon Papers, an elaborate secret history of the U.S. government's involvement in the Vietnam War (1965–1975). The secret documents had been obtained illegally by a disillusioned former Pentagon official. The government wanted a court order to bar publication of the documents, arguing that national security was threatened and that the documents had been stolen. The newspapers argued that the public had a right to know the information contained in the papers and that the press had the right to inform the public. The Supreme Court ruled six to three in favor of the newspapers' right to publish the information. This case affirmed the no-prior-restraint doctrine.

The Protection of Symbolic Speech

Not all expression is in words or in writing. Articles of clothing, gestures, and other forms of nonverbal expressive conduct are considered **symbolic speech.** Such speech is given substantial protection today by our courts. For example, in a landmark decision issued in 1969, *Tinker v. Des Moines School District,*[14] the United States Supreme Court held that the wearing of black armbands by students in protest against the Vietnam War was a form of speech protected by the First Amendment.

Flag Burning. In 1989, the Supreme Court ruled that state laws that prohibited the burning of the American flag as part of a peaceful protest also violated the freedom of expression protected by the First Amendment.[15] Congress responded by passing the Flag Protection Act of 1989, which was ruled unconstitutional by the Supreme Court in 1990.[16] Congress and President George H. W. Bush immediately pledged to work for a constitutional amendment to "protect our flag"—an effort that has yet to be successful.

Cross Burning. In 2003, the Supreme Court concluded in a Virginia case that a state, consistent with the First Amendment, may ban cross burnings carried out with the intent to intimidate. The Court reasoned that historically, cross burning was a sign of impending violence, and a state has the right to ban threats of violence. The Court also ruled, however, that the state must prove intimidation and cannot infer it from the cross burnings themselves. In an impassioned dissent, Justice Clarence Thomas, who is African American and usually one of the Court's most conservative members, argued that cross burnings should be automatic evidence of intent to intimidate.[17]

The Protection of Commercial Speech

Commercial speech usually is defined as advertising statements. Can advertisers use their First Amendment rights to prevent restrictions on the content of commercial advertising? Until the 1970s, the Supreme Court held that such speech was not protected at all by the First Amendment. By the mid-1970s, however, more and more commercial speech had been brought under First Amendment protection. According to Justice Harry A. Blackmun, "Advertising, however tasteless and excessive it sometimes may seem, is nonetheless

---

13. 403 U.S. 713 (1971).
14. 393 U.S. 503 (1969).
15. *Texas v. Johnson,* 488 U.S. 884 (1989).
16. *United States v. Eichman,* 496 U.S. 310 (1990).
17. *Virginia v. Black,* 538 U.S. 343 (2003).

Learning Outcome **3:**

Specify the limited circumstances in which the national and state governments may override the principles of free speech and freedom of the press.

symbolic speech

Expression made through articles of clothing, gestures, movements, and other forms of nonverbal conduct. Symbolic speech is given substantial protection by the courts.

commercial speech

Advertising statements, which increasingly have been given First Amendment protection.

Apic/Getty Images

Image 4–6 This ad for cigarettes appeared in 1946. Despite protection of commercial speech, it would be impossible for such an ad to appear today. **Why?**

dissemination of information as to who is producing and selling what product for what reason and at what price."[18] Nevertheless, the Supreme Court will consider a restriction on commercial speech valid as long as it (1) seeks to implement a substantial government interest, (2) directly advances that interest, and (3) goes no further than necessary to accomplish its objective. In particular, a business engaging in commercial speech can be subject to liability for factual inaccuracies in ways that do not apply to noncommercial speech.

Attempts to Ban Subversive or Advocacy Speech

Over the past hundred years, the United States Supreme Court has established, in succession, a number of doctrines regarding language allegedly subversive to the public order.

The Clear and Present Danger Test. In 1919, the Supreme Court ruled that when a person's remarks create a clear and present danger to the peace or public order, they can be curtailed constitutionally. Justice Oliver Wendell Holmes used this reasoning when ratifying the conviction of a socialist who had been charged with violating the Espionage Act by distributing a leaflet that opposed the military draft.[19] According to the *clear and present danger test*, expression may be restricted if evidence exists that such expression would cause a dangerous condition, actual or imminent, that Congress has the power to prevent.

The Bad Tendency Rule. Over the course of the twentieth century, the Supreme Court modified the clear and present danger rule, limiting the constitutional protection of free speech in 1925 and 1951, and then broadening it substantially in 1969. In *Gitlow v. New York*,[20] the Court reintroduced the earlier *bad tendency rule,* which placed greater restrictions on speech than are found in Justice Holmes's formulation. According to this rule, speech may be curtailed if there is a possibility that such expression might lead to some "evil."

In the *Gitlow* case, a member of a left-wing group was convicted of violating New York State's criminal anarchy statute when he published and distributed a pamphlet urging the violent overthrow of the U.S. government. In its majority opinion, the Supreme Court held that the First Amendment afforded protection against state incursions on freedom of expression—the first time that the First Amendment was ever invoked against a state government. Nevertheless, Gitlow could be punished legally because his expression would tend to bring about evils that the state had a right to prevent.

---

18. *Virginia State Board of Pharmacy v. Virginia Citizens Consumer Council, Inc.,* 425 U.S. 748 (1976).
19. *Schenck v. United States,* 249 U.S. 47 (1919).
20. 268 U.S. 652 (1925).

The Imminent Lawless Action Test. Some claim that the United States did not achieve true freedom of political speech until 1969. In that year, in *Brandenburg v. Ohio,*[21] the Supreme Court overturned the conviction of a Ku Klux Klan leader for violating a state statute. The statute prohibited anyone from advocating "the duty, necessity, or propriety of sabotage, violence, or unlawful methods of terrorism as a means of accomplishing industrial or political reform." The Court held that the guarantee of free speech does not permit a state "to forbid or proscribe [disallow] advocacy of the use of force or of law violation except where such advocacy is directed to inciting or producing imminent [immediate] lawless actions and is likely to incite or produce such action." The **imminent lawless action test** enunciated by the Court is a difficult one for prosecutors to meet. As a result, the Court's decision significantly broadened the protection given to advocacy speech.

The Eclipse of Obscenity as a Legal Category

Traditionally, state and federal statutes made it a crime to disseminate obscene materials. But what is *obscenity*? Justice Potter Stewart once stated that even though he could not define obscenity, "I know it when I see it." The legal system needs a more precise definition than that, however.

The Rise and Fall of *Miller v. California*. In 1973, in *Miller v. California,*[22] Chief Justice Warren Burger created a list of requirements that must be met for material to be legally obscene. Material is obscene if (1) the average person finds that it violates contemporary community standards, (2) the work taken as a whole appeals to a prurient interest in sex, (3) the work shows patently offensive sexual conduct, and (4) the work lacks serious redeeming literary, artistic, political, or scientific merit. The definition of *prurient interest* would be determined by "community standards," thus leaving the definition to local and state authorities.

The Court's ruling came down at a time when popular attitudes toward obscenity were undergoing a revolution. A few years earlier, literary works regarded as masterpieces by critics could be banned from the U.S. mail, from import, and from sale. Such works included *Lady Chatterley's Lover* by D. H. Lawrence and *Ulysses* by James Joyce. By the 1980s, however, it was possible in almost every corner of the country to buy or rent pornographic videotapes that left nothing to the imagination.

Internet Pornography. The rise of the Internet in the 1990s sealed the fate of obscenity as a useful legal category. Conventional pornography on the Internet was essentially impossible to police. Congress attempted to spare children from exposure to Internet pornography by laws passed in 1996 and 1998, but the Court found this legislation to be unconstitutional.[23] In 2000, Congress was more successful with the Children's Internet Protection Act, which requires public schools and libraries to install filtering software to prevent children from viewing websites with "adult" content. This law was upheld.[24] Young people today, however, are not dependent on libraries for Internet access. Free Wi-Fi, for use by laptops, tablets, and smartphones, is available almost everywhere.

Remaining Restrictions. Pornography can still be limited by the private sector— for example, most mainstream movie theaters will not show a film that has received a "no [child] 17 or under admitted" (NC-17) rating from the Motion Picture Association of America. The government also retains the right to place restrictions on media it controls,

---

21. 395 U.S. 444 (1969).
22. 413 U.S. 5 (1973).
23. *Reno v. American Civil Liberties Union*, 521 U.S. 844 (1997); *American Civil Liberties Union v. Ashcroft*, 542 U.S. 646 (2004).
24. United States v. American Library Association, 539 U.S. 194 (2003).

imminent lawless action test
The current standard established by the Supreme Court for evaluating the legality of advocacy speech. Such speech can be forbidden only when it is "directed to inciting . . . imminent lawless action."

Image 4–7

iStockphoto.com/Tom Nulens

such as the broadcast spectrum. Therefore, restrictions on radio and broadcast television remain.

Pornography That Exploits Minors. The government has also successfully outlawed materials that show sexual performance by minors. In 1990, the Court ruled that states can criminalize the possession of child pornography. The Court reasoned that the ban on private possession is justified because owning the material constitutes a form of child abuse.[25] This legal reasoning, however, reveals just how barren the concept of obscenity had become. Child abuse was the crime—not obscenity. As a result, the law makes no attempt to ban depictions of sexual performance by children in literary works such as Vladimir Nabokov's *Lolita* or in obvious cartoons such as Japanese *hentai*. Novels and cartoons do not involve the exploitation of actual, identifiable children.

Unprotected Speech: Slander

Can you say anything you want about someone else? Not really. Individuals are protected from **defamation of character,** which is defined as wrongfully hurting a person's good reputation. The law imposes a general duty on all persons to refrain from making false, defamatory statements about others. Breaching this duty orally is the wrongdoing called *slander.* Breaching it in writing is the wrongdoing called *libel,* which we discuss later. The government itself does not bring charges of slander or libel. Rather, the defamed person may bring a civil suit (as opposed to a criminal action) for damages.

Legally, **slander** is the public uttering of a false statement that harms the good reputation of another. Public uttering means that the defamatory statement is made to, or within the hearing of, a person other than the defamed party. If one person calls another dishonest, manipulative, and incompetent to his or her face when no one else is around, that does not constitute slander. If, however, a third party accidentally overhears defamatory statements, the courts have generally held that this constitutes a public uttering and may therefore be slander.

Student Speech

In recent years, high school and university students at public institutions have faced a variety of free speech challenges. Court rulings on these issues have varied by the level of school involved. Elementary schools, in particular, have great latitude in determining what kinds of speech are appropriate for their students. High school students have more free speech rights than do elementary students, and college students have the most speech rights of all.

Rights of Public School Students. High schools can impose restrictions on speech that would not be allowed in a college setting or in the general society. For example, high school officials may censor publications such as newspapers and yearbooks produced by the school's students. Courts have argued that a school newspaper is an extension of the school's educational mission, and thus subject to control by the school administration.

One of the most striking rulings to illustrate the power of school officials was handed down by the Supreme Court in 2007. An Alaska high school student had displayed a banner reading "Bong Hits 4 Jesus" on private property across from the school as students on the school grounds watched the Winter Olympics torch relay. The school

defamation of character

Wrongfully hurting a person's good reputation. The law imposes a general duty on all persons to refrain from making false, defamatory statements about others.

slander

The public uttering of a false statement that harms the good reputation of another. The statement must be made to, or within the hearing of, a person other than the defamed party.

25. *Osborne v. Ohio,* 495 U.S. 103 (1990).

principal crossed the street, seized the banner, and suspended the student from school. The Supreme Court later held that the school had an "important—indeed, perhaps compelling—interest" in combating drug use, which allowed it to suppress the banner.[26] The Court's decision was widely criticized.

Campus Speech and Behavior Codes.

Another free speech issue is the legitimacy of campus speech and behavior codes at some state universities. These codes prohibit so-called hate speech—abusive speech attacking persons on the basis of their ethnicity, race, or other criteria. For example, a University of Michigan code banned "any behavior, verbal or physical, that stigmatizes or victimizes an individual on the basis of race, ethnicity, religion, sex, sexual orientation, creed, national origin, ancestry, age, marital status, handicap," or Vietnam-veteran status. A federal court found that the code violated students' First Amendment rights.[27] Although the courts generally have held, as in the University

Image 4–8 A student at the University of Texas is part of a project to track Internet censorship around the world. He and other concerned students then help people in various countries to bypass the censors. *Can the Internet be a force for freedom? Why or why not?*

of Michigan case, that campus speech codes at state institutions are unconstitutional restrictions on the right to free speech, such codes continue to exist.

A variety of incidents in 2015 raised additional questions about free speech. At the University of Oklahoma (OU), a video surfaced that showed members of a fraternity chanting a song that was highly insulting to African Americans and even referred to lynching. OU expelled two students and closed the fraternity. Some observers thought that these steps violated the students' First Amendment rights, but the students in question did not contest their punishment.

"Political Correctness" on Campus.

Free speech on campus becomes a somewhat more complicated issue when students, as opposed to the school administration, undertake controversial actions. At the University of Missouri, following a series of racially charged incidents, protesting students tried to prevent campus reporters from covering their activities. While journalists everywhere sided with the reporters, there are circumstances when citizens have a right to demand that reporters leave them alone. Students have also been accused of "political correctness" when they condemn language that may be insensitive or even racist. Of course, criticizing other people's speech is also a way to exercise one's own freedom of speech.

The Right to Assemble and to Petition the Government

The First Amendment prohibits Congress from making any law that abridges "the right of the people peaceably to assemble, and to petition the Government for a redress of grievances." Inherent in such a right is the ability of private citizens to communicate their ideas on public issues to government officials, as well as to other individuals. The Supreme Court has often put this freedom on a par with freedom of speech and freedom of the press. Nonetheless, it has allowed municipalities to require permits for parades, sound

---

26. *Morse v. Frederick*, 551 U.S. 393 (2007).
27. *Doe v. University of Michigan*, 721 F.Supp. 852 (1989).

trucks, and demonstrations so that public officials can control traffic or prevent demonstrations from turning into riots.

The freedom to demonstrate became a major issue in 1978 when the American Nazi Party sought to march through Skokie, Illinois, a largely Jewish suburb with many Holocaust survivors. The Supreme Court let stand a lower court's ruling that the city of Skokie had violated the Nazis' First Amendment guarantees by denying them a permit to march.[28]

Freedom of the Press

Freedom of the press can be regarded as a special instance of freedom of speech. Of course, at the time of the framing of the Constitution, the press meant only newspapers, pamphlets, magazines, and books. As technology has modified the ways in which we disseminate information, the laws touching on freedom of the press have been modified. What can and cannot be printed still occupies an important place in constitutional law, however.

Defamation in Writing. **Libel** is defamation in writing or in pictures, signs, films, or any other communication. As with slander, libel occurs only if the defamatory statements are observed by a third party. If one person sends a private communication to another wrongfully accusing him or her of embezzling funds, that does not constitute libel.

A 1964 case, *New York Times Co. v. Sullivan*,[29] explored an important question regarding libelous statements made about public officials. The Supreme Court held that only when a statement against a public official is made with **actual malice**—that is, with either knowledge of its falsity or a reckless disregard for the truth—can damages be obtained.

The standard set by the Court in the *New York Times* case has since been applied to **public figures** generally. Public figures include not only public officials but also any persons, such as movie stars, who are generally in the public limelight. Statements made about public figures usually are related to matters of general public interest. They are made about people who substantially affect all of us. Furthermore, public figures generally have some access to a public medium for answering disparaging falsehoods about themselves, whereas private individuals do not. For these reasons, public figures have a greater burden of proof in defamation cases than do private individuals.

The Internet has vastly expanded the number of published statements by the general citizenry, including anonymous comments. Today, as a result, libelous statements can be hard even to track down, much less prosecute.

Libel is easier to prove in many other countries than in the United States. Britain requires that a person accused of libel prove that his or her statements are not libelous, rather than putting the burden of proof on the offended party. British courts have also been willing to hear cases in which the alleged libel occurred in some other country. That has resulted in the practice of "libel tourism," in which foreigners travel to Britain to bring libel suits.

Films, Radio, and TV. As we have noted, in only a few cases has the Supreme Court upheld prior restraint of published materials. The Court's reluctance to accept prior restraint is less evident with respect to motion pictures. In the first half of the twentieth century, films were routinely submitted to local censorship boards. Only in 1952 did the Court find that motion pictures were covered by the First Amendment.[30] In contrast, the Court extended full protection to the Internet almost immediately by striking down provisions of the 1996 Telecommunications Act.[31] Cable TV received broad protection in 2000.[32]

Image 4–9 Los Angeles soccer star David Beckham did not succeed in his libel suit against *In Touch* magazine. *What legal standard makes it more difficult for a celebrity to win a libel suit?*

libel
A written defamation of a person's character, reputation, business, or property rights.

actual malice
Either knowledge of a defamatory statement's falsity or a reckless disregard for the truth.

public figure
A public official or any other person, such as a movie star, known to the public because of his or her position or activities.

---

28. *Smith v. Collin*, 439 U.S. 916 (1978).
29. 376 U.S. 254 (1964).
30. *Joseph Burstyn, Inc. v. Wilson*, 343 U.S. 495 (1952).
31. *Reno v. American Civil Liberties Union*, 521 U.S. 844 (1997).
32. *United States v. Playboy Entertainment Group*, 529 U.S. 803 (2000).

While the Court has held that the First Amendment is relevant to broadcast radio and television, it has never extended full protection to these media. The Court has used a number of arguments to justify this stand—initially, the scarcity of broadcast frequencies. The Court later held that the government could restrict "indecent" programming based on the "pervasive" presence of broadcasting in the home.[33] On this basis, the Federal Communications Commission (FCC) has the authority to fine broadcasters for indecency or profanity.

The Right to Privacy

No explicit reference is made anywhere in the Constitution to a person's right to privacy. Until the second half of the 1900s, the courts did not take a very positive approach toward this right. In the 1960s, the highest court began to change its views. In 1965, in *Griswold v. Connecticut*,[34] the Supreme Court overturned a Connecticut law that effectively prohibited the use of contraceptives, holding that the law violated the right to privacy. Justice William O. Douglas formulated a unique way of reading this right into the Bill of Rights. He claimed that the First, Third, Fourth, Fifth, and Ninth Amendments created "penumbras, formed by emanations [shadows, formed by the light] from those guarantees that help give them life and substance," and he went on to describe zones of privacy that are guaranteed by these rights.

When we read the Ninth Amendment, we can see the foundation for his reasoning: "The enumeration in the Constitution, of certain rights, shall not be construed to deny or disparage [belittle] others retained by the people." In other words, just because the Constitution, including its amendments, does not specifically talk about the right to privacy does not mean that this right is denied to the people.

Privacy Rights and Abortion

Historically, abortion was not a criminal offense before the "quickening" of the fetus (the first movement of the fetus in the uterus, usually between the sixteenth and eighteenth weeks of pregnancy). During the latter half of the nineteenth century, however, state laws became more severe. By 1973, performing an abortion at any time during pregnancy was a criminal offense in a majority of the states.

Roe v. Wade. In 1973, in *Roe v. Wade*,[35] the United States Supreme Court accepted the argument that the laws against abortion violated "Jane Roe's" right to privacy under the Constitution. The Court held that during the first trimester (three months) of pregnancy, abortion was an issue solely between a woman and her physician. The state could not limit abortions except to require that they be performed by licensed physicians. During the second trimester, to protect the health of the mother, the state was allowed to specify the conditions under which an abortion could be performed. During the final trimester, the state could regulate or even outlaw abortions except when they were necessary to preserve the life or health of the mother.

Learning Outcome 4:

Provide the constitutional basis of the right to privacy, and explain how the principle has been applied to the abortion and right-to-die controversies.

Image 4–10 This protester stands in front of the Planned Parenthood center in Aurora, Illinois. *What limits are placed on anti-abortion protesters?*

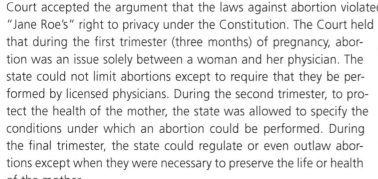

---

33. *FCC v. Pacifica Foundation*, 438 U.S. 726 (1978). In this case, the Court banned seven swear words (famously used by the late comedian George Carlin) during hours when children could hear them.

34. 381 U.S. 479 (1965).

35. 410 U.S. 113 (1973). Jane Roe was not the real name of the woman in this case. It is a common legal pseudonym used to protect a person's privacy.

After the *Roe* case, the Supreme Court issued decisions in a number of cases defining and redefining the boundaries of state regulation of abortion. During the 1980s, the Court twice struck down laws that required a woman who wished to have an abortion to undergo counseling designed to discourage abortions. In the late 1980s and early 1990s, however, the Court took a more conservative approach. For example, in 1989 the Court upheld a Missouri statute that, among other things, banned the use of public hospitals or other taxpayer-supported facilities for performing abortions.[36] In 1992, the Court upheld a Pennsylvania law that required preabortion counseling, a waiting period of twenty-four hours, and, for girls under the age of eighteen, parental or judicial permission.[37] As a result, abortions are now more difficult to obtain in some states than others, as noted in the chapter-opening *What If . . .* feature.

It is worth noting that while the Court has placed limits on what the national and state governments can do to restrict the availability of abortions, governments retain the right to discourage the procedure. Governments as well as individuals enjoy freedom of speech and have the right to condemn abortion. A state can issue "right-to-life" license plates without offering ones that support "freedom of choice." No level of government is required to fund abortions, and such government funding is in fact banned by the federal government and a majority of the states.

Protests at Abortion Clinics. Because of several episodes of violence attending protests at abortion clinics, in 1994 Congress passed the Freedom of Access to Clinic Entrances Act. The act prohibits protesters from blocking entrances to such clinics. The Supreme Court has upheld laws requiring "buffer zones" around abortion clinics. In 2014, however, the Court found that a thirty-five-foot buffer zone established by Massachusetts was excessive.[38]

Partial-Birth Abortion. Another issue in the abortion controversy concerns "partial-birth" abortion. A partial-birth abortion, which physicians call intact dilation and extraction, is a procedure that can be used during the second trimester of pregnancy. Abortion rights advocates claim that in limited circumstances the procedure is the safest way to perform an abortion and that the government should never outlaw specific medical procedures. Opponents argue that the procedure has no medical merit and that it ends the life of a fetus that might be able to live outside the womb. In 2000, the Supreme Court invalidated a Nebraska law on the ground that the law could be used to ban other abortion procedures and contained no provisions for protecting the health of the pregnant woman.[39]

In 2003, legislation similar to the Nebraska statute was passed by the U.S. Congress and signed into law by President George W. Bush. In 2007, the Supreme Court, with several changes in membership since the 2000 ruling, upheld the federal law in a five-to-four vote, effectively reversing its position on partial-birth abortions.[40]

Privacy Rights and the "Right to Die"

A 1976 case involving Karen Ann Quinlan was one of the first publicized "right-to-die" cases.[41] The parents of Quinlan, a young woman who had been in a coma for nearly a year and who had been kept alive during that time by a respirator, wanted her respirator

36. *Webster v. Reproductive Health Services*, 492 U.S. 490 (1989).

37. *Planned Parenthood v. Casey*, 505 U.S. 833 (1992).

38. *Hill v. Colorado*, 530 U.S. 703 (2000) and *McCullen v. Coakley*, ___ U.S. ___ (2014).

39. *Stenberg v. Carhart*, 530 U.S. 914 (2000).

40. *Gonzales v. Carhart*, 550 U.S. 124 (2007).

41. 70 N.J. 10 (1976).

removed. The ruling of the New Jersey Supreme Court, *In re Quinlan,* was that the right to privacy includes the right of a patient to refuse treatment and that patients unable to speak can exercise that right through a family member or guardian. In 1990, the Supreme Court took up the issue. In *Cruzan v. Director, Missouri Department of Health,*[42] the Court stated that a patient's life-sustaining treatment can be withdrawn at the request of a family member only if there is "clear and convincing evidence" that the patient did not want such treatment.

AP Images/Charles Dharapak

Image 4–11 Physician-assisted suicide continues to be an emotional issue for many Americans. Only three states allow such action by physicians. *Does the Constitution give any guidelines about the "right-to-die" controversy?*

What If There Is No Living Will?

Since the 1976 *Quinlan* decision, most states have enacted laws permitting people to designate their wishes concerning life-sustaining procedures in "living wills" or durable health-care powers of attorney. These laws and the Supreme Court's *Cruzan* decision have resolved the right-to-die controversy for situations in which the patient has drafted a living will. Disputes are still possible if there is no living will.

An example is the case of Terri Schiavo. The husband of the Florida woman, who had been in a persistent vegetative state for more than a decade, sought to have her feeding tube removed on the basis of oral statements that she would not want her life prolonged in such circumstances. Schiavo's parents fought this move in court but lost on the ground that a spouse, not a parent, is the appropriate legal guardian for a married person. Although the Florida legislature passed a law allowing Governor Jeb Bush to overrule the courts, the state supreme court held that the law violated the state constitution.[43] The federal courts agreed with the Florida state courts, and Schiavo died shortly thereafter.

Physician-Assisted Suicide.

In the 1990s, another issue surfaced: Do privacy rights include the right of terminally ill people to end their lives through physician-assisted suicide? Until 1996, the courts consistently upheld state laws that prohibited this practice. In 1996, after two federal appellate courts ruled that state laws banning assisted suicide were unconstitutional, the issue reached the United States Supreme Court.

In 1997 the Court stated that the liberty interest protected by the Constitution does not include a right to commit suicide, with or without assistance. In effect, the Supreme Court left the decision as to whether to permit the practice to the states.[44] Since then, assisted suicide has been allowed in Montana, New Mexico, Oregon, Vermont, and Washington. In 2006, the Supreme Court upheld Oregon's physician-assisted suicide law against a challenge from the George W. Bush administration.[45]

---

42. 497 U.S. 261 (1990).

43. *Bush v. Schiavo,* 885 So.2d 321 (Fla. 2004).

44. *Washington v. Glucksberg,* 521 U.S. 702 (1997).

45. *Gonzales v. Oregon,* 546 U.S. 243 (2006).

Civil Liberties versus Security Issues

As former Supreme Court justice Thurgood Marshall once said, "Grave threats to liberty often come in times of urgency, when constitutional rights seem too extravagant to endure." Not surprisingly, antiterrorist legislation since the attacks on September 11, 2001, has eroded certain basic rights, in particular the Fourth Amendment protections against unreasonable searches and seizures.

The USA Patriot Act

The most significant piece of antiterrorism legislation, the USA Patriot Act, was passed in 2001 and renewed in 2006. Many in government believed that a lack of cooperation among government agencies was a major reason for the failure to anticipate the 9/11 attacks. One goal of the Patriot Act was to lift such barriers to cooperation. Under the Patriot Act, law enforcement officials can also secretly search a suspect's home and monitor a suspect's Internet activities, phone conversations, and financial records. The government can even open a suspect's mail. While many believe that the Patriot Act is a necessary safety measure to prevent future terrorist attacks, others argue that it endangers civil liberties.

Roving Wiretaps

One civil liberties issue involves legislation that allows the government to conduct "roving" wiretaps. Previously, only specific telephone numbers, cell phone numbers, or computers could be tapped. Now a person under suspicion can be monitored electronically no matter what form of electronic communication he or she uses. Such roving wiretaps appear to be inconsistent with the Fourth Amendment, which requires a judicial warrant to describe the *place* to be searched, not just the person. As an unavoidable side effect, the government has access to the conversations and e-mail of many innocent people.

National Security Agency Surveillance

Shortly after September 11, 2001, President George W. Bush issued an executive order authorizing the National Security Agency (NSA) to conduct secret surveillance without court warrants, even warrants from special security courts. The NSA was to monitor phone calls and other communications between foreign parties and persons within the United States when one of the parties had suspected links to terrorist organizations. News of the secret program came out in December 2005. The program was intensely criticized by civil liberties groups. In 2007, Congress passed a law to authorize the warrantless NSA wiretaps. The law was reauthorized in 2008.

Recent Revelations of NSA Activity

In June 2013, leaks provided by Edward Snowden, a federal contractor, revealed that NSA surveillance was far more extensive than previously assumed. Among the most striking discoveries was that the NSA gathers information on *every* domestic land-line phone call made in the United States and certain other countries. The NSA does not record the contents of U.S. domestic calls, but rather the *metadata,* which includes the time of the call, the number of the caller, and the number of the phone that was called.

Collecting Actual Data. Under a second program, PRISM, the NSA has collected information from the websites of corporations, including Apple, Google, Facebook, Microsoft, Skype, and others. This data collection was undertaken without the knowledge of the companies involved. A third revelation was of NSA espionage actions against European countries. These included bugging the offices of the European Union in advance of trade talks between the United States and that organization. The NSA also bugged the cell phones of a wide variety of world leaders, including Brazil's president Dilma Rousseff and Germany's chancellor Angela Merkel.

Consequences of the Revelations. Snowden fled to Russia. Meanwhile, reports based on the materials he released resulted in an outcry by U.S. civil libertarians. The Obama administration defended the NSA programs, noting—correctly—that they had been authorized by secret courts. In addition, former NSA director Michael Hayden bluntly stated that the Fourth Amendment, which prohibits unreasonable searches, "is not an international treaty." Foreigners, in other words, had no privacy rights that the U.S. government was bound to respect.

As you might imagine, citizens of foreign countries, especially in Europe, found such statements to be alarming. Several nations announced initiatives aimed at protecting the privacy of data belonging to their own citizens. Such steps could cut into the sales of American high-tech firms. Currently, through "cloud computing" services, U.S. companies such as Google and Microsoft store vast amounts of data belonging to people and corporations not just in America, but around the world. In the future, individuals and firms in Germany, for example, might limit their use of cloud computing to servers located in Germany.

Image 4–12 Opponents of national security surveillance support Edward Snowden, the leaker who exposed NSA activities. *Is Snowden a hero or a traitor? In either case, why?*

Apple and Microsoft versus Government Surveillance. The question of whether government surveillance threatened high-tech businesses led to several confrontations in 2016. One was a dispute between Apple and the FBI over iPhone security. In December 2015, domestic Islamist terrorists killed fourteen people and seriously injured twenty-two in an attack in San Bernardino, California. The alleged terrorists then died in a shootout with police. They left behind a locked iPhone that the FBI sought to crack. It obtained a court order demanding that Apple create a special version of the iPhone operating system that would bypass security controls. Apple refused, arguing that such a step would undermine the privacy of all iPhone users. In March, however, the FBI found a way to crack the iPhone without Apple's help.

One tool used by the government in the years since 9/11 has been national security orders (NSOs), which are subpoenas issued by the FBI without judicial oversight. Individuals, financial institutions, and Internet service providers are banned from speaking about the NSOs with anyone. Other than constitutional issues, this practice raises the concern that no one would be allowed to blow the whistle on abuses of the government's powers. A U.S. district court has found NSOs to be unconstitutional, but thousands are still issued every year. In April 2016, Microsoft sued the Justice Department, claiming that NSO "gag orders" violated the First and Fourth Amendments. In both the Apple and Microsoft cases, a serious concern existed that government powers first exercised in the war against terror would quickly be employed in general law enforcement.

National Security and the Civil Liberties of Immigrants

For many U.S. citizens, immigration—especially unauthorized or illegal immigration—is a national security issue. The terrorist attacks on September 11, 2001, reinforced the belief that the civil liberties of noncitizens should be limited. Among the most obvious

Why should you care about CIVIL LIBERTIES?

The Bill of Rights includes numerous provisions that protect persons who are suspected of criminal activity. You may be the most law-abiding person in the world, but that will not guarantee that you will never be stopped, searched, or arrested by the police. Sooner or later, the great majority of all citizens will have some kind of interaction with the police. People who do not understand their rights or how to behave toward law enforcement officers can find themselves in serious trouble. The advice in the *How You Can Make a Difference* feature at the end of this chapter therefore provides key survival skills for life in the modern world.

characteristics of the terrorists who perpetrated the 9/11 attacks is that they were all foreign citizens. Still, legal immigrants who are not citizens have rights. The Bill of Rights contains no language that limits its protections to citizens. The Fourteenth Amendment specifies that all *persons* (as opposed to all *citizens*) shall enjoy "due process of law."

Illegal immigrants are subject to deportation. In 1903, however, the Supreme Court ruled that the government could not deport someone without a hearing that meets constitutional due process standards.[46] Today, most people facing deportation are entitled to a hearing before an immigration judge, to representation by a lawyer, and to the right to see the evidence presented against them. The government must prove that its grounds for deportation are valid.

Limits to the Rights of Deportees: Due Process. Despite the language of the Fourteenth Amendment, the courts have often deferred to government assertions that noncitizens cannot make constitutional claims. The Antiterrorism and Effective Death Penalty Act passed by Congress in 1996 was especially restrictive. The government was given the right to deport noncitizens for alleged terrorism without any court review of the deportation order. Further, the government is now allowed to deport noncitizens based on secret evidence that the deportee is not permitted to see.

Limits to the Rights of Deportees: Freedom of Speech. A case in 1999 involved a group of noncitizens associated with the Popular Front for the Liberation of Palestine (PFLP). The PFLP had carried out terrorist acts in Israel, but there was no evidence of criminal conduct by the group arrested in the United States. In this case, the Supreme Court ruled that aliens have no First Amendment rights to object to deportation, even if the deportation is based on their political associations.[47] This ruling also covers permanent residents—noncitizens with "green cards" that allow them to live and work in the United States on a long-term basis.

Limits to the Rights of Deportees: *Ex Post Facto* Laws. Article I, Section 9, of the Constitution prohibits *ex post facto* laws—laws that inflict punishments for acts that were not illegal when they were committed. This provision may not apply in deportation cases, however. The 1996 law mentioned earlier provided mandatory deportation for noncitizens convicted of an aggravated felony, even if the crime took place before 1996. Under the 1996 law, permanent residents have been deported to nations that they left when they were small children. In some cases, deported persons did not even speak the language of the country to which they were deported.

The Great Balancing Act: The Rights of the Accused versus the Rights of Society

Learning Outcome **6:**

Identify the constitutional rights of those who are accused of a crime, explain the *Miranda* and exclusionary rules, and describe the current status of the death penalty.

The United States has one of the highest murder rates in the industrialized world. It is not surprising, therefore, that many citizens have extremely strong opinions about the rights of those accused of violent crimes. When an accused person, especially one who has confessed to some criminal act, is set free because of an apparent legal "technicality," many

46. *Yamataya v. Fisher,* 189 U.S. 86 (1903).
47. *Reno v. Arab-American Anti-Discrimination Committee,* 525 U.S. 471 (1999).

people believe that the rights of the accused are being given more weight than the rights of society and of potential or actual victims. Why, then, give criminal suspects rights? The answer is partly to avoid convicting innocent people, but mostly because due process of law and fair treatment benefit everyone who comes in contact with law enforcement or the courts.

The courts and the police must constantly engage in a balancing act of competing rights. The basis of all discussions about the appropriate balance is, of course, the U.S. Bill of Rights. The Fourth, Fifth, Sixth, and Eighth Amendments deal specifically with the rights of criminal defendants.

Rights of the Accused

The basic rights of criminal defendants are outlined below. When appropriate, the specific constitutional provision or amendment on which a right is based is also given.

Limits on the Conduct of Police Officers and Prosecutors.

- No unreasonable or unwarranted searches and seizures (Amendment IV).
- No arrest except on probable cause (Amendment IV).
- No coerced confessions or illegal interrogation (Amendment V).
- No entrapment.
- On questioning following an arrest, a suspect must be informed of her or his rights.

Defendant's Pretrial Rights.

- Writ of *habeas corpus* (Article I, Section 9).
- Prompt **arraignment** (Amendment VI).
- Legal counsel (Amendment VI).
- Reasonable bail (Amendment VIII).
- To be informed of charges (Amendment VI).
- To remain silent (Amendment V).

Trial Rights.

- Speedy and public trial before a jury (Amendment VI).
- Impartial jury selected from a cross section of the community (Amendment VI).
- Trial atmosphere free of prejudice, fear, and outside interference.
- No compulsory self-incrimination (Amendment V).
- Adequate counsel (Amendment VI).
- No cruel and unusual punishment (Amendment VIII).
- Appeal of convictions.
- No double jeopardy (Amendment V).

Extending the Rights of the Accused

During the 1960s, the Supreme Court, under Chief Justice Earl Warren, significantly expanded the rights of accused persons. In *Gideon v. Wainwright,*[48] a case decided in 1963, the Court held that if a person is accused of a felony and cannot afford an attorney, an attorney must be made available to the accused person at the government's expense. Although the Sixth Amendment to the Constitution provides for the right to counsel, the

arraignment

The first act in a criminal proceeding, in which the defendant is brought before a court to hear the charges against him or her and enter a plea of guilty or not guilty.

---

48. 372 U.S. 335 (1963).

Image 4–13 Police arrest a young suspect. *For what reasons can the police arrest someone?*

Court had previously held that only criminal defendants in capital (death penalty) cases automatically had a right to free legal counsel.

Miranda v. Arizona. In 1966, the Court issued its decision in *Miranda v. Arizona.*[49] The case involved Ernesto Miranda, who was charged with the kidnapping and rape of a young woman. After questioning, Miranda confessed and was later convicted. Miranda's lawyer appealed his conviction, arguing that the police had never informed Miranda that he had a right to remain silent and a right to be represented by counsel. The Court, in ruling in Miranda's favor, enunciated the now-familiar *Miranda* rights. Today, *Miranda* rights statements typically take the following form:

> *You have the right to remain silent. Anything you say can and will be used against you in a court of law. You have the right to speak to an attorney. If you cannot afford an attorney, one will be appointed for you. Do you understand these rights as they have been read to you?*

Exceptions to the *Miranda* Rule. As part of a continuing attempt to balance the rights of accused persons against the rights of society, the Supreme Court has made a number of exceptions to the *Miranda* rule. As one example, in an important 1991 decision, the Court stated that a suspect's conviction will not be automatically overturned if the suspect was coerced into making a confession. If the other evidence admitted at trial is strong enough to justify the conviction without the confession, then the fact that the confession was obtained illegally can effectively be ignored.[50]

The Exclusionary Rule

At least since 1914, judicial policy has prohibited the admission of illegally seized evidence at trials in federal courts. This is the so-called **exclusionary rule.** Improperly obtained evidence, no matter how telling, cannot be used by prosecutors. This includes evidence obtained by police in violation of a suspect's *Miranda* rights or of the Fourth Amendment. The Fourth Amendment protects against unreasonable searches and seizures and provides that a judge may issue a search warrant to a police officer only on *probable cause* (a demonstration of facts that permit a reasonable belief that a crime has been committed). The courts must determine what constitutes an "unreasonable" search and seizure.

The reasoning behind the exclusionary rule is that it forces police officers to gather evidence properly, in which case their due diligence will be rewarded by a conviction. Nevertheless, the exclusionary rule has always had critics who argue that it permits guilty persons to be freed because of innocent procedural errors by the police.

Adjustments to the Exclusionary Rule. This rule was first extended to state court proceedings in a 1961 United States Supreme Court decision, *Mapp v. Ohio.*[51] In this case, the Court overturned the conviction of Dollree Mapp for the possession of obscene materials. Police found pornographic books in her apartment after searching it without a search warrant and despite her refusal to let them in. Under the Fourth Amendment,

---

exclusionary rule

A judicial policy prohibiting the admission at trial of illegally obtained evidence.

49. 384 U.S. 436 (1966).

50. *Arizona v. Fulminante,* 499 U.S. 279 (1991).

51. 367 U.S. 643 (1961).

search warrants must describe the persons or things to be seized. Nonetheless, officers are entitled to seize items not mentioned in the search warrant if the materials are in "plain view" and reasonably appear to be contraband or evidence of a crime.[52]

During the past several decades, the Supreme Court has diminished the scope of the exclusionary rule by creating exceptions to its applicability. For example, the Court has created the "good faith" exception to the exclusionary rule. In 2009, the Court found that the good faith exception applies when an officer makes an arrest based on an outstanding warrant in another jurisdiction, even if the warrant in question was based on a clerical error.[53]

The Exclusionary Rule and New Technology. The Supreme Court has also attempted to update the exclusionary rule to make it compatible with the latest technology. In 2014, for example, a unanimous Court found it unconstitutional for officers to search and seize the digital contents of a cell phone without a search warrant. According to the Court, smartphones now contain such vast quantities of private data that they are "worthy of the protection for which the Founders fought."[54] A topic that is sure to reach the Court in the future is the use of drones for surveillance by law enforcement. Under what circumstances does the use of drones violate our Fourth Amendment protections?

The Death Penalty

Capital punishment remains one of the most debated aspects of our criminal justice system. Those in favor of the death penalty maintain that it serves as a deterrent to serious crime and satisfies society's need for justice and fair play. Those opposed to the death penalty do not believe it has any deterrent value and hold that it constitutes a barbaric act in an otherwise civilized society.

Cruel and Unusual Punishment? The Eighth Amendment prohibits "cruel and unusual punishment." Throughout history, the phrase referred to torture and to executions that prolonged the agony of dying. The Supreme Court has never interpreted "cruel and unusual" as prohibiting all forms of capital punishment in all circumstances. Many people came to believe, however, that the imposition of the death penalty was random and arbitrary, and in 1972 the Supreme Court agreed, in *Furman v. Georgia*.[55]

The Supreme Court's 1972 decision stated that the death penalty, as then applied, violated the Eighth and Fourteenth Amendments. The Court also ruled that capital punishment is not necessarily cruel and unusual if the criminal has killed or attempted to kill someone. In its opinion, the Court invited the states to enact more precise laws so that the death penalty would be applied more consistently. By 1976, twenty-five states had adopted a two-stage, or *bifurcated*, procedure for capital cases. In the first stage, a jury determines the guilt or innocence of the defendant for a crime that has been determined by statute to be punishable by death. If the defendant is found guilty, the jury reconvenes in the second stage and considers all relevant evidence to decide whether the death sentence is, in fact, warranted.

In 1976, in *Gregg v. Georgia*,[56] the Supreme Court ruled in favor of Georgia's bifurcated process, holding that the state's legislative guidelines had removed the ability of a jury to "wantonly and freakishly impose the death penalty." The Court upheld similar procedures in Texas and Florida, establishing a "road map" for all states to follow that would assure them protection from lawsuits based on Eighth Amendment grounds.

The Death Penalty Today. Today, thirty-one states and the federal government have capital punishment laws based on the guidelines established by the *Gregg* case (see

Image 4–14 Front page of the *New York Daily News*, April 23, 2013. Dzhokhar Tsarnaev was accused of bombing the Boston Marathon on April 15. Three died and 264 were injured, many badly. *Is revenge a legitimate reason for imposing the death penalty?*

---

52. *Texas v. Brown*, 460 U.S. 730 (1983); and *Horton v. California*, 496 U.S. 128 (1990).
53. *Herring v. United States*, 555 U.S. 135 (2009).
54. *Riley v. California*, 134 S.Ct. 2473 (2014).
55. 408 U.S. 238 (1972).
56. 428 U.S. 153 (1976).

Figure 4–1). State governments are responsible for almost all executions in this country. At this time, there are about 3,100 prisoners on death row across the nation.

The number of executions per year reached a high in 1998 at ninety-eight and then began to fall. Twenty-eight people were executed in 2015 in six states. Some believe that the declining number of executions reflects the waning support among Americans for the imposition of the death penalty. In 1994, polls indicated that 80 percent of Americans supported the death penalty in cases involving murder. Recent polls, however, suggest that this number has dropped to below 60 percent.

Recently, DNA testing has shown that some innocent people may have been convicted unjustly of murder. Since 1973, more than 150 prisoners have been freed from death row after new evidence suggested that they were convicted wrongfully.

Methods of Execution. The most recent controversy concerning the death penalty is whether execution by injecting the condemned prisoner with lethal drugs is a cruel and unusual punishment. Lethal injection is currently used in almost all executions. Evidence exists that when performed incompetently, death by lethal injection can be extremely painful. Some death penalty opponents have claimed that the procedure is painful in so many instances that it constitutes cruel and unusual punishment. The United States Supreme Court took up this matter in a Kentucky case in 2007. In 2008, it ruled by a seven-to-two margin that Kentucky's method of execution by lethal injection was constitutional.[57] It issued a similar ruling in a 2015 Oklahoma case.[58]

---

57. *Baze v. Rees*, 553 U.S. 35 (2008).
58. *Glossip v. Gross*, 576 U.S. ____ (2015).

Figure 4–1 The States and the Death Penalty: Executions since 1976 and the Death Row Population

Today, as shown in this figure, nineteen states have abolished the death penalty. Delaware was the most recent, in 2016. The District of Columbia, Puerto Rico, Guam, and the U.S. Virgin Islands also have no death penalty. In Connecticut and New Mexico, abolition of the death penalty was not retroactive. Therefore, these states still have inmates on death row. *Why might some Americans have become more skeptical about the death penalty?*

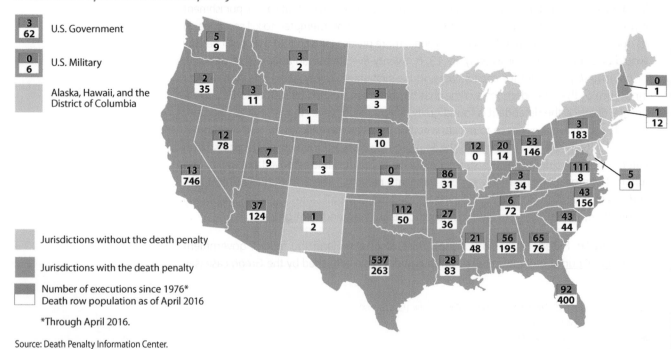

3 / 62	U.S. Government
0 / 6	U.S. Military
	Alaska, Hawaii, and the District of Columbia

Jurisdictions without the death penalty

Jurisdictions with the death penalty

Number of executions since 1976*
Death row population as of April 2016

*Through April 2016.

Source: Death Penalty Information Center.

Despite Supreme Court approval, states have confronted other difficulties in carrying out capital punishment. One has been opposition to the death penalty by state governors. In Colorado, Oregon, Pennsylvania, and Washington, governors have refused to permit any executions during their terms of office. A second issue is the availability of the necessary lethal drugs. More than twenty pharmaceutical companies in the United States and Europe have refused to sell or even manufacture drugs used in executions. In May 2016, Pfizer, the last company to sell such drugs, announced sweeping measures to prevent its products from being used in executions. This step could lead some death penalty states to consider older forms of execution, such as hanging or electrocution.

 How you can make a difference

How should you behave if you are stopped by police officers?

- Your civil liberties protect you from having to provide information other than your name and address.

- Normally, even if you have not been placed under arrest, the officers have the right to frisk you for weapons, and you must let them proceed. The officers cannot, however, check your person or your clothing further if, in their judgment, no weaponlike object is produced.

- The officers may search you only if they have a search warrant or probable cause to believe that a search will likely produce incriminating evidence. What if the officers do not have probable cause or a warrant? Physically resisting their attempt to search you can lead to disastrous results. It is best simply to refuse orally to give permission for the search, if possible in the presence of a witness.

- Being polite is better than acting out of anger and making the officers irritable. It is usually advisable to limit what you say to the officers. If you are arrested, it is best to keep quiet until you can speak with a lawyer.

- If you are in your car and are stopped by the police, the same fundamental rules apply. Always be ready to show your driver's license and car registration.

- You may be asked to get out of the car. The officers may use a flashlight to peer inside if it is too dark to see otherwise. None of this constitutes a search. A true search requires either a warrant or probable cause.

- No officer has the legal right to search your car simply to find out if you may have committed a crime. Police officers can conduct searches that are incident to lawful arrests, however.

- If you are in your home and a police officer with a search warrant appears, you can ask to examine the warrant before granting entry. A warrant that is correctly made out will state the place or persons to be searched, the object sought, and the date of the warrant (which should be no more than ten days old). It will also bear the signature of a judge or magistrate. If the warrant is in order, you need not make any statement.

- If you believe the warrant to be invalid, or if no warrant is produced, you should make it clear orally that you have not consented to the search, if possible in the presence of a witness. If the search later is proved to be unlawful, normally any evidence obtained cannot be used in court.

- Officers who attempt to enter your home without a search warrant can do so only if they are pursuing a suspected felon into the house. Rarely is it advisable to give permission for a warrantless search.

- You, as the resident, must be the one to give permission if any evidence obtained is to be considered legal. A landlord, manager, or head of a college dormitory cannot give legal permission. A roommate, however, can give permission for a search of his or her room, which may allow the police to search areas where you have belongings.

- If you are a guest in a place that is being legally searched, you may be legally searched as well. But unless you have been placed under arrest, you cannot be compelled to go to the police station or get into a squad car.

KEY TERMS

actual malice **100**

arraignment **107**

bill of attainder **88**

commercial speech **95**

defamation of
  character **98**

establishment clause **89**

ex post facto law **88**

exclusionary rule **108**

free exercise clause **89**

imminent lawless action
  test **97**

incorporation theory **88**

libel **100**

prior restraint **94**

public figure **100**

slander **98**

symbolic speech **95**

writ of *habeas corpus* **87**

CHAPTER SUMMARY

Learning Outcome 1 Originally, the Bill of Rights limited only the power of the national government, not that of the states. Gradually and selectively, however, the Supreme Court accepted the incorporation theory, under which no state can violate most provisions of the Bill of Rights. Several of our rights are also guaranteed by the main body of the Constitution.

Learning Outcome 2 The First Amendment protects against government interference with freedom of religion by requiring a separation of church and state (under the establishment clause) and by guaranteeing the free exercise of religion. Controversial issues that arise under the establishment clause include school prayer, the teaching of evolution versus creationism, and the placement of religious displays on public property. The government can interfere with the free exercise of religion only when religious practices work against public policy or the public welfare.

Learning Outcome 3 The First Amendment protects against government interference with freedom of speech, which includes symbolic speech (expressive conduct). The Supreme Court has been especially critical of government actions that impose prior restraint on expression. Restrictions on expression are permitted when the expression may incite imminent lawless action. The First Amendment protects against government interference with the freedom of the press, which can be regarded as a special instance of freedom of speech.

Learning Outcome 4 Under the Ninth Amendment, rights not specifically mentioned in the Constitution are not necessarily denied to the people. Among these unspecified rights protected by the courts is a right to privacy, which has been inferred from the First, Third, Fourth, Fifth, and Ninth Amendments. Whether an individual's privacy rights include a right to an abortion or a "right to die" continues to provoke controversy.

Learning Outcome 5 Another major challenge concerns the extent to which Americans must forfeit civil liberties to control terrorism. Partially in response to alleged national security concerns, the civil rights of noncitizens in deportation cases are quite limited.

Learning Outcome 6 The Constitution includes protections for the rights of persons accused of crimes. Under the Fourth Amendment, no one may be subject to an unreasonable search or seizure or be arrested except on probable cause. Under the Fifth Amendment, an accused person has the right to remain silent. Under the Sixth Amendment, an accused person must be informed of the reason for his or her arrest. In *Miranda v. Arizona* (1966), the Supreme Court held that criminal suspects, before interrogation by law enforcement personnel, must be informed of the right to remain silent and the right to be represented by counsel. The exclusionary rule forbids the admission in court of illegally obtained evidence. Under the Eighth Amendment, cruel and unusual punishment is prohibited. Whether the death penalty is cruel and unusual punishment continues to be debated.

ADDITIONAL RESOURCES

The debate over civil liberties versus national security is a heated one. In the 2015–2016 school year, the National Federation of State High School Associations (NFHS) chose as its policy debate topic "Resolved: The United States federal government should substantially curtail its domestic surveillance." National Public Radio and Intelligence Squared U.S. sponsored a debate on this topic. Search for "Does Spying Keep Us Safe?" to find a broadcast version of the debate or to download a transcript in PDF format. For a YouTube video version, search for "Spy on Me, I'd Rather Be Safe." When you are done with the debate, decide who you think won. You can compare your verdict with the opinions of audience members.

Online Resources

- A key asset in learning about our civil liberties is the website of the American Civil Liberties Union (ACLU). Find it at **aclu.org**.

- The largest group advocating robust Second Amendment rights is the National Rifle Organization (NRA). Its website is at **nra.org**.

Books

Breyer, Stephen, and John Bessler (ed.). *Against the Death Penalty*. Washington: Brookings Institution Press, 2016. United States Supreme Court Justice Stephen Breyer makes the case against capital punishment along with John Bessler, a professor at the University of Baltimore Law School.

Gellman, Barton. *Dark Mirror: Edward Snowden and the American Surveillance State*. New York: Penguin, 2016. An in-depth look at the Snowden revelations by a journalist who has won the Pulitzer Prize three times.

Witte, John Jr., and Joel A. Nichols. *Religion and the American Constitutional Experiment* (4th ed.). New York: Oxford University Press, 2016. The authors are law professors, Witte at Emory University and Nichols at the University of St. Thomas. They describe the origins, theoretical background, and legal history of the First Amendment's religion clauses.

Video

Assaulted: Civil Rights under Fire—Released in 2013, this film, narrated by the rapper Ice-T, presents arguments against gun control legislation. In an unusual twist, Ice-T describes how African Americans have been denied access to weapons throughout U.S. history.

Citizenfour—A documentary showing the actual events surrounding the Edward Snowden revelations. Laura Poitras, the director, was one of the few journalists that Snowden trusted.

Quiz

Multiple Choice and Fill-Ins

Learning Outcome 1 Identify the rights listed in the original Constitution, describe the Bill of Rights, and discuss how it came to be applied to state governments as well as the national government.

1. As originally intended, the Bill of Rights limited the powers of:
   a. only the state governments.
   b. both the national government and the state governments.
   c. only the national government.

2. Since 1925, the Supreme Court has gradually accepted the _____ _____ and has therefore extended the Bill of Rights to cover state governments under the Fourteenth Amendment's due process clause.

Learning Outcome 2 Explain how the First Amendment's establishment clause and free exercise clause guarantee our freedom of religion.

3. Religious displays on public property are:
   a. always acceptable.
   b. never acceptable.
   c. acceptable as part of a broader display that contains non-religious elements.

4. Our freedom of religion is based on two clauses in the First Amendment. These are the _____ ___ _____ _____ clauses.

Learning Outcome 3 Specify the limited circumstances in which the national and state governments may override the principles of free speech and freedom of the press.

5. If you utter a false statement that harms the good reputation of another, it is called slander, and such expression is:
   a. always protected under the First Amendment.
   b. unprotected speech and a potential basis for a lawsuit.
   c. prosecuted as a felony in most states.

6. When governments attempt to ban certain types of clothing, gestures, and other forms of expressive conduct, they are attempting to ban _____ _____.

Learning Outcome 4 Provide the constitutional basis of the right to privacy, and explain how the principle has been applied to the abortion and right-to-die controversies.

7. The right to privacy:
   a. is explicitly guaranteed by the original text of the Constitution.
   b. is explicitly guaranteed by the Fifth Amendment to the Constitution.
   c. has been inferred from other rights by the Supreme Court.

8. The Supreme Court has ruled that the decision as to whether to permit the practice of assisted suicide must be left to the _____.

Learning Outcome 5 Cite examples of how recent security concerns have affected our civil liberties.

9. The Supreme Court has significantly limited the rights of non-citizens in cases that involve:
   a. deportation.
   b. employment.
   c. freedom of religion.

10. The most significant antiterrorism legislation is the _____ _____ _____.

Learning Outcome 6 Identify the constitutional rights of those who are accused of a crime, explain the *Miranda* and exclusionary rules, and describe the current status of the death penalty.

11. Illegally seized evidence is not admissible at trial because of the:
    a. exclusionary rule.
    b. *Miranda* rule.
    c. writ of *habeas corpus*.

12. Cruel and unusual punishment is prohibited by the _____ _____.

Essay Questions

1. The courts have never held that the provision of military chaplains by the armed forces is unconstitutional, despite the fact that chaplains are religious leaders who are employed by and under the authority of the U.S. government. What arguments might the courts use to defend the military chaplain system?

2. In a surprisingly large number of cases, arrested individuals do not choose to exercise their right to remain silent. Why might a person not exercise his or her *Miranda* rights?

Answers to multiple-choice and fill-in questions: 1. c, 2. incorporation theory, 3. c, 4. establishment and free exercise, 5. b, 6. symbolic speech, 7. c, 8. states, 9. a, 10. USA Patriot Act, 11. a, 12. Eighth Amendment.

CIVIL RIGHTS 5

Children celebrate the fiftieth anniversary of the March on Washington, where the Reverend Dr. Martin Luther King, Jr., delivered his world-famous "I Have a Dream" speech. *What are the children trying to say with their "My Voice Matters" placards?*

Joseph Sohm/Shutterstock.com

These six **LEARNING OUTCOMES** *below are designed to help improve your understanding of this chapter:*

1: Summarize the historical experience of African Americans, state how the separate-but-equal doctrine was abolished, and describe the consequences of the civil rights movement.

2: Define the different levels of scrutiny used by the Supreme Court in civil rights cases, and describe recent rulings on affirmative action.

3: Discuss the history and current status of Latinos, American Indians, and Asian Americans.

4: Contrast the goals of the women's suffrage movement with the goals of modern feminism.

5: Summarize the recent revolution in the rights enjoyed by gay men and lesbians.

6: Evaluate the rights and status of juvenile citizens.

What if...

We Deported Most Unauthorized Immigrants?

Background

Today, about 11 million unauthorized—or illegal—immigrants live in the United States. For years, Congress has made various attempts at resolving the illegal immigrant issue. Yet nothing has happened. Many proposals have involved programs to move illegal immigrants onto a path that ends in legal status or even citizenship. In contrast, Republican presidential candidates Donald Trump and Ted Cruz advocated the deportation of all 11 million. The hostility of Trump and other Republicans to illegal immigration has pushed Latino voters toward the Democrats. President Obama, however, has in practice taken a hard line on undocumented workers. He has deported 2 million persons, more than any other president. As a result of these deportations and the lack of jobs due to the recent Great Recession, the number of illegal immigrants has been stable for several years.

What If We Deported Most Unauthorized Immigrants?

Suppose that the federal government expanded its current deportation effort into a program aimed at identifying and deporting every last unauthorized immigrant. If this were to be a two-year project, as Trump proposed, we would need to deport more people every month than we now do in a year. That is more than ten times the current deportation effort. By one study, we would need at least ten times as many immigration officers, ten times as many prison beds, and many more immigration courts and federal lawyers. Physically moving the deportees would require 84 buses and 47 chartered flights every day for two years.

The total cost would be about $400 billion. Immigration opponents argue that we could keep the costs down by making life so unpleasant for unauthorized immigrants that they leave under their own power. The study just mentioned, however, already assumes that about 20 percent of those eligible for deportation would leave voluntarily. It's not clear how much higher this percentage could go.

Surprise—Such a Program Might Kill Jobs

Deportation proponents argue that with fewer illegal immigrants, American citizens would have access to more jobs. Most economists disagree. The number of jobs in the economy is not fixed. When the economy grows, the number of jobs rises. Legal and illegal immigrants alike add to net employment because they not only work, they also spend. They buy lodging, food, and entertainment. This spending adds to the demand for goods and services, which leads to more employment, not less.

Major industries such as agriculture are dependent on undocumented workers. A team at the University of Alabama recently estimated that Alabama's stiff immigration law may cost the state almost $2.5 billion per year. A study at UCLA predicted that mass deportation would reduce California tax revenues by 8.5 percent and would shrink the state economy by tens of billions of dollars per year. Nationwide, the reduced economic activity resulting from mass deportation could trigger an economic recession. By one estimate, the reduction in economic activity could exceed $1 trillion per year.

The Effect on Civil Rights

A successful mass deportation effort would require that police have the ability to "stop and ask." Everyone would have to produce proof of legal status. Questioning could not be limited to unauthorized immigrants. Latinos who are U.S. citizens would be singled out. Many non-Hispanic citizens might be caught in the net as well.

For Critical Analysis

▶ **If mass deportations were initiated, what might happen to the cost of farm produce?**

▶ **Why has the immigration issue remained a political "hot potato" for decades?**

Image 5–1 Thousands demonstrate against new anti-immigration legislation in Madison, Wisconsin, in 2016. *Can states enact anti-immigration legislation that contradicts the policies of the federal government?*

AAraujo/Shutterstock.com

E quality is at the heart of the concept of civil rights. Generally, the term **civil rights** refers to the rights of all Americans to equal protection under the law, as provided by the Fourteenth Amendment to the Constitution. Although the terms *civil rights* and *civil liberties* are sometimes used interchangeably, scholars make a distinction between the two. As discussed in Chapter 4, civil liberties are basically limitations on government. They specify what the government *cannot* do. Civil rights, in contrast, specify what the government *must* do to ensure equal protection and freedom from discrimination.

The history of civil rights in America is the story of the struggle of various groups to be free from discriminatory treatment. In this chapter, we look at several movements that had significant consequences for civil rights in America: the civil rights movement of the 1950s and 1960s, the women's movement, and the movement to gain equal rights for gay men and lesbians. Each of these movements resulted in legislation and court rulings that secured important basic rights for all Americans.

Most of the 11 million unauthorized immigrants in the United States come from Latin America. In this chapter, we look at some of the issues facing Latino Americans, and also American Indians and Asian Americans. In addition, other groups have suffered—and continue to suffer—from discrimination of one kind or another. These include Muslim Americans, persons with disabilities, and older Americans. The fact that any group is not singled out for special attention in the following pages should not be construed to mean that its struggle for equality is any less significant than the struggles of those groups that we do discuss.

The African American Experience and the Civil Rights Movement

Before 1863, the Constitution protected slavery and made equality impossible in the sense in which we use the word today. The system of slavery, however, did not survive the American Civil War (1861–1865).

Ending Servitude

With the emancipation of the slaves by President Abraham Lincoln's Emancipation Proclamation in 1863 and the passage of the Thirteenth, Fourteenth, and Fifteenth Amendments during the Reconstruction period (1865–1877) following the Civil War, constitutional inequality was ended.

Constitutional Amendments. The Thirteenth Amendment (1865) states that neither slavery nor involuntary servitude shall exist within the United States. The Fourteenth Amendment (1868) tells us that *all* persons born or naturalized in the United States are citizens of the United States. It states, furthermore, that "[n]o State shall make or enforce any law which shall abridge the privileges or immunities of citizens of the United States; nor shall any State deprive any person of life, liberty, or property, without due process of law; nor deny to any person within its jurisdiction the equal protection of the laws." Note the use of the terms *citizen* and *person* in this amendment. *Citizens* have political rights, such as the right to vote and run for political office. Citizens also have certain privileges or immunities (see Chapter 3). All *persons,* however, including noncitizen immigrants, have a right to due process of law and equal protection under the law. We discuss the Fourteenth Amendment in greater detail later in this chapter.

Finally, the Fifteenth Amendment (1870) reads as follows: "The right of citizens of the United States to vote shall not be denied or abridged by the United States or by

Learning Outcome 1:

Summarize the historical experience of African Americans, state how the separate-but-equal doctrine was abolished, and describe the consequences of the civil rights movement.

civil rights

Generally, all rights rooted in the Fourteenth Amendment's guarantee of equal protection under the law.

Image 5–2 Harriet Tubman was a leader of the "underground railroad" that smuggled slaves to freedom. During the Civil War, she served as a nurse, spy, and scout for the Union army. *Why has the Treasury Department decided to put her image on the twenty-dollar bill?*

Library of Congress Prints and Photographs Division Washington, D.C. [LC-US262-7816]

any State on account of race, color, or previous condition of servitude." The right to vote is also known as **suffrage**, or the franchise. Another term is *enfranchisement,* which means "granting the right to vote."

The Civil Rights Acts of 1865 to 1875. From 1865 to 1875, Congress passed a series of civil rights acts to enforce the Thirteenth, Fourteenth, and Fifteenth Amendments. The Civil Rights Act of 1866 implemented the extension of citizenship to anyone born in the United States and gave African Americans full equality before the law. The Enforcement Act of 1870 set out specific criminal penalties for interfering with the right to vote as protected by the Fifteenth Amendment and by the Civil Rights Act of 1866.

Equally important was the Civil Rights Act of 1872, known as the Anti–Ku Klux Klan Act. This act made it a federal crime for anyone to use law or custom to deprive an individual of rights, privileges, and immunities secured by the Constitution or by any federal law. The Second Civil Rights Act, passed in 1875, declared that everyone is entitled to full and equal enjoyment of public accommodations, theaters, and other places of public amusement, and it imposed penalties on violators.

The Ineffectiveness of the Early Civil Rights Laws

The Reconstruction statutes, or civil rights acts, ultimately did little to secure equality for African Americans. Both the *Civil Rights Cases* and the case of *Plessy v. Ferguson* (discussed next) effectively nullified these acts. Additionally, various barriers were erected that prevented African Americans from exercising their right to vote.

The *Civil Rights Cases.* The United States Supreme Court invalidated the 1875 Second Civil Rights Act when it held, in the *Civil Rights Cases*[1] of 1883, that the enforcement clause of the Fourteenth Amendment (which states that "[n]o State shall make or enforce any law which shall abridge the privileges or immunities of citizens") was limited to correcting official actions by states. Thus, the discriminatory acts of *private* citizens were not illegal. ("Individual invasion of individual rights is not the subject matter of the Amendment.")

The 1883 Supreme Court decision met with widespread approval by whites throughout most of the United States. Twenty years after the Civil War, the white majority was all too willing to forget about the Civil War amendments to the U.S. Constitution and the civil rights legislation of the 1860s and 1870s. The other civil rights laws that the Court did not specifically invalidate became dead letters in the statute books, although they were never officially repealed by Congress.

Plessy v. Ferguson: Separate but Equal. A key decision during this period concerned Homer Plessy, who was one-eighth African American. In 1892, he boarded a train in New Orleans. The conductor made him leave the car, which was restricted to whites, and directed him to a car for nonwhites. At that time, Louisiana had a statute providing for separate railway cars for whites and African Americans.

Plessy went to court, claiming that such a statute was contrary to the Fourteenth Amendment's equal protection clause. In 1896, the United States Supreme Court rejected Plessy's contention in *Plessy v. Ferguson*.[2] The Court concluded that the Fourteenth

suffrage

The right to vote; the franchise.

1. 109 U.S. 3 (1883).
2. 163 U.S. 537 (1896).

Amendment "could not have been intended to abolish distinctions based upon color, or to enforce social . . . equality." The Court stated that segregation alone did not violate the Constitution: "Laws permitting, and even requiring, their separation in places where they are liable to be brought into contact do not necessarily imply the inferiority of either race to the other." So was born the **separate-but-equal doctrine.**

Plessy v. Ferguson became the judicial cornerstone of racial discrimination throughout the United States. The result was a system of racial segregation, particularly in the South—supported by state and local "Jim Crow" laws. (Jim Crow was an insulting term for African Americans derived from a song-and-dance show.) These laws required separate drinking fountains; separate seats in theaters, restaurants, and hotels; separate public toilets; and separate waiting rooms for the two races. "Separate" was indeed the rule, but "equal" was never enforced, nor was it a reality.

Image 5–3 Segregated drinking fountains were common in southern states in the late 1800s and during the first half of the twentieth century. *What landmark Supreme Court case made such segregated facilities legal?*

Voting Barriers. The brief voting enfranchisement of African Americans ended after 1877, when the federal troops that occupied the South during the Reconstruction era were withdrawn. White supremacist politicians regained control of state governments and, using everything except race as a formal criterion, passed laws that effectively deprived African Americans of the right to vote. By using the ruse that political parties were private entities, the Democratic Party managed to keep black voters from its primaries. The **white primary** was upheld by the Supreme Court until 1944, when the Court ruled it a violation of the Fifteenth Amendment.[3]

Another barrier to African American voting was the **grandfather clause,** which restricted voting to those who could prove that their ancestors had voted before 1867. **Poll taxes** required the payment of a fee to vote. Thus, poor African Americans—as well as poor whites—who could not afford to pay the tax were excluded from voting. Not until the Twenty-fourth Amendment to the Constitution was ratified in 1964 was the poll tax eliminated as a precondition to voting. **Literacy tests** were also used to deny the vote to African Americans. Such tests asked potential voters to read, recite, or interpret complicated texts, such as a section of the state constitution, to the satisfaction of local registrars—who were, of course, almost never satisfied with the responses of African Americans.

Extralegal Methods of Enforcing White Supremacy.

The second-class status of African Americans was also a matter of social custom, especially in the South. In their interactions with southern whites, African Americans were expected to observe an informal but detailed code of behavior that confirmed their inferiority. The code was backed up by the common practice of *lynching*—mob action to murder an accused individual, usually by hanging and sometimes accompanied by torture. Of course, lynching was illegal, but southern authorities rarely prosecuted these cases, and white juries would not convict.

separate-but-equal doctrine

The doctrine holding that separate-but-equal facilities do not violate the equal protection clause of the Fourteenth Amendment to the U.S. Constitution.

white primary

A state primary election that restricted voting to whites only. It was outlawed by the Supreme Court in 1944.

grandfather clause

A device used by southern states to disenfranchise African Americans. It restricted voting to those whose ancestors had voted before 1867.

poll tax

A special tax that had to be paid as a qualification for voting. In 1964, the Twenty-fourth Amendment to the Constitution outlawed the poll tax in national elections, and in 1966 the Supreme Court declared it unconstitutional in state elections as well.

literacy test

A test administered as a precondition for voting, often used to prevent African Americans from exercising their right to vote.

3. *Smith v. Allwright*, 321 U.S. 649 (1944).

Image 5–4 Sisters Linda and Terry Lynn Brown sit on a fence outside of their racially segregated elementary school in Topeka, Kansas, in 1953. At that time, the Supreme Court had yet to decide *Brown v. Board of Education*, the landmark civil rights case that banned segregation in public schools. *What were the immediate results of this decision?*

The End of the Separate-but-Equal Doctrine

As early as the 1930s, several court rulings began to chip away at the separate-but-equal doctrine. The United States Supreme Court did not explicitly overturn *Plessy v. Ferguson* until 1954, however, when it issued one of the most famous judicial decisions in U.S. history.

In 1951, Oliver Brown decided that his eight-year-old daughter, Linda Carol Brown, should not have to go to an all-nonwhite elementary school twenty-one blocks from her home, when there was a white school only seven blocks away. The National Association for the Advancement of Colored People (NAACP), formed in 1909, decided to support Oliver Brown.[4] The outcome would have a monumental impact on American society.

Brown v. Board of Education of Topeka.
The 1954 unanimous decision of the Supreme Court in *Brown v. Board of Education of Topeka*[5] established that the segregation of races in the public schools violates the equal protection clause of the Fourteenth Amendment. Chief Justice Earl Warren said that separation implied inferiority, whereas the majority opinion in *Plessy v. Ferguson* had said the opposite.

The following year, in *Brown v. Board of Education*[6] (sometimes called the second *Brown* decision), the Court declared that the lower courts needed to ensure that African Americans would be admitted to schools on a nondiscriminatory basis "with all deliberate speed."

Reactions to School Integration.
The white South did not let the Supreme Court ruling go unchallenged. Governor Orval Faubus of Arkansas used the state's National Guard to block the integration of Central High School in Little Rock in September 1957. Finally, President Dwight Eisenhower had to federalize the Arkansas National Guard and send in the Army's 101st Airborne Division to quell the violent resistance. Central High became integrated.

Universities in the South remained segregated. When James Meredith, an African American student, attempted to enroll at the University of Mississippi in 1962, violence flared there, as it had in Little Rock. The riot by whites was so intense that President John F. Kennedy was forced to send in 30,000 U.S. combat troops, a larger force than the one then stationed in Korea. Ultimately, peace was restored, and Meredith began attending classes.

De Jure and De Facto Segregation

The kind of segregation faced by Linda Carol Brown and James Meredith is called **de jure segregation,** because it is the result of discriminatory laws or government actions.

de jure segregation

Racial segregation that occurs because of laws or administrative decisions by public agencies.

4. *NAACP* is pronounced "N-double A-C-P."

5. 347 U.S. 483 (1954).

6. 349 U.S. 294 (1955).

(*De jure* is Latin for "by law.") A second kind of public school segregation was common in many northern communities—***de facto* segregation.** This term refers to segregation that is not due to an explicit law but results from other causes, such as residential patterns. Neighborhoods inhabited almost entirely by African Americans naturally led to *de facto* segregation of the public schools.

Discrimination was still involved. In many communities, landlords would only rent to African Americans in specific districts, and realtors would not allow them to view houses for sale outside of these zones. In other words, nongovernmental discrimination confined African Americans to all-black districts, which became known as *ghettos.*[7]

de facto segregation

Racial segregation that occurs because of past social and economic conditions and residential racial patterns.

civil disobedience

A nonviolent, public refusal to obey allegedly unjust laws.

The Civil Rights Movement

The *Brown* decisions applied only to public schools. Not much else in the structure of existing segregation was affected. In December 1955, an African American woman, Rosa Parks, boarded a public bus in Montgomery, Alabama. When the bus became crowded, Parks was asked to move to the rear of the bus, the "colored" section. She refused and was arrested. But that was not the end of the matter. For an entire year, African Americans boycotted the Montgomery bus system. The protest was headed by a twenty-seven-year-old Baptist minister, Dr. Martin Luther King, Jr. In 1956, a federal district court issued an injunction prohibiting the segregation of buses in Montgomery. The era of civil rights protests had begun.

King's Philosophy of Nonviolence. In the following year, 1957, King formed the Southern Christian Leadership Conference (SCLC). King advocated nonviolent **civil disobedience** as a means to achieve racial justice. The SCLC used tactics such as demonstrations and marches, as well as nonviolent, public disobedience of unjust laws. King's followers successfully used these methods to gain wider public acceptance of their cause.

Nonviolent Demonstrations. For the next decade, African Americans and sympathetic whites engaged in sit-ins, freedom rides, and freedom marches. In the beginning, such demonstrations were often met with violence, and the contrasting image of nonviolent African Americans and violent, hostile whites created strong public support for the civil rights movement. When African Americans in Greensboro, North Carolina, were refused service at a Woolworth's lunch counter, they organized a sit-in that was aided day after day by other African Americans and by sympathetic whites. Within six months of the first sit-in at the Greensboro Woolworth's, hundreds of lunch counters throughout the South were serving African Americans. The sit-in technique also was successfully used to integrate interstate buses and their

UniversalImagesGroup/Getty Images

Image 5–5 In 1955, Rosa Parks was arrested for refusing to give up her seat on a Montgomery, Alabama, bus and move to the colored section. *What happened after her arrest?*

7. *Ghetto* was originally the name of a district in Venice, Italy, in which Venetian Jews were required to live.

Image 5–6 Leaders of the March on Washington for Jobs and Freedom on August 28, 1963. The Reverend Dr. Martin Luther King, Jr., is front and center. The march provided the setting for King's "I Have a Dream" speech. *Why might many religious leaders have supported this movement?*

terminals, as well as railroads engaged in interstate transportation.

The March on Washington. In August 1963, African American leaders A. Philip Randolph and Bayard Rustin organized the massive March on Washington for Jobs and Freedom. Before nearly a quarter-million white and African American spectators and millions watching on television, Dr. Martin Luther King, Jr., told the world: "I have a dream that my four little children will one day live in a nation where they will not be judged by the color of their skin but by the content of their character."

Another Approach—Black Power. Not all African Americans agreed with King's philosophy of nonviolence. Black Muslims and other African American separatists advocated a more militant stance and argued that desegregation should not result in cultural assimilation. During the 1950s and 1960s, when King was spearheading nonviolent protests and demonstrations to achieve civil rights for African Americans, black power leaders such as Malcolm X insisted that African Americans should "fight back" instead of turning the other cheek. Indeed, some would argue that without the fear generated by black militants, a "moderate" such as King would not have garnered such widespread support from white America.

Modern Civil Rights Legislation

Attacks on demonstrators using police dogs, cattle prods, high-pressure water hoses, beatings, and bombings—plus the March on Washington—all led to an environment in which Congress felt compelled to act on behalf of African Americans. The second era of civil rights acts, sometimes referred to as the second Reconstruction period, was under way.

The Civil Rights Act of 1964. The Civil Rights Act of 1964, the most far-reaching bill on civil rights in modern times, banned discrimination on the basis of race, color, religion, gender, or national origin. The major provisions of the act were as follows:

- It outlawed arbitrary discrimination in voter registration.

- It barred discrimination in public accommodations, such as hotels and restaurants, which have operations that affect interstate commerce.

- It authorized the federal government to sue to desegregate public schools and facilities.

- It expanded the power of the Civil Rights Commission, which had been created in 1957, and extended its life.

- It provided for the withholding of federal funds from programs administered in a discriminatory manner.

- It established the right to equality of opportunity in employment.

Title VII of the Civil Rights Act of 1964 is the cornerstone of employment-discrimination law. It prohibits discrimination in employment based on race, color, religion, gender, or national origin. Under Title VII, executive orders were issued that banned employment discrimination by firms that received any federal funding. The 1964 Civil Rights Act created the Equal Employment Opportunity Commission (EEOC) to administer Title VII. It was not until 1972, however, that Congress gave the EEOC the right to sue employers, unions, and employment agencies. Litigation then became an important agency activity.

The Voting Rights Act of 1965. As late as 1960, only 29 percent of African Americans of voting age were registered in the southern states, in stark contrast to 61 percent of whites. The Voting Rights Act of 1965 addressed this issue. The act had two major provisions. The first outlawed discriminatory voter-registration tests. The second authorized federal registration of voters and federally administered voting procedures in any political subdivision or state that discriminated electorally against a particular group. The act also provided that certain political subdivisions could not change their voting procedures and election laws without federal approval—a provision greatly weakened by the Supreme Court in 2013.

The act targeted counties, mostly in the South, in which fewer than 50 percent of the eligible population were registered to vote. Federal voter registrars were sent to those areas to register African Americans who had been kept from voting by local registrars. Within one week after the act was passed, forty-five federal examiners were sent to the South. A massive voter-registration drive covered the country.

Urban Riots. Even as the civil rights movement was experiencing its greatest victories, a series of riots swept through African American inner-city neighborhoods. The riots were primarily civil insurrections, although these disorders were accompanied by large-scale looting of stores. Inhabitants of the affected neighborhoods attributed the riots to racial discrimination. The riots dissipated much of the goodwill toward the civil rights movement that had been built up earlier in the decade among northern whites. Together with widespread student demonstrations against the Vietnam War (1965–1975), the riots pushed many Americans toward conservatism.

The Civil Rights Act of 1968 and Other Housing Reform Legislation. Martin Luther King, Jr., was assassinated on April 4, 1968. Despite King's message of peace, his death was followed by the most widespread rioting to date. Nine days after King's death, President Lyndon Johnson signed the Civil Rights Act of 1968, which banned discrimination in most housing and provided penalties for those attempting to interfere with individual civil rights (giving protection to civil rights workers, among others). Subsequent legislation added enforcement provisions to the federal government's rules against discriminatory mortgage-lending practices.

Consequences of Civil Rights Legislation

As a result of the Voting Rights Act of 1965 and its amendments, and the large-scale voter-registration drives in the South, the number of African Americans registered to vote climbed dramatically. By 1980, 56 percent of African Americans of voting age in the South were registered. In recent national elections, turnout by African American voters has come very close to the white turnout. In 2008, with an African American on the presidential ballot, African American turnout exceeded that of whites for the first time in history.[8]

Political Participation by African Americans. Today, there are more than ten thousand African American elected officials in the United States. The movement of African American citizens into high elected office has been sure, if exceedingly slow. Notably, recent polling data show that most Americans do not consider race a significant factor

---

8. One widely reported study claimed that African American turnout did not quite match that of whites, but this conclusion was based on an overestimate of the number of African Americans eligible to vote.

Image 5–7 A police officer confronts a demonstrator who tried to chain the doors to Chicago police headquarters during a protest over the death of seventeen-year-old Laquan McDonald. An officer who shot McDonald sixteen times was charged with murder more than one year after the incident. *Why are police officers rarely convicted in such cases?*

in choosing a president. In 1958, when a Gallup poll first asked whether respondents would be willing to vote for an African American as president, only 38 percent of the public said yes. By 2008, this number had reached 94 percent.

This high figure may have been attained, at least in part, because of the emergence of African Americans of presidential caliber. Of course, Barack Obama, first elected president in 2008 on the Democratic ticket, is African American. Republican African American presidential candidates have earned support in recent primary election seasons. These include businessman Herman Cain, who ran in the 2011–2012 cycle, and neurosurgeon Ben Carson, a candidate in 2016. Neither secured the Republican nomination.

Differing Perspectives. Even today, however, race consciousness continues to divide African Americans and white Americans. Whether we are talking about media stereotyping, racial profiling, or academic achievement, the black experience is different from the white one. As a result, African Americans often view the nation and many specific issues differently than their white counterparts do. In survey after survey, when blacks are asked whether they have achieved racial equality, few believe that they have. In contrast, whites are much more likely than blacks to believe that racial equality has been achieved.

One of the most troubling contrasts between the races is their differing experiences with the criminal justice system. African Americans, especially men, are far more likely to be arrested and imprisoned than whites. It is true that African Americans, young men especially, are disproportionately likely to be involved in violent crime. But they are also far more likely than whites to be arrested and convicted even when they do *not* commit a particular offense more often than whites. About the same number of blacks and whites admit to using illegal drugs. Yet African Americans are three times more likely than whites to be arrested on drug charges, and they are far more likely to wind up in prison. Black youth in some urban neighborhoods report that they are stopped by police—for no particular reason—as often as once a month. We take a further look at black–police relations in this chapter's *Which Side Are You On?* feature.

One proposed way of addressing police conduct is to equip police officers with video cameras, so that supervisors and the general public can see exactly what happened in disputed interactions. In fact, many departments have recently installed such cameras in police cars. Some have even distributed small cameras that officers carry on their persons. It remains to be seen whether such programs are helpful.

Civil Rights and the Courts

Learning Outcome **2:**

Define the different levels of scrutiny used by the Supreme Court in civil rights cases, and describe recent rulings on affirmative action.

The Fourteenth Amendment to the U.S. Constitution, adopted in 1869 following the Civil War, is the main constitutional basis for civil rights legislation and court decisions. In Chapter 4, we discussed the due process clause of the Fourteenth Amendment:

Which side are you on?

Do Police Use Excessive Force against African Americans?

In recent years, police behavior toward minority group members—in particular, black men—has become a major political issue. Unarmed black men have died as a result of interactions with police officers in Baltimore, Chicago, Cleveland, and many other places. A loose alliance of activists opposed to the alleged excessive use of force has grown up under the label "Black Lives Matter." Are the activists responding to a real problem—or is the excessive use of force by police largely a myth?

Police Behavior Is Almost Always Appropriate

The first point when considering law enforcement behavior is that the United States is a relatively violent country. Americans have a constitutional right to bear arms for personal protection, and millions do just that. U.S. police know there is a good chance that anyone they stop or arrest may have a firearm—and may be prepared to use it. That is a problem that police in Europe or Japan simply don't face.

Supporters of the police contend that they use appropriate force given what they are up against. The greater use of force against African Americans simply reflects their disproportionate participation in violent crime. Such participation may be caused by the disastrous conditions in which so many young black men grow up, but that does not change participants' culpability. African Americans commit murder at almost eight times the rate of other races.

In the *National Review*, David French states that the numbers back up the police. We only have data from a limited number of departments, but in 2015 police on those forces fatally shot 965 individuals. Of these, 564 were armed with a gun and 289 had another weapon. Only 90 were unarmed. In 75 percent of the shootings, the "police were under attack or defending someone who was." Rogue officers exist, but for the most part the police are just doing their jobs.

Too Many Officers Are Quick on the Trigger

Writing in *Current Affairs*, Nathan Robinson finds French's statistical reasoning ludicrous. In effect, French argues that we have no problem if police shootings are justified, say, 96 percent of the time. But if the other 4 percent were murder, the fact that 96 percent "were *not murder* wouldn't make the slightest bit of difference." True, African Americans are disproportionately involved in violent crime. But black teens are over twenty times more likely to be killed by police than are white teens. It is not acceptable to kill black people simply because they may have committed a crime. Also, possession of a weapon is not in itself a crime. The Second Amendment applies to all citizens, regardless of race.

Further, police killings are only the tip of the iceberg. Three out of five black people report that they personally have been mistreated by police. This often takes place during *investigatory stops*—stops made without evidence of a crime. African Americans refer to these stops as the "crime of driving while black." Whites almost never experience these stops. According to Robinson, those who condemn Black Lives Matter seem to believe that "African Americans are delusional about their own first-person memories." Police personnel are rarely prosecuted and almost never convicted for excessive use of force. We need to change this system.

For Critical Analysis

▷ If police behavior is sometimes abusive, how would that affect the willingness of African Americans to come forward with information about crimes they have witnessed?

No State shall . . . *deprive any person of life, liberty, or property, without due process of law. . . .*

This language mirrors that of the Fifth Amendment, which binds the federal government:

No person shall . . . *be deprived of life, liberty, or property, without due process of law. . . .*

The due process clause was crucial to extending the civil liberties contained in the Bill of Rights to cover the actions of the individual states. The courts have made use of this clause

strict scrutiny

A judicial standard for assessing the constitutionality of a law or government action when the law or action threatens to interfere with a fundamental right or potentially discriminates against members of a suspect classification.

suspect classification

A classification, such as race, religion, or national origin, that triggers strict scrutiny by the courts when a law or government action potentially discriminates against members of the class.

intermediate, or exacting, scrutiny

The standard used by the courts to determine whether a law or government action improperly discriminates against women.

in civil rights cases as well. As a guarantee of civil rights, however, the next clause in the Fourteenth Amendment is at least as important:

> *. . . nor deny to any person within its jurisdiction the equal protection of the laws.*

The principal effect of *Plessy v. Ferguson,* described earlier, was to make the equal protection clause almost a dead letter in cases involving discrimination against individuals. Today, in contrast, the equal protection clause serves as the foundation of a sizable body of law.

Standards for Judicial Review

Federal courts use three standards when engaging in judicial review of laws or executive actions. The most exacting of these, **strict scrutiny,** is employed when fundamental rights are at stake, such as those guaranteed by the Bill of Rights. Strict scrutiny also comes into play when laws are based on a **suspect classification.** The original suspect class was race. As these terms suggest, the courts are suspicious of, and will strictly scrutinize, any attempt by a government body to treat persons of different races in different ways. A recent study suggested that 70 percent of all legal challenges based on strict scrutiny have succeeded in striking down the law or action in question. Religion and national origin are also suspect classifications. To be acceptable under the strict scrutiny standard, a law must pass three tests:

- It must be justified by a *compelling government interest.* National security is an example of such an interest.

- It must be *narrowly tailored* to meet that interest.

- It must be the *least restrictive means* of accomplishing the goal in question. In other words, restrictions on rights such as freedom of speech must not exceed what is absolutely necessary.

The Supreme Court introduced the standard of strict scrutiny in 1944 in *Korematsu v. United States.* This was the case in which the Court ruled that the federal government had the right to force West Coast Japanese Americans into detention camps purely on the basis of race. National security was cited as the compelling government interest.[9] The irony could hardly be greater—the Court established the standard of strict scrutiny in the course of approving one of the greatest acts of racial discrimination in American history. In later years, however, the Court would use the standard as a major tool in outlawing racial discrimination. *Brown v. Board of Education* was only one of many rulings that employed strict scrutiny on behalf of civil rights.

Why should you care about **CIVIL RIGHTS?**

Why should you, as an individual, care about civil rights? Some people may think that discrimination is a problem only for members of racial or ethnic minorities. Actually, almost everyone can be affected. Consider that in some instances, white men have actually experienced "reverse discrimination"—and have obtained redress for it. Also, discrimination against women is common, and women constitute half the population. Even if you are male, you probably have female friends or relatives whose well-being is of interest to you.

Intermediate, or Exacting, Scrutiny. As you will learn in a subsequent section, the women's movement that arose in the 1960s led to a large number of suits claiming that various laws, policies, and government actions improperly discriminated against women. The courts were often sympathetic to such arguments. Still, the Supreme Court was reluctant to define sex or gender as a suspect classification equivalent to race. The Court therefore established a new standard—**intermediate, or exacting, scrutiny**—in a 1976 ruling. In that case, the Court ruled that Oklahoma could not ban men from drinking

---

9. 323 U.S. 214 (1944). Fred Korematsu's conviction was overturned in 1983. In 1988, the U.S. Congress apologized for the internments and granted $20,000 in compensation to each surviving prisoner.

127
Chapter 5 | *Civil Rights*

low-alcohol beer until they turned twenty-one, while women were allowed to drink this type of beer at the age of nineteen.[10]

To pass the intermediate scrutiny test, a law or government action "must further an important government interest by means that are substantially related to that interest." This standard is easier to meet than the standard established for strict scrutiny. In later years, the Court tightened the test by requiring an "exceedingly persuasive justification" for gender-based discrimination.[11]

Rational Basis Review.

In cases where neither strict scrutiny nor intermediate scrutiny are appropriate, the courts use **rational basis review** as a standard. This test requires that an action or law be "rationally related" to a "legitimate government interest." The legitimate interest does not have to be an interest cited by the government. If the courts can imagine a possible legitimate interest, the law stands. Rational basis review does not involve assessing the usefulness of laws. As Justice Thurgood Marshall observed, "The Constitution does not prohibit legislatures from enacting stupid laws."[12]

If a court can find no legitimate interest at all, however, a law or action can fail even this test. For example, courts have found that certain laws penalizing gay men and lesbians fail the rational basis test. Rational basis review was introduced in a 1938 decision in which the Court affirmed the right of the federal government to ban a dairy product known as *filled milk* from interstate commerce.[13]

The Courts Address Affirmative Action

As noted earlier in this chapter, the Civil Rights Act of 1964 prohibited discrimination against any person on the basis of race, color, national origin, religion, or gender. The act also established the right to equal opportunity in employment. A basic problem remained, however: minority groups and women, because of past discrimination, often lacked the education and skills to compete effectively in the marketplace. In 1965, the federal government attempted to remedy this problem by implementing the concept of affirmative action. **Affirmative action** policies attempt to "level the playing field" by giving special preferences in educational admissions and employment decisions to groups that have been discriminated against in the past.

Implementing Affirmative Action.

In 1965, President Lyndon Johnson issued an executive order that mandated affirmative action policies to remedy the effects of past discrimination. All government agencies, including those of state and local governments, were required to implement such policies. Additionally, affirmative action requirements were imposed on companies that sell goods or services to the federal government and on institutions that receive federal funds, such as universities. Affirmative action policies were also required whenever an employer had been ordered to develop such a plan by a court or by the Equal Employment

Image 5–8 Affirmative action supporters in front of the Supreme Court building during arguments on *Fisher v. University of Texas*. In June 2016, the Court ruled that the university's limited affirmative action program was constitutional. *What considerations must the Court take into account when deciding such cases?*

rational basis review
The standard used by the courts to determine the constitutionality of a law or government action if neither strict scrutiny nor intermediate scrutiny applies.

affirmative action
A policy in educational admissions and job hiring that gives special attention or compensatory treatment to traditionally disadvantaged groups in an effort to overcome present effects of past discrimination.

10. *Craig v. Boren*, 429 U.S. 190 (1976).

11. *Mississippi University for Women v. Hogan*, 458 U.S. 718 (1982).

12. As quoted in Justice Stevens's concurrence to *New York State Board of Elections v. Lopez Torres*, 552 U.S. 196 (2008).

13. *United States v. Carolene Products Company*, 304 U.S. 144 (1938). *Filled milk* is milk in which the dairy fat has been replaced by other fats, typically vegetable oils. This product was frequently banned in the 1920s and 1930s. It is legal today, however, and it is widely used in ice cream and baked goods.

Opportunity Commission because of evidence of past discrimination. Finally, labor unions that had been found to discriminate against women or minorities in the past were required to establish and follow affirmative action plans.

Affirmative action programs have been controversial because they allegedly result in discrimination against "majority" groups, such as white males (or discrimination against other minority groups that may not be given preferential treatment under a particular affirmative action program). At issue in the current debate over affirmative action programs is whether such programs, because of their discriminatory nature, violate the equal protection clause of the Fourteenth Amendment to the Constitution.

The *Bakke* Case.

The first Supreme Court case addressing the constitutionality of affirmative action examined a program at the University of California at Davis. Allan Bakke, a white student who had been turned down for medical school at the Davis campus, discovered that his academic record was better than those of some of the minority applicants who had been admitted to the program. He sued the University of California regents, alleging **reverse discrimination.** The UC Davis School of Medicine had held sixteen places out of one hundred for educationally "disadvantaged students" each year, and the administrators at that campus admitted to using race as a criterion for admission for those particular slots.

In 1978, the Supreme Court handed down its decision in *Regents of the University of California v. Bakke.*[14] The Court did not rule against affirmative action programs. Rather, it held that Bakke must be admitted to the medical school because its admissions policy had used race as the sole criterion for the sixteen "minority" positions. Justice Lewis Powell, speaking for the Court, indicated that while race can be considered "as a factor" among others in admissions (and presumably hiring) decisions, race cannot be the sole factor. So affirmative action programs, but not quota systems, were upheld as constitutional.

Additional Limits on Affirmative Action.

A number of cases decided during the 1980s and 1990s placed further limits on affirmative action programs. In a landmark decision in 1995, *Adarand Constructors, Inc. v. Peña,*[15] the Supreme Court held that any federal, state, or local affirmative action program that uses racial or ethnic classifications as the basis for making decisions is subject to the strict scrutiny standard. The Court's opinion in the *Adarand* case means that an affirmative action program cannot make use of quotas or preferences for unqualified persons. In addition, once the program has succeeded in achieving the purpose it was tailored to meet, the program must be changed or dropped.

In 2003, in two cases involving the University of Michigan, the Supreme Court indicated that limited affirmative action programs continued to be acceptable and that diversity was a legitimate goal. The Court struck down the affirmative action plan used for undergraduate admissions at the university, which automatically awarded a substantial number of points to applicants based on minority status.[16] At the same time, it approved the admissions plan used by the law school, which took race into consideration as part of a complete examination of each applicant's background.[17]

The End of Affirmative Action?

Despite the position taken by the Supreme Court in the University of Michigan Law School case, affirmative action is subject to serious threats. In 2007, the Supreme Court tightened the guidelines for permissible affirmative action programs. In rejecting school integration plans in Seattle, Washington, and

reverse discrimination

The situation in which an affirmative action program discriminates against those who do not have minority status.

14. 438 U.S. 265 (1978).
15. 515 U.S. 200 (1995).
16. *Gratz v. Bollinger,* 539 U.S. 244 (2003).
17. *Grutter v. Bollinger,* 539 U.S. 306 (2003).

Louisville, Kentucky, the Court found that race could not be used as a "tiebreaker" when granting admission to a school.[18] Many observers thought that the Supreme Court might end affirmative action programs altogether in *Fisher v. University of Texas,* a 2013 case. In deciding *Fisher,* the Court made no significant alterations to the law and handed the case back to the lower courts. In 2016, however, *Fisher* was back before the Court. In June of that year, the Court ruled in favor of the university. It found that the goal of diversity was legitimate, and that the university's admissions policies were (as the law requires) "narrowly tailored" to meet that goal.[19]

Affirmative action may face a greater danger from the states. Seven states have now banned state-level affirmative action programs, though voters in Colorado rejected such a measure in 2008. In 2014, the Supreme Court ruled in favor of Michigan's affirmative action ban, effectively upholding the law in six other states.[20]

Experiences of Other Minority Groups

In a single chapter, it is not possible to describe the experiences of all groups of Americans who have had to struggle for civil rights. Still, three of the largest groups deserve mention: Hispanic Americans, or Latinos, are now the nation's largest minority group by population. Asian Americans are the third largest group, after African Americans. American Indians are notable for their unusual and troubled history, and of course because they were here first.

Latinos and the Immigration Issue

The most striking characteristic of Latinos is that many of them are relatively recent immigrants. A century ago, most immigrants to the United States came from Europe. Today, most come from Latin America and Asia. In the last five years, immigrants from Asian nations have begun to outnumber Hispanic immigrants. This change is largely due to a drop in the number of Hispanics rather than an increase in the number of Asians. Still, immigrants from Spanish-speaking countries have significantly increased the Hispanic proportion of the U.S. population. Table 5–1 shows the leading countries of origin for the foreign-born population in the United States.

The law recognizes that Latinos have been subjected to many of the same forms of ill treatment as African Americans. Therefore, Latinos are usually grouped with African Americans and American Indians in laws and programs that seek to protect minorities from discrimination or to address the results of past discrimination.

Political Participation by Hispanics. The civil rights movement focused primarily on the rights of African Americans, but the legislation resulting from the movement ultimately benefited nearly all minority groups. The Civil Rights Act of 1964, for example, prohibits discrimination against any person because of race, color, or national origin. Subsequent amendments to the Voting Rights Act of 1965 extended its protections to Latino Americans, Asian Americans, Native Americans, and Native Alaskans. Latino political participation has increased in recent years, and they have gained political power in several states. Latinos do not vote at the same rate as African Americans, in large part because many Hispanics are immigrants who are not yet citizens. Still, there are now about five thousand Latino elected officials in the United States.

Learning Outcome **3:**

Discuss the history and current status of Latinos, American Indians, and Asian Americans.

Table 5–1 Top Ten Countries of Origin for the Foreign-Born Population

Hispanic countries are shown in red.
Why are there no European countries on this list?

Mexico	11,585,000
China	2,384,000
India	2,035,000
Philippines	1,844,000
Vietnam	1,281,000
El Salvador	1,252,000
Cuba	1,144,000
Korea	1,070,000
Dominican Republic	991,000
Guatemala	902,000
ALL COUNTRIES	41,348,000

Source: U.S. Bureau of the Census. Figures are for 2013.

18. *Parents Involved in Community Schools v. Seattle School District No. 1,* 551 U.S. 701 (2007).
19. 133 S.Ct. 2411 (2013) and *Fisher v. U. Texas,* 579 U.S. ____ (2016).
20. *Schuette v. Coalition to Defend Affirmative Action,* 572 U.S. ____ (2014).

Unauthorized Immigration. Illegal immigration—or unauthorized immigration, to use the language of the Department of Homeland Security—has been a major national issue for many years. Latinos, especially those migrating from Mexico, constitute the majority of individuals entering the United States without permission. In addition, many unauthorized immigrants enter the country legally, as tourists or students, and then fail to return home when their visas expire.

Naturally, the unauthorized population is hard to count. The Pew Research Hispanic Trends Project believes that the population has stabilized at about 11 million in recent years. Unauthorized immigrants typically come to the United States to work, and until the economic crisis of 2008 their labor was in high demand. Before the Immigration Reform and Control Act of 1986, there was no law against hiring foreign citizens who lacked proper papers. We list the top ten countries of birth for unauthorized immigrants to the United States in Table 5–2, and the top ten countries for legal immigrants in Table 5–3.

Characteristics of the Undocumented Population. Studies of unauthorized immigrants have revealed that a large share of them eventually return to their home countries, where they frequently set up small businesses or retire. Many send remittances back to relatives in their homeland. In 2015, Mexico received about $25 billion in such remittances. In these ways, unauthorized immigrants are acting as immigrants to the United States always have. Throughout American history, immigrants frequently returned home or sent funds to relatives in the "old country."

Table 5–2 Top Ten Countries of Birth for Unauthorized Immigrants

Of necessity, these figures are rough estimates. Hispanic countries are shown in red. *Given high rates of poverty in Africa, why don't more Africans come to America?*

Mexico	6,194,000
Guatemala	704,000
El Salvador	436,000
Honduras	317,000
China	285,000
India	284,000
Philippines	197,000
Korea	192,000
Ecuador	196,000
Colombia	137,000
ALL COUNTRIES	11,022,000

Source: Migration Policy Institute. Figures are for 2013.

Table 5–3 Top Ten Countries of Origin for Legal Immigrants

The following figures are for a single year only. Legal immigrants are persons obtaining official permanent resident status in that year. Hispanic countries are shown in red. Immigrants from Asia each year now outnumber Latinos. *Why might that be so?*

Mexico	134,052
India	77,908
China	76,089
Philippines	49,996
Cuba	46,679
Dominican Republic	44,577
Vietnam	30,283
South Korea	20,423
El Salvador	19,273
Iraq	19,153
ALL COUNTRIES	1,016,518

Source: U.S. Department of Homeland Security. Figures are for 2014.

Unauthorized immigrants often live in mixed households, in which one or more members of a family have lawful resident status, but others do not. A woman from Guatemala with permanent resident status, for example, might be married to a Guatemalan man who is in the country illegally. Often, the parents in a family are unauthorized, while the children, who were born in the United States, possess American citizenship. Mixed families mean that deporting the illegal immigrant will either break up a family or force one or more American citizens into exile.

In some circumstances, though, immigrants actually choose to separate their families. In 2014 and 2015, large numbers of unaccompanied children from violence-torn Central American countries turned themselves in to U.S. authorities at the Mexican border. Because these children claimed the internationally recognized right of asylum, they could not be immediately deported.

Exemptions from Deportation. In recent years, the debate over whether unauthorized immigrants should be allowed to normalize their status has been intense. Normalization would provide legal residency, if not citizenship. Immigration reform was blocked in Congress, however. During President Obama's first term, his administration actually increased the enforcement of immigration laws. In June 2012, with the November elections approaching, Obama issued an executive order providing relief to many young immigrants. Most unauthorized immigrants who came to the United States under the age of sixteen could apply for an indefinite deportation deferral and obtain work permits.

In November 2014, Obama issued another executive order extending protection to the parents of children who were citizens or legal residents. This second order was challenged in court. Opponents argued that the order would subvert the separation of powers by creating a new program without Congressional approval. Supporters pointed out that the government does not currently have the resources to deport millions of people. Therefore, Obama should be able to decide who is subject to deportation, and who is allowed to stay.

The Fifth Circuit Court ruled against the administration, and the Supreme Court then took up the case. The Court's decision came in June 2016, after the death of Justice Antonin Scalia left the Court with only eight members. In this case, the Court split four to four. The result upheld the circuit court's decision, but without establishing a precedent.[21]

The Agony of the American Indian

Whether living on rural reservations or in urban neighborhoods, American Indians have long experienced high rates of poverty. There is much history behind this problem. (In recent years, a majority of American Indians have come to prefer the term *American Indian*—or even, simply, *Indian*—to *Native American*. Still, both terms are in use.)

The Demographic Collapse. During the years after Columbus arrived in America, native population numbers—both in the future United States and in the Americas generally—experienced one of the most catastrophic collapses in human history. The Europeans brought with them Old World diseases to which Native Americans had no immunity. A person who was able to resist one disease might die from another. By one estimate, 90 percent of the inhabitants of the New World died. For their part, the Europeans had no idea what caused diseases and did not understand what was happening. When the Pilgrims landed at Plymouth in 1620, the coast of New England was lined with empty Indian village sites. The villages had been abandoned because of an epidemic touched off by shipwrecked French sailors in 1616.

Image 5–9 This member of the Ute tribe attends a ceremony for Ute and Comanche leaders. *About how many Native Americans are there today?*

---

21. *United States v. Texas*, 579 U.S. ____ (2016).

American Indians in the Nineteenth and Twentieth Centuries. In the United States, the American Indian population continued to decrease through the nineteenth century—a time when the European American and African American populations were experiencing explosive growth. The decrease was largely due to the concentration of Native Americans into ever-smaller territories. The U.S. Indian population bottomed out at 250,000 at the end of the nineteenth century. Since that time, however, it has recovered substantially. The figure is about 3.2 million today, possibly close to the number living here before Columbus.

American Indians faced additional challenges. A federal policy of "assimilation" adopted in the late 1880s resulted in further loss of territory and the suppression of traditional cultures. Indians did not become U.S. citizens until 1924.

In the late twentieth century, some native tribes hit upon a new strategy for economic development—gambling casinos on reservation lands. This strategy was possible because the U.S. Constitution grants the responsibility for Indian relations to the national government. As a result, reservations are not subject to the full authority of the states in which they are located.

Asian Americans

Asian Americans are probably better integrated into the broader society than any other racial minority. Collectively, Americans with ancestors from China, India, Japan, Korea, the Philippines, and Vietnam have above-average incomes. (Some smaller national groups, however, continue to struggle economically.)

As a result of these successes, it may be hard for today's students to realize just how powerful anti-Asian prejudice was a century ago. For example, Justice John Marshall Harlan, in his dissent to *Plessy v. Ferguson,* stated just a few paragraphs after his famous words that our Constitution is "color-blind" that Chinese people are members of "a race so different from our own" that it is permissible to deny them citizenship. In fact, Chinese American immigrants and their children were denied citizenship throughout the nineteenth century. Only in 1898 did the Supreme Court rule that Chinese Americans born in the United States must be recognized as citizens, in accordance with the Fourteenth Amendment.[22]

The Chinese Exclusion Act. Immigrants from China began arriving in California at the time of the 1849 Gold Rush. Almost all were young men who worked in mines and in railroad construction. The absence of women meant that the Chinese American population grew very slowly. Hostility among white Californians was severe, and anti-Chinese riots were common. In time, Chinese Americans became confined largely to urban Chinatowns and to menial labor. In 1882, the Chinese Exclusion Act banned all further immigration from China. The act was not repealed until 1943.

The Japanese in America. Immigration from Japan was banned in 1924. By that time, Japanese Americans had become a major ethnic group in Hawaii. In California, some Japanese Americans were able to advance economically by setting up businesses or becoming truck farmers. Almost all of these businesses were lost after 1942, however, when West Coast Japanese were forced into internment camps. Of those interned, 62 percent were U.S. citizens. Japanese Americans were not allowed to leave until 1945, near the end of World War II. The Supreme Court justified the internment in *Korematsu v. United States*, described earlier.

Asian Americans and College Admissions. A current issue faced by Asian Americans is the question of admissions to highly selective colleges and universities. Princeton sociologist Thomas Espenshade has calculated that for Asian Americans to obtain equal consideration at elite colleges, they must outperform whites on SAT tests by 140

---

22. *United States v. Wong Kim Ark,* 169 U.S. 649 (1898).

points (out of 1600). Top schools deny that they employ quotas. Still, in one way or another, these schools appear to be limiting the number of Asian Americans in their student bodies.

Lingering Social and Economic Disparities

According to census data, social and economic disparities between U.S. racial and ethnic groups persist. Mean incomes in black households are only 59 percent of the incomes in non-Hispanic white households, and incomes of Hispanic households are just 69 percent of those of non-Hispanic whites. White adults were also more likely than black and Hispanic adults to have college degrees and to own their own homes. We examine some of these disparities in this chapter's *Consider the Source* feature.

Consider the source

Measuring Poverty and Wealth by Race and Ethnicity

As you can see in Figure 5–1, blacks, Hispanics, and American Indians are more likely than whites or Asians to have incomes below the poverty line. Children are substantially more likely than adults to live in low-income families.

Figure 5–2 shows median household wealth for Hispanics and for non-Hispanic whites, blacks, and Asians. (We do not have good data on American Indian wealth.)

Differences in wealth are much greater than differences in income. Note also that while Asian Americans have a median household income greater than that of whites—$66,000 versus $54,000—they have less wealth. It takes years for income to translate into wealth, and on average Asian Americans haven't been saving and investing for nearly as many years as their white neighbors.

The Source: The Census

The Constitution requires a census every ten years, which is conducted by the Bureau of the Census. The Bureau also conducts regular studies of communities, governments, businesses, and much else. The decennial census, however, is by far the most complete of these studies, and it yields a vast collection of data. As a result, for many questions we have better information for 2010 than for any year since. The data will not be refreshed until 2020.

For Critical Analysis

▶ **Why has it been so hard for African Americans and Hispanics to accumulate wealth?**

Figure 5–1 Persons in Poverty in the United States by Race and Hispanic Origin

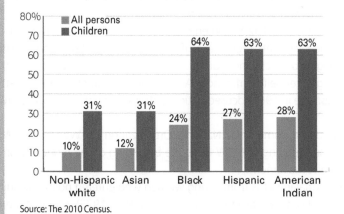

Source: The 2010 Census.

Figure 5–2 Median Household Wealth in the United States by Race and Hispanic Origin

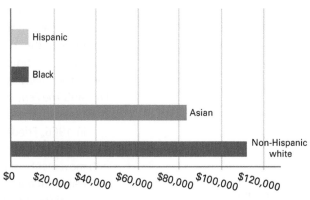

Source: The 2010 Census.

Learning Outcome **4:**

Women's Struggle for Equal Rights

Contrast the goals of the women's suffrage movement with the goals of modern feminism.

Like African Americans and other minorities, women have had to struggle for equality. During the first phase of this struggle, the primary goal of women was to obtain the right to vote.

Early Women's Political Movements

In 1848, Lucretia Mott and Elizabeth Cady Stanton organized the first women's rights convention in Seneca Falls, New York. The three hundred people who attended approved a Declaration of Sentiments: "We hold these truths to be self-evident: that all men and women are created equal."

Women's Suffrage Associations. In 1869, after the Civil War, Susan B. Anthony and Stanton formed the National Woman Suffrage Association. In their view, women's *suffrage*—the right to vote—was a means to achieve major improvements in the economic and social situation of women in the United States. In other words, the vote was to be used to seek broader goals.

Lucy Stone, however, a key founder of the rival American Woman Suffrage Association, believed that the vote was the only major issue. In 1880, the two organizations joined forces. The resulting National American Woman Suffrage Association had only one goal—the enfranchisement of women—but it made little progress.

Image 5–10 Women did not get the right to vote throughout the United States until 1920. Before that, though, there was a strong women's suffrage movement. This cardboard poster is asking voters to support candidates who favor women's right to vote.

The Nineteenth Amendment. The Congressional Union, founded in the early 1900s by Alice Paul, adopted a national strategy of obtaining an amendment to the U.S. Constitution. The Union employed militant tactics. It sponsored large-scale marches and civil disobedience—which resulted in hunger strikes, arrests, and jailings. Finally, in 1920, the Nineteenth Amendment was passed: "The right of citizens of the United States to vote shall not be denied or abridged by the United States or by any State on account of sex." (Today, the word *gender* is typically used instead of *sex.*)

The Modern Women's Movement

Historian Nancy Cott contends that the word *feminism* first began to be used around 1910. At that time, **feminism** meant, as it does today, political, social, and economic equality for women—a radical notion that gained little support then.

After gaining the right to vote in 1920, women engaged in little independent political activity until the 1960s. The civil rights movement of that decade resulted in a growing awareness of rights for all groups, including women. Increased participation in the workforce gave many women greater self-confidence. Additionally, the publication of Betty Friedan's *The Feminine Mystique* in 1963 focused national attention on the unequal status of women in American life.

In 1966, Friedan and others formed the National Organization for Women (NOW). Many observers consider the founding of NOW to be the beginning of the modern women's movement—the feminist movement.

Feminism gained additional impetus from young women who entered politics to support the civil rights movement or to oppose the Vietnam War (1965–1975). Many of them found that despite the egalitarian principles of these movements, women remained in

feminism
The movement that supports political, economic, and social equality for women.

David Frent/Getty Images

second-class positions. These young women sought their own movement. In the late 1960s, "women's liberation" organizations began to spring up on college campuses. Women also began organizing independent "consciousness-raising groups" in which they discussed how gender issues affected their lives. The new women's movement experienced explosive growth, and by 1970 it had emerged as a major social force.

The Equal Rights Amendment. The initial focus of the modern women's movement was to eradicate gender inequality through a constitutional amendment. The proposed Equal Rights Amendment (ERA), which was first introduced in Congress in 1923 by leaders of the National Women's Party (a successor to the Congressional Union), states as follows: "Equality of rights under the law shall not be denied or abridged by the United States or by any state on account of sex." For years, the amendment was not even given a hearing in Congress, but finally it was approved by both chambers and sent to the state leg-

Image 5–11 Long-time feminist leader Gloria Steinem receives the Presidential Medal of Freedom from President Obama at the White House. *What successes has the feminist movement enjoyed?*

islatures for ratification in 1972. The necessary thirty-eight states failed to ratify the ERA within the time specified by Congress, however. To date, efforts to reintroduce the amendment have not succeeded.

During the national debate over the ratification of the ERA, a women's countermovement emerged. Some women perceived the goals pursued by NOW and other liberal women's organizations as a threat to their way of life. The "Stop ERA" campaign found significant support among fundamentalist religious groups and other conservative organizations.

Additional Women's Issues. While NOW concentrated on the ERA, other women's groups, many of them entirely local, addressed a spectrum of added issues. One of these was *domestic violence*—that is, assaults within the family. Typically, this meant husbands or boyfriends assaulting their wives or girlfriends. During the 1970s, feminists across the country began opening *battered women's shelters* to house victims of abuse.

Abortion soon emerged as a key concern. Almost the entire organized women's movement united behind the "freedom-of-choice" position, at the cost of alienating potential women's rights supporters who favored the "right-to-life" position instead. Because abortion was a national issue, the campaign was led by national organizations such as NARAL Pro-Choice America, formerly the National Abortion and Reproductive Rights Action League.

Another issue—pornography—tended to divide the women's movement rather than unite it. While a majority of feminists found pornography demeaning to women, many were also strong supporters of free speech. Others believed that pornography was so central to the subjugation of women that First Amendment protections should not apply.

Challenging Gender Discrimination in the Courts. When ratification of the ERA failed, women's rights organizations began a campaign to establish national and state laws that would guarantee the equality of women. This more limited campaign met with much success. Women's rights organizations also challenged discriminatory statutes and policies in the federal courts, contending that **gender discrimination** violated the Fourteenth Amendment's equal protection clause. Employing the intermediate scrutiny

gender discrimination

Any practice, policy, or procedure that denies equality of treatment to an individual or to a group because of gender.

Image 5–12 This woman, a senior airman in the U.S. Air Force, is stationed at Manas Air Base in the nation of Kyrgyzstan, central Asia. Through 2014, Kyrgyzstan allowed the United States to use this base to resupply its forces in Afghanistan. Since 2013, women have been able to serve in combat units. *Is this a positive development?*

standard, the United States Supreme Court has invalidated many such statutes and policies. For example, in 1977 the Court held that police and firefighting units cannot establish arbitrary rules, such as height and weight requirements, that tend to keep women from participating in those occupations.[23] In 1983, the Court ruled that life insurance companies cannot charge different rates for women and men.[24]

Gender Equality on Campus. Congress sought to guarantee equality of treatment in education by passing Title IX of the Education Amendments of 1972, which states: "No person in the United States shall, on the basis of sex, be excluded from participation in, be denied the benefits of, or be subjected to discrimination under any education program or activity receiving Federal financial assistance." Title IX's best-known and most controversial impact has been on high school and collegiate athletics, although the original statute made no reference to athletics.

In 2011, the Department of Education issued a statement clarifying that sexual harassment on campus, including rape, violated Title IX. Investigations by the Obama administration suggested that many schools were not taking such violations seriously. Dozens of schools were potentially subject to penalties. As a result, many colleges and universities launched efforts to address the issue.

Women in the Military. One of the most controversial issues involving women's rights has been the role of women in the armed forces. Many believe that the ERA failed because of the fear that women might be drafted (forced) into military service. Currently, no draft exists, but to this day young American men must register for it. Women do not face such a requirement.

A recent issue has been whether women should be allowed to serve in military combat units. In the past, women were not allowed to join such units. Due to the fluid nature of modern combat, however, women in support positions have often found themselves in firefights anyway. In January 2013, the Department of Defense lifted the Combat Exclusion Policy, and in the future women will be able to compete for assignment to combat units. Participation in such units is usually a requirement for promotion to top military positions.

Women in Politics Today

The efforts of women's rights advocates have helped to increase the number of women holding political offices at all levels of government.

Women in Congress. Although a men's club atmosphere still prevails in Congress, the number of women holding congressional seats has increased significantly in recent years. In 2001, for the first time, a woman was elected to a leadership post in Congress—Nancy Pelosi of California became the Democrats' minority whip in the U.S. House of Representatives. In 2002, she was elected minority leader. In 2006, she was chosen to be the first woman Speaker of the House in the history of the United States—although she was forced to drop back to minority leader again in 2010 when the Republicans regained control of the House.

Women in the Executive and Judicial Branches. In 2008, Hillary Clinton mounted a major campaign for the Democratic presidential nomination, and Sarah Palin

---

23. *Dothard v. Rawlinson*, 433 U.S. 321 (1977).
24. *Arizona v. Norris*, 463 U.S. 1073 (1983).

became the Republican nominee for vice president. Recent Gallup polls show that close to 90 percent of Americans said they would vote for a qualified woman for president if she was nominated by their party. Increasing numbers of women are also being appointed to cabinet posts.

More women are sitting on federal judicial benches as well. President Ronald Reagan (1981–1989) was credited with a historic first when he appointed Sandra Day O'Connor to the United States Supreme Court in 1981. (O'Connor retired in 2006.) President Bill Clinton also appointed a woman, Ruth Bader Ginsburg. In 2009, President Obama named Sonia Sotomayor to the Court. She became the third woman and first Hispanic to serve. In 2010, Obama appointed Elena Kagan, bringing the number of women currently serving on the Court to three.

Gender-Based Discrimination in the Workplace

Traditional cultural beliefs concerning the proper role of women in society continue to be evident not only in the political arena but also in the workplace. Since the 1960s, however, women have gained substantial protection against discrimination through laws that require equal employment opportunities and equal pay.

Title VII of the Civil Rights Act of 1964. Title VII of the Civil Rights Act of 1964 prohibits gender discrimination in employment and has been used to strike down employment policies that discriminate against employees on the basis of gender. In 1978, Congress amended Title VII to expand the definition of gender discrimination to include discrimination based on pregnancy.

Sexual Harassment. The United States Supreme Court has also held that Title VII's prohibition of gender-based discrimination extends to **sexual harassment** in the workplace. One form of sexual harassment occurs when job opportunities, promotions, salary increases, and the like are given in return for sexual favors. Another form of sexual harassment is called hostile-environment harassment. It occurs when an employee is subjected to sexual conduct or comments that interfere with the employee's job performance or are so pervasive or severe as to create an intimidating, hostile, or offensive environment.

Wage Discrimination. Although Title VII and other legislation since the 1960s has mandated equal employment opportunities for men and women, women continue to earn less, on average, than men do.

The Equal Pay Act, which was enacted in 1963, basically requires employers to provide equal pay for substantially equal work. In other words, males cannot legally be paid more than females who perform essentially the same job.

The Equal Pay Act did not address the fact that certain types of jobs traditionally held by women pay lower wages than the jobs usually held by men. For example, more women than men are salesclerks and nurses, whereas more men than women are construction workers and truck drivers. Even if all clerks performing substantially similar jobs for a company earned the same salaries, they typically would still be earning less than the company's truck drivers.

When Congress passed the Equal Pay Act in 1963, a woman, on average, made 59 cents for every dollar earned by a man. By the mid-1990s, this amount had risen to 75 cents. Figures recently released by the U.S. Department of Labor indicate, though, that since then there has been little change. By 2017, women were still earning, on average, 79 cents for every dollar earned by men.

Everett Collection/Shutterstock.com

Image 5–13 Alaska governor Sarah Palin ran for vice president on the Republican ticket in 2008. *Why do conservatives find it important to promote women to leadership positions?*

sexual harassment

Unwanted physical or verbal conduct or abuse of a sexual nature that interferes with a recipient's job performance, creates a hostile work environment, or carries with it an implicit or explicit threat of adverse employment consequences.

Election 2016

Women and Minority Group Members

For women in office, the 2016 elections were a mixed bag. The number of women in the U.S. Senate was now twenty-one, up one. The number of female representatives, however, declined by two to eighty-three. A woman—Hillary Clinton—became the first female major-party candidate for president of the United States. She did not, however, become the first woman president. (Bill Clinton, therefore, did not become the nation's first "First Gentleman.")

Still, the women who were elected were more diverse than ever. The new Congress contained a record number of minority group women, including thirty-five Democrats and three Republicans. Catherine Cortez Masto of Nevada became the nation's first Latina senator. Representative Stephanie Murphy (D., Fla.) became the first Vietnamese American woman in Congress. One of the more inspiring examples was the election of Representative Tammy Duckworth (D., Ill.) to the U.S. Senate. Duckworth, a veteran who lost both legs in the Iraq War when her helicopter was shot down, was the first disabled woman elected to Congress and the first member of Congress to be born in Thailand. Another example was Kamala Harris of California. With an African American father and a mother from India, she was the first Indian American and second African American woman elected to the Senate. By now, only Mississippi and Vermont have never sent a woman to Congress.

Male as well as female minority group members experienced gains. The number of minority-group senators rose by three, for a total of ten. The number in the House rose by six, for a total of ninety. Finally, in 2016 all six openly gay or lesbian members of Congress were reelected.

The Rights and Status of Gay Males and Lesbians

Learning Outcome 5:

Summarize the recent revolution in the rights enjoyed by gay men and lesbians.

On June 27, 1969, patrons of the Stonewall Inn, a New York City bar popular with gay men, lesbians, and transgender women, responded to a police raid. They threw beer cans and bottles because they were angry at what they felt was unrelenting police harassment. In the ensuing riot, which lasted two nights, hundreds of gay men, lesbians, and transgender women fought with police. Before Stonewall, the stigma attached to homosexuality and the resulting fear of exposure had tended to prevent most gay men and lesbians from engaging in activism. In the months after Stonewall, however, the Gay Liberation Front and the Gay Activist Alliance were formed, and similar groups sprang up in other parts of the country.

Growth in the Gay Male and Lesbian Rights Movement

The Stonewall incident marked the beginning of the movement for gay and lesbian rights. Since then, gay men and lesbians have formed thousands of organizations to exert pressure on legislatures, the media, schools, churches, and other organizations to recognize their right to equal treatment.

To a great extent, lesbian and gay groups have succeeded in changing public opinion—and state and local laws—that pertain to their status and rights. Nevertheless, they continue to struggle against age-old biases against homosexuality, often rooted in deeply held religious beliefs, and the rights of gay men and lesbians remain an extremely divisive issue in American society.

In time, the lesbian and gay rights movement came to include bisexuals and transgender people—that is, individuals who experience a gender identity at odds with their biology at the time of their birth. The popular acronym LGBT signifies this broader movement.

Today, thirty-four states, the District of Columbia, and more than 180 cities and counties have enacted laws protecting lesbians and gay men from discrimination in employment in at least some workplaces. Many of these laws also ban discrimination in housing, in public accommodation, and in other contexts. Nineteen states extend private-sector employment rights to transgender individuals.

State and Local Laws Targeting Gay Men and Lesbians

Before the Stonewall incident, forty-nine states had sodomy laws that made various kinds of sexual acts, including homosexual acts, illegal (Illinois, which had repealed its sodomy law in 1962, was the only exception). During the 1970s and 1980s, more than half of these laws were either repealed or struck down by the courts.

Lawrence v. Texas. The states—mostly in the South—that resisted the movement to abolish sodomy laws received a boost in 1986 with the Supreme Court's decision in *Bowers v. Hardwick*.[25] In that case, the Court upheld a Georgia law that made homosexual conduct between two adults a crime. In 2003, however, the Court reversed its earlier position with its decision in *Lawrence v. Texas*.[26] In this case, the Court held that laws against sodomy violate the due process clause of the Fourteenth Amendment. The Court stated: "The liberty protected by the Constitution allows homosexual persons the right to choose to enter upon relationships in the confines of their homes and their own private lives and still retain their dignity as free persons." *Lawrence v. Texas* invalidated the sodomy laws that remained on the books in fourteen states.

Ben Hider/Getty Images

Image 5–14 In the summer of 1969, gay men and lesbians who frequented a New York City bar called the Stonewall Inn had had enough. They were tired of unrelenting police harassment. For two nights, they fought with police. *What movement resulted from the riots?*

The Gay Community and Politics. Politicians at the national level have not overlooked the potential significance of homosexual issues in American politics. While conservative politicians generally have been critical of efforts to secure gay and lesbian rights, liberals, by and large, have been speaking out for gay rights in the past thirty years. In 1980, the Democratic platform included a gay rights section for the first time. It is a fact, however, that discrimination against LGBT individuals in housing, employment, and public accommodations remains legal in a majority of U.S. jurisdictions.

Gay Men and Lesbians in the Military

Until recently, the armed forces viewed homosexuality as incompatible with military service. In 1993, however, President Bill Clinton announced a new policy, described as "don't ask,

25. 478 U.S. 186 (1986).
26. 539 U.S. 558 (2003).

Image 5–15 Air Force Lieutenant Colonel Sean Hackbart (left) and his partner, Mike Culver, celebrate the official end of the military's "don't ask, don't tell" policy. *Do such officers still need to worry about how their sexual orientation might affect their careers?*

don't tell." Enlistees would not be asked about their sexual orientation, and gay men and lesbians would be allowed to serve in the military so long as they did not declare that they were gay men or lesbians or commit homosexual acts. The new policy was a compromise—Clinton had promised during his presidential campaign to repeal outright the long-standing ban on lesbian and gay military service. Despite the new policy, large numbers of gay men and lesbians were expelled from the military in subsequent years.

During his 2008 presidential campaign, Barack Obama promised to repeal "don't ask, don't tell" and allow lesbians and gay men to serve openly. Still, Congress failed to act on legislation that would repeal the policy. By December 2010, however, respondents in a public opinion poll supported the right of gay men and lesbians to serve openly by a margin of 77 to 21 percent. In September 2010, a U.S. district court judge ruled that "don't ask, don't tell" was unconstitutional.[27] In December, Congress finally passed the gradual repeal legislation that had been tied up for most of 2010. "Don't ask, don't tell" was phased out in 2011.

Same-Sex Marriage

Given the rampant hostility toward gay men and lesbians that existed throughout most of American history, legal same-sex marriage was beyond imagination for most Americans. Still, some same-sex couples celebrated their unions with private, unofficial ceremonies.

In 2015, however, the Supreme Court endorsed nationwide recognition of same-sex marriage. This landmark decision was part of one of the most rapid and profound extensions of civil rights in history—the recognition of equal rights regardless of sexual orientation. In Chapter 3, you learned about the most recent legal developments in the campaign for marriage equality. Here, we will provide some of the background to these events.

The Defense of Marriage Act (DOMA). Controversy over this issue first flared up in 1993 when the Hawaii Supreme Court ruled that denying marriage licenses to gay couples might violate the equal protection clause of the Hawaii constitution.[28] In response, the U.S. Congress passed the Defense of Marriage Act of 1996, which banned federal recognition of lesbian and gay male couples and allowed state governments to ignore same-sex marriages performed in other states.

Civil Unions. In 1999, the Vermont Supreme Court ruled that gay couples were entitled to the same benefits of marriage as opposite-sex couples.[29] The Vermont legislature then passed a law permitting gay and lesbian couples to form *civil unions*. Partners

27. *Log Cabin Republicans v. United States,* 716 F.Supp.2d 884 (C.D. Cal. 2010).

28. *Baehr v. Lewin,* 852 P.2d 44 (Hawaii 1993).

29. *Baker v. Vermont,* 744 A.2d 864 (Vt. 1999).

forming civil unions could receive all state benefits available to married couples. The law did not, however, entitle those partners to receive benefits provided to married couples under federal law. Later, a number of other states adopted civil unions before moving on to full recognition of same-sex marriage.

State Recognition of Same-Sex Marriages. Massachusetts was the first state to recognize gay marriage. In November 2003, the Massachusetts Supreme Judicial Court ruled that same-sex couples have a right to civil marriage under the Massachusetts state constitution.[30] For four years, Massachusetts stood alone in approving such marriages. From 2008 on, however, more and more states began to accept same-sex marriage. Initially, state courts took the lead. In 2009, state legislatures began authorizing the practice. In 2012, for the first time, voters in three states endorsed same-sex marriage through a referendum or initiative. By May 2013, same-sex marriage had been endorsed by thirteen states and the District of Columbia.

Constitutional End Game. In June 2013, the Supreme Court refused to rule on a California case, and as a result, a lower-court ruling that legalized same-sex marriage went into effect in that state.[31] More importantly, on the same day the Court found, in *United States v. Windsor*, that the provision of the Defense of Marriage Act that banned federal recognition of same-sex marriages performed by the states was unconstitutional.[32] From December 2013 on, ever-larger numbers of state and federal judges used arguments contained in *Windsor* to overturn same-sex marriage bans. Finally, in June 2015, the Supreme Court overturned the remaining state-level prohibitions in *Obergefell v. Hodges*.[33]

---

30. *Goodridge v. Department of Public Health*, 798 N.E.2d 941 (Mass. 2003).
31. *Hollingsworth v. Perry*, 133 S.Ct. 2652 (2013).
32. 570 U.S. ___ (2013).
33. 135 S.Ct. 2584 (2015).

Image 5-16 Rainbow-colored lights shine on the White House to celebrate the Supreme Court ruling in favor of same-sex marriage in June 2015. The Court ruled that the Constitution guarantees a right to same-sex marriage in all fifty states. *Why has public opinion on same-sex marriage changed so quickly and dramatically?*

Mark Wilson/Getty Images

Image 5–17 Demonstrators in Asheville, North Carolina, protest the state's new law that restricts the rights of transgender persons to use the toilet facilities that they believe are appropriate to their gender. *Why has this question become a political issue?*

The Rights of Transgender Individuals

The question of who is a woman and who is a man is not as open-and-shut as many people once assumed. Thousands of people grow up convinced that their bodies are lying to them. They may have been born with the physical characteristics of one sex, but in their hearts they know they belong to the other. The existence of such **transgender persons** has been known for many years and has led to the practice of reassigning gender through surgery. Not all transgender persons undergo such an invasive process, however. Indeed, some transgender persons find that they cannot identify either as men *or* women. In June 2016, an Oregon court became the first in the nation to recognize such a nonaligned status.

Forty-six states allow birth certificates to be amended or replaced to change a person's recorded sex. Twenty-eight states, however, allow such a change only following surgery. Discrimination against transgender individuals in employment and other fields is widespread. In recent years, such persons have increasingly come out into the open and demanded equal rights.

In 2015 and 2016, however, various states and localities passed laws banning transgender persons from using public restrooms that did not accord with the sex listed on their birth certificates. A common argument was that trans women (born men) would use their access to women's restrooms to sexually harass or attack women. Despite this fear, there is no recorded case of such an incident ever happening, and if it did it would be a felony under existing laws. In response to North Carolina legislation, in May 2016 the Obama administration announced that any such ban in a public school would threaten the school's access to federal funding. Eleven states sued the administration in an attempt to reverse this decision.

transgender persons

Persons who experience a mismatch between their gender identity and the gender assigned to them at birth.

The Rights and Status of Juveniles

Learning Outcome **6:**

Evaluate the rights and status of juvenile citizens.

Approximately 75 million Americans—about 24 percent of the total population—are under eighteen years of age. Depending on the topic, the definition of *child* can range from a person under age sixteen to a person under age twenty-one. However defined, children in the United States have fewer rights and protections than adults.

The reason for this lack of rights is the presumption of society that children basically are protected by their parents. This is not to say that children are the property of the parents. Rather, an overwhelming case *against* allowing parents to control the actions of a child must be presented before that child or the state can act on the child's behalf without regard to the parents' wishes.

Supreme Court decisions affecting children's rights began a process of slow evolution with *Brown v. Board of Education of Topeka,* the landmark civil rights case of 1954 discussed earlier in this chapter. In the *Brown* case, the Court granted children the status of rights-bearing persons. In the 1967 case *In re Gault,*[34] the Court expressly held that children have a constitutional right to be represented by counsel at the government's expense in a criminal action. Five years later, the Court acknowledged that "children are 'persons' within the meaning of the Bill of Rights. We have held so over and over again."[35]

Voting Rights and the Young

The Twenty-sixth Amendment to the Constitution, ratified on July 1, 1971, reads as follows:

> *The right of citizens of the United States, who are eighteen years of age or older, to vote shall not be denied or abridged by the United States or by any State on account of age.*

Before this amendment was ratified, the age at which citizens could vote was twenty-one in most states. One of the arguments used for granting suffrage to eighteen-year-olds was that, because they could be drafted to fight in the country's wars, they had a stake in public policy. At the time, the example of the Vietnam War was paramount.

The Rights of Children in Civil and Criminal Proceedings

Civil law relates to such matters as contracts among private individuals, domestic relations, and business transactions. **Criminal law** relates to crimes against society that are defined by legislatures and prosecuted by a public official, such as a district attorney. Different procedural rules and judicial safeguards apply under civil and criminal laws.

The Rights of Juveniles in Civil Proceedings. The rights of children in civil cases are defined by state laws. The legal definition of **majority**—the age at which a person is entitled by law to the right to manage his or her own affairs—varies from eighteen to twenty-one years of age, depending on the state. As a rule, an individual who is legally a minor cannot be held responsible for contracts that he or she forms with others. In most states, only contracts entered into for so-called *necessaries* (things necessary for subsistence, such as food and clothing) can be enforced against minors. Also, when minors engage in negligent behavior, typically their parents are liable. If, for example, a minor destroys a neighbor's fence, the neighbor may bring a suit against the child's parent rather than the child.

civil law

The law regulating conduct between private persons over noncriminal matters, including contracts, domestic relations, and business interactions.

criminal law

The law that defines crimes and provides punishment for violations. In criminal cases, the government is the prosecutor.

majority

The age at which a person is entitled by law to the right to manage her or his own affairs.

---

34. 387 U.S. 1 (1967).
35. *Wisconsin v. Yoder,* 406 U.S. 205 (1972).

Image 5–18 When children are at risk, local or state agencies sometimes take over their care. *Under what circumstances might the government take such an action?*

Civil law also encompasses the area of child custody. Child-custody rulings traditionally have given little weight to the wishes of the child. Courts have maintained the right to act on behalf of the child's "best interests" but have sometimes been constrained from doing so by the "greater" rights possessed by adults. For instance, a widely publicized Supreme Court ruling awarded legal custody of a two-and-a-half-year-old Michigan resident to an Iowa couple, the child's biological parents. A Michigan couple, who had cared for the child since shortly after her birth and who had petitioned to adopt the child, lost out in the custody battle. The Court agreed that the law allowed it to consider only the parents' rights and not the child's best interests.[36]

Children's rights and their ability to articulate their rights for themselves in custody matters were strengthened, however, by several rulings involving older children. For example, an eleven-year-old Florida boy filed suit in his own name to terminate his relationship with his biological parents and to have the court affirm his right to be adopted by foster parents. The court granted his request, although it did not agree procedurally with the method by which the boy initiated the suit.[37]

Criminal Rights of Juveniles. One of the main requirements for an act to be criminal is intent. The law has given children certain defenses against criminal prosecution because of their presumed inability to have criminal intent. Under the **common law,** children up to seven years of age were considered incapable of committing a crime because they did not have the moral sense to understand that they were doing wrong. Children between the ages of seven and fourteen were also presumed to be incapable of committing a crime, but this presumption could be challenged by showing

common law

Judge-made law that originated in England from decisions shaped according to prevailing customs. Decisions were applied to similar situations and thus gradually became common to the nation.

---

36. *DeBoer by Darrow v. DeBoer,* 509 U.S. 1301 (1993).
37. *Kingsley v. Kingsley,* 623 So.2d 780 (Fla.App. 1993).

that the child understood the wrongful nature of the act. Today, states vary in their approaches. Most states retain the common law approach, although age limits vary from state to state. Other states have simply set a minimum age for criminal responsibility.

Juvenile Court Systems. All states have juvenile court systems that handle children below the age of criminal responsibility who commit delinquent acts. The aim of juvenile courts is allegedly to reform rather than to punish. In states that retain the common law approach, children who are above the minimum age but are still juveniles can be turned over to the criminal courts if the juvenile court determines that they should be treated as adults. Children sent to juvenile court do not have the right to trial by jury or to post bail.

Felony Cases. Although minors usually do not have the full rights of adults in criminal proceedings, they have certain advantages. In felony cases, which include, among others, cases involving manslaughter, murder, armed robbery, and assault, juveniles traditionally were not tried as adults. (A **felony** is a serious crime punishable in most jurisdictions by a prison sentence longer than one year.) They were often sentenced to probation or "reform" school for a relatively short term regardless of the seriousness of their crimes. Today, however, most states allow juveniles to be tried as adults for certain crimes, such as murder.

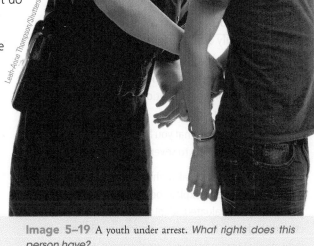

Image 5–19 A youth under arrest. *What rights does this person have?*

Juveniles who are tried as adults may also face adult penalties. Formerly, these included the death penalty. In 2005, however, the United States Supreme Court ruled that executing persons who were under the age of eighteen when they committed their crimes would constitute cruel and unusual punishment.[38] In 2010, the Court also ruled that juveniles who commit crimes in which no one is killed may not be sentenced to life in prison without the possibility of parole.[39]

felony

A serious crime punishable in most jurisdictions by a prison sentence longer than one year.

---

38. *Roper v. Simmons*, 543 U.S. 551 (2005).

39. *Graham v. Florida*, 130 S.C.t 2011 (2010).

How you can make a difference

Anyone applying for a job may be subjected to a variety of possibly discriminatory practices based on race, gender, religion, age, sexual preference, or disability. Tests may have a discriminatory effect. The government continues to monitor the fairness and validity of criteria used in screening job applicants. As a result, there are ways of addressing the problem of discrimination.

If you believe that you have been discriminated against by a potential employer, consider the following steps:

1. Evaluate your own capabilities, and determine if you are truly qualified for the position.
2. Analyze the reasons why you were turned down. Would others agree with you that you have been the object of discrimination, or would they uphold the employer's claim?
3. If you still believe that you have been treated unfairly, you have recourse to several agencies and services.

You should first speak to the human resources director of the company and explain politely that you believe you have not been evaluated adequately. If asked, explain your concerns clearly. If necessary, go into explicit detail, and indicate that you may have been discriminated against.

If a second evaluation is not forthcoming, contact your local state employment agency. If you still do not obtain adequate help, contact one or more of the following state agencies, usually listed in your telephone directory under "State Government":

- If a government entity is involved, a state ombudsperson or citizen aide may be available to mediate.
- You can contact the state civil rights commission, which at least should give you advice, even if it does not wish to take up your case.
- The state attorney general's office normally has a division dealing with discrimination and civil rights.
- There may be a special commission or department specifically set up to help you, such as a women's status commission or a commission on Hispanics or Asian Americans. If you are a woman or a member of such a minority group, contact these commissions.
- At the national level, you can contact the Equal Employment Opportunity Commission (eeoc.gov).

KEY TERMS

affirmative action 127
civil disobedience 121
civil law 143
civil rights 117
common law 144
criminal law 143
de facto segregation 121

de jure segregation 120
felony 145
feminism 134
gender discrimination 135
grandfather clause 119
intermediate, or exacting, scrutiny 126

literacy test 119
majority 143
poll tax 119
rational basis review 127
reverse discrimination 128
separate-but-equal doctrine 119

sexual harassment 137
strict scrutiny 126
suffrage 118
suspect classification 126
transgender persons 142
white primary 119

CHAPTER SUMMARY

Learning Outcome 1 Before the Civil War, African American slavery was protected by the Constitution. Constitutional amendments after the Civil War ended slavery, and African Americans gained citizenship, the right to vote, and other rights. This protection was largely a dead letter by the 1880s, however.

Segregation was declared unconstitutional by the Supreme Court in *Brown v. Board of Education of Topeka* (1954), in which the Court stated that separation implied inferiority. In 1955, the modern civil rights movement began. The Civil Rights Act of 1964 banned discrimination on the basis of race, religion, gender, or national origin in employment and public accommodations. The Voting Rights Act of 1965 outlawed discriminatory voter-registration tests and authorized federal voter registration.

Learning Outcome 2 Civil rights are protected by the due process and equal protection clauses of the Fourteenth Amendment to the U.S. Constitution. The courts have developed a series of tests to use when considering cases of possible discrimination. Strict scrutiny applies to classifications such as race, religion, and national origin. Intermediate, or exacting, scrutiny is employed in cases involving women's rights. Rational basis review, used when strict or exacting scrutiny does not apply, is the easiest test to meet.

Affirmative action programs have been controversial because they may lead to reverse discrimination against majority groups or even other minority groups. Supreme Court decisions have limited affirmative action programs, and several states now ban state-sponsored affirmative action.

Learning Outcome 3 Today, most immigrants come from Asia and Latin America, especially Mexico. Many are unauthorized (or illegal) immigrants. Latinos and American Indians benefit from the same antidiscrimination measures as African Americans. American Indians suffered a demographic collapse upon the arrival of the Europeans in the New World. They continue to face high levels of poverty. Asian Americans have frequently enjoyed economic success, despite severe past prejudice.

Learning Outcome 4 In the early history of the United States, women had no political rights. After the first women's rights convention in 1848, the women's movement gained momentum. Not until 1920, however, with the Nineteenth Amendment, did women obtain the right to vote nationwide. The modern women's movement began in the 1960s in the wake of the civil rights and anti–Vietnam War movements. Efforts to secure the ratification of the Equal Rights Amendment failed, but the women's movement has been successful in obtaining new laws, changes in social customs, and increased political representation for women.

Federal government efforts to eliminate gender discrimination in the workplace include Title VII of the Civil Rights Act of 1964, which prohibits gender-based discrimination, including sexual harassment on the job.

Learning Outcome 5 In 2003, a United States Supreme Court decision invalidated all remaining sodomy laws (which criminalized specific sexual practices). Many states and cities have laws prohibiting at least some types of discrimination based on sexual orientation. In 2011, lesbians and gays won the right to serve openly in the military. In 2015, the Supreme Court legalized same-sex marriage nationwide. Recently, the rights of transgender persons have become a major issue.

Learning Outcome 6 Children have few rights and protections, in part because it is presumed that their parents protect them. The Twenty-sixth Amendment grants the right to vote to those ages eighteen or older. Minors have some defense against criminal prosecution because of their presumed inability to have criminal intent below certain ages.

ADDITIONAL RESOURCES

Online Resources

- An excellent source of information on issues facing African Americans is the website of the National Association for the Advancement of Colored People (NAACP). Find it at **naacp.org**.

- The National Organization for Women (NOW) offers online information and updates on the status of women's rights. You can locate its website at **now.org**.

Books

Adichie, Chimamanda Ngozi. *We Should All Be Feminists*. New York: Anchor, 2015. In this brief work, Adichie, a prize-winning Nigerian American novelist, makes the case for feminism.

Coates, Ta-Nehisi. *Between the World and Me*. New York: Spiegel & Grau, 2015. Coates, a correspondent for *The Atlantic,* explains the dangers of life as an African American in a series of letters to his son. Few books in 2015 were more widely acclaimed.

Faderman, Lillian. *The Gay Revolution: The Story of the Struggle*. New York: Simon & Schuster, 2015. An in-depth history by an award-winning author.

Video

Eyes on the Prize: America's Civil Rights Years 1954–1965—Narrated by civil rights veteran Julian Bond, this six-hour television series is one of the most highly regarded video histories of the civil rights movement ever. It was released in 2010.

Miss Representation—This highly acclaimed 2011 documentary shows how the media's emphasis on youth and beauty makes it harder for women to gain equality and to win leadership positions. The all-star cast includes Margaret Cho, Katie Couric, Geena Davis, Rachel Maddow, Nancy Pelosi, Condoleezza Rice, and Gloria Steinem.

Quiz

Multiple Choice and Fill-Ins

Learning Outcome 1 Summarize the historical experience of African Americans, state how the separate-but-equal doctrine was abolished, and describe the consequences of the civil rights movement.

1. The separate-but-equal doctrine was announced by the Supreme Court:
   a. in *Plessy v. Ferguson*.
   b. in *Roe v. Wade*.
   c. nowhere, because the Supreme Court never addressed the issue.

2. Past barriers to African American voting included grandfather clauses, poll taxes, and _____
   _____.

Learning Outcome 2 Define the different levels of scrutiny used by the Supreme Court in civil rights cases, and describe recent rulings on affirmative action.

3. Affirmative action programs have assisted groups that were discriminated against in the past. In educational admissions and employment, these programs have:
   a. awarded preferences to minority group members.
   b. relied on numerical quotas to improve outcomes.
   c. involved federal grants to complying institutions.

4. The Fourteenth Amendment requires that no state shall deprive any person of life, liberty, or property, without
   _____ _____ __ _____.

Learning Outcome 3 Discuss the history and current status of Latinos, American Indians, and Asian Americans.

5. In the years following the European discovery of America, the number of Native Americans:
   a. rose because of the introduction of new foodstuffs.
   b. fell because of the introduction of new diseases.
   c. remained about the same for many years.

6. Currently, the country providing the largest number of immigrants to the United States is _____.

Learning Outcome 4 Contrast the goals of the women's suffrage movement with the goals of modern feminism.

7. The Equal Rights Amendment today requires:
   a. that women be treated equally to men.
   b. that women be treated equally in the labor market.
   c. nothing at all, because the Equal Rights Amendment never passed.

8. Among the most controversial issues raised by the modern feminist movement are whether pornography should be banned and whether women should have the right to
   _____ __ _____.

Learning Outcome 5 Summarize the recent revolution in the rights enjoyed by gay men and lesbians.

9. The Defense of Marriage Act (DOMA) provided for all of the following except:
   a. states were not required to recognize same-sex marriages conducted in other states.
   b. states were not required to recognize divorces obtained in other states.
   c. the federal government was barred from recognizing same-sex marriages when awarding benefits or collecting taxes.

10. Since 2011, _____ _____ ___ _____ can openly serve in the U.S. military.

Learning Outcome 6 Evaluate the rights and status of juvenile citizens.

11. Very young children may not be charged with crimes because:
    a. they lack the ability to form criminal intent.
    b. their parents must be charged instead.
    c. such charges would not be in the best interest of the child.

12. In 1971, because of the _____ _____, citizens eighteen and older were given the right to vote.

Essay Questions

1. Not all African Americans agreed with the philosophy of nonviolence espoused by Dr. Martin Luther King, Jr. Advocates of black power called for a more militant approach. Can militancy make a movement more effective (possibly by making a more moderate approach seem like a reasonable compromise), or is it typically counterproductive? Either way, why?

2. The prevention of terrorist acts committed by adherents of radical Islamism is a major policy objective today. Can we defend ourselves against such acts without abridging the civil rights and liberties of American Muslims and immigrants from predominantly Muslim countries? What measures that might be undertaken by the authorities are legitimate? Which are not?

Answers to multiple-choice and fill-in questions: 1. a, 2. literacy tests, 3. a, 4. due process of law, 5. b, 6. Mexico, 7. c, 8. obtain an abortion, 9. b, 10. gay men and lesbians, 11. a, 12. Twenty-sixth Amendment.

PUBLIC OPINION AND POLITICAL SOCIALIZATION

Actress America Ferrera talks to high school students about the importance of voting in North Las Vegas, Nevada. *What effect can celebrities have on the political process?*
Ethan Miller/Getty Images

These four **LEARNING OUTCOMES** *below are designed to help improve your understanding of this chapter:*

1: Define *public opinion, consensus,* and *divided opinion,* and discuss major sources of political socialization, including the family, the schools, the media, and political events.

2: Identify the effects of various influences on opinion, including education, income, religion, race/ethnicity, gender, and geography.

3: Describe the characteristics of a scientific opinion poll, and list some of the problems pollsters face in obtaining accurate results.

4: Consider the effect that public opinion may have on the political process.

What if...

Politicians Really Listened to the Polls?

Background

How do we know about popular opinion? For the most part, we must rely on public opinion polling. Of course, politicians are aware of public opinion. Indeed, many of them use polling to determine what positions they should take during an election campaign. Once elected, though, it is not clear how much senators and members of the House really do listen to public opinion.

On a few issues, politicians clearly do respond to popular opinion. On others, however, the Washington, D.C., political elites—politicians, columnists, think tank experts, major fund-raisers, and others—take a different approach. On these issues, rather than paying attention to polls, elites are apparently drawing their own conclusions about what is good for the country. Policymaking might be more conservative on some issues—and more liberal on others—if politicians really tried to respond to popular opinion.

What If Politicians Really Listened to the Polls?

According to the Pew Research Center, 75 percent of those polled believe that it would be positive for our society if more Americans were religious. About the same percentage believe that religion is losing its influence on American life. Almost three quarters believe that the state of U.S. moral values is getting worse.

About 60 percent of Americans believe that progressives have gone too far in trying to keep religion out of the schools and government. If politicians really listened to these polls, they would find ways to allow more religion in our public school systems. Three quarters of Americans favor a constitutional amendment to allow "voluntary prayer" in the public schools—that is, prayer led by teachers from which students could theoretically opt out. Yet somehow, this amendment never seems to make it to the floor of the House or Senate.

What Should We Do to Cut the Deficit?

If Americans are more conservative than political elites on religion in the schools, they are more liberal on a few economic issues. Polls regularly report that voters want to reduce the deficit—the excess of the federal government's spending over and above its income. It's widely believed among elites that we therefore need to cut rates of "entitlement spending," programs such as Social Security and Medicaid. Newspapers such as the *Washington Post* regularly report this need as if it were a fact, not an opinion. Pew Research, however, in a poll on the deficit, reported that 41 percent of respondents wanted to *increase* Social Security spending. Only 10 percent wanted to see it cut. A majority of those polled opposed cutting *anything* except foreign aid.

A unique poll by the Program for Public Consultation at the University of Maryland let respondents work through an interactive budget exercise in which they were forced to confront the realities of taxing and spending. Respondents did cut the deficit. Still, a majority also increased Social Security benefits slightly. It was the only program so treated. Respondents supported large cuts to defense spending—and major tax increases on the wealthy. These are not policies with much elite support.

For Critical Analysis

◗ Often, groups of voters believe that politicians are ignoring them on an issue—when the simple truth is that neither they nor their elected representatives have enough votes to win their preferred policy. How does our system of checks and balances make it hard to pass new laws?

◗ Why do you think a majority of voters oppose cuts to most federal government programs?

Image 6–1 A canvasser queries a businessman in front of the U.S. Capitol. *How might businesspeople respond to issues such as religion in the schools and funding social security?*

Cameron Whitman/Shutterstock.com

In a democracy, the ability of the people to freely express their opinions is fundamental. Americans can express their opinions in many ways. They can write letters to newspapers. They can share their ideas in online forums on Facebook, blogs, and tweets. They can organize politically. They can vote. They can respond to opinion polls.

Leaders of the Republican Party were reminded of the importance of public opinion during the 2016 Republican primary elections, won by businessman Donald Trump. Most Republican leaders supported a conservatism based on small government and free markets. Tax rate cuts for the richest Americans were the number-one issue. Spending on programs such as Social Security and Medicare should be controlled, if not cut. Foreign trade was a blessing, and quite a few believed that compromise on immigration was at least conceivable. These positions matched the preferences of the *donor class*—the multimillionaires who provide much Republican campaign funding. Many ordinary Republicans, however, had other ideas. Often, they depended on programs such as Social Security. Many believed, with some reason, that imports damaged the lives of American workers, despite the benefits to the overall economy. With less reason, they believed that immigration was damaging as well. For Trump, these were the beliefs that won the primaries, to the shock of traditional small-government conservatives.

There is no doubt that public opinion can be powerful. The extent to which public opinion affects policymaking is not always so clear, however. For example, suppose that public opinion strongly supports a certain policy. If political leaders adopt that position, is it because they are responding to public opinion or because they share the public's beliefs?

Image 6–2 Representatives John Conyers (D., Mich.) and Donna Edwards (D., Md.) speak during a rally to promote more generous Social Security benefits. Labor unions were major sponsors of this event. *Why would organized labor want to expand Social Security?*

Public Opinion and Political Socialization

There is no single public opinion, because there are many different "publics." In a nation of 320 million people, there may be innumerable gradations of opinion on an issue. What we do is describe the distribution of opinions about a particular question. Thus, we define **public opinion** as the aggregate of individual attitudes or beliefs shared by some portion of the adult population.

Consensus and Divided Opinion

Typically, public opinion is distributed among several different positions, and the distribution of opinion can tell us how divided the public is on an issue and whether compromise is possible. When polls show that a large proportion of the American public appears to express the same view on an issue, we say that a **consensus** exists, at least at the moment the poll was taken. Figure 6–1 shows a pattern of opinion that might be called consensual. Issues on which the public holds widely differing attitudes result

Learning Outcome **1:**

Define *public opinion,* *consensus,* **and** *divided opinion,* **and discuss major sources of political socialization, including the family, the schools, the media, and political events.**

public opinion
The aggregate of individual attitudes or beliefs shared by some portion of the adult population.

consensus
General agreement among the citizenry on an issue.

Figure 6–1   Consensus Opinion

Question: How much more needs to be done in order to achieve racial equality? (Asked of African Americans.) *Based on what you learned in Chapter 5, what steps might African Americans advocate to achieve racial equality?*

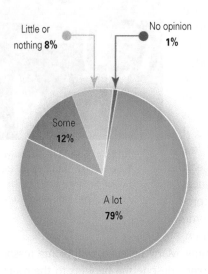

Source: Pew Research Center for the People and the Press, "On MLK Day, a Look at Black and White America," January 19, 2015.

Figure 6–2   Divided Opinion

Question: How much more needs to be done in order to achieve racial equality? (Asked of non-Hispanic whites.) *If some whites believe that achieving racial equality actually means doing more for white people, how might they respond to this question?*

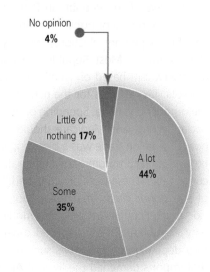

Source: Pew Research Center for the People and the Press, "On MLK Day, a Look at Black and White America," January 19, 2015.

in **divided opinion** (see Figure 6–2). Sometimes, a poll shows a distribution of opinion indicating that most Americans either have no information about the issue or do not care enough about the issue to formulate a position.

An interesting question arises as to when private opinion becomes public opinion. Everyone probably has a private opinion about the competence of the president, as well as about more personal concerns, such as the state of a neighbor's lawn. We say that private opinion becomes public opinion when the opinion is publicly expressed and concerns public issues. When someone's private opinion becomes so strong that the individual is willing to take action, then the opinion becomes public opinion.

Forming Public Opinion: Political Socialization

Most Americans are willing to express opinions on political issues when asked. How do people acquire these opinions and attitudes? Typically, views that are expressed as political opinions are acquired through the process of **political socialization.** By this, we mean that people acquire their political beliefs and values, often including their political party identification, through relationships with their families, friends, and co-workers.

The most important early sources of political socialization are the family and the schools. Individuals' basic political orientations are formed in the family if other family members hold strong views. When the adults in a family view politics as relatively unimportant and describe themselves as independent voters or disaffected from the political system, however, children may receive very little political socialization.

In the past few decades, more and more sources of information about politics have become available to all Americans, especially to young people through the Internet. Thus, although their basic outlook on the political system still may be formed by early family

divided opinion

Public opinion that is polarized between two quite different positions.

political socialization

The process by which people acquire political beliefs and values.

influences, young people are now exposed to many other sources of information about issues and values. This greater access to information may explain why young Americans are often more liberal than their parents on certain social issues, such as gay rights.

The Family. Not only do our parents' political beliefs, values, and actions affect our opinions, but the family also links us to other factors that affect opinion, such as race, social class, educational environment, and religious beliefs. How do parents transmit their political values to their offspring?

Studies suggest that the influence of parents is due to two factors: communication and receptivity. Parents communicate their feelings and preferences to their children constantly. Because children have such a strong need for parental approval, they are very receptive to their parents' views.

Children are less likely to influence their parents, because parents expect deference from their children.[1] Nevertheless, other studies show that if children are exposed to political ideas at school and in the media, they will share these ideas with their parents, giving the parents what some scholars call a "second chance" at political socialization.

Education as a Source of Political Socialization. From the early days of the republic, schools were perceived to be important transmitters of political information and attitudes. Children in the primary grades learn about their country mostly in patriotic ways. They learn about the Pilgrims, the flag, and some of the nation's presidents. In

---

1. Barbara A. Bardes and Robert W. Oldendick, *Public Opinion: Measuring the American Mind,* 4th ed. (Belmont, Calif.: Wadsworth Publishing Co., 2012), p. 73.

Image 6–3 A Maryland voter holds her daughter as she participates in early voting. *How much of an effect might early voting programs have on voter turnout?*

Image 6–4 His Holiness Pope Francis at the Cathedral Basilica of Saints Peter and Paul in Philadelphia. *Why might this pope be an opinion leader for many people who are not Catholic?*

the middle grades, children learn additional historical facts and come to understand the structure of government and the functions of the president, judges, and Congress. By high school, students have a more complex understanding of the political system.

Generally, the more education a person receives, the more likely it is that the person will be interested in politics, be confident in his or her ability to understand political issues, and be an active participant in the political process.

Peers and Peer Group Influence. Once a child enters school, the child's friends become an important influence on behavior and attitudes. For children and for adults, friendships and associations in **peer groups** affect political attitudes. We must, however, separate the effects of peer group pressure on opinions and attitudes in general from the effects of peer group pressure on political opinions. For the most part, associations among peers are nonpolitical. Political attitudes are more likely to be shaped by peer groups when those groups are involved directly in political activities. Individuals who share an ethnic identity, for example, may find a common political bond through working for the group's civil liberties and rights.

Opinion Leaders' Influence. We are all influenced by those with whom we are closely associated or whom we hold in high regard—friends at school, family members and other relatives, and teachers. In a sense, these people are **opinion leaders,** but on an *informal* level. That is, their influence on our political views is not necessarily intentional or deliberate. We are also influenced by *formal* opinion leaders, such as presidents, lobbyists, congresspersons, news commentators, and religious leaders, who have as part of their jobs the task of swaying people's views.

The Media and Public Opinion

Clearly, the **media**—newspapers, television, radio, and Internet sources—strongly influence public opinion. This is because the media inform the public about the issues and events of our times and thus have an **agenda-setting** effect. Consider Bernard Cohen's classic statement about the media and public opinion: the media may not be successful in telling people what to think, but they are "stunningly successful in telling their audience what to think about."[2] The media's influence will be discussed in more detail in Chapter 10.

The Popularity of the Media. Today, many contend that the media's influence on public opinion has grown to equal that of the family. For example, in her analysis of the role played by the media in American politics, media scholar Doris A. Graber points out that high school students, when asked where they obtain the information on which they base their views, mention the mass media far more than they mention their families, friends, and teachers.[3]

peer group

A group whose members share common social characteristics. These groups play an important part in the socialization process, helping to shape attitudes and beliefs.

opinion leader

One who is able to influence the opinions of others because of position, expertise, or personality.

media

The channels of mass communication.

agenda setting

Determining which public-policy questions will be debated or considered.

2. Bernard C. Cohen, *The Press and Foreign Policy* (Princeton, N.J.: Princeton University Press, 1963; repr. 2016), p. 81.

3. Doris A. Graber, *On Media: Making Sense of Politics* (Boulder, Colo.: Paradigm Publishers, 2011).

The Impact of the New Media. The extent to which new forms of media have supplanted older ones—such as newspapers and the major broadcast networks—has been a major topic of discussion for several years. New forms include not only the Internet, but also talk radio and cable television. Talk radio would seem to be a very dated medium, given that radio first became important early in the twentieth century. Between 1949 and 1987, however, the Federal Communications Commission (FCC) enforced the **Fairness Doctrine,** which required radio and television to present controversial issues in a manner that was (in the FCC's view) honest, equitable, and balanced. Modern conservative talk radio took off only after the Fairness Doctrine was abolished.

The impact of the various forms of new media appears to vary considerably. Talk radio and cable networks such as Fox News have given conservatives new methods for promoting their views and socializing their audiences. It is probable, however, that such media mostly strengthen the beliefs of those who are already conservative, rather than recruiting new members to the political right. A similar observation is often made about political blogs on the Internet, although in this medium liberals may be even better represented than conservatives. Blogs appear to radicalize their readers, rather than turn conservatives into liberals or vice versa. Indeed, cable news, talk radio, and political blogs are widely blamed for the increased polarization that has characterized American politics in recent years.

The impact of social-networking sites is more ambiguous. Facebook, for example, does have strongly political "pages" that, in effect, are political blogs. Many interactions on Facebook, however, are between members of peer groups, such as students who attend a particular school or individuals who work in the same profession. Members of such groups are more likely to hold a variety of views than are members of groups explicitly organized around a political viewpoint. Social media, in other words, may enhance peer group influence.

Kobby Dagan/Shutterstock.com

Image 6–5 Facebook founder Mark Zuckerberg marches with his employees in San Francisco's Gay Pride Parade. *How are leaders of the new media different from leaders of the old?*

Political Events and Public Opinion

Generally, older Americans tend to be somewhat more conservative than younger Americans—particularly on social issues but also, to some extent, on economic issues. This effect probably occurs because older adults are likely to retain the social values that they learned years ago when various kinds of inequality were more widely accepted. The experience of marriage and raising a family also has a measurable conservatizing effect. Young people, especially today, are more liberal than their grandparents on social issues, such as the rights of gay men and lesbians, as well as racial and gender equality. Nevertheless, a more important factor than a person's age is the impact of momentous political events that shape the political attitudes of an entire generation. When events produce such a long-lasting result, we refer to it as a **generational effect** (also called a *cohort effect*).

Historical Events. Working class voters who grew up in the 1930s during the Great Depression were likely to form lifelong attachments to the Democratic Party, the party of Franklin D. Roosevelt. In the 1960s and 1970s, the war in Vietnam, the *Watergate break-in,* and the subsequent presidential cover-up fostered widespread cynicism toward government. (The Watergate break-in was the 1972 illegal entry into Democratic National Committee offices by members of President Richard Nixon's reelection organization.)

Fairness Doctrine

A Federal Communications Commission rule enforced between 1949 and 1987 that required radio and television to present controversial issues in a manner that was (in the commission's view) honest, equitable, and balanced.

generational effect

The long-lasting effect of the events of a particular time on the political opinions of those who came of political age at that time.

There is evidence that the years of economic prosperity under President Ronald Reagan during the 1980s led many young people to identify with the Republican Party. The high levels of support that younger voters gave to Barack Obama during his presidential campaigns may be good news for the Democratic Party in future years, even if it did not help the Democrats during midterm elections when the president was not on the ballot.

Generational effects can be complicated by the widely recognized phenomenon of nostalgia. Throughout recorded history, older individuals have tended to view the world of their youth more positively than the world in which they currently live. As a presidential candidate, Donald Trump appealed to this tendency with the slogan "Make America Great Again." Was the United States a greater place years ago? We examine that question in this chapter's *Which Side Are You On?* feature.

Which side are you on?

Were the "Good Old Days" Really That Great?

At one time or another, almost all of us have heard older people reminiscing about the good old days. Indeed, in a poll by the Pew Research Center in 2016, almost half of registered voters said that life in America today is worse than it was fifty years ago "for people like them." Voters who supported Donald Trump in the primary elections were much more likely to believe this—at a rate of 75 percent, compared with 63 percent for supporters of Senator Ted Cruz (R., Tex.), 54 percent for supporters of Ohio governor John Kasich, 34 percent of those supporting Senator Bernie Sanders (D., Vt.), and 22 percent for backers of former secretary of state Hillary Clinton. Trump's slogan "Make America Great Again" clearly meant something to his followers. Clinton's supporters, many of whom were African Americans or older women, had a different view of the past. So, were the good old days really that great? Or do many people view the past through rose-tinted glasses?

The Times Weren't So Great Back Then

Anyone who imagines travelling back in time to the fifties or even the sixties must realize how much they would have to give up. There was no Internet. Long-distance phone calls cost a fortune. Medical science could do essentially nothing for those suffering from heart disease. Many of the older folks most given to nostalgia would *die* if they went back then. If you were a success in life, you faced a top federal marginal income tax of 91 percent. If you were a businessman (yes, man) your ability to manage your corporation was limited by an aggressive, unionized workforce. Oh, and by the way, the food was terrible.

Are you a woman? In those days, your employment opportunities would have been quite limited. Many people still believed that your place was in the kitchen. Married women could not get loans or credit cards in their own names. If you are African American, you really would have been in trouble. Leave aside Jim Crow laws and denial of the right to vote—black people also earned 40 percent less than their white counterparts.

Yet Some People Have Reasons to Be Nostalgic

Yet nostalgia for the past is understandable for certain groups. After all, we had just emerged from World War II as the strongest nation on earth. We experienced a period of economic growth not seen before or since. Between 1947 and 1973, the median family income doubled. Staying home might have been an imposition on suburban housewives, but not for their children. With so many eyes looking after them, suburban children could roam freely in ways that are no longer allowed.

One group above all did well. In 1950, a young white man, whether he went to college or not, could easily get and keep a job in, say, the auto industry. He could then meet typical mortgage payments with about 14 percent of his take-home pay. The high top tax rates and the unionized workforce of the time meant trouble for business, but they were a benefit to the white working man. As a citizen of the greatest nation on earth, his superiority over other nations, other races, and women was guaranteed. Should it be a surprise that some people might long for the past?

For Critical Analysis

▷ If you had to pick a time in the history of the United States in which to live, what period would it be and why?

The Political Mood. A number of political scientists believe that they can make some broad generalizations about events that tug voters to the political right or the political left. One such proposition is that the public mood swings in a more liberal direction when the federal government is successful, especially in handling economic issues. Presumably, the identification of liberalism with active government means that the image of liberalism improves when the government is successful. Likewise, the trend is toward conservatism during periods of perceived governmental failure.[4] The presidencies of Republican Gerald Ford (1974–1977) and Democrat Jimmy Carter (1977–1981) provide examples of failure. In those years, the government appeared to be incapable of addressing huge rises in prices, gasoline shortages, and other problems. The resulting trend toward conservatism culminated in the election of Republican Ronald Reagan (1981–1989) as president.

A second apparent tendency is that when the government seems to be introducing conservative policies—which usually means that a Republican is president—public sentiment drifts to the left. When governance is perceived to be liberal—which typically means there is a Democratic president—opinion moves to the right. This tendency and the success/failure dynamic just mentioned can reinforce each other or balance each other out. As an example, Reagan's presidency was both conservative and successful. As a result, the public mood, which was quite conservative at the time that Reagan was first elected, shifted back toward the center during his two terms in office. Eventually, voters picked Democrat Bill Clinton (1993–2001) as president.

Political Preferences and Voting Behavior

Learning Outcome **2:**

A major indicator of voting behavior is, of course, party identification. In addition, a variety of socioeconomic and demographic factors also appear to influence political preferences. These factors include education, income and **socioeconomic status,** religion, race/ethnicity, gender, geographic region, and similar traits. People who share the same religion, occupation, or any other demographic trait are likely to influence one another and may also have common political concerns that follow from the common characteristic.

Other factors, such as perception of the candidates and issue preferences, are closely connected to the electoral process itself. Table 6–1 illustrates the impact of some of these variables on voting behavior.

Identify the effects of various influences on opinion, including education, income, religion, race/ethnicity, gender, and geography.

Party Identification and Demographic Influences

With the possible exception of race, party identification has been the most important determinant of voting behavior in national elections. Party affiliation is influenced by family and peer groups, by generational effects, by the media, and by the voter's assessment of candidates and issues.

In the middle to late 1960s, party attachment began to weaken. Whereas independent voters were only a little more than 20 percent of the eligible electorate during the 1950s, they constituted more than 30 percent of all voters by the mid-1990s, and their numbers have grown since that time. New voters are likely to identify themselves as independent voters, although they may be more ready to identify with one of the major parties by their mid-thirties. There is considerable debate among political scientists over whether those who call themselves independents are truly so: when asked, a majority say that they are "leaning" toward one party or the other. (For further discussion of party affiliation, see Chapter 8.)

socioeconomic status
The value assigned to a person due to occupation or income. An upper-class person, for example, has high socioeconomic status.

---

4. For data on the public mood, see James A. Stimpson, *Public Opinion in America: Moods, Cycles, and Swings,* 2d ed. (Boulder, Colo.: Westview Press, 1999), plus annual updates through 2014 at stimson.web.unc.edu/data.

Table 6–1 Voters by Groups in Presidential Elections, 2000–2016 (in Percentages)

Why do African Americans and Hispanics tend to support Democrats?

	2000		2004		2008		2012		2016	
	Gore (Dem.)	Bush (Rep.)	Kerry (Dem.)	Bush (Rep.)	Obama (Dem.)	McCain (Rep.)	Obama (Dem.)	Romney (Rep.)	Clinton (Dem.)	Trump (Rep.)
Total Vote	48	48	48	51	53	46	50	48	48	48
Gender										
Men	42	53	44	55	49	48	45	52	41	53
Women	54	43	51	48	56	43	55	44	54	42
Race										
White	42	54	41	58	43	55	39	59	37	58
Black	90	8	88	11	95	4	93	6	88	8
Hispanic	67	31	58	40	67	31	71	27	65	29
Educational Attainment										
Not a high school graduate[1]	59	39	50	50	63	35	64	35	45	51
High school graduate[2]	48	49	47	52	52	46	51	48	43	52
College graduate	45	51	46	52	50	48	47	51	49	45
Postgraduate education	52	44	54	45	58	40	55	42	58	37
Religion										
White Protestant[3]	34	63	32	68	34	65	30	69	37	60
Catholic	49	47	47	52	54	45	50	48	45	52
Jewish	79	19	75	24	78	21	69	30	71	24
White evangelical	NA	NA	21	79	24	74	21	78	16	81
Union Status										
Union household	59	37	59	40	59	39	58	40	51	43
Family Income										
Under $15,000	57	37	63	37	73	25	NA	NA	NA	NA
$15,000–29,000[4]	54	41	57	41	60	37	63	35	53	41
$30,000–49,000	49	48	50	49	55	43	57	42	51	42
Over $50,000	45	52	43	56	49	49	45	53	47	49
Size of Place of Residence										
Population over 500,000[5]	71	26	60	40	70	28	69	29	59	35
Population 50,000 to 500,000[6]	57	40	50	50	59	39	58	40	45	50
Population 10,000 to 50,000	38	59	48	51	45	53	42	56	NA	NA
Rural	37	59	39	60	45	53	37	61	34	62

Note: Figures do not necessarily sum to 100 because of "other" or "no response" answers. NA = Not asked.
1. In 2016, "high school or less."
2. In 2016, "some college."
3. In 2012 and 2016, Protestant or "other Christian."

4. In 2012 and 2016, below $30,000.
5. In 2016, "urban."
6. In 2016, "suburban."
Sources: The National Election Pool, as reported by CBS, the *New York Times,* CNN, Fox News, and Politico.

Demographic influences reflect the individual's personal background and place in society. Some factors, such as race and (for most people) religion, have to do with the family into which a person was born. Others may be the result of choices made throughout an individual's life. They include place of residence, educational achievement, and profession.

It is also clear that many of these factors are interrelated. People who have more education typically have higher incomes and may hold professional jobs. Similarly, children born into wealthier families are far more likely to complete college than are children from poor families. A number of other interrelationships are not so immediately obvious. For example, many people might not realize that 79 percent of African Americans report that religion is very important in their lives, compared with only 56 percent of the total population.

Educational Achievement. In the past, having a college education tended to be associated with voting for Republicans. In recent years, however, this correlation has become weaker. In particular, individuals with a postgraduate education—more than a bachelor's degree—have become predominantly Democratic. Many people with postgraduate degrees are professionals, such as physicians, attorneys, and college instructors. Usually, a postgraduate degree is an occupational requirement for professionals.

Despite the recent popularity of the master of business administration (MBA) degree, businesspersons are more likely to have only a bachelor's degree or no degree at all. They are also much more likely to vote Republican.

In the 2016 primary elections, many observers remarked on the tendency of less-well-educated Republicans to support Donald Trump. Some even saw Trump as representing the white working class as a whole, using education as a marker for socioeconomic status. There are plenty of less-well-educated white Democrats, however. Such persons were more likely to vote for Democrat Bernie Sanders than any other candidate.

Economic Status. Family income is a strong predictor of economic liberalism or conservatism. Those with low incomes tend to favor government action to benefit the poor or to promote economic equality. Those with high incomes tend to oppose government intervention in the economy or to support it only when it benefits business. On political issues, therefore, the traditional political spectrum shown in Chapter 1, Table 1–1 is a useful tool. The rich often tend toward the right, and the poor often lean toward the left.

If we examine cultural as well as economic issues, however, the four-cornered ideological grid provided in Chapter 1, Figure 1–1 becomes important. It happens that upper-class voters are more likely to endorse cultural liberalism and lower-class individuals are more likely to favor cultural conservatism. Support for the right to have an abortion, for example, rises with income. It follows that libertarians—those who oppose government action on both economic and social issues—are concentrated among the wealthier members of the population. (Libertarians constitute the upper-right-hand corner of the grid in Figure 1–1 in Chapter 1.) Those who favor government action both to promote traditional moral values and to promote economic equality—economic liberals, cultural

Mario Tama/Getty Images

Image 6–6 Some sections of the U.S. have high levels of poverty, such as in Owsley County, Kentucky, where this auto mechanic lives. *How does family income influence feelings about government?*

conservatives—are concentrated among groups that are less well off. (This group fills up the lower-left-hand corner of the grid.) As you might conclude from the chapter-opening *What If . . .* feature, those who are economic liberals and cultural conservatives tend to lack political clout.

That said, it remains generally true that the higher a person's income, the more likely that person will be to vote Republican. Manual laborers, factory workers, and especially union members are more likely to vote Democratic. There are no hard-and-fast rules, however. Many very poor individuals are devoted Republicans, just as some extremely wealthy people support the Democratic Party.

Religious Denomination. Traditionally, scholars have examined the impact of religion on political attitudes by dividing the population into such categories as Protestant, Catholic, and Jewish. In recent decades, however, such a breakdown has become less valuable as a means of predicting someone's political preferences. It is true that Jewish voters, as they were in the past, are notably more liberal than members of other groups, on both economic and cultural issues. Persons reporting no religion are very liberal on social issues but have mixed economic views.

Protestants and non-Hispanic Catholics, however, have grown closer to each other politically in recent years. This represents something of a change—in the late 1800s and early 1900s, northern Protestants were distinctly more likely to vote Republican, and northern Catholics were more likely to vote Democratic. Even now, in a few parts of the country, Protestants and Catholics tend to line up against each other when choosing a political party.

Image 6–7 Three generations in a synagogue. *Do most Jewish voters prefer liberal or conservative candidates?*

Fuse/Getty Images

Religious Commitment and Beliefs. Today, two factors turn out to be major predictors of political attitudes among members of the various Christian denominations. One factor is the degree of religious commitment, as measured by such actions as regular churchgoing. The other is the degree to which the voter adheres to religious beliefs that (depending on the denomination) can be called conservative, evangelical, or fundamentalist. High scores on either factor are associated with cultural conservatism on political issues—that is, with beliefs that place a high value on social order. (See Chapter 1 for a discussion of the contrasting values of order and liberty.)

Voters who are more devout, regardless of their church affiliation, tend to vote Republican, while voters who are less devout are more often Democrats. In the 2012 presidential elections, for example, Protestants who attended church weekly cast 70 percent of their votes to Republican candidate Mitt Romney, compared with 55 percent of those who attended church less often. Among Catholics, there was a similar pattern: 57 percent of Catholics who attended church weekly voted for Romney, while 42 percent of Catholics who were not regular churchgoers voted for him. Exit polls following the 2014 congressional elections showed the same pattern. There is an exception to this trend: African Americans of all religious tendencies have been strongly supportive of Democrats.

The politics of white Protestant Americans who can be identified as holding evangelical or fundamentalist beliefs deserve special attention. Actually, a majority of American Protestants can be characterized as evangelical. Beliefs common to evangelicals include the ultimate authority of the Bible, the importance of a conversion experience (being "born again"), and that God's gift of salvation is limited to those who accept Christ. Not all evangelicals are politically conservative. Some are politically liberal, such as former Democratic presidents Jimmy Carter and Bill Clinton.

Fundamentalists are a subset of evangelicals who believe in a number of doctrines not held by all evangelicals. In particular, fundamentalists believe in biblical inerrancy—that is, that every word of the Bible is literally true. In politics, fundamentalists are notably more conservative than other evangelicals. Liberal fundamentalists are rare indeed.[5]

Race and Ethnicity. African Americans, on average, are somewhat conservative on certain cultural issues, such as gay rights and abortion. Yet they tend to be more liberal than whites on social-welfare matters, civil liberties, and even foreign policy. African Americans voted principally for Republicans until Democrat Franklin Roosevelt's New Deal in the 1930s. Since then, they have largely identified with the Democratic Party. Indeed, Democratic presidential candidates have received, on average, more than 80 percent of the African American vote since 1956. Barack Obama's support among African Americans was overwhelming, and the same was true of Hillary Clinton.

Most Asian American groups lean toward the Democrats, although Vietnamese Americans are strongly Republican. Most Vietnamese Americans left Vietnam because of the Communist victory in the Vietnam War, and their strong anticommunism translates into conservative politics.

Muslim American immigrants and their descendants make up an interesting category.[6] In 2000, a majority of Muslim Americans of Middle Eastern ancestry voted for Republican George W. Bush because they shared his cultural conservatism. By 2012, the issues of Muslim civil liberties and discrimination against Muslims had turned Islamic voters into one of the nation's most Democratic blocs.

The Hispanic Vote. The diversity among Hispanic Americans has resulted in differing political behavior. The majority of Hispanic Americans vote Democratic. Cuban Americans, however, are often Republican. Most Cuban Americans left Cuba because of Fidel Castro's Communist regime. As in the example of the Vietnamese, anticommunism leads to political conservatism. By 2016, however, increasing numbers of young Cuban Americans were supporting the Democrats.

In 2004, Republican presidential candidate George W. Bush may have received almost 40 percent of the Latino vote. In 2008, however, Barack Obama won more than two-thirds of the Latino vote. Why did Latino support for the Republicans fall so greatly? In a word: immigration. Bush favored a comprehensive immigration reform that would have granted unauthorized immigrants a path to citizenship. Most Republicans in Congress refused to support Bush on this issue. The harsh rhetoric of some Republicans convinced many Latinos that the Republicans were hostile to Hispanic interests.

Image 6—8 A Latino woman and her eighteen-month-old daughter march to the White House in support of immigration reform. *How is the daughter acquiring political values by attending a rally with her mother?*

---

5. Douglas A. Sweeney, *The American Evangelical Story: A History of the Movement.* (Grand Rapids, Mich.: Baker Academic, 2005).

6. At least one-third of U.S. Muslims actually are African Americans whose ancestors have been in this country for a long time. In terms of political preferences, African American Muslims are more likely to resemble other African Americans than to resemble Muslim immigrants from the Middle East.

gender gap

The difference between the percentage of women who vote for a particular candidate and the percentage of men who vote for the candidate.

In 2012, according to one poll, Obama's support among Hispanics reached 75 percent, an all-time high. At the same time, Hispanics were a growing share of the voting population—10 percent, up from 9 percent in 2008 and 8 percent in 2004. These trends were widely seen as a serious problem for the Republican Party. Following the 2012 elections, some Republicans advocated a more welcoming line toward unauthorized immigrants in hopes of winning Hispanic support. Most Republicans rejected this proposal, however. In 2016, Republicans nominated Donald Trump as their presidential candidate, and Trump's hostility toward illegal immigrants may alienate Latinos from the Republicans for years to come.

The Gender Gap. Women won the right to vote in all states in 1920, and all the way through the 1960 elections they gave somewhat more support to Republicans than men did. From 1964 through 1976, women did not demonstrate a clear partisan preference. Beginning in 1980, however, with the election of Ronald Reagan, scholars began to detect a **gender gap**. Women were now favoring the Democrats, as you can see in Figure 6–3. In 2016, 54 percent of women voted for Democrat Hillary Clinton, compared with 41 percent of men, a gap of 13 percentage points. Clinton, of course, was the first female major-party candidate for president in U.S. history, and Republican Donald Trump was famous for his rude remarks toward women.

Women's attitudes also appear to differ from those of their male counterparts on a range of issues other than presidential preferences. They are much more likely than men to oppose capital punishment and the use of force abroad. Studies also have shown that women are more concerned about risks to the environment, more supportive of social welfare, and more in agreement with extending civil rights to gay men and lesbians than are men.

Geographic Region. Finally, where you live can influence your political attitudes. In 2012, many commentators suggested that the white working class was hostile to Obama. This conclusion was not entirely accurate. In a pre-election poll by the Public Religion Research Institute, neither Obama nor Romney held a statistically significant lead among white working class voters in the East, Midwest, or West. In the South, however, Romney's margin was 62 percent to 22 percent (16 percent were undecided). Regardless of region, opposition to

---

Figure 6–3 The Gender Gap in Presidential Elections

The gender gap is the difference between the percentage of women and the percentage of men voting for a given candidate, conventionally the Democrat. From 1980 on, women have always given more of their votes to the Democrats than men do. *Why might men be more attracted to Republicans?*

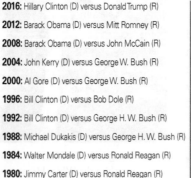
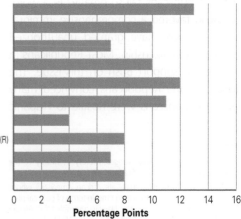

2016: Hillary Clinton (D) versus Donald Trump (R)
2012: Barack Obama (D) versus Mitt Romney (R)
2008: Barack Obama (D) versus John McCain (R)
2004: John Kerry (D) versus George W. Bush (R)
2000: Al Gore (D) versus George W. Bush (R)
1996: Bill Clinton (D) versus Bob Dole (R)
1992: Bill Clinton (D) versus George H. W. Bush (R)
1988: Michael Dukakis (D) versus George H. W. Bush (R)
1984: Walter Mondale (D) versus Ronald Reagan (R)
1980: Jimmy Carter (D) versus Ronald Reagan (R)

Percentage Points

Source: Center for American Women and Politics

Obama was strongest among those who saw themselves culturally as Southerners—that is, as persons who identified with the losing side in the American Civil War.

The split between the city and the country is almost as important as the one between the North and the South. In 2012, Obama did far better than Romney in large cities. The northern states that Romney carried were often heavily rural.

Election-Specific Factors

Factors such as perception of the candidates and issue preferences may have an effect on how people vote in particular elections. Candidates and issues can change greatly, and voting behavior can therefore change as well.

Perception of the Candidates. A candidate's image seems to be important in a voter's choice, especially for a presidential candidate. To some extent, voter attitudes toward candidates are based on emotions (such as trust) rather than on any judgment about experience or policy. In some years, voters have been attracted to a candidate who appeared to share their concerns and worries. In other years, voters have sought a candidate who

Image 6–9 Florida women support Senator Ted Cruz (R., Tex.) for president. The rally took place shortly before the Florida presidential primaries. *What influence does geographical region have on political preferences?*

appeared to have high integrity and honesty. Voters have been especially attracted to these candidates in elections that follow a major scandal, such as Richard Nixon's Watergate scandal (1972–1974) or Bill Clinton's sex scandal (1998–1999). Perceptions of candidates were especially important in 2016. In that year, Hillary Clinton suffered from a strong perception that she was untrustworthy. For his part, Donald Trump's negative ratings in polls set new records. It appeared that many voters would have to decide which candidate they disliked the least.

Issue Preferences. Issues make a difference in presidential and congressional elections. Although personality or image factors may be very persuasive, most voters have some notion of how the candidates differ on basic issues or at least know which candidates want a change in the direction of government policy.

Historically, economic concerns have been among the most powerful influences on public opinion. When the economy is doing well, it is very difficult for a challenger, especially at the presidential level, to defeat the incumbent. In contrast, inflation, unemployment, or high interest rates are likely to work to the disadvantage of the incumbent.

Measuring Public Opinion

Learning Outcome **3:**

Describe the characteristics of a scientific opinion poll, and list some of the problems pollsters face in obtaining accurate results.

In a democracy, people express their opinions in a variety of ways, as mentioned in this chapter's introduction. One of the most common means of gathering and measuring public opinion on specific issues is through the use of **opinion polls.**

The History of Opinion Polls

During the 1800s, certain American newspapers and magazines spiced up their political coverage by conducting face-to-face polls or mail surveys of their readers' opinions. In the early twentieth century, the magazine *Literary Digest* mailed large numbers of questionnaires to individuals, many of whom were its own subscribers, to determine their political opinions. From 1916 to 1932, more than 70 percent of the magazine's election predictions were accurate.

opinion poll

A method of systematically questioning a small, selected sample of respondents who are deemed representative of the total population.

In 1936, however, the magazine predicted that Republican Alfred Landon would defeat Democrat Franklin D. Roosevelt in the presidential race. Landon won in only two states. A major problem was that in 1936, several years into the Great Depression, the *Digest*'s subscribers were considerably wealthier than the average American. In other words, they did not accurately represent all of the voters in the U.S. population.

Several newcomers to the public opinion poll industry accurately predicted Roosevelt's landslide victory. These newcomers are still active in the poll-taking industry today: the Gallup poll of George Gallup and the Roper poll founded by Elmo Roper. Gallup and Roper, along with Archibald Crossley, developed the modern polling techniques of market research. Using personal interviews with small samples of selected voters (fewer than two thousand), they showed that they could predict with relative accuracy the behavior of the total voting population.

Sampling Techniques

How can interviewing fewer than two thousand voters tell us what tens of millions of voters will do? Clearly, it is necessary that the sample of individuals be representative of all voters in the population.

The Principle of Randomness. The most important principle in sampling is randomness. Every person should have a known chance, and in particular an *equal chance,* of being sampled. If sampling follows this principle, then a small sample should be representative of the whole group, both in demographic characteristics (age, religion, race, region, and the like) and in opinions. The ideal way to sample the voting population of the United States would be to put all voter names into a jar—or a computer file—and randomly sample, say, two thousand of them. Because this is too costly and inefficient, pollsters have developed other ways to obtain good samples. One technique is simply to randomly select telephone numbers and interview the respective households. This technique used to produce a relatively accurate sample at a low cost.

The Statistical Nature of Polling. Universally, when the results of an opinion poll are announced, the findings are reported as specific numbers. A poll might find, for example, that 10 percent of those surveyed approve of the job performance of Congress. Such precise figures can mislead you as to the essential nature of polling. In reality, it makes more sense to consider the results of a particular survey question as a range of numbers, not a single integer. That would mean that the question about Congress's job performance yielded an answer that fell somewhere between 7 percent and 13 percent. The reported figure of 10 percent is only the midpoint of the possible spread—the most probable result. If we had been able to question all members of the public, what are the chances that they would give Congress a 10 percent rating? The chances are not high. Even if the pollster in this case employed the best possible practices, the

Image 6–10 Polling expert Nate Silver (center) with his colleagues Michah Cohen and Harry Enton. Silver was almost alone in saying that Trump could win despite the polls. His Fivethirtyeight blog is now sponsored by ESPN. *In what ways do politics resemble sports?*

odds are better than 50-50 that the true answer is not exactly 10 percent, but some other number in the 7–13 percent range.

Sampling Error. Reputable polling firms report the margin of error associated with their results. The results of a carefully conducted poll that surveys a large number of respondents—say, two thousand people—might have a 95 percent chance of falling within a 3 percent margin of error. The 95 percent figure is an industry standard. What this means, however, is that the pollster believes that any given poll result has a 5 percent chance of landing four or more percentage points away from the true answer, which we would get if we really could interview everyone. In the example of the question about Congress, there is a 5 percent chance—one chance in twenty—that the approval rating is actually below 7 percent or above 13 percent.

These variations are called **sampling error.** They follow from the fact that the poll taker is examining a sample and not the entire population. Sampling error is one reason that knowledgeable poll watchers disregard small variations in poll results. Gallup, for example, polls the public on its approval of the president's job performance every day. Such continuous polls are known as *tracking polls*. Let us say that on Monday, the tracking poll shows that the president has a 45 percent approval rating. On Tuesday, it is 47 percent, on Wednesday 46 percent, and on Thursday 43 percent. Was the president really more popular on Tuesday and Wednesday? Almost certainly not. These variations are simply artifacts of the polling process—so much "statistical noise."

The Difficulty of Obtaining Accurate Results

Reputable polling organizations devote a substantial amount of effort to ensuring that their samples are truly random. If they succeed, then the accuracy of their results should be limited only by sampling error. Unfortunately, obtaining a completely random sample of the population is difficult. Poll takers must consider that women are more likely to answer the telephone than men. Some kinds of people, such as students and low-income individuals, are relatively hard to contact.

Weighting the Sample. Polling firms address this problem of obtaining a true random sample by weighting their samples. That is, they correct for differences between the sample and the public by adding extra "weight" to the responses of underrepresented groups. For example, 20 percent of the respondents in a survey might state that they are evangelical Christians. Based on other sources of information, however, the poll taker believes that the true share of evangelicals in the target population is 25 percent. Therefore, the responses of the evangelical respondents receive extra weight so that they make up 25 percent of the reported result.

It is relatively easy to correct a sample for well-known demographic characteristics, such as education, gender, race, ethnicity, religion, and geography. It is much harder—and more risky—to adjust for political ideology, partisan preference, or likelihood of voting. The formulas that firms use to weight their responses are typically trade secrets and are not disclosed to the public or the press.

House Effects. One consequence of the use of secret in-house weighting schemes is that the results reported by one polling firm may

The New Yorker Collection/The Cartoon Bank

Image 6–11 *"No, I don't want to know what my approval rating is."*

house effect

In public opinion polling, an effect in which one polling organization's results consistently differ from those reported by other poll takers.

systematically differ from those reported by another. Pollster A might consistently rate the chances of Republican candidates as 2 percentage points higher than does pollster B. This could happen because pollster A thinks that turnout among Republican voters will be high, whereas pollster B predicts a lower turnout. Alternatively, pollster A may simply believe that there are more Republicans in the electorate. A consistent difference in polling results between firms is known as a **house effect.** (*House* here means the organization or firm, as when referring to casinos.) House effects are measured by comparing a firm's results with the average results of all other poll takers.

Some polling organizations have ties to one of the major political parties. Not surprisingly, many such firms have house effects that favor their parties. Such relationships do not always exist, however. Some party-linked pollsters exhibit no discernible house effect, and some firms that are known for their independence do demonstrate such an effect. Further, a house effect does not mean that a firm's results are in error. It could be noticing something important that its rivals have missed.

How Accurate Are the Results? We show the historical accuracy record of Gallup, perhaps the most famous pollster, in Figure 6–4. Despite all of the practical difficulties involved in poll taking, the major polling organizations have usually enjoyed a good record in predicting the outcome of presidential contests. Many major firms have predicted the outcome of recent presidential elections with considerable accuracy. Some poll takers, however, reported results that were embarrassingly inaccurate. Figure 6–5 shows the 2016 predictions of several prominent pollsters.

Additional Problems with Polls

Public opinion polls are snapshots of opinions and preferences at a specific moment in time and as expressed in response to a specific question. Given that definition, it is fairly easy to understand situations in which the polls are wrong. For example, opinion polls leading up to the 1980 presidential elections showed President Jimmy Carter defeating challenger Ronald Reagan. Only a few analysts noted the large number of "undecided" respondents a week before the elections. Those voters shifted massively to Reagan at the last minute, and Reagan won the election.

The famous photo of Harry Truman showing the front page of the newspaper that declared his defeat in the 1948 presidential election is another example of the potential weakness of polling. Again, the poll that predicted his defeat was taken more than a week before Election Day. Truman won the election with 49.9 percent of the vote.

Figure 6–4 Gallup Poll Accuracy Record

This chart compares the percentage of the vote received by the winning presidential candidate with Gallup's final prediction. *Is Gallup still the "gold standard" among poll takers? Why or why not?*

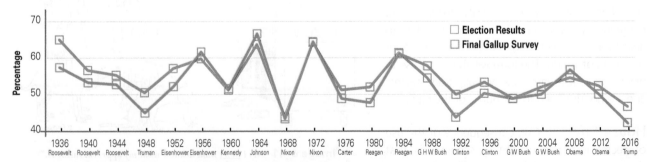

Sources: *The Gallup Poll Monthly,* November 1992; *Time,* November 21, 1994; *The Wall Street Journal,* November 6, 1996; and authors' updates. Gallup did not track the presidential race in 2016—the final survey number that year is the Real Clear Politics polling average.

Poll Questions. It makes sense to expect that the results of a poll will reflect the questions that are asked. Depending on what question is asked, voters could be said either to support a particular proposal or to oppose it. One of the problems with many polls is the yes/no answer format. For example, suppose that a poll question asks, "Do you support President Obama's policies toward Syria?" Respondents who have a complicated view of these events, as many people do, have no way of indicating their true position because "yes" and "no" are the only possible answers.

How a question is phrased can change the polling outcome dramatically. The Roper polling organization once asked a double-negative question that was very hard to understand: "Does it seem possible or does it seem impossible to you that the Nazi extermination of the Jews never happened?" The survey results showed that 20 percent of Americans seemed to doubt that the Holocaust ever occurred. When the Roper organization rephrased the question more clearly, the percentage of doubters dropped to less than 1 percent.

Respondents' answers are also influenced by the order in which questions are asked, by the possible answers from which the respondents are allowed to choose, and, in some cases, by their interaction with the interviewer. To a certain extent, people try to please the interviewer.

Figure 6–5 Donald Trump's Predicted Margin of Victory over Hillary Clinton in the 2016 Presidential Elections

The eleven polls on this chart were conducted immediately before the elections. Only one pollster got the outcome right. (Note that Clinton narrowly carried the popular vote.) *Why might Trump have done better than many pollsters predicted?*

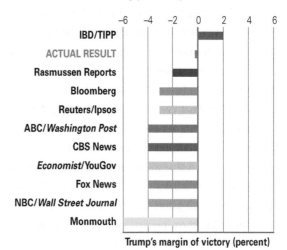

Trump's margin of victory (percent)

Source: RealClearPolitics blog. Popular vote as of November 9, 2016.

Unscientific and Fraudulent Polls. A perennial issue is the promotion of surveys that are unscientific or even fraudulent. All too often, a magazine or website asks its readers to respond to a question—and then publishes the answers as if they were based on a scientifically chosen random sample. Other news media may then publicize the survey as if it were a poll taken by such reliable teams as Gallup, CBS and the *New York Times,* or the *Wall Street Journal* and NBC. Critical consumers should watch out for surveys with self-selected respondents and other types of skewed samples. These so-called polls may be used to deliberately mislead the public.

In recent years, polling experts have made a number of allegations of outright polling fraud. In these cases, so-called polling firms have been accused of reporting results

Image 6–12 President Harry Truman holds up the front page of the *Chicago Daily Tribune* issue that predicted his defeat on the basis of a Gallup poll. Truman, of course, defeated Dewey. *Why would a newspaper today be unlikely to make such an inaccurate prediction and put it on newsstands?*

AP Images/Byron Rollins

Election 2016

Polling Accuracy in the 2016 Elections

Note from Figure 6–5 that almost all poll takers missed the presidential outcome in 2016. Responses crowded around a Hillary Clinton advantage of 3 to 4 percentage points. Such unanimity suggests that some pollsters might be engaged in "herding," that is, adjusting their assumptions to produce a result closer to what everyone else is reporting. With so many polls off, it was inevitable that poll aggregators were off as well. Aggregators average large numbers of polls in the belief that the average will have more predictive power than any single poll, usually a sound expectation. What differentiated the aggregators was the degree of certainty they claimed for their predictions. Sam Wang of the Princeton Election Consortium put Clinton's odds of victory at a stunning 99 percent. Only one aggregator sounded a

note of caution. Nate Silver's Fivethirtyeight blog listed Trump's chances at almost one in three. Silver warned of possible industry-wide polling error. His team took a lot of guff for this uncertainty, but they were right. A one-in-three chance will materialize, after all, one-third of the time. Why were the polls off? A close look shows that the state-level polls were fairly accurate in most parts of the country. The exception was in a block of Midwestern states—precisely the region that handed Trump his victory. Here, pollsters underestimated the turnout by Trump supporters. Trump drew many new believers into the political process. Poll takers use "likely voter" screens to weed out respondents who are unlikely to actually vote. Such screens usually improve accuracy, but in 2016 they did the reverse.

without ever conducting any actual surveys. The numbers have been simply made up, out of thin air. After a challenge by polling experts, one such company ceased issuing polls and quietly disappeared. Another poll taker was sued by its largest customer, a major political blog. The blogger claimed that the pollster was making up its results. (The case was settled out of court.)

Push Polls. Some campaigns have used "push polls," in which the respondents are given misleading information in the questions asked to persuade them to vote against a candidate. The practice has spread throughout all levels of U.S. politics—local, state, and federal. In 1996, in a random survey of forty-five candidates, researchers found that thirty-five of them claimed to have been victimized by negative push-polling techniques used by their opponents.[7] Now even advocacy groups, as well as candidates for political offices, are using push polls. Push polling was prevalent during the congressional campaigns in 2014, and in the 2012 and 2016 presidential and congressional campaigns.

Technology and Opinion Polls

Public opinion polling is based on scientific principles, particularly the principle of randomness. Today, technological advances allow polls to be taken over the Internet, but serious questions have been raised about the ability of pollsters to obtain truly random samples

---

7. Karl T. Feld, "When Push Comes to Shove: A Polling Industry Call to Arms," *Public Perspective*, September/October 2001, p. 38.

using this medium. The same was said not long ago when another technological break-through changed public opinion polling—the telephone.

The Advent of Telephone Polling. During the 1970s, telephone polling began to predominate over in-person polling. Obviously, telephone polling is less expensive than sending interviewers to poll respondents in their homes. Additionally, telephone interviewers do not have to worry about safety problems, which is particularly important for interviewers working in high-crime areas. Finally, telephone interviews can be conducted relatively quickly. They allow politicians or the media to poll one evening and report the results the next day.

In recent years, many polling firms that rely on the telephone have begun employing automatic scripts read by a machine, the so-called *robopolls*. Polls of this type are much cheaper and easier to set up than traditional polls using live interviewers. Many observers also believe, however, that robopolls are substantially less accurate than traditional surveys.

Telephone Polling Problems. Somewhat ironically, the success of telephone polling has created major problems for the technique. The telemarketing industry in general has become so pervasive that people increasingly refuse to respond to telephone polls. More than 40 percent of households now use either caller ID or some other form of call screening. This has greatly reduced the number of households that polling organizations can reach.

For most telephone polls, the nonresponse rate has increased to as high as 90 percent. Such a high nonresponse rate undercuts confidence in the survey results. In most cases, polling only 10 percent of those on the list cannot lead to a random sample. Even more important for politicians is the fact that polling organizations are not required to report their response rates.

The Cell Phone Problem. An additional problem for telephone polling is the popularity of cell phones. Cellular telephone numbers are not listed in telephone directories. Furthermore, pollsters cannot legally use robopolling to contact cell phone users. Also, individuals with cell phones may be located anywhere, thus confounding attempts to reach people in a particular area. More people, and especially younger Americans, choose to use only a cell phone and do not have a landline at all. These individuals are ignored by many polls.

A final problem for telephone pollsters that results from new technologies: many savvy Internet users now rely on Skype and other voice-over-Internet services for their telephone calls. Skype allows users to see each other through the camera built into modern

Image 6–13 College fraternity members wait to meet Republican presidential candidate Donald Trump at a campaign rally in Albany, New York. *How might young Republicans view issues differently from older ones?*

laptop computers, tablets, and cell phones. Currently, *no* polling firm has discovered a way to survey voice-over-Internet users.

Enter Internet Polling. Obviously, Internet polling is not done on a one-on-one basis, because there is no voice communication. In spite of the potential problems, the Harris Poll, a widely respected national polling organization, conducts online polls. This organization believes that proper weighting of the results will achieve the equivalent of a random-sample poll.

Public opinion experts, however, argue that the Harris Poll procedure violates the mathematical basis of random sampling. Even so, the Internet population is looking more like the rest of America: almost as many women go online as men (84 percent of women and 85 percent of men), 80 percent of African American adults are online, and so are 80 percent of Hispanics (compared with 97 percent of non-Hispanic whites).[8]

<table>
<tr><td>

Learning Outcome **4:**

Consider the effect that public opinion may have on the political process.

</td><td>

Public Opinion and the Political Process

Public opinion affects the political process in many ways. Politicians, whether in office or in the midst of a campaign, see public opinion as important to their careers. The president, members of Congress, governors, and other elected officials realize that strong support by the public as expressed in opinion polls is a source of power in dealing with other politicians. It is more difficult for a senator to say no to the president if the president is immensely popular and if polls show approval of the president's policies. Public opinion also helps political candidates identify voters' most important concerns and may help them shape their campaigns successfully.

</td></tr>
</table>

Political Culture and Public Opinion

Americans are divided into a multitude of ethnic, religious, regional, and political subgroups. Given the diversity of American society and the wide range of opinions contained within it, how is it that the political process continues to function without falling into chaos?

One explanation is rooted in the concept of the American political culture, which can be described as a set of attitudes and ideas about the nation and the government.

Why should you care about **PUBLIC OPINION?**

Knowing what makes a poll accurate is important if you ever plan to participate in politics, even at the local level. Successful participation depends on knowing what your fellow citizens are thinking. If large numbers of other people agree with you that a particular policy needs to be changed, there may be a good chance that the policy can actually be altered. If almost no one agrees with you on a particular issue, there may be no point in trying to change policy immediately. The best you can do is to try to sway the opinions of others, in the hope that someday enough people will agree with you to make policy changes possible.

As discussed in Chapter 1, our political culture is widely shared by Americans of many different backgrounds. To some extent, it consists of symbols, such as the American flag, the Liberty Bell, and the Statue of Liberty. The elements of our political culture also include certain shared beliefs about the most important values in the American political system, including liberty, equality, and property.

The political culture provides a general environment of support for the political system. If the people share certain beliefs about the system and a reservoir of good feeling exists toward the institutions of government, the nation will be better able to weather periods of crisis. The political culture also helps Americans evaluate their government's performance. We examine one measure of popular attitudes toward government performance in this chapter's *Consider the Source* feature.

political trust

The degree to which individuals express trust in the government and political institutions, usually measured through a specific series of survey questions.

8. Pew Internet and American Life Project, August 2013 survey.

Consider the source

Political Trust

Poll takers have used a variety of questions to measure **political trust,** the degree to which individuals express trust in political institutions. One of these is whether the respondent is satisfied with "the way things are going in the United States." Figure 6–6 shows the responses to this question over time.

During the successful presidency of Republican Ronald Reagan (1981–1989), satisfaction levels rose from a fairly dismal 20 percent range to around 50 percent. Republican George H. W. Bush (1989–1993) enjoyed high levels of satisfaction until 1992, when rates fell back to the 20 percent range. This fall reflected the economic problems and other difficulties that handed the presidency to Democrat Bill Clinton.

Clinton's two terms appear to have been mostly a success, as satisfaction levels rose to as high as 70 percent. Under Republican George W. Bush (2001–2009), however, satisfaction levels slowly fell. In October 2008, at the peak of the crisis in the financial industry, satisfaction rates bottomed out at an unprecedented 7 percent. They have since recovered. Yet with more than two-thirds of Americans still saying that they were dissatisfied with "the way things are going," it is not surprising that outsiders such as Donald Trump and Bernie Sanders did well in the 2016 primary elections.

The Source: Gallup

The Gallup Poll is the most famous polling organization and one of the oldest. It has not always been among the most accurate, however. For example, in the 2012 presidential elections, Gallup seriously overestimated voter turnout among Republicans and underestimated Democratic turnout. Gallup made major corrections at the last minute when it became clear that its models were inaccurate but still predicted that Republican Mitt Romney would win. He did not. Still, Gallup has one major advantage over other pollsters. It has been asking Americans a standardized set of questions for decades, as shown in Figure 6–6. Other firms simply can't match this historical depth.

For Critical Analysis

▶ **Satisfaction hit a minor peak of 33 percent on Election Day 2012, briefly enough that it is not fully reflected in the figure. Why might satisfaction have been greater on that day?**

Figure 6–6 Political Satisfaction Trend

Question: In general, are you satisfied or dissatisfied with the way things are going in the United States at this time?

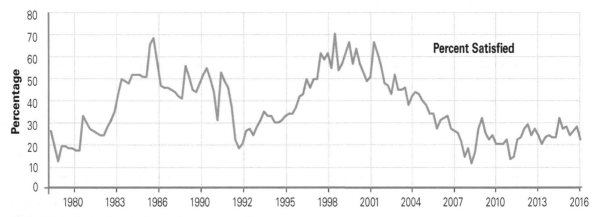

Source: Gallup polls, 1979 through 2016. Percentages are quarterly averages.

Public Opinion about Government

A vital component of public opinion in the United States is the considerable ambivalence with which the public regards many major national institutions. Figure 6–7 shows trends from 1993 to 2014 in opinion polls asking respondents how much confidence they had in the institutions listed. Over the years, military and religious organizations have ranked highest. Note, however, the decline in confidence in churches in 2002 following sex-abuse allegations against a number of Catholic priests. The public has consistently had more confidence in the military than in any of the other institutions shown in Figure 6–7. In 2002 and 2003, confidence in the military soared even higher, most likely because of the military's role in the war on terrorism.

Confidence in Other Institutions. The United States Supreme Court and the public schools have scored well over time. Less confidence is expressed in television, organized labor, and big business. From 2007 on, confidence in Congress almost disappeared. By 2015, the figure was down to 8 percent, close to an all-time low.

At times, popular confidence in all institutions may rise or fall, reflecting optimism or pessimism about the general state of the nation. For example, a Gallup poll in 2008 following the onset of the Great Recession showed that the level of national satisfaction with the state of the nation had dropped to 14 percent—the lowest rating since 1992.

The Most Important National Problems. Although people may not have much confidence in government institutions, they nonetheless turn to government to solve what they perceive to be the major problems facing the country. Table 6–2, which is based on Gallup polls conducted from the years 1992 to 2016, shows that the leading problems have changed over time. The public tends to emphasize problems that are immediate and that have been the subject of many stories in the media. When coverage of a particular problem increases suddenly, the public is more likely to see that as the most important problem. Thus, the fluctuations in the "most important problem" cited in Table 6–2 may, at times, be attributed to media agenda setting. In other years, however, the nation's leading problem has been so obvious that media attention is a minor factor. The Great Recession, which began in December 2007, is one example.

Figure 6–7 Confidence in Institutions Trend

Question: I am going to read a list of institutions in American society. Please tell me how much confidence you, yourself, have in each one: a great deal, quite a lot, some, or very little?

Why might the Supreme Court and public schools be at least moderately popular?

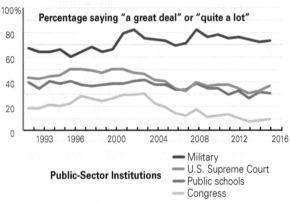

Public-Sector Institutions
— Military
— U.S. Supreme Court
— Public schools
— Congress

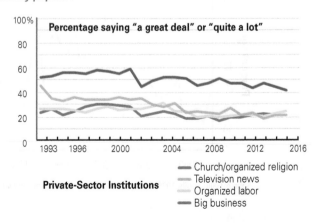

Private-Sector Institutions
— Church/organized religion
— Television news
— Organized labor
— Big business

Source: Gallup polls over time.

Table 6–2 Most Important Problem Trend, 1992 to Present

2016	Government, economy	2003	Terrorism, economy
2015	Government, economy	2002	Terrorism, economy
2014	Government, economy	2001	Economy, education
2013	Economy, unemployment	2000	Morals, family decline
2012	Economy, unemployment	1999	Crime, violence
2011	Economy, unemployment	1998	Crime, violence
2010	Economy, unemployment	1997	Crime, violence
2009	Economy	1996	Budget deficit
2008	Economy, war in Iraq	1995	Crime, violence
2007	War in Iraq, health care	1994	Crime, violence, health care
2006	War in Iraq, terrorism	1993	Health care, budget deficit
2005	War in Iraq	1992	Unemployment, budget deficit
2004	War in Iraq, economy		

Source: Gallup polls, 1992 through 2016. This poll is usually conducted in January.

Public Opinion and Policymaking

If public opinion is important for democracy, are policymakers really responsive to public opinion? A classic study by political scientists Benjamin I. Page and Robert Y. Shapiro in the early 1990s suggested that in fact the national government is somewhat responsive to the public's demands for action.[9] More recently, scholars have contended that these studies overstate the effect of public opinion on public policy, in part because on many of the issues taken up by policymakers, the public has no clear opinions.[10]

Setting Limits on Government Action. Although opinion polls cannot give exact guidance on what the government should do in a specific instance, the opinions measured in polls may set an informal limit on government action. For example, consider the controversial issue of unauthorized immigration. A majority of Americans are moderates on this issue. They disapprove of illegal immigration and believe that undocumented immigrants have violated the rules. At the same time, they express sympathy for unauthorized immigrants. Yet sizable groups of people express very intense feelings on this topic. Some are outraged at the number of unauthorized immigrants in the country. Others are passionate about the suffering caused by deportations. Politicians and political party platforms take firm positions on this issue.

The strong words, however, are not matched with strong actions. Changes to the nation's immigration laws would require a degree of consensus that does not exist. At a minimum, new legislation would require the support of a majority in both chambers of Congress, plus the support of the president. A government divided between the parties

---

9. Benjamin I. Page and Robert Y. Shapiro, *The Rational Public: Fifty Years of Trends in Americans' Policy Preferences* (Chicago: University of Chicago Press, 1992).

10. Paul Burstein, "Why Estimates of the Impact of Public Opinion on Public Policy Are Too High: Empirical and Theoretical Implications," *Social Forces*, Vol. 84, No. 4, June 2006, pp. 2273–2289.

has made such consensus impossible. In this example, as in many others, public opinion does not make public policy. Rather, it leads to inaction. Only if one political party were to gain control of the presidency and the Congress are we likely to see changes to the immigration laws.

The Public versus the Policymakers. To what degree should public opinion influence policymaking? It would appear that members of the public view this issue differently than policy leaders do. Polls indicate that whereas a majority of the public feel that public opinion should have a great deal of influence on policy, a majority of policy leaders hold the opposite position. Why would a majority of policy leaders not want to be strongly influenced by public opinion? One answer to this question is that public opinion polls can provide only a limited amount of guidance to policymakers.

The Limits of Polling. Policymakers cannot always be guided by opinion polls. In the end, politicians must make their own choices. When they do so, their choices necessarily involve trade-offs. If politicians vote for increased spending to improve education, for example, by necessity fewer resources are available for other worthy projects. Moreover, to make an informed policy choice requires an understanding not only of the policy area but also of the consequences of any given choice. Public opinion polls very rarely ensure that those polled have such information.

Finally, government decisions cannot be made simply by adding up individual desires. Politicians regularly engage in "horse trading" with each other. Politicians also know that they cannot satisfy every desire of every constituent. Therefore, each politician attempts to maximize the net benefits to his or her constituents, while keeping within the limits of whatever the politician believes the government can afford.

A Policy Example: Contraception Insurance

One policy issue that demonstrates the limits of public opinion first surfaced in 2012. Should employers be required to include coverage for birth control methods—contraception—in the insurance plans offered to employees? Under the Affordable Care Act, it was left to the executive branch to define which medical services must be covered by qualifying plans. The Obama administration ruled that religious bodies such as churches that opposed birth control did not need to pay for insurance plans that covered contraception. Hospitals and schools owned or controlled by churches, however, would have to provide coverage like all other employers.

The Controversy. The Obama ruling was denounced by religious bodies, including the Catholic Church, that oppose contraception and also control hospitals and colleges. Defenders of the ruling argued that exempting religiously owned hospitals and schools from the requirement would mean that employers could force their own religious principles on their employees. In the end, the government came up with a compromise: contraception would be covered by insurance, but religiously controlled institutions would not have to pay for the coverage. Some institutions accepted this plan, but the Catholic bishops and a number of Catholic institutions did not.

The Supreme Court Addresses the Issue. The controversy resulted in two major Supreme Court cases. The first did not deal directly with the question of religiously controlled institutions. Rather, the issue was whether a family-owned corporation could claim rights similar to those of a religiously controlled institution. In *Burwell v. Hobby Lobby* (2014), the Court found that the Hobby Lobby chain of stores could in fact obtain exemption from paying for certain types of contraception that the owners rejected on religious grounds.[11]

The Court took up the rights of religiously controlled institutions in 2016. The Little Sisters of the Poor, an order of Catholic nuns, runs a number of nursing homes for the elderly. The order argued that its religious liberty was infringed in two ways: it had to claim exemption on an official form, and even though it did not pay for birth control services, its insurance policies still covered them. The Court was closely divided on the merits of this case. In May 2016, it sent the case back to the lower courts in the hope that the parties to the suit could reach a compromise.[12]

Public Opinion and the Controversy. Public opinion on this dispute was split. A major question was whether the issue at stake was religious freedom—or the right of women to reproductive health care. An initial CBS News/*New York Times* poll asked whether insurance plans of religiously affiliated institutions should be required to cover contraception. Respondents supported coverage by 61 percent to 31 percent. One month later, a second poll added the language "opt out based on religious and moral objections." This time, respondents agreed by 57 percent to 36 percent that the institutions should be able to opt out.

These differing survey results emphasize the importance of **framing.** The public response to a particular issue may depend largely on how the question is framed—in this example, whether the issue is framed as a question of women's health rights or a question of religious freedom. Indeed, the contraception insurance issue soon became a political battle to determine which frame would predominate.

---

11. 134 S.Ct. 2751 (2014).
12. *Zubik v. Burwell*, 578 U.S. ___ (2016).

framing

Establishing the context of a polling question or a media report. Framing can mean fitting events into a familiar story or activating preconceived beliefs.

Image 6–14 Catholic nuns often run schools and hospitals. *Should those institutions be required to offer contraception as part of their employees' health care plans?*

How you can make a difference

As a critical consumer, you need to be aware of what makes one set of public opinion poll results valid and other results useless or even dangerously misleading.

- Pay attention only to opinion polls that are based on scientific, or random, samples. In these samples, a known probability is used to select each person interviewed.

- Do not give credence to the results of opinion polls that consist of shopping-mall interviews or the like. The main problem with this kind of opinion taking is that not everyone has an equal chance of being in the mall when the interview is conducted. Also, it is almost certain that the people in the mall are not a reasonable cross section of a community's entire population.

- Pay attention as well to how people were contacted for the poll—by mail, by telephone, in person in their homes, or in some other way. Because of their lower cost, polling firms

have turned more and more to "robocalls"—automated telephone interviews. This method can produce accurate results, but it has its disadvantages—as discussed earlier in this chapter.

- Results from mailed questionnaires should usually be disregarded. Only a small percentage of people send them back. Also, when viewers or listeners tuned in to television or radio shows are encouraged to call in their opinions to an 800 telephone number, the polling results are meaningless.

- Users of the Internet also have an easy way to make their views known. Only people with access to the Internet will be able to respond, however, and that group may not be representative of the general public.

KEY TERMS

agenda setting **154**
consensus **151**
divided opinion **152**
Fairness Doctrine **155**
framing **175**

gender gap **162**
generational effect **155**
house effect **166**
media **154**
opinion leader **154**

opinion poll **163**
peer group **154**
political socialization **152**
political trust **170**
public opinion **151**

sampling error **165**
socioeconomic status **157**

CHAPTER SUMMARY

Learning Outcome 1 Public opinion is the aggregate of individual attitudes or beliefs shared by some portion of the adult population. A consensus exists when a large proportion of the public appears to express the same view on an issue. Divided opinion exists when the public holds widely different attitudes on an issue. Sometimes, a poll shows a distribution of opinion indicating that most people either have no information about an issue or are not interested enough in the issue to form a position on it.

People's opinions are formed through the political socialization process. Important factors in this process are the family, educational experiences, peer groups, opinion leaders, the media, and political events.

Learning Outcome 2 Party identification is one of the most important indicators of voting behavior. Voting behavior is

also influenced by demographic factors, such as education, economic status, religion, race and ethnicity, gender, and geographic region. Finally, voting behavior is influenced by election-specific factors, such as perception of the candidates and issue preferences.

Learning Outcome 3 Most descriptions of public opinion are based on the results of opinion polls. An accurate poll includes a representative sample of the population being polled and ensures randomness in the selection of respondents.

Problems with polls include sampling error, the difficulty of persuading people to participate, badly weighted samples, and questions that are poorly worded. "Polls" that rely on self-selected respondents are inherently inaccurate and should be discounted.

Advances in technology have changed polling techniques over the years. During the 1970s, telephone polling became widely used. Today, largely because of extensive telemarketing, people often refuse to answer calls, and nonresponse rates in telephone polling have skyrocketed. Many poll takers also fail to include cell phone users. Due to the difficulty of obtaining a random sample in the online environment, Internet polls are often "nonpolls."

Learning Outcome 4 The political culture provides a general environment of support for the political system, allowing the nation to weather periods of crisis. The political culture also helps Americans to evaluate their government's performance.

Public opinion also plays an important role in policymaking. Politicians, however, cannot always be guided by opinion polls. This is because the respondents often do not understand the costs and consequences of policy decisions or the trade-offs involved in making such decisions. How issues are framed has an important influence on popular attitudes.

ADDITIONAL RESOURCES

Online Resources

- The Polling Report website offers polls and their results organized by topic. It is up to date and easy to use. To find it, go to **www.polling report.com**.

- The Pew Research Center, a major public opinion research group, sponsors projects on journalism, the Internet, religion, Hispanics, global attitudes, and other topics. For a home page with links to all projects, visit **www.pewresearch.org**.

- Real Clear Politics is known for its "poll of polls," which aggregates results from leading pollsters in the run-up to elections. Although the site is run by conservatives, it offers opinion pieces from multiple media sources on its home page. Go to **www.realclearpolitics.com**.

Books

Burstein, Paul. *American Public Opinion, Advocacy, and Policy in Congress: What the Public Wants and What It Gets.* New York: Cambridge University Press, 2014. Burstein, a sociology professor at the University of Washington, attempts to determine the effect of popular opinion on legislation by "working backward." He first chooses a representative sample of bills, and then estimates how much influence the public had on the outcome.

Holbrook, Thomas M. *Altered States: Changing Populations, Changing Parties, and the Transformation of the American Political Landscape.* New York: Oxford University Press, 2016. A study of how changes in public opinion have altered popular support for the two major political parties. Holbrook is a professor of government at University of Wisconsin–Milwaukee.

Khoury, Rana B. *As Ohio Goes: Life in the Post-Recession Nation.* Kent, Ohio: Kent State University Press, 2016. Intimate stories of Ohio citizens reacting to economic threats. Khoury is a Ph.D. student at Northwestern University.

Video

Purple State of Mind—A 2009 film, in which two old friends, college roommates, take different political roads—one left, the other right. They meet again and explore their differences.

Inside Islam: What a Billion Muslims Really Think—A 2014 documentary about a world-wide Gallup opinion poll of Muslims. Topics addressed include gender equality, democracy, and terrorism.

Quiz

Multiple Choice and Fill-Ins

Learning Outcome 1 Define *public opinion, consensus opinion,* and *divided opinion,* and discuss major sources of political socialization, including the family, schools, the media, and political events.

1. We can best define *public opinion* as:
   a. beliefs held by moderate voters.
   b. beliefs shared by both Republicans and Democrats.
   c. the aggregate of individual beliefs shared by some por-tion of adults.

2. If you are influenced in your political attitudes by your friends and co-workers, that means that a _____ _____ affects your attitudes.

Learning Outcome 2 Identify the effects of various influences on voting behavior, including education, income, religion, race/ethnicity, gender, and geography.

3. The gender gap refers to:
   a. the difference in college attendance rates for males and females.
   b. the tendency for women to be more likely to vote for a particular candidate than men.
   c. the tendency for men to dominate the political process.

4. With the possible exception of race, _____ _____ is the most important determinant of voting behavior in national elections.

Learning Outcome 3 Describe the characteristics of a scientific opinion poll, and list some of the problems pollsters face in obtaining accurate results.

5. One way to compensate for underrepresented groups in a polling sample is to:
   a. eliminate all answers from those who are part of the underrepresented group.
   b. reduce the weight given to the underrepresented group so that it does not count excessively.
   c. compensate by adding extra weight to the responses of the underrepresented group.

6. When one polling organization's results consistently differ from those of other poll takers, we call this the _____ effect.

Learning Outcome 4 Consider the effect that public opinion may have on the political process.

7. The trend in political satisfaction in this country has:
   a. always been very high.
   b. fallen since around 2001.
   c. risen since around 2001.

8. The same polling question can result in different responses depending on how that question is _____.

Essay Questions

1. Years ago, people with postgraduate degrees were more likely to vote for Republican than Democratic candidates, but in recent years, highly educated voters have been trending Democratic. Why might physicians and lawyers have become more likely to vote Democratic? For what reasons might college professors lean Democratic?

2. Why do you think the American people express a relatively high degree of confidence in the military as an institution? Why do people express less confidence in Congress than in other major institutions? Could people be holding various institutions to different standards, and if so, what might these standards be?

Answers to multiple-choice and fill-in questions: 1. c, 2. peer group, 3. b, 4. party identification, 5. c, 6. house, 7. b, 8. framed.

INTEREST 7 GROUPS

Demonstrators await a United States Supreme Court opinion on whether new Texas laws regulating abortion clinics place an undue burden on a woman's right to seek an abortion. The Court ruled that the laws were, in fact, unconstitutional. *What has the Court said about abortion in previous years?*

Rena Schild/Shutterstock.com

These five **LEARNING OUTCOMES** *below are designed to help improve your understanding of this chapter:*

1: Describe the basic characteristics of interest groups, and provide three major reasons why Americans join them.

2: List the major types of interest groups, especially those with economic motivations.

3: Evaluate the factors that make some interest groups especially effective.

4: Discuss direct and indirect interest group techniques.

5: Describe the main ways in which lobbyists are regulated.

What if...

We Let More People Live in Big Cities?

The news out of the Bay Area is sometimes strange. Back in 2013, demonstrators began protesting Google's use of buses to ferry employees from San Francisco to Silicon Valley. Bus opponents believed that well-paid tech workers moving into the city were driving up rents and forcing out existing residents. (Such a process is called *gentrification*.) Indeed, San Francisco, Seattle, New York City, and other booming central cities have experienced a major housing shortage, which inevitably has driven up the cost of housing.

The housing shortage in the nation's most attractive central cities has had another effect. Many young people seeking to establish families and careers have discovered that it makes no sense to move to where the best-paid jobs are. Instead, they are heading for cities in states such as Texas, where rents are lower. Of course, pay is also lower in these cities. Some economists have calculated that the resulting low population growth in the nation's most productive regions is costing us hundreds of billions of dollars every year. Is there a solution to this problem? Some people contend that there is.

What If We Let More People Live in Big Cities?

How could we let more people live in the nation's most attractive big cities? Those who know economics can answer that question. If something is expensive because it is in short supply, produce *more* of it. If there is not enough "San Francisco" to keep housing prices from skyrocketing, create more San Francisco. Keep building until prices start to fall. The city now has a population density half that of Brooklyn, which is not a part of New York City famous for high-rises. There is no need to knock down any of San Francisco's famous "painted ladies," its architecturally significant Victorian houses. San Francisco contains many hundreds of relatively low-rise buildings that are undistinguished—if not positively ugly. These buildings could be replaced with residential high-rises. In other Bay Area cities, unremarkable ranch houses could be replaced by row houses or even apartment buildings. If all parts of the Bay Area became a little more dense, the problem would be solved without destroying the character of any municipality.

Not in My Back Yard

Some new housing is going up in the Bay Area, but not nearly enough to keep prices under control. Why not? The answer is that existing residents in every community form a powerful interest group that is, by and large, opposed to new development. This is the *NIMBY* phenomenon—"not in my back yard." NIMBY can be a very potent force in local politics. After all, if you already own a house, escalating housing values make you richer. If you are a renter, you may still treasure your existing community and may not want it to change. If you have a great view of a bridge, new development may block that view. Those who lose out are not organized. Many are not even around—they're living in Fort Worth or El Paso.

In Housing, "Trickle Down" Works

It's common for antidevelopment activists to argue that supply and demand don't work in housing. New construction typically consists of upscale condos or co-ops aimed at the rich. Build these, they say, and you'll just have more rich people. In fact, the supply of rich people is not infinite. Also, in a free country, there is no way to keep the rich out of San Francisco. If there are no shiny new condos and co-ops for them, they will simply take up the next-best housing and renovate it. That will drive out middle-class people, who will then take over—and smarten up—housing that's now occupied by the poor. In an economic competition such as this, the poor always lose. Some will have to double up, live with relatives, or leave the area altogether. In the end, there is only one solution to a cost-of-housing crisis: more housing.

For Critical Analysis

▶ Why don't high-tech firms consider moving to cities where housing is cheap, such as Detroit?

▶ San Francisco anti-NIMBY activists recently founded the Bay Area Renters Federation (BARF). Does this group have any chance of success? Why or why not?

Image 7–1 Low-income housing under construction. *Is housing designed specifically for low-income families enough to resolve the so-called rent crisis in highly desirable metro areas? Why or why not?*

Paul D. Smith/Shutterstock.com

The structure of American government invites the participation of **interest groups** at various stages of the policymaking process. Americans can form groups in their neighborhoods or cities and lobby the city council or their state government around issues such as the one discussed in the chapter-opening *What If . . .* feature. They can join statewide groups or national groups and try to influence government policy through Congress or through one of the executive agencies or cabinet departments. Representatives of large corporations may seek to influence members of Congress or the president personally at social events or fund-raisers. When attempts to influence government through the executive and legislative branches fail, interest groups can turn to the courts, filing suits in state or federal courts to achieve their political objectives.

The large number of "pressure points" in American government helps to explain why there are so many—more than one hundred thousand—interest groups at work in our society. Another reason for the multitude of interest groups is that the right to join a group is protected by the First Amendment to the U.S. Constitution (see Chapter 4). Not only are all people guaranteed the right "peaceably to assemble," but they are also guaranteed the right "to petition the Government for a redress of grievances." This constitutional provision encourages Americans to form groups and to express their opinions to the government or to their elected representatives as members of these groups. The constitutional protection of groups is one reason that it would be very difficult to satisfy the occasional demand that **lobbyists**—persons hired to represent interest groups to the government—be banned.

Mark Reinstein/Getty Images

Image 7–2 The rotunda and main lobby of the capitol building in Topeka, Kansas. Lobbyists and state legislators meet one another here, outside the chambers of the Kansas House. *Why does lobbying have constitutional protection?*

Interest Group Fundamentals

Learning Outcome 1:

Describe the basic characteristics of interest groups, and provide three major reasons why Americans join them.

Alexis de Tocqueville observed in the early 1830s that "in no country of the world has the principle of association been more successfully used or applied to a greater multitude of objectives than in America."[1] The French traveler was amazed at the degree to which Americans formed groups to solve civic problems, establish social relationships, and speak for their economic or political interests. Perhaps James Madison, when he wrote *Federalist Paper* No. 10 (see Appendix C), had already judged the character of his country's citizens similarly. He supported the creation of a large republic with many states to encourage the formation of multiple interests. The multitude of interests, in Madison's view, would work to discourage the formation of an oppressive majority interest.

Poll data show that more than two-thirds of all Americans belong to at least one group or association. Although the majority of these affiliations could not be classified as "interest groups" in the political sense, Americans certainly understand the principles of working in groups.

Today, interest groups range from the elementary school parent-teacher association to the statewide association of insurance agents. They include small groups such as local environmental organizations and national groups such as the American Civil Liberties

interest group

An organized group of individuals sharing common objectives who actively attempt to influence policymakers.

lobbyist

An organization or individual who is employed to influence legislation and the administrative decisions of government.

1. Alexis de Tocqueville, *Democracy in America*, Vol. 1 [1835], ed. Phillips Bradley (New York: Knopf, 1980), p. 191.

Image 7–3 Campaigners for woman suffrage in San Francisco, 1915. *Did they have many supporters at that time?*

Union, the National Education Association, and even the Association of Government Relations Professionals, formerly the American League of Lobbyists.

Interest Groups and Social Movements

Interest groups may be spawned by mass **social movements.** Such movements represent demands by a large segment of the population for change in the political, economic, or social system. A social movement is often the first expression of latent discontent with the existing system. It may be the authentic voice of weaker or oppressed groups in society that do not have the means or standing to organize as interest groups. For example, the women's movement of the early 1800s suffered disapproval from most mainstream political and social leaders. Because women were unable to vote or take an active part in the political system, it was difficult for women who desired greater freedoms to organize formal groups. After the Civil War, when more women became active in professional life, organizations seeking to win women the right to vote came into being.

African Americans found themselves in an even more disadvantaged situation after the end of the Reconstruction period (1865–1877). They were unable to exercise political rights in many southern states, and their participation in any form of organization could lead to economic ruin, physical harassment, or even death. The civil rights movement of the 1950s and 1960s was clearly a social movement. To be sure, several formal organizations worked to support the movement—including the Southern Christian Leadership Conference, the National Association for the Advancement of Colored People, and the Urban League—but only a social movement could generate the kinds of civil disobedience that took place in hundreds of towns and cities across the country.

Social movements may generate interest groups with specific goals. In the example of the women's movement of the 1960s, the National Organization for Women was formed in part out of a demand to end gender-segregated job advertising in newspapers.

Why Do Americans Join Interest Groups?

One puzzle that has fascinated political scientists is why some people join interest groups, while many others do not. Everyone has some interest that could benefit from government action. For many individuals, however, those concerns remain unorganized interests, or **latent interests.**

According to political theorist Mancur Olson,[2] it simply may not be rational for individuals to join most groups. In his classic work on this topic, Olson introduced the idea of the "collective good." This concept refers to any public benefit that, if available to any member of the community, cannot be denied to any other member, whether or not he or she participated in the effort to gain the good.

Although collective benefits are usually thought of as coming from such goods as clean air and national defense, benefits are also bestowed by the government on subsets of the public. Price subsidies to dairy farmers and loans to college students are examples.

social movement

A movement that represents the demands of a large segment of the public for political, economic, or social change.

latent interests

Public-policy interests that are not recognized or addressed by a group at a particular time.

2. Mancur Olson, *The Logic of Collective Action* (Cambridge, Mass.: Harvard University Press, 1965).

Olson used economic theory to propose that it is not rational for interested individuals to join groups that work for *group* benefits. In fact, it is often more rational for the individual to wait for others to procure the benefits and then share them. How many community college students, for example, join the American Association of Community Colleges, an organization that lobbies the government for increased financial aid to students? The difficulty interest groups face in recruiting members when the benefits can be obtained without joining the groups is referred to as the **free rider problem.**

If so little incentive exists for individuals to join together, why are there thousands of interest groups lobbying in Washington? According to the logic of collective action, if the contribution of an individual *will* make a difference to the effort, then it is worth it to the individual to join. Thus, smaller groups, which seek benefits for only a small proportion of the population, are more likely to enroll members who will give time and funds to the cause. Larger groups, which represent general public interests (the women's movement or the American Civil Liberties Union, for example), will find it relatively more difficult to persuade individuals to join. People need an incentive—material or otherwise—to participate.

Solidary Incentives. Interest groups offer **solidary incentives** for their members. Solidary benefits include companionship, a sense of belonging, and the pleasure of associating with others. Although the National Audubon Society was originally founded to save the snowy egret from extinction, today most members join to learn more about birds and to meet and share their pleasure with other individuals who enjoy bird-watching as a hobby. Even though the incentive might be solidary for many members, this organization nonetheless also pursues an active political agenda, working to preserve the environment and to protect endangered species. Still, most members may not play any part in working toward larger, more national goals unless the organization can convince them to take political action or unless some local environmental issue arises.

Material Incentives. For other individuals, interest groups offer direct **material incentives.** A case in point is AARP (formerly the American Association of Retired Persons), which provides discounts, insurance plans, and organized travel opportunities for its members. (You can find information about these benefits at the AARP home page.) Because of its exceptionally low dues ($16 annually) and the benefits gained through membership, AARP has become the largest—and a very powerful—interest group in the United States. AARP can claim to represent the interests of millions of senior citizens and can show that they actually have joined the group. For most seniors, the material incentives outweigh the membership costs.

Another example of such an interest group is the American Automobile Association (AAA). Most people who join this organization do so for its emergency roadside assistance and trip planning. Many members may not realize that the AAA is also a significant interest group seeking to shape laws that affect drivers.

Purposive Incentives. Interest groups also offer the opportunity for individuals to pursue political, economic, or social goals through joint action. **Purposive incentives** offer individuals the satisfaction of taking action when the goals of a group correspond to their beliefs or principles. The individuals who belong to a group focusing on the abortion issue or gun control, for example, do so because they feel strongly enough about the issues to support the group's work with money and time.

free rider problem

The difficulty interest groups face in recruiting members when the benefits they achieve can be gained without joining the group.

solidary incentive

A reason or motive that follows from the desire to associate with others and to share with others a particular interest or hobby.

material incentive

A reason or motive based on the desire to enjoy certain economic benefits or opportunities.

purposive incentive

A reason for supporting or participating in the activities of a group that is based on agreement with the goals of the group. For example, someone with a strong interest in human rights might have a purposive incentive to join Amnesty International.

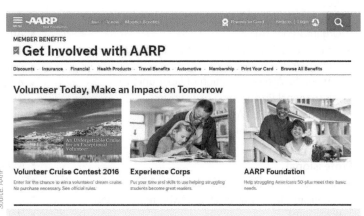

Source: AARP

Image 7–4

Some scholars have argued that many people join interest groups simply for the discounts, magazine subscriptions, and other tangible benefits and are not really interested in the political positions taken by the groups. According to William P. Browne, however, research shows that people really do care about the policy stance of an interest group. Representatives of a group seek people who share the group's views and then ask them to join. As one group leader put it, "Getting members is about scaring the hell out of people."[3] People join the group and then feel that they are doing something about a cause that is important to them.

Learning Outcome 2:

List the major types of interest groups, especially those with economic motivations.

Types of Interest Groups

Thousands of groups exist to influence government. Among the major types of interest groups are those that represent the main sectors of the economy. In addition, a number of environmental groups and "public-interest" organizations have been formed to protect the environment and represent the needs of the general citizenry. Other types of groups include many "single-issue" groups, ideological groups, and groups based on race, sex, or sexual orientation. The interests of foreign governments and foreign businesses are represented in the American political arena as well. The names of some major interest groups are shown in Table 7–1.

3. William P. Browne, *Groups, Interests, and U.S. Public Policy* (Washington, D.C.: Georgetown University Press, 1998), p. 23.

Table 7–1 A List of Effective Interest Groups

Do you know people who are members of any of these groups?

Business
- American Bankers Association
- American Farm Bureau Federation
- American Hospital Association
- America's Health Insurance Plans
- Business Roundtable
- Chamber of Commerce of the United States
- National Association of Home Builders
- National Association of Manufacturers (NAM)
- Pharmaceutical Research and Manufacturers of America

Labor
- American Federation of Labor–Congress of Industrial Organizations (AFL-CIO)
- American Federation of State, County, and Municipal Employees (AFSCME)
- Change to Win (a federation of labor unions)
- International Brotherhood of Teamsters
- National Education Association (NEA)
- Service Employees International Union

Professional
- American Association for Justice (trial lawyers)
- American Medical Association (AMA, representing physicians)
- National Association of Realtors

Identity
- AARP (formerly the American Association of Retired Persons)
- League of United Latin American Citizens (LULAC)
- National Association for the Advancement of Colored People (the NAACP, representing African Americans)
- National Organization for Women (NOW)

Environmental
- National Audubon Society
- National Wildlife Federation
- Nature Conservancy
- Sierra Club

Other
- American Civil Liberties Union (ACLU)
- American Israel Public Affairs Committee (AIPAC)
- American Legion (veterans)
- American Society for the Prevention of Cruelty to Animals (ASPCA)
- Amnesty International USA (human rights)
- Consumers Union
- The Brady Campaign to Prevent Gun Violence
- Mothers Against Drunk Driving (MADD)
- NARAL Pro-Choice America
- National Rifle Association (NRA)
- National Right to Life Committee

Economic Interest Groups

More interest groups are formed to represent economic interests than any other set of interests. The variety of economic interest groups mirrors the complexity of the American economy.

Business Interest Groups. Thousands of business groups and trade associations work to influence government policies that affect their respective industries. "Umbrella groups" represent collections of businesses or other entities. For example, the National Association of Manufacturers is an umbrella group that represents manufacturing concerns. Some business groups are decidedly more powerful than others. Consider the U.S. Chamber of Commerce, which represents about 3 million member companies. It can bring constituent influence to bear on every member of Congress. Studies have shown that business groups—especially those representing specific industries such as banking or filmmaking—are exceptionally successful in winning beneficial legislation.

Business influence has been especially conspicuous in negotiations over international trade, such as the Trans-Pacific Partnership (TPP), provisionally concluded in February 2016. Nations that are party to this agreement include the United States, Australia, Canada, Japan, Mexico, Vietnam, and six others. Earlier trade agreements typically focused on reducing tariffs (taxes on imports). While the TPP would cut tariffs, it also covers intellectual property and disputes between investors and governments.

The intellectual property clauses of the TPP would essentially impose U.S. trademark, copyright, and patent laws on other nations. Such a step would be of great benefit to drug companies and to Hollywood. The Walt Disney Company, for example, has long fought to ensure that its rights to Mickey Mouse never expire. The TPP would protect Disney's control of Mickey Mouse until at least 2036. Some economists have argued that lengthy copyright and patent protections discourage innovation and hurt the overall economy.

The dispute resolution clauses would let investors sue governments in international tribunals that are not subject to national control and are staffed by business professionals. The nature of these tribunals alarmed defenders of national sovereignty. (It is true, though, that the United States has rarely lost a case brought before such tribunals.) All in all, the TPP would benefit U.S. business interests, and it would strengthen ties among countries worried about the growing influence of China. It was less clear whether the deal would benefit ordinary U.S. citizens. In any event, there was no chance of the U.S. Congress approving the TPP before the 2016 elections.

Agricultural Interest Groups. American farmers and their employees represent less than 1 percent of the U.S. population. In spite of this, farmers' influence on legislation beneficial to their interests has been significant. Farmers have very strong interest groups. For example, the American Farm Bureau Federation, or Farm Bureau, established in 1919, represents more than 5.5 million families (a majority of whom are not actually farm families).

Agricultural interest groups are among the most successful in obtaining subsidies from American taxpayers. The most recent "farm bill" was passed in 2014. This legislation provides $19 billion per year to the nation's farmers. The new bill did abolish direct

Image 7–5 A young farmer inspects his grain crop. *Why is it hard to become a farmer if you were not raised in a farm family?*

labor movement
The economic and political expression of working-class interests.

payments—sums that formerly went to growers of corn, cotton, rice, soybeans, and wheat regardless of whether they actually planted the crops. Almost all of the funds saved were added back as crop insurance subsidies, however.

As expensive as U.S. agricultural supports may be, many other nations provide their farmers with even greater subsidies. We provide some figures in this chapter's *Beyond Our Borders* feature.

Labor Interest Groups. Interest groups representing the **labor movement** date back to at least 1886, when the American Federation of Labor (AFL) was formed. In 1955, the AFL joined forces with the Congress of Industrial Organizations (CIO). Today, the combined AFL-CIO is a large federation with a membership of about 10 million workers and an active political arm called the Committee on Political Education. In a sense, the AFL-CIO is a union of unions.

Beyond our borders

How Foreign Countries Subsidize Agriculture

U.S. agricultural subsidies have often been controversial. In the 1930s, when subsidies began, many farmers were seriously impoverished. With today's large farms, this is no longer true. It is worth noting, however, that the United States is far from the greatest sinner in the farm subsidy game. Most wealthy nations and some middle-income nations provide larger subsidies. Figure 7–1 shows the size of farm subsidies as a percentage of total agricultural production. We give a single figure for the European Union, a confederation of twenty-eight countries with a Common Agricultural Policy (CAP). While the CAP is generous, it was more so in the past. In the 1980s, it paid out subsidies worth 40 percent of production.

For Critical Analysis

◗ **Some African countries tax farmers to support people who live in cities. If those countries were on this chart, their figures would actually be negative. Why might such nations have policies so different from those of wealthier countries?**

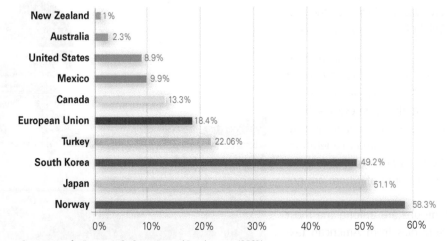

Figure 7–1 Agricultural Subsidies as a Percent of Production Value

Country	Percent
New Zealand	1%
Australia	2.3%
United States	8.9%
Mexico	9.9%
Canada	13.3%
European Union	18.4%
Turkey	22.06%
South Korea	49.2%
Japan	51.1%
Norway	58.3%

Source: Organisation for Economic Co-Operation and Development (OECD).

The AFL-CIO remained the predominant labor union organization for fifty years. In 2005, however, four key unions left the federation and formed the Change to Win Coalition. Today, Change to Win has a membership of about 4 million workers.

Labor's Decline. The role of unions in American society has been waning, as witnessed by the decline in union membership (see Figure 7–2). In the age of automation and with the rise of the **service sector,** traditionally unionized blue-collar workers in basic industries (auto, steel, and the like) represent a smaller and smaller percentage of the total working population.

As a result, unions are looking to other areas for their membership, including migrant farmworkers, service workers, and especially public employees. These include police officers, firefighting personnel, teachers, college professors, and even graduate assistants. Indeed, public-sector unions make up an ever-greater share of the labor movement.

Image 7–6 Fast-food, home-health-care, and other low-wage workers rally in Chicago on behalf of the Fight for $15, a campaign that calls for better wages and working conditions. *Why would organized labor favor a higher minimum wage for all workers, not just union members?*

Public Employee Unions. The degree of unionization in the private sector has declined over the past fifty years, but this decline has been partially offset by growth in the unionization of public employees. With a total membership of more than 7 million, public-sector unions are a powerful force. Figure 7–2 displays the growth in public-sector unionization. (Note that the percentage of the workforce that consists of union members, as shown on

service sector

The sector of the economy that provides services—such as health care, banking, and education—in contrast to the sector that produces goods.

Figure 7–2   Decline in Union Membership, 1948 to Present

The percentage of the total workforce that consists of labor union members has declined greatly over the past forty years. The percentage of government workers who are union members, however, increased significantly in the 1960s and 1970s and has remained stable since. *Why could it be easier to organize a union in the public sector than in the private sector?*

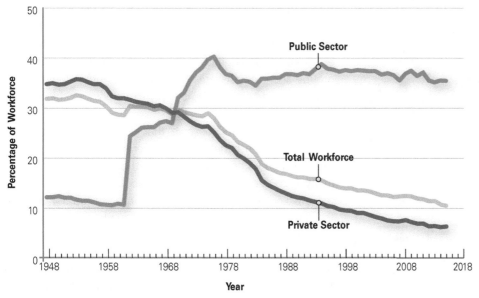

Source: Bureau of Labor Statistics.

this graph, is several points lower than the percentage of workers represented by a union, because most unions represent some nonmembers.)

Over the years, public employee unions have sometimes been involved in strikes. Most of these strikes are illegal, because almost no public employees have the right to strike. In recent years, conservatives have taken a strong stand against public employee unions, particularly teachers' unions such as the National Education Association and the American Federation of Teachers. In some states, mostly in the South, bargaining with public sector unions is prohibited. In 2011 and 2012, Republican governors in several Midwestern states—notably Ohio and Wisconsin—attempted to restrict or abolish the bargaining rights of public employees. The cost of public employee pension funds has also been an issue.

The Political Environment Faced by Labor. The success or failure of attempts to form unions depends greatly on popular attitudes. Many business-oriented conservatives have never accepted unions as legitimate institutions. In states where this position is widely held, local laws and practices can make it hard for labor to organize. For example, Georgia and North Carolina are major manufacturing states, but the percentages of union members in these two conservative states are 4.0 percent and 3.0 percent, respectively. States where the voting public is more sympathetic to labor, such as California and New York, have unionization rates of 15.9 percent and 24.7 percent, respectively. These rates are more typical of the world's wealthy nations than are the rates in conservative southern states.

One way a state can make it more difficult to form unions is by adopting "right-to-work" laws. Such legislation bans contracts that require all employees to pay union dues or fees. The result is a free-rider problem for the unions. Twenty-five states have such laws. Indiana, Michigan, and Wisconsin are the most recent states to adopt them.

Interest Groups of Professionals.

Many professional organizations exist, including the American Bar Association, the Associated General Contractors of America, the Institute of Electrical and Electronics Engineers, and others. Some professional groups, such as those representing lawyers and physicians, are more influential than others because of their ability to restrict entry into their professions. Lawyers have a unique advantage—a large number of members of Congress share their profession.

Image 7–7 Pat Capon, an advocate for low-income people who are also dealing with mental illness. *What kinds of problems could cause an individual to fall into poverty?*

David Cooper/Getty Images

The Unorganized Poor.

Some have argued that the system of interest group politics leaves out poor Americans. If they are members of the working poor, they may hold two or more jobs just to survive, leaving them no time to participate in interest groups. Consequently, some scholars suggest that interest groups and lobbyists are the privilege of upper-middle-class Americans and those who belong to unions or other special groups.

Others, however, observe that the low-income population does obtain benefits from government. Without federal tax and spending programs aimed at low-income persons, as many as 25 percent of U.S. families would have incomes below the official poverty line. If you take into account all benefits that low-income families obtain, that number drops to about 10 percent. True, the poor cannot easily represent themselves. But for decades, liberal groups and, especially, religious groups have campaigned on behalf of those suffering from poverty. These interest groups have done for the poor what the poor cannot do for themselves.

Environmental Groups

Environmental interest groups are not new. We have already mentioned the National Audubon Society, which was founded in 1905 to protect the snowy egret from the commercial demand for hat decorations. The patron of the Sierra Club, John Muir, worked for the creation of national parks more than a century ago. But the blossoming of environmental groups with mass memberships did not occur until the 1970s.

Today's Environmental Groups. Since the first Earth Day, organized in 1972, many interest groups have sprung up to protect the environment in general or unique ecological niches. The groups range from the National Wildlife Federation, with a membership of more than 4 million, to the more elite Environmental Defense Fund, with a membership of five hundred thousand. Another group, the Nature Conservancy, uses members' contributions to buy up threatened natural areas and then either gives them to state or local governments or manages them itself. Other groups include the more radical Greenpeace Society and Earth First.

Climate Change. The topic of climate change, or global warming, has become a major focus for environmental groups in recent years. This issue has pitted environmentalists against other interest groups to a much greater degree than in the past. Environmentalists often find themselves in opposition to economic interests representing industries that promote warming by releasing "greenhouse" gases into the atmosphere. Indeed, the reaction against environmentalism has been strong enough in such coal-oriented states as West Virginia to transform them politically. Once a Democratic bastion, West Virginia now usually supports Republicans in presidential contests.

Public-Interest Groups

Public interest is a difficult term to define because, as we noted in Chapter 6, there are many publics in our nation of about 320 million. It is almost impossible for one particular public policy to benefit everybody, which in turn makes it practically impossible to define the public interest. Nonetheless, over the past few decades, a variety of lobbying organizations have been formed "in the public interest."

The Consumer Movement. As an organized movement, consumerism began in 1936 with the founding of the Consumers Union, which continues to publish the popular magazine *Consumer Reports*. The movement had antecedents dating back to the earliest years of the twentieth century, when investigative journalists known as "muckrakers" exposed exploitative working conditions and unsafe products in a variety of industries. Upton Sinclair's 1906 novel *The Jungle,* which revealed abuses of the workforce and unsanitary conditions in the meatpacking industry, was a classic of this genre.

Consumerism took off during the 1960s, a time of social ferment marked by the civil rights, antiwar, and feminist movements. Ralph Nader, who gained notice by exposing unsafe automobiles, was a key figure in the consumer movement. Nader was a major sponsor of a series of new organizations. These included the Public Interest Research Groups (PIRGs)—campus organizations that emerged in the early 1970s and continue to provide students with platforms for civic engagement. Other new groups included the Consumer Federation of America (1968) and Public Citizen (1971).

Partly in response to the variety of consumer groups, several conservative public-interest legal foundations have sprung up that are often pitted against liberal groups in court. Some of these are the Pacific Legal Foundation, the Institute for Justice, and the Mid-Atlantic Legal Foundation.

public interest
The best interests of the overall community; the national good, rather than the narrow interests of a particular group.

Other Public-Interest Groups. One of the largest public-interest groups is Common Cause, founded in 1968. Its goal is to reorder national priorities toward "the public" and to make governmental institutions more responsive to the needs of the public. Another public-interest group is the League of Women Voters, founded in 1920. Although officially nonpartisan, it has lobbied for the Equal Rights Amendment and for government reform.

Other Interest Groups

A number of interest groups focus on just one issue. Single-interest groups, being narrowly focused, may be able to call attention to their causes because they have simple, straightforward goals and because their members tend to care intensely about the issues. Thus, such groups can easily motivate their members to contact legislators or to organize demonstrations in support of their policy goals.

The abortion debate has created groups opposed to abortion (such as the National Right to Life Committee) and groups in favor of abortion rights (such as NARAL Pro-Choice America). Further examples of single-issue groups are the National Rifle Association of America, the National Right to Work Committee (an antiunion group), and the American Israel Public Affairs Committee (a pro-Israel group).

Ideological Groups. Among the most important interest groups are those that unite citizens around a common ideological viewpoint. Americans for Democratic Action, for example, was founded in 1947 as a home for liberals who were explicitly anti-Communist. On the political right, Americans for Tax Reform, organized by Grover Norquist, has been successful in persuading almost all leading Republicans to sign a pledge promising never to vote to raise taxes. The various organizations making up the Tea Party movement are widely seen as ideological interest groups. (Some observers, however, believe that the movement is better considered as a faction of the Republican Party rather than a series of interest groups.)

Image 7–8 Grover Norquist of Americans for Tax Reform displays a pledge against tax increases that most Republicans in Congress have signed. The mask is of Guy Fawkes, who tried to blow up the English Parliament in 1605. *Was Fawkes a terrorist?*

Identity Groups. Still other groups represent Americans who share a common identity, such as membership in a particular race or ethnic group. The NAACP, founded in 1909 as the National Association for the Advancement of Colored People, represents African Americans. The National Organization for Women (NOW) has championed women's rights since 1966.

Elderly Americans can be considered to have a common identity. AARP is one of the most powerful interest groups in Washington, D.C. It is the nation's largest interest group, with a membership of about 40 million. AARP played a significant role in the creation of Medicare and Medicaid, as well as in obtaining annual cost-of-living increases in Social Security payments. (Medicare pays for medical expenses incurred by those who are at least sixty-five years of age; Medicaid provides health-care support for the poor.) In 2009 and 2010, AARP strongly supported the Democratic health-care reform bills.

Foreign Interest Groups. Homegrown interest groups are not the only players in the game. Washington, D.C., is also the center for lobbying by foreign governments as well as private foreign interests. The governments of the largest U.S. trading partners, such as Canada, the European Union (EU) countries, Japan, and South Korea, maintain substantial research and lobbying staffs. Even smaller nations, such as those in the Caribbean, engage lobbyists when vital legislation affecting their trade interests is considered.

Why should you care about **INTEREST GROUPS?**

Some interest groups focus on issues that concern only a limited number of people. Others, however, are involved in causes in which almost everyone has a stake. Gun control is an issue that concerns a large number of people. The question of whether the possession of handguns should be regulated is at the heart of a long-running, heated battle among organized interest groups. The fight is fueled by the 1 million gun incidents occurring in the United States each year—murders, suicides, assaults, accidents, and robberies in which guns are involved. If you are interested in strengthening—or weakening—the nation's gun control laws, check out the chapter-ending *How You Can Make a Difference* feature.

The Influence of Interest Groups

Learning Outcome 3:

Evaluate the factors that make some interest groups especially effective.

At any time, thousands of interest groups are attempting to influence state legislatures, governors, Congress, and members of the executive branch of the U.S. government. How powerful are these groups—and what influence do they have on policy and our democratic institutions?

What Makes an Interest Group Powerful?

What characteristics make some interest groups more powerful than others and more likely to have influence over government policy? Generally, interest groups attain a reputation for being powerful through their membership size, financial resources, leadership, and cohesiveness.

Size and Resources. No legislator can deny the power of an interest group that includes thousands of his or her own constituents among its members. Labor unions and organizations such as AARP and the American Automobile Association are able to claim voters in every congressional district. Having a large membership—about 10 million in the case of the AFL-CIO—carries a great deal of weight with government officials. AARP now has about 40 million members and a budget of more than a billion dollars for its operations. In addition, AARP claims to represent all older Americans, who constitute close to 20 percent of the population, whether they join the organization or not.

Having a large number of members, even if the individual membership dues are relatively small, provides an organization with a strong financial base. Those funds pay for lobbyists, television advertisements, e-mailings to members, a website, pages on Facebook, Twitter feeds, and many other resources that help an interest group make its point to politicians. The business organization with the largest membership is probably the U.S. Chamber of Commerce, which represents about 3 million businesses. The Chamber uses its members' dues to pay for staff and lobbyists, as well as a sophisticated communications network so that it can contact members in a timely way. All of the members can check the Chamber's website to get updates on the latest legislative proposals.

Other organizations may have fewer members but nonetheless can muster significant financial resources. The pharmaceutical lobby, which represents many of the major drug manufacturers, is one of the most powerful interest groups in Washington due to its financial resources. This interest group has more than 1,250 registered lobbyists and spent large sums in the 2015–2016 election cycle for lobbying and campaign expenditures.

Leadership. Money is not the only resource that interest groups need. Strong leaders who can develop effective strategies are also important. For example, the American Israel Public Affairs Committee (AIPAC) has long benefited from strong leadership. AIPAC lobbies Congress and the executive branch on issues related to U.S.-Israeli relations, as well as general foreign policy in the Middle East. AIPAC has been successful in promoting the close relationship that the two nations have enjoyed, which includes foreign aid that the United States annually bestows on Israel, now about $3.1 billion per year. Despite its modest membership size, AIPAC has won bipartisan support for its agenda and is consistently ranked among the most influential interest groups in America.

Cohesiveness. Regardless of an interest group's size or the amount of funds in its coffers, the motivation of an interest group's members is a key factor in determining how powerful it is. If the members of a group hold their beliefs strongly enough to send letters

Image 7–9 Democratic presidential candidate Hillary Clinton at the annual conference of the American Israel Public Affairs Committee (AIPAC). *Why does Israel have so much support among Americans?*

to their representatives, join a march on Washington, or work together to defeat a candidate, that group is considered powerful.

Although groups that oppose abortion rights have had modest success in influencing policy, they are considered powerful because their members are vocal and highly motivated. Of course, the existence of countervailing pro-choice groups limits their influence. Other measures of cohesion include the ability of a group to persuade its members to contact Washington quickly or to give extra funds when needed. The U.S. Chamber of Commerce excels at both of these strategies. In comparison, AARP cannot claim that it can induce many of its 40 million members to contact their congressional representatives, but it does seem to have some influence on the opinions of older Americans and their views of political candidates.

Interest Groups and Representative Democracy

The role played by interest groups in shaping national policy has caused many to question whether we really have a democracy at all. Most interest groups have a middle-class or upper-class bias. Members of interest groups can afford to pay the membership fees, are generally fairly well educated, and normally participate in the political process to a greater extent than the "average" American.

Furthermore, leaders of interest groups tend to constitute an "elite within an elite" in the sense that they usually are from a higher social class than other group members. The most powerful interest groups—those with the most resources and political influence—are primarily business, trade, and professional groups. In contrast, public-interest groups and civil rights groups make up only a small percentage of the interest groups lobbying Congress.

Interest Groups: Elitist or Pluralist? Remember from Chapter 1 that the elite theory of politics presumes that most Americans are uninterested in politics and are willing to let a small, elite group of citizens make decisions for them. Pluralist theory, in contrast, views politics as a struggle among various interest groups to gain benefits for their members. The pluralist approach views compromise among various competing interests as the essence of political decision making. In reality, neither theory fully describes American politics. If interest groups led by elite, upper-class individuals are the dominant voices in Congress, then what we see is a conflict among elite groups—which would lend as much support to the elitist theory as to the pluralist approach.

The Impact of Interest Groups. The results of lobbying efforts—congressional bills—do not always favor the interests of the most powerful groups, however. In part, this is because not all interest groups have an equal influence on government. Each group has a different combination of resources to use in the policymaking process. While some groups are composed of members who have high social status and significant economic resources, such as the National Association of Manufacturers, other groups derive influence from their large memberships. AARP, for example, has more members than any other interest group. Still other groups, such as environmentalists, have causes that can claim strong public support even from people who have no direct stake in the issue. Groups such as the National Rifle Association are well organized and have highly motivated members. This enables them to channel a stream of letters, e-mails, and tweets toward Congress with a few days' effort.

Even the most powerful interest groups do not always succeed in their demands. The U.S. Chamber of Commerce may be accepted as having a justified interest in the question of business taxes. Yet many legislators might feel that the group should not engage in the debate over the future of Social Security. In other words, groups are seen as having a legitimate concern in the issues closest to their interests but not necessarily in

Image 7–10 A gun-control advocate from Code Pink holds up a banner at a press conference by Wayne LaPierre, executive vice president of the National Rifle Association (NRA). *What makes the NRA an effective interest group?*

Chip Somodevilla/Getty Images

broader issues. This may explain why some of the most successful groups are those that focus on very specific issues—such as tobacco farming, funding of abortions, and handgun control—and do not get involved in larger conflicts.

Complicating the question of interest group influence is the fact that many groups' lobbyists are former colleagues, friends, or family members of current members of Congress.

Concentrated Benefits, Dispersed Costs.

We noted earlier that when an interest is shared by a small number of individuals, it may be easier to organize them into a group. One reason for this effect is known as *concentrated benefits and dispersed costs*. If a special law, such as a tax break, helps a relatively small number of people, those who receive the benefit will fight hard to keep or enlarge it. Other citizens, who pay for the benefit, may have little motivation to oppose it. For members of the majority, after all, the cost can be a matter of pennies. In other words, there is an *enthusiasm gap* between supporters and opponents of any given subsidy or tax break.

Sugar producers, for example, benefit greatly from restrictions on sugar imports. They work hard to ensure that these restrictions continue. Yet for sugar consumers—all the rest of us—the price of sugar is a trivial matter. End users of sugar have little incentive to organize. Still, when many interest groups are able to obtain benefits, the total impact on our representative democracy can be large.

It is also possible that a new type of enterprise may impose serious costs on existing businesses—for example, by taking away their customers. The businesses that are losing out can fight for government action to protect their interests, but they may find that they are not strong enough to prevail. We examine one such contest in this chapter's *Which Side Are You On?* feature.

Interest Groups and the Political Parties

Political scientists draw a distinction between interest groups and political parties. Parties nominate candidates for office, contest elections, and seek to operate the government. Interest groups do not seek to operate the government, even though they often support candidates who will promote their interests if elected.

Interest Groups and Party Coalitions. The separation between interest groups and political parties is not as sharp as some political models suggest, however. A party, after all, consists not only of candidates for office, elected officials, party officials, and party activists. A party also includes all of the people who identify with and support that party. Party supporters include millions of ordinary, unaffiliated citizens—and these supporters include interest groups as well.

A large number of interest groups are closely linked to one or another of the major political parties. To examine the broad coalition that normally supports the Democrats, for example, you need to consider labor unions, organized minority groups, ideological organizations, and many other interests. Take labor. Although the percentage of workers who

Which side are you on?

Should We Let Uber and Lyft Pick Up Passengers?

It was only a matter of time. Smartphone apps have become powerful and popular. Many people in big cities need to summon a taxicab or hire a car service. Why not create an app to let people order such services? That is exactly what has happened in major cities around the world. Uber was the first "transportation network company" to harness the power of mobile apps to arrange on-demand ridesharing. Lyft followed suit. Other competitors have joined this growing business.

To become an Uber or Lyft driver, you must pass a criminal background check and show that your car is safe and clean. To become a customer, all you have to do is download the app and furnish a credit-card number.

That is not the end of the story, however. Licensed taxis have been fighting Uber, Lyft, and their competitors, and in some cases winning. Many states, cities, and even countries have banned Uber altogether. Others have severely regulated it. So, should Uber, Lyft, and others be able to freely compete against traditional taxi companies and drivers?

It's the Twenty-First Century—Get Used to It

The Global Positioning System (GPS) is not going to go away. Smartphones are here to stay. Together, they can form the basis of a new transportation service. Whoever is providing this service, you cannot stop it. Drivers like it because they can earn extra money—provided they have a decent car, a pleasant demeanor, and free time to do the work. Drivers are rated by customers, so the bad ones are weeded out. Because payments are processed through a credit card, drivers are no longer sitting ducks for armed robbery.

True, Uber and Lyft pose a competitive threat to existing taxi companies. But the new companies are also expanding the size of the market. People are simply taking more rides. Taxicab company owners are the only people truly hurt by Uber and Lyft. Thousands of ordinary cabdrivers have found it makes sense to drive for the new firms instead of the old ones.

Unfair and Unsafe Competition

Uber, Lyft, and the like may provide a cool way to hail a cab. Taxicab companies, however, argue that this is not the real reason the new companies are successful. Rather, they are taking advantage of a new business model to escape regulations imposed on taxis. These regulations impose costs, but there are good reasons for them. Regulatory compliance is important to passenger safety. Too little is known about Uber drivers. There have actually been instances of drivers attacking passengers. Drivers can register online and pay off a shady mechanic to certify the safety of the cars. Drivers may also buy ordinary auto insurance. Doing so is a scam— commercial vehicle insurance is more expensive because claims are more frequent. Is it fair for Uber and Lyft to compete against licensed taxi services without paying these costs?

For Critical Analysis

▶ At times, Uber and Lyft use "surge pricing" to balance supply and demand. On New Year's Eve, for example, ride prices are much higher than normal. Is this a problem? Why or why not?

---

belong to a labor union has declined, unions continue to support sympathetic candidates for Congress and for state office. The AFL-CIO and many individual unions have large political budgets, which they use to help Democratic candidates nationwide. Labor can offer a candidate (such as Hillary Clinton) a corps of volunteers in addition to campaign contributions.

On the Republican side, major business groups such as the U.S. Chamber of Commerce are normally considered to be part of the Republican coalition. Other members include ideological groups such as Americans for Tax Reform and various Tea Party organizations.

Nonpartisan Interest Groups. Years ago, business interests would endorse friendly Democrats, and unions could and did endorse many sympathetic Republicans. With today's polarized politics, however, the number of labor-friendly Republican candidates approaches zero, and the number of Democrats who can win business endorsements is down as well.

Nevertheless, even today, many interest groups maintain their independence. These groups stay nonpartisan for several reasons. A group such as AIPAC hopes to win support for Israel from members of both parties. Other interest groups may find that they are not in full agreement with either major party. A Catholic organization, for example, might favor the Republicans to oppose abortion, but ally with the Democrats to support those in poverty. In short, like individual Americans, interest groups can be Republican, Democratic, or independent.

Learning Outcome **4:**

Discuss direct and indirect interest group techniques.

Interest Group Strategies

Interest groups employ a wide range of techniques and strategies to promote their policy goals. Although few groups are successful at persuading Congress and the president to endorse their programs completely, many are able to block—or at least weaken—legislation injurious to their members. The key to success for interest groups is access to government officials. To gain such access, interest groups and their representatives try to cultivate long-term relationships with legislators and government officials. The best of these relationships are based on mutual respect and cooperation. The interest group provides the official with sources of information and assistance, and the official in turn gives the group opportunities to express its views.

The techniques used by interest groups can be divided into direct and indirect techniques. With **direct techniques,** the interest group and its lobbyists approach officials personally to present their case. With **indirect techniques,** in contrast, the interest group uses the general public or individual constituents to influence the government on behalf of the interest group.

Direct Techniques

Lobbying, publicizing ratings of legislative behavior, building alliances, and providing campaign assistance are four direct techniques used by interest groups.

The Rule of Lobbyists. As you might have guessed, the term *lobbying* comes from the activities of private citizens regularly congregating in the lobbies of legislative chambers to petition legislators. In the latter part of the 1800s, railroad and industrial groups openly bribed state legislators to pass legislation beneficial to their interests, giving lobbying a well-deserved bad name. Most lobbyists today are professionals. They are either consultants to a company or interest group or members of one of the Washington, D.C., law firms that specialize in providing lobbying services. Such firms employ hundreds of former members of Congress and former government officials who are valued for their network of contacts in Washington. As Ed Rollins, a former White House aide, put it, "I've got many friends who are all through the agencies and equally important, I don't have many enemies. . . . I tell my clients I can get your case moved to the top of the pile."[4] Lobbyists of all types are becoming more numerous. The number of lobbyists in Washington, D.C., has more than doubled since 2000.

Lobbying Techniques. Lobbyists engage in an array of activities to influence legislation and government policy. These activities include the following:

- Meeting privately with public officials. Although they are acting on behalf of their clients, lobbyists often furnish needed information to senators and representatives (and

direct technique

An interest group activity that involves personal interaction with government officials to further the group's goals.

indirect technique

A strategy employed by interest groups that uses third parties to influence government officials.

---

4. As quoted in H. R. Mahood, *Interest Groups in American National Politics: An Overview* (New York: Prentice Hall, 2000), p. 51.

government agency appointees). It is to the lobbyists' advantage to provide useful information so that the policymakers will rely on them in the future.

- Testifying before congressional committees for or against proposed legislation.

- Testifying before executive rulemaking agencies—such as the Federal Trade Commission or the Consumer Product Safety Commission—for or against proposed rules.

- Assisting legislators or bureaucrats in drafting legislation or prospective regulations. Especially at the state level, lobbying firms have been known to write up the complete text of a bill, which is then passed by the legislature.

- Inviting legislators to social occasions, such as cocktail parties, boating expeditions, and other events, including conferences at exotic locations.

- Providing political information to legislators and other government officials. Sometimes, the lobbyists have better information than the party leadership about how other legislators are going to vote.

- Suggesting nominations for federal appointments to the executive branch.

AP Images/Jason Getz/Atlanta Journal-Constitution

Image 7–11 Georgia governor Nathan Deal (on the left) meets with a lobbyist during a session of that state's legislature. *Why would a governor willingly be photographed with lobbyists?*

The Ratings Game. Many interest groups attempt to influence the overall behavior of legislators through their rating systems. Each year, these interest groups identify the legislation that they consider most important to their goals and then monitor how legislators vote on it. Legislators receive scores based on their votes. The usual ratings scheme ranges from 0 to 100 percent. In the scheme of the liberal Americans for Democratic Action, for example, a rating of 100 means that a member of Congress voted with the group on every issue and is, by that measure, very liberal.

Building Alliances. Another direct technique used by interest groups is to form a coalition with other groups concerned about the same legislation. Often, these groups will set up a paper organization with an innocuous name to represent their joint concerns. For example, the Coalition for the Future American Worker is an umbrella coalition of grassroots organizations and professional groups. Members argue that immigration is harming American workers.

Members of such a coalition share expenses and multiply the influence of their individual groups by combining their efforts. Other advantages of forming a coalition are that it blurs the specific interests of the individual groups involved and makes it appear that larger public interests are at stake. These alliances also are efficient devices for keeping like-minded groups from duplicating one another's lobbying efforts.

Campaign Assistance. Groups recognize that the greatest concern of legislators is to be reelected, so they focus on the legislators' campaign needs. Associations with large memberships, such as labor unions, are able to provide workers for political campaigns, including precinct workers to get out the vote, volunteers to put up posters and pass out literature, and people to staff telephone banks at campaign headquarters.

ClassicStock/Alamy

Image 7–12 A cartoon from 1889 contends that the United States Senate is dominated by corporate interests. The term *trust* refers to a type of monopoly. Prior to the 1914 elections, members of the Senate were elected by state legislatures. *Was such a body more likely to be corrupt than one elected directly by the people? Why or why not?*

Candidates vie for the groups' endorsements in a campaign. Gaining those endorsements may be automatic, or it may require that the candidates participate in debates or interviews with the interest groups. An interest group usually publicizes its choices in its membership publication, and the candidate can use the endorsement in her or his campaign literature.

Citizens United v. FEC. In 2010, the United States Supreme Court shook up the campaign-finance system when it issued its opinion in *Citizens United v. FEC.*[5] The Court ruled that corporations (and, implicitly, unions) may spend freely to support or oppose political candidates, so long as they do not contribute directly to candidate campaigns. The new freedom to make "independent expenditures" eases decades-old limits on corporate participation in federal elections. The Court held that the independent expenditures were a form of constitutionally protected free speech. The Court's decision was criticized by President Obama and many others. Some critics argued that the Court was granting to corporations rights that should only be given to flesh-and-blood humans. As it turned out, the main beneficiaries of the new rules were not corporations, but ideological interest groups that were often funded by extremely wealthy individuals. You will learn much more about campaign finance in Chapter 9.

Indirect Techniques

Interest groups can also try to influence government policy by working through others, who may be constituents or members of the general public. Indirect techniques mask an interest group's own activities and make the effort appear to be spontaneous. Furthermore, legislators and government officials are often more impressed by contacts from constituents than from an interest group's lobbyist.

5. 130 S.Ct. 876 (2010).

Generating Public Pressure. In some instances, interest groups try to produce a "groundswell" of public pressure to influence the government. Such efforts may include advertisements online and in newspapers, mass mailings, television publicity, and demonstrations. The Internet and social media make communication efforts even more effective. Interest groups may commission polls to find out what the public's sentiments are and then publicize the results. The intent of this activity is to convince policymakers that public opinion supports the group's position.

Some corporations and interest groups also engage in a practice that might be called **climate control.** With this strategy, public relations efforts are aimed at improving the public image of the industry or group and are not necessarily related to any specific political issue. Contributions by corporations and groups in support of public television programs, sponsorship of special events, and commercials extolling the virtues of corporate research are some ways of achieving climate control. For example, to improve its image in the wake of litigation against tobacco companies, Philip Morris began advertising its assistance to community agencies, including halfway houses for teen offenders and shelters for battered women. By building a reservoir of favorable public opinion, groups believe that their legislative goals will be less likely to encounter opposition from the public.

Using Constituents as Lobbyists. An interest group may also use constituents of elected officials to lobby for the group's goals. In the "shotgun" approach, the interest group tries to mobilize large numbers of constituents to write, phone, or send e-mails and tweets to their legislators or to the president. Often, the group provides language that constituents can use in the communication, thus sparing people from the need to compose a message of their own. These efforts are effective on Capitol Hill only when the number of responses is very large. Legislators know that the voters did not initiate the communications on their own when many communications use exactly the same wording. Artificially manufactured grassroots activity has been aptly labeled *astroturf lobbying.*

A more powerful variation of this technique uses only important constituents. With this approach, known as the "rifle" technique or the "Utah plant manager theory," the interest group might, for example, ask the manager of a local plant in Utah to contact the senator from Utah. Because the constituent is seen as influential and responsible for many jobs, the legislator is more likely to listen carefully to the constituent's concerns about legislation than to a paid lobbyist.

Unconventional Forms of Pressure. Sometimes, interest groups may employ forms of pressure that are outside the ordinary political process. These can include marches, rallies, or demonstrations. Such assemblies, as long as they are peaceful, are protected by the First Amendment. In Chapter 5, we described the civil disobedience techniques of the African American civil rights movement in the 1950s and 1960s. The 1963 March on Washington in support of civil rights was one of the most effective demonstrations ever organized. The women's suffrage movement of the early 1900s also employed marches and demonstrations to great effect.

Demonstrations, however, are not always peaceable. Violent demonstrations have a long history in America, dating back to the antitax Boston Tea Party described in Chapter 2. The Vietnam War (1965–1975) provoked a continuous series of demonstrations, some of which were violent. Violent demonstrations can be counterproductive—instead of putting pressure on the authorities, they may simply alienate the public. For instance, historians continue to debate whether the demonstrations against the Vietnam War were effective or counterproductive. The same question has been raised in response to demonstrations against presidential candidate Donald Trump.

climate control

The use of public relations techniques to create favorable public opinion toward an interest group, industry, or corporation.

Image 7–13 Actors from the movie *Selma* wear T-shirts at the New York Public Library to protest the death of Eric Garner, who died of asphyxiation during an arrest in Staten Island. *How effective are demonstrations?*

Another unconventional form of pressure is the **boycott**—a refusal to buy a particular product or deal with a particular business. To be effective, boycotts must command widespread support. One example was the African American boycott of buses in Montgomery, Alabama, in 1955, described in Chapter 5. Another was the boycott of California grapes that were picked by nonunion workers, as part of a campaign to organize Mexican American farmworkers. The first grape boycott lasted from 1965 to 1970. A series of later boycotts was less effective. Recent attempts to boycott Israel due to its occupation of Palestinian territories have been extremely controversial.

Regulating Lobbyists

Learning Outcome **5:**

Describe the main ways in which lobbyists are regulated.

Congress made its first attempt to control lobbyists and lobbying activities through Title III of the Legislative Reorganization Act of 1946, otherwise known as the Federal Regulation of Lobbying Act. The law actually provided for public disclosure more than for regulation, and it neglected to specify which agency would enforce its provisions. The 1946 legislation defined a *lobbyist* as any person or organization that received funds to be used principally to influence legislation before Congress. Such persons and organizations were supposed to "register" their clients and the purposes of their efforts, and to report quarterly on their activities.

The legislation was tested in a 1954 Supreme Court case and was found to be constitutional.[6] The Court agreed that the lobbying law did not violate due process, freedom of speech or of the press, or the freedom to petition. The Court narrowly con-

boycott

A form of pressure or protest—an organized refusal to purchase a particular product or deal with a particular business.

6. *United States v. Harris,* 347 U.S. 612 (1954).

strued the act, however, holding that it applied only to lobbyists who were influencing federal legislation *directly*.

The Results of the 1946 Act

The immediate result of the act was that a minimal number of individuals registered as lobbyists. National interest groups, such as the National Rifle Association and the American Petroleum Institute, could employ hundreds of staff members who were, of course, working on legislation but register only one or two lobbyists who were engaged *principally* in influencing Congress. There were no reporting requirements for lobbying the executive branch, federal agencies, or congressional staff. Approximately seven thousand individuals and organizations registered annually as lobbyists, although most experts estimated that ten times that number were actually employed in Washington to exert influence on the government.

The Reforms of 1995

The reform-minded Congress of 1995–1996 overhauled the lobbying legislation, fundamentally changing the ground rules for those who seek to influence the federal government. The Lobbying Disclosure Act, passed in 1995, included the following provisions:

- A *lobbyist* is defined as anyone who spends at least 20 percent of his or her time lobbying members of Congress, their staffs, or executive-branch officials.

- Lobbyists must register with the clerk of the House and the secretary of the Senate.

- Semiannual reports must disclose the general nature of the lobbying effort.

- The requirements exempt "grassroots" lobbying efforts and those of tax-exempt organizations, such as religious groups.

Also in 1995, both the House and the Senate adopted new rules on gifts and travel expenses provided by lobbyists. The House adopted a flat ban on gifts, while the Senate established limits—senators were prohibited from accepting any gift with a value of more than $50 and from accepting gifts worth more than $100 from a single source in a given year. These gift rules stopped the broad practice of taking members of Congress to lunch or dinner at high-priced restaurants, but the various exemptions and exceptions have allowed much gift giving to continue.

The Reforms of 2007

In September 2007, President George W. Bush signed the Honest Leadership and Open Government Act. Under the new law, lobbyists must report quarterly, and the registration threshold is $10,000 in spending per quarter. Organizations must report coalition activities if they contribute more than $5,000 to a coalition. The House and the Senate must now post lobbying information in a searchable file on the Internet.

In a significant alteration to legislative practices, "earmarked" expenditures, commonly called "pork," must now be identified and made public. This last change may not have immediately had its intended effect of reducing earmarks, however. Many legislators are actually proud of their pork and happy to tell the folks back home all about it. In 2011, the Republican majority in the House banned earmarks that benefit a particular business, but this rule tended to drive pork underground rather than eliminating it completely.

How you can make a difference

Almost every year, Congress and the various state legislatures debate measures that would alter gun laws for the nation or for the individual states. As a result, there are plenty of opportunities to get involved.

- Issues in the debate include child-safety features on guns and the regulation of gun dealers who sell firearms at gun shows. Proponents of gun control seek safety locks and more restrictions on gun purchases.

- Proponents of firearms claim that possessing firearms is a constitutional right and meets a vital defense need for individuals. They contend that the problem lies not in the sale and ownership of weapons but in their use by criminals.

- The Coalition to Stop Gun Violence takes the position that handguns "serve no valid purpose, except to kill people." In contrast, the National Rifle Association (NRA) of America supports the rights of gun owners. The NRA, founded in 1871, is currently one of the most powerful single-issue groups in the United States. The NRA believes that gun laws will not reduce the number of crimes. It is illogical to assume, according to the NRA, that persons who refuse to obey laws prohibiting rape, murder, and other crimes will obey a gun law.

- In recent years, gun rights advocates have been strikingly successful in accomplishing their objectives. One sign of this is the affirmation by the United States Supreme Court that individuals have a constitutional right to bear arms.

- The NRA and other organizations have also been effective in winning state laws that allow citizens to carry concealed weapons in an ever-greater number of environments, including college campuses.

- To find out more about the NRA's positions, go to www.nra.org.

- Organizations that advocate gun controls include the Coalition to Stop Gun Violence and the Brady Campaign to Prevent Gun Violence. You can locate the first of these organizations at csgv.org and the second at www.bradycampaign.org.

KEY TERMS

boycott 200	indirect technique 196	lobbyist 181	service sector 187
climate control 199	interest group 181	material incentive 183	social movement 182
direct technique 196	labor movement 186	public interest 189	solidary incentive 183
free rider problem 183	latent interests 182	purposive incentive 183	

CHAPTER SUMMARY

Learning Outcome 1 An interest group is an organization whose members share common objectives and actively attempt to influence government policy. Interest groups proliferate in the United States because they can influence government at many points in the political structure and because they offer solidary, material, and purposive incentives to their members. Interest groups are often created out of social movements.

Learning Outcome 2 Major types of economic interest groups include business, agricultural, labor, public employee, and professional groups. Other important groups include environmental, public-interest, single-interest, ideological, and identity groups. In addition, foreign governments and corporations lobby our government.

Learning Outcome 3 Factors that can help make an interest group effective include membership size, financial resources, strong leadership, and cohesion around specific issues. The existence of interest groups has been seen as confirming both the elite theory and the pluralist theory of American politics.

Many groups are considered to be part of the coalitions that support the two major parties.

Learning Outcome 4 Interest groups use direct and indirect techniques to influence government. Direct techniques include testifying before committees and rulemaking agencies, providing information to legislators, rating legislators' voting records, building alliances, and aiding political campaigns. Indirect techniques to influence government include campaigns to rally public sentiment, letter-writing campaigns, efforts to influence the climate of opinion, and the use of constituents to lobby for the group's interest. Unconventional methods of applying pressure include demonstrations and boycotts.

Learning Outcome 5 The 1946 Legislative Reorganization Act was the first attempt to control lobbyists and their activities through registration requirements. In 1995, Congress approved new legislation requiring anyone who spends 20 percent of his or her time influencing legislation to register as a lobbyist. Also, any organization spending more than a set amount and any individual who is paid significantly for his or her work must register. Semiannual reports must include the names of clients, the bills in which they are interested, and the branches of government contacted. Grassroots and tax-exempt organizations are exempt from the rules.

In 2007, Congress tightened rules and increased reporting requirements for lobbyists. Under the 2007 reform legislation, lobbyists now have to report contributions to coalition efforts. Congress has created a searchable online database of lobbying information.

ADDITIONAL RESOURCES

Online Resources

- You can learn more about the labor movement by visiting the AFL-CIO's site at **www.aflcio.org**. For a business perspective, try the U.S. Chamber of Commerce at **www.uschamber.com**.

- AARP (formerly the American Association of Retired Persons) can be found at **www.aarp.org**.

Books

Day, Christine L. *AARP: America's Largest Interest Group and Its Impact.* Westport, Conn.: Praeger, 2016. The history and successes of the nation's largest membership organization. Day is a political science professor at the University of New Orleans.

Moss, Michael. *Salt Sugar Fat: How the Food Giants Hooked Us.* New York: Random House Trade Paperbacks, 2014. An investigative reporter for the *New York Times,* Moss argues that while food safety is heavily regulated, the government has been industry's best partner in encouraging Americans to become more dependent on processed foods.

Rolf, David. *The Fight for Fifteen: The Right Wage for a Working America.* New York: The New Press, 2016. Rolf, a leader of the Service Employees International Union, describes the ongoing fight for a higher minimum wage.

Video

Sixty Minutes: The Lobbyist's Playbook—Jack Abramoff, the notorious former lobbyist, spent more than three years in prison for his crimes. In this 2011 excerpt from the well-known CBS News show, Leslie Stahl interviews Abramoff.

Moyers & Company: United States of ALEC—The American Legislative Exchange Council (ALEC) is an alliance of corporations and conservative state politicians that designs model laws for states to adopt. In this 2012 episode, journalist Bill Moyers contends that ALEC's legislation promotes corporate profits at the public's expense.

Quiz

Multiple Choice and Fill-Ins

Learning Outcome 1 Describe the basic characteristics of interest groups, and provide three major reasons why Americans join them.

1. When individuals benefit by the actions of an interest group but do not support that group, they are:
   a. free riders.
   b. freeloaders.
   c. usually just waiting to join the group.

2. When individuals have definite interests, but choose not to become a member of an interest group that represents these interests, their concerns are called _____ interests.

Learning Outcome 2 List the major types of interest groups, especially those with economic motivations.

3. Union membership in the United States has:
   a. been growing, especially since 2000.
   b. stayed about the same since the Great Depression.
   c. been declining in recent years, except in the public sector.

4. The U.S. Chamber of Commerce is an example of a _____ interest group.

Learning Outcome 3 Evaluate the factors that make some interest groups especially effective.

5. Some factors that make an interest group powerful include:
   a. urban location and financial resources.
   b. membership size, financial resources, and cohesion of its members on key issues.
   c. membership size and attention to a broad range of interests.

6. Interest groups have been described as examples of both the _____ and _____ theories of politics.

Learning Outcome 4 Discuss direct and indirect interest group techniques.

7. Direct interest group techniques include:
   a. using constituents as lobbyists and organizing demonstrations.
   b. meeting with officials and making campaign contributions.
   c. organizing boycotts and filing lawsuits.

8. Some interest groups hire public relations firms to improve the public image of an industry or a group. This is called _____ _____.

Learning Outcome 5 Describe the main ways in which lobbyists are regulated.

9. A difficulty in limiting the effect of lobbying is:
   a. opposition to new legislation by Democratic members of Congress.
   b. opposition to new legislation by Republican presidents.
   c. many legislators are proud of "pork" spending and are happy to tell their constituents all about it.

10. Most lobbying today is undertaken by _____, who often work in Washington, D.C., law firms.

Essay Questions

1. "If guns are outlawed, only outlaws will have guns." This is a key slogan used by opponents of gun control. How much truth do you think there is to this slogan? Explain your reasoning.

2. About half of the paid lobbyists in Washington are former government staff members or former members of Congress. Why would interest groups employ such people? Why might some reformers want to limit the ability of interest groups to employ them? On what basis might an interest group argue that such limits are unconstitutional?

POLITICAL 8 PARTIES

In American politics, the donkey is the symbol for the Democrats. It was first used in 1828. The elephant is the symbol for the Republicans. It was first used in 1874.

Found Image Holdings Inc/Getty Images

These five **LEARNING OUTCOMES** *below are designed to help improve your understanding of this chapter:*

1: Cite some of the major activities of U.S. political parties, and discuss how they are organized.

2: Explain how the history of U.S. political parties has led to the two major parties that exist today.

3: Summarize key differences between the policies and supporters of the major parties.

4: Give reasons why the two-party system has endured in America, and evaluate the impact of third parties on U.S. politics.

5: Discuss some of the ways in which support for the parties can change, and explain the increasing importance of independents.

What if... the Democrats Behaved More Like the Republicans?

The Republicans are the conservative party, and the Democrats lean liberal. Conservatism and liberalism are powerful traditions. Neither party is about to abandon these beliefs. Yet ideology is not the only way in which Democrats and Republicans differ.

Pundits—newspaper columnists and "talking heads" on TV—often describe the major parties as mirror images of each other. True, both parties have ideologies. Both are supported by various interest groups. In other ways, however, the parties are quite different. In recent decades, conservative ideology has been central to the Republican identity. Interest groups are much more important to the Democrats.

Why aren't Democrats the ideological party and Republicans the party more attuned to interests? That might make as much sense as what we have now. Further, there are Democrats who wish their party were more ideological. One of them is Bernie Sanders. What would it be like if Bernie had his way?

What If the Democrats Behaved More Like the Republicans?

Ideological consistency among Republican legislators is not something that "just happened." Republicans in Congress know that if they do not toe the ideological line, they will face opposition in Republican primary elections. Their opponents will brand them as *RINOs* (Republicans in name only). Scores of Republican officeholders have gone down to defeat in recent years because they were seen as insufficiently conservative.

If the Democrats were to become an equally ideological party, they would have to start defeating "*DINOs*" in the Democratic primaries. That would require something of a political revolution, of course, but that is what Bernie has advocated. According to Bernie, a more ideological Democratic Party would inspire ordinary voters. Young people would be more likely to turn out and vote. It is not enough to have a long list of small steps, as Hillary Clinton did. The Democrats need "big ideas" such as Medicare for everyone and tuition-free college.

Yet big ideas are very difficult to implement given our system of checks and balances.

Even if the Democrats managed to gain the presidency and both chambers of Congress, they would still be limited by their most conservative members. Big ideas that fail will just frustrate people.

What If the Republicans Were More Like the Democrats?

Consider the Republicans. By 2016, that party had become a study in popular frustration. In 2010, Republicans took control of the U.S. House. In 2014, they added the Senate. Republican leaders promised major results. Yet Obama was still president. He had the power to veto any new Republican legislation. Republican radicals hoped to override the president by shutting down the government. The problem was that such a step was hugely unpopular—and unpopular with major Republican interests, such as business groups. Despite the grand promises to Republican voters, nothing much happened.

Or rather, nothing much happened in Congress. The 2016 Republican presidential primaries were another matter. Donald Trump, the winner, did adopt various conservative positions to mollify his new party. Unlike the vast majority of Republican elected officials, however, he had no time for traditional small-government conservatism. Trump demonstrated that major Republican groups—such as the conservative wing of the white working class—were not actually that committed to the party ideology. They wanted a government that would *do* something for them, regardless of whether it squared with ideology. In the future, if the Republicans hope to satisfy these voters, they may need to be a bit more like the Democrats. They may need to find practical ways to address the interests of ordinary Republicans.

For Critical Analysis

◗ **Would you rather have a government dominated by one party that could get something done? Or is it better if the parties share government and balance each other? In either case, why?**

◗ **Why might the Republicans have become the more ideological party?**

Gino Santa Maria/Shutterstock.com

Image 8–1 Presidential candidate Bernie Sanders (D., Vt.) at a campaign rally in Missouri in 2016. *Is there any way in which Sanders could have won the Democratic nomination?*

Every two years, the media concentrate on the state of the political parties. Prior to an election, a typical poll usually asks the following question: "Do you consider yourself to be a Republican, a Democrat, or an independent?" For many years, Americans were divided fairly evenly among these three choices. Today, more than 40 percent of all voters call themselves **independents,** although in fact three-quarters or more of all independents lean toward either the Republicans or the Democrats.

After the elections are over, the media publish the election results. Among other things, Americans learn which party will control the presidency and how many Democrats and Republicans will be sitting in the House of Representatives and the Senate when the new Congress convenes. These results can have consequences, as we showed in the chapter-opening *What If . . .* feature.

Still, hardly anyone actually "belongs" to a political party in the sense of being a card-carrying member. To become a member of a political party, you do not have to pay dues, pass an examination, or swear an oath of allegiance. Therefore, we can ask an obvious question: If it takes almost nothing to be a member of a political party, what, then, is a political party?

independent

A voter or candidate who does not identify with a political party.

political party

A group of political activists who organize to win elections, operate the government, and determine public policy.

policy demanders

Individuals or interest group members who participate in political parties with the intent to see that certain policies are adopted or specific groups favored.

Political Parties in the United States

> Learning Outcome **1:**

A **political party** might be formally defined as a group of political activists who organize to win elections, operate the government, and determine public policy. Political parties are thus quite different from interest groups, which seek to influence, not run, the government.

As we explain later, a party includes elected officials who ran under the party's banner, officers of the party organization itself, and party supporters. These supporters may be ordinary citizens who do nothing more than regularly vote for the party's candidates. Supporters also include individuals and interest groups who are much more active than that. In *The Party Decides*, a modern classic book, a team of political scientists has argued that **policy demanders** are a key part of any major party. Policy demanders are interest group members or other ideologically motivated individuals who participate in parties with the intent to see that certain policies are adopted, or at least specific groups favored.[1]

Cite some of the major activities of U.S. political parties, and discuss how they are organized.

Functions of Political Parties in the United States

Political parties in the United States engage in a wide variety of activities, many of which are discussed in this chapter. Through these activities, parties perform a number of functions for the political system. These functions include the following:

1. *Recruiting candidates for public office.* Because it is the goal of parties to gain control of government, they must work to recruit candidates for all elective offices.

Emmanuel Dunand/Getty Images

Image 8–2 Republican Party supporters at the Republican National Convention. *What does it take to become a member of a U.S. political party?*

---

1. Marty Cohen et al., *The Party Decides: Presidential Nominations before and after Reform* (Chicago: University of Chicago Press, 2008).

party-in-the-electorate

Those members of the general public who identify with a political party or who express a preference for one party over another.

party organization

The formal structure and leadership of a political party, including election committees; local, state, and national executives; and paid professional staff.

2. *Organizing and running elections.* Although elections are a government activity, political parties actually organize voter-registration drives, recruit volunteers to work at the polls, provide much of the campaign activity to stimulate interest in the election, and work to increase voter participation.

3. *Presenting alternative policies to the electorate.* Parties focus on a political program, which is typically detailed in the *party platform.* Party members, when elected, usually try to implement that program.

4. *Accepting responsibility for operating the government.* When a party elects the president or governor—or the majority of the members of a legislative body—it accepts the responsibility for running the government. This includes developing linkages among elected officials in the various branches of government to gain support for policies and their implementation.

5. *Acting as the organized opposition to the party in power.* The "out" party, or the one that does not control the government, is expected to articulate its own policies and oppose the winning party when appropriate.

The major functions of American political parties are carried out by a small, relatively loose-knit nucleus of party activists. This arrangement is quite different from the more highly structured, mass-membership organization typical of many European parties. American parties concentrate on winning elections rather than on signing up large numbers of deeply committed, dues-paying members who believe passionately in the party's program.

The Three Faces of a Party

Although American parties are known by a single name and, in the public mind, have a common historical identity, each party really has three major components. The first component is the **party-in-the-electorate.** This phrase refers to all those individuals who claim an attachment to the political party. They need not participate in election campaigns. Rather, the party-in-the-electorate is the large number of Americans who feel some loyalty to the party or who use partisanship as a cue to decide who will earn their vote. Party membership is not really a rational choice. Rather, it is an emotional tie somewhat analogous to identifying with a region or a baseball team.

The second component, the **party organization,** provides the structural framework for the political party by recruiting volunteers to become party leaders, identifying potential candidates, and organizing caucuses, conventions, and election campaigns for its candidates, as will be discussed in more detail shortly. It is the party organization and its active workers that keep the party functioning between elections, as well as ensure that the party puts forth electable candidates. If the party-in-the-electorate declines in numbers and loyalty, the party organization must try to find a strategy to rebuild the grassroots following.

Allison Shelley/Getty Images

Image 8–3 In June 2016, House members undertook an overnight sit-in on the House floor in an attempt to force a vote on gun control legislation. From left to right are John Lewis (D., Ga.), James Clyburn (D., S.C.), Maxine Waters (D., Calif.), and Charles Rangel (D., N.Y.). *Why is gun legislation so hard to pass?*

The **party-in-government** is the third component of American political parties. The party-in-government consists of those elected and appointed officials who identify with a political party. Generally, elected officials do not also hold official party positions within the formal organization, although they often have the informal power to appoint party executives.

The Party-in-the-Electorate

The party-in-the-electorate consists of everyone who identifies with the party in question who is not an elected official or part of the formal party organization. The party-in-the-electorate does not just consist of ordinary Americans, however, but of elites—motivated interests, media personalities, fund-raisers, and prominent figures of all types. These are people who identify with a party but who are not part of its formal organization and are not elected officials.

As we have noted, the party-in-the-electorate includes policy demanders. In the Democratic Party, for example, teachers' unions function as policy demanders who favor increased spending on education and policies that benefit teachers. Among the Republicans, a variety of policy demanders oppose legislation that would grant legal status to unauthorized immigrants.

Another elite group is opinion leaders. Radio talk show host Rush Limbaugh, for example, holds no office in the government or the Republican Party, but his ideological influence is substantial. Other Republican opinion leaders include Fox News commentator Bill O'Reilly, *Washington Post* columnist George Will, and Erick Erickson of the Resurgent blog. Democratic opinion leaders include MSNBC commentator Rachel Maddow, *New York Times* economics columnist Paul Krugman, and Markos Moulitsas of the Daily Kos blog.

Other elite individuals include fund-raisers and large-scale contributors. In recent years, a majority of the truly famous individual fund-raisers have been Republicans. They include organizers, such as Karl Rove of American Crossroads, and persons who are major contributors all by themselves, such as the brothers Charles and David Koch. Finally, one elite group is heavily Democratic—entertainment celebrities ranging from Leonardo DiCaprio and Natalie Portman through Beyoncé and Bruce Springsteen.

The Party Organization

American political parties are sometimes seen as hierarchical, but this perception is not accurate. In reality, the formal structure of each party—the party organization—reflects a high degree of decentralization. The political parties have a confederal structure, in which each unit has significant autonomy and is linked only loosely to the other units.

The National Party Organization. Each party has a national organization, the most conspicuous part of which is the **national convention,** held every four years. The convention is used to officially nominate the presidential and vice-presidential candidates. In addition, the **party platform** is developed at the national convention. The platform sets forth the party's position on the issues and makes promises to initiate certain policies if the party wins control of the government.

After the convention, the platform sometimes is neglected or ignored when party candidates disagree with it. Still, once elected,

party-in-government

All of the elected and appointed officials who identify with a particular political party.

national convention

The meeting held every four years by each major party to select presidential and vice-presidential candidates, write a platform, choose a national committee, and conduct party business.

party platform

A document drawn up at each national convention, outlining the policies, positions, and principles of the party.

Image 8–4 Reince Priebus is the chairperson of the Republican National Committee. *Do you think he's like the head of a big corporation?*

Image 8–5 Donna Brazile became the interim chair of the Democratic National Committee during the July 2016 Democratic National Convention. The previous chair, Representative Debbie Wasserman Schultz of Florida, resigned after Russian hackers released committee emails that suggested bias against Bernie Sanders.

the parties very often do try to carry out platform promises, and many of the promises eventually become law. Of course, some general goals, such as economic prosperity, are included in the platforms of both parties.

Convention Delegates. The party convention provides a striking illustration of the differences between the ordinary members of a party, or party identifiers, and party activists. Delegates to the Democratic National Convention often take stands on issues that are far more liberal than the positions of ordinary Democratic voters. Delegates to the Republican National Convention are often more conservative than ordinary Republicans. Why does this happen? In part, it is because a person who wishes to become a delegate must be appointed by party leaders or gather votes in a primary election from party members who care enough to vote in a primary. Voter turnout in primary elections is often quite low, and those who do vote are likely to be among the most committed and ideological members of the party.

The National Committee. At the national convention, each of the parties formally chooses a national standing committee, elected by the individual state parties. This **national committee** directs and coordinates party activities during the following four years.

One of the jobs of the national committee is to ratify the presidential nominee's choice of a national chairperson, who in principle acts as the spokesperson for the party. The national chairperson and the national committee plan the next campaign and the next convention, obtain financial contributions, and publicize the national party.

The National Chairperson. In general, the party's presidential candidate chooses the national chairperson. (If that candidate loses, however, the chairperson is often changed.) The national chairperson performs such jobs as establishing a national party headquarters, raising campaign funds and distributing them to state parties and to candidates, and appearing in the media as a party spokesperson. The national chairperson, along with the national committee, attempts to maintain some sort of communication among the different levels of the party organization.

The State Party Organization.
Every state party is unique. Nonetheless, state parties have several organizational features in common. Each state party has a chairperson, a committee, and a number of local organizations. In theory, the role of the **state central committee**—the principal organized structure of each political party within each state—is similar in the various states. The committee has responsibility for carrying out the policy decisions of the party's state convention.

Also, like the national committee, the state central committee has control over the use of party campaign funds during political campaigns. Usually, the state central committee has little, if any, influence on party candidates once they are elected.

Local Party Machinery: The Grassroots.
The lowest layer of party machinery is the local organization, supported by district leaders, precinct or ward captains, and party workers.

Patronage and City Machines. In the 1800s, the institution of **patronage**—the rewarding of the party faithful with government jobs or contracts—held the local organization together. For immigrants and the poor, the political machine often furnished

national committee
A standing committee of a national political party established to direct and coordinate party activities between national party conventions.

state central committee
The principal organized structure of each political party within each state. This committee is responsible for carrying out policy decisions of the party's state convention.

patronage
The rewarding of faithful party workers and followers with government employment or contracts.

important services and protections. The big-city machine was the archetypal example. The last big-city political machine to exercise substantial power was run by Chicago mayor Richard J. Daley (1955–1978), who was also an important figure in national Democratic politics. City machines are now dead, mostly because their function of providing social services (and reaping the reward of votes) has been taken over by state and national agencies.

divided government
A situation in which one major political party controls the presidency and the other controls one or more chambers of Congress, or in which one party controls a state governorship and the other controls part or all of the state legislature.

Local Party Organizations Today. Local political organizations are still able to provide the foot soldiers of politics—individuals who pass out literature and get out the vote on Election Day, which can be crucial in local elections. In many regions, local Democratic and Republican organizations still exercise some patronage, such as awarding courthouse jobs, contracts for street repair, and other lucrative construction contracts. The Supreme Court, however, has ruled that firing or failing to hire individuals because of their political affiliation is an infringement of the employees' First Amendment rights to free expression.[2] Local party organizations are also the most important vehicles for recruiting young adults into political work.

The Party-in-Government

After the election is over and the winners are announced, the focus of party activity shifts from getting out the vote to organizing and controlling the government. As you will see in Chapter 11, party membership plays an important role in the day-to-day operations of Congress, with partisanship determining everything from office space to committee assignments and power on Capitol Hill. For the president, the political party furnishes a pool of qualified applicants for political appointments to run the government. (Although it is uncommon to do so, presidents can and occasionally do appoint executive personnel, such as cabinet members, from the opposition party.) Judicial appointments also offer a great opportunity to the winning party. For the most part, presidents are likely to appoint federal judges from their own party.

Divided Government. All of these party appointments suggest that the winning political party, whether at the national, state, or local level, has a great deal of control in the American system. The degree of control that a winning party can actually exercise, however, depends on several factors. At the national level, an important factor is whether the party controls both the executive and the legislative branches of government. This situation existed while the Republicans controlled both the legislative and the executive branches of government from January 2003 to January 2007, and when the Democrats controlled the government in the two years following Obama's inauguration in January 2009.

The winning party has less control over the government when the government is divided. A **divided government** is one in which the executive and legislative branches are controlled by different parties. After the 2010 elections, this was the situation facing the nation. Even though the Democrats still controlled the presidency and the U.S. Senate, they could not

Image 8–6 Senator Amy Klobuchar (D., Minn.) participates in the Twin Cities Gay Pride Parade in Minneapolis. *What positions do leaders of the major parties usually take on gay rights?*

2. *Rutan v. Republican Party of Illinois*, 497 U.S. 62 (1990).

Image 8–7 Republican Nikki Haley is the governor of South Carolina. Her parents immigrated from India, but she was born in the United States. *How can Republicans maximize their support among Asian Americans?*

State of South Carolina

pass legislation unless it was also supported by the Republicans in the House. Although House Republicans could not pass legislation either, they energetically sought to use what bargaining power they had.

Party Polarization. In recent years, it has become increasingly difficult for legislators in either party to obtain support for important legislation from members of the other party. More and more, voting takes place strictly along party lines. Discipline within the party caucuses has never been greater. The Republicans, who took the lead in the development of party unity, presented a united front throughout much of the 1990s. By 2009, the Democrats had largely caught up. One reason for party-line voting is that political overlap between the two parties has essentially vanished. Political scientists calculated that by 2009, the most conservative Democrat in the House was still more liberal than the most liberal Republican—if a term such as *liberal Republican* still makes any sense.

For much of the twentieth century, however, liberal Republicans were a real presence in the nation's politics, and so were extremely conservative Democrats. Millions of Americans formed their party attachments not through ideology, but on the basis of tradition and sentiment. Old-stock New England Yankees were Republicans because New England Yankees had always been Republicans. White southerners were, by and large, Democrats because that party affiliation was part of what it meant to be a southerner. Ideologically, however, most of the southerners were well to the right of the average Yankee. Likewise, Yankee Republicans were, on average, more liberal than most southern Democrats. Today, liberal Yankees are usually Democrats, and conservative southerners are Republicans.

Blocking Tactics. One effect of the new polarization is that interpersonal relationships between members of the parties have deteriorated. True, some senators and representatives are able to maintain friendships across party lines, but such friendships have become less common. A second effect is the growing tactic of blocking bills to make the other party appear ineffective, without any attempt to reach a compromise. Republicans pioneered this tactic in the 1990s under House Speaker Newt Gingrich in an attempt to embarrass Democratic president Bill Clinton, and they tried it again under President Obama with varying degrees of success.

A History of Political Parties in the United States

Learning Outcome **2:**

Explain how the history of U.S. political parties has led to the two major parties that exist today.

two-party system

A political system in which only two parties have a reasonable chance of winning.

The United States has a **two-party system,** and that system has been around since before 1800. The function and character of the political parties, as well as the emergence of the two-party system itself, have much to do with the unique historical forces operating from this country's beginning as an independent nation.

Generally, we can divide the evolution of our nation's political parties into seven periods:

1. The formation of parties, from 1789 to 1816.
2. The era of one-party rule, from 1816 to 1828.
3. The period from Andrew Jackson's presidency to the eve of the Civil War, from 1828 to 1856.

4. The Civil War and post–Civil War period, from 1856 to 1896.
5. The Republican ascendancy and the progressive period, from 1896 to 1932.
6. The New Deal period, from 1932 to about 1968.
7. The modern period, from approximately 1968 to the present.

The Formative Years:
Federalists and Anti-Federalists

The first political division in the United States occurred before the adoption of the Constitution. As you will recall from Chapter 2, the Federalists were those who pushed for the adoption of the Constitution, whereas the Anti-Federalists were against ratification.

In September 1796, George Washington, who had served as president for two terms, decided not to run again. In his farewell address, he made a somber assessment of the nation's future. Washington felt that the country might be destroyed by the "baneful [harmful] effects of the spirit of party." He viewed parties as a threat to both national unity and the concept of popular government.

Nevertheless, in the years after the ratification of the Constitution, Americans came to realize that some permanent mechanism would be necessary to identify candidates for office and represent political differences among the people. The result was two political parties.

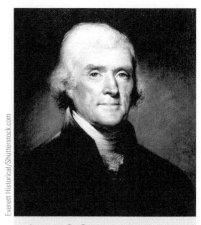

Image 8–8 Thomas Jefferson was particularly adamant about his dislike of political parties. Nonetheless, he helped create a new party that we call the Jeffersonian Republicans. *Why did he find it necessary to engage in party politics?*

Federalists and Republicans. One party was the Federalists, which included John Adams, the second president (1797–1801). The Federalists represented commercial interests such as merchants and large planters. They supported a strong national government.

Thomas Jefferson led the other party, which came to be called the Republicans, or Jeffersonian Republicans. (These Republicans should not be confused with the later Republican Party of Abraham Lincoln.[3]) Jefferson's Republicans represented artisans and farmers. They strongly supported states' rights. In 1800, when Jefferson defeated Adams in the presidential contest, one of the world's first peaceful transfers of power from one party to another was achieved.

The One-Party Interlude. From 1800 to 1820, a majority of U.S. voters regularly elected Jeffersonian Republicans to the presidency and to Congress. By 1816, the Federalist Party had nearly collapsed, and two-party competition did not really exist at the national level. Because there was no real political opposition to the Republicans and thus little political debate, the administration of James Monroe (1817–1825) came to be known as the *era of good feelings.*

Democrats and Whigs

Organized two-party politics returned after 1824. Following the election of John Quincy Adams as president, the Jeffersonian Republican Party split in two. The supporters of Adams called themselves National Republicans. The supporters of Andrew Jackson, who defeated Adams in 1828, formed the **Democratic Party.** Later, the National Republicans took the name **Whig Party,** which had been a traditional name for British liberals. The Whigs stood for, among other things, federal spending on "internal improvements," such as roads.

The Democrats opposed this policy. The Democrats, who were the stronger of the two parties, favored personal liberty and opportunity for the "common man." It was understood implicitly that the "common man" was a white man—hostility toward African Americans was an important force holding the disparate Democratic groups together.[4]

Democratic Party

One of the two major American political parties evolving out of the Republican Party of Thomas Jefferson.

Whig Party

A major party in the United States during the first half of the nineteenth century, formally established in 1836. The Whig Party was anti-Jackson and represented a variety of regional interests.

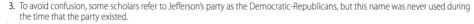

3. To avoid confusion, some scholars refer to Jefferson's party as the Democratic-Republicans, but this name was never used during the time that the party existed.
4. Edward Pessen, *Jacksonian America: Society, Personality, and Politics* (Homewood, Ill.: Dorsey Press, 1969). See especially pages 246–247. The small number of free blacks who could vote were overwhelmingly Whig.

Image 8–9 Andrew Jackson earned the name "Old Hickory" for his exploits during the War of 1812. In 1828, Jackson was elected president as the candidate of the new Democratic Party. *What policies held the new party together?*

Image 8–10 Abraham Lincoln ran on the Republican ticket for president in 1860. *What political groups banded together to form the modern Republican party?*

The Civil War Crisis

In the 1850s, hostility between the North and the South over the issue of slavery divided both parties. The Whigs were the first to split in two. The Whigs had been the party of an active federal government, but white Southerners had come to believe that "a government strong enough to build roads is a government strong enough to free your slaves." The southern Whigs therefore ceased to exist as an organized party. In 1854, the northern Whigs united with antislavery Democrats and members of the radical antislavery Free Soil Party to found the modern **Republican Party.**

The Post–Civil War Period

After the Civil War, the Democratic Party was able to heal its divisions. Southern resentment of the Republicans' role in defeating the South and fears that the federal government would intervene on behalf of African Americans ensured that the Democrats would dominate the white South for the next century. It was in this period that the Republicans adopted the nickname **GOP,** which stands for "grand old party."

Cultural Politics. Northern Democrats feared a strong government for other reasons. The Republicans thought that the government should promote business and economic growth, but many Republicans also wanted to use the power of government to impose evangelical Protestant moral values on society. Democrats opposed what they saw as culturally coercive measures. Many Republicans wanted to limit or even prohibit the sale of alcoholic beverages. They favored the establishment of public schools—with a Protestant curriculum. As a result, Catholics were strongly Democratic.

The Triumph of the Republicans. In this period, the parties were very evenly matched in strength. In the 1890s, however, the Republicans gained a decisive edge. In that decade,

Republican Party

One of the two major American political parties. It emerged in the 1850s as an antislavery party and consisted of former northern Whigs and antislavery Democrats.

GOP

A nickname for the Republican Party; stands for "grand old party."

the Populist movement emerged in the West and South to champion the interests of small farmers, who were often greatly in debt. Populists supported inflation, which benefited debtors by reducing the real value of outstanding debts. In 1896, when William Jennings Bryan became the Democratic candidate for president, the Democrats embraced populism.

As it turned out, the few western farmers who were drawn to the Democrats by this step were greatly outnumbered by urban working class voters who believed that inflation would reduce the purchasing power of their paychecks and who therefore became Republicans. William McKinley, the Republican candidate, was elected with a solid majority of the votes. You can see the states taken by Bryan and McKinley in this chapter's *Consider the Source* feature. Political scientists use the term *realignment* to refer to this

Consider the source

Presidential Election Results

One of the most fascinating ways to examine American political history is through a series of maps showing presidential election outcomes by state. We cannot include all of these maps here, but we do show one of the most important years—1896.

The Election of 1896

In 1896, the agrarian populist appeal of Democrat William Jennings Bryan (red states) won western states for the Democrats at the cost of losing more populous eastern states to Republican William McKinley (blue states). McKinley won the electoral college vote by 271–176. This pattern held in subsequent presidential elections. Note that in 1896, Alaska, Hawaii, Arizona, New Mexico, and Oklahoma were not yet states. Also, the District of Columbia did not yet have representation in the electoral college.

It happens that the partisan division among the states in 1896 was an almost exact reversal of the pattern seen in the

twenty-first century. Except for Washington, every state that supported Bryan in 1896 supported Republican George W. Bush in 2000 and 2004. This reversal parallels the transformation of the Democrats from an anti–civil rights to a pro–civil rights party, and from a party that supported limited government to a party that favors positive government action.

The Source

The number of websites with historical maps of presidential elections is large. The map in Figure 8–1 is taken from one of the best—Dave Leip's Atlas of U.S. Presidential Elections, at uselectionatlas.org. As you will have noticed, one peculiarity of Leip's site is that he reverses the typical color scheme used to depict the two major parties. Leip also shades the colors to indicate intensity of support. In Vermont, the most Republican state, McKinley won more than 80 percent of the vote. In Democratic Mississippi, Bryan's vote exceeded 90 percent. It is worth remembering that almost no African Americans could vote in Mississippi in 1896.

In addition to historical maps, Leip's site also includes an electoral college calculator. This feature lets you play around with possible election outcomes. Do you think a Republican could carry Colorado, Florida, New Hampshire, and Pennsylvania? The calculator lets you find out what would happen in that case.

Figure 8-1 The 1896 Presidential Elections

Note that the colors on this map reverse the usual pattern—here, blue is Republican and red is Democratic.

For Critical Analysis

⊙ Go to uselectionatlas.org and play with the calculator. If a Republican presidential candidate added the four states just mentioned to the states carried by Mitt Romney in 2012, would that have been enough to win? What other election outcomes might be possible?

kind of large-scale change in support for the two major parties. (Realignment is discussed in more detail later in this chapter.) From 1896 until 1932, the GOP was successful in presenting itself as the party that knew how to manage the economy.

The Progressive Interlude

In the early 1900s, a spirit of political reform arose in both major parties. Called *progressivism,* this spirit was compounded of a fear of the growing power of large corporations and a belief that honest, impartial government could regulate the economy effectively. In 1912, the Republican Party temporarily split as former Republican president Theodore Roosevelt campaigned for the presidency on a third-party Progressive ticket. The Republican split permitted the election of Woodrow Wilson, the Democratic candidate, along with a Democratic Congress.

Like Roosevelt, Wilson considered himself a progressive, although he and Roosevelt did not agree on how progressivism ought to be implemented. Wilson's progressivism marked the beginning of a radical change in Democratic policies. Dating back to its very foundation, the Democratic Party had been the party of limited government. Under Wilson, the Democrats became for the first time at least as receptive as the Republicans to government action in the economy. (Wilson's progressivism did not extend to race relations—African Americans found the Wilson administration to be unremittingly hostile to their interests.)

Image 8–11 President Woodrow Wilson (1913–1921) at baseball opening day in 1916. Wilson considered himself a progressive. *How did he change Democratic policies?*

The New Deal Era

The Republican ascendancy resumed after Wilson left office. It ended with the election of 1932, in the depths of the Great Depression. Republican Herbert Hoover was president when the Depression began in 1929. Although Hoover took some measures to fight the Depression, they fell far short of what the public demanded. Significantly, Hoover opposed federal relief for the unemployed and the destitute. In 1932, Democrat Franklin D. Roosevelt was elected president by an overwhelming margin. As with the election of 1896, the vote in 1932 constituted a major political realignment.

The Great Depression shattered the working class belief in Republican economic competence. Under Roosevelt, the Democrats began to make major interventions in the economy in an attempt to combat the Depression and to relieve the suffering of the unemployed. Roosevelt's New Deal relief programs were open to all citizens, both black and white. As a result, African Americans began to support the Democratic Party in large numbers—a development that would have stunned any American politician of the 1800s.

Roosevelt's political coalition was broad enough to establish the Democrats as the new majority party, in place of the GOP. In the 1950s, Republican Dwight D. Eisenhower, the leading U.S. general during World War II, won two terms as president. Otherwise, with minor interruptions, the Democratic ascendancy lasted until about 1968.

An Era of Divided Government

The New Deal coalition managed the unlikely feat of including both African Americans and whites who were hostile to African American advancement. This balancing act came to an end in the 1960s, a decade that was marked by the civil rights movement, by several years of "race riots" in major cities, and by increasingly heated protests against the Vietnam War (1965–1975). For many economically moderate, socially conservative voters, especially in the South, social issues had become more important than economic ones, and these individuals left the Democratic Party. These voters outnumbered the new voters who joined the Democrats—newly enfranchised African Americans and former liberal Republicans in New England and the upper Midwest.

The Parties in Balance. The result, after 1968, was a slow-motion realignment that left the nation almost evenly divided in politics. In presidential elections, the Republicans had more success than the Democrats. Until the 1990s, Congress remained Democratic, but official party labels can be misleading. Some of the Democrats were southern conservatives who normally voted with the Republicans on issues. As these conservative Democrats retired, they were largely replaced by Republicans. In 1994, Republicans were able to take control of both the House and the Senate for the first time in many years.

Red State, Blue State. Nothing demonstrated the nation's close political divisions more clearly than the 2000 presidential elections. Democratic presidential candidate Al Gore won the popular vote, but lost the electoral college by a narrow margin to Republican George W. Bush. The closeness of the vote in the electoral college led the press to repeatedly publish the map of the results state by state. Commentators discussed at length the supposed differences between the Republican "red states" and the Democratic "blue states."[5]

The Two Major U.S. Parties Today

Learning Outcome **3:**

Summarize key differences between the policies and supporters of the major parties.

Not only was the presidential election of 2000 very close, but the partisan balance in the U.S. Congress was also very close in the opening years of the twenty-first century. It is true that from 1995 until the elections of 2006, the Republicans generally controlled Congress. Their margins of control, however, were very narrow.

A Series of Wave Elections

From time to time, voters demonstrate that they are relatively dissatisfied with the performance of one or another of the major parties. This dissatisfaction can produce a "wave" of support for the other party. Unlike realignments, the effects of a **wave election** are temporary. The first decade of the twenty-first century was marked by a series of wave elections in which the voters punished first one party and then the other.

Wave Elections Sweep Out the Republicans. By 2006, ever-larger numbers of voters came to believe that U.S. intervention in Iraq had been a mistake. In the 2006 midterm elections, the Democrats took control of the U.S. House and Senate in a wave election. In September 2008, a worldwide financial panic turned what had been a modest recession into the greatest economic downturn since the Great Depression of the 1930s. The political consequences were inevitable. In November, Democratic presidential candidate Barack Obama was elected with one of the largest margins in recent years.

wave election

An election in which voters display dissatisfaction with one of the major parties through a "wave" of support for the other. In contrast to a realigning election, the results of a wave election are not permanent.

---

5. The use of red for Republicans and blue for Democrats is a twenty-first century development. It originated in the colors used by TV networks to display the results of presidential elections. This color scheme reverses the typical international pattern, which assigns red to the political left and blue to the right. Red is the traditional color of socialist and communist parties, and the U.S. color reversal was a deliberate attempt to avoid implying that Democrats were socialists.

Wave Elections Threaten the Democrats. As you learned in Chapter 1, in 2010 a wave election returned control of the House to the Republicans. Many voters were convinced that Democrats were expanding government to an unacceptable degree. The uncompromising politics of many of the new Republicans in Congress, however, may have helped President Obama win reelection in 2012. Still, the Republicans retained control of the House, even though Democratic House candidates won more votes nationwide than Republican candidates. The 2014 midterm elections appeared to be another Republican wave. After the elections, the Republicans enjoyed larger majorities in the House and in state legislatures than in any year since 1928.

Two Electorates? While the Republican triumph in 2014 was undeniable, some observers began to question whether that success was really due to the kind of political waves seen in 2008 and 2010. It was hard to identify issues that could have drawn large numbers of people to vote for the Republicans or against the Democrats. In fact, voter turnout in 2014 was only 36.4 percent, lower than any year since the elections of 1942 (which were held in the middle of World War II). Clearly, many people were not motivated to vote at all.

Indeed, low turnout may have been the key to the 2014 midterm elections. Many minority and youthful voters failed to vote in the midterms. In 2014, only 13 percent of voters were aged 18 to 29, compared with 19 percent in 2012. One characteristic of the Obama years has been a striking political divergence between the old and the young. As a result, the nation may be moving into a pattern in which the Democrats usually do better in presidential years, while the Republicans normally have the majority in the midterms.

Election 2016

Partisan Trends in the 2016 Elections

Once upon a time, the Democrats were the party of the white working class. That ceased to be true of the South in the 1960s, and by 2016 it was no longer really true in the North. Much has been made of Trump's appeal to the white working class, defined as white persons without a college education. Trump gained much more support among such voters than among voters with a college degree. (It is also true, however, that Clinton won a majority of the votes of all Americans with incomes below $50,000.) You can see the state-by-state outcome of the 2016 presidential elections in Figure 8–2.

Analysts found that support for Trump was not based in the most troubled parts of the white working class. Such people were likely not to vote at all. The heart of the Trump vote, rather, was among those who were somewhat better off, but who saw their communities unraveling around them. Trump supporters had a bleak view of the future, while Clinton voters were optimistic. A black president, increased immigration, gay marriage, the predicted transition of the United States to a majority-minority nation by 2050—all were signs that the traditional world valued by Trump supporters was in danger.

Trump's victory raised major issues for the Republicans. "White identity politics" may have been a winning strategy in 2016, but it could not win indefinitely. Trump's nationalism, further, was different from the small-government conservatism advocated by most Republican leaders. Many questioned whether the two types of Republicans could hold together. The reality was, however, that as the slogan from the American Revolution put it, if they did not hang together, they would surely hang separately. The Democratic Party had little appeal for either group.

Figure 8–2 The 2016 Presidential Elections

In the 2016 presidential elections, Donald Trump received a majority of the electoral college votes, outdoing Hillary Clinton by a convincing margin. The map is somewhat different than in the presidential election years 2000 through 2012 because of Trump's breakthrough in the Midwest. *Why might Trump have done so well in that region?*

■ Won by Hillary Clinton in 2016.
■ Won by Donald Trump in 2016.
■ Won by Obama in 2012 and Trump in 2016.

The Parties' Core Constituents

Who are the people that support the two major parties? You learned in Chapter 6 how demographic factors affect support for the two parties. Democrats receive disproportionate support not only from the least well-educated voters but also from individuals with advanced degrees. Businesspersons are much more likely to vote Republican than are labor union members. The Jewish electorate is heavily Democratic. White evangelical Christians who are regular churchgoers tend to be Republicans. Hispanics are strongly Democratic, and African Americans are overwhelmingly so. City dwellers tend to be Democrats, and rural people tend to be Republicans.

Core Democratic Groups. In the 1930s, the Democratic Party became something that it had never been before—a party representing the working class. In those years, President Franklin D. Roosevelt implemented new social programs, including Social Security and unemployment insurance. These New Deal programs were in part an attempt to reverse the effects of the Great Depression, which had brought hard times to Americans. Roosevelt's new legislation was particularly beneficial to labor, racial minorities, and lower-income persons in general. Social programs to benefit such groups continue to be key planks in the Democratic Party platform.

As we explained earlier in this chapter, the civil rights movement of the 1950s and 1960s resulted in changes to the Democratic coalition. Culturally conservative Democrats, including many Southerners and some Northern members of the working class, abandoned their party and found a new home with the Republicans. This movement, strongest in the years 1964 through 1980, has been called a "rolling realignment," that is, a realignment not tied to any specific election year. In turn, African Americans, who in the 1950s still cast about a third of their votes for Republicans, became overwhelmingly Democratic.

Image 8–12 Donald Trump and Mike Pence with their families behind them after accepting the Republican nominations for president and vice president at the Republican National Convention in Cleveland in July 2016. *Can a candidate for vice president really help the ticket? Why or why not?*

A history of appealing to groups—labor, African Americans, and later environmentalists, women, and the LGBT community—has shaped the character of the Democratic Party to this day.

Core Republican Values. Like the Democrats, the Republicans are a coalition of interests that sometimes compete with one another. As we explained in the chapter-opening *What If . . .* feature, however, the Republican coalition rests on different principles than the Democratic coalition. Conservatism, as a philosophy, is central to the Republican Party and a powerful force for party unity. Liberalism—or progressivism—simply does not play an equivalent role among the Democrats. According to political scientists Matt Grossman and David Hopkins, "the Republican Party is primarily the agent of an ideological movement whose supporters prize doctrinal purity, while the Democratic Party is better understood as a coalition of social groups seeking concrete government action."[6] Given such traditions, it is understandable that Donald Trump's primary victories in 2016 should have come as a major shock to Republican leaders.

Divisions within the Parties

For much of American history, the two major political parties included individuals with widely varying political beliefs. Today, however, supporters of the major parties demonstrate a striking degree of political convergence. Despite this unity, the parties are made up of a variety of different kinds of people.

Different Kinds of Democrats. In addition to members of the working class and various racial and ethnic minority groups, the Democrats have long included middle-class to upper-middle-class "reform" elements that are drawn to specific issues. By the late twentieth century, these Democrats were likely to be antiwar or interested in the environment, women's rights, or other causes. During the Vietnam War (1965–1975), differences between "regulars" and antiwar insurgents almost tore the Democrats apart. Typically, Democratic regulars with working class appeal have beaten issue-oriented liberals in presidential nomination contests. As noted, however, many white working class Democrats have become Republicans, even as the number of well-educated liberals in the party has grown.

Obama versus Clinton in 2008. In the 2008 Democratic primaries, Barack Obama appealed to the middle-class reform element while Hillary Clinton did best among working class regulars. Obama, after all, had opposed the war in Iraq, while Clinton had supported it. In previous years, that would have guaranteed Clinton a victory, but Obama also gained strong support among African American voters. A black–reform coalition was just enough to put him over the top.

Clinton versus Sanders in 2016. In 2016, it was Clinton who swept the black vote on the way to victory. Bernie Sanders, her chief opponent, somewhat resembled

6. Matt Grossman and David A. Hopkins, "Ideological Republicans and Group Interest Democrats: The Asymmetry of American Party Politics," *Perspectives on Politics* 13, no. 1 (March 2015), pp. 119–139.

the middle-class reform insurgents who had gone down to defeat in so many earlier Democratic primary contests. Unlike earlier reformers, however, Sanders's pitch was almost entirely based on economic inequality. As a result, he was able to outdraw Clinton among white working class voters. While many reform-movement veterans also supported Sanders, Clinton was able to win over much of the middle class, especially women. The sharpest difference between Sanders and Clinton supporters was that Sanders did very well among younger voters, while older ones tended to prefer Clinton. Sanders supporters perceived themselves as more radical than those backing Clinton. Yet the two candidates were clearly headed in the same progressive direction. They were separated by strategy, not ideology.

Different Kinds of Republicans.

Observers have distinguished several kinds of Republicans. One bloc of GOP voters, often called the Religious Right, is energized by conservative religious beliefs. These conservatives are often evangelical Protestants but may also be Catholics, Mormons, or adherents of other faiths. In the recent past, moral issues such as abortion and gay marriage have been important for these voters.

Business-Oriented Republicans. Another group of Republicans is more oriented toward economic issues and business concerns. These voters often are small-business owners or have some other connection to commercial enterprise. Such voters oppose high tax rates and are concerned about government regulations that interfere with the conduct of business. Business interests and the Religious Right have different concerns, but in the past it was relatively easy for a Republican politician to appeal to both with a platform that was both culturally conservative and pro-business.

Libertarian Republicans. A third type of Republican, however, is strongly libertarian. These voters dislike government regulation of social issues as well as economic ones. They may also oppose U.S. intervention in foreign conflicts. This group is much smaller than the Religious Right or the pro-business bloc and has little influence on party policy. Republican politicians with national ambitions may find that they must play down any libertarian tendencies they actually embrace.

Conservative Nationalists. The rise of Donald Trump exposed an additional type of Republican—conservative nationalists. Opposition to immigration and foreign imports were key issues for this group. These positions put them in direct conflict with the business wing of the party, which supported free trade and relatively open immigration. Trump supporters were disproportionately working class, but many of them were small-business owners and others who had been relatively successful in life.

While Trump supporters reported comparatively high levels of economic anxiety, an even stronger predictor of Trump support was a feeling of racial resentment. This characteristic is often measured by asking whether racism against whites is more of a problem than racism toward blacks or other minority groups. Trump backers were distinctly more likely than supporters of other Republicans to agree that racism against whites is a major concern. Such attitudes pose a continuing problem for Republican leaders,

Tom Williams/CQ Roll Call

Image 8–13 Democratic presidential nominee Hillary Clinton and her running mate Senator Tim Kaine (D., Va.) celebrate at the Democratic National Convention in Philadelphia in July 2016. *In what ways do the national conventions serve the parties?*

many of whom have sought ways to make conservative ideology appealing to minority group members.

Radicals and Moderates.

In the twenty-first century, differences within the parties often pitted moderates against radicals. The contest between Hillary Clinton and Bernie Sanders was an example of this tendency. The division between radicals and moderates was particularly conspicuous among the Republicans during Obama's presidency. In 2010 and 2012, Tea Party activists and other ideological groups sought to purge the Republicans of so-called RINOs (Republicans in name only).

In the 2014 Republican primaries, for example, Eric Cantor (R., Va.)—the majority leader in the House, who had a strong conservative reputation—was defeated by a little-known economics professor running on a more radical platform. In September 2015, House Speaker John Boehner (R., Ohio) announced that he would retire from politics, largely due to frustration with the Tea Party oriented Liberty Caucus and other radicals in the House. The rise of Trump scrambled the division between radicals and moderates, at least for a time. Responses to his candidacy did not follow existing party divisions.

Cultural Politics and Party Loyalty

Cultural values have played a growing role in defining the beliefs of the two major parties. For example, in 1987 Democrats were almost as likely to favor stricter abortion laws (40 percent) as Republicans were (48 percent). Today, Republicans are twice as likely as Democrats to favor stricter abortion laws (50 percent to 25 percent). Cultural forces and economic interests do not always pull in the same direction. In the long run, however, most voters find themselves supporting both the cultural and economic positions of their party, even if they were initially attracted primarily by economics or by cultural issues.

Changing Points of View.

We remarked earlier that cultural conservatism propelled some white working class voters out of the Democratic Party and into the Republican ranks. A number of these voters may initially have retained certain progressive economic ideas. Yet it is not comfortable to hold progressive economic views while supporting a conservative party. The impulse toward political unity becomes conspicuous when an issue that previously was nonpartisan becomes partisan. Climate change can serve as an example. As recently as fifteen years ago, opinions on this topic crossed ideological lines. Today, almost all progressives believe that climate change is a problem, and almost all conservatives believe that it is not.

In the past, progressives often assumed that greater levels of education might change people's minds on an issue such as climate change. After all, a strong scientific consensus exists that climate change is real, man-made, and a serious problem. As it turns out, better-educated Republicans are *more* skeptical of the importance of climate change, not less. If you are better educated, you are more likely to know what your party's position is on an issue such as this. You may also have more familiarity with the arguments advanced by party leaders to defend the party's stand. Climate-change skeptics have produced a substantial body of work that defends their positions. A well-educated person is

Image 8–14 *"I think it was an election year."*

Danny Shanahan The New Yorker Collection/The Cartoon Bank

much more likely to have read these articles and books, or at least to have picked up the main points from fellow conservatives who have read the literature.

Motivated Reasoning. It is very common for people to first establish what it is that they want to believe, and only then assemble data and arguments to back up their conclusions. This is backward reasoning, of course, but it is a kind of reasoning that is important to life as a social animal. For most people, maintaining social relationships is far more important than taking a particular position on an issue. Psychologists refer to this process of working backwards from a preferred conclusion as **motivated reasoning**. This behavior is not limited to one political party. For instance, it can be difficult for a progressive to defend crops altered by genetic engineering (GMO crops) even though the scientific evidence is that such crops are harmless. Motivated reasoning is a strong force for party unity, even if it does not promote rational analysis of the issues.

Why Has the Two-Party System Endured?

Learning Outcome **4:**

There are several reasons why two major parties have dominated the political landscape in the United States for almost two centuries. These reasons have to do with (1) the historical foundations of the system, (2) political socialization and practical considerations, (3) the winner-take-all electoral system, and (4) state and federal laws favoring the two-party system.

Give reasons why the two-party system has endured in America, and evaluate the impact of third parties on U.S. politics.

The Historical Foundations of the Two-Party System

As we have seen, at many times in American history one preeminent issue or dispute has divided the nation politically. In the beginning, Americans were at odds over ratifying the Constitution. After the Constitution went into effect, the power of the federal government became the major national issue. Thereafter, the dispute over slavery divided the nation, North versus South. At times—for example, in the North after the Civil War—cultural differences have been important, with advocates of government-sponsored morality (such as banning alcoholic beverages) pitted against advocates of personal liberty.

During much of the twentieth century, economic differences were preeminent. In the New Deal period, the Democrats became known as the party of the working class, while the Republicans became known as the party of the middle and upper classes and commercial interests. In situations like these, when politics is based on an argument between two opposing points of view, advocates of each viewpoint can mobilize most effectively by forming a single, unified party. The result is a two-party system. When such a system has been in existence for almost two centuries, it becomes difficult to imagine an alternative.

Political Socialization and Practical Considerations

Given that the majority of Americans identify with one of the two major political parties, it is not surprising that most children learn at a fairly young age to think of themselves as either Democrats or Republicans. This generates a built-in mechanism to perpetuate a two-party system. Also, most politically oriented people who aspire to work for change consider that the only realistic way to capture political power in this country is to be either a Republican or a Democrat.

The Winner-Take-All Electoral System

At almost every level of government in the United States, the outcome of elections is based on the **plurality,** winner-take-all principle. In a plurality system, the winner is the person who obtains the most votes, even if that person does not receive a majority (more

motivated reasoning
The process of beginning with the conclusion you want, and only then assembling data and arguments to back up your conclusions.

plurality
A number of votes cast for a candidate that is greater than the number of votes for any other candidate but not necessarily a majority.

than 50 percent) of the votes. Whoever gets the most votes gets everything. Most legislators in the United States are elected from single-member districts in which only one person represents the constituency, and the candidate who finishes second in such an election receives nothing for the effort.

Presidential Voting. The winner-take-all system also operates in the election of the U.S. president. Recall that the voters in each state do not vote for a president directly but vote for electoral college delegates who are committed to the various presidential candidates. These delegates are called *electors*.

Why should you care about **POLITICAL PARTIES?**

Political parties play an important role at the state and local level, in addition to their importance in national politics. A state legislature controlled by the Democrats will create and implement different policies than one controlled by the Republicans, and vice versa. These policies can affect the amount of tuition you pay, the speed limits on your state's highways, and much else.

In all but two states (Maine and Nebraska), if a presidential candidate wins a plurality in the state, then *all* of the state's electoral votes go to that candidate. This is known as the *unit rule*. For example, suppose that the electors pledged to a particular presidential candidate receive a plurality of 40 percent of the votes in a state. That presidential candidate will receive all of the state's votes in the electoral college. Minor parties have a difficult time competing under such a system. Because voters know that minor parties cannot win any electoral votes, they often will not vote for minor-party candidates, even if the candidates are in tune with them ideologically.

Popular Election of the Governors and the President. In most of Europe, the chief executive (usually called the prime minister) is elected by the legislature, or parliament. If the parliament contains three or more parties, as is usually the situation, two or more of the parties can join together in a coalition to choose the prime minister and the other leaders of the government. In the United States, however, the people elect the president and the governors of all fifty states. There is no opportunity for two or more parties to negotiate a coalition. Here, too, the winner-take-all principle discriminates powerfully against any third party.

Proportional Representation. Many other nations use a system of proportional representation. If, during the national election, party X obtains 12 percent of the vote, party Y gets 43 percent of the vote, and party Z gets the remaining 45 percent of the vote, then party X gets 12 percent of the seats in the legislature, party Y gets 43 percent of the seats, and party Z gets 45 percent of the seats.

Some nations implement proportional representation by creating districts that elect multiple representatives. Such a system, however, can require the creation of districts that are uncomfortably large. The nation of Israel, for example, is a single, large electoral district. Every party runs nationwide.

An alternative system is to let voters choose both a local representative and a preferred party. Germany uses such a system to elect members of the Bundestag, its lower house of parliament. Suppose that the Green Party wins the support of 10 percent of the voters in a particular German state, but only a few Greens win in their local districts. If this happens, enough Greens will be added from the party's statewide list of candidates to boost its Bundestag delegation to 10 percent of the total from that state. Regardless of how proportional representation is implemented, the system gives smaller parties a greater incentive to organize than in the United States.

State and Federal Laws Favoring the Two Parties

Many state and federal election laws offer a clear advantage to the two major parties. In some states, the established major parties need to gather fewer signatures to place their candidates on the ballot than minor parties or independent candidates do. The criterion for determining how many signatures will be required is often based on the total party vote in the last general election, thus penalizing a new political party that did not compete in that election.

At the national level, minor parties face different obstacles. All of the rules and procedures of both chambers of Congress divide committee seats, staff members, and other privileges on the basis of party membership. A legislator who is elected on a minor-party ticket, such as the Conservative Party of New York, must choose to be counted with one of the major parties to obtain a committee assignment.

The Federal Election Commission (FEC) rules for campaign financing also place restrictions on minor-party candidates for president. Such candidates are not eligible for federal matching funds in either the primary or the general election. In the 1980 elections, John Anderson, running for president as an independent, sued the FEC for campaign funds. The commission finally agreed to repay part of his campaign costs after the election in proportion to the votes he received. Giving funds to a candidate when the campaign is over is, of course, much less helpful than providing funds while the campaign is still under way.

Image 8–15 Congressional pages carry the electoral college votes to the House chamber where the election of Barack Obama as the forty-fourth president of the United States was certified on January 8, 2009. *What effect does the electoral college have on the political system?*

The Role of Minor Parties in U.S. Politics

For the reasons just discussed, minor parties have a difficult, if not impossible, time competing within the American two-party political system. Still, minor parties have played an important role in our political life. Parties other than the Republicans or Democrats are usually called **third parties.** (Technically, of course, there could be fourth, fifth, or sixth parties as well, but we use the term *third party* because it has endured.) Third parties can come into existence in a number of ways. They may be founded from scratch by individuals or groups who are committed to a particular interest, issue, or ideology. They can split off from one of the major parties when a group becomes dissatisfied with the major party's policies. Finally, they can be organized around a particular charismatic leader and serve as that person's vehicle for contesting elections.

Frequently, third parties have acted as barometers of change in the political mood, forcing the major parties to recognize new issues or trends in the thinking of Americans. Political scientists believe that third parties have acted as safety valves for dissident groups, preventing major confrontations and political unrest. In some instances, third parties have functioned as way stations for voters en route from one of the major parties to the other. Table 8–1 lists significant third-party presidential campaigns in American history, and Table 8–2 provides a brief description of third-party beliefs.

Ideological Third Parties. The longest-lived third parties have been those with strong ideological foundations that are typically at odds with the majority mind-set. The Socialist Party is an example. The party was founded in 1901 and lasted until 1972, when it was finally dissolved. (A smaller party later took up the name.) The Socialists were never very popular in the United States. Conservatives recently revived the term

third party

A political party other than the two major political parties (Republican and Democratic).

Table 8–1   The Most Successful Third-Party Presidential Campaigns since 1864

The following list includes all third-party candidates winning more than 5 percent of the popular vote or any electoral votes since 1864. (We ignore isolated "unfaithful electors" in the electoral college who failed to vote for the candidate to which they were pledged.)

Year	Major Third Party	Third-Party Presidential Candidate	Percent of the Popular Vote	Electoral Votes	Winning Presidential Candidate and Party
1892	Populist	James Weaver	8.5	22	Grover Cleveland (D)
1912	Progressive	Theodore Roosevelt	27.4	88	Woodrow Wilson (D)
	Socialist	Eugene Debs	6.0	—	
1924	Progressive	Robert LaFollette	16.6	13	Calvin Coolidge (R)
1948	States' Rights	Strom Thurmond	2.4	39	Harry Truman (D)
1960	Independent Democrat	Harry Byrd	0.4	15*	John F. Kennedy (D)
1968	American Independent	George Wallace	13.5	46	Richard Nixon (R)
1980	National Union	John Anderson	6.6	—	Ronald Reagan (R)
1992	Independent	Ross Perot	18.9	—	Bill Clinton (D)
1996	Reform	Ross Perot	8.4	—	Bill Clinton (D)

*Byrd received fifteen electoral votes from unpledged electors in Alabama and Mississippi.

Source: *Dave Leip's Atlas of U.S. Presidential Elections* at **www.uselectionatlas.org.**

socialist as an insult directed at President Obama. Given that, it was somewhat surprising that Bernie Sanders did so well as a presidential candidate in 2016 running as a democratic socialist. We take a look at the socialist label in this chapter's *Beyond Our Borders* feature.

Ideology has at least two functions in such parties. First, the members of the party regard themselves as outsiders and look to one another for support—ideology provides great psychological cohesiveness. Second, because the rewards of ideological commitment are partly psychological, these parties do not think in terms of immediate electoral success. A poor showing at the polls therefore does not dissuade either the leadership or the grassroots participants from continuing their quest for change in American government (and, ultimately, American society).

Today's active ideological parties include the Libertarian Party and the Green Party. As you learned in Chapter 1, the Libertarian Party supports a *laissez-faire* ("let it be") capitalist economic program, together with a hands-off policy on regulating matters of moral conduct. The Green Party began as a grassroots environmentalist organization with affiliated political parties across North America and Western Europe. It was established in the United States as a national party in 1996 and nominated Ralph Nader to run for president in 2000. Nader campaigned against what he called "corporate greed," advocated universal health insurance, and promoted environmental concerns. (He ran again for president as an independent in 2004 and 2008.)

splinter party

A new party formed by a dissident faction within a major political party. Often, splinter parties have emerged when a particular personality was at odds with the major party.

Splinter Parties.   Some of the most successful minor parties have been those that split from major parties. The impetus for these **splinter parties,** or factions, has usually been a situation in which a particular personality was at odds with the major party. The

Table 8–2 Policies of Selected American Third Parties since 1864

Populist: This pro-farmer party of the 1890s advocated progressive reforms. It also advocated replacing gold with silver as the basis of the currency in hopes of creating a mild inflation in prices. (It was believed by many that inflation would help debtors and stimulate the economy.)

Socialist: This party advocated a "cooperative commonwealth" based on government ownership of industry. It was pro-labor, often antiwar, and in later years, anti-Communist. It was dissolved in 1972 and replaced by nonparty advocacy groups.

Communist: This left-wing breakaway from the Socialists was the U.S. branch of the worldwide Communist movement. The party was pro-labor and advocated full equality for African Americans. It was also closely aligned with the Communist-led Soviet Union, which provoked great hostility among most Americans.

Progressive: This name was given to several successive splinter parties built around individual political leaders. Theodore Roosevelt, who ran in 1912, advocated federal regulation of industry to protect consumers, workers, and small businesses. Robert LaFollette, who ran in 1924, held similar views.

American Independent: Built around George Wallace, this party opposed any further promotion of civil rights and advocated a militant foreign policy. Wallace's supporters were mostly former Democrats who were soon to be Republicans.

Libertarian: This party opposes most government activity.

Reform: The Reform Party was initially built around businessman H. Ross Perot but later was taken over by others. Under Perot, the party was a middle-of-the-road group opposed to federal budget deficits. Under Patrick Buchanan, it came to represent right-wing nationalism and opposition to free trade.

Green: The Greens are a left-of-center pro-environmental party. They are also generally hostile to globalization.

most successful of these splinter parties was the "Bull Moose" Progressive Party, formed in 1912 to support Theodore Roosevelt for president. The Republican national convention of that year denied Roosevelt the nomination, despite the fact that he had won most of the primaries. He therefore left the GOP and ran against Republican "regular" William Howard Taft in the general election. Although Roosevelt did not win the election, he did split the Republican vote so that Democrat Woodrow Wilson became president.

Third parties have also been formed to back individual candidates who were not rebelling against a particular party. H. Ross Perot, for example, who challenged Republican George H. W. Bush and Democrat Bill Clinton for the presidency in 1992, had not previously been active in a major party. Perot's supporters probably would have split their votes between Bush and Clinton had Perot not been in the race. In theory, Perot ran in 1992 as a nonparty independent. In practice, he had to create a campaign organization. By 1996, Perot's organization was formalized as the Reform Party.

The Impact of Minor Parties. Third parties have rarely been able to affect American politics by actually winning elections. (One exception is that third-party and independent candidates have occasionally won races for state governorships—for example, Jesse Ventura was elected governor of Minnesota on the Reform Party ticket in 1998.) Instead, the impact of third parties has taken two forms. First, third parties can influence one of the major parties to take up one or more issues. Second, third parties can determine the outcome of a particular election by pulling votes from one of the major-party candidates in what is called the "spoiler effect."

Influencing the Major Parties. One of the most clear-cut examples of a major party adopting the issues of a minor party took place in 1896, when

Image 8–16 Eugene V. Debs was the nation's most popular socialist ever—at least until Senator Bernie Sanders (D., Vt.). Debs ran for president five times from 1900 to 1920, the last time from a prison cell. He had been convicted of speaking out against World War I. *Why would such a conviction be impossible today?*

Library of Congress Prints and Photographs Division Washington, D.C. 20540 USA

Beyond our borders

Is Denmark Socialist?

For older Americans, the word *socialism* brings to mind such nations as Cuba, the former Soviet Union, or today's Venezuela. These are not countries that most Americans would want to emulate. Still, from the start of his political career, Vermont senator Bernie Sanders has described himself as a democratic socialist. This identification doesn't seem to have done him any harm in Vermont. The socialist label also doesn't appear to have hurt him much during his campaign for president. Of course, Sanders never named the Soviet Union or Cuba as role models. Rather, when asked what socialism meant to him, his answer was simply "Denmark." There may be much to admire about Denmark, but is it really a socialist country?

The Socialist Tradition in Europe

In response, Danish prime minister Lars Løkke Rasmussen said, "Denmark is far from a socialist planned economy. Denmark is a market economy." Yet Denmark is not quite like the United States, either. Businesses may be lightly regulated, but Denmark has one of the world's most generous welfare systems, with matching high taxes. This system is largely due to the influence of the Social Democrats, Denmark's largest political party for most of the twentieth century. Like the British Labour Party, the French Socialist Party, and the Social Democratic Party of Germany, the Danish Social Democrats are descended from the worldwide socialist movement.

A hundred years ago, all of these parties were much more radical than they are today. Most called for the abolition of capitalism. Instead, the state, democratically elected by the people, would own the factories and shops, the banks and railroads. (Some socialists advocated ownership by employee cooperatives instead.) Time and experience, however, revealed that government ownership of businesses was not helpful. In the years following World War II, one by one the socialist parties gave up the goal of replacing capitalism. What remains is a commitment to a strong welfare state and to the labor movement.

Socialism and Social Democracy

Communists have also described their system as socialist (communism is a goal for the far future). Countries such as Denmark, however, are nothing like that. How should we distinguish Denmark from the old Soviet Union? One answer is to describe Denmark as a *social democracy*. If by *democratic socialist* Bernie really means *social democrat*, he may be on target.

For Critical Analysis

◯ *Socialism* is one of those words that can mean many different things, depending on who is talking. Many other political terms are also highly flexible. Try identifying multiple meanings of words such as *democracy* or *freedom*.

---

the Democratic Party took over the Populist demand for "free silver"—that is, a policy of coining enough new money to create an inflation. As you learned earlier in this chapter, however, absorbing the Populists cost the Democrats votes overall.

Affecting the Outcome of an Election. The presidential elections of 2000 were one instance in which a minor party may have altered the outcome. Green Party candidate Ralph Nader received almost one hundred thousand votes in Florida, a majority of which would probably have gone to Democrat Al Gore if Nader had not been in the race.

The real question, however, is not whether the Nader vote had an effect—clearly, it did—but whether the effect was important. The problem is that in elections as close as the presidential elections of 2000, any factor with an impact on the outcome can be said to have determined the results.

Mechanisms of Political Change

Learning Outcome **5:**

Discuss some of the ways in which support for the parties can change, and explain the increasing importance of independents.

In the future, could one of the two parties decisively overtake the other and become the "natural party of government"? The Republicans held this status from 1896 until 1932, and the Democrats enjoyed it for many years after the election of Franklin D. Roosevelt in 1932.

Realignment

One mechanism by which a party might gain dominance is **realignment.** In this process, major constituencies shift their allegiance from one party to another, creating a long-term alteration in the political environment. Realignment has often been associated with particular elections, called *realigning elections.* The election of 1896, which established a Republican ascendancy, was clearly a realigning election. So was the election of 1932, which made the Democrats the leading party.

Realignments in American Politics. A number of myths exist about the concept of realignment. One is that in realignment a newly dominant party must replace the previously dominant party. Actually, realignment could easily strengthen an already dominant party. Alternatively, realignment could result in a tie. This has happened—twice. One example was the realignment of the 1850s, which resulted in Abraham Lincoln's election as president in 1860. After the Civil War, the Republicans and the Democrats were almost evenly matched nationally.

The most recent realignment—which also resulted in two closely matched parties—was a gradual process that took place over many years. In 1968, Republican presidential candidate Richard Nixon adopted a "southern strategy," aimed at drawing dissatisfied southern Democrats into the Republican Party.[7] At the presidential level, the strategy was an immediate success, although years would pass before the Republicans could gain dominance in the South's delegation to Congress or in state legislatures. Another milestone in the progress of the Republican realignment was Ronald Reagan's sweeping victory in the presidential elections of 1980.

Is Realignment Still Possible? The sheer size of our nation, combined with the inexorable pressure toward a two-party system, has resulted in parties made up of voters with conflicting interests or values. The pre–Civil War party system involved two parties—Whigs and Democrats—with support in both the North and the South. This system could survive only by burying, as deeply as possible, the issue of slavery. We should not be surprised that the structure eventually collapsed. The Republican ascendancy of 1896–1932 united capitalists and industrial workers under the Republican banner, despite serious economic conflicts between the two. The New Deal Democratic coalition after 1932 brought African Americans and ardent segregationists into the same party.

For realignment to occur, a substantial body of citizens must come to believe that their party can no longer represent their interests or values. The problem must be fundamental and not attributable to the behavior of an individual politician. It is not easy to identify large groups of Republicans or Democrats today who might reach such a conclusion.

In recent years, however, a number of small-scale realignments have taken place. Chapter 7 described a state-level realignment in West Virginia. Many West Virginia voters switched from the Democrats to the Republicans in the belief that Democratic environmentalists were "anti-coal." Muslims of Middle Eastern ancestry provide another

realignment

A process in which a substantial group of voters switches party allegiance, producing a long-term change in the political landscape.

---

7. The classic work on Nixon's southern strategy is Kirkpatrick Sales, *The Emerging Republican Majority* (New Rochelle, N.Y.: Arlington House, 1969).

dealignment

A decline in party loyalties that reduces long-term party commitment.

party identification

Linking oneself to a particular political party.

straight-ticket voting

Voting exclusively for the candidates of one party.

split-ticket voting

Voting for candidates of two or more parties for different offices, such as voting for a Republican presidential candidate and a Democratic congressional candidate.

small-scale example. This group formerly had a Republican majority, but during the last decade, most Muslim Republicans decided that the Democrats were more likely to protect Muslim rights and interests.

Dealignment

Among political scientists, one common argument has been that realignment is no longer likely because voters are not as committed to the two major parties as they were in the 1800s and early 1900s. In this view, called **dealignment** theory, large numbers of independent voters may result in political volatility, but the absence of strong partisan attachments means that it is no longer easy to "lock in" political preferences for decades.

Independent Voters. Figure 8–3 shows trends in **party identification,** as measured by standard polling techniques from 1944 to the present. The chart displays a rise in the number of independent voters throughout the period combined with a fall in support for the Democrats from the mid-1960s on. The decline in Democratic identification may be due to the consolidation of Republican support in the South since 1968, a process that by now is substantially complete. In any event, the traditional Democratic advantage in party identification has largely vanished.

Not only has the number of independents grown over the last half century, but voters have also been less willing to vote a straight ticket—that is, to vote for all the candidates of one party. In the early twentieth century, **straight-ticket voting** was nearly universal. By midcentury, 12 percent of voters engaged in **split-ticket voting**—voting for candidates of two or more parties for different offices, such as voting for a Republican presidential candidate and a Democratic congressional candidate. By the 1970s and 1980s, 25 to 30 percent of all ballots cast in presidential election years were split-ticket. A major reason was that many voters, especially in the South, were pairing a Republican for president with a conservative Democrat for Congress. In recent years, however, conservative Democrats have become scarce, and the incidence of split-ticket voting has ranged only from 17 to 19 percent.

Figure 8–3   Party Identification from 1944 to the Present

Why would people who usually support one of the two major parties still call themselves independents?

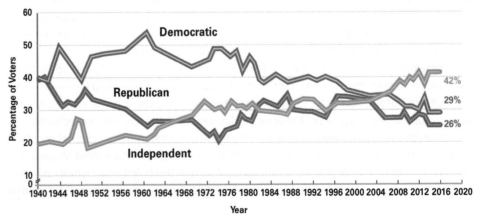

Sources: *Gallup Report,* August 1995; *New York Times*/CBS poll, June 1996; *Gallup Report,* February 1998; The Pew Research Center for the People and the Press, November 2003; Gallup polls, 2004 through 2016.

Not-So-Independent Voters. A problem with dealignment theory is that many of the "independent" voters are not all that independent. Political scientists have long known that a majority of self-identified independents reliably support one or another of the major political parties. When it comes to voting, these political *leaners* are every bit as loyal to their preferred party as those who accept a party label. As you can see in Figure 8–3, in a recent Gallup poll, 42 percent of those polled described themselves as independents. Yet 16 percent of all respondents admitted that they were independents who leaned Republican, and another 16 percent were independents who leaned Democratic. This left only 10 percent of the total who were true **swing voters** who could swing between the parties.

The relatively modest number of true independents raises a strategic question for the parties. Is it more important to sway the independents, or can a party obtain better results by improving voter turnout among its natural supporters? The answer to that question has varied by election.

Tipping

Political transformation can also result from changes in the composition of the electorate. Even when groups of voters never change their party preferences, if one group becomes more numerous over time, it can become dominant for that reason alone. We call this kind of demographically based change **tipping.**

Tipping in Massachusetts and California. Consider Massachusetts, where for generations Irish Catholics confronted Protestant Yankees in the political arena. Most of the Yankees were Republicans, and most of the Irish were Democrats. The Yankees were numerically dominant from the founding of the state until 1928. In that year, for the first time, Democratic Irish voters came to outnumber the Republican Yankees. Massachusetts, which previously had been one of the most solidly Republican states, became one of the most reliably Democratic states in the nation.

California may have experienced a tipping effect during the 1990s. From 1952 through 1988, California normally supported Republican presidential candidates. Since 1992, however, no GOP presidential candidate has managed to carry California. The improved performance of the Democrats in California is almost certainly a function of demography. In 1999, California became the third state, after Hawaii and New Mexico, in which non-Hispanic whites do not make up a majority of the population.

Tipping in the Twenty-First Century? It is possible that states other than California may tip to a different party in future years. John B. Judis and Ruy Teixeira have argued that the Democrats are poised to become the new majority party due to a growth in the number of liberal professionals and Hispanic immigrants.[8] This thesis attracted much ridicule prior to 2006, as the Republicans continued to triumph in midterm and presidential elections.

By 2008, however, the thesis had become more credible. In that year, a growing Hispanic vote clearly pushed several southwestern states, such as Nevada and Colorado, into the Democratic column, while larger numbers of upscale urban voters in the suburbs of Washington, D.C., helped Obama carry the traditionally Republican state of Virginia. Time will tell how important the tipping effect turns out to be in the long run.

swing voters
Voters who frequently swing their support from one party to another.

tipping
A phenomenon that occurs when a group that is becoming more numerous over time grows large enough to change the political balance in a district, state, or country.

8. John B. Judis and Ruy Teixeira, *The Emerging Democratic Majority* (New York: Scribner, 2004).

How you can make a difference

How would you like to exercise a small amount of real political power yourself—power that goes beyond simply voting in an election? You might be able to become a delegate to a county, district, or even state party convention.

- Many of these conventions nominate candidates for various offices. For example, in Michigan, the state party conventions nominate the candidates for the Board of Regents of the state's three top public universities. The regents set university policies, so these are nominations in which students have an obvious interest. In Michigan, if you are elected as a party precinct delegate, you can attend your party's state convention.

- In much of the country, there are more openings for precinct-level delegates than there are people willing to serve. In such circumstances, almost anyone can become a delegate by collecting a handful of signatures on a nominating petition or by mounting a small-scale write-in campaign.

- You are then eligible to take part in one of the most educational political experiences available to an ordinary citizen. You will get a firsthand look at how political persuasion takes place, how resolutions are written and passed, and how candidates seek out support among their fellow party members.

- If you are interested in committing yourself, check with your local county committee about the rules you must follow.

KEY TERMS

dealignment 230	party identification 230	political party 207	third party 225
Democratic Party 213	party-in-government 209	realignment 229	tipping 231
divided government 211	party-in-the-electorate 208	Republican Party 214	two-party system 212
GOP 214	party organization 208	splinter party 226	wave election 217
independent 207	party platform 209	split-ticket voting 230	Whig Party 213
motivated reasoning 223	patronage 210	state central committee 210	
national committee 210	plurality 223	straight-ticket voting 230	
national convention 209	policy demanders 207	swing voters 231	

CHAPTER SUMMARY

Learning Outcome 1 A political party is a group of political activists who organize to win elections, operate the government, and determine public policy. Political parties recruit candidates for public office, organize and run elections, present alternative policies to the voters, assume responsibility for operating the government, and act as the opposition to the party in power.

A political party consists of three components: the party-in-the-electorate, the party organization, and the party-in-government. Each party component maintains linkages to the others to keep the party strong. Each level of the party—local, state, and national—has considerable autonomy. The national party organization is responsible for holding the national convention in presidential election years, writing the party platform, choosing the national committee, and conducting party business.

The party-in-government comprises all of the elected and appointed officeholders of a party. Increased ideological coherence in both major parties has resulted in growing political polarization.

Learning Outcome 2 The evolution of our nation's political parties can be divided into seven periods: (a) the formation of political parties from 1789 to 1816; (b) the era of one-party rule from 1816 to 1828; (c) the period from Andrew Jackson's presidency to the eve of the Civil War, from 1828 to 1856; (d) the Civil War and post–Civil War period, from 1856 to 1896; (e) the Republican ascendancy and the progressive period, from 1896 to 1932; (f) the New Deal period, from 1932 to about 1968; and (g) the modern period, from approximately 1968 to the present. Throughout most of the modern period, the Republican and Democratic parties have been closely matched in strength.

Learning Outcome 3 Many of the differences between the two parties date from the time of Franklin D. Roosevelt's New Deal. The Democrats have advocated government action to help labor and minorities, and the Republicans have championed self-reliance and limited government. While the two major parties are made up of various types of voters, both have become more politically unified in recent years.

Learning Outcome 4 Two major parties have dominated the political landscape in the United States for almost two centuries. The reasons for this include (a) the historical foundations of the system, (b) political socialization and practical considerations, (c) the winner-take-all electoral system, and (d) state and federal laws favoring the two-party system. For these reasons, minor parties have found it extremely difficult to win elections.

Minor, or third, parties have emerged from time to time, sometimes as dissatisfied splinter groups from within major parties, and have acted as barometers of change in the political mood. Third parties can affect the political process (even if they do not win) if major parties adopt their issues or if they help determine which major party wins an election.

Learning Outcome 5 One mechanism of political change is realignment, in which major blocs of voters switch allegiance from one party to another. Realignments were manifested in the elections of 1896 and 1932. Some scholars speak of dealignment—that is, the loss of strong party attachments. In fact, the share of the voters who describe themselves as independents has grown. Many independents actually vote as if they were Democrats or Republicans, however. Demographic change can also "tip" a district or state from one party to another.

ADDITIONAL RESOURCES

Online Resources

- The political parties all have websites. You can locate the Republican National Committee at **www.gop.com** and the Democratic National Committee at **www.democrats.org**.
- The two leading third parties are the Libertarian Party and the Green Party. Find their websites at **www.lp.org** and **www.greenparty.org**, respectively.

Books

Gairdner, William D. *The Great Divide: Why Liberals and Conservatives Will Never, Ever Agree.* New York: Encounter Books, 2015. Gairdner argues that the divide between liberalism and conservatism has grown so great that liberals and conservatives can barely speak to one another. A Canadian businessman, Gairdner draws his examples from Europe as well as North America.

Geismer, Lily. *Don't Blame Us: Suburban Liberals and the Transformation of the Democratic Party.* Princeton, N.J., Princeton University Press, 2014. Geismer traces the reorientation of modern liberalism and the Democratic Party away from their roots in labor union halls of northern cities to white-collar professionals in postindustrial high-tech suburbs. Geismer is a history professor at Claremont McKenna College.

Masket, Seth. *The Inevitable Party: Why Attempts to Kill the Party System Fail and How They Weaken Democracy.* New York: Oxford University Press, 2016. Masket argues that antiparty reforms in U.S. history have reduced transparency and accountability. A widely regarded analyst, he is a political science professor at the University of Denver.

Video

House of Cards—This celebrated series premiered in 2013 on the streaming service Netflix. Kevin Spacey stars as Frank Underwood, a ruthless and conniving Democratic member of the U.S. House. By 2014, *House of Cards* had received more than thirty recognitions, including nominations for the Emmy, Writer's Guild, and Golden Globe awards.

A Third Choice—An award-winning 2011 PBS documentary, *A Third Choice* provides a colorful look at the history of third parties and how they changed America.

Quiz

Multiple Choice and Fill-Ins

Learning Outcome 1 Cite some of the major activities of U.S. political parties, and discuss how they are organized.

1. The three faces of a political party include:
   a. the party-in-the-electorate, the party organization, and the members of the party.
   b the party organization, the party-in-government, and the party-in-the-electorate.
   c. the party-in-government, the party-in-the-electorate, and the lobbyists for that party.

2. Both political parties have _____ _____ that direct and coordinate party activities during the four years after each presidential election.

Learning Outcome 2 Explain how the history of U.S. political parties has led to the two major parties that exist today.

3. The New Deal era under Democratic president Franklin D. Roosevelt occurred:
   a. at the beginning of the twentieth century.
   b. during the 1960s.
   c. during the Great Depression of the 1930s.

4. The first organized political parties in the United States were the _____ and the _____ _____.

Learning Outcome 3 Summarize key differences between the policies and supporters of the major parties.

5. Two major types of Republicans are:
   a. members of the Religious Right and business-oriented economic conservatives.
   b. members of the Religious Right and organized labor.
   c. supporters of the Tea Party movement and Hispanics.

6. When voters are temporarily dissatisfied with the performance of one or another of the major parties, the result may be a _____ election.

Learning Outcome 4 Give reasons why the two-party system has endured in America, and evaluate the impact of third parties on U.S. politics.

7. At almost every level of government in this country, the outcome of elections is based on the plurality voting system, which means that:
   a. the candidate with the largest number of votes wins, even if the winner does not receive 50 percent or more of the votes.
   b. when no one receives 50 percent of the vote, a runoff election is held.
   c. there is no need for everyone to vote in each election.

8. The two most important third parties that remain active today are the _____ and _____ parties.

Learning Outcome 5 Discuss some of the ways in which support for the parties can change, and explain the increasing importance of independents.

9. The presidential elections of 1932, in which Democrat Franklin D. Roosevelt carried all but six states, were an example of:
   a. political dealignment.
   b. the establishment of divided government.
   c. a realigning election.

10. In an election, when a voter casts ballots for candidates of two or more parties, we call this _____-_____ voting.

Essay Questions

1. Do you support (or lean toward) one of the major political parties today? If so, would you have supported the same party in the late 1800s—or would you have supported a different party? Explain your reasoning.

2. In America, party candidates for national office are typically chosen through primary elections. In some other countries, a party's central committee picks the party's candidates. How might primary elections limit the ability of parties to present a united front on the issues?

CAMPAIGNS AND ELECTIONS

Supporters of presidential candidates Hillary Clinton (left) and Donald Trump hold up signs outside a Democratic unity rally where Senator Bernie Sanders (D., Vt.) endorsed Clinton. *Is it appropriate for a supporter of one candidate to demonstrate at a rally held by another candidate?*
Boston Globe/Getty Images

These five **LEARNING OUTCOMES** *below are designed to help improve your understanding of this chapter:*

1: Discuss who runs for office and how campaigns are managed.

2: Describe the current system of campaign finance.

3: Summarize the process of choosing a president of the United States.

4: Explain the mechanisms through which voting takes place on Election Day.

5: Discuss voter turnout in the United States and the types of people most likely to vote.

What if...

We Elected the President by Popular Vote?

Background

When you vote for president, the names of the candidates appear before you on the ballot. You don't, however, choose one of these candidates directly. You vote for a slate of electors who are pledged to support a particular candidate. There are 538 electors, one for each member of Congress plus three for the District of Columbia. Although the electors never gather together in one place, they are known collectively as the electoral college. This body was created by the founders in the hopes that the people would delegate the choice of president to a group of notables. The plan did not survive contact with reality. Electors publicly pledged themselves to candidates almost from the start, and so voters knew who they were choosing for president.

While the electoral college system has not prevented the people from choosing the president, it does have some side effects. It is possible for a candidate to become president without obtaining a majority of the popular vote. Perhaps more distressing is the possibility that a presidential candidate could win a majority of the popular votes but still lose the election. Some citizens believe, therefore, that the existing electoral college system should be abolished.

What If We Elected the President by Popular Vote?

Presidents who did not win an absolute majority of the popular vote include Abraham Lincoln, Woodrow Wilson, Harry Truman, John F. Kennedy, Richard Nixon (in 1968), and Bill Clinton. Candidates have also been elected even though an opposing candidate received a *larger* share of the popular vote. This occurred on five occasions—in the elections of John Quincy Adams in 1824, Rutherford B. Hayes in 1876, Benjamin Harrison in 1888, George W. Bush in 2000, and Donald Trump in 2016.

Under the current system, in all but two small states, the winner of the state's popular vote takes all of the state's electoral votes. This winner-take-all provision is called the *unit rule*. As a consequence, presidential candidates have little reason to campaign in states where they are certain either to win or to lose by a large margin. During the last presidential elections, major campaigns took place in only ten key

states, such as Florida, Ohio, and Virginia. States with minimal campaigns—the "spectator" states—included some of the nation's most populous, such as California, Illinois, New York, and Texas. If presidential candidates had to win a majority of the popular vote, they would be forced to campaign in every state.

Some believe, however, that without the electoral college and the unit rule, small states would be ignored. Also, the current system typically encourages certainty in elections by exaggerating the winner's margin of victory. Finally, under the existing system, if the election is close and votes must be recounted, the recounts will take place in only a few jurisdictions. If the popular vote determined the winner, votes might have to be recounted in every corner of the country.

How a Popular Vote System Could Be Established

Abolishing the electoral college would mean amending the Constitution, and that is very difficult. As an alternative, some people have proposed a National Popular Vote Interstate Compact that would allow presidents to be elected by popular vote. Under the proposal, participating states would award their electoral votes to the candidate who wins the national popular vote. The plan would go into effect when enough states joined to control the electoral college. So far, ten states and the District of Columbia have joined. Among the most recent are California and New York. Participants in the interstate compact now have 61 percent of the electoral votes needed to put the compact into effect.

For Critical Analysis

◗ Would the National Popular Vote Interstate Compact need approval by Congress to go into effect? Why or why not? (Hint: In the U.S. Constitution, see Article I, Section 10, Clause 3.)

◗ Critics of the system argue that it prevents us from ever electing a third-party presidential candidate. Do you agree? Why or why not? And is this really a problem?

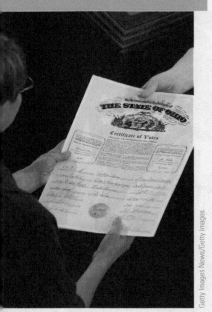

Getty Images News/Getty Images

Image 9–1 A congressional clerk presents the electoral college certificate from Ohio. Electoral votes are tallied in the House of Representatives chamber. *Would bypassing the electoral college be a good idea? Why or why not?*

Free elections are the cornerstone of the American political system. Voters choose one candidate over another to hold political office by casting ballots in local, state, and federal elections. In 2016, the voters chose Republicans Donald Trump and Mike Pence to be president and vice president of the United States for the following four years. Voters also elected all of the members of the House of Representatives and one-third of the members of the Senate. The campaigns were bitter, long, and expensive.

Voters and candidates frequently criticize the American electoral process. It is said to favor wealthier candidates, to further the aims of special interest groups, and to be dominated by older voters and those with better education and higher incomes. Campaign fund-raising has grown by leaps and bounds as the United States Supreme Court has progressively reduced limits on the fund-raising process. Does all that mean that there is a better way to choose the U.S. president? We looked at this question in the chapter-opening *What If . . .* feature.

The Twenty-First-Century Campaign

Learning Outcome **1:**

There are thousands of elective offices in the United States. Although the major political parties strive to provide a slate of candidates for every election, recruiting candidates is easier for some offices than for others. Political parties may have difficulty finding candidates for the board of the local water control district, for example, but they generally find a sufficient number of candidates for county commissioner or sheriff. The "higher" the office and the more prestige attached to it, the more candidates are likely to want to run. In many areas of the country, however, one major party may be considerably stronger than the other. In those situations, the minority party may have difficulty finding nominees for elections in which victory is unlikely.

Discuss who runs for office and how campaigns are managed.

The presidential campaign provides the most colorful and exciting look at candidates and how they prepare to compete for office—in this instance, the highest office in the land. The men and women who wanted to be their party's candidate in the 2016 presidential campaign faced a long and obstacle-filled path. First, they needed to tour the nation, particularly the states with early **presidential primaries,** to see if they had enough local supporters. They needed to create an organization and win primary votes. Finally, when nominated as the party's candidate, the winner required funds to finance a successful campaign for president. Always, at every turn, there was the question of whether there were enough funds to effectively compete against primary opponents, and eventually against the candidate of the other party in the general election.

Who Is Eligible?

There are few constitutional restrictions on who can be elected to national office in the United States. As detailed in the Constitution, the formal requirements are as follows:

1. *President*. Must be a natural-born citizen, have attained the age of thirty-five years, and be a resident of the country for fourteen years by the time of inauguration.
2. *Vice president*. Must meet the same requirements as the president and also not be a resident of the same state as the president.[1]
3. *Senator*. Must be a citizen for at least nine years, have attained the age of thirty by the time of taking office, and be a resident of the state from which elected.
4. *Representative*. Must be a citizen for at least seven years, have attained the age of twenty-five by the time of taking office, and be a resident of the state from which elected.

presidential primary
A statewide primary election of delegates to a political party's national convention, held to determine a party's presidential nominee.

---

1. Technically, a presidential and vice-presidential candidate on the same ticket can be from the same state, but if they are, one of the two must forfeit the electoral votes of his or her home state.

Image 9–2 Democratic presidential candidate Hillary Clinton campaigns in Los Angeles. *What kinds of voters supported Clinton?*

Image 9–3 Republican presidential candidate Donald Trump campaigns in Virginia. *How was Trump different from past Republican nominees?*

The qualifications for state legislators are set by the state constitutions and likewise include age, place of residence, and citizenship. (Usually, the requirements for the upper chamber of a legislature are somewhat higher than those for the lower chamber.) The legal qualifications for serving as governor or in other state offices are similar.

Who Runs?

In spite of these minimal legal qualifications for office at both the national and the state levels, a quick look at the slate of candidates in any election—or at the current members of Congress—will reveal that not all segments of the population enjoy these opportunities equally. Holders of political office in the United States are predominantly white and male. Until the twentieth century, presidential candidates were exclusively of northern European origin and of Protestant heritage.[2] Laws that effectively denied voting rights made it impossible to elect African American public officials in many areas in which African Americans constituted a significant portion of the population. As a result of the passage of major civil rights legislation in the 1960s, however, the number of African American public officials has increased throughout the United States, and in a groundbreaking vote, the nation elected an African American president in 2008.

Women as Candidates. Until recently, women generally were considered to be appropriate candidates only for lower-level offices, such as state legislator or school board member. The past twenty-five years have seen a tremendous increase in the number of women who run for office, not only at the state level but for the U.S. Congress as well. Figure 9–1 shows the increase in female candidates. In 2016, 183 women ran for the House or Senate on major-party tickets, and 89 were elected. Today, a majority of Americans say they would vote for a qualified woman for president of the United States. Indeed, Hillary Clinton came close to winning the Democratic presidential nomination in 2008, and she succeeded in 2016.

---

2. A number of early presidents were Unitarian. The Unitarian Church is not Protestant, but it is historically rooted in the Protestant tradition.

Figure 9–1 Women Running for Congress (and Winning)

Why are women still well in the minority in both chambers of Congress?

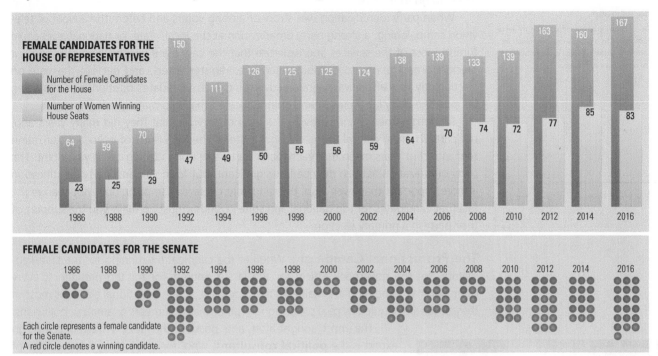

Professional Status. Political campaigning and officeholding are easier for some occupational groups than for others, and political involvement can make a valuable contribution to certain careers. Lawyers, for example, have more flexible schedules than do many other professionals, can take time off for campaigning, and can leave their jobs to hold public office full time. Furthermore, holding political office is good publicity for their professional practice. Perhaps most important, many jobs that lawyers aspire to—federal or state judgeships, state's attorney offices, or work in a federal agency—can be attained by political appointment.

Managing the Campaign

After the candidates have been nominated, typically through a **primary election,** the most exhausting and expensive part of the election process begins—the **general election** campaign, which actually fills the offices at stake. Political campaigns are becoming more complex and more sophisticated with every election. Even with the most appealing of candidates, today's campaigns require a strong organization with (1) expertise in political polling and marketing, (2) professional assistance in fund-raising, accounting, and financial management, and (3) technological capabilities in every aspect of the campaign.

The Changing Campaign. The goal is the same for all campaigns—to convince voters to choose a candidate or a slate of candidates for office. In recent decades, the typical campaign for high office has no longer been centered on the party but on the candidate. The candidate-centered campaign emerged in response to changes in the electoral system, the increased importance of television in campaigns, technological innovations such as the Internet, and the increased cost of campaigning.

To run a successful and persuasive campaign, the candidate's organization must be able to raise funds for the effort, obtain coverage from the media, and produce and pay for political commercials and advertising. In addition, the organization needs to schedule

primary election

An election in which political parties choose their candidates for the general election.

general election

An election open to all eligible voters, normally held on the first Tuesday in November, that determines who will fill various elected positions.

political consultant

A paid professional hired to devise a campaign strategy and manage a campaign.

focus group

A small group of individuals who are led in discussion by a professional consultant in order to gather opinions on and responses to candidates and issues.

the candidate's time effectively, convey the candidate's position on the issues to the voters, and conduct research on the opposing candidate. Finally, the campaign must get the voters to go to the polls.

When party identification was stronger among voters and before the advent of television campaigning, a strong party organization at the local, state, or national level could furnish most of the services and expertise that the candidate needed. Parties used their precinct organizations to distribute literature, register voters, and get out the vote on election day. Less effort was spent on advertising each candidate's positions and character, because the party label presumably communicated that information to many voters.

Modern parties cannot provide the level of services that they did many years ago, but parties remain central to the elections system. The high levels of political polarization seen in recent years mean that each major party is a strong ideological rallying point. The party organization as such may be less significant, but for politicians, party identification is more important than ever. Also, the candidate-centered campaign does not change the fact that candidates for top national and state positions must normally win the support of their party in a primary election.

The Professional Campaign. Whether the candidate is running for the state legislature, for the governor's office, for the U.S. Congress, or for the presidency, every campaign has some fundamental tasks to accomplish. Today, in national elections most of these tasks are handled by paid professionals rather than volunteers or amateur politicians.

The most sought-after and possibly the most criticized campaign expert is the **political consultant,** who, for a large fee, takes charge of the candidate's campaign. Political consultants began to displace volunteer campaign managers in the 1960s, about the same time that television became a force in campaigns. The paid consultant devises a campaign strategy and theme, oversees advertising, and plans media appearances. The consultants and the firms they represent are not politically neutral. Most will work only for candidates from one party.

Image 9–4 Political consultant Paul Manafort was Donald Trump's campaign manager for several months until he was fired in August 2016. Earlier, Manafort worked for pro-Russian Ukrainian leader Viktor Yanukovych, who was forced from power in 2014 by an anti-Russian popular movement. It was reported that Yanukovych's party may have paid Manafort more than $12 million. This news did not result in Manafort's dismissal, however. Rather, the cause was Manafort's opposition to the "let Trump be Trump" campaign strategy. *What consequences could follow from Trump's admiration of Russian President Vladimir Putin?*

Tom Williams/CQ Roll Call

The Use of Opinion Polls. One of the major sources of information for both the media and the candidates is opinion polls. Poll taking is widespread during the primaries. Presidential hopefuls have private polls taken to make sure that there is at least some chance they could be nominated and, if nominated, elected. During the presidential campaign itself, polling is even more frequent. Polls are taken not only by the regular pollsters—Gallup, Pew Research, and others—but also privately by each candidate's campaign organization. These private polls are for the exclusive and confidential use of the candidate and his or her campaign organization. As the election approaches, many candidates use *tracking polls,* which are polls taken almost every day, to find out how well they are competing for votes. Tracking polls enable consultants to fine-tune advertising and the candidate's speeches in the last days of the campaign.

Focus Groups. Another tactic used by campaign organizations to gain insights into public perceptions of the candidate is the **focus group.** The ten to fifteen ordinary citizens who make up the group discuss the candidate or certain political issues. Professional consultants, who conduct the discussion, select focus group members from specific target groups in the population—for example, working women, blue-collar men, senior citizens, or young voters. Recent campaigns have tried to reach groups such as "soccer moms," "Walmart shoppers," or "NASCAR dads."[3] The group discusses personality traits of the candidate, political advertising, and other candidate-related issues. Focus groups can reveal more emotional responses to candidates or the deeper anxieties of voters—feelings that consultants believe often are not tapped by more impersonal telephone surveys. The campaign then can shape its messages to respond to those feelings and perceptions.

Financing the Campaign

Learning Outcome **2:**

Describe the current system of campaign finance.

The connection between money and elections is a sensitive issue in American politics. The belief is widespread that large campaign contributions by special interests corrupt the political system. Indeed, spending reached unprecedented heights during the 2015–2016 election cycle. In 2016, total spending for the presidential races alone reached $1.6 billion. These funds had to be provided by the candidates and their families, borrowed, or raised by contributions from individuals, organizations, or **political action committees (PACs).** PACs are committees set up under federal or state law for the express purpose of making political donations.

The way campaigns are financed has changed dramatically in the past several years. For decades, candidates and political parties had to operate within the constraints imposed by complicated laws regulating campaign financing. Some of these constraints still exist, but recent developments have opened up the process to a striking degree. Today, there are no limits on how much any person or institution can invest in the political process, and only modest limits on how this spending can take place.

The Evolution of the Campaign Finance System

Throughout much of early American history, campaign financing was unregulated. No limits existed on contributions, and no data were collected on campaign funding. During the twentieth century, however, a variety of federal corrupt practices acts were adopted to regulate campaign financing. The first, passed in 1925, contained many loopholes and proved to be ineffective. The **Hatch Act** (Political Activities Act) of 1939 is best known for restricting the political activities of civil servants. The act also made it unlawful for a political group to spend more than $3 million in any campaign and limited individual contributions to a campaign committee to $5,000. Of course, such restrictions were easily circumvented by creating additional political organizations.

The Federal Election Campaign Act. The Federal Election Campaign Act (FECA) of 1971, which became effective in 1972, replaced all past laws. The act restricted the amount that could be spent on campaign advertising. It also limited the amount that candidates could contribute to their own campaigns and required disclosure of all contributions and expenditures over $100. In principle, the FECA limited the role of labor unions and corporations in political campaigns.

Amendments to the FECA passed in 1974 created the **Federal Election Commission (FEC).** This commission consists of six bipartisan administrators whose duty is to enforce compliance with the requirements of the act. The 1974 amendments also placed limits on the sums that individuals and committees could contribute to candidates.

The principal role of the FEC today is to collect data on campaign contributions. Candidate committees must file periodic reports with the FEC listing who contributed, how much was spent, and for what it was spent. As an enforcement body, however, the FEC is

political action committee (PAC)

A committee set up by and representing a corporation, labor union, or special-interest group. PACs raise and give campaign donations.

Hatch Act

An act passed in 1939 that restricted the political activities of government employees. It also prohibited a political group from spending more than $3 million in any campaign and limited individual contributions to a campaign committee to $5,000.

Federal Election Commission (FEC)

The federal regulatory agency with the task of enforcing federal campaign laws. As a practical matter, the FEC's role is largely limited to collecting data on campaign contributions.

---

3. NASCAR stands for the National Association for Stock Car Auto Racing.

Image 9–5 Charles Koch is head of Koch Industries. With his brother David, he runs one of the largest fundraising operations in American politics. The brothers consider themselves libertarians and contribute to Republicans. *Are super PACs a problem in American politics? Why or why not?*

conspicuously ineffective and typically does not determine that a campaign has violated the rules until the elections are over, if then.

The original FECA of 1971 limited the amount that each individual could spend on his or her own behalf. The Supreme Court overturned the provision in 1976, in *Buckley v. Valeo,*[4] stating that it was unconstitutional to restrict in any way the amount congressional candidates could spend on their own behalf. The Court later extended this principle to state elections as well.

Political Action Committees. Changes to the FECA in 1974 and 1976 allowed corporations, labor unions, and other interest groups to set up political action committees (PACs) to raise funds for candidates. PACs can contribute up to $5,000 to each candidate in each election. Each corporation or each union is limited to one PAC. The number of PACs grew significantly after 1976, as did the amounts that they spent on elections. Since the 1990s, however, the number of traditional PACs has leveled off because interest groups and activists have found alternative mechanisms for funneling resources into campaigns.

Issue Advocacy Advertising. Business corporations, labor unions, and other interest groups have also developed ways of making independent expenditures that are not coordinated with those of a candidate or political party. A common tactic is **issue advocacy** advertising, which promotes positions on issues rather than candidates. Although promoting issue positions aligns very closely with promoting candidates who support those positions, the courts repeatedly have held that interest groups have a First Amendment right to advocate their positions. Political parties may also make independent expenditures on behalf of candidates.

Soft Money. Interest groups and PACs hit upon the additional strategy of generating **soft money**—that is, campaign contributions to political parties that escaped the limits of federal or state election law. No limits existed on contributions to political parties for activities such as voter education and voter-registration drives. This loophole enabled the parties to raise millions of dollars from corporations and individuals.

The Rise and Fall of the McCain-Feingold Act. The Bipartisan Campaign Reform Act of 2002, also known as the McCain-Feingold Act after its chief sponsors in the Senate, took effect on the day after the midterm elections of 2002. The law sought to regulate the new campaign finance practices developed since the passage of the FECA. It banned soft money at the federal level, but it did not ban such contributions to state and local parties. It attempted to curb issue advocacy advertising, but also increased the sums that individuals could contribute directly to candidates.

The constitutionality of the 2002 act was immediately challenged. In December 2003, the Supreme Court upheld almost all of the clauses of the act.[5] In 2007, however, the Court eased the act's restrictions on issue advocacy ads when it ruled that only those ads "susceptible of no reasonable interpretation other than as an appeal to vote for or against a specific candidate" could be restricted prior to an election.[6] Finally, in 2010, *Citizens*

---

issue advocacy

Advertising paid for by interest groups that support or oppose a candidate's position on an issue without mentioning voting or elections.

soft money

Campaign contributions unregulated by federal or state law, usually given to parties and party committees to help fund general party activities.

---

4. 424 U.S. 1 (1976).

5. *McConnell v. FEC,* 540 U.S. 93 (2003).

6. *FEC v. Wisconsin Right to Life,* 551 U.S. 449 (2007).

United v. FEC[7] swept away almost all remaining restrictions on independent expenditures, leading to the system we have today.

The Current Campaign Finance Environment

As of 2016, political campaigns are financed in two distinct ways. One of these is spending by the candidate's own committee. Contributions made directly to a candidate's committee are subject to limitations: An individual can donate no more than $2,500 to a candidate in a single election, and contributions by committees are limited as well. In exchange for these limits, candidates have almost complete control over how their own campaign money is spent.

Another way in which campaigns are financed is through **independent expenditures.** These funds may be spent on advertising and other political activities, but in theory the expenditures cannot be coordinated with those of a candidate. No limits exist on how much can be spent in this fashion. This two-part system is the direct result of the 2010 *Citizens United v. FEC* ruling by the Supreme Court.

Image 9–6 *"Most of all, I want to thank the people of my district for their unflagging support and disturbingly short term memories."*

Citizens United v. FEC. In January 2010, the Supreme Court ruled that corporations, unions, and nonprofits may spend freely to support or oppose candidates, so long as the expenditures are made independently and are not coordinated with candidate campaigns. The ruling overturned campaign-finance laws dating back decades. Democrats, plus many journalists and bloggers, accused the Court of granting corporations rights that ought to be exercised only by flesh-and-blood humans. Republicans and others defended the ruling as protecting freedom of speech. Two months later, a federal court of appeals held that it was not possible to limit contributions to independent-expenditure groups based on the size of the contribution.[8]

Super PACs. These rulings led directly to a new type of political organization: the **super PAC.** Traditional PACs, which continue to exist, are set up to represent a corporation, labor union, or special interest group. The super PAC, in contrast, is established to aggregate unlimited contributions by individuals and organizations and then funnel these sums into independent expenditures. By 2011, every major presidential candidate had a super PAC. It soon became clear that the supposed independence of these organizations is a fiction. Presidential super PACs are usually chaired by individuals who are closely associated with the candidate. Frequently, the chair is a former top member of the candidate's campaign. A variety of other super PACs were established as well. These groups were often oriented toward a party, rather than a candidate.

One interesting development has been the tendency for super PACs to be supported primarily by very wealthy individuals, rather than by corporations or other organizations. The Koch brothers provide a striking example of this phenomenon.[9] For years, Charles and David Koch have been famous for their large contributions to Republican campaigns. A political network overseen by the brothers spent almost $400 million during the 2012

independent expenditures

Nonregulated contributions from PACs, organizations, and individuals. The funds may be spent on advertising or other campaign activities, so long as those expenditures are not coordinated with those of a candidate.

super PAC

A political organization that aggregates unlimited contributions by individuals and organizations to be spent independently of candidate committees.

---

7. 558 U.S. 310 (2010).

8. *Speechnow v. FEC,* 599 F.3d 686 (D.C.Cir. 2010).

9. The name is pronounced *coke.*

Image 9–7 Hedge fund manager Tom Steyer opposes a California proposition supported by oil companies. Steyer is one of the Democrats' largest donors. *Why might a billionaire Democrat be more interested in the environment than, say, the minimum wage?*

election cycle, a huge sum at the time. For 2016, the network established a spending goal of $889 billion. That would almost match the sums raised by the candidate committees of Barack Obama or Mitt Romney in 2012.

This plan, however, ran into trouble when Donald Trump became the Republican presidential nominee. Trump was not acceptable to the libertarian-minded Koch brothers, who decided to devote whatever funds they could raise to the campaigns of "down-ticket" Republican candidates running for the Senate, House, and state-level positions. Trump's ability to win the Republican primaries while spending very little money poses the question: Just how important is campaign finance, really? We look at that question in this chapter's *Which Side Are You On?* feature.

The 527 Organization. Well before *Citizens United,* interest groups realized that they could set up new organizations outside the parties to encourage voter registration and to run issue ads aimed at energizing supporters. So long as these committees did not endorse candidates, they faced no limits on fund-raising. These tax-exempt groups, called 527 organizations after the section of the tax code that provides for them, first made a major impact during the 2003–2004 election cycle. Since then, they have largely been replaced by super PACs, but a number continue to be active to the present day.

The 501(c)4 Organization. In the 2007–2008 election cycle, campaign-finance lawyers began recommending a new type of independent group—the 501(c)4 organization, which, like the 527 organization, is named after the relevant provision of the tax code. A 501(c)4 is ostensibly a "social welfare" group and, unlike a 527, is not required to disclose the identity of its donors or to report spending to the FEC.

Lawyers then began suggesting that 501(c)4 organizations claim a special exemption that would allow such an organization to ask people to vote for or against specific candidates as long as a majority of the group's effort was devoted to issues. Only those funds spent directly to support candidates had to be reported to the FEC, and the 501(c)4 could continue to conceal its donors.

One result was to make it all but impossible to determine exactly how much was spent by independent groups in elections since 2008. Critics claimed that 501(c)4s were being used illegally. The FEC has never ruled on their validity, however. Like the 527 organizations, 501(c)4 groups were eclipsed by super PACs from 2011–2012 on, but they continue to be a valuable tool for those donors who prefer to conceal their political contributions. For the top independent committees contributing to federal candidates in 2016, see Table 9–1.

Candidate Committees. Despite limits on contributions to candidate committees, they continue to collect large sums. The committees of major-party presidential nominees, such as Barack Obama and Mitt Romney, were able to amass beyond $1 billion each. Hillary Clinton raised about $700 million and Donald Trump brought in only $250 million.

Candidate committees at all levels received a boost in April 2014 as a result of the Supreme Court's latest ruling on campaign finance. The Court continued to hold that limits on the amount that any one individual could contribute to any one candidate were

Which side are you on?

Can Money Buy Elections?

The 2010 Supreme Court decision *Citizens United v. FEC* allowed corporations, unions, and individuals to donate unlimited sums to entities that are "independent" of the candidates. So was born the super PAC. A super PAC can raise sums without limit. Some very rich people donated millions of dollars to various super PACs in the years following that decision. During the 2011–2012 presidential election cycle, outside groups spent an estimated $1.3 billion. Super PACs were back in action during the 2015–2016 election cycle. Of course, the presidential campaigns themselves also raise vast sums, typically even more than what super PACs take in. Does all this money corrupt the political process?

Just Another Way for Big Money to Rule America

Those who are critical of the role of money in our elections argue that no one would give such large sums unless they expect to benefit in return. Candidates are perfectly well aware of who their largest contributors are. Often enough, they have spent time pleading with these people for donations. Super PACs are supposed to be independent, but in reality, most are run by candidates' former staff members. Hillary Clinton's super PAC, Priorities USA Action, is led by Guy Cecil, who was political director of Clinton's 2008 presidential campaign. Candidates are just as aware of who has donated to their super PACs as they are of donors to their actual campaigns.

Almost all the advertising purchased by super PACs is negative—the candidates can remain upbeat while their super PACs do the dirty work. These attack ads are themselves a corruption of the political process. Finally, due to the rise of 501(c)4 organizations, some groups manage to hide the identity of many of their donors. A number of

public-interest groups have called for constitutional amendment to overturn *Citizens United*. We need some such action to keep the United States from becoming a republic of the rich, by the rich, and for the rich.

Money Alone Can't Buy Elections

Those who support the current system argue that people should have the right to say whatever they want. Corporations and unions are made up of individuals, and so organizations as well as individuals should be able to express their views by donating to campaign organizations.

Does money buy elections? The dollars did not seem to have made that much difference in 2012. Casino owner Sheldon Adelson and his wife spent almost $100 million, including $20 million to Republican presidential candidate Newt Gingrich (he lost), and $20 million in the general election to support Mitt Romney (he lost, too).

Consider also Donald Trump's presidential campaign. In many key primary states, Trump ran no television ads at all, relying instead on social media and nonstop cable news coverage. In contrast, former Florida governor Jeb Bush raised about $130 million for his primary effort with almost nothing to show for it. Trump also planned to spend relatively little on his general election campaign. The 2016 elections, therefore, were a test of how important campaign money really is. Many political scientists expected that its impact would be surprisingly small.

For Critical Analysis

○ Some have argued that limits on campaign spending violate First Amendment guarantees of freedom of speech. How strong is this argument?

permissible. An overall cap on the total amount that an individual could contribute, however, was unconstitutional. In other words, there can be no limit on the number of different candidates a wealthy individual can support. A billionaire could, for example, give the $2,600 maximum contribution to every single candidate of a particular party running for the U.S. Congress. The ruling also freed up the amounts that individuals could give to the political parties.[10] The likely consequence will be to divert some funds away from super PACs and to candidate and party committees.

10. *McCutcheon v. FEC*, 572 U.S. ___ (2014).

Table 9–1 The Fifteen Top Groups Making Independent Expenditures during the 2016 Cycle

Independent expenditures only. Some groups, such as the party committees, have designated only a small part of their total fundraising as independent expenditures. *Does this list suggest that either of the two major parties has an advantage?*

Committee	Affiliation	Raised by October 2016	Type	Disclosure of Contributors
Priorities USA Action	Hillary Clinton	$117,047,422	Super PAC	full
Right to Rise USA	Jeb Bush	$86,817,138	Super PAC	full
Senate Leadership Fund	Republican	$60,834,460	Super PAC	full
Senate Majority PAC	Democratic	$60,629,235	Super PAC	full
Democratic Congressional Campaign Committee	Democratic	$59,877,326	Party committee	full
National Republican Congressional Committee	Republican	$58,848,634	Party committee	full
Conservative Solutions PAC	Marco Rubio	$55,443,483	Super PAC	full
Get Our Jobs Back	Donald Trump	$50,010,166	Super PAC	full
NRA & NRA Institute for Legislative Action	gun rights	$49,719,389	501c, Super PAC	partial
Democratic Senatorial Campaign Committee	Democratic	$46,290,452	Party committee	full
National Republican Senatorial Committee	Republican	$35,254,013	Party committee	full
House Majority PAC	Democratic	$33,412,267	Super PAC	partial
Congressional Leadership Fund	Republican	$29,984,123	Super PAC	partial
Freedom Partners Action Fund	Koch brothers (libertarian)	$29,718,852	Super PAC	full
US Chamber of Commerce	business	$28,021,319	501c	none
Women Vote!	Democratic	$26,388,017	Super PAC	partial
Club for Growth & Club for Growth Action	anti-tax	$21,623,133	Super PAC, 501c	partial
NextGen Climate Action & NextGen California Action Committee	Tom Steyer (environmental)	$21,309,977	Super PACs	partial
Granite State Solutions	Sen. Kelly Ayotte	$18,799,608	Super PAC	full
America Leads	Chris Christie	$18,578,852	Super PAC	full

Source: Center for Responsive Politics.

The Decline and Fall of Public Financing. From 1976 through 2004, most presidential candidates relied on a system of public funding financed by a checkoff on federal income tax forms. This system provided funds to match what a candidate could raise during the primary season. During the general election campaign, the system would pay for a candidate's entire campaign. Publicly funded candidates, however, could not raise funds independently for the general election or exceed the program's overall spending limits.

The system began to break down after 2000, when many candidates rejected public support during the primaries in the belief that they could raise larger sums privately. In 2008, Barack Obama became the first candidate since the program was founded to opt out of federal funding for the general elections as well. By 2012, the public financing system was essentially out of business. None of the major candidates in either party was willing to use it. Public funds continued to be available to support the parties' national conventions, but in 2012 Congress revoked funding for conventions in future election years.

From 2012 on, a division of effort developed between candidate committees and outside organizations such as super PACs. Candidate committees would run positive advertisements that portrayed the candidate to best advantage. Independent organizations would run negative ads aimed at tearing down the candidate's opponents. The belief was that because super PACs and other groups were technically independent, a candidate could deny responsibility for the negative campaign. Over time, however, such denials grew less and less credible.

Running for President: The Longest Campaign

Learning Outcome 3:

Summarize the process of choosing a president of the United States.

The American presidential election is the culmination of two different campaigns: the presidential primary campaign and the general election campaign following the party's national convention. Traditionally, both the primary campaigns and the final campaigns take place during the first ten months of an election year. Increasingly, though, the states are holding their primaries earlier in the year, which has motivated the candidates to begin their campaigns earlier as well. Indeed, candidates in the 2016 presidential races began campaigning in early 2015, thus launching one of the longest presidential campaigns to date.

Primary elections were first organized in 1904 in Wisconsin for choosing state officials. The purpose of the primary was to open the nomination process to ordinary party members and to weaken the influence of party bosses. Until 1968, however, there were fewer than twenty primary elections for the presidency. They were often *beauty contests,* in which the candidates competed for popular votes but the results did not control the selection of delegates to the national convention. National conventions were meetings of the party elite—legislators, mayors, county chairpersons, and loyal party workers—who were mostly appointed to their delegations. The leaders of large blocs of delegates could direct their delegates to support a favorite candidate.

Reforming the Presidential Primaries

In recent decades, the character of the presidential primary process and the makeup of the national convention have changed dramatically. The public, rather than party elites, now generally controls the nomination process. After the disruptive riots outside the doors of the 1968 Democratic convention in Chicago, many party leaders pushed for serious reforms of the convention system.

The Power of Elected Delegates. The Democratic National Committee appointed a special commission to study the problems of the presidential primary system. During the next several years, the group—called the McGovern-Fraser Commission—formulated new rules for delegate selection that had to be followed by state Democratic parties beginning in 1972.

The reforms instituted by the Democratic Party, which were mostly imitated by the Republicans, revolutionized the nomination process for the presidency. The most important changes require that a majority of the convention delegates be elected by the voters

Election 2016

Campaign Finance in 2016

Political fundraising has risen for many years, but the 2016 elections were somewhat of an exception. The Center for Responsive Politics estimated that the total cost of the 2016 elections would reach $6.6 billion, only modestly more than in 2012. Presidential primary candidates, congressional hopefuls, and independent committees all spent more. For example, the Senate race in Pennsylvania cost a cool $139 million. Still, the presidential candidate committees—directly under candidate control—spent less. Clinton raised about $700 million and Trump a mere $250 million. A problem for Trump was that major Republican donors boycotted his campaign. For example, a network organized by the Koch brothers had planned to raise almost $890 million. In the end, Koch fundraising was limited to $250 million, much of which went to Senate and House Republicans.

in primary elections, in caucuses held by local parties, or at state conventions. Delegates are normally pledged to a particular candidate, although the pledge is not always formally binding at the convention. The delegation from each state must also include a proportion of women, younger party members, and representatives of the minority groups within the party. At first, almost no special privileges were given to party leaders and elected party officials, such as senators and governors. In 1984, however, many of these individuals returned to the Democratic convention as **superdelegates.**

The Role of the Superdelegates. In 2016, the number of Democratic superdelegates attending the party's national convention was 717 out of a total delegate count of 4,768. Unpledged superdelegates therefore amounted to about 15 percent of the convention. In addition to elected officials and former officials, they included 437 members of the Democratic National Committee. (Exact numbers change from year to year.) Republicans had an equivalent category of delegates, although the number of such persons could not exceed 150 out of a delegate total of 2,472. Unlike Democratic superdelegates, the Republicans were pledged to support the nominee who carried their state in the primaries.

The role of Democratic superdelegates became an issue in 2016, when most superdelegates with a preferred candidate lined up behind Hillary Clinton. Bernie Sanders claimed that the convention was therefore rigged against him. Of course, Clinton also outdid Sanders in electing regular delegates, so Sanders's charge was somewhat beside the point. Still, some Democrats recommended reducing the number of superdelegates in future years—especially the number who were merely members of the national committee. Other Democrats argued that superdelegates could prevent a takeover of the party's convention by a complete outsider such as Donald Trump.

The Invisible Primary

Before the primary season even begins, presidential candidates must begin lining up as much support within their party as is possible. This process has been called the **invisible primary**, because much of the action occurs behind closed doors. Potential candidates try to win supporters among elected officials, fund-raisers, interest groups,

superdelegate

A party leader or elected official who is given the right to vote at the party's national convention. Superdelegates are not selected at the state level.

invisible primary

The pre-primary campaign to win supporters among elected officials, fund-raisers, interest groups, and opinion leaders.

and opinion leaders. If a candidate can "win" the invisible primary, his or her chances in the actual primaries go way up. Historically, Republicans have been even more ready than Democrats to rally around the presumptive candidate. This process was described in *The Party Decides*, a widely acclaimed 2008 work of political science.[11]

As it happens, the 2015–2016 election cycle featured the primary election victories of Donald Trump, who had almost no support among the party leaders who typically participate in the invisible primary. The resulting joke: "The party decides—except when it doesn't." Studies of why Trump was victorious will surely provide political scientists with years of research opportunities.

Trump was not the first candidate ever to win a party's nomination after decisively losing the invisible primary, though such a result has not been seen in decades. Democratic candidates George McGovern and Jimmy Carter managed that feat in 1972 and 1976, respectively. These were, however, the first two Democratic contests after the party reforms of 1972, and it may have taken that long for Democratic elders to adjust to the new system.

Primaries and Caucuses

Various types of primaries are used by the states. One notable difference is between proportional and winner-take-all primaries. Another important consideration is whether independent voters can take part in a primary. Some states also use caucuses and conventions to choose candidates for various offices.

Direct and Indirect Primaries. A **direct primary** is one in which voters decide party nominations by voting directly for candidates. In an **indirect primary,** voters instead choose convention delegates, and the delegates determine the party's candidate in the

---

11. Marty Cohen et al., *The Party Decides: Presidential Nominations before and after Reform* (Chicago: University of Chicago Press, 2008).

direct primary

A primary election in which voters decide party nominations by voting directly for candidates.

indirect primary

A primary election in which voters choose convention delegates, and the delegates determine the party's candidate in the general election.

Joseph Sohm/Shutterstock.com

Image 9–8 Supporters of presidential candidate Senator Ted Cruz (R., Tex.) at a rally in Las Vegas the night before the 2016 Nevada presidential caucuses. *Do rallies really help a candidate? Why or why not?*

Image 9–9 UC Davis students line up at a campus polling place in Davis, California, on Election Day. *Should students vote where they attend school or where their parents live? In either case, why?*

general election. Delegates may be pledged to a particular candidate. Indirect primaries are rare except when choosing a presidential candidate. Most candidates in state and local elections are chosen by direct primaries.

Proportional and Winner-Take-All Primaries. Most primaries are *winner-take-all*. *Proportional* primaries are used mostly to elect delegates to the national conventions of the two major parties—delegates who are pledged to one or another candidate for president. Under the proportional system, if one candidate for president wins 40 percent of the vote in a primary, that candidate receives about 40 percent of the pledged delegates.

In recent years, the Democrats have used the proportional system for all of their presidential primaries and caucuses. For the most part, the Republicans have relied on the winner-take-all principle. In 2012, however, the Republican National Committee began requiring that early primaries be proportional. Republicans made even greater use of proportional primaries in 2016. Following Trump's victories in that year, several members of the Republican National Committee recommended that all Republican primaries should be proportional beginning in 2020.

Closed Primary. A closed primary is one of several types of primaries distinguished by how independent voters are handled. In a **closed primary,** only declared members of a party can vote in that party's primary. In other words, voters must declare their party affiliation, either when they register to vote or at the primary election. In a closed-primary system, voters cannot cross over into the other party's primary in order to nominate the weakest candidate of the opposing party or to affect the ideological direction of that party.

Open Primary. In an **open primary,** any voter can vote in either party's primary without declaring a party affiliation. Basically, the voter makes the choice in the privacy of the voting booth. The voter must, however, choose one party's list from which to select candidates.

Blanket Primary. A *blanket primary* is one in which the voter can vote for candidates of more than one party. Until 2000, a few states, including Alaska, California, and Washington, had blanket primaries. In 2000, however, the United States Supreme Court abolished the system. The Court ruled that the blanket primary violated political parties' First Amendment right of association. Because the nominees represent the party, party members—not the general electorate—should have the right to choose the party's nominee.[12]

Run-Off Primary. Some states have a two-primary system. If no candidate receives a majority of the votes in the first primary, the top two candidates must compete in another primary, called a *run-off primary*.

The "Top-Two" Primary. Louisiana has long used a special type of primary for filling some offices. Under the system, all candidates appear on a single ballot. A party cannot

closed primary

A type of primary in which the voter is limited to choosing candidates of the party of which he or she is a member.

open primary

A primary in which any registered voter can vote (but must vote for candidates of only one party).

12. *California Democratic Party v. Jones,* 530 U.S. 567 (2000).

prevent a candidate from appearing on the primary ballot—an insurgent Republican, for example, could appear on the ballot alongside the party-supported Republican. The two candidates receiving the most votes, regardless of party, then move on to the general election. Following the abolition of the blanket primary, the state of Washington adopted this system. In 2008, the Supreme Court upheld the new plan.[13] In 2010, Californians voted to use this type of primary, beginning in 2012.

The assumption is that in a top-two primary, candidates would take more moderate stands to appeal to independents or members of the other party. For example, in a conservative district, two Republican candidates might be forced to compete on the basis of who could add the most independent and even Democratic voters to their Republican support.

According to Ron Nehring, a former chair of the California Republican Party, "It's a misnomer to call this an open primary. It's the abolition of primaries." Indeed, a top-two election is not really a partisan primary—it is not a way in which parties can decide whom to support. Rather, it can be viewed as the first half of a two-part general election process. Still, under the top-two system, political parties continue to have the right to endorse candidates for the various offices. The parties can publicize these candidates and can spend, within legal limits, as much as they wanted in campaigning for them. The parties cannot, however, automatically place their preferred candidates on the November ballot.

Image 9–10 Supporters of Republican presidential candidate Donald Trump recite the Pledge of Allegiance at the 2016 Western Conservative Summit in Denver. *What kind of conservatism does Trump represent?*

Conventions. While primary elections are the most common way in which a party's candidates are selected, there are other procedures in use. State party conventions may nominate candidates for various offices. Those who attend meetings below the statewide level may participate in nominating candidates as well. The most famous of such meetings are the caucuses that help nominate a party's candidate for president of the United States.

Caucuses. In 2016, fifteen states relied at least in part on **caucuses** for choosing delegates to the Republican and Democratic national conventions. Some of these states used a combined system. Strictly speaking, the caucus system is actually a convention system. In North Dakota, for example, local citizens, who need not be registered as party members, gather in party meetings, called caucuses, at the precinct level. They choose delegates to district conventions. The district conventions elect delegates to the state convention, and the state convention actually chooses the delegates to the national convention. The national delegates, however, are pledged to reflect the presidential preferences that voters expressed at the caucus level.

Front-Loading the Primaries

When potential presidential candidates realized that winning as many primary elections as possible guaranteed them the party's nomination for president, their tactics changed dramatically. Candidates began to concentrate on building organizations in states that held early, important primary elections. By the 1970s, candidates recognized that winning early

caucus
A meeting of party members to select candidates and propose policies.

13. *Washington State Grange v. Washington State Republican Party*, 552 U.S. 442 (2008).

Image 9–11 A Texas delegate at the Democratic National Convention. *What kinds of Americans tended to support the Democratic candidate?*

contests, such as the Iowa caucuses and the New Hampshire primary election (both now held in January), meant that the media instantly would label the winner as the **front-runner,** thus increasing the candidate's media exposure and escalating the pace of contributions to his or her campaign.

The Rush to Be First. The state political parties began to see that early primaries had a much greater effect on the outcome of the presidential contest than did later ones. Accordingly, in successive presidential elections, more and more states moved their primaries into the first months of the year, a process known as **front-loading** the primaries. One result was a series of "Super Tuesdays," when multiple states held simultaneous primaries. In 2008, twenty-four states held their primaries or caucuses on February 5, making it the largest Super Tuesday ever. So many states were in play on February 5 that it was impossible for the candidates to campaign strongly in all of them. Rather than winning more attention, many Super Tuesday states found that they were ignored. Because the Democratic race was not decided until the very end of the process in June, the later Democratic primaries, such as those in Indiana, North Carolina, Ohio, Pennsylvania, and Texas, were hotly contested.

Front-loading, in short, had become counterproductive. As a result, in 2012 Super Tuesday was held on March 6, a month later than in 2008. Ten states participated instead of twenty-four. In 2016, Super Tuesday was on March 1, and twelve states participated.

The National Parties Seek to Regain Control. The process of front-loading the primaries alarmed many observers, who feared that a frontrunner might wrap up the nomination before voters were able to make a thorough assessment of the candidates. In response, the national Democratic and Republican parties took steps to regain control of the primary schedule. Such steps included a ban on primaries or caucuses held before a specified date. States would need special permission to choose delegates before that date. Traditional lead-off states such as Iowa and New Hampshire were allowed to go first, and a limited number of other states also received such permission. At first, a few states were unwilling to follow the official schedule, and as a result they were penalized by the national parties. By 2016, however, all states were obeying the rules.

On to the National Convention

Presidential candidates have been nominated by the convention method in every election since 1832. Extra delegates are allowed from states that had voting majorities for the party in the preceding elections. Parties also accept delegates from the District of Columbia, the territories, and U.S. citizens living abroad.

Seating the Delegates. At the convention, each political party uses a **credentials committee** to determine which delegates may participate. Controversy may arise when rival groups claim to be the official party organization. For example, the Mississippi Democratic Party split in 1964 at the height of the civil rights movement, and two sets of delegates were selected. After much debate, the credentials committee seated the mixed-race, pro–civil rights delegation and excluded those who represented the traditional "white" party.

Convention Activities. Most delegates arrive at the convention committed to a presidential candidate. No convention since 1952 has required more than one ballot to choose a nominee. Conventions normally last four days, but in both 2008 and 2012 the Republican convention was shortened to three days due to hurricanes. On each night,

front-runner

The presidential candidate who appears to be ahead at a given time in the primary season.

front-loading

The practice of moving presidential primary elections to the early part of the campaign to maximize the impact of these primaries on the nomination.

credentials committee

A committee used by political parties at their national conventions to determine which delegates may participate. The committee inspects the claim of each prospective delegate to be seated as a legitimate representative of his or her state.

featured speakers seek to rally the party faithful and draw in uncommitted voters who are watching on television.

A major goal of the conventions is to unite each party around the winning candidate. Party members who supported losing candidates must be encouraged to switch their support to the winner. In 2016, both major party conventions were successful in this effort—ordinary party members largely rallied around the winners. The Democrats, however, were more successful in uniting their party. Most supporters of Bernie Sanders were willing to endorse Hillary Clinton. On the Republican side, a number of the party's officeholders failed even to attend the convention and some refused to back Donald Trump. Candidates normally receive a positive "bump" in polls following their convention, and both Trump and Clinton did receive such a bump. Trump's advantage was temporary, however. The increase in support for Clinton appeared to be more lasting.

The Electoral College

Some people who vote for the president and vice president think that they are voting directly for a candidate. In actuality, they are voting for **electors** who will cast their ballots in the electoral college. Article II, Section 1, of the Constitution outlines in detail the method of choosing electors for president and vice president. The framers of the Constitution did not want the president and vice president to be selected by the "excitable masses." Rather, they wished the choice to be made by a few supposedly dispassionate, reasonable men (but not women).

The Choice of Electors. Electors are selected during each presidential election year. The selection is governed by state laws. After the national party convention, the electors are pledged to the candidates chosen. Each state's number of electors equals that state's number of senators (two) plus its number of representatives. The total number of electors today is 538, equal to 100 senators, 435 members of the House, and 3 electors for the District of Columbia. (The Twenty-third Amendment, ratified in 1961, added electors for the District of Columbia.)

The Electors' Commitment. A plurality of voters in a state chooses a slate of electors (except in Maine and Nebraska, where electoral votes are partly based on congressional districts). A *plurality* is the largest number, but not necessarily a majority. Those electors are pledged to cast their ballots on the first Monday after the second Wednesday in December in the state capital for the presidential and vice-presidential candidates of their party. The Constitution does not, however, *require* the electors to cast their ballots for the candidates of their party, and on rare occasions so-called *faithless electors* have voted for a candidate to whom they were not pledged.

The ballots are counted and certified before a joint session of Congress early in January. The candidates who receive a majority (270) of the electoral votes are certified as president-elect and vice president–elect. According to the Constitution, if no candidate receives a majority of the electoral votes, the election of the president is decided in the House of Representatives from among the candidates with the three highest numbers of votes, with each state having one vote (decided by a plurality of each state delegation). The selection of the vice president is determined by the Senate in a choice between the two candidates with the most votes, each senator having one vote. The House was required to choose the president in 1801 (Thomas Jefferson) and again in 1825 (John Quincy Adams).

Problems with the Electoral College System. It is possible for a candidate to become president without obtaining a majority of the popular vote. In fact, there have been many presidents in our history who did not win a majority of the popular vote. Such an event becomes more likely when there are important third-party candidates. The

elector

A member of the electoral college, which selects the president and vice president. Each state's electors are chosen in each presidential election year according to state laws.

possibility also exists that a candidate might be elected even though an opposing candidate receives a plurality of the popular vote. This has occurred on five occasions. Such results have led to calls for replacing the electoral college with a popular-vote system. We discussed that issue in the chapter-opening *What If . . .* feature.

How Are Elections Conducted?

The United States uses the **Australian ballot**—a secret ballot that is prepared, distributed, and counted by government officials at public expense. Since 1888, all states have used the Australian ballot. Before that, many states used oral voting or differently colored ballots prepared by the parties. Obviously, knowing which way a person was voting made it easy to apply pressure on the person to change his or her vote, and vote buying was common.

Office-Block and Party-Column Ballots

Two types of Australian ballots are used in the United States in general elections. The first, called an **office-block ballot,** or sometimes a **Massachusetts ballot,** groups all the candidates for a particular elective office under the title of that office. Parties dislike the office-block ballot because it places more emphasis on the office than on the party. It discourages straight-ticket voting—voting for all the candidates of a particular party—and encourages split-ticket voting instead. Most states now use this type of ballot.

A **party-column ballot** is a form of general election ballot in which all of a party's candidates are arranged in one column under the party's label and symbol. It is also called an **Indiana ballot.** In some states, it allows voters to vote for all of a party's candidates for local, state, and national offices by simply marking a single "X" or by pulling a single lever. Because it encourages straight-ticket voting, the two major parties favor this form. When a party has an exceptionally strong presidential or gubernatorial candidate to head the ticket, the use of the party-column ballot increases the **coattail effect** (the influence of a popular candidate on the success of other candidates on the same party ticket).

Australian ballot

A secret ballot prepared, distributed, and tabulated by government officials at public expense. Since 1888, all states have used the Australian ballot rather than an open, public ballot.

office-block, or Massachusetts, ballot

A form of general election ballot in which candidates for elective office are grouped together under the title of each office. It emphasizes voting for the office and the individual candidate, rather than for the party.

party-column, or Indiana, ballot

A form of general election ballot in which all of a party's candidates for elective office are arranged in one column under the party's label and symbol. It emphasizes voting for the party, rather than for the office or individual.

coattail effect

The influence of a popular candidate on the success of other candidates on the same party ticket.

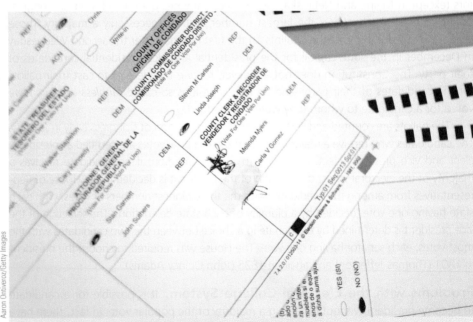

Aaron Ontiveroz/Getty Images

Image 9–12 A badly marked ballot for a very close local race in Colorado. *Would you count this ballot as a vote for the first of the two candidates? Why or why not?*

Voting by Mail

Voting by mail has been accepted for absentee ballots for many decades (for example, for individuals who are doing business away from home or for members of the armed forces). Recently, several states have offered mail ballots to all of their voters. The rationale for using the mail ballot is to make voting easier for the voters and increase turnout. Oregon has gone one step further: since 1998, that state has employed postal ballots exclusively, and there are no polling places. (Voters who do not prepare their ballot in time for the U.S. Postal Service to deliver it can drop off their ballots at drop boxes on Election Day.) All counties in Washington State began using postal ballots for the 2012 elections. Colorado adopted the practice in 2014. Voter turnout in these states exceeds the national average, especially in midterm elections when participation rates typically drop.

Voting Fraud and Voter ID Laws

Voting fraud is something regularly suspected but seldom proved. Voting in the 1800s, when secret ballots were rare and people had a cavalier attitude toward the open buying of votes, was probably much more conducive to fraud than modern elections are. Still, some observers claim that the potential for voting fraud is high in many states, particularly through the use of phony voter registrations and absentee ballots. Other observers claim, however, that errors due to fraud are trivial in number and that a few mistakes are inevitable in a system involving millions of voters. These people argue that an excessive concern with voting fraud makes it harder for minorities and poor people to vote.

Image 9–13 Senator Charles Schumer (D., N.Y.) points to a blowup of a flyer with misleading voting information. Schumer cosponsored a bill to make the distribution of fraudulent election material a federal offense. *How likely is it that a voter would be misled by such a flyer?*

Voter ID Requirements. In recent years, many states have adopted laws requiring enhanced proof of identity before voters can cast their ballots. Indiana imposed what was then the nation's toughest voter identification (ID) law in 2005. Indiana legislators claimed that they were motivated by a desire to prevent voting fraud, but critics argued that they were really trying to suppress voter turnout among minority group members and the poor—the individuals least likely to possess adequate identification. In 2008, the United States Supreme Court upheld the Indiana voter ID law.[14]

Voting Restrictions. In the years since 2008, dozens of states have moved to tighten voter ID requirements. Republicans provided almost all of the support for the new ID laws. By 2016, twenty-one states had enacted new laws that made it more difficult to vote. Cumbersome voter ID rules were the most common, but other new laws limited early voting or absentee ballots. In some states, however, state or federal courts overturned some of the new laws. In a few states, they were repealed by the voters.

In Texas, acceptable forms of ID included concealed carry permits for guns, but not student IDs, even those issued by state universities. Persons without acceptable forms of ID could obtain free Texas ID cards, but only through an in-person application at a limited number of state offices during normal business hours. In July 2016, however, the Texas ID law was ruled unconstitutional by a U.S. appeals court.

---

14. *Crawford v. Marion County Election Board*, 553 U.S. 181 (2008).

voter turnout

The percentage of citizens taking part in the election process; the number of eligible voters that actually "turn out" on election day to cast their ballots.

midterm elections

National elections in which candidates for president are not on the ballot. In midterm elections, voters choose all members of the U.S. House of Representatives and one-third of the members of the U.S. Senate.

Until 2013, most southern states with a history of racial discrimination had to obtain preclearance from the federal government for any significant change to their voting laws and procedures under the 1965 Voting Rights Act. The Department of Justice refused to preclear voter ID laws in South Carolina and Texas on the ground that the laws impose a greater burden on minority voters than on whites. As we explain in a later section of this chapter, however, in June 2013 the United States Supreme Court effectively suspended the preclearance procedure. As a result, many southern states were able to implement strict voter ID laws in time for the 2014 elections.

The Impact of Restrictive Voting Laws on Voter Turnout. In any election, the number of Americans who fail to vote is very large. Any factor that affects voter turnout, therefore, can have a major impact on election results. Heavy voter turnout among conservatives, for example, made 2010 a banner year for the Republicans. In 2012, a belief by minority group members that their voting rights were at risk seems to have increased minority turnout measurably. If the new voting laws really were meant to reduce the Democratic vote in 2012, they apparently backfired. In the 2014 midterm elections, however, several jurisdictions with new restrictive laws reported substantial drops in turnout compared with the 2010 midterms.

Learning Outcome **5:**

Discuss voter turnout in the United States and the types of people most likely to vote.

Turning Out to Vote

In 2014, the number of Americans eligible to vote was about 227.2 million people. Of that number, about 83.3 million, or 36.7 percent of the eligible population, actually cast a ballot. When voter turnout is this low, it means, among other things, that the winner of a close election may be voted in by a very small share of those eligible to vote.

Figure 9–2 shows **voter turnout** for presidential and **midterm elections** from 1910 to 2014. Each of the peaks in the figure represents voter turnout in a presidential election.

Figure 9–2 Voter Turnout for Presidential and Midterm Elections, 1910–2014

The peaks represent voter turnout in presidential election years; the troughs represent voter turnout in off-presidential election years.

Why might voter turnout have picked up in recent years?

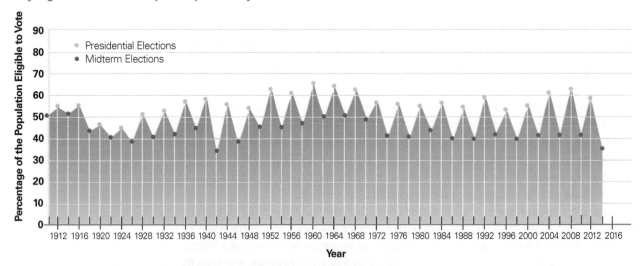

Note: Prior to 1948, the voting-age population is used as a proxy for the population eligible to vote.

Sources: Historical Data Archive, Inter-university Consortium for Political and Social Research; Michael P. McDonald and Samuel L. Popkin, "The Myth of the Vanishing Voter," *American Political Science Review,* Vol. 95, No. 4 (December 2001), p. 966; and the United States Elections Project.

Thus, we can also see that turnout for congressional elections is influenced greatly by whether there is a presidential election in the same year. Whereas voter turnout during the presidential elections of 2012 was 58.7 percent, it was, as noted, only 36.7 percent in the midterm elections of 2014.

The same is true at the state level. When there is a race for governor, more voters participate in the elections than when only state legislators are on the ballot. Voter participation rates in gubernatorial elections are also greater in presidential election years. The average turnout in state elections is about 14 percentage points higher when a presidential election is held.

Now consider local elections. In races for mayor, city council, county auditor, and the like, it is fairly common for only 25 percent or less of the electorate to vote. Is something amiss here? It would seem that people should be more likely to vote in elections that directly affect them. At the local level, each person's vote counts more (because there are fewer voters). Furthermore, the issues—crime control, school bonds, sewer bonds, and the like—touch the immediate interests of the voters. In reality, however, potential voters are most interested in national elections when a presidential choice is involved. Otherwise, voter participation in our representative government is very low (and, as we have seen, it is not overwhelmingly high even in presidential elections). You can find more information about voter turnout in this chapter's *Consider the Source* feature.

voting-age population

The number of people of voting age living in the country at a given time, regardless of whether they have the right to vote.

vote-eligible population

The number of people who, at a given time, enjoy the right to vote in national elections.

NEWS) *Consider the source*

The Voting-Age Population and the Vote-Eligible Population

In the past, the press and even many political scientists calculated voter turnout by taking the number of people who vote as a percentage of the nation's **voting-age population**. Until about 1972, this was a reasonable way to obtain an approximate figure for turnout. In recent decades, however, turnout figures based on the voting-age population have become less and less reliable. The problem is that the voting-age population is not the same as the population of eligible voters, the **vote-eligible population**. The figure for the voting-age population includes felons and ex-felons who have lost the right to vote. Above all, it includes a large number of new immigrants who are not yet citizens. Finally, it does not include Americans living abroad, who can cast absentee ballots.

In 2014, the voting-age population included 3.4 million ineligible felons and ex-felons and an estimated 20.6 million noncitizens. It did not include 5.3 million Americans abroad. The voting-age population in 2014 was 245.7 million people. The number of eligible voters, however, was only 227.2 million. If we calculated 2014 voter turnout based on the larger voting-age population, turnout would appear to be 33.9 percent, not 36.7 percent.

As you learned earlier, the United States has experienced high rates of immigration in recent decades. The very low voter turnout reported for several decades after 1972 may have been a function of the increasing size of the ineligible population, chiefly due to immigration.

The Source

The argument that low voter turnout might be largely due to immigration was first made by political scientists Michael P. McDonald and Samuel L. Popkin (see the source note for Figure 9–2). In the years since, McDonald and his students have developed the nation's premier website for tracking voter turnout—the United States Election Project. You can find it at www.electproject.org. You'll note that we do not report turnout figures for the 2016 elections in this chapter. While it is usually possible to determine who won an election within days, full information on voter turnout is not available until the following year. What was voter turnout like in 2016? Find out by visiting www.electproject.org and clicking on "Voter Turnout Data."

For Critical Analysis

○ **How likely is it that a person who is out of the country during elections will vote? Explain your reasoning.**

Factors Influencing Who Votes

A clear association exists between voter participation and the following characteristics: age, educational attainment, income level, minority status, and ideology.

- *Age.* Look at Figure 9–3, which shows the breakdown of voter participation by age group for the 2014 elections. It would appear from these figures that age is a strong factor in determining voter turnout on Election Day. The reported turnout increases with older age groups. Older voters are more settled in their lives, are already registered, and have had more time to experience voting as an expected activity.

- *Educational attainment.* Education also influences voter turnout. In general, the more education you have, the more likely you are to vote. This pattern is clearly evident in the 2014 election results, as you can see in Figure 9–4.

- *Income level.* Differences in income also correlate with differences in voter turnout. Wealthier people tend to be overrepresented among voters who turn out on Election Day. In recent presidential elections, voter turnout for those with the highest annual family incomes has approached three times the turnout of those with the lowest annual family incomes.

- *Minority status.* African Americans and Hispanics traditionally have not turned out to vote at the same rate as non-Hispanic whites. Minority group members, however, tend to have less education and lower incomes than non-Hispanic whites. On average, minority group members are younger. Many Latinos are immigrants who have not yet obtained citizenship. If, however, we correct for such factors as socioeconomic status, age, citizenship, and loss of the right to vote due to a felony conviction, the difference in turnout due to minority status largely disappears.

- *Ideology.* Depending on the issues at stake in a particular election year, political ideology may have a large impact on turnout. Either Republicans or Democrats may be discouraged from voting in a year that looks especially good for the other party. In 2008, for example, turnout among conservatives was relatively low for a presidential

Figure 9–3 Voting in the 2014 Elections by Age Group

Turnout is given as a percentage of the voting-age citizen population. *What could be done to make young people more likely to vote?*

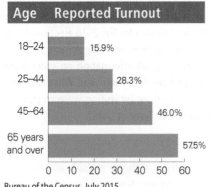

Source: U.S. Bureau of the Census, July 2015.

Figure 9–4 Voting in the 2014 Elections by Education Level

Turnout is given as a percentage of the voting-age citizen population. *Are there steps we could take that would encourage the less well educated to vote?*

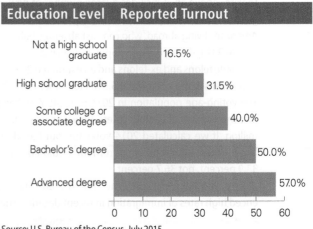

Source: U.S. Bureau of the Census, July 2015.

election year. In contrast, conservatives voted in very large numbers in 2010 and 2014, while more liberal voters, especially young people, often stayed home.

Legal Restrictions on Voting

Legal restrictions on voter registration have existed since the founding of our nation. Most groups in the United States have been concerned with the suffrage (the right to vote, also called the franchise) issue at one time or another. In colonial times, only white males who owned property with a certain minimum value were eligible to vote, leaving more Americans ineligible to take part in elections than were eligible.

Property Requirements. Many government functions concern property rights and the distribution of income and wealth, and some of the founders of our nation believed it was appropriate that only people who had an interest in property should vote on these issues. The idea of extending the vote to all citizens was, according to Charles Pinckney, a South Carolina delegate to the Constitutional Convention, merely "theoretical nonsense."

The writers of the Constitution allowed the states to decide who should vote. Thus, women were allowed to vote in Wyoming in 1870 but not in the entire nation until the Nineteenth Amendment was ratified in 1920. By about 1850, most white adult males in nearly all the states could vote without any property qualification. North Carolina was the last state to eliminate its property test for voting—in 1856.

Further Extensions of the Franchise. Extension of the franchise to black males occurred with the passage of the Fifteenth Amendment in 1870. This enfranchisement was short lived, however, as the "redemption" of the South by white supremacists had rolled back those gains by the end of the century. It was not until the 1960s that African Americans, both male and female, were able to participate in the electoral process in all states. Women received full national voting rights with the Nineteenth Amendment in 1920. The most recent extension of the franchise occurred when the voting age was reduced to eighteen by the Twenty-sixth Amendment in 1971. One result of lowering the voting age was to depress voter turnout beginning in 1972, as you can see in Figure 9–2. Young people are less likely to vote than older citizens.

Why should you care about ELECTIONS?

Why bother to vote? After all, the electorate is large and many elections are not close. If you do vote, however, you increase the amount of attention that politicians pay to people like you. When Congress, state legislatures, or city councils consider new laws and regulations, these bodies typically give more weight to the interests of groups that are more likely to vote. Your vote adds, to a small degree, to the voter turnout for your constituency. It therefore increases the chances of legislation that benefits you or that meets with your approval.

Is the Franchise Still Too Restrictive? There continue to be certain classes of people who do not have the right to vote. These include noncitizens and, in many states, convicted felons who have been released from prison. They also include current prison inmates, election law violators, and people who are mentally incompetent. Also, no one under the age of eighteen can vote. A number of political activists have argued that some of these groups should be allowed to vote. Most other democracies do not prevent convicts from voting after they have completed their sentences. In the 1800s, many states let noncitizen immigrants vote.

One discussion concerns the voting rights of convicted felons who are no longer in prison or on parole. According to the American Civil Liberties Union, ten states currently prevent felons from voting after they have completed their sentences. (The number used to be higher, but recently some states have relaxed their laws.) The Sentencing Project reports that several states prohibit 6 to 11 percent of their electorate from voting. In three states—Florida, Kentucky, and Virginia—more than 20 percent of African Americans of voting age have lost the right to vote. Barring felons from the polls injures minority groups because they make up a disproportionate share of former prison inmates.

Image 9–14 Ex-felons in Baltimore celebrate a new Maryland law that has restored their right to vote. *Which party are these people likely to support?*

Current Eligibility and Registration Requirements.
Voting generally requires **registration,** and to register, a person must satisfy the following voter qualifications, or legal requirements: (1) citizenship, (2) age (eighteen or older), and (3) residency. Since 1972, states cannot impose residency requirements of more than thirty days.

Each state has different laws for voting and registration. In 1993, Congress passed the "motor voter" bill, which requires that states provide voter-registration materials when people receive or renew driver's licenses, that all states allow voters to register by mail, and that voter-registration forms be made available at a wider variety of public places and agencies.

In 2015, Oregon passed a new law under which any citizen who obtains an Oregon driver's license is automatically registered to vote. Anyone who does not want to be registered can opt out, but doing so requires an explicit act by the nonvoter. Automatic voter registration quickly took off around the country. California, Vermont, and West Virginia adopted similar legislation. By mid-2016, twenty-five additional states and the District of Columbia were considering such laws, though few were in place in time for the 2016 elections.

In general, a person must register well in advance of an election, although voters in eleven states are allowed to register up to, or even on, Election Day.[15] North Dakota has no voter registration at all.

Not all voting reforms have a positive impact on turnout. Studies of early voting have generally found no effect on turnout. One recent study actually found that early voting can lower turnout, largely by reducing the publicity associated with Election Day. In contrast, Election Day registration can increase turnout by several percent.[16]

Some argue that registration requirements are responsible for much of the nonparticipation in our political process. There also is a partisan dimension to the debate over registration and nonvoting. Republicans generally fear that an expanded electorate would help to elect more Democrats—because more Democrats than Republicans are the kinds of persons who have trouble registering.

Voter-Registration Drives.
Given the registration system, voter-registration drives are a familiar part of the political landscape. In the year leading up to any presidential or midterm election, public-interest groups and political organizations fan out across the land to register new voters. Registration drives are particularly common on college campuses and in low-income neighborhoods, where large numbers of unregistered voters may be found.

Long seen as noncontroversial, voter-registration drives suddenly became a political issue in 2010, when Acorn, a community-organizing group, was accused of violating election laws in its campaigns. Conservatives claimed that Acorn posed a major threat to the

---

registration

The entry of a person's name onto the list of registered voters for elections. To register, a person must meet certain legal requirements of age, citizenship, and residency.

15. Election-day registration is available in Colorado, Connecticut, Idaho, Illinois, Iowa, Maine, Minnesota, Montana, New Hampshire, Wisconsin, Wyoming, and the District of Columbia. Rhode Island has election-day registration for presidential elections. Vermont implemented the system in 2017 and Hawaii in 2018.

16. Barry C. Burden et al., "Election Laws, Mobilization, and Turnout: The Unanticipated Consequences of Election Reform," *American Journal of Political Science*, Vol. 58, No. 1 (January 2014), pp. 95–109.

integrity of the voting process. Liberals contended that the controversy was overblown. Still, Acorn was forced to dissolve in 2010. Many former members later organized new groups.

In 2011 and 2012, Republican-controlled legislatures in a number of states tightened the laws governing voter-registration drives. Florida adopted the most stringent of these laws. In that state, organizations conducting registration drives were required to hand in all new registrations within forty-eight hours on penalty of a $50 fine for each late form. No allowance was made for days when state offices are closed—thus restricting voter registration on Fridays and any Saturday falling in a three-day weekend. Early voting days were also drastically curtailed. As a result, the League of Women Voters and Rock the Vote, major sponsors of voter-registration drives, suspended activities in Florida and sued to block the new law. The political parties, however, vowed to press on. In May 2012, a federal district judge suspended most of the voter registration requirements.

Image 9–15 In Washington, D.C., Republican presidential candidate Dr. Ben Carson greets Georgetown University students. Carson, a retired pediatric neurosurgeon, was unsuccessful as a candidate. *Should persons who have never held elected office run for president? Why or why not?*

Changes in the Voting Rights Act. The Voting Rights Act was enacted in 1965 to ensure that African Americans had equal access to the polls. Section 5 of the act requires that new voting practices or procedures in jurisdictions with a history of discrimination in voting have to be approved by the national government before being implemented.

In June 2013, in *Shelby County v. Holder*, the Supreme Court effectively invalidated the requirement that changes to voting procedures in covered states and districts receive preclearance.[17] The Court did not throw out Section 5. Rather, it overturned Section 4, which determined those states and localities that should be covered by Section 5. The Court contended that Section 4, which dated back to the 1960s, was obsolete. In principle, Congress could adopt a new set of Section 4 formulas based on more current conditions. The chances of such legislation making its way through a polarized Congress, however, seemed slight.

African American and liberal leaders accused the Court of engaging in one of the most sweeping examples of conservative judicial activism ever. The Voting Rights Act had been reaffirmed by Congress in 2006, with the House supporting it by 390 to 33 and the Senate by 98 to 0.

Even with the suspension of the preclearance system, the federal government retained the power under the Voting Rights Act to sue states and localities after a change to voting procedures was implemented. Such suits are far less effective than preclearance. The then attorney general Eric Holder, however, announced that the Department of Justice would sponsor such lawsuits whenever necessary.

---

17. 570 U.S. ___ (2013).

How you can make a difference

What do you have to do to register and cast a vote?

- In general, you must be a citizen of the United States, at least eighteen years old on or before Election Day, and a resident of the state in which you intend to register.

- A number of states require that you meet a minimum-residency requirement. The minimum-residency requirement is very short in some states. No state requires more than thirty days. Thirty states do not have any minimum-residency requirement.

- Nearly every state also specifies a closing date by which you must be registered before an election. You may not be able to vote if you register too close to the day of the election. The closing date for registration varies from Election Day itself to thirty days before the election. In North Dakota, no registration is necessary.

- In most states, your registration can be revoked if you do not vote within a certain number of years or do not report a change of address. Federal regulations place limits on how purges of the voting rolls are conducted.

- Look at voter registration in Texas as an example. If you live in Texas, you may have registered to vote when you obtained your Texas driver's license. If not, you can find a voter registration form online by searching on "texas vrapp."

- You must mail the application to the voter registrar in your county. (The registrar's address appears on the form after you finish filling it out.) Applications are also available at post offices, libraries, and other government offices. Your application must be postmarked thirty days before Election Day.

KEY TERMS

Australian ballot **254**	front-loading **252**	office-block, or Massachusetts, ballot **254**	registration **260**
caucus **251**	front-runner **252**		soft money **242**
closed primary **250**	general election **239**	open primary **250**	superdelegate **248**
coattail effect **254**	Hatch Act **241**	party-column, or Indiana, ballot **254**	super PAC **243**
credentials committee **252**	independent expenditures **243**	political action committee (PAC) **241**	vote-eligible population **257**
direct primary **249**	indirect primary **249**		voter turnout **256**
elector **253**	invisible primary **248**	political consultant **240**	voting-age population **257**
Federal Election Commission (FEC) **241**	issue advocacy **242**	presidential primary **237**	
focus group **240**	midterm elections **256**	primary election **239**	

CHAPTER SUMMARY

Learning Outcome 1 The legal qualifications for holding political office are minimal at the national, state, and local levels, but holders of political office still are predominantly white and male and are likely to be from the professional class.

American political campaigns are lengthy and extremely expensive. In the past decade, they have become more candidate centered in response to technological innovations and decreasing party identification. Candidates tend to rely on paid professional consultants to perform the various tasks necessary to wage a political campaign, which include devising a campaign strategy. Candidates use public opinion polls and focus groups to gauge their popularity and to test the mood of the country.

Learning Outcome 2 Under current conditions, finance for federal campaigns is supplied in two ways: candidate committees and independent expenditures. Candidate committees are under the complete control of the candidate. They have few limits on how they can spend their resources, but individual and organizational contributions to the committees face strict limits. Presidential candidate committees formerly accepted public financing, but candidates no longer participate in that system because they can raise more funds on their own. Independent organizations are not allowed to coordinate their expenditures with candidate campaigns, although this restriction is something of a fiction. These groups, which include super PACs and 501(c)4 organizations, can raise unlimited sums. Modern independent groups are the result of a 2010 Supreme Court ruling, *Citizens United v. FEC*.

Learning Outcome 3 After the Democratic convention of 1968, the McGovern-Fraser Commission formulated new rules for primaries, which were adopted by Democrats and, in most cases, by Republicans. These reforms opened up the nomination process for the presidency to all voters.

A presidential primary is a statewide election to help a political party determine its presidential nominee at the national convention. Some states use the caucus method of choosing convention delegates. The primary campaign recently has been shortened to the first few months of the election year.

A voter technically does not vote directly for president but instead chooses between slates of presidential electors. In most states, the slate that wins the most popular votes throughout the state gets to cast all the electoral votes for the state. The candidate receiving a majority (270) of the electoral votes wins.

Learning Outcome 4 The United States uses the Australian ballot, a secret ballot that is prepared, distributed, and counted by government officials. In recent years, several states have passed laws requiring photo IDs in order to vote and imposing other restrictions on voting. These laws have been very controversial.

Learning Outcome 5 Voter participation in the United States is often considered to be low, especially in elections that do not feature a presidential contest. Turnout is lower when measured as a percentage of the voting-age population than it is when measured as a percentage of the population actually eligible to vote. There is an association between voter turnout and a person's age, education, and income level.

In colonial times, only white males with a certain minimum amount of property were eligible to vote. The suffrage issue has concerned, at one time or another, most groups in the United States. Today, to register to vote, a person must satisfy citizenship, age, and residency requirements. Each state has different qualifications.

ADDITIONAL RESOURCES

Online Resources

- To locate excellent reports on where campaign money comes from and how it is spent, be sure to view the site of the Center for Responsive Politics at **www.opensecrets.org**.

- Another website for investigating voting records and campaign financing information is run by Project Vote Smart. Find it at **www.votesmart.org**.

Books

Johnson, Dennis W. *Democracy for Hire: A History of American Political Consulting*. New York: Oxford University Press, 2016. The most sweeping history of the political consulting profession to date. Johnson, a political science professor at George Washington University, has also worked in various political campaigns.

Mattes, Kyle, and David P. Redlawsk. *The Positive Case for Negative Campaigning*. Chicago, University of Chicago Press, 2015. In this comprehensive treatment, the authors make the case that negative campaigning provides voters with valuable information. The authors are professors of political science, Mattes at the University of Iowa and Redlawsk at Rutgers.

Mayer, Jane. *Dark Money: The Hidden History of the Billionaires Behind the Rise of the Radical Right*. New York: Doubleday, 2016. Mayer argues that current campaign finance laws hugely benefit conservative causes. A staff writer for *The New Yorker,* Mayer has written several best sellers on political topics.

Video

Scandal—A celebrated ABC drama series, *Scandal* stars Kerry Washington as political consultant Olivia Pope. Pope, a former presidential staff member, runs a crisis management firm that tries to protect the public images of the nation's political elite. Pope is usually successful, but we the viewers learn all the real dirt.

Veep—This award-winning series premiered in 2012 on HBO. *Veep* is a comedy starring Julia Louis-Dreyfus as U.S. vice president Selina Meyer. The hapless vice president, a former and possibly future presidential candidate, is forever one step away from catastrophe.

Quiz

Multiple Choice and Fill-Ins

Learning Outcome 1 Discuss who runs for office and how campaigns are managed.

1. To be eligible to serve as president of the United States, you must be:
   a. a natural-born citizen, a resident of the country for twenty-five years, and at least forty-two years old.
   b a naturalized citizen, a resident of the country for twenty-five years, and at least thirty-five years old.
   c. at least thirty-five years old, a natural-born citizen, and a resident of the country for fourteen years.

2. The most sought-after (and most criticized) campaign expert is the _____ _____, who for a large fee takes over the candidate's campaign.

Learning Outcome 2 Describe the current system of campaign finance.

3. Today, presidential candidates do not accept matching public funds because:
   a. candidates can raise far more outside of the public system than they would receive if they participated in it.
   b. once candidates accept public funds for the primaries, they must match public funds in a ratio of two to one for the general elections.
   c. public funds are no longer available.

4. The Supreme Court ruling that was most important in creating our current campaign finance system was _____ *v. FEC*.

Learning Outcome 3 Summarize the process of choosing a president of the United States.

5. In an indirect primary:
   a. voters decide party nominations by voting directly for candidates.
   b. voters make no decisions directly about convention delegates.
   c. voters choose convention delegates, and those delegates determine the party's candidate in the general election.

6. In a/an _____ _____, any voter can vote in either party primary without declaring a party affiliation.

Learning Outcome 4 Explain the mechanisms through which voting takes place on Election Day.

7. In the United States today, all states use secret ballots that are prepared, distributed, and counted by government officials at public expense. This system is called:
   a. the Australian ballot.
   b. the Massachusetts ballot.
   c. the office-block ballot.

8. A/an _____ - _____ ballot groups all the candidates for a particular elective office under the title of that office.

Learning Outcome 5 Discuss voter turnout in the United States and the types of people most likely to vote.

9. In colonial times, the right to vote was typically limited to persons who were:
   a. of English ancestry.
   b. adult white males.
   c. adult white males who owned some property.

10. In statistics on voter participation, the voting-age population is typically larger than the _____ - _____ population.

Essay Questions

1. Many observers believe that holding so many presidential primary elections at such an early point in an election year is a serious problem. How might the problem be resolved? Also, is it fair and appropriate that New Hampshire always holds the first presidential primary and Iowa always conducts the first caucuses? Why or why not?

2. Some people are more likely to vote than others. Older persons vote more frequently than younger people. Wealthy voters make it to the polls more often than poor voters. What might cause older and wealthier individuals to exhibit greater turnout?

Answers to multiple-choice and fill-in questions: 1. c, 2. political consultant, 3. a, 4. *Citizens United*, 5. c, 6. open primary, 7. a, 8. office-block, 9. c, 10. vote-eligible.

THE MEDIA

SiriusXM radio staff sit down with Politico reporters at the Republican National Convention in Cleveland, Ohio, in July 2016. *Should the major networks give the national party conventions "gavel-to-gavel" coverage?*
Kirk Irwin/Getty Images

These four **LEARNING OUTCOMES** *below are designed to help improve your understanding of this chapter:*

1: Describe the different types of media and the changing roles that they play in American society.

2: Summarize the impact of the media on the political process.

3: Explain the relationship between the government and the media, and in particular the Internet.

4: Discuss the question of opinion and bias in the mainstream media and alternative media such as talk radio.

What if...

There Were No Newspapers?

Background

At the end of the Revolutionary War, Americans could buy any of a total of forty-three newspapers. By 1910, newspapers throughout the country looked much as they do today. Currently, however, many newspapers face extinction. Great newspapers in Chicago, Minneapolis, Philadelphia, and other cities have filed for bankruptcy protection. Some, such as the *Baltimore Examiner* and the *Cincinnati Post*, have folded completely. Some people have speculated that, ultimately, newspapers will disappear altogether. What would such a world look like?

What If There Were No Newspapers?

The trend is already here. Since 1994, the share of Americans saying they read a daily newspaper has dropped from almost 60 percent to around 30 percent. If this trend continues, newspapers could for the most part vanish. Gone, too, would be their reporters and management.

By 2010, for the first time, more people obtained their national and international news from the Internet than from newspapers. Obviously, without newspapers, everyone would obtain their news from the Internet, broadcast and cable television, and to a lesser extent, news magazines. Without newspapers, these other sources of news would increase in size, scope, and availability.

The Death of the Standard News Package

When you open a metropolitan newspaper today, it has a "newspaper look." When you visit that newspaper's website, it often has the same look, one that dates back a hundred years. You'll find a mixture of local, national, business, sports, and international news, plus weather forecasts. What you see online is not much different from what is in print, although it may be easier to access.

If newspapers disappeared, the conventional news package also would disappear. People would find their news using online portals such as Yahoo and Google News. Their news format consists of headlines, a sentence, and a link. Such operations are cheap to run. Google News has no editors as such—everything is automated. Of course, if newspapers disappeared, Google News would not be able to access newspaper stories. Such stories would have to be found elsewhere online.

News Blogs and Cable News Channels Would Gain Viewers

Without newspapers, news blogs would grow. Already, the Huffington Post (nicknamed HuffPost) has a total staff of 850. It has an unpaid army of thousands of bloggers.

As of 2016, Fox News was the most popular cable news channel, but we also have MSNBC, CNN, and others. Without newspapers, more people would obtain some of their news from these cable sources. New cable news channels might pop up to serve niche audiences.

Local News Without Newspapers

Newspaper owners claim that it is not possible to obtain local news without the services of a local newspaper. Yet start-up companies are now creating "hyperlocal" news sites. These sites let people zoom in on what is happening in their neighborhoods. Check out www.berkeleyside.com for coverage of Berkeley, California; www.arlnow.com for Arlington, Virginia; or www.everyblock.com for Chicago. These sites collect links to articles and blogs and often obtain data from municipal governments and other local sources.

For Critical Analysis

▶ Would the quality of news gathering diminish if newspapers no longer existed?

▶ Many news blogs are definitely biased and often proud of it. Should this attitude worry us? Why or why not?

Image 10–1 A businesswoman consults her laptop while her male colleague reads a newspaper. *Why are so many young people giving up on newspapers?*

bikeriderlondon/Shutterstock.com

The study of people and politics must take into account the role played by the media. Historically, the print media played the most important role in informing public debate. The print media developed, for the most part, our understanding of how news is to be reported. Today, however, 55 percent of Americans use television news as their primary source of information. In addition, the Internet has become a major source for news, political communication, and fund-raising. The Internet is now the second most widely used source of information—22 percent of all persons consider it their primary source of news. Only 9 percent of the public currently relies on print publications as a primary news source, and newspapers are facing serious problems, as you can see from the chapter-opening *What If . . .* feature.

The Roles of the Media

Learning Outcome **1:**

Describe the different types of media and the changing roles that they play in American society.

The mass media perform a number of different functions in any country. In the United States, we can list at least six media functions. Almost all of them can have political implications, and some are essential to the democratic process. These functions are: (1) entertaining the public, (2) reporting the news, (3) identifying public problems, (4) socializing new generations, (5) providing a political forum, and (6) making profits.

Entertaining the Public

By far the greatest number of radio and television hours are dedicated to entertaining the public. The battle for prime-time ratings indicates how important successful entertainment is to the survival of networks and individual stations. A number of network shows have a highly political content. Many younger people have reported that they get much of their political information from the *Daily Show* on the Comedy Central network. Long the home of comedian Jon Stewart, the *Daily Show* is now run by Trevor Noah. An equally important personality is John Oliver, who hosts *Last Week Tonight* on HBO. Oliver combines off-color humor with serious investigative journalism.

For many Americans, especially younger ones, the Internet has replaced television as a source of entertainment. While much time on the Internet may be spent chatting with friends on Skype or watching television programs online, politics is often a topic. YouTube, in particular, offers a large number of politically oriented videos, many of which are satirical. Talk radio and television shows that feature talk-radio personalities are another form of politically oriented entertainment—one that is dominated by the political right.

Reporting the News

A primary function of the mass media in all their forms is the reporting of news. The media provide words and pictures about events, facts, personalities, and ideas. The protections of the First Amendment are intended to keep the flow of news as free as possible, because it is an essential part of the democratic process. If citizens cannot obtain unbiased information about the state of their communities and their leaders' actions, how can they make voting decisions? One of the most incisive comments about the importance of the media was made by James Madison, who said, "A popular government without popular information or the means of acquiring it, is but a prologue to a farce or a tragedy or perhaps both."[1]

Image 10–2 MSNBC personality Rachel Maddow speaks at the Times Center Stage about the 2016 elections. Maddow is one of the most popular liberals on television. *How might a network gain viewers by adopting a particular political line?*

1. James Madison, "Letter to W. T. Barry" (August 4, 1822), in Gaillard P. Hunt, ed., *The Writings of James Madison*, Vol. 1 (New York: G. P. Putnam's Sons, 1910).

Slaven Vlasic/Getty Images Entertainment/Getty Images

Image 10–3 Commentator Bill O'Reilly is one of the stars of Fox News. Fox is known for its conservative slant on the news, and it is more popular than its competitors. *Why might this be?*

Identifying Public Problems

The power of the media is important not only in revealing what the government is doing but also in determining what the government ought to do—in other words, in setting the **public agenda.** The mass media identify public issues. American journalists also have a long tradition of uncovering public wrongdoing, corruption, and bribery, and of bringing such wrongdoing to the public's attention. For its part, the enormous collection of political sites on the Internet is filled with policy proposals representing every point of view.

Agenda setting by the media is enhanced by the various ways in which they can present the news. Earlier in this text, we introduced the concept of *framing*. The media can affect the public response to a particular issue by how they frame the issue—that is, by embedding the issue in a particular story line. Attitudes toward government spending on the poor, for example, can be altered by stories that present poor people who are victims of bad luck—or who are suffering mostly due to their own behavioral problems. A similar concept is **priming**, that is, altering the public's reaction to a story by reporting it together with facts that support a particular interpretation. Take popular attitudes toward a state tax, for instance. The press might compare a state's tax rate to taxes in states with high tax rates—or states with low rates. If a reporter chooses a high-tax state for the comparison, the local state tax will appear more reasonable.

Socializing New Generations

The media strongly influence the beliefs and opinions of Americans. Because of this influence, the media play a significant role in the political socialization of the younger generation and of immigrants to this country. Through the transmission of historical information (sometimes fictionalized), the presentation of American culture, and the portrayal of the diverse regions and groups in the United States, the media teach young people and immigrants about what it means to be an American. Many children's television shows are designed not only to entertain young viewers but also to instruct them in the moral values of American society.

On the Internet, young Americans participate in political forums, obtain information for writing assignments, and, in general, acquire much of their political socialization.

Providing a Political Forum

As part of their news function, the media also provide a political forum for leaders and the public. Candidates for office use news reporting to sustain interest in their campaigns, while officeholders use the media to gain support for their policies or to present an image of leadership. Presidential trips abroad are one way for the chief executive to get colorful, positive, and exciting news coverage that makes the president look "presidential." The media also offer ways for citizens to participate in public debate, through letters to the editor, blog posts, Twitter, and other channels.

public agenda

Issues that are perceived by the political community as meriting public attention and governmental action.

priming

A way in which the media can alter public perceptions of an issue—by choosing which facts they include in the reporting.

Making Profits

Most of the news media in the United States are private, for-profit corporate enterprises. In general, profits are made as a result of charging for advertising. Advertising revenues usually are related directly to circulation or to listener/viewer ratings.

Several well-known media outlets, in contrast, are publicly owned—public television stations in many communities and National Public Radio. These operate without extensive commercials, are locally supported, and are often subsidized by the government and corporations.

Pressure by Advertisers. For the most part, however, the media depend on advertisers to obtain revenues to make profits. Consequently, reporters may feel pressure from media owners and from advertisers. If an important advertiser does not like the political bent of a particular newspaper reporter, for example, the reporter could be asked to alter his or her "style" of writing.

In one example, a harsh review of a country singer was removed from the website of an alternative weekly when concert promoters threatened never to advertise in the weekly again. In another instance, advertiser pressure on a firearms industry trade magazine led to the firing of a columnist and the resignation of the magazine's editor. The columnist had contended that Second Amendment rights are subject to regulation.

Newspapers in Crisis. Lately, newspapers have found it increasingly difficult to make a profit. Newspaper revenues have fallen because online services such as Craigslist have taken over a greater share of classified advertising. The recent economic crisis, which depressed advertising spending, pushed many large daily newspapers over the edge. Newspapers in Chicago, Denver, and Seattle went out of business. Even some famous papers, such as the *New York Times,* the *Chicago Tribune,* and the *Boston Globe,* were in serious financial trouble.

Although all major newspapers are now online, they have found it difficult to turn a profit on their Web editions. News sites typically cannot sell enough advertising to meet their costs. For an example, see the HP ad in Image 10–4 showing the *New York Times* website (which appears behind a paywall). In response to this problem, many newspapers have begun charging for online access, a process dubbed *retreating behind a paywall.* Access charges, however, reduce the number of users who are willing to view a site. Major publications such as the *Wall Street Journal* have been able to set up paywalls without losing an excessive number of customers, but less famous newspapers have not been so successful.

Content Providers versus Aggregators. On the Internet, news organizations that employ reporters and create articles are known as **content providers**, because they provide original content. Unfortunately for the content providers, they collect only a small share of the total revenue from online advertising. Most ad revenue goes to **aggregators**, such as Google, that provide search and aggregation services but generate little or no original content. We compare Google's ad revenues with those of print media in this chapter's *Consider the Source* feature.

content provider

On the Internet, an individual or organization that generates original content.

aggregator

A website that provides search and aggregation services, but creates little or no original content.

Image 10–4 An image from the *New York Times* website. *Does it make sense for the Times to charge for access to its site?*

Consider the source

Ad Revenues

To assess the financial pressure that online firms are exerting on newspapers and magazines, let's look at advertising revenues. Figure 10–1 shows such revenues for 2015 in billions of U.S. dollars.

As you can see from the chart, Google collects slightly more than half of all U.S. online ad revenue. In fact, its ad revenue now exceeds the total ad revenue of all newspapers and magazines in the nation put together. Print media are doing somewhat better in the rest of the world, but online firms are advancing quickly. In other words, there is no absolute shortage of ad revenue—the problem is that it goes to the aggregators, not the content providers. Of course, without content providers, there is nothing to aggregate.

The Source

Ironically, the best gateway to information about ad revenue for Google and the rest of the industry is Google itself. No single website provides all the data we want. You can find the reports listed in "Sources" under the chart by searching for the report names using Google or another online search engine. Financial results for Google itself come from Google's own investor relations website. Google doesn't break out its U.S. ad revenue number—we use an estimate by Brian Wieser of Pivotal Research, as reported by the Bloomberg Technology website. For interesting stories about advertising, you can also check out the website of *Advertising Age* at adage.com.

For Critical Analysis

▷ After visiting adage.com and reading one or two of the more interesting-looking stories, describe what you have learned.

Figure 10–1 Advertising Revenue, 2015

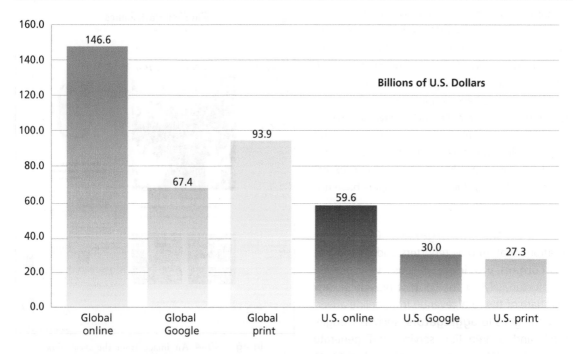

Sources: McKinsey & Company, *Global Media Report 2015;* Interactive Advertising Bureau, *IAB Internet Advertising Revenue Report, 2015 Full Year Results;* and Bloomberg Technology, "Google and Facebook Lead Digital Ad Industry to Revenue Record," April 22, 2016.

Television versus the New Media

As we explained earlier, new forms of media are displacing older ones as sources of information on politics and society in general. Although it is only recently that newspapers have experienced severe economic difficulties, they were losing ground to television as early as the 1950s. Today, the Internet has begun to displace television.

New Patterns of Media Consumption.

Not everyone, however, migrates to new media at the same rate. Among Americans older than sixty-five years of age, only 6 percent obtained the greatest amount of information about political campaigns in 2016 by going online. In this older generation, 11 percent still relied on a printed daily newspaper, down from 58 percent in 2000. A full 70 percent found cable, network, or local television to be most helpful. Among 18- to 29-year-olds, in contrast, social media came first with 35 percent, followed by news websites or apps with 18 percent.[2]

Image 10–5 Don Lemon is the host of CNN *Tonight,* a prime time news show. *Does CNN have a political bias? If so, what is it?*

The media consumption patterns of *early adopters* of new technology are simply different from the past. Some older high-income persons are among the early adopters, but the new media are most popular among youth. Indeed, many younger people have abandoned e-mail, relying on Facebook, texting, and other systems for messages. Many have moved on from Facebook to newer, more innovative social-networking platforms. Television becomes something to watch only if you cannot find online the program you want to see.

Young early adopters may find much of the offline media irrelevant to their lives. Yet television news, cable networks, talk radio, and other forms of media are not irrelevant to American politics. Older voters outnumber younger ones by a wide margin. As of 2016, about 111 million Americans were age fifty or older. U.S. residents age eighteen through twenty-nine were less than half that number. Older voters are more likely to make it to the polls—and many early adopters of new media technology are too young to vote. It follows that television remains essential to American politics.

The Continuing Influence of Television.

Television's continuing influence on the political process today is recognized by all who engage in that process. Television news is often criticized for being superficial, particularly compared with the detailed coverage available in newspapers, magazines, and online articles. In fact, television news is constrained by its technical characteristics, the most important being the limitations of time—stories must be reported in only a few minutes.

The most interesting aspect of television—and of online video—is that it relies on pictures rather than words to attract the viewer's attention. Therefore, video that is chosen for a particular political story has exaggerated importance. Viewers do not know what other photos may have been taken or what other events may have been recorded—they see only those appearing on their screens. Video clips, whether they appear on network news or YouTube, can also use well-constructed stories to exploit the potential for drama. Some critics suggest that there is pressure to produce television news that has a story line, like a novel or movie. The story should be short, with exciting pictures and a clear plot.

---

2. Pew Research Center for the People & the Press, "The 2016 Presidential Campaign—a News Event That's Hard to Miss," February 4, 2016.

In extreme cases, the news media are satisfied with a **sound bite,** a several-second comment selected or crafted for its immediate impact on the viewer.

It has been suggested that these formatting characteristics of video increase its influence on political events. As you are aware, real life is usually not dramatic, nor do all events have a plot that is neat or easily understood. Political campaigns are continuing events, lasting perhaps as long as two years. The significance of their daily turns and twists is only apparent later. The "drama" of Congress, with its 535 players and dozens of important committees and meetings, is also difficult for the media to present. Television requires, instead, dozens of daily three-minute stories.

Learning Outcome **2:**

Summarize the impact of the media on the political process.

The Media and Political Campaigns

All forms of the media—television, newspapers, radio, magazines, online services—have a significant political impact on American society. It is not too much of an exaggeration to say that almost all national political figures, starting with the president, plan every public appearance and statement to attract media coverage.

Television Coverage

As we have explained, although younger voters get a relatively small share of their news from television, it remains the primary news source for older voters. Therefore, candidates and their consultants spend much of their time devising strategies that use television to their benefit. Three types of TV coverage are generally employed in campaigns for the presidency and other offices: political advertising (including negative ads), management of news coverage, and campaign debates.

Political Advertising. Political advertising has become increasingly important for the profitability of television station owners. Hearst Television, for example, obtains more than 10 percent of its revenues from political ads during an election year. During the 2012 presidential elections, total spending exceeded $7 billion. Among other expenses, candidates purchased more than 3 million campaign advertisements.

Negative Advertising. Perhaps one of the most effective political ads of all time was a thirty-second spot created by President Lyndon Johnson's media adviser in 1964. Johnson's opponent in the campaign was Barry Goldwater, a conservative Republican candidate known for his expansive views on the role of the U.S. military. In this ad, a little girl stood in a field of daisies. As she held a daisy, she pulled the petals off and quietly counted to herself. Suddenly, when she reached number ten, a deep bass voice cut in and began a countdown: "10, 9, 8, 7, 6 . . . ." When the voice intoned "zero," the mushroom cloud of an atomic bomb began to fill the screen. Then President Johnson's voice was heard: "These are the stakes. To make a world in which all of God's children can live, or to go into the dark. We must either love each other or we must die." At the end of the commercial, the message read, "Vote for President Johnson on November 3."

Since the daisy girl advertisement, negative advertising has come into its own. In recent elections, an ever-increasing percentage of political ads have been negative in nature.

The public claims not to like negative advertising, but as one consultant put it, "Negative advertising works." Negative ads can backfire, however, when there are three or more candidates in the race, a typical state of affairs in the early presidential primaries. If one candidate attacks another, the attacker as well as the candidate who is attacked may come to be viewed negatively by the public. A candidate who "goes negative" may thus

sound bite

A brief, memorable comment that easily fits into news broadcasts.

Image 10–6 These are stills of a short television advertisement used by presidential candidate Lyndon Johnson in 1964. The daisy girl ad contrasted the innocence of childhood with the horror of an atomic bomb. *How effective was this negative TV ad?*

Doyle, Dane, Bernbach

unintentionally boost the chances of a third candidate who is not part of the exchange. The 2016 Republican presidential primaries provided one example. New Jersey governor Chris Christie effectively criticized Florida senator Marco Rubio for repeating lines in an almost robotic fashion. While Christie's comment hurt Rubio, it did Christie himself no good at all.

Management of News Coverage. Using political advertising to get a message across to the public is a very expensive tactic. Coverage by the news media, however, is free. The campaign simply needs to ensure that coverage takes place. In recent years, campaign managers have shown increasing sophistication in creating newsworthy events for journalists to cover. Uniquely, in 2015 and 2016 Donald Trump had no need of a campaign manager to help him attract free media coverage. Trump's personal talent for winning media attention was unprecedented.

The campaign staff uses several methods to try to influence the quantity and type of coverage the campaign receives. First, with an understanding of the technical aspects of media coverage—camera angles, necessary equipment, timing, and deadlines—the staff plans political events to accommodate the press. Second, the campaign organization is aware that political reporters and their sponsors—networks, newspapers, or blogs—are in competition for the best stories and can be manipulated through the granting of favors, such as a personal interview with the candidate. Third, the scheduler in the campaign has the important task of planning events that will be photogenic and interesting enough for the evening news.

A related goal, although one that is more difficult to attain, is to convince reporters that a particular interpretation of an event is true. Today, the art of putting the appropriate

Image 10–7 A family watches the 1960 Kennedy-Nixon debates on television. After the debate, TV viewers thought Kennedy had won, whereas radio listeners thought Nixon had the edge. *Why have televised presidential debates become major media events?*

spin on a story or event is highly developed. Press advisers, often referred to as **spin doctors,** try to convince journalists that the advisers' interpretations of the political events are correct. For instance, the Obama administration and Republicans in Congress engaged in a major spinning duel over Obama's executive order in 2014 that would allow certain classes of illegal immigrants to remain in the country. Republicans sought to portray the order as overreach by an imperial presidency. Republicans in the House tried—unsuccessfully—to overturn the order by refusing to fund the Department of Homeland Security. Democrats then argued that Republicans were acting irresponsibly and threatening our national security. (The order was blocked by the Supreme Court in 2016.)

Going for the Knockout Punch—Televised Presidential Debates.

In presidential elections, perhaps just as important as political advertisements and general news coverage is the performance of the candidate in televised presidential debates. Consider the first such debate in 1960, in which John Kennedy, the young senator from Massachusetts, took on the vice president of the United States, Richard Nixon. Many observers concluded that Kennedy's performance in these debates provided the edge he needed to win a very close contest. Thereafter, candidates became aware of the great potential of television for changing the momentum of a campaign. In general, challengers have much more to gain from debating than do incumbents. Challengers hope that the incumbent will make a mistake in the debate and undermine the "presidential" image. Incumbent presidents are loath to debate their challengers because it puts their opponents on an equal footing with them, but the debates have become so widely anticipated that it is difficult for an incumbent to refuse to participate.

The 2015–2016 Primary Debates.

With the pending retirement of President Obama, both major parties held important presidential debates. The Republicans sponsored twelve debates and nine forums in 2015 and 2016. The most notable feature of these events was the very large number of participants—seventeen at the initial debate. These were not the only Republicans to run. Dozens more did so but did not receive enough support in opinion polls to earn a debate invitation from the Republican National Committee. Because of the large number of participants, the debaters were divided into two teams, based on their poll standings. A main "varsity" debate with ten candidates was preceded by a secondary "junior varsity" event with an additional seven contenders. The first varsity debate, sponsored by Fox News in August, had twenty-four million viewers, making it the most-watched live broadcast for a nonsporting event in the history of cable TV. Each of the subsequent main debates was seen by at least eleven million viewers.

The Republican Debates: An Unexpected Outcome.

Despite the large field, most Republican leaders assumed that the debates would lead to results similar to those in the presidential primary campaigns of 2011–2012. In 2011, a series of strongly conservative candidates rose up to challenge Mitt Romney, the "invisible primary" favorite. Each insurgent candidate had problems, however, and each one faded. Romney triumphed in the end.

spin

An interpretation of campaign events or election results that is favorable to the candidate's campaign strategy.

spin doctor

A political campaign adviser who tries to convince journalists of the truth of a particular interpretation of events.

The 2015–2016 primary race, however, was completely different. Party leaders never settled on a favorite, although several candidates did have establishment backing. These included former Florida governor Jeb Bush, Florida senator Marco Rubio, and Wisconsin governor Scott Walker. Despite his considerable fund-raising advantage, however, Bush dropped out in February. Walker did not make it to the third debate. Unlike four years before, the insurgent candidate with an early lead in the polls never faded. That candidate was real estate mogul Donald Trump. Even though Trump was not a particularly strong debater, he was able to communicate his message to restive Republican voters effectively. He therefore succeeded where other insurgent candidates in 2012 and 2016 had failed.

The Democratic Debates: A Civil Campaign. The Democrats held nine debates and thirteen forums in 2015 and 2016. The first of these, on CNN, had almost sixteen million viewers, but later debates had an audience of less than half that. In contrast to the Republicans, whose exchanges were often remarkably sharp, the Democratic candidates tended to avoid personal attacks. Five Democrats were on hand for the first debate, but by February the field was down to two candidates: former secretary of state Hillary Clinton and Vermont senator Bernie Sanders.

Image 10–8 Republican presidential candidates Donald Trump, left, and Senator Ted Cruz (R., Tex.) in a debate sponsored by Fox News in March 2016 in Detroit. *Why do you think Trump beat Cruz (who came in second in the primaries)?*

Clinton was the overwhelming favorite of party elders, but Sanders managed to turn the campaign into a serious race. Sanders emphasized a series of major themes, such as breaking up large banks, Medicare for everyone, and tuition-free education at public colleges and universities. Despite winning large margins among younger voters, in the end Sanders was unable to overcome Clinton's natural advantages.

Clinton-Trump Debates. The first presidential debates, between John F. Kennedy and Richard Nixon in 1960, may have determined the outcome of that race. Later debates were less consequential. The 2016 debates between Hillary Clinton and Donald Trump were crucial, however. Viewership reached an unprecedented 80 million for the first debate, not including people who watched on their computers or smart phones. Trump refused to prepare, and it showed. After an initial vigorous presentation on immigration, he lapsed into near-incoherence. Clinton, in contrast, appeared calm and knowledgeable. She knew that Trump was relatively thin-skinned, and therefore she ended the debate by criticizing Trump for "fat-shaming" a Miss Universe winner. Trump took the bait and denounced the beauty queen for days thereafter. Going into the first debate, Clinton's margin in the polls was very narrow. After all three debates, her margin approached 7 percent.

The Internet, Blogging, and Podcasting

Today, the campaign staff of every candidate running for a significant political office includes an Internet campaign strategist—a professional hired to create and maintain the campaign website, social media accounts, blogs, and podcasts (blogs and podcasts will be discussed shortly). The work of this strategist includes designing a user-friendly and attractive website for the candidate; managing the candidate's e-mail, Twitter, and Facebook communications; tracking campaign contributions made through the site; hiring bloggers to push the candidate's agenda on the Internet; and monitoring websites for favorable or unfavorable comments or video clips about the candidate.

Additionally, all major interest groups in the United States now use the Internet to promote their causes. Prior to elections, various groups engage in issue advocacy from their websites. At little or no cost, they can promote positions taken by favored candidates and solicit contributions.

Online Fund-raising. Two politicians stand out as pioneers of online fund-raising. The first of these was Ron Paul, a Republican member of Congress from Texas, who ran for president several times on a strongly libertarian platform. Paul's support was especially strong among heavy Internet users, and these supporters introduced the idea of the *moneybomb.* The San José *Mercury News* described a moneybomb as "a one-day fund-raising frenzy." Two moneybomb events in late 2007 raised more than $10 million for the Paul campaign.

Paul's fund-raising success was overshadowed in 2008, however, by Barack Obama's online fund-raising machine. In that year, Obama obliterated every political fund-raising and spending record in history. In total, his campaign raised more than $650 million, much of it in small donations solicited through the Internet. A key characteristic of successful Internet campaigns has been decentralization. The nature of the Internet has allowed candidates to assemble thousands of individual activists who serve as fund-raisers.

In the 2015–2016 election cycle, the online fund-raising champion was Bernie Sanders. By the end of the primary season, Sanders had raised $222 million. Most of this sum was raised online, and about two-thirds of the total came in donations of less than $200. Hillary Clinton raised slightly more—$229 million—but three-quarters of her total came in larger donations, many of them collected at fund-raising events. Republicans were even less effective at playing the online fund-raising game during the 2016 primaries. The largest Republican fund-raiser was Texas senator Ted Cruz, who came in second to Donald Trump in the Republican delegate count. He brought in a total of about $80 million. (Jeb Bush raised more than that, mostly from large donors, but he gave about half of it back when he dropped out.) Roughly half of the $63 million that Donald Trump raised through June consisted of personal loans to his own campaign, loans that conceivably could be paid back.

Blogging. Within the past few years, politicians have also felt obligated to post regular blogs on their websites. The word **blog** comes from *Web log,* a regular updating of one's ideas at a specific website. Of course, many people besides politicians are also posting blogs. Not all of the millions of blogs posted daily are political in nature. Many are, though, and they can have a dramatic influence on events, giving rise to the term *blogosphere politics.*

Blogs are clearly threatening the mainstream media. They can be highly specialized, highly political, and highly entertaining. And they are cheap. The *Washington Post* requires thousands of employees, paper, and ink to generate its offline product and incurs delivery costs to get it to readers. A relatively large blogging organization such as Vox can generate its content with only about twenty reporters.

Blogs versus Magazines. Originally, blogs were the work of a single individual, describing that person's opinions and experiences. The Conscience of a Liberal, Paul Krugman's blog on economics and politics, is a modern example. (Visiting it through Twitter will get you past the *New York Times* paywall.) Today, however, most of the highly popular political blogs are team efforts. In many cases, they were founded by an individual blogger who later hired additional contributors. It can be hard to distinguish such blogs from online magazines, given that a magazine and a team blog both contain original content from multiple writers. Indeed, some sites are divided into two parts: one designated as a magazine and the other as a collection of blog posts.

blog

From *Web log.* A website where an individual or group posts regular updates on their ideas or experiences.

A further complication is the difficulty in distinguishing between a blog with multiple authors and an aggregation site. The largest political site on the Internet, the Huffington Post, is visited by more than 100 million individuals each month. The Huffington Post (www.huffingtonpost.com) gained fame as an aggregator of material from mainstream news organizations, but today its 850 employees generate large amounts of original material. The site is also famous for its veritable army of unpaid bloggers. Is the "HuffPost" an aggregator, an online newsmagazine, or a blogging site? It appears to be all three. We list a variety of interesting blogs in Table 10–1.

Comments. Many, but not all, blog posts—and also articles in online newspapers and magazines—allow readers to comment on the post or article. Comments can be a way to build a community around a small blog, enhancing its influence. Sites with a huge readership drawn from the general public, however, experience problems with comments. They can quickly deteriorate into "flame wars," in which partisans of the left and right insult each other instead of entering useful observations. Even a blog with a relatively small readership, such as The Reality-Based Community (www.samefacts.com), can face this problem if it deals with a controversial topic such as policies toward illegal drugs. Short of shutting down the comments sections, one solution is to *moderate* the comments—to publish only those comments approved by a moderator. For most blogs, however, this procedure involves an unacceptable amount of effort.

Podcasting. Once blogs—written words—became well established, it was only a matter of time before they ended up as spoken words. Enter **podcasting,** so called because the first Internet-communicated spoken blogs were downloaded onto Apple's iPods. Podcasts, though, can be heard on a computer or downloaded onto any portable listening device. Podcasting can also include videos. Hundreds of thousands of podcasts are now generated every day. Basically, anyone who has an idea can easily create a podcast and make it available for downloading. Like blogs, podcasting threatens traditional media sources. Publications that sponsor podcasts find it hard to make them profitable.

Although politicians have been slower to adopt this form of communication, many now are using podcasts to keep in touch with their constituents, and there are currently tens of thousands of political podcasts.

Trump's Use of Twitter. One characteristic of the 2016 elections was the enhanced role of Twitter. With 310 million active users in 2016, Twitter is not the largest social media service. Famously, "tweets" are limited to 140 characters. Still, Twitter proved to be an ideal platform for Donald Trump, who reveled in his ability to issue short, colorful statements. Trump's Twitter presence was backed up by a veritable army of supporters who retweeted each of his observations to thousands of additional people. These supporters were also quite willing to organize massive trolling campaigns against anyone who criticized their candidate. Trump's tweets often provoked controversy. His campaign devoted little time to screening its sources, some of which turned out to be highly questionable.

Table 10–1 Selected Political Blog Sites

Which of these sites could also be called an online magazine?

Progressive	Conservative
The American Prospect prospect.org	American Thinker www.americanthinker.com
The Conscience of a Liberal https://twitter.com/paulkrugman	Breitbart News Network www.breitbart.com
The Daily Kos www.dailykos.com	The Daily Caller dailycaller.com
Mother Jones www.motherjones.com	National Review Online www.nationalreview.com
TalkingPointsMemo talkingpointsmemo.com	PJ Media pjmedia.com
ThinkProgress thinkprogress.org	Townhall townhall.com

podcasting

A method of distributing multimedia files, such as audio or video files, for downloading onto mobile devices or personal computers.

Learning Outcome **3:**

Explain the relationship between the government and the media, and in particular the Internet.

Government Regulation of the Media

The United States has one of the freest presses in the world. Nonetheless, regulation of the media, particularly of the electronic media, does exist. In addition to First Amendment rights, we have the issue of concentrated ownership of the media.

Concentrated Ownership of the Media

Many rules by the Federal Communications Commission (FCC) have dealt with ownership of news media, such as how many TV stations a network can own. In 1996, Congress passed legislation that had far-reaching implications for the communications industry—the Telecommunications Act. The act ended the rule that kept telephone companies from entering the cable business and other communications markets. What this means is that a single corporation—whether Time Warner or Disney—can offer long-distance and local telephone services, cable television, satellite television, Internet services, and, of course, libraries of films and entertainment. The act opened the door to competition and led to more options for consumers, who now can choose among multiple competitors for all of these services delivered to the home. At the same time, it launched a race among competing companies to control media ownership.

Many media outlets are now owned by corporate conglomerates. A single entity may own a television network; the studios that produce shows, news, and movies; and the means to deliver that content to the home via cable, satellite, or the Internet. The question to be faced in the future is how to ensure competition in the delivery of news so that citizens have access to multiple points of view from the media.

Today, all of the prime-time television networks are owned by major American corporations and are part of corporate conglomerates. The Turner Broadcasting/CNN network was purchased by a major corporation, Time Warner. Fox Broadcasting Company has always been a part of Rupert Murdoch's publishing and media empire. Many of these companies have also formed partnerships with computer software makers, such as Microsoft, for joint electronic-publishing ventures.

The greatest concern advanced by observers of concentrated media ownership is that it could lead to a decline in democratic debate. Also, media owners might use their power to steer the national agenda in a direction that they prefer. Indeed, several news organizations have clear conservative or liberal viewpoints. Among the most famous and successful of these is Fox News, part of Rupert Murdoch's operation. Murdoch's U.S. newspapers and networks have not been shy about promoting conservative politics. Some observers, however, believe that the emergence of independent news websites, blogs, and podcasts provides an ample counterweight to the advocacy of media moguls.

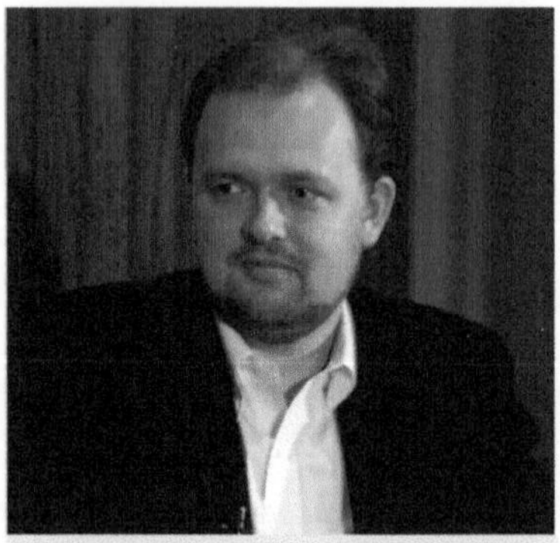

WENN Ltd/Alamy

Image 10–9 Ross Douthat is a conservative *New York Times* blogger and columnist. His conservatism is strongly influenced by his Catholic faith. ***How do you think he might have reacted to Donald Trump's candidacy?***

Government Control of Content

The First Amendment does not mention electronic media, which did not exist when the Bill of Rights was written. For many reasons, the government has much greater control over electronic media than it does over print media. The Federal Communications Commission (FCC) regulates communications by radio, television, wire, and cable. For many years, the FCC has controlled the number of radio stations, even though technologically we could have many more radio stations than now exist. Also, the FCC created the environment in which for many decades the three major TV networks (NBC, CBS, and ABC) dominated broadcasting.

On the face of it, the First Amendment would seem to apply to all media. In fact, the United States Supreme Court has often been slow to extend free speech and free press guarantees to new media. For example, in 1915 the Court held that "as a matter of common sense," free speech protections did not apply to movies. Only in 1952 did the Court find that motion pictures were covered by the First Amendment.[3] In contrast, the Court extended full protection to the Internet almost immediately by striking down provisions of the 1996 Telecommunications Act.[4]

The Issue of Net Neutrality

The Internet is widely regarded as a triumph of unregulated enterprise, but it has been tied to the federal government from the start. The Internet is directly descended from ARPAnet, a project of the Advanced Research Projects Agency within the Department of Defense. Initially, ARPAnet linked computers at four universities—the first message to cross the net was sent in October 1969 from UCLA to Stanford. Only in 1988 was the Internet opened up to commercial users.

Image 10–10 *"Leak to the press that my Administration won't stand for any more leaks."*

Even though the federal government was responsible for the Internet's creation, Internet pioneers were remarkably successful in preventing the government from imposing regulations that might limit the freedom of users. For example, websites and communication services are largely exempt from responsibility for the actions of their users, just as a telephone company is not liable when users commit crimes using telephones. Could the actions of foreign governments impair Internet freedom? We examine that question in this chapter's *Beyond Our Borders* feature.

Who Pays for the Internet? Almost all funding for the Internet comes from the individuals and organizations that connect to it. An individual or organization may purchase connectivity from an **Internet service provider (ISP)**. The ISP then purchases connectivity from an intermediate ISP, which in turn purchases connectivity from an Internet *backbone*, often provided by a telephone company. Funds flow in one direction: from the periphery—end users or servers—through ISPs to the backbones. Major Internet destinations such as Amazon or Google must, of course, purchase vast amounts of connectivity. In the past, however, they have not usually had to pay extra fees to ISPs (though there have been exceptions).

Network Neutrality. The principle of **network neutrality,** or net neutrality, is that an ISP should treat all traffic equally. It should not block or degrade access to websites, for example ones that compete with the ISP's own telephone or TV services. Nor should it create special "fast lanes" that allow favored content to load more quickly than the rest. The fundamental structure of the Internet has tended to enforce the network neutrality principle. If an ISP attempted to block access to a site, for example, angry users would switch to a different ISP. Congress has never written the network neutrality principle into law, however.

Monopoly ISPs. Back in the days when people connected to the Internet using dial-up modems, users often had dozens of ISPs vying for their business. Today, however, for many customers high-speed broadband service is available only from a cable TV company such as Comcast that has a local monopoly, and cell phone providers such as Verizon Wireless. Secure in the knowledge that it would be difficult for their customers to switch to a different company, large ISPs have explored the possibility of charging services such as Netflix for expedited transit. Recently, in fact, Netflix agreed to pay for a special dedicated high-volume line connecting it with Comcast. Under these arrangements, Internet funding no longer flows only from the periphery toward the center, but also from one Internet customer to another.

Internet service provider (ISP)
A company or organization that provides Internet connectivity to end users or to servers.

network neutrality
The principle that an ISP should treat all Internet traffic equally.

---

3. *Joseph Burstyn, Inc. v. Wilson*, 343 U.S. 495 (1952).
4. *Reno v. American Civil Liberties Union*, 521 U.S. 844 (1997).

Beyond our borders

Does the United Nations Threaten the Internet?

One of the major reasons that the Internet has experienced explosive worldwide growth is that in general, governments do not control it. To be sure, every country with an authoritarian regime tries, with more or less success, to control its citizens' Internet access. Witness China, home of the so-called Great Firewall of China. A huge number of foreign websites are blocked. Bloggers and tweeters can be certain that government censors are analyzing their political statements.

The one government that has maintained some control of the Internet is the U.S. government, which makes sense given that it was the Internet's initial sponsor. For example, the Internet Corporation for Assigned Names and Numbers (ICANN) has been responsible to the U.S. Commerce Department. ICANN oversees the system of assigning Internet domain names and addresses worldwide. In 2014, however, the Obama administration announced that it would give up control of ICANN to an international body.

The Edge of the Wedge

A controversy erupted. Some feared that if the U.S. government did not control ICANN, a United Nations (UN) body such as the International Telecommunication Union (ITU) might assume control instead. The ITU, however, is controlled by governments. This includes authoritarian regimes such as China, Iran, and Russia. Such governments might try to ban website addresses of dissident groups. These governments have been able to keep their citizens from accessing unapproved websites, but currently they cannot undermine access to the Internet in other countries. That might change

if the ITU were involved—authoritarian governments could form a coalition to restrict access to the Internet. Already, the ITU has voted to let governments close off their own citizens' access to the global Internet. China and Russia want the ITU to ban anonymity on the Internet and to tax international access to sites such as Google and Facebook.

The Fate of ICANN

ICANN gets much attention because nontechnical people can understand its job of distributing names. Yet other Internet bodies may be more important. For example, the Internet Engineering Taskforce (IETF), a group mainly of engineers, develops standards for Internet protocols and is not affiliated with any government. The World Wide Web Consortium (W3C) is another nongovernmental group that helps to maintain international standards for the Web. Still other groups help the Internet run fluidly and efficiently without government interference.

In response to criticisms of its plans for ICANN, the Obama administration postponed action. In 2016, however, ICANN finally adopted new governance rules. The organization is now controlled by a nongovernmental "geek squad," just like the IETF and the W3C. Governments will have almost no input into ICANN decisions. In particular, the ITU is frozen out.

For Critical Analysis

▶ **What would happen if governments tried to tax access to Google or Facebook?**

Net Neutrality and the Federal Communications Commission (FCC).

Net neutrality has become a partisan issue, with congressional Republicans favoring the ISPs while Democrats champion the major Internet firms such as Facebook and Netflix. Under President Obama, the FCC has tried to use the government's regulatory authority to defend net neutrality. In 2014, however, the D.C. Circuit Court ruled that the FCC could not impose the necessary regulations on the ISPs as long as they were considered information services rather than "common carriers," that is, utilities.[5] In the past, the FCC had been reluctant to classify ISPs as utilities, but in 2015 it adopted the utility framework. In June 2016, the D.C. Circuit Court endorsed the FCC's new position.[6] The ISPs hoped to appeal to the Supreme Court. We discuss that issue in this chapter's *Which Side Are You On?* feature.

5. *Verizon v. FCC*, 740 F.3d 623 (D.C. Cir. 2014).

6. *U.S. Telecom Association v. FCC and USA*, ___ F.3d ___ (D.C. Cir. 2016).

Which side are you on?

Should Net Neutrality Be Enforced by Law?

California has a network of freeways. As the name suggests, they are free—without tolls. A few highways impose tolls, however. When traffic is stalled on the freeways, some drivers reroute and opt to pay for a less-crowded and thus faster toll road, presuming one is available.

Should a similar pricing system be provided on the Internet? Already, some people have faster connections because they pay more for an upgraded broadband connection. Another way to serve those who want higher-speed downloads and uploads would be to charge high-volume websites such as Netflix more for better connections. Internet service providers (ISPs) that provide Netflix downloads would be able to charge Netflix more than other users because Netflix "crowds" our Internet highways.

Such a policy would violate the principle of net neutrality. Under net neutrality, all Internet service providers must treat all traffic equally. ISPs should not allow favored content to load more quickly than other content. Should we allow such a system on the Internet—or enforce net neutrality instead?

Net Neutrality Means Less Investment in the Internet

Major ISPs such as Comcast and Verizon oppose net neutrality. They are especially concerned about a Federal Communication Commissions (FCC) ruling in early 2015. That ruling gave the FCC the right to regulate the Internet as if it were a utility. The FCC intends to use its new powers to promote net neutrality. ISPs argue that this ruling has provoked a significant drop in investment in Internet infrastructure. After all, it costs billions to improve quality and speed through, for example, fiber optic networks. If companies that seek to invest in improving the Internet cannot charge a price sufficient to justify the investment, they will invest less. If Netflix clogs up the Internet, shouldn't ISPs be able to charge it more (and Netflix will, in turn, charge its customers more)? Shouldn't some content providers be able to pay ISPs higher prices to get faster downloads? It is really a simple question of freedom—freedom for consumers to choose, and freedom for companies to invest in the best products and services.

Net Neutrality Helps Internet Start-Ups

Major Internet content providers and aggregators are almost universally in favor of net neutrality. Could Facebook, YouTube, and DropBox have succeeded if they faced discriminatory pricing by ISPs? Quite possibly not. Certainly, from their statements, companies such as Facebook, Google, and Twitter doubt that they could have succeeded. Net neutrality guarantees that the next Facebook will not have to ask special permission of Comcast or Verizon or any other ISP to initiate and develop an innovative service.

Net neutrality guarantees that once a website is created, it is automatically available from any Internet-connected computer in the world, and that is essential. Innovation on the Internet depends on net neutrality, which prevents barriers to entry for new websites and Internet applications. Net neutrality supporters contend that any recent fall in investment is trivial and not due to the FCC's ruling. Current rules provide ISPs with plenty of investment funds. We should not let ISPs start overpricing Internet access.

For Critical Analysis
▶ Why is net neutrality a political issue?

Opinion and Bias in the Media

Learning Outcome 4:

Almost every news operation has an opinion section. Traditionally, newspapers and other media have tried carefully to separate opinion pieces from "straight news." Newer media may blur the distinction. In recent years, many media observers have worried that opinion is "taking over" and displacing news sources that try to be objective. Many blogs, for example, are almost pure opinion, even if in the course of delivering that opinion they

Discuss the question of opinion and bias in the mainstream media and alternative media such as talk radio.

Image 10–11 Rush Limbaugh is perhaps one of the most listened to talk-radio hosts in America. At times, he has been considered the spokesperson for American conservatives. *Should the Federal Communications Commission be able to regulate what he says?*

also provide some facts. Another media format in which opinion is dominant is talk radio, which we describe in the following section. A final concern is whether media that purport to report the facts, including network news, cable news, and newspaper websites, are free of bias.

Talk Radio

The most conspicuous characteristic of talk radio is that it is almost completely dominated by conservatives, many of whom are quite radical. Most of the top twenty radio talk shows feature conservative politics. None of the top talk-show hosts are liberal. Talk-show hosts do not pretend to be reporters or journalists. Rather, they are entertainment personalities who entertain their audiences with red-meat politics. Exaggeration for effect is typical, and language that would be unacceptable in other contexts is commonplace.

Repeal of the Fairness Doctrine. Talk radio as it exists today would be impossible if the FCC had not repealed the *fairness doctrine* in 1987. Under the doctrine, anyone holding a broadcast license had to present controversial issues of public importance in a way that was (in the view of the FCC) honest, equitable, and balanced. With such a rule, it would be almost impossible for a radio network to broadcast anything like the *Rush Limbaugh Show*, even if it were matched with a liberal counterpart.

The Talk-Radio Style Migrates to Television. Until recently, television networks, including cable networks, saw the rhetoric typical of talk-radio hosts as unacceptable. That sense of propriety has retreated in the last several years. Some credit the *Glenn Beck* show on Fox News for breaking down the barriers to uninhibited speech. Beck's emotional style and apocalyptic views helped make him one of the nation's most politically polarizing figures. Beck is no longer with Fox, but remains a significant radio and television personality. Another major radio host who has extended his reach to television is Sean Hannity.

The Impact of Talk Radio. It has been said that conservative talk radio was the Tea Party before there was a Tea Party movement. Certainly, talk radio has played a role in pushing the Republican Party to the right. Hosts such as Limbaugh and Michael Savage have devoted much energy to hunting *RINOs*, that is, "Republicans in Name Only."

As you will learn shortly, many conservatives believe that progressives dominate the "mainstream media." The overwhelming conservative dominance of talk radio, however, makes it harder to argue that the media as a whole has a liberal bias. No other media format can match the partisan vehemence of talk radio.

In 2009, after the Democratic sweep in the 2008 elections, a number of liberals raised the question of whether the fairness doctrine ought to be reinstated. President Obama and the Democratic leadership in Congress, however, quickly put an end to this notion. True, the Supreme Court has held that the fairness doctrine is constitutional.[7] Yet most Americans today would consider its reestablishment to be a serious violation of the right to free speech. Conservative talk radio, in short, is here to stay.

Bias in the Media

For decades, the contention that the mainstream media have a liberal **bias** has been repeated time and again. Bernard Goldberg, formerly a CBS broadcaster and now a commentator for Fox News, is among the most prominent of these critics. Goldberg argues

bias

An inclination or preference that interferes with impartial judgment.

7. *Red Lion Broadcasting v. FCC*, 395 U.S. 367 (1969).

that liberal bias, which "comes naturally to most reporters," has given viewers reason to distrust the big news networks.

A number of studies appear to back up this claim. For example, research at the University of Connecticut has shown that journalists consider themselves Democrats three times as often as they identify with the Republicans. A recent Gallup poll reports that 47 percent of the public think that the news media are too liberal, while 13 percent see the media as too conservative. These views are strongly associated with the politics of the respondent: 75 percent of Republicans believe the media are too liberal, while only 20 percent of Democrats think that is true.

Other observers claim that, on the whole, the media actually have a conservative bias, especially in their coverage of economic issues. In an analysis of visual images on television news, political scientist Maria Elizabeth Grabe concluded that "image bites" (as opposed to sound bites) more often favor the Republicans.[8]

Other Theories of Media Bias. Some writers have concluded that the mainstream media are really biased toward stories that involve conflict and drama—the better to attract viewers. Still others contend the media are biased against "losers," and when a candidate falls behind in a race, his or her press quickly becomes negative. In the 2015–2016 election cycle, one Republican presidential candidate after another experienced dismissive news coverage as their poll numbers slipped. Of course, media coverage of Donald Trump was negative from the very start, but such coverage did not appear to hurt him much in the primaries. It is possible that most of Trump's voters had already written off the mainstream media as irredeemably hostile to their candidate.

Bias and Professionalism. While many journalists may be Democrats at heart, most operate under a code of professional ethics that dictates "objectivity" and a commitment to the truth. Journalists may not always succeed in living up to such a code, but it helps that it exists.

As we have observed, many media outlets have an explicit political point of view. This is especially common in the blogosphere, but it is true of some cable news channels as well. Fox News, for example, takes pride in avoiding what it sees as the liberal bias of the mainstream media.

Some progressives, however, have accused Fox and other conservative outlets of allowing politics to interfere with their objectivity. They argue that conservatives find liberal bias even in reporting that is scrupulously accurate. In the words of humorist Stephen Colbert, "Reality has a well-known liberal bias." An example was the widespread refusal of conservative media to believe opinion polls that showed Barack Obama leading in the 2012 presidential race.

Other observers contend that the issue of media bias is declining in importance due to the rise of the Internet. Today's technologically savvy media consumers can easily find information from a wide variety of sources, mainstream and alternative, liberal and conservative. The best answer to bias may be a willingness to consult a wide range of sources.

Why should you care about THE MEDIA?

Television, print media, and the Internet provide a wide range of choices for Americans who want to stay informed. Still, a substantial amount of what you read and see is colored either by the subjectivity of editors and bloggers or by the demands of profit making. Even when journalists themselves are relatively successful in an attempt to remain objective, they will of necessity give airtime to politicians and interest group representatives who are far from impartial. You need the ability to determine what motivates the players in the political game and to what extent they are "shading" the news or even propagating outright lies. You also need to determine which news sources are reliable.

8. Maria Elizabeth Grabe and Erik Page Bucy, *Image Bite Politics: News and the Visual Framing of Elections* (New York: Oxford University Press, 2009).

How you can make a difference

To become a critical news consumer, you must develop a critical eye and ear.

- For example, ask yourself what stories are given prominence at the top of a newspaper website.

- For a contrast to most daily papers, visit the sites of publications with explicit points of view, such as the *National Review* (search on "national review") or the *New Republic* (search on "tnr"). Take note of how they handle stories.

- Sources such as blogs often have strong political preferences, and you should try to determine what these are. Does a blog merely give opinions, or does it back up its arguments with data? It is possible to select anecdotes to support almost any argument—does a particular anecdote represent typical circumstances, or is it a rare occurrence highlighted to make a point?

- Watching the evening news can be far more rewarding if you look at how much the news depends on video

effects. You will note that stories on the evening news tend to be no more than three minutes long, that stories with excellent videos get more attention, and that considerable time is taken up with "happy talk" or human interest stories.

- Another way to critically evaluate news coverage is to compare how the news is covered by different outlets. For example, you might compare the coverage of events on Fox News with the presentation on MSNBC, or compare the radio commentary of Rush Limbaugh with that of National Public Radio's *All Things Considered*.

- Fairness and Accuracy in Reporting is a media watchdog with a strong liberal viewpoint. Visit it at fair.org.

- Accuracy in Media takes a combative conservative position on media issues. Find its site at www.aim.org.

KEY TERMS

aggregator 269	Internet service	priming 268	spin 274
bias 282	provider (ISP) 279	public agenda 268	spin doctor 274
blog 276	network neutrality 279	sound bite 272	
content provider 269	podcasting 277		

CHAPTER SUMMARY

Learning Outcome 1 The media are enormously important in American politics today. They perform a number of functions, including (a) entertaining the public, (b) news reporting, (c) identifying public problems, (d) socializing new generations, (e) providing a political forum, and (f) making profits.

Learning Outcome 2 The political influence of the media is most obvious during political campaigns. Today's campaigns use political advertising and expert management of news coverage. For presidential candidates, how they appear in presidential debates is of major importance. Internet blogs, podcasts, tweets, and websites such as YouTube are transforming today's political campaigns.

Learning Outcome 3 Despite the First Amendment and our free speech traditions, the U.S. government has always engaged in at least some regulation of the media. Past regulation has sought to address concentrated ownership and the content of broadcast media. A current issue is whether the government should enforce net neutrality on the Internet.

Learning Outcome 4 Frequently, the mainstream media have been accused of liberal bias, although some observers contend that these accusations result from true stories that offend conservatives. Other possible media biases include a bias against political "losers." For many, the dominance of opinion over reporting in blogs and on talk radio is also a matter of concern.

ADDITIONAL RESOURCES

Online Resources

The Internet offers great opportunities to those who want to access the news. All of the major news organizations, including radio and television stations and newspapers, are online. Even foreign sources can now be accessed online within a few seconds. To gain an international perspective on the news, you can check foreign news websites in English. The following sites all have broad worldwide coverage:

- For the British Broadcasting Corporation, go to www.bbc.com.

- For the Japan Broadcasting Corporation, visit **www3.nhk.or.jp/ nkhworld**.

- Al Jazeera is the Arab world's number-one television news network. See it at **www.aljazeera.com**.

- The German magazine *Der Spiegel* is online at **www.spiegel.de/ international**.

Books

Cassino, Dan. *Fox News and American Politics: How One Channel Shapes American Politics and Society*. New York: Routledge, 2016. Cassino, a political science professor at Fairleigh Dickinson University, provides detailed evidence of the importance of Fox News.

Highfield, Tim. *Social Media and Everyday Politics*. Boston: Polity, 2016. A wide-ranging study of how ordinary people around the world express themselves politically through social media. Highfield is a fellow at Queensland University of Technology.

Schroeder, Alan. *Presidential Debates: Risky Business on the Campaign Trail*, 3rd ed. New York: Columbia University Press, 2016. Schroeder, a journalism professor at Northeastern University, enlivens the history of presidential debates with illustrations and intrigue.

Video

All the President's Men—A film, produced by Warner Bros. in 1976, starring Dustin Hoffman and Robert Redford as the two *Washington Post* reporters, Carl Bernstein and Bob Woodward, who broke the story on the Watergate scandal. The film is an excellent portrayal of the *Washington Post* newsroom and the decisions that editors make in such situations.

The Social Network—In this 2010 Hollywood blockbuster, director David Fincher tells the story of Facebook founder Mark Zuckerberg. The film received eight Academy Award nominations and won three Oscars, including one for best-adapted screenplay. It swept the Golden Globe awards, winning for best drama, best director, and best screenplay.

Quiz

Multiple Choice and Fill-Ins

Learning Outcome 1 Describe the different types of media and the changing roles that they play in American society.

1. Television remains a key medium in American politics because:
   a. it is the number-one source of information for older voters, who dominate the electorate.
   b. young people are avoiding the Internet as a source of information.
   c. television advertisements are not that expensive to buy.

2. A major problem facing newspapers today is that they cannot collect enough online _____ _____.

Learning Outcome 2 Summarize the impact of the media on the political process.

3. The first televised major-party presidential debates were held between:
   a. Democrat Lyndon Johnson and Republican Barry Goldwater in 1964.
   b. Democrat Jimmy Carter and Republican Ronald Reagan in 1980.
   c. Democrat John F. Kennedy and Republican Richard Nixon in 1960.

4. A campaign press advisor who tries to convince reporters of a particular interpretation of an event is called a _____ _____.

Learning Outcome 3 Explain the relationship between the government and the media, and in particular the Internet.

5. The United States Supreme Court found that the First Amendment applied to motion pictures:
   a. in 1915, shortly after the movies were invented.
   b. in 1952.
   c. in 1996, when it struck down provisions of the Telecommunications Act.

6. The principle that all traffic on the Internet should be treated equally is called _____ _____.

Learning Outcome 4 Discuss the question of opinion and bias in the mainstream media and alternative media such as talk radio.

7. Critics of the mainstream media have often accused it of exhibiting which of the following forms of bias:
   a. bias against conservatives, bias against losers, and bias in favor of conflict and drama.
   b. bias against Democrats, bias in favor of religion, and bias in favor of whoever is president.
   c. bias against science, bias against entertainment figures, and bias in favor of minority group members.

8. For more than two decades, the most popular conservative radio talk-show host has been _____ _____.

Essay Questions

1. Individuals who respond to blog posts sometimes enter comments that are deliberately designed to foster disruption. Why might people engage in such behavior? (Consider also the prevalence of hostile and even threatening responses to posts by women on controversial topics.)

2. Conservatives have long accused traditional media outlets of having a liberal bias. Are they correct? If so, to what degree? Regardless of whether this particular accusation is correct, what other kinds of bias might affect the reporting of prominent journalists? To the extent that the press exhibits political bias, what factors might cause this bias?

Answers to multiple-choice and fill-in questions: 1. a, 2. ad revenue, 3. c, 4. spin doctor, 5. b, 6. net neutrality, 7. a, 8. Rush Limbaugh.

THE CONGRESS

President Barack Obama delivers his last State of the Union address to a joint session of Congress. Obama spoke on climate change, gun control, immigration, and income inequality. *How much influence can a president have on a Congress controlled by the other party?*
Alex Wong/Getty Images

These five **LEARNING OUTCOMES** *below are designed to help improve your understanding of this chapter:*

1: Describe the various roles played by Congress and the constitutional basis of its powers.

2: Explain some of the differences between the House and the Senate and some of the privileges enjoyed by members of Congress.

3: Examine the implications of apportioning House seats.

4: Describe the committee structure of the House and the Senate and the key leadership positions in each chamber.

5: Discuss the process by which a bill becomes law and how the federal government establishes its budget.

What if...

We Used Proportional Representation to Elect the House?

Background

It used to be that Americans chose their representatives. Today, though, representatives seem to be choosing their voters, through *gerrymandering*. In most states, district lines are drawn after each census by party leaders in the state legislature. If one party dominates, it will maximize the number of safe seats for its members. As we have noted, 2010 was a good year for the Republicans—and 2010 was a census year. Republicans, therefore, controlled a majority of the state legislatures. As you might expect, the resulting gerrymanders favored the Republicans.

In 2012, Democratic candidates for the U.S. House in Pennsylvania received about 70,000 more votes than the Republicans. Still, Pennsylvania elected thirteen Republicans and only five Democrats. Nationally, the Republicans kept control of the U.S. House even though they received fewer votes overall than the Democrats. In other years, the Democrats have been responsible for their own egregious gerrymanders. Such outcomes have caused some to call for nonpartisan state boards to draw congressional districts. There is another solution, however, used around the world.

What If We Used Proportional Representation to Elect the House?

Proportional representation (PR) is designed to ensure that the number of candidates elected from each major party matches the popular vote for that party. PR is an alternative to the pure "first-past-the-post" system used in Britain, Canada, and the United States. In our system, the candidate with the largest number of votes—a *plurality*—always wins. If a party with substantial support is in the minority everywhere, it will elect no representatives.

Many forms of PR exist, but let's look at one of the simplest. Congress could pass a law creating, say, two hundred new seats in the House. These seats would be distributed among the states as the Constitution requires, but no new districts would be created. Each of the new seats would be filled on a statewide basis. Voters would not fill these seats directly. Instead, the extra seats would be filled based on how many votes each party won in the *district* seats, with the goal of making the statewide result proportional. (This plan would not yield perfect proportional representation, but it would be close.)

Immediate Consequences

One result of such a system would be to make gerrymandering pointless. That, of course, is what PR is designed to do. A second result would be more Republicans elected from Democratic states, and more Democrats from Republican ones. Some might hope that would have a moderating effect. If at-large candidates were selected in partisan primaries, though, they would probably resemble the district candidates. Another result is that a large state such as California would almost surely elect some Green and Libertarian candidates based on the statewide vote for these parties.

A Bigger House

If we implemented PR by adding two hundred seats to the House, it would have 635 members, not 435. You might consider that a large chamber, but by international standards it is not. The British House of Commons has 650 members, the German Bundestag has 620, and the French National Assembly has 577. A U.S. House with 635 members would fit right in. One result: we might see more of our representatives, because there would be more of them.

For Critical Analysis

▶ How would members of the existing House react to a proposal to substantially increase the size of their chamber?

▶ Would a PR system such as the one described be constitutional? (Hint: See Clause 1, Section 4, Article I, of the Constitution.)

Tom Williams/Getty Images

Image 11–1 A congressional intern learns how to play the Redistricting Game, a simulation that shows how the manipulation of district boundaries (gerrymandering) can yield victory for either party. *How much of a problem is gerrymandering?*

Most Americans view Congress in a less-than-flattering light. In recent years, Congress has appeared to be deeply split, highly partisan in its conduct, and not very responsive to public needs. Polls show that recently, as few as 7 percent of the public have had a favorable opinion about Congress as a whole. In one poll, respondents rated traffic jams, root canal operations, and cockroaches more favorably than Congress. (Congress did beat Fidel Castro, meth labs, and the Ebola virus.) Yet individual members of Congress often receive much higher approval ratings from the voters in their districts. This is one of the paradoxes of the relationship between the people and Congress. Members of the public hold the institution in relatively low regard compared with the satisfaction they express with their individual representatives.

Part of the explanation for these seemingly contradictory appraisals is that members of Congress spend considerable time and effort serving their **constituents.** If the federal bureaucracy makes a mistake that affects a legislator's constituent, that senator or representative tries to resolve the issue. On a personal level, what most Americans see, therefore, is the work of these local representatives in their home states.

Congress, however, was created to work not just for local constituents but also for the nation as a whole. As shown in the chapter-opening *What If . . .* feature, changes might be possible in the way we elect members of Congress that could encourage members to consider the national interest more closely. Understanding the nature of the institution and the process of lawmaking is an important part of understanding how the policies that shape our lives are made. In this chapter, we describe the functions of Congress, including constituent service, representation, lawmaking, and oversight of the government. We review how the members of Congress are elected and how Congress organizes itself when it meets. We also examine how bills pass through the legislative process and become laws, and how the federal budget is established.

The Nature and Functions of Congress

Learning Outcome 1:

Describe the various roles played by Congress and the constitutional basis of its powers.

The founders of the American republic believed that the bulk of the power that would be exercised by a national government should be in the hands of the legislature. The leading role envisioned for Congress in the new government is apparent from its primacy in the Constitution. Article I deals with the structure, the powers, and the operation of Congress.

Bicameralism

The **bicameralism** of Congress—its division into two legislative houses—was in part the result of the Connecticut Compromise, which tried to balance the large-state population advantage, reflected in the House, and the small-state demand for equality in policymaking, which was satisfied in the Senate. Beyond that, the two chambers of Congress also reflected the social class biases of the founders. They wished to balance the interests and the numerical superiority of the common citizens with the property interests of the less numerous landowners, bankers, and merchants.

They achieved this goal by providing that members of the House of Representatives should be elected directly by "the People," whereas members of the Senate were to be chosen by the elected representatives sitting in state legislatures, who were more likely to be members of the elite. (The latter provision was changed in 1913 by the passage of the Seventeenth Amendment, which provides that senators are also to be elected directly by the people.)

constituent

A person represented by a legislator or other elected or appointed official.

bicameralism

The division of a legislature into two separate assemblies.

lawmaking

The process of establishing the legal rules that govern society.

earmarks

Special provisions in legislation to set aside funds for projects that have not passed an impartial evaluation by agencies of the executive branch. Also known as *pork*.

representation

The function of members of Congress as elected officials representing the views of their constituents as well as larger national interests.

trustee

A legislator who acts according to her or his conscience and the broad interests of the entire society.

The logic of the bicameral Congress was reinforced by differences in length of tenure. Members of the House are required to face the electorate every two years, whereas senators can serve for a much more secure term of six years—even longer than the four-year term provided for the president. Furthermore, the senators' terms are staggered so that only one-third of the senators face the electorate every two years, along with all of the House members.

The bicameral Congress was designed to perform certain functions for the political system. These functions include lawmaking, representation, service to constituents, oversight (regulatory supervision), public education, and conflict resolution. Of these, the two most important and the ones that most often interfere with each other are lawmaking and representation.

The Lawmaking Function

The principal and most obvious function of any legislature is **lawmaking.** Congress is the highest elected body in the country, charged with making binding rules for all Americans. This does not mean, however, that Congress initiates most of the ideas for legislation that it eventually considers. A majority of the bills that Congress acts on originate in the executive branch. Many other bills are traceable to interest groups and political party organizations. In dealing with legislation, members engage in compromise and *logrolling* (offering to support a fellow member's bill in exchange for that member's promise to support your bill in the future). Through such tactics, as well as debate and discussion, backers of legislation attempt to fashion a winning majority coalition.

Traditionally, logrolling often involved agreements to support another member's legislative **earmarks,** also known as *pork*. Earmarks are special provisions in legislation to set aside funds for projects that have not passed an impartial evaluation by agencies of the executive branch. (Normal spending projects pass through such evaluations.) Recent attempts to curtail pork have not succeeded in eliminating the process altogether but have significantly reduced its frequency.

The Representation Function

Representation includes both representing the desires and demands of the constituents in the member's home district or state and representing larger national interests, such as the nation's security. Because the interests of constituents in a specific district may be at odds with the demands of national policy, the representation function is often a source of conflict for lawmakers. For example, although it may be in the interest of the nation to reduce defense spending by closing certain military bases, such closures are not in the interest of the states and districts that will lose jobs and local spending. Every legislator faces votes that set local representational issues against lawmaking realities.

How should the legislators fulfill the representation function? There are several views on how this task should be accomplished.

The Trustee View of Representation. One approach to the question of how representation should be achieved is that legislators should act as **trustees** of the broad interests of the entire society. They should vote

Image 11–2 Senator Elizabeth Warren (D., Mass.) listens as then-Federal Reserve chair Ben Bernanke answers a question at a hearing of the Senate Banking, Housing, and Urban Affairs Committee. *Why might Warren's strong criticisms of banks be popular?*

Bloomberg/Contributor/Getty Images

against the narrow interests of their constituents if their conscience and their perception of national needs so dictate. For example, in 2011 Congress approved trade agreements with Colombia, Panama, and South Korea, despite the widely held belief that such agreements cost specific Americans their jobs.

The Instructed-Delegate View of Representation. Directly opposed to the trustee view of representation is the notion that members of Congress should behave as **instructed delegates.** That is, they should mirror the views of the majority of the constituents who elected them.

Generally, most legislators hold neither a pure trustee view nor a pure instructed-delegate view. Typically, they combine both perspectives in a pragmatic mix.

Service to Constituents. Individual members of Congress are expected by their constituents to act as brokers between private citizens and the federal government. This function of providing service to constituents usually takes the form of **casework.** The legislator and her or his staff spend a considerable portion of their time in casework activities, such as explaining the meaning of particular bills to people who may be affected by them, promoting a local business interest, or interceding with a regulatory agency on behalf of constituents who disagree with proposed agency regulations.

This **ombudsperson** role strongly benefits the members of Congress. A government characterized by a large, confusing bureaucracy and complex public programs offers innumerable opportunities for legislators to come to the assistance of (usually) grateful constituents.

The Oversight Function

Oversight of the bureaucracy is essential if the decisions made by Congress are to have any force. **Oversight** is the process by which Congress follows up on the laws it has enacted to ensure that they are being enforced and administered in the way Congress intended. This is done by holding committee hearings and investigations, changing the size of an agency's budget, or cross-examining high-level presidential nominees to head major agencies. In part, oversight is related to the concept of constituency service, particularly when Congress investigates alleged arbitrariness or wrongdoing by bureaucratic agencies.

A problem with oversight is that it has become entangled in partisan politics. Members of Congress have tended to ease up on oversight whenever the president is of their political party. In contrast, oversight can become intense, and even excessive, when the president faces a chamber of Congress that is controlled by the other party. For example, in 2015 and 2016 the Republicans launched a series of investigations of former secretary of state Hillary Clinton. The thinly disguised reason was that she was expected to be the Democratic candidate for president in 2016. A committee unsuccessfully tried to find improper conduct by Clinton during and after an attack on the U.S. consulate in Benghazi, Libya. A more promising line of questioning opened up after the FBI criticized Clinton for using a private e-mail server instead of a federal computer system while she was secretary of state.

The Public-Education Function

Educating the public is a function that Congress performs whenever it holds public hearings, exercises oversight of the bureaucracy, or engages in committee and floor debate on such major issues and topics as immigration, firearms, and the concerns of small businesses. In so doing, Congress presents a range of viewpoints on pressing national questions. Congress also decides what issues will come up for discussion and decision. This **agenda setting** is a major facet of its public-education function.

instructed delegate

A legislator who is an agent of the voters who elected him or her and who votes according to the views of constituents regardless of personal beliefs.

casework

Personal work for constituents by members of Congress.

ombudsperson

A person who hears and investigates complaints by private individuals against public officials or agencies. (From the Swedish word *ombudsman,* meaning "representative.")

oversight

The process by which Congress follows up on laws it has enacted to ensure that they are being enforced and administered in the way Congress intended.

agenda setting

Determining which public-policy questions will be debated or considered.

The Conflict-Resolution Function

Congress is commonly seen as an institution for resolving conflicts within American society. Organized interest groups and spokespersons for different racial, religious, economic, and ideological interests look on Congress as an access point for airing their grievances and seeking help. This view of Congress puts it in the position of trying to resolve the differences among competing points of view by passing laws to accommodate as many interested parties as possible. To the extent that Congress meets pluralist expectations in accommodating competing interests, it tends to build support for the entire political process. Failure, however, tends to bring the political process into disrepute.

The Powers of Congress

The Constitution is both highly specific and extremely vague about the powers that Congress may exercise. The first seventeen clauses of Article I, Section 8, specify most of the **enumerated powers** of Congress—that is, powers expressly given to that body.

Enumerated Powers. The enumerated, or expressed, powers of Congress include the right to:

- Impose a variety of taxes, including tariffs on imports.
- Borrow funds.
- Regulate interstate commerce and international trade.
- Establish procedures for naturalizing citizens.
- Make laws regulating bankruptcies.
- Coin (and print) currency, and regulate its value.
- Establish standards of weights and measures.
- Punish counterfeiters.
- Establish post offices and post roads.
- Regulate copyrights and patents.
- Establish the federal court system.
- Punish illegal acts on the high seas.
- Declare war.
- Raise and regulate an army and a navy.
- Call up and regulate the state militias to enforce laws, to suppress insurrections, and to repel invasions.
- Govern the District of Columbia.

The most important of the domestic powers of Congress, listed in Article I, Section 8, are the rights to impose taxes, to spend, and to regulate commerce. The most important foreign policy power is the power to declare war. Other sections of the Constitution allow Congress to establish rules for its own members, to regulate the electoral college, and to override a presidential veto. Congress may also regulate the extent of the Supreme Court's authority to review cases decided by the lower courts, regulate relations among states, and propose amendments to the Constitution.

Powers of the Senate. Some functions are restricted to one chamber. The Senate must advise on, and consent to, the ratification of treaties and must accept or reject presidential nominations of ambassadors, Supreme Court justices, other federal judges, and "all other

enumerated power

A power specifically granted to the national government by the Constitution. The first seventeen clauses of Article I, Section 8, specify most of the enumerated powers of Congress.

Officers of the United States." But the Senate may delegate to the president or lesser officials the power to make lower-level appointments.

These specific powers granted to the Senate mean that the Senate is a more powerful chamber than the House. The United States is unique among the world's economically advanced nations in that its "upper house"— the Senate—is more powerful than the "lower house." In every nation with a parliamentary system, the lower house in effect chooses the nation's chief executive officer, the prime minister. The ability to exercise that power inevitably causes the upper house to have little real power.

Constitutional Amendments. Amendments to the Constitution provide for other congressional powers. Congress must certify the election of a president and a vice president or itself choose those officers if no candidate has a majority of the electoral vote (Twelfth Amendment). It may levy an income tax (Sixteenth Amendment) and determine who will be acting president in case of the death or incapacity of the president or vice president (Twentieth Amendment and Twenty-fifth Amendment).

Image 11–3 New U.S. citizens say the Pledge of Allegiance during a naturalization ceremony at the Smithsonian Institute. Congress, which has responsibility under the Constitution for naturalization, has allowed veterans to speed up the naturalization process. *Why would Congress pass such legislation?*

The Necessary and Proper Clause. Beyond these numerous specific powers, Congress enjoys the right under Clause 18 of Article I, Section 8 (the "elastic," or "necessary and proper," clause), "to make all Laws which shall be necessary and proper for carrying into Execution the foregoing Powers [of Article I], and all other Powers vested by this Constitution in the Government of the United States, or in any Department or Officer thereof." This vague statement of congressional responsibilities has provided, over time, the basis for a greatly expanded national government. It has also constituted, at least in theory, a check on the expansion of presidential powers.

House–Senate Differences and Congressional Perks

Learning Outcome **2:**

Explain some of the differences between the House and the Senate and some of the privileges enjoyed by members of Congress.

Congress is composed of two markedly different—but co-equal—chambers. Although the Senate and the House of Representatives exist within the same legislative institution, each has developed certain distinctive features that clearly distinguish one from the other. A summary of these differences is given in Table 11–1.

Size and Rules

The central difference between the House and the Senate is simply that the House is much larger than the Senate. The House has 435 voting representatives, plus delegates from the District of Columbia, Puerto Rico, Guam, American Samoa, and the Virgin Islands, compared with just 100 senators. This size difference means that a greater number of formal rules are needed to govern activity in the House, whereas correspondingly looser procedures can be followed in the less-crowded Senate.

Table 11–1 Differences between the House and the Senate

Some of these differences are provided for in the Constitution, while others are not. **Can you tell which ones are from the Constitution?**

House	Senate
Members chosen from local districts	Members chosen from an entire state
Two-year term	Six-year term
Originally elected by voters	Originally (until 1913) elected by state legislatures
May impeach (indict) federal officials	May convict federal officials of impeachable offenses
Larger (435 voting members)	Smaller (100 members)
More formal rules	Fewer rules and restrictions
Debate limited	Debate extended
Less prestige and less individual notice	More prestige and more media attention
Originates bills for raising revenues	Has power to advise the president on, and to consent to, presidential appointments and treaties
Local or narrow leadership	National leadership
Highly partisan	Somewhat less party loyalty

This difference is most obvious in the rules governing debate on the floors of the two chambers. The Senate usually permits extended debate on all issues that arise before it. In contrast, the House generally operates with an elaborate system in which its **Rules Committee** proposes time limitations on debate for any bill, and a majority of the entire body accepts or modifies those suggested time limits. As a consequence of its stricter time limits on debate, the House, despite its greater size, often is able to act on legislation more quickly than the Senate.

An additional practice in the House that affects its ability to legislate is the **Hastert rule,** which is named after a former Speaker. Under this rule, a Republican Speaker of the House will not allow a bill to reach the floor for a vote unless it has the support of a "majority of the majority." That means that the Speaker will block a bill that could pass with votes from both parties if that bill is not supported by at least half of the Republican members. Although the Hastert rule is a Republican concept, Democratic Speakers have also blocked legislation that did not have the support of a majority of the Democrats. Further, even Republican Speakers will violate the rule when it is absolutely necessary. Then-Speaker John Boehner, for example, abandoned the Hastert rule to end a government shutdown in October 2013.

As a consequence of the larger size of the House, representatives generally cannot achieve as much individual recognition and public prestige as can members of the Senate. Senators are better able to gain media exposure and to establish careers as spokespersons for large national constituencies.

Debate and Filibustering

The Senate tradition of the **filibuster,** or the use of unlimited debate as a blocking tactic, dates back to 1790.[1] In that year, a proposal to move the U.S. capital from New York to Philadelphia was stalled by such time-wasting maneuvers. This unlimited-debate tradition—which also existed in the House until 1811—is not absolute, however.

Cloture. Under Senate Rule 22, debate may be ended by invoking *cloture.* Cloture shuts off discussion on a bill. Amended in 1975 and 1979, Rule 22 states that debate may be closed off on a bill if sixteen senators sign a petition requesting it and if, after two days have elapsed, three-fifths of the entire membership (sixty votes, assuming no vacancies) vote for cloture. After cloture is invoked, each senator may speak on a bill for a maximum of one hour before a vote is taken.

Increased Use of the Filibuster. Traditionally, filibusters were rare, and the tactic was employed only on issues of principle. Filibustering senators spoke for many hours,

Rules Committee

A standing committee of the House of Representatives that provides special rules under which specific bills can be debated, amended, and considered by the House.

Hastert rule

A rule adopted by Republicans in the U.S. House, under which a Republican Speaker will not bring a measure to the floor for a vote unless it has the support of a majority of the Republican members.

filibuster

The use of the Senate's tradition of unlimited debate as a delaying tactic to block a bill.

---

1. *Filibuster* comes from a Spanish word for pirate, which in turn came from the Dutch term *vrijbuiter,* or freebooter. The word was first used in 1851 to accuse senators of pirating or hijacking debate.

sometimes reading names from a telephone book. By the twenty-first century, however, filibusters could be invoked without such speeches, and senators were threatening to filibuster almost every significant piece of legislation to come before the body. The threats were sufficient to create a new, ad hoc rule that important legislation needed the support of sixty senators, not fifty. As a result of the increased use of the filibuster, some senators have called for its abolition. We discuss that topic in this chapter's *Which Side Are You On?* feature.

reconciliation

A special rule that can be applied to budget bills sent from the House of Representatives to the Senate. Reconciliation measures cannot be filibustered.

Reconciliation. An additional way of bypassing the filibuster is known as **reconciliation.** Budget bills sent from the House of Representatives to the Senate can be handled under special reconciliation rules that do not permit filibusters. Under the rules, reconciliation can be used *only* to handle budgetary matters. Also, in principle, the procedure is to be invoked only for measures that would have the net effect of reducing the federal deficit. This last restriction, however, has frequently been avoided by misleading bookkeeping.

One of the most striking examples of reconciliation took place in March 2010, when the Democrats used the procedure to make a series of amendments to the just-passed Affordable Care Act, also known as Obamacare. Reconciliation was necessary because

Which side are you on?

Is It Time to Get Rid of the Filibuster?

It is not in the Constitution, but it is an important institution. It is the filibuster, and it follows from Senate Rule 22, which allows for unlimited debate. Throughout American history, senators could tie up the Senate's business by talking indefinitely. In 1975, Rule 22 was revised. Since that year, a vote by sixty senators is required to stop floor debate instead of the previous sixty-seven. A second significant change in Senate practice developed, however—today, senators don't actually have to *talk* to hold a filibuster. All they have to do to maintain a filibuster is to announce that a filibuster exists. Some want the filibuster abolished. Others do not agree.

The Filibuster Is Not Even Constitutional

Critics of the filibuster argue that it has no constitutional basis and implicitly violates many actual provisions of the Constitution. After all, the Constitution requires a *super-majority*—more than a simple majority—only for special situations such as ratifying treaties, proposing constitutional amendments, overriding presidential vetoes, and convicting impeached officials.

Consider this statement by Alexander Hamilton in *Federalist Paper* No. 75: "All provisions which require more than a majority of any [legislative] body to its resolutions have a direct tendency to embarrass the operations of the

government and an indirect one to subject the sense of the majority to that of the minority." Hamilton was writing about a proposal to require that more than half of a chamber's members be present to convene a session, but his argument certainly applies to whether a body should need more than a majority of its members to take a vote.

The Filibuster as Damage Control

True, filibusters today are not as colorful as they were before 1975, when senators were forced to read out of a telephone book or even wear diapers to keep a filibuster going. Yet supporters of the current filibuster system argue that it continues to provide an important protection for minority rights. Why shouldn't Congress be forced to obtain broad support for important legislation? It would be dangerous to allow major taxation and spending measures to be decided by a bare majority. Opinion polling has shown that the filibuster is quite popular among the public at large. Clearly, Americans see the importance of slowing down legislation created by only a single party in Congress. The filibuster still serves a useful purpose, so let's keep it.

For Critical Analysis

⊙ What would be likely to happen if the filibuster were abolished?

at the end of January, the Republicans won a special U.S. Senate election, thus reducing the number of Democratic senators to fifty-nine.

The Nuclear Option. It takes sixty senators to invoke cloture. Senate rules, however, can be changed by a simple majority vote. It is possible, therefore, to limit or abolish the filibuster by a majority vote. Such an act has been dubbed the *nuclear option*, in comparison to the most extreme option in warfare. In the past, such an act would have been considered an unthinkable violation of Senate tradition. In the polarized Congress of the twenty-first century, however, very few procedural tricks are still unthinkable.

In 2005, after Democratic senators blocked a vote on a series of Republican judicial candidates, the Republican leadership threatened to employ the nuclear option. A bipartisan group arranged a compromise. Filibusters of nominees were to be reserved for "extraordinary circumstances."

In November 2013, Democrats contended that Republicans had violated this understanding. At that time, fifty-nine executive branch nominees and seventeen judicial nominees were awaiting confirmation. No compromise was reached, and so Democrats voted to abolish filibusters against all executive branch nominees and judicial nominees other than to the Supreme Court. The rules change did not affect use of the filibuster against proposed legislation. Despite the change, Republican senators were still able to delay Democratic nominees through various procedural maneuvers. In January 2015, Republicans took control of the Senate. They were then able to block President Obama's nominees without using special tactics.

Congresspersons and the Citizenry: A Comparison

Members of the Senate and the House of Representatives are not typical American citizens. Members of Congress are older than most Americans, partly because of constitutional age requirements and partly because a good deal of political experience normally is an advantage in running for national office. Members of Congress are also disproportionately white, male, and trained in high-status occupations. Lawyers are by far the largest occupational group among congresspersons, although the proportion of lawyers in the House is lower now than it was in the past.

Compared with the average American citizen, members of Congress are well paid. Annual congressional salaries are now $174,000. Increasingly, members of Congress are also much wealthier than the average citizen. Table 11–2 summarizes selected characteristics of the members of Congress.

Perks and Privileges

Legislators have many benefits that are not available to most people. These range from subsidized meals in the congressional dining rooms to free postage to free parking at Washington, D.C., airports.

Permanent Professional Staffs. More than thirty thousand people are employed on Capitol Hill. About half of them are personal and committee staff members. The personal staff includes office clerks and assistants;

Image 11–4 Senator Marco Rubio (R., Fla.) ran in the 2016 Republican presidential primaries but lost. Had he won, he would have been the first Hispanic presidential candidate from a major party. *Could Rubio's ethnicity have an impact on his political positions?*

Philip Scott Andrews/The New York Times/Redux Pictures

Table 11–2 Characteristics of the 115th Congress, 2017–2019

Why might it be difficult to determine the wealth of a member of Congress?

Characteristic	U.S. Population	House	Senate
Age (median)	36.8	61.3	59.9
Percentage minority	34.9	20.7	10
Religion			
Percentage church or synagogue members	66.4	88.5	88
Percentage Roman Catholic	23.9	30.8	24
Percentage Protestant	51.3	48.2	55
Percentage Jewish	1.7	5.1	9
Percentage female	50.7	19.1	21
Percentage with advanced degrees Persons age 25 or above only	10.1	61.3	74
Occupation Percentage lawyers of those employed	0.8	35.9	54
Family income Percentage of families earning over $50,000 annually	44.9	100.0	100
Median Net Worth*	$45,000	$860,000	$2,900,000

*113th Congress.

Sources: Census Bureau; Association of Religion Data Archives; *Congressional Quarterly*; and authors' updates.

professionals who deal with media relations, draft legislation, and satisfy constituency requests for service; and staffers who maintain local offices in the member's home district or state.

The average Senate office on Capitol Hill employs about thirty staff members, and twice that number work on the personal staffs of senators from the most populous states. House office staffs typically are about half as large as those of the Senate.

Congress also benefits from the expertise of the professional staffs of agencies that were created to produce information for members of the House and Senate. For example, the Congressional Research Service, the Government Accountability Office, and the Congressional Budget Office all provide reports, audits, and policy recommendations for review by members of Congress.

Congressional Caucuses: Another Source of Support. The typical member of Congress is part of a variety of caucuses. The most important caucuses are those established by the parties in each chamber. These Democratic and Republican meetings provide information to the members and devise legislative strategy for the party. Other caucuses have been founded, such as the Democratic Study Group and the

Image 11–5 Senator Ted Cruz (R., Tex.) was a candidate for president in 2016. Like Senator Marco Rubio, Cruz is Cuban American. *Why do so many U.S. Senators run for president?*

Congressional Black Caucus, to support subgroups of members. Many caucuses are established to promote special interests, such as the Potato Caucus and the Sportsmen's Caucus. These caucuses deal with a limited range of legislation. Ideological caucuses, in contrast, may take up any issue. Two of the most important ideological caucuses are the conservative Freedom Caucus and the liberal Progressive Caucus, both in the House.

Privileges and Immunities under the Law. Members of Congress also benefit from a number of special constitutional protections. Under Article I, Section 6, of the Constitution, for example, "for any Speech or Debate in either House, they shall not be questioned in any other Place." The "speech or debate" clause means that a member may make any allegations or other statements he or she wishes in connection with official duties and normally not be sued for libel or slander or otherwise be subject to legal action.

Congressional Elections and Apportionment

Learning Outcome 3:

Examine the implications of apportioning House seats.

The process of electing members of Congress is decentralized. Congressional elections are conducted by the individual state governments. The states, however, must conform to the rules established by the U.S. Constitution and by federal statutes. The Constitution states that representatives are to be elected every second year by popular ballot, and the number of seats awarded to each state is to be determined every ten years by the results of the census. Each state has at least one representative, with most congressional districts having about 750,000 residents. Senators are elected by popular vote every six years. Approximately one-third of the seats are chosen every two years. Each state has two senators.

Under Article I, Section 4, of the Constitution, state legislatures are given control over "the Times, Places and Manner of holding Elections for Senators and Representatives"; however, "the Congress may at any time by Law make or alter such Regulations."

Only states can elect members of Congress. Therefore, territories such as Puerto Rico and Guam are limited to electing nonvoting delegates to the House. The District of Columbia is also represented only by a nonvoting delegate.

Candidates for Congressional Elections

Congressional campaigns have changed considerably in the past two decades. Like all other campaigns, they are much more expensive, with the average cost of a winning Senate campaign now $10.5 million and a winning House campaign averaging almost $1.7 million. In addition, large sums are spent on congressional campaigns by independent committees. Once in office, legislators spend time almost every day raising funds for their next campaign. We provide information about how to locate your congressional district in this chapter's *Consider the Source* feature.

Image 11–6 Representative Marcy Kaptur is the most senior member of Ohio's congressional delegation as well as the longest-serving woman in the House. *How strongly are representatives motivated by the desire to win reelection?*

Presidential Effects. Congressional candidates are always hopeful that a strong presidential candidate will sweep in other members of their party. (In fact, in some presidential elections "coattail effects" have not materialized at all.) One way to measure the coattail effect is to look at the subsequent midterm elections, held in the even-numbered years following the presidential contests. In these years, voter turnout falls sharply. The party controlling the White House frequently loses seats in Congress in the midterm elections, in part because the coattail effect ceases to apply. Table 11–3 shows the pattern for midterm elections since 1946.

Table 11–3 Midterm Gains and Losses by the Party of the President, 1946–2014

What effect might voter turnout have had on these numbers?

Seats Gained or Lost by the Party of the President in the House of Representatives					
Year	President's Party	Outcome	Year	President's Party	Outcome
1946	D.	−55	1982	R.	−26
1950	D.	−29	1986	R.	−5
1954	R.	−18	1990	R.	−8
1958	R.	−47	1994	D.	−52
1962	D.	−4	1998	D.	+5
1966	D.	−47	2002	R.	+5
1970	R.	−12	2006	R.	−30
1974	R.	−48	2010	D.	−64
1978	D.	−15	2014	D.	−15

Consider the source

Finding Your Congressional District

The districts from which we elect members of the U.S. House are often wildly malformed. Commonly, their shapes make few if any concessions to established local boundaries, such as county lines and city limits. What logic they do possess is typically due to political considerations. Consider the boundaries of Ohio's Eleventh Congressional District, as shown in Figure 11–1. The Eleventh District is located in Cuyahoga and Summit counties. More precisely, it is mostly made up of the east side of Cleveland and of central Akron. What these two areas have in common is that they have African American majorities. The Republican majority in the Ohio state legislature thus created the most Democratic district in Ohio and the nineteenth most Democratic district in the nation. With so many Democrats concentrated in this district and a few others, Republicans were guaranteed victory in the rest of the state.

Figure 11–1

Cengage Learning

The Source

Because districts are so oddly shaped, you may have trouble locating your own. The GovTrack website, a project of Civic Impulse, has a service that can help you. Go to www.govtrack.us/congress/members/map and enter your street address. The website will bring up a map of your district together with the names of your House member and senators. The map in Figure 11–1 is from GovTrack. After viewing the district boundaries, you can go to a Wikipedia page to learn more about the district. For the Ohio example just given, in Wikipedia enter "Ohio's 11th Congressional District."

For Critical Analysis

◗ **Can you explain the boundaries of your district in terms of the political leanings of local people? If so, provide your reasoning.**

The Power of Incumbency. The power of incumbency in the outcome of congressional elections cannot be overemphasized. Figure 11–2 shows that a sizable majority of representatives and senators who decide to run for reelection are successful. This conclusion holds for both presidential-year and midterm elections. Even in 2010 and 2014, when the Republicans made very large gains, most incumbents were safe.

Apportionment of the House

Two of the most complicated aspects of congressional elections are apportionment issues—**reapportionment** (the allocation of seats in the House to each state after a census) and **redistricting** (the redrawing of the boundaries of the districts within each state). In a landmark six-to-two vote in 1962, the United States Supreme Court made the creation of state legislative districts a *justiciable* (that is, a reviewable) *question*.[2] The Court did so by invoking the Fourteenth Amendment principle that no state can deny to any person "the equal protection of the laws." In 1964, the Court held that both chambers of a state legislature must be designed so that all districts are equal in population.[3] That same year, the Court applied this "one person, one vote" principle to U.S. congressional districts on the basis of Article I, Section 2, of the Constitution, which requires that members of the House be chosen "by the People of the several States."[4]

reapportionment

The allocation of seats in the House of Representatives to each state after a census.

redistricting

The redrawing of the boundaries of the congressional districts within each state.

2. *Baker v. Carr*, 369 U.S. 186 (1962). The word *justiciable* is pronounced juhs-*tish*-a-buhl.

3. *Reynolds v. Sims*, 377 U.S. 533 (1964).

4. *Wesberry v. Sanders*, 376 U.S. 1 (1964).

Figure 11–2 The Power of Incumbency

The chart shows senators and representatives together. You can see a small increase in the number of legislators who failed to be reelected in 2010. *What happened in that year?*

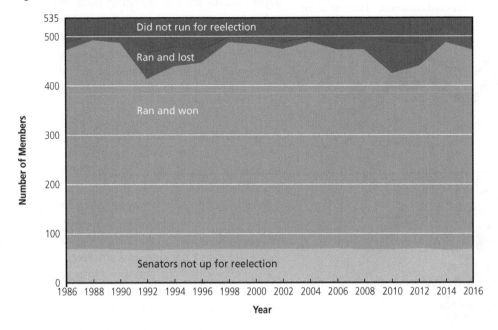

Sources: Norman Ornstein, Thomas E. Mann, and Michael J. Malbin, *Vital Statistics on Congress, 2001–2002* (Washington, D.C.: The AEI Press, 2002); and authors' updates.

Severe malapportionment of congressional districts before 1964 had resulted in some districts containing two or three times the population of other districts in the same state, thereby diluting the effect of a vote cast in the more populous districts. This system generally benefited the conservative residents of rural areas and small towns and harmed the interests of the more heavily populated and liberal cities.

Gerrymandering. Although the general issue of apportionment has been dealt with fairly successfully by the one person, one vote principle, the **gerrymandering** issue has not yet been resolved. This term refers to the legislative-boundary-drawing tactics that were used under Elbridge Gerry, the governor of Massachusetts, in the 1812 elections. (See Figure 11–3.) A district is said to have been gerrymandered when its shape is altered substantially in an attempt to determine which party will win it.

Gerrymandering and the Supreme Court. In 1986, the Supreme Court heard a case that challenged gerrymandered congressional districts in Indiana. The Court ruled for the first time that redistricting for the political benefit of one group could be challenged on constitutional grounds.[5] In this specific case, however, the Court did not agree that the districts had been drawn unfairly. According to the Court, it could not be proved that a group of voters would consistently be deprived of influence at the polls as a result of the new districts.

In 2004, the United States Supreme Court reviewed an obviously political redistricting scheme in Pennsylvania. The Court concluded, however, that the federal judiciary would not address purely political gerrymandering claims.[6] Two years later, the Supreme

gerrymandering

The drawing of legislative district boundary lines for the purpose of obtaining partisan advantage. A district is said to be gerrymandered when its shape is manipulated to determine which party will win it.

---

5. *Davis v. Bandemer*, 478 U.S. 109 (1986).

6. *Vieth v. Jubelirer*, 541 U.S. 267 (2004).

Figure 11-3 The Original Gerrymander

In 1812, the Massachusetts legislature carved out of Essex County a district that had a dragonlike contour. When the painter Gilbert Stuart saw the misshapen district, he penciled in a head, wings, and claws and exclaimed, "That will do for a salamander!" Editor Benjamin Russell replied, "Better say a Gerrymander."

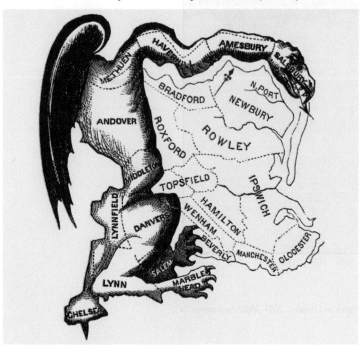

Source: *Congressional Quarterly's Guide to Congress*, 3d ed. (Washington, D.C.: Congressional Quarterly Press, 1982), p. 695.

Court reached a similar conclusion with respect to most of the new congressional districts created by the Republicans in the Texas legislature in 2003. Again, except for one district in Texas, the Court refused to intervene in what was clearly a political gerrymandering plan.[7] Still, gerrymandering is widely seen as unfair. For that reason several states have passed laws aimed at abolishing the process by establishing nonpartisan redistricting boards.

How Gerrymandering Works. Congressional and state legislative redistricting decisions are often made by a small group of political leaders within a state legislature. Typically, their goal is to shape voting districts in such a way as to maximize their party's chances of winning state legislative seats, as well as seats in Congress. Two of the techniques in use are called **packing** and **cracking**. Through the use of powerful computers and software, voters supporting the opposing party are "packed" into as few districts as possible or the opposing party's supporters are "cracked" into different districts.

Figure 11–4 illustrates the redistricting process. In these three examples, sixty-four individuals must be distributed among four districts, each of which has a population of sixteen. Two political parties are involved: the O Party and the X Party.

In Example 1, supporters of the two parties are sorted so that each differently colored district contains only one kind of voter. Such a pattern sometimes appears when the members of a state legislature are most interested in preserving the seats of incumbents, regardless of party. In this example, it would be almost impossible to dislodge a sitting member in a general election. Example 2 is the reverse case. Every district is divided evenly between the parties, and even a very slight swing toward one of the parties could give that party all four seats.

Example 3 is a classic partisan gerrymander benefiting the X Party. The orange district in the lower right is an example of packing—the maximum possible number of supporters of the O Party are packed into that district. The other three districts are examples of cracking. The O Party supporters are cracked so that they do not have a majority in any of the three districts. In these districts, the X Party has majorities of eleven to five, ten to six, and eleven to five.

"Minority–Majority" Districts. Under the mandate of the Voting Rights Act of 1965, the Justice Department issued directives to states after the 1990 census instructing them to create congressional districts that would maximize the voting power of minority groups—that is, create districts in which minority group voters were the majority. The result was a number of creatively drawn congressional districts.

Many of these "minority–majority" districts were challenged in court by citizens who claimed that creating districts based on race or ethnicity alone violates the equal protection clause of the Constitution. In 2001, for example, the Supreme Court reviewed, for a second time, a case involving North Carolina's Twelfth District.

packing

In gerrymandering, packing as many voters as possible of the opposing party into a single district.

cracking

In gerrymandering, splitting the opposing party's voters into many different districts.

7. *League of United Latin American Citizens v. Perry*, 548 U.S. 399 (2006).

Figure 11–4 Examples of Districting

Why might a nonpartisan redistricting board tend to favor solutions such as example 2?

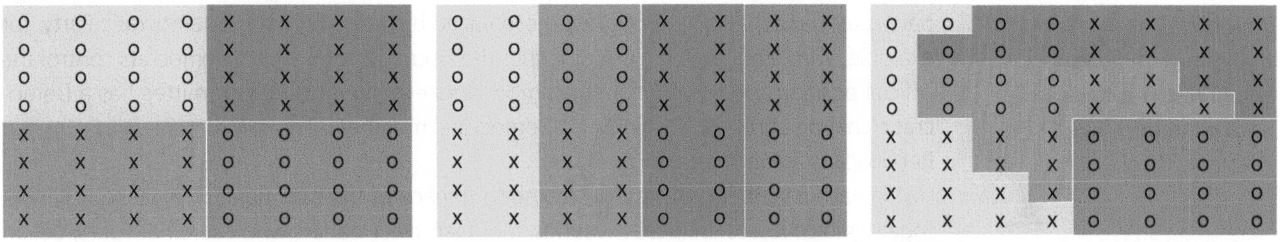

Example 1. A "bipartisan gerrymander" aimed at protecting incumbents in both the O Party and the X Party.

Example 2. An unstable system. All districts have the same number of supporters in each party.

Example 3. A classic partisan gerrymander. The X Party is almost guaranteed to carry three out of the four districts.

The district was 165 miles long, following Interstate 85 for the most part. In 1996, the Supreme Court had held that the district was unconstitutional because race had been the dominant factor in drawing the district's boundaries. Shortly thereafter, the boundaries were redrawn, but the district was again challenged as a racial gerrymander. In 2001, however, the Supreme Court held that there was insufficient evidence that race had been the dominant factor when the boundaries were redrawn.[8] The Twelfth District's boundaries remained in place.

8. *Easley v. Cromartie*, 532 U.S. 234 (2001).

Election 2016

Party Control of Congress after the 2016 Elections

The 2016 elections produced little change in the party balance in Congress. Democrats posted a net gain of eight House seats, far less than what they would have needed to control that chamber. They gained two seats in the Senate, but they would have needed four to win a majority. That also assumes that Democratic vice presidential candidate Tim Kaine had been elected and could break ties. Indeed, if Hillary Clinton had been able to win the White House, she probably would have swelled the Democratic vote by enough to ensure victory by two or more additional Senate Democrats in states such as Pennsylvania and Wisconsin.

With the presidency and a majority in both chambers, it would appear that the Republicans were poised to do whatever they wanted. Congress could repeal Obamacare and much else. One institutional barrier stood in the Republicans'

way, however—the filibuster. With only fifty-two senators, Republicans were far short of the sixty that were required to end a filibuster. Democrats could use the filibuster to protest an extremely conservative Supreme Court nominee. They could use it to block most legislation. That assumes, however, that the filibuster survived. In this chapter, you learned about the "nuclear option," under which the filibuster could be abolished by a simple majority vote. As of 2016, the filibuster no longer applied to most presidential nominees (the Supreme Court excepted). If Republicans abolished it altogether, they really would be able to do almost anything. One of the most important questions facing the 115th Congress, therefore, was whether there were enough Republican traditionalists in the Senate to keep that party from abolishing the filibuster. Time would tell.

How Congress Is Organized

The limited amount of centralized power that exists in Congress is exercised through party-based mechanisms. Congress is organized by party. When the Democratic Party, for example, wins a majority of seats in either the House or the Senate, Democrats control the official positions of power in that chamber, and every important committee has a Democratic chairperson and a majority of Democratic members. The same process holds when Republicans are in the majority.

In each chamber of Congress, members of each of the two major political parties meet together in *caucuses*. In these meetings, members elect leaders who coordinate party action and negotiate with the other chamber and with the president. Still, much of the actual work of legislating is performed by the committees and subcommittees within Congress.

Thousands of bills are introduced in every session of Congress, and no single member can possibly be adequately informed on all the issues that arise. The committee system is a way to provide for specialization, or a division of the legislative effort. Members of a committee can concentrate on just one area or topic—such as taxation or energy—and develop sufficient expertise to draft appropriate legislation when needed. The flow of legislation through both the House and the Senate is determined largely by the speed with which the members of these committees act on bills and resolutions.

The Power of Committees

Sometimes called "little legislatures," committees usually have the final say on pieces of legislation.[9] Committee actions may be overturned on the floor by the House or Senate, but this rarely happens. Legislators normally defer to the expertise of the chairperson and other members of the committee who speak on the floor in defense of a committee decision. Chairpersons of committees exercise control over the scheduling of hearings and formal actions on bills. They also decide which subcommittee will act on legislation falling within

---

9. The term *little legislatures* is from Woodrow Wilson, *Congressional Government* (Mineola, N.Y.: Dover Books, 2006 [first published in 1885]).

Image 11–7 Bob Corker (R., Tenn.), chair of the Senate Foreign Relations Committee, at hearings on North Korea that addressed human rights issues and North Korea's nuclear weapons program. *Years ago it was said that "politics stops at the water's edge." Is this still true?*

their committee's jurisdiction. Committees normally have the power to kill proposed legislation by refusing to act on it—that is, by never sending it to the entire chamber for a vote.

Committees only very rarely are deprived of control over bills—although this kind of action is provided for in the rules of each chamber. In the House, if a bill has been considered by a standing committee for thirty days, the signatures of a majority (218) of the House membership on a **discharge petition** can pry the bill out of the uncooperative committee's hands. From 1909 to 2016, however, although more than nine hundred such petitions were initiated, only slightly more than two dozen resulted in successful discharge efforts. Of those, twenty resulted in bills that passed the House.[10]

Types of Congressional Committees

Over the past two centuries, Congress has created several different types of committees, each of which serves particular needs of the institution.

Standing Committees. By far, the most important committees in Congress are the **standing committees**—permanent bodies that are established by the rules of each chamber and that continue from session to session. A list of the standing committees of the 115th Congress is presented in Table 11–4. In addition, most of the standing committees have created subcommittees to carry out their work. For example, the 115th

---

10. Congressional Quarterly, Inc., *Guide to Congress*, 7th ed. (Washington, D.C.: CQ Press, 2012) and authors' updates.

discharge petition
A procedure by which a bill in the House of Representatives can be forced (discharged) out of a committee that has refused to report it for consideration by the House. The petition must be signed by an absolute majority (218) of representatives and is used only on rare occasions.

standing committee
A permanent committee in the House or Senate that considers bills within a certain subject area.

Table 11–4 Standing Committees of the 115th Congress, 2017–2019

In 2011, House Republicans changed the name of the Committee on Education and Labor to the Committee on Education and the Workforce. *Why do you think that Republicans objected to the word "labor"?*

House Committees	Senate Committees
Agriculture	Agriculture, Nutrition, and Forestry
Appropriations	Appropriations
Armed Services	Armed Services
Budget	Banking, Housing, and Urban Affairs
Education and the Workforce	Budget
Energy and Commerce	Commerce, Science, and Transportation
Ethics	Energy and Natural Resources
Financial Services	Environment and Public Works
Foreign Affairs	Finance
Homeland Security	Foreign Relations
House Administration	Health, Education, Labor, and Pensions
Judiciary	Homeland Security and Governmental Affairs
Natural Resources	Judiciary
Oversight and Government Reform	Rules and Administration
Rules	Small Business and Entrepreneurship
Science, Space, and Technology	Veterans' Affairs
Small Business	
Transportation and Infrastructure	
Veterans' Affairs	
Ways and Means	

Congress has 73 subcommittees in the Senate and 104 in the House. Each standing committee is given a specific area of legislative policy jurisdiction, and almost all legislative measures are considered by the appropriate standing committees.

Because of the importance of their work and the traditional influence of their members in Congress, certain committees are considered to be more prestigious than others. Seats on standing committees that handle spending issues are especially sought after because members can use these positions to benefit their constituents. Committees that control spending include the Appropriations Committee in either chamber and the Ways and Means Committee in the House. Members also normally seek seats on committees that handle matters of special interest to their constituents. A member of the House from an agricultural district, for example, will have an interest in joining the House Agriculture Committee.

Select Committees. In principle, a **select committee** is created for a limited time and for a specific legislative purpose. For example, a select committee may be formed to investigate a public problem, such as child nutrition or aging. In practice, a select committee, such as the Select Committee on Intelligence in each chamber, may continue indefinitely. Select committees rarely create original legislation.

Joint Committees. A **joint committee** is formed by the concurrent action of both chambers of Congress and consists of members from each chamber. Joint committees, which may be permanent or temporary, have dealt with the economy, taxation, and the Library of Congress.

Conference Committees. Special joint committees—**conference committees**—are formed for the purpose of achieving agreement between the House and the Senate on the exact wording of legislative acts when the two chambers pass legislative proposals in different forms. No bill can be sent to the White House to be signed into law unless it first passes both chambers in identical form. Conference committees are in a position to make significant alterations to legislation and frequently become the focal point of policy debates.

The House Rules Committee. Due to its special "gatekeeping" power over the terms on which legislation will reach the floor of the House of Representatives, the House Rules Committee holds a uniquely powerful position. A special rule by the committee sets the time limit on debate and determines whether and how a bill may be amended. The Rules Committee has the unusual power to convene while the House is meeting as a whole, to have its resolutions considered immediately on the floor, and to initiate legislation on its own.

The Selection of Committee Members

In both chambers, members are appointed to standing committees by the steering committee of their party. The majority-party member with the longest term of continuous service on a standing committee is given preference when the committee selects its chairperson. The most senior member of the minority party is called the *ranking committee member* for that party. This **seniority system** is not required by law but is an informal, traditional process, and it applies to other significant posts in Congress as well. The system provides a predictable means of assigning positions of power within Congress.

The general pattern until the 1970s was that members of the House or Senate who represented safe seats would be reelected repeatedly and eventually could accumulate

---

Why should you care about **CONGRESS?**

Many people pay little attention to political races below the presidential level, but the legislation that Congress passes—or fails to pass—can directly affect your life. For instance, federally guaranteed student loans are a major issue. By 2017, outstanding student loans amounted to $1.3 trillion, substantially larger than U.S. credit-card debt. Student loans cannot be discharged through bankruptcy. Despite partisan gridlock, Congress has recently made a number of adjustments beneficial to students, yet more could be done. Yet no such reforms are possible without congressional action—so it matters a great deal who is elected to Congress.

---

select committee

A temporary legislative committee established for a limited time period and for a special purpose.

joint committee

A legislative committee composed of members from both chambers of Congress.

conference committee

A special joint committee appointed to reconcile differences when bills pass the two chambers of Congress in different forms.

seniority system

A custom followed in both chambers of Congress specifying that the member of the majority party with the longest term of continuous service will be given preference when a committee chairperson (or a holder of some other significant post) is selected.

Image 11–8 Republican Paul Ryan of Wisconsin, left, became Speaker of the House in October 2015 after Ohio's John Boehner resigned. Kevin McCarthy, center, became House majority leader in June 2014 after the previous majority leader lost a Republican primary election. Democrat Nancy Pelosi of California, right, formerly the Speaker, became House minority leader after the 2010 elections. These three leaders were expected to be reelected by their colleagues in the leadership elections held in late November 2016.

enough years of continuous committee service to enable them to become the chairpersons of their committees. In the 1970s, reforms of the chairperson selection process somewhat modified the seniority system in the House. The reforms introduced the use of a secret ballot in electing House committee chairpersons and allowed for the possibility of choosing a chairperson on a basis other than seniority. The Democrats immediately replaced three senior chairpersons who were out of step with the rest of their party. In 1995, under Speaker Newt Gingrich, the Republicans chose relatively junior House members as chairpersons of several key committees, thus ensuring conservative control of the committees. The Republicans also passed a rule limiting the term of a chairperson to six years.

Leadership in the House

The House leadership is made up of the Speaker, the majority and minority leaders, and the party whips.

The Speaker. The foremost power holder in the House of Representatives is the **Speaker of the House.** The Speaker's position is technically a nonpartisan one, but in fact, for the better part of two centuries, the Speaker has been the official leader of the majority party in the House. When a new Congress convenes in January of odd-numbered years, each party nominates a candidate for Speaker. All Republican members of the House are expected to vote for their party's nominee, and all Democrats are expected to support their candidate. The vote to organize the House is the one vote in which representatives are expected to vote with their party. In a sense, this vote defines a member's partisan status.

The major formal powers of the Speaker include the following:

- Presiding over meetings of the House.

- Appointing members of joint committees and conference committees.

- Scheduling legislation for floor action.

Speaker of the House

The presiding officer in the House of Representatives. The Speaker is always a member of the majority party and is the most powerful and influential member of the House.

majority leader of the House
The party leader elected by the majority party in the House of Representatives.

minority leader of the House
The party leader elected by the minority party in the House.

whip
A member of Congress who aids the majority or minority leader of the House or the Senate.

- Deciding points of order and interpreting the rules with the advice of the House parliamentarian.

- Referring bills and resolutions to the appropriate standing committees of the House.

A Speaker may take part in floor debate and vote, as can any other member of Congress, but recent Speakers usually have voted only to break a tie.

In the years since 2011, when the Republicans took control of the House, the Speaker's job has often been difficult. Speaker John Boehner was forced to confront insurgent conservatives who were willing to shut down the government if that was what it took to attain their policy goals. In October 2015, Boehner decided that enough was enough, and he resigned. After a brief period of political turbulence, Republicans settled on Paul Ryan of Wisconsin as his replacement.

The Majority Leader. The **majority leader of the House** is elected by the caucus of the majority party to foster cohesion among party members and to act as a spokesperson for the party. The majority leader influences the scheduling of debate and acts as the chief supporter of the Speaker. The majority leader cooperates with the Speaker and other party leaders, both inside and outside Congress, to formulate the party's legislative program and to guide that program through the legislative process in the House. The parties have often recruited future Speakers from those who hold the position of majority leader.

The Minority Leader. The **minority leader of the House** is the candidate nominated for Speaker by the caucus of the minority party. Like the majority leader, the leader of the minority party has as her or his primary responsibility the maintaining of cohesion within the party's ranks. The minority leader works for cooperation among the party's members and speaks on behalf of the president if the minority party controls the White House. In relations with the majority party, the minority leader consults with both the Speaker and the majority leader on recognizing members who wish to speak on the floor, on House rules and procedures, and on the scheduling of legislation. Minority leaders have no actual power in these areas, however.

Whips. The leadership of each party includes assistants to the majority and minority leaders, known as **whips**.[11] The whips are members of Congress who assist the party leaders by passing information down from the leadership to party members and by ensuring that members show up for floor debate and cast their votes on important issues. Whips conduct polls among party members about the members' views on legislation, inform the leaders about whose vote is doubtful and whose is certain, and may exert pressure on members to support the leaders' positions.

Leadership in the Senate

The Senate is less than one-fourth the size of the House. This fact alone probably explains why a formal, complex, and centralized leadership structure is not as necessary in the Senate as it is in the House.

The two highest-ranking formal leadership positions in the Senate are essentially ceremonial in nature. Under the

Image 11–9 After the Republicans took control of the U.S. Senate in the 2014 elections, Republican senator Mitch McConnel of Kentucky, left, was elected Senate majority leader. Democratic senator Charles Schumer of New York, right, was expected to become the minority leader in January 2017 as a result of the retirement of Nevada senator Harry Reid. Both senators had to be confirmed in the caucus leadership elections held in late November 2016.

11. *Whip* comes from "whipper-in," a fox-hunting term for someone who keeps the hunting dogs from straying.

Constitution, the vice president of the United States is the president (that is, the presiding officer) of the Senate and may vote to break a tie. The vice president, however, is only rarely present for a meeting of the Senate. The Senate elects instead a **president pro tempore** ("pro tem") to preside over the Senate in the vice president's absence. Ordinarily, the president pro tem is the member of the majority party with the longest continuous term of service in the Senate. As mentioned, the president pro tem is mostly a ceremonial position. More junior senators take turns actually presiding over the sessions of the Senate.

The real leadership power in the Senate rests in the hands of the **Senate majority leader,** the **Senate minority leader,** and their respective whips. The Senate majority and minority leaders have the right to be recognized first in debate on the floor and generally exercise the same powers available to the House majority and minority leaders. They control the scheduling of debate on the floor in conjunction with the majority party's policy committee, influence the allocation of committee assignments for new members or for senators attempting to transfer to a new committee, influence the selection of other party officials, and participate in selecting members of conference committees.

The leaders are expected to mobilize support for partisan legislative or presidential initiatives. They act as liaisons with the White House when the president is of their party, try to obtain the cooperation of committee chairpersons, and seek to facilitate the smooth functioning of the Senate through the senators' unanimous consent. The majority and minority leaders are elected by their respective party caucuses.

Senate party whips, like their House counterparts, maintain communication within the party on platform positions and try to ensure that party colleagues are present for floor debate and important votes. The Senate whip system is far less elaborate than its counterpart in the House, because there are fewer members to track and senators have a greater tradition of independence. A list of the candidates expected to become the formal party leaders of the 115th Congress is presented in Table 11–5.

president pro tempore
The temporary presiding officer of the Senate in the absence of the vice president.

Senate majority leader
The chief spokesperson of the majority party in the Senate, who directs the legislative program and party strategy.

Senate minority leader
The party officer in the Senate who commands the minority party's opposition to the policies of the majority party and directs the legislative program and strategy of his or her party.

Table 11–5 Party Leaders in the 115th Congress, 2017–2019

The named individuals were the leading contenders for the various positions in the 2016 leadership elections. Note that the Republican caucuses are formally known as conferences. *Why might joining the leadership sometimes make a member of Congress less popular in his or her home district?*

Position	Incumbent	Party/State	Leader Since
House			
Speaker	Paul Ryan	R., Wisc.	Oct. 2015
Majority leader	Kevin McCarthy	R., Calif.	June 2014
Majority whip	Steve Scalise	R., La.	June 2014
Chair of the Republican Conference	Cathy McMorris Rogers	R., Wash.	Jan. 2013
Minority leader	Nancy Pelosi	D., Calif.	Jan. 2011
Minority whip	Steny Hoyer	D., Md.	Jan. 2011
Assistant minority leader	James Clyburn	D., S.C.	Jan. 2011
Chair of the Democratic Caucus	Xavier Becerra	D., Calif.	Jan. 2013
Senate			
President pro tempore	Orrin Hatch	R., Utah	Jan. 2015
Majority leader	Mitch McConnell	R., Ky.	Jan. 2015
Majority whip	John Cornyn	R., Tex.	Jan. 2015
Chair of the Republican Conference	John Thune	R., S.D.	Jan. 2015
Minority leader	Charles Schumer	D., N.Y.	Jan. 2017
Minority whip	Dick Durbin	D., Ill.	Jan. 2015
Chair of the Democratic Caucus	Charles Schumer	D., N.Y.	Jan. 2017

Lawmaking and Budgeting

Discuss the process by which a bill becomes law and how the federal government establishes its budget.

Each year, Congress and the president propose and approve many laws. Some are budget and appropriations laws that require extensive bargaining but must be passed for the government to continue to function. Other laws are relatively free of controversy and are passed with little dissension. Still other proposed legislation is extremely controversial and reaches to the roots of differences between Republicans and Democrats.

Figure 11–5 shows that each law begins as a bill, which must be introduced in either the House or the Senate. Often, similar bills are introduced in both chambers. A budget bill, however, must start in the House. In each chamber, the bill follows similar steps. It is referred to a committee and its subcommittees for study, discussion, hearings, and markup (rewriting). When the bill is reported out to the full chamber, it must be scheduled for debate (by the Rules Committee in the House and by the leadership in the Senate). After the bill has been passed in each chamber, if the two versions of the bill contain different provisions, a conference committee is formed to write a compromise bill, which must be approved by both chambers before it is sent to the president to sign or veto.

How Much Will the Government Spend?

The Constitution is very clear about where the power of the purse lies in the national government: all taxing or spending bills must originate in the House of Representatives.

Image 11–10 Senator Orrin Hatch (R., Utah) is the most senior Republican in the Senate and holds the honorary post of president pro tem. *What are the benefits of the seniority system?*

Today, much of the business of Congress is concerned with approving government expenditures through the budget process and with raising the revenues to pay for government programs.

From 1922 until 1974, Congress required the president to prepare and present to the legislature an **executive budget.** Still, the congressional budget process was so disjointed that it was difficult to visualize the total picture of government finances. The president presented the executive budget to Congress in January. It was broken down into thirteen or more appropriations bills. Some time later, after all of the bills had been debated, amended, and passed, it was more or less possible to estimate total government spending for the next year.

Frustrated by the president's ability to impound, or withhold, funds and dissatisfied with the entire budget process, Congress passed the Budget and Impoundment Control Act of 1974 to regain some control over the nation's spending. The act required the president to spend the funds that Congress had

executive budget

The budget prepared and submitted by the president to Congress.

Figure 11–5 How a Bill Becomes Law

This illustration shows the most typical way in which proposed legislation is enacted into law. Most legislation begins as similar bills introduced into the House and the Senate. The process is illustrated here with two hypothetical bills, House bill No. 100 (HR 100) and Senate bill No. 200 (S 200). The path of HR 100 is shown on the left and that of S 200 on the right. *Where does the filibuster fit into this process?*

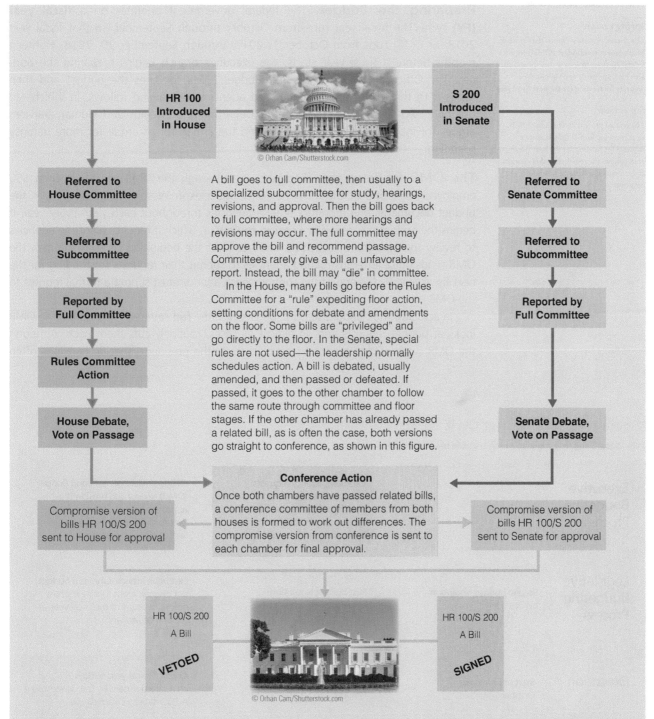

A compromise bill approved by both houses is sent to the president, who can sign it into law or veto it and return it to Congress. Congress may override a presidential veto by a two-thirds majority in both chambers. The bill then becomes law without the president's signature.

fiscal year (FY)
A twelve-month period that is used for bookkeeping, or accounting, purposes. Usually, the fiscal year does not coincide with the calendar year. For example, the federal government's fiscal year runs from October 1 through September 30.

spring review
The annual process in which the Office of Management and Budget (OMB) requires federal agencies to review their programs, activities, and goals and submit their requests for funding for the next fiscal year.

fall review
The annual process in which the OMB, after receiving formal federal agency requests for funding for the next fiscal year, reviews the requests, makes changes, and submits its recommendations to the president.

appropriated, ending the president's ability to kill programs by withholding funds. The other major result of the act was to force Congress to examine total national taxing and spending at least twice in each budget cycle. (See Figure 11–6 for a graphic illustration of the budget cycle.)

Preparing the Budget. The federal government operates on a **fiscal year (FY)** cycle. The fiscal year runs from October through September, so that fiscal year 2018, or FY18, runs from October 1, 2017, through September 30, 2018. Eighteen months before a fiscal year starts, the executive branch begins preparing the budget. The Office of Management and Budget (OMB) outlines the budget and then sends it to the various departments and agencies. Bargaining follows, in which—to use only two of many examples—the Department of Health and Human Services argues for more antipoverty spending, and the armed forces argue for more defense spending.

The OMB Reviews the Budget. Even though the OMB has fewer than 550 employees, it is one of the most powerful agencies in Washington. It assembles the budget documents and monitors federal agencies throughout each year. Every year, it begins the budget process with a **spring review,** in which it requires all of the agencies to review their programs, activities, and goals. At the beginning of each summer, the OMB sends out a letter instructing agencies to submit their requests for funding for the next fiscal year. By the end of the summer, each agency must submit a formal request to the OMB.

In actuality, the "budget season" begins with the **fall review.** At this time, the OMB looks at budget requests and, in almost all cases, routinely cuts them back. Although the OMB works within guidelines established by the president, specific decisions often

Figure 11–6 The Budget Cycle

Why does Congress have so much trouble meeting its deadlines?

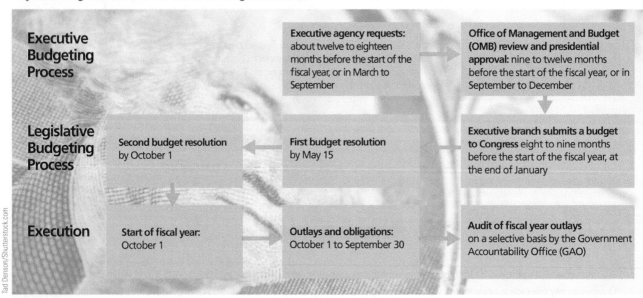

Executive Budgeting Process

Executive agency requests: about twelve to eighteen months before the start of the fiscal year, or in March to September

Office of Management and Budget (OMB) review and presidential approval: nine to twelve months before the start of the fiscal year, or in September to December

Legislative Budgeting Process

Second budget resolution by October 1

First budget resolution by May 15

Executive branch submits a budget to Congress eight to nine months before the start of the fiscal year, at the end of January

Execution

Start of fiscal year: October 1

Outlays and obligations: October 1 to September 30

Audit of fiscal year outlays on a selective basis by the Government Accountability Office (GAO)

Tad Denson/Shutterstock.com

are left to the OMB director and the director's associates. By the beginning of November, the director's review begins. The director meets with cabinet secretaries and budget officers. Time becomes crucial. The budget must be completed by January so that it can be included in the *Economic Report of the President.*

The Election-Year Budget. The schedule just described cannot apply to a year in which the voters elect a new president or to a year in which a new president is inaugurated. In 2008, George W. Bush did not engage in a fall review of the FY 2010 budget, because he would no longer be in office when the budget went into effect in October 2009. Barack Obama could hardly have undertaken the fall review either, given that he was still campaigning for the presidency.

Following the election of a new president, the budget process is compressed into the first months of the new administration. Indeed, Barack Obama released a budget document for FY 2010 on February 26, 2009, barely a month after he was inaugurated.

Image 11–11 "**I sincerely regret if our actions had the appearance of being partisan, discriminatory, or in any way Congressional.**"

Congress Faces the Budget

In January, nine months before the fiscal year starts, the president takes the OMB's proposed budget, approves it, and submits it to Congress. Then the congressional budgeting process takes over. The budgeting process involves two steps: authorization and appropriation.

The Authorization Process. First, Congress must authorize funds to be spent. The **authorization** is a formal declaration by the appropriate congressional committee that a certain amount of funding may be available to an agency. Congressional committees and subcommittees look at the proposals from the executive branch and the Congressional Budget Office in making the decision to authorize funds.

The Appropriation Process. After the funds have been authorized, they must be appropriated by Congress. The appropriations committees of both the House and the Senate forward spending bills to their respective bodies. The **appropriation** of funds occurs when the final bill is passed. In this process, large sums are in play. Representatives and senators who chair key committees have traditionally found it easy to slip additional spending proposals into a variety of bills. These proposals may have nothing to do with the ostensible purpose of the bill. Such *earmarked* appropriations, known as "pork," have their defenders. Many members of Congress believe that they have a better understanding of the needs of their districts than does any executive branch agency.

authorization

A formal declaration by a legislative committee that a certain amount of funding may be available to an agency. Some authorizations terminate in a year; others are renewable automatically without further congressional action.

appropriation

The passage, by Congress, of a spending bill specifying the amount of authorized funds that actually will be allocated for an agency's use.

Evading the Ban on Earmarks. In March 2010, the Republican-controlled House implemented rules designed to eliminate earmarks benefiting individuals or corporations. The new rules have substantially reduced the amount of pork inserted into appropriations bills, but lawmakers have been creative in attempting to circumvent the ban. In some instances, legislators have simply denied that a particular funding request is actually an earmark. More commonly, members have lobbied the various executive agencies to include projects that benefit their districts. According to the OMB definition, spending requested by executive agencies is not pork. Further, the White House itself frequently inserts special requests into the executive budget, thus making the president the biggest "porkmeister" of all.

Budget Resolutions and Crises

The **first budget resolution** by Congress is due each May. It sets overall revenue goals and spending targets. Spending and tax laws that are drawn up over the summer are supposed to be guided by the first budget resolution. By September, Congress is scheduled to pass its **second budget resolution,** one that will set binding limits on taxes and spending for the fiscal year beginning October 1.

The Continuing Resolution. In actuality, Congress has finished the budget on time in only three years since 1977. As mentioned earlier, the budget is usually broken into a series of appropriations bills. If Congress has not passed one of these bills by October 1, it normally passes a **continuing resolution** that allows the affected agencies to keep on doing whatever they were doing the previous year with the same amount of funding.

The Federal Debt Ceiling. In recent years, the budgeting process has included a series of crises marked by confrontations between the Republicans and Democrats. Several of these confrontations involved the federal *debt ceiling*.

If the federal government runs a budget deficit—if it spends more than it takes in—it must issue new debt. The government has, in fact, run a deficit in most recent years. Under current law, the national government is limited in the amount of debt it can issue, and if the federal debt approaches the legal ceiling, Congress must raise the limit to allow additional debt. Many people mistakenly believe that raising the ceiling is a prerequisite for new, future spending, but that is not the case. If the debt ceiling is not raised as needed, the government might be forced to default on its existing obligations.

Traditionally, members of Congress often "grandstanded" by voting against the debt ceiling hike, even though passage was never in doubt. In 2011, however, House Republicans, for the first time, sought to use the ceiling as a tool to force Democrats to accept spending cuts. At the last minute, House Republicans and the Democrats under President Obama reached a deal that involved significant cuts.

In 2013, Republicans attempted to use the debt ceiling tactic again. Democrats, believing that the Republicans had taken advantage of them in 2011, refused to negotiate. At the same time, the government was about to run out of funding because no continuing resolution had been passed. On October 1, parts of the federal government were forced to shut down. Following intense pressure from the public and from business interests, the Republicans caved in. On October 16, they raised the debt ceiling and passed a continuing resolution. That vote marked the end of the debt ceiling tactic.

Xinhua News Agency/Getty Images

Image 11–12 Democratic presidential candidate and former Secretary of State Hillary Clinton testifies before the House Select Committee on Benghazi in 2015. Clinton's defense of her actions was regarded by her supporters as successful. *Why would a congressional committee pursue such an issue?*

How you can make a difference

To contact a member of Congress, start by going to the websites of the U.S. House of Representatives (www.house.gov) and the U.S. Senate (www.senate.gov).

- Although you can communicate easily with your representatives by e-mail, using it has some drawbacks. Representatives and senators receive large volumes of e-mail from constituents, which they rarely read themselves. They have staff members who read and respond to e-mail instead. Many interest groups argue that U.S. mail, or even express mail or a phone call, is more likely to capture the attention of a representative than e-mail.

- You can contact your representatives and senators using one of the following addresses or phone numbers:

  United States House of Representatives
  Washington, DC 20515
  202-224-3121

  United States Senate
  Washington, DC 20510
  202-224-3121

- Interest groups track the voting records of members of Congress and rate the members on the issues. Project Vote Smart tracks the performance of more than thirteen thousand political leaders, including their campaign finances, issue positions, and voting records. You can locate the website of Project Vote Smart at www.votesmart.org.

- Finally, if you want to know how your representatives funded their campaigns, contact the Center for Responsive Politics (CRP), a research group that tracks money in politics, campaign fund-raising, and similar issues. You can see the CRP site by visiting www.opensecrets.org.

KEY TERMS

CHAPTER SUMMARY

Learning Outcome 1 The authors of the Constitution believed that the bulk of national power should be in the legislature. The Connecticut Compromise established a balance, with the membership in the House of Representatives based on population and the membership in the Senate based on the equality of states.

The functions of Congress include (a) lawmaking, (b) representation, (c) service to constituents, (d) oversight, (e) public education, and (f) conflict resolution.

The Constitution specifies most of the enumerated, or expressed, powers of Congress, including the right to impose taxes, to borrow funds, to regulate commerce, and to declare war. Congress also enjoys the right, under the elastic, or necessary and proper, clause, to make all laws necessary and proper for executing the various powers of the national government.

Learning Outcome 2 There are 435 voting members in the House of Representatives and 100 members in the Senate. Owing to its larger size, the House has a greater number of formal rules. The Senate tradition of unlimited debate has been used over the years to frustrate the passage of bills. Budget bills can be exempt from a filibuster, and in 2013 most presidential nominations became exempt as well.

Members of Congress are not typical American citizens. They are older and wealthier than most Americans, disproportionately white and male, and more likely to be lawyers.

Learning Outcome 3 Most incumbent representatives and senators who run for reelection are successful. Apportionment is the allocation of legislative seats to constituencies. The Supreme Court's "one person, one vote" rule means that the populations of legislative districts must be effectively equal.

The process of gerrymandering, however, often lets party leaders determine the political leanings of particular districts.

Learning Outcome 4 Most of the work of legislating is performed by committees and subcommittees within Congress. Legislation introduced into the House or Senate is assigned to standing committees for review. Joint committees are formed by the action of both chambers and consist of members from each. Conference committees are joint committees set up to achieve agreement between the House and the Senate on the exact wording of legislative acts that were passed by the chambers in different forms. The seniority rule, which is usually followed, specifies that the longest-serving member of the majority party will be the chairperson of a committee.

The foremost power holder in the House of Representatives is the Speaker of the House. Other leaders are the House majority leader, the House minority leader, and the majority and minority whips. Formally, the vice president is the presiding officer of the Senate. Actual leadership in the Senate rests with the majority leader, the minority leader, and their whips.

Learning Outcome 5 A bill becomes law by progressing through both chambers of Congress and their appropriate standing and joint committees before submission to the president.

The budget process for a fiscal year begins with the preparation of an executive budget by the president. This is reviewed by the Office of Management and Budget and then sent to Congress, which is supposed to pass a final budget by the end of September. Since 1978, Congress generally has not followed its own time rules.

ADDITIONAL RESOURCES

Online Resources

- *RollCall*, the newspaper of the Capitol, is available at **www.rollcall.com**.

- You can find Politico, a major website of political news, at **www.politico.com**.

- *The Hill,* a newspaper that investigates various activities of Congress, can be found at **thehill.com**.

Books

Lee, Frances E. *Insecure Majorities: Congress and the Perpetual Campaign.* Chicago: University of Chicago Press, 2016. Lee argues that much of the partisanship in Congress is due to close party divisions and the possibility that the majority party could lose its control. She is a professor of political science at the University of Maryland.

Mann, Thomas E., and Norman J. Ornstein. *It's Even Worse Than It Looks: How the American Constitutional System Collided with the New Politics of Extremism.* New York: Basic Books, First Trade Paper Edition, 2013. The authors, political scientists with positions at Washington "think tanks," contend that the political polarization that has tied up Congress endangers the nation. Mann is a Democrat and Ornstein is a Republican, but they agree that extremism among Republicans is the greater threat.

McConnell, Mitch. *The Long Game: A Memoir.* New York: Sentinel, 2016. Mitch McConnell became the minority leader in the Senate in 2007, and the majority leader in January 2015 after the Republicans took control of the Senate. The title of his memoir says it all—in a surprisingly candid book by a sitting politician, McConnell explains why for him conservative politics is a long game.

Video

Charlie Wilson's War—One of the best movies of 2007, starring Tom Hanks and Julia Roberts. This hilarious film is based on the true story of how Wilson, a hard-living, hard-drinking representative from Texas, almost single-handedly wins a billion dollars in funding for the Afghans who are fighting a Russian invasion. When equipped with heat-seeking missiles, the Afghans win. The late Philip Seymour Hoffman steals the show portraying a rogue CIA operative.

House of Cards—This political drama was the first original series to be commissioned by Netflix, the online streaming-video company. Kevin Spacey stars as Frank Underwood, a scheming member of the House who eventually manages to become president. As of 2016, it had received thirty-three Emmy nominations and eight Golden Globe nominations.

Quiz

Multiple Choice and Fill-Ins

Learning Outcome 1 Describe the various roles played by Congress and the constitutional basis of its powers.

1. The bicameralism of Congress means that:
   a. every district has two members.
   b. every state has two senators.
   c. Congress is divided into two legislative bodies.

2. The process of compromise in which members of Congress support each other's bills is called _____.

Learning Outcome 2 Explain some of the differences between the House and the Senate and some of the privileges enjoyed by members of Congress.

3. The central difference between the House and the Senate is that:
   a. the House is much larger than the Senate.
   b. the Senate is much larger than the House.
   c. the Senate meets only occasionally, but the House meets all of the time.

4. In contrast to the House, only the Senate has the power to accept or reject _____ with foreign nations.

Learning Outcome 3 Examine the implications of apportioning House seats.

5. Congressional redistricting often involves gerrymandering, which means that the redistricting:
   a. results in an equal number of Democratic and Republican districts.
   b. results in strange-shaped districts designed to favor one party.
   c. results in districts that have almost no representation.

6. A high percentage of senators and representatives are reelected, and we describe this as due to the power of _____.

Learning Outcome 4 Describe the committee structure of the House and the Senate and the key leadership positions in each chamber.

7. There are several types of committees in Congress. They include:
   a. standing committees, sitting committees, and joint committees.
   b. sitting committees, joint committees, and select committees.
   c. standing committees, select committees, and joint committees.

8. The representative with the most power in the House is the _____ ___ ___ _____ because he or she is the official leader of the majority party.

Learning Outcome 5 Discuss the process by which a bill becomes law and how the federal government establishes its budget.

9. When an appropriations bill has not been passed on time, Congress may pass a temporary funding law called:
   a. a continuing resolution.
   b. a second budget resolution.
   c. a temporary authorization.

10. In contrast to the calendar year, which starts January 1 and ends on December 31, the federal government's _____ year runs from October 1 through September 30.

Essay Questions

1. The District of Columbia is not represented in the Senate and has a single, nonvoting delegate to the House. Should the District of Columbia be represented in Congress by voting legislators? Why or why not? If it should be represented, how? Would it make sense to admit it as a state? To give it back to Maryland? Explain your reasoning.

2. Identify some advantages to the nation that might follow when one party controls the House, the Senate, and the presidency. Identify some of the disadvantages that might follow from such a state of affairs.

THE PRESIDENT

Donald Trump prepares to address the 2016 Republican National Convention in Cleveland. *What were some of the reasons he won the presidential election?*
Alex Wong/Getty Images

These five **LEARNING OUTCOMES** *below are designed to help improve your understanding of this chapter:*

1: Identify the types of people who typically undertake serious campaigns for the presidency.

2: Distinguish among the major roles of the president, including head of state, chief executive, commander in chief, chief diplomat, chief legislator, party chief, and politician.

3: Describe some of the special powers of the president, and tell how a president can be removed from office.

4: Explain the organization of the executive branch and, in particular, the executive office of the president.

5: Evaluate the role of the vice president, and describe what happens if the presidency becomes vacant.

What if... a New President Tore Up Our Trade Agreements?

Background

Whatever you thought of Donald Trump's presidential bid, he has certainly been an endless source of what-if-style questions. Hostility to imports is central to Trump's nationalism. He has consistently denounced existing trade deals with other countries. That includes the North American Free Trade Agreement (NAFTA) between the United States, Canada, and Mexico. Trump stated that either this agreement must be completely rewritten in America's favor or he would simply withdraw from the pact. Such a statement raises the question: does the U.S. president even have the power to tear up a trade treaty? As we explain later in this chapter, Supreme Court rulings appear to confirm that the president *can* withdraw from a treaty unilaterally, without the consent of Congress—even though agreeing to a treaty requires a two-thirds vote by the Senate.

Trump also threatened to impose tariffs (taxes) on Chinese imports of up to 45 percent. Such tariffs would require congressional assent—although the president does have some powers to impose tariffs due to previous bills passed by Congress. Trump's surprise victory in 2016 meant that he was now in a position to take serious actions.

What If a New President Tore Up Our Trade Agreements?

This most important point to understand about foreign trade is that it is a two-way street. We import goods and services—but we export them as well. True, the United States imports more by value than it exports, but that only works because foreign nations have been eager to pile up savings in safe U.S. dollars. In other words, we export dollars as well as goods and services, and the books must balance. Everything we import is paid for by exporting something, and everything we export is paid for by importing something. If we slash our imports, sooner or later foreign nations will run out of the U.S. dollars they need to import goods and services from us. Cutting imports eventually means cutting exports.

Foreign leaders, however, are not going to wait until their nations run out of dollars. They will immediately curb imports from the United States, through tariffs or other mechanisms. That would hurt everyone who depends on U.S. exports. Boeing, which makes airplanes, is a huge exporter. It also competes with Airbus, a European firm. If we are in a "trade war" with China or other countries, why would they ever consider buying from Boeing instead of Airbus? China would buy every shipment of soybeans it possibly could from Brazil before considering soybeans from U.S. farmers. A trade war would cost thousands of Americans their jobs, and many others would lose large sums in lost business.

Could a Trade War Spark a Recession?

In principle, jobs lost to vanishing exports could be made up by new jobs producing the items we no longer import. In practice, it is not likely to be that simple. Manufacturing jobs have migrated to China and Mexico because workers there earn much lower wages than American workers. If these jobs came back to the United States, they would still be badly paid.

Nor can we assume that these manufacturing jobs would even return. The United States makes many more goods than ever before—manufacturing continues to grow even as factory employment falls. When the price of labor is an issue, industries add more machines, robots included. Increased taxes (tariffs) would also hurt the economy. A trade war could thus mean a fall in employment and a major recession. Many economists believe that there are policies that could counteract such a disaster, but Congress is unlikely to adopt them, because they would involve an increase in the federal budget deficit.

For Critical Analysis

▷ What would happen to Walmart's prices if the federal government imposed a steep tariff on Chinese goods?

▷ America's position in the world isn't just a matter of economics, but of national security as well. What impact could a trade war have on our relations with our strategic allies?

Image 12–1 A farmer holds soybean seeds. *Why is U.S. agriculture a major export industry?*

JOAT/Shutterstock.com

The writers of the Constitution had no models to follow when they created the presidency of the United States. Nowhere else in the world was there an elected head of state. What the founders did not want was a king. The two initial plans considered by the founders—the Virginia and New Jersey plans—both called for an executive elected by Congress. Other delegates, especially those who had witnessed the need for a strong leader in the Revolutionary Army, believed a strong executive would be necessary for the new republic. The delegates, after much debate, created a chief executive who had enough powers granted in the Constitution to balance those of Congress.

In this chapter, after looking at who can become president and at the process involved, we examine closely the nature and extent of the constitutional powers held by the president. These constitutional powers are at their strongest in the area of foreign policy, a topic that we discussed in the chapter-opening *What If. . .* feature.

Who Can Become President?

Learning Outcome **1:**

Identify the types of people who typically undertake serious campaigns for the presidency.

The requirements for becoming president, as outlined in Article II, Section 1, of the Constitution, are not overwhelmingly stringent:

> *No person except a natural born Citizen, or a Citizen of the United States, at the time of the Adoption of this Constitution, shall be eligible to the Office of President; neither shall any Person be eligible to that Office who shall not have attained to the Age of thirty-five Years, and been fourteen Years a Resident within the United States.*

The president receives a salary of $400,000, plus $169,000 for expenses and a vast array of free services, beginning with residence in the White House.

A "Natural Born Citizen"

The only question that arises about the constitutional requirements relates to the term *natural born Citizen*. Does that mean only citizens born in the United States and its territories? What about a child born to U.S. citizens visiting or living in another country? Although the question has not been dealt with directly by the Supreme Court, it is reasonable to expect that someone would be eligible if her or his parents were Americans.

These questions were debated when George Romney, who was born in Chihuahua, Mexico, to American parents, made a serious bid for the Republican presidential nomination in the 1960s.[1] The issue came up again when opponents of President Barack Obama claimed that Obama was not a natural born citizen. In fact, Obama was born in Honolulu, Hawaii, in 1961, two years after Hawaii became a state. Those who disputed Obama's birth claimed that his birth certificate was a forgery—despite the fact that Obama's birth was also recorded by two Honolulu newspapers. It's also worth noting that Senator Ted Cruz of Texas, a Republican presidential candidate in 2016, was born in Canada to an American mother.

Presidential Characteristics

The American dream is symbolized by the statement that "anybody can become president of this country." It is true that in modern times, presidents have included a haberdasher (Harry Truman), the owner of a peanut warehouse (Jimmy Carter), and an actor (Ronald Reagan). But if you examine the list of presidents in Appendix F at the end of

---

1. George Romney was governor of Michigan from 1963 to 1969. Romney was not nominated for the presidency, and the issue remains unresolved. George Romney was the father of Mitt Romney, the 2012 Republican presidential candidate.

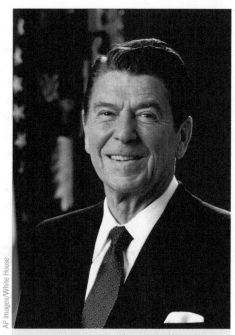

Image 12–2 The youngest president ever elected was John F. Kennedy (1961–1963). Despite his youth, Kennedy had serious health problems that he kept secret. *Could a presidential candidate do such a thing today?*

Image 12–3 The oldest president ever elected was Ronald Reagan (1981–1989). *Could Reagan's age have helped him with some voters?*

this book, you will see that the most common previous occupational field of presidents in this country has been the law. Out of forty-four presidents, twenty-six have been lawyers, and many have been wealthy.

Although the Constitution states that the minimum-age requirement for the presidency is thirty-five years, most presidents have been much older than that when they assumed office. John F. Kennedy, at the age of forty-three, was the youngest elected president, and the oldest was Ronald Reagan, at age sixty-nine. The average age at inauguration has been fifty-four. There has clearly been a demographic bias in the selection of presidents. All have been male, white, and from the Protestant tradition, except for John F. Kennedy, a Roman Catholic, and Barack Obama, an African American.

The Process of Becoming President

Major and minor political parties nominate candidates for president and vice president at national conventions every four years. As noted previously, the nation's voters do not elect a president and vice president directly but rather cast ballots for presidential electors, who then vote for president and vice president in the electoral college.

Because victory goes to the candidate with a majority in the electoral college, it is conceivable that someone could be elected to the office of the presidency without having a plurality of the popular vote cast. In elections in which more than two candidates were running for office, many presidential candidates have won with less than 50 percent of the total popular votes cast for all candidates—including Abraham Lincoln, Woodrow Wilson, Harry Truman, John F. Kennedy, Richard Nixon, and, in 1992, Bill Clinton.

Thus far, on two occasions the electoral college has failed to give any candidate a majority. At that point, the House of Representatives takes over, and the president is then chosen from among the three candidates having the most electoral college votes. In 1800, Thomas Jefferson and Aaron Burr tied in the electoral college. This happened because the Constitution had not been explicit in indicating which of the two electoral votes was for president and which was for vice president. In 1804, the **Twelfth Amendment** clarified the matter by requiring that the president and vice president be chosen separately. In 1824, the House again had to make a choice, this time among William H. Crawford, Andrew Jackson, and John Quincy Adams. It chose Adams, even though Jackson had more electoral and popular votes.

Twelfth Amendment

An amendment to the Constitution, adopted in 1804, that requires the separate election of the president and the vice president by the electoral college.

head of state

The role of the president as ceremonial head of the government.

The Many Roles of the President

Learning Outcome **2:**

The Constitution speaks briefly about the duties and obligations of the president. Based on this brief list of powers and on the precedents of history, the presidency has grown into a very complicated job that requires balancing at least five constitutional roles. These are (1) head of state, (2) chief executive, (3) commander in chief of the armed forces, (4) chief diplomat, and (5) chief legislator of the United States. In addition to these constitutional roles, the president serves as the leader of his or her political party. Of course, the president is also the nation's most prominent and successful politician. Here we examine each of these significant presidential functions, or roles. It is worth noting that one person plays all these roles simultaneously and that the needs of the roles may at times come into conflict.

Distinguish among the major roles of the president, including head of state, chief executive, commander in chief, chief diplomat, chief legislator, party chief, and politician.

Head of State

Every nation has at least one person who is the ceremonial head of state. In most democratic nations, the role of **head of state** is given to someone other than the chief executive, who leads the executive branch of government. In Britain, for example, the head of state is the queen. In much of Europe, the head of state is a relatively powerless president. The prime minister is the chief executive. But in the United States, the president is both chief executive and head of state.

The president, as head of state, engages in a number of activities that are largely symbolic or ceremonial. Some students of the American political system believe that having the president serve as both the chief executive and the head of state drastically limits the time available to do "real" work. Not all presidents have agreed with this conclusion, however—particularly those presidents who have skillfully blended these two roles with their role as a politician. Being head of state gives the president tremendous public exposure, which can be an important asset in a campaign for reelection. When that exposure is positive, it helps the president deal with Congress over proposed legislation and increases the chances of being reelected—or getting the candidates of the president's party elected.

George Skadding/Getty Images

Image 12–4 American president Harry Truman (1945–1953), right, stands with General Dwight Eisenhower in 1951. A year later, Eisenhower successfully ran for president. *Why might a general make a good president?*

Chief Executive

According to the Constitution, "The executive Power shall be vested in a President of the United States of America. . . . [H]e may require the Opinion, in writing, of the principal Officer in each of the executive Departments, upon any Subject relating to the Duties of their respective Offices . . . and he shall nominate, and by and with the Advice and Consent of the Senate, shall appoint . . . Officers of the

chief executive

The role of the president as head of the executive branch of the government.

civil service

A collective term for the body of employees working for the government. Generally, "civil service" is understood to apply to all those who gain government employment through a merit system.

appointment power

The authority vested in the president to fill a government office or position. Positions filled by presidential appointment include those in the executive branch and the federal judiciary, commissioned officers in the armed forces, and members of the independent regulatory commissions.

United States. . . . [H]e shall take Care that the Laws be faithfully executed." As **chief executive,** the president is constitutionally bound to enforce the acts of Congress, the judgments of federal courts, and treaties signed by the United States.

The Powers of Appointment and Removal. To assist in the various tasks of the chief executive, the president has a federal bureaucracy that currently consists of 2.0 million federal civilian employees, not counting the U.S. Postal Service (493,000 employees). You might think that the president, as head of the largest bureaucracy in the United States, wields enormous power. The president, however, only nominally runs the executive bureaucracy. Most government positions are filled by **civil service** employees, who generally gain government employment through a merit system rather than presidential appointment. Therefore, even though the president has important **appointment power,** it is limited to cabinet and subcabinet jobs, federal judgeships, agency heads, and several thousand lesser jobs—about eight thousand positions in total.

This means that most of the 2.5 million employees of the executive branch (USPS included) owe no political allegiance to the president. They are more likely to owe loyalty to congressional committees or to interest groups representing the sector of the society that they serve. Table 12–1 shows what percentage of the total employment in each executive department is available for political appointment by the president.

Table 12–1 Total Civilian Positions in Cabinet Departments Available for Political Appointment by the President

Why might the State Department have a large number of political appointees?

Executive Department	Total Number of Employees	Political Appointments Available	Percentage
Agriculture	86,525	363	0.42
Commerce	45,308	284	0.63
Defense	731,152	598	0.08
Education	4,244	207	4.88
Energy	15,040	558	3.71
Health and Human Services	85,974	536	0.62
Homeland Security	188,844	304	0.16
Housing and Urban Development	8,063	177	2.20
Interior	62,893	302	0.48
Justice	115,424	485	0.42
Labor	15,720	189	1.20
State	12,890	557	4.32
Transportation	54,697	264	0.48
Treasury	100,425	235	0.23
Veterans Affairs	368,109	447	0.12

Sources: *Policy and Supporting Positions* (Washington, D.C.: Government Printing Office, 2012). This text, known as the "Plum Book," is published after each presidential election. Also, U.S. Office of Personnel Management. Figures are for March 2016.

The president's power to remove from office those officials who are not doing a good job or who do not agree with the president is not explicitly granted by the Constitution and has been limited. In 1926, however, a Supreme Court decision prevented Congress from interfering with the president's ability to fire those executive-branch officials whom the president had appointed with Senate approval.[2] There are ten agencies whose directors the president can remove at any time. These agencies include the Commission on Civil Rights, the Environmental Protection Agency, the General Services Administration, and the Small Business Administration. In addition, the president can remove all heads of cabinet departments, all individuals in the Executive Office of the President, and all of the political appointees listed in Table 12–1.

Harry Truman spoke candidly of the difficulties a president faces in trying to control the executive bureaucracy. On leaving office, he referred to the problems that Dwight Eisenhower, as a former general of the army, was going to have: "He'll sit here and he'll say do this! do that! and nothing will happen. Poor Ike—it won't be a bit like the Army. He'll find it very frustrating."[3]

Image 12–5 President Obama and Hillary Clinton wave to the crowd as they campaign in Charlotte, North Carolina. *When Clinton was secretary of state, what was her relationship with the president?*

The Power to Grant Reprieves and Pardons. Section 2 of Article II of the Constitution gives the president the power to grant **reprieves** and **pardons** for offenses against the United States except in cases of impeachment. All pardons are administered by the Office of the Pardon Attorney in the Department of Justice.

The Supreme Court upheld the president's power to grant reprieves and pardons in a 1925 case concerning a pardon granted by the president to an individual convicted of contempt of court. A federal circuit court had contended that only judges had the authority to convict individuals for contempt of court when court orders were violated and that the courts should be free from interference by the executive branch. The Supreme Court simply stated that the president could grant reprieves or pardons for all offenses "either before trial, during trial, or after trial, by individuals, or by classes, conditionally or absolutely, and this without modification or regulation by Congress."[4]

President Andrew Johnson set the record for the largest number of persons ever pardoned in 1868 when he issued a blanket amnesty to all former Confederate soldiers. In 1974, in a controversial decision, President Gerald Ford pardoned former president Richard Nixon for his role in the Watergate affair before any charges were brought in court. In 1977, President Jimmy Carter issued a blanket pardon to Vietnam War–era draft resisters, a group that probably included more than 100,000 persons.

Commander in Chief

The president, according to the Constitution, "shall be Commander in Chief of the Army and Navy of the United States, and of the Militia of the several States, when called into the

reprieve

A formal postponement of the execution of a sentence imposed by a court of law.

pardon

A release from the punishment for, or legal consequences of, a crime. A pardon can be granted by the president before or after a conviction.

---

2. *Meyers v. United States,* 272 U.S. 52 (1926).

3. Quoted in Richard E. Neustadt, *Presidential Power: The Politics of Leadership* (New York: Wiley, 1960), p. 9. Note that Truman may not have considered the amount of politics involved in decision making in the upper ranks of the army.

4. *Ex parte Grossman,* 267 U.S. 87 (1925).

actual Service of the United States." In other words, the armed forces are under civilian, rather than military, control.

Wartime Powers. Those who wrote the Constitution had George Washington in mind when they made the president the **commander in chief.** Although we do not expect our president to lead the troops into battle, presidents as commanders in chief have wielded dramatic power. Harry Truman made the fateful decision to drop atomic bombs on Hiroshima and Nagasaki in 1945 with the goal of forcing Japan to surrender and thus bring World War II to an end. Lyndon Johnson ordered bombing missions against North Vietnam in the 1960s, and he personally selected some of the targets. Richard Nixon decided to invade Cambodia in 1970. Ronald Reagan sent troops to Lebanon and Grenada in 1983 and ordered U.S. fighter planes to attack Libya in 1986. George H. W. Bush sent troops to Panama in 1989 and to the Middle East in 1990. Bill Clinton sent troops to Haiti in 1994 and to Bosnia in 1995, ordered missile attacks on alleged terrorist bases in 1998, and sent American planes to bomb Serbia in 1999. George W. Bush ordered the invasion of Afghanistan in 2001 and of Iraq in 2003, and most recently, Barack Obama ordered additional troops into Afghanistan in 2009 and authorized air strikes in Libya in 2011.

The president is the ultimate decision maker in military matters. Everywhere the president goes, so too goes the "football"—a briefcase filled with all of the codes necessary to order a nuclear attack. Only the president has the power to order the use of nuclear force.

As commander in chief, the president exercises more authority than in any other role. Constitutionally, Congress has the sole power to declare war, but the president can send the armed forces into situations that are certainly the equivalent of war. Harry Truman dispatched troops to Korea in 1950. Johnson and Nixon waged an undeclared war in Southeast Asia, where more than 58,000 Americans were killed and 300,000 were wounded. In neither of these situations had Congress declared war. Should the new president take additional military actions against ISIS? We discuss that question in this chapter's *Which Side Are You On?* feature.

Power over the National Guard. One of the president's powers as commander in chief is the right to assume authority over National Guard units—that is, state militias. Throughout American history, presidents have "nationalized" the Guard to handle domestic problems such as natural disasters or severe social disturbances, including strikes or urban riots. President George W. Bush sent 6,000 members of the National Guard to the Mexican border in 2006–2008 to assist the Border Patrol, and in 2010 President Obama sent 1,200 Guard troops to the border for the same purpose.

The president also has the ability to send National Guard units abroad to supplement the regular armed forces. Both Bush and Obama sent Guard forces abroad on a massive scale. In 2005, National Guard troops comprised a larger percentage of frontline fighting forces than in any war in U.S. history—about 43 percent in Iraq and 55 percent in Afghanistan. Since then, the number of National Guard troops sent abroad has declined substantially.

commander in chief

The role of the president as supreme commander of the military forces of the United States and of the state National Guard units when they are called into federal service.

War Powers Resolution

A law passed in 1973 spelling out the conditions under which the president can commit troops without congressional approval.

The War Powers Resolution. In an attempt to gain more control over such military activities, in 1973 Congress passed the **War Powers Resolution**—over President Nixon's veto—requiring that the president consult with Congress when sending American forces into action. Once they are sent, the president must report to Congress within forty-eight hours. Unless Congress approves the use of troops within sixty days or extends the sixty-day time limit, the forces must be withdrawn.

In spite of the War Powers Resolution, the effective powers of the president as commander in chief are more extensive today than they were in the past. The so-called war on

Which side are you on?

Should the New President Do More to Fight ISIS?

Compared with other presidents, Barack Obama was somewhat reluctant to commit the United States military to foreign interventions. That does not mean that America was at peace in the Obama years. U.S. troops continued to fight in Afghanistan. Obama employed U.S. air power in Iraq, Libya, and Syria. Military drones took out terrorist targets in Pakistan, Yemen, and elsewhere. Still, Obama won the 2008 Democratic presidential primaries in part because he opposed George W. Bush's war in Iraq. His opponent, Hillary Clinton, supported that war. As secretary of state, Clinton advocated hawkish positions within the Obama administration, while Vice President Joe Biden spoke up for the doves. From his campaign rhetoric, Trump might be more of a hawk than President Obama. But how much of a hawk? Are there steps that we should take to counteract ISIS beyond those that Obama has already taken?

ISIS Must Be Destroyed

Hawks say that whether it is called ISIS, ISIL, the Islamic State, or by the Arabic term Daesh, we are confronting a group that is a major threat to world peace. ISIS has tried to carve out a new country uniting Iraq and Syria. It terrorizes the populations under its control. Women who belong to the wrong religion or even the wrong Islamic denomination are enslaved. ISIS propagates a world view of unprecedented viciousness. It delights in posting videos in which its soldiers chop off the heads of Christians and other "infidels." It has begun sponsoring major terrorist attacks in Western nations.

Destroying ISIS does not necessarily mean deploying U.S. infantry, the famous "boots on the ground." It could mean more air strikes and less worry about civilian deaths. We could introduce more U.S. special forces to train ISIS opponents and help identify targets for air power. We could set up a "no-fly zone" in which Syrian civilians can find protection both from ISIS and from the vicious regime of the dictator Bashar al Assad.

This Is Not Our Fight

Those who oppose additional military action ask why we should take responsibility for what happens in Syria—or for that matter Iraq. The troubles in Syria, where almost half a million people have died and millions have been driven from their homes, have led to massive refugee flows into Turkey and Europe. If Syria needs straightening out, why should the United States do it—and not these other countries? To be sure, our armed forces are powerful enough that we could quickly take over all ISIS-held territory. We would then be foreign occupiers, hated by every Syrian patriot. We don't need that.

Furthermore, current policies are showing signs of success. ISIS has lost territory in both Syria and Iraq, and it will lose more. Its finances have been cut in half. The terrorist attacks ISIS organized in Paris, Brussels, Baghdad, and Ankara, Turkey—and the ones it inspired in San Bernardino, Orlando, and Nice—are signs of weakness. ISIS is reverting to terrorism because it cannot hold real estate. Sooner or later, ISIS will fall.

For Critical Analysis

▷ Should we cooperate with Syrian dictator Bashar al Assad against ISIS? Why or why not?

---

terror, which began after the terrorist attacks of September 11, 2001, led to an especially notable increase in presidential powers.

Chief Diplomat

The Constitution gives the president the power to recognize foreign governments and to make treaties with the **advice and consent** of the Senate. The president also nominates U.S. ambassadors to other countries. As **chief diplomat,** the president dominates American foreign policy, a role that has been supported many times by the Supreme Court.

advice and consent
Terms in the Constitution describing the U.S. Senate's power to review and approve treaties and presidential appointments.

chief diplomat
The role of the president in recognizing foreign governments, making treaties, and effecting executive agreements.

Image 12–6 President George H. W. Bush (1989–1993) is the father of President George W. Bush (2001–2009). Here, he is shown meeting with the foreign minister of Saudi Arabia. *Why would a president spend time in such a meeting?*

Diplomatic Recognition.
An important power of the president as chief diplomat is that of **diplomatic recognition,** or the power to recognize—or to refuse to recognize—foreign governments as legitimate. In the role of ceremonial head of state, the president has always received foreign diplomats. In modern times, the simple act of receiving a foreign diplomat has been equivalent to accrediting the diplomat and officially recognizing his or her government. Such recognition of the legitimacy of another country's government is a prerequisite to diplomatic relations or treaties between that country and the United States.

Deciding when to recognize a foreign power is not always simple. The United States, for example, did not recognize the Soviet Union until 1933—sixteen years after the Russian Revolution of 1917. It was only after all attempts to reverse the effects of that revolution—including military invasion of Russia and diplomatic isolation—had proved futile that Franklin D. Roosevelt extended recognition to the Soviet government. In December 1978, long after the Communist victory in China in 1949, President Jimmy Carter granted official recognition to the People's Republic of China.[5]

Proposal and Ratification of Treaties.
The president has the sole power to negotiate treaties with other nations. These treaties must be presented to the Senate. A two-thirds vote is required in the Senate for approval, or *ratification.* After ratification, the president can approve the treaty as adopted by the Senate. Approval poses a problem when the Senate has tacked on substantive amendments or reservations to a treaty, particularly when such changes may require reopening negotiations with the other signatory governments. Sometimes, a president may decide to withdraw a treaty if the senatorial changes are too extensive—as Woodrow Wilson did with the Versailles Treaty in 1919, which concluded World War I. Wilson believed that the senatorial reservations would weaken the treaty so much that it would be ineffective.

Ratifying a treaty may be a difficult process, but revoking a treaty appears to be easier. The Constitution says nothing about how a treaty can be terminated, and on at least two occasions presidents have revoked treaties unilaterally, without the approval of Congress. One of these terminations was challenged by a lawsuit. Ultimately, the Supreme Court refused to overrule the president's decision.[6]

Executive Agreements.
Presidential power in foreign affairs is enhanced greatly by the use of **executive agreements** made between the president and other heads of state. Such agreements do not require Senate approval, although the House and the Senate

diplomatic recognition

The formal acknowledgment of a foreign government as legitimate.

executive agreement

An international agreement made by the president, without senatorial ratification, with the head of a foreign state.

5. The Nixon administration first encouraged new relations with the People's Republic of China by allowing a cultural exchange of table tennis teams.

6. *Goldwater v. Carter,* 444 U.S. 996 (1979).

may refuse to appropriate the funds necessary to implement them. Whereas treaties are normally binding on succeeding administrations, executive agreements require each new president's consent to remain in effect.

Among the advantages of executive agreements are speed and secrecy. The former is essential during a crisis. The latter is important when the administration fears that open senatorial debate may be detrimental to the best interests of the United States or to the interests of the president.[7] There have been far more executive agreements (about nine thousand) than treaties (about thirteen hundred). Many executive agreements contain secret provisions calling for American military assistance or other support.

The Constitution makes no mention—explicit or implicit—of executive agreements. The Supreme Court, however, has given executive agreements the same legal weight as formal treaties.[8] This conclusion follows from earlier cases in which the Court found the president's powers in the international realm to be "plenary and exclusive." Executive agreements are clearly an attractive way for a president to bypass Congress when making foreign policy. President Obama used an executive agreement when endorsing the nuclear arms deal with Iran and five other world powers in 2015. Some have argued, however, that even if the president can bypass Congress, doing so is not good practice.

Chief Legislator

Constitutionally, presidents must recommend to Congress legislation that they judge necessary and expedient. Not all presidents have wielded their powers as **chief legislator** in the same manner. Some presidents have been almost completely unsuccessful in getting their legislative programs implemented by Congress. Presidents Franklin Roosevelt (1933–1945) and Lyndon Johnson (1963–1969), however, saw much of their proposed legislation put into effect.

Creating the Congressional Agenda. In modern times, the president has played a dominant role in creating the congressional agenda. In the president's annual **State of the Union message,** which is required by the Constitution (Article II, Section 3) and is usually given in late January shortly after Congress reconvenes, the president presents a legislative program. The message gives a broad, comprehensive view of what the president wishes the legislature to accomplish during its session. It is as much a message to the American people and to the world as it is to Congress. Its impact on public opinion can determine the way in which Congress responds to the president's agenda.

Since 1913, the president has delivered the State of the Union message in a formal address to Congress. Today, this address is one of the great ceremonies of American governance, and many customs have grown up around it. For example, one cabinet member, the "designated survivor," stays away to ensure that the country will always have a president, even if someone manages to blow up the Capitol building. Everyone gives the president an initial standing ovation out of respect for the office, but this applause does not necessarily represent support for the individual who holds the office. During the speech, senators and House members either applaud or remain silent to indicate their opinion of the policies that the president announces.

Getting Legislation Passed. The president can propose legislation, but Congress is not required to pass—or even introduce—any of the administration's bills. How, then, does the president get those proposals made into law? One way is by exercising the power of persuasion. The president writes to, telephones, and meets with various congressional

chief legislator
The role of the president in influencing the making of laws.

State of the Union message
An annual message to Congress in which the president proposes a legislative program. The message is addressed not only to Congress but also to the American people and to the world.

---

7. The Case Act of 1972 requires that all executive agreements be transmitted to Congress within sixty days after the agreement takes effect. Secret agreements are transmitted to the foreign relations committees as classified information.

8. *United States v. Belmont*, 301 U.S. 324 (1937) and *United States v. Pink*, 315 U. S. 203 (1942).

veto message

The president's formal explanation of
a veto when legislation is returned to
Congress.

pocket veto

A special veto exercised by the chief executive after a legislative body has adjourned.
Bills not signed by the chief executive die
after a specified period of time. If Congress
wishes to reconsider such a bill, it must be
reintroduced in the following session of
Congress.

leaders. He or she makes public announcements to influence public opinion. Finally, as head of a party, the president exercises leadership over the party's members in Congress. A president whose party holds a majority in both chambers of Congress usually has an easier time getting legislation passed than does a president who faces a hostile Congress.

Saying No to Legislation. The president has the power to say no to legislation through use of the veto,[9] by which the White House returns a bill unsigned to Congress with a **veto message** attached. Because the Constitution requires that every bill passed by the House and the Senate be sent to the president before it becomes law, the president must act on each bill:

1. If the bill is signed, it becomes law.
2. If the bill is not sent back to Congress after ten congressional working days, it becomes law without the president's signature.
3. The president can reject the bill and send it back to Congress with a veto message setting forth objections. Congress then can change the bill, hoping to secure presidential approval, and repass it. Or Congress can simply reject the president's objections by overriding the veto with a two-thirds roll-call vote of the members present in both the House and the Senate.
4. If the president refuses to sign the bill and Congress adjourns within ten working days after the bill has been submitted to the president, the bill is killed for that session of Congress. This is called a **pocket veto.** If Congress wishes the bill to be reconsidered, the bill must be reintroduced during the following session.

Presidents employed the veto power infrequently until after the Civil War, but it has been used with increasing vigor since then (see Table 12–2). The total number of vetoes from George Washington's administration through the end of Barack Obama's administration was 2,572, with about two-thirds of those vetoes being exercised by Grover Cleveland, Franklin Roosevelt, Harry Truman, and Dwight Eisenhower.

George W. Bush was the first president since Martin Van Buren (1837–1841) to serve a full term in office without exercising the veto power. Bush, who had the benefit of a Republican Congress, did not veto any legislation during his first term. Only in the summer of 2006 did Bush finally issue a veto, saying "no" to stem-cell research legislation passed by Congress. After the Democrats took control of Congress in January 2007, however, the president issued eleven vetoes, plus an additional four that were overridden. President Obama, who for two years also enjoyed a Congress dominated by his own party, issued a similar number of vetoes while in office.

Congress's Power to Override Presidential Vetoes. A veto is a clear-cut indication of the president's dissatisfaction with congressional legislation. Congress, however, can override a presidential veto, although it rarely exercises this power. Consider that two-thirds of the members of each chamber who are present must vote to override the president's veto in a roll-call vote. This means that if only one-third plus one of the members voting in one of the chambers of Congress do not agree to override the veto, the veto holds. In American history, only about 4 percent of all vetoes have been overridden.

Image 12–7 President George W. Bush (2001–2009) gives a State of the Union address while Vice President Dick Cheney and Speaker of the House Nancy Pelosi listen. *Where is that address given?*

Charles Dharapak/AP Images

---

9. *Veto* in Latin means "I forbid."

Table 12–2 Presidential Vetoes, 1789 to Present

If the president and Congress are of different parties, what effect might that have on the number of presidential vetoes?

Years	President	Regular Vetoes	Vetoes Overridden	Pocket Vetoes	Total Vetoes
1789–1797	Washington	2	0	0	2
1797–1801	J. Adams	0	0	0	0
1801–1809	Jefferson	0	0	0	0
1809–1817	Madison	5	0	2	7
1817–1825	Monroe	1	0	0	1
1825–1829	J. Q. Adams	0	0	0	0
1829–1837	Jackson	5	0	7	12
1837–1841	Van Buren	0	0	1	1
1841–1841	Harrison	0	0	0	0
1841–1845	Tyler	6	1	4	10
1845–1849	Polk	2	0	1	3
1849–1850	Taylor	0	0	0	0
1850–1853	Fillmore	0	0	0	0
1853–1857	Pierce	9	5	0	9
1857–1861	Buchanan	4	0	3	7
1861–1865	Lincoln	2	0	5	7
1865–1869	A. Johnson	21	15	8	29
1869–1877	Grant	45	4	48	93
1877–1881	Hayes	12	1	1	13
1881–1881	Garfield	0	0	0	0
1881–1885	Arthur	4	1	8	12
1885–1889	Cleveland	304	2	110	414
1889–1893	Harrison	19	1	25	44
1893–1897	Cleveland	42	5	128	170
1897–1901	McKinley	6	0	36	42
1901–1909	T. Roosevelt	42	1	40	82
1909–1913	Taft	30	1	9	39
1913–1921	Wilson	33	6	11	44
1921–1923	Harding	5	0	1	6
1923–1929	Coolidge	20	4	30	50
1929–1933	Hoover	21	3	16	37
1933–1945	F. Roosevelt	372	9	263	635
1945–1953	Truman	180	12	70	250
1953–1961	Eisenhower	73	2	108	181
1961–1963	Kennedy	12	0	9	21
1963–1969	L. Johnson	16	0	14	30
1969–1974	Nixon	26*	7	17	43
1974–1977	Ford	48	12	18	66
1977–1981	Carter	13	2	18	31
1981–1989	Reagan	39	9	39	78
1989–1993	G. H. W. Bush	29	1	15	44
1993–2001	W. Clinton	36†	2	1	37
2001–2009	G. W. Bush	12	4	0	12
2009–2017	Obama	10	1	0	10
TOTAL		1,506	111	1,066	2,572

*Two pocket vetoes by President Nixon, overruled in the courts, are counted here as regular vetoes.
†President Clinton's line-item vetoes are not included.
Sources: United States Senate.

The President as Party Chief and Superpolitician

Presidents are by no means above political partisanship, and one of their many roles is that of chief of party. Although the Constitution says nothing about the function of the president within a political party (the mere concept of political parties was abhorrent to most of the authors of the Constitution), today presidents are the actual leaders of their parties.

The President as Chief of Party. As party leader, the president chooses the national committee chairperson and can try to discipline party members who fail to support presidential policies. One way of exerting political power within the party is through **patronage**—rewarding the faithful by appointing them to government or public jobs. This power was more extensive in the past, before the establishment of the civil service in 1883, but the president still retains important patronage power. As we noted earlier, the president can appoint several thousand individuals to jobs in the cabinet, the White House, and the federal regulatory agencies.

Perhaps the most important partisan role that the president has played in the 1990s and 2000s has been that of fund-raiser. The president is able to raise large sums for the party through appearances at dinners, speaking engagements, and other social occasions. President Clinton may have raised more than half a billion dollars for the Democratic Party during his two terms. President George W. Bush was even more successful than Clinton. Barack Obama's spectacular success in raising funds for his presidential campaigns (particularly via the Internet) indicates that he carried on this fund-raising tradition.

Presidents have a number of other ways of exerting influence as party chief. The president may make it known that a particular congressperson's choice for federal judge will not be appointed unless that member of Congress is more supportive of the president's legislative program. The president may agree to campaign for a particular program or for a particular candidate. Presidents also reward loyal members of Congress with support for the funding of local projects, tax breaks for regional industries, and other forms of "pork."

Presidential Constituencies. Presidents have many constituencies. In principle, they are beholden to the entire electorate—the public of the United States—even those who did not vote. Presidents are certainly beholden to their party, because its members helped to put them in office. The president's constituencies also include members of the opposing party whose cooperation the president needs. Finally, the president must take into consideration a constituency that has come to be called the *Washington community* (also known as those "inside the beltway").[10] This community consists of individuals who—whether in or out of political office—are intimately familiar with the workings of government, thrive on gossip, and measure on a daily basis the political power of the president.

Public Approval. All of these constituencies are impressed by presidents who maintain a high level of public approval, partly because doing so is very difficult to accomplish. Presidential popularity, as measured by national polls, gives the president an extra political resource to use in persuading legislators to pass legislation. A president who

---

Why should you care about **THE PRESIDENCY?**

The president can influence many issues that directly affect your life. For example, in recent years, many people have raised the question of whether anything could be done soon about reforming the nation's immigration policies. To succeed, any change to immigration policies would need strong support from the president. Immigration might be a topic on which you have strong opinions. If you have opinions on a subject such as this, you may well want to "cast your vote" by adding your e-mail to the many others that the president receives on the issue.

---

patronage

The practice of rewarding faithful party workers and followers with government employment and contracts.

---

10. The *beltway* refers to Interstate 495, which circles the capital, passing through Maryland and Virginia suburbs.

suffers a dramatic loss of popularity will have trouble getting legislation through Congress. In such circumstances, a president can even fail to be reelected. That was the fate of President Jimmy Carter (1977–1981), who lost to Ronald Reagan after a disastrous collapse in popular support.

As you can see from Figure 12–1, President George W. Bush enjoyed spectacularly high approval ratings immediately after the terrorist attacks of 9/11. Bush's popularity declined steadily after 9/11. Obama's popularity figures were also high right when he took office. Some of that initial popularity came from Republicans, however, and could not survive the partisan battles that began in 2009. Thereafter, Obama's job approval ratings fluctuated, usually falling between 40 and 50 percent. He was more popular than that toward the end of his presidency, however.

"Going Public." Since the early 1900s, presidents have spoken more to the public and less to Congress. In the 1800s, only 7 percent of presidential speeches were addressed to the public. Since 1900, 50 percent have been addressed to the public. Presidents frequently go over the heads of Congress and the political elites, taking their cases directly to the people.

This strategy, dubbed "going public," gives the president additional power through the ability to persuade and manipulate public opinion. By identifying their own positions so clearly, presidents can weaken the legislators' positions. In times when the major political parties are highly polarized, however, the possibility of compromise with the opposition party may actually be reduced if the president openly takes a strong position. If the opposition party dominates Congress, it may argue that its democratic legitimacy trumps that of the president. We examine this issue in the *Beyond Our Borders* feature.

Image 12–8 President Jimmy Carter addresses a town hall meeting. Carter lost resoundingly to Republican Ronald Reagan in 1980. *For what reasons can a sitting president lose popularity?*

Figure 12–1 Public Popularity of Modern Presidents

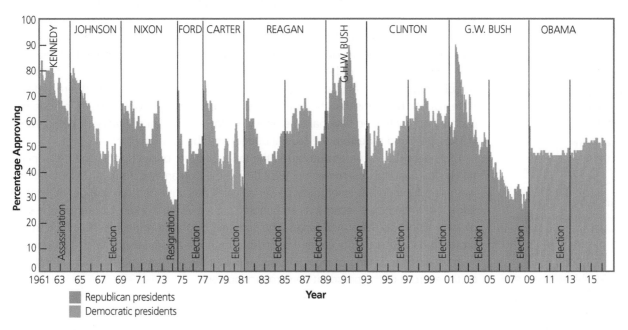

- Republican presidents
- Democratic presidents

Sources: Adapted from the Roper Center for Public Opinion Research: Gallup and *USA Today*/CNN polls, March 1992 through July 2016.

Learning Outcome **3:**

Describe some of the special powers of the president, and tell how a president can be removed from office.

Presidential Powers

Presidents have at their disposal a variety of special powers and privileges not available in the other branches of the U.S. government. The powers of the president discussed earlier in this chapter in the section on the roles of the president are called **constitutional powers,** because their basis lies in the Constitution. In addition, Congress has established by law, or statute, numerous other presidential powers—such as the ability to declare national emergencies. These are called **statutory powers.** Both constitutional and statutory powers have been labeled the **expressed powers** of the president, because they are expressly written into the Constitution or into law.

Presidents also have what have come to be known as **inherent powers.** These depend on the statements in the Constitution that "the executive Power shall be vested in a President" and that the president should "take Care that the Laws be faithfully executed." The most common example of inherent powers is those emergency powers invoked by a president during wartime. Franklin Roosevelt, for example, used his inherent powers to move Japanese Americans living on the West Coast into internment camps for the duration of World War II. President George W. Bush often justified expanding the powers of his presidency by saying that such powers were necessary to fight the war on terrorism.

Emergency Powers

If you were to read the Constitution, you would find no mention of the additional powers that the executive office may exercise during national emergencies. Indeed, the Supreme Court has stated that an "emergency does not create power."[11] But it is clear that presidents have made strong use of their inherent powers during times of emergency, particularly in the realm of foreign affairs. The **emergency powers** of the president were first enunciated in the Supreme Court's decision in *United States v. Curtiss-Wright Export Corp.*[12] In that case, President Franklin Roosevelt, without authorization by Congress, ordered an embargo on the shipment of weapons to two warring South American countries. The Court recognized that the president may exercise inherent powers in foreign affairs and that the national government has primacy in these affairs.

Examples of emergency powers are abundant, coinciding with crises in domestic and foreign affairs. Abraham Lincoln suspended civil liberties at the beginning of the Civil War (1861–1865) and called the state militias into national service. These actions and his subsequent governance of conquered areas—and even of areas of northern states—were justified by claims that they were essential to preserve the Union. Franklin Roosevelt declared an "unlimited national emergency" following the fall of France in World War II (1939–1945) and mobilized the federal budget and the economy for war.

President Harry Truman authorized the federal seizure of steel plants and their operation by the national government in 1952 during the Korean War. Truman claimed that he was using his inherent emergency power as chief executive and commander in chief to safeguard the nation's security, as an ongoing strike by steelworkers threatened the supply of weapons to the armed forces. The Supreme Court did not agree, holding that the president had no authority under the Constitution to seize private property or to legislate such action.[13] According to legal scholars, this was the first time a limit had been placed on the exercise of the president's emergency powers.

constitutional power
A power vested in the president by Article II of the Constitution.

statutory power
A power created for the president through laws enacted by Congress.

expressed power
A power of the president that is expressly written into the Constitution or into statutory law.

inherent power
A power of the president derived from the statements in the Constitution that "the executive Power shall be vested in a President" and that the president should "take Care that the Laws be faithfully executed"; defined through practice rather than through law.

emergency power
An inherent power exercised by the president during a period of national crisis.

11. *Home Building and Loan Association v. Blaisdell,* 290 U.S. 398 (1934).
12. 299 U.S. 304 (1936).
13. *Youngstown Sheet and Tube Co. v. Sawyer,* 343 U.S. 579 (1952).

Beyond our borders

Presidents in Latin America

You learned in Chapter 2 about the parliamentary system, a form of democratic government that is an alternative to our system. Many countries, however, do have systems much like ours, in which the president and congress are elected separately. Most countries in Latin America have presidential systems. One characteristic of a presidential system is that both the president and the congress can claim democratic legitimacy. Both, after all, were elected by the people.

President versus Congress in Latin America

A presidential system would seem to call for compromise between the president and congress. That, however, does not always happen. In 2009 in Honduras, the military, acting for the supreme court and congress, seized the president and flew him into exile. In 2012 in Paraguay, a congress dominated by conservatives impeached and convicted a liberal president on purely political grounds. Paraguay's neighbors treated this act as a coup d'état. In contrast, presidents in Argentina and Venezuela have dominated their nations in ways that clearly threaten democracy.

Jose Antonio Cheibub, a political scientist, has calculated that the average parliamentary regime lasts 73 years—and the average presidential regime just 21 years. Political scientist Juan Linz has observed that "the only presidential democracy with a long history of constitutional continuity is the United States."

The U.S. Exception

The United States enjoys the longest-lived political system on earth (with the possible exception of Britain). The weight of constitutional tradition in this country is enormous. We will not end up like Paraguay or Venezuela. Yet there are worrying signs. Linz argued that the ideological diversity of U.S. political parties traditionally prevented formation of a congressional leadership that rejects the legitimacy of the president. But we don't have parties like that anymore. Our parties are now ideologically unified.

In recent crises, Republicans in the House have argued that they, not the president, represent the will of the American people. Meanwhile, on issues such as bombing Libya, immigration, and controlling carbon dioxide emissions by power plants, Obama has sought to act unilaterally. A congress that harasses the executive, and a president who engages in unilateral action whenever he or she can get away with it—in the future, these may be common themes of U.S. politics.

For Critical Analysis

◗ **Some people argue that it is a good thing when Congress and the president keep each other in check. When might this checking be an advantage, and when might it be a disadvantage?**

Executive Orders

Congress allows the president (as well as administrative agencies) to issue *executive orders* that have the force of law. These executive orders can do the following: (1) enforce legislative statutes, (2) enforce the Constitution or treaties with foreign nations, and (3) establish or modify rules and practices of executive administrative agencies.

An executive order, then, represents the president's legislative power. The only apparent requirement is that under the Administrative Procedure Act of 1946, all executive orders must be published in the **Federal Register,** a daily publication of the U.S. government. Executive orders have been used to implement national affirmative action regulations, to restructure the White House bureaucracy, and, under emergency conditions, to ration consumer goods and to administer wage and price controls. They have also been used to classify government information as secret, to regulate the export of restricted items, and to establish military tribunals for suspected terrorists.

President George W. Bush made use of such orders in executing the war on terrorism, and more generally in expanding presidential powers. President Obama's executive orders have

Federal Register

A publication of the U.S. government that prints executive orders, rules, and regulations.

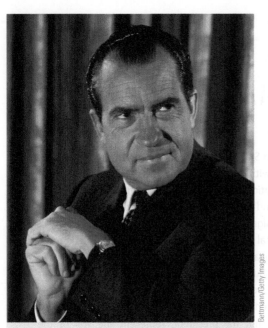

Image 12–9 President Richard Nixon (1969–1974). Nixon resigned on August 9, 1974, as a result of the Watergate scandal. *What happened to Nixon's attempt to defend himself by invoking executive privilege?*

covered such matters as raising the fuel efficiency standards of cars and trucks, permitting federal grants to international organizations that support abortion, and lifting restrictions on the federal funding of embryonic stem-cell research.

Executive Memorandums. An innovation during the Obama administration has been the issuance of *executive memorandums.* Obama has written more of these than any president in history. Memorandums and orders are effectively indistinguishable. Taking executive orders and memorandums together, Obama has issued more such statements than other recent presidents, but not by a large margin.

Obama's Orders on Unauthorized Immigrants. Regardless of the number, Republicans have argued strongly that Obama's executive actions exceeded his constitutional authority. It is possible that the courts may agree. In 2014, Obama issued two orders that would have protected more than 4 million unauthorized immigrants from deportation. The orders were blocked by a U.S. appeals court in 2015, and in 2016 the Supreme Court, on a four-to-four vote, failed to lift the blockage.[14]

Executive Privilege

Another inherent executive power that has been claimed by presidents concerns the right of the president and the president's executive officials to withhold information from or refuse to appear before Congress or the courts. This is called **executive privilege,** and it relies on the constitutional separation of powers for its basis.

Invoking Executive Privilege. Presidents have frequently invoked executive privilege to avoid having to disclose information to Congress about actions of the executive branch. Executive privilege rests on the assumption that a certain degree of secrecy is essential to national security. Critics of executive privilege believe that it can be used to shield from public scrutiny actions of the executive branch that should be open to Congress and to the American citizenry.

Limiting Executive Privilege. Limits to executive privilege went untested until the Watergate affair in the early 1970s. Five men had broken into the headquarters of the Democratic National Committee and were caught searching for documents that might damage the candidacy of the Democratic nominee, George McGovern. Later investigation showed that the break-in had been planned by members of Richard Nixon's campaign committee and that Nixon and his closest advisers had devised a strategy for impeding the investigation of the crime. After it became known that all conversations held in the Oval Office had been recorded on a secret system, Nixon was ordered to turn over the tapes to the special prosecutor in charge of the investigation.

Nixon refused to do so, claiming executive privilege. He argued that "no president could function if the private papers of his office, prepared by his personal staff, were open to public scrutiny." In 1974, in one of the Supreme Court's most famous cases, *United States v. Nixon,*[15] the justices unanimously ruled that Nixon had to hand over the tapes. The Court held that executive privilege could not be used to prevent evidence from being heard in criminal proceedings.

executive privilege
The right of executive officials to withhold information from or to refuse to appear before a legislative committee.

14. *United States v. Texas,* 579 U.S. ___ (2016).
15. 318 U.S. 683 (1974).

Signing Statements

Is the president allowed to refuse to enforce certain parts of legislation if he or she believes that they are unconstitutional? This question came to the forefront in recent years because of President George W. Bush's extensive use of signing statements. A **signing statement** is a written declaration that a president may make when signing a bill into law regarding the law's enforcement.

Presidents have been using such statements for decades, but President Bush used 161 statements to invalidate more than one thousand provisions of federal law. No president before Bush used signing statements to make such sweeping claims on behalf of presidential power. Earlier presidents often employed statements to serve notice that parts of bills might be unconstitutional, but they were just as likely to issue statements that were purely rhetorical. For example, statements might praise Congress and the measure it just passed—or denounce the opposition party. During his campaign, Barack Obama criticized Bush's use of signing statements. As president, Obama's statements were more in line with tradition. About half of his statements were entirely rhetorical.

Abuses of Executive Power and Impeachment

Presidents normally leave office either because their first term has expired and they have not sought (or won) reelection or because, having served two full terms, they are not allowed to be elected for a third term (owing to the Twenty-second Amendment, passed in 1951). Eight presidents have died in office. But there is still another way for a president to leave office—by **impeachment** and conviction. Articles I and II of the Constitution authorize the House and Senate to remove the president, the vice president, or other civil officers of the United States for committing "Treason, Bribery, or other high Crimes and Misdemeanors." According to the Constitution, the impeachment process begins in the House, which impeaches (accuses) the federal officer involved. If the House votes to impeach the officer, it draws up articles of impeachment and submits them to the Senate, which conducts the actual trial.

Why should you care about **THE PRESIDENCY?**

There may also be issues on which the president refuses to consider popular opinion. President George W. Bush refused to be swayed by the public about the war in Iraq, even after the voters turned Congress over to the Democrats, and President Obama did not consult opinion polls when pushing through health-care reform. The determination of these presidents should remind you of the importance of learning about presidential candidates and their positions on important issues, and then making sure to vote. Once a candidate is elected, it is possible that neither public opinion nor Congress will be able to alter presidential policies on certain issues.

Presidents Andrew Johnson and Richard Nixon. In the history of the United States, no president has ever actually been impeached and also convicted—and thus removed from office—by means of this process. President Andrew Johnson (1865–1869), who succeeded to the office after the assassination of Abraham Lincoln, was impeached by the House but acquitted by the Senate. More than a century later, the House Judiciary Committee approved articles of impeachment against President Richard Nixon for his involvement in the cover-up of the Watergate break-in of 1972. Informed by members of his own party that he had no hope of surviving the trial in the Senate, Nixon resigned on August 9, 1974, before the full House voted on the articles. Nixon is the only president to have resigned from office.

President Bill Clinton. The second president to be impeached by the House but not convicted by the Senate was President Bill Clinton. In September 1998, the Republican House approved two charges against Clinton: lying to a grand jury about his affair with White House intern Monica Lewinsky and obstruction of justice. The articles of impeachment were then sent to the Senate, which acquitted Clinton. The attempt to

signing statement

A written declaration that a president may make when signing a bill into law. Such statements may point out sections of the law that the president deems unconstitutional.

impeachment

An action by the House of Representatives to accuse the president, vice president, or other civil officers of the United States of committing "Treason, Bribery, or other high Crimes and Misdemeanors."

cabinet

An advisory group selected by the president to aid in making decisions. The cabinet includes the heads of fifteen executive departments and others named by the president.

kitchen cabinet

The informal advisers to the president.

remove Clinton was very unpopular, although the allegations against him did damage his popularity as well. Part of the problem for Clinton's Republican opponents was that the charges against the president essentially boiled down to his lying about sex. As one observer put it, "Everyone lies about sex." Of course, not everyone lies about sex when under oath.

The Executive Organization

Gone are the days when presidents answered their own mail, as George Washington did. It was not until 1857 that Congress authorized a private secretary for the president, to be paid by the federal government. Woodrow Wilson typed most of his correspondence, even though he did have several secretaries. At the beginning of Franklin Roosevelt's long tenure in the White House, the entire staff consisted of thirty-seven employees. With the New Deal and World War II, however, the presidential staff became a sizable organization.

The Cabinet

Although the Constitution does not include the word *cabinet,* it does state that the president "may require the Opinion, in writing, of the principal Officer in each of the executive Departments." Since the time of George Washington, these officers have formed an advisory group, or **cabinet,** to which the president turns for counsel.

Image 12–10 Bill Clinton (1993–2001) campaigns for the presidency in Cleveland, Ohio. *Why was Clinton not forced to leave office because of his impeachment?*

Joseph Sohm/Shutterstock.com

Members of the Cabinet. Originally, the cabinet consisted of only four officials—the secretaries of state, treasury, and war and the attorney general. Today, the cabinet numbers fourteen department secretaries and the attorney general. (See Table 12–1 for the names of the cabinet departments.)

The cabinet may include others as well. The president at his or her discretion can, for example, ascribe cabinet rank to the vice president, the head of the Office of Management and Budget, the national security adviser, and additional officials. Under President Barack Obama, the additional members of the cabinet were the following:

- The vice president.
- The White House chief of staff.
- The administrator of the Environmental Protection Agency.
- The director of the Office of Management and Budget.
- The U.S. trade representative.
- The U.S. ambassador to the United Nations.
- The chair of the Council of Economic Advisers.
- The administrator of the Small Business Administration.

Often, a president will use a **kitchen cabinet** to replace the formal cabinet as a major source of advice. The term *kitchen cabinet* originated during the presidency of Andrew Jackson, who relied on the counsel of close friends who allegedly met with him in the kitchen of the White House. A kitchen cabinet is a very informal group of advisers. Usually, they are friends with whom the president worked before being elected.

Image 12–11 Members of the national security team receive an update on the mission against Osama bin Laden in the Situation Room of the White House on May 1, 2011. Those present included Vice President Joe Biden (left), President Barack Obama (second left), Secretary of State Hillary Clinton (second right), and Secretary of Defense Robert Gates (right). *What happened to bin Laden?*

Presidential Use of Cabinets. Because neither the Constitution nor statutory law requires the president to consult with the cabinet, its use is purely discretionary. Some presidents have relied on the counsel of their cabinets more than others. Dwight Eisenhower was used to the team approach to solving problems from his experience as supreme allied commander during World War II, and therefore he frequently turned to his cabinet for advice on a wide range of issues. More often, presidents have solicited the opinions of their cabinets and then have done what they wanted to do anyway. Lincoln supposedly said—after a cabinet meeting in which a vote was seven nays against his one aye—"Seven nays and one aye, the ayes have it."

It is not surprising that presidents tend to disregard their cabinet members' advice. Often, the departmental heads are more responsive to the wishes of their own staffs or to their own political ambitions than they are to the president. They may be more concerned with obtaining resources for their departments than with achieving the goals of the president. So there is often a conflict of interest between presidents and their cabinet members.

The Executive Office of the President

When President Franklin Roosevelt appointed a special committee on administrative management, he knew that the committee would conclude that the president needed help. Indeed, the committee proposed a major reorganization of the executive branch. Congress did not approve the entire reorganization, but it did create the **Executive Office of the President (EOP)** to provide staff assistance for the chief executive and to help coordinate the executive bureaucracy. Since that time, a number of agencies have been created within the EOP to supply the president with advice and staff help. Presidents reorganize the EOP and the White House Office constantly, and any table of

Executive Office of the President (EOP)

An organization established by President Franklin Roosevelt to assist the president in carrying out major duties.

organization is therefore temporary. As of 2016, the EOP agencies under Barack Obama were the following:

- Council of Economic Advisers.
- Council on Environmental Quality.
- Executive Residence.
- National Security Council.
- Office of Administration.
- Office of Management and Budget.
- Office of National Drug Control Policy.
- Office of Science and Technology Policy.
- Office of the United States Trade Representative.
- Office of the Vice President.
- White House Office.

Many staff members within the EOP are assigned to specific policy areas, and the number of such individuals grew noticeably during Obama's administration. Popularly referred to as "czars," they included a cyber security czar, an urban affairs czar, and even an Asian carp czar, who coordinated efforts to keep Asian carp out of the Great Lakes. Unlike cabinet officers and many other top executive officials, czars are not subject to confirmation by the U.S. Senate. This exemption has been a source of controversy.

The White House Office. The **White House Office** includes most of the key personal and political advisers to the president. Among the jobs held by these aides are those of legal counsel to the president, secretary, press secretary, and appointments secretary. Often, the individuals who hold these positions are recruited from the president's campaign staff. Their duties—mainly protecting the president's political interests—are similar to campaign functions. In 2016, the White House Office was made up of the following units:

- Domestic Policy Council.
- National Security Adviser.
- National Economic Council.
- Office of Cabinet Affairs.
- Office of the Chief of Staff.
- Office of Communications.
- Office of Digital Strategy.
- Office of the First Lady.
- Office of Legislative Affairs.
- Office of Management and Administration.
- Oval Office Operations.
- Office of Presidential Personnel.
- Office of Public Engagement and Intergovernmental Affairs.
- Office of Scheduling and Advance.
- Office of the Staff Secretary.
- Office of the White House Counsel.

In all recent administrations, one member of the White House Office has been named **chief of staff.** This person, who is responsible for coordinating the office, is also one of the president's chief advisers.

The White House Military Office. In addition to civilian advisers, the president is supported by a large number of military personnel, who are organized under the White House Military Office. These members of the military provide communications, transportation, medical care, and food services to the president and the White House staff.

White House Staff Influence. White House staff members are closest to the president and may have considerable influence over the administration's decisions. Often, when presidents are under fire for their decisions, the staff is accused of keeping the chief executive too isolated from criticism or help. Presidents insist that they will not allow the staff to become too powerful, but, given the difficulty of the office, each president eventually turns to staff members for loyal assistance and protection.

White House Office

The personal office of the president, which tends to presidential political needs and manages the media.

chief of staff

The person who is named to direct the White House Office and advise the president.

The Office of Management and Budget. The **Office of Management and Budget (OMB)** was originally the Bureau of the Budget, which was created in 1921 within the Department of the Treasury. Recognizing the importance of this agency, Franklin Roosevelt moved it into the White House Office in 1939. Richard Nixon reorganized the Bureau of the Budget in 1970 and changed its name to reflect its new managerial function. It is headed by a director, who drafts the annual federal budget that the president presents to Congress each January for approval. In principle, the director of the OMB has broad fiscal powers in planning and estimating various parts of the federal budget, because all agencies must submit their proposed budget to the OMB for approval. In reality, it is not so clear that the OMB truly can affect the greater scope of the federal budget. The OMB may be more important as a clearinghouse for legislative proposals initiated in the executive agencies.

Image 12–12 *"Time to rake up the leaflets."*

The National Security Council. The **National Security Council (NSC)** is a link between the president's key foreign and military advisers and the president. Its members consist of the president, the vice president, and the secretaries of state and defense, plus other informal members. The NSC is managed by the president's assistant for national security affairs, also known as the national security adviser.

The Vice Presidency

Learning Outcome **5:**

Evaluate the role of the vice president, and describe what happens if the presidency becomes vacant.

The Constitution does not give much power to the vice president. The only formal duty is to preside over the Senate—which is rarely necessary. This obligation is fulfilled when the Senate organizes and adopts its rules and also when the vice president is needed to decide a tie vote. In all other cases, the president pro tem manages parliamentary procedures in the Senate. (The president pro tem is the longest-serving senator of the majority party.) The vice president is expected to participate only informally in senatorial deliberations, if at all.

The Vice President's Job

Vice presidents have traditionally been chosen by presidential nominees to balance the ticket by attracting groups of voters or appeasing party factions. If a presidential nominee is from the North, it is not a bad idea to have a vice-presidential nominee who is from the South. If the presidential nominee is from a rural state, perhaps someone with an urban background would be most suitable as a running mate. Presidential nominees who are strongly conservative or strongly liberal would do well to have vice-presidential nominees whose views lie more in the middle of the political road.

Strengthening the Ticket. In recent presidential elections, however, vice presidents have often been selected for other reasons. Barack Obama picked Joe Biden to be his running mate in 2008 and 2012 to add gravitas (seriousness) and foreign policy experience to the ticket. In 2012, Republican presidential candidate Mitt Romney chose Representative Paul Ryan of Wisconsin as his running mate. Ryan, the author of conservative House budget proposals, was greeted with enthusiasm by Republicans who were skeptical of Romney's right-wing credentials.

Office of Management and Budget (OMB)

A division of the Executive Office of the President. The OMB assists the president in preparing the annual budget, clearing and coordinating departmental agency budgets, and supervising the administration of the federal budget.

National Security Council (NSC)

An agency in the Executive Office of the President that advises the president on national security.

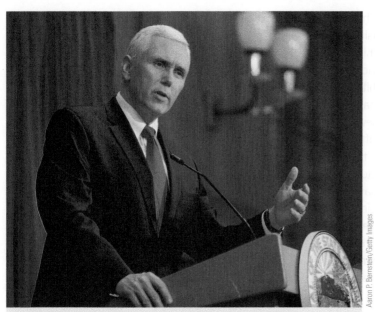

Image 12–13 Vice President Mike Pence when he was governor of Indiana. *What are the official duties of the vice president?*

Aaron P. Bernstein/Getty Images

In 2016, Republican candidate Donald Trump picked Indiana governor Mike Pence to be his running mate. Pence was a fairly conventional conservative Republican. By choosing him, Trump sought to rally Republicans who were uncomfortable with Trump's insurgent politics. For her part, Democrat Hillary Clinton selected Virginia senator Tim Kaine, a moderate from a vital swing state. Kaine is also fluent in Spanish. The apparent plan was that Kaine could help with independent voters, who were essential to Clinton's election.

Supporting the President. Traditionally, the job of the vice president has not been very demanding. In recent years, however, presidents have granted their running mates increased responsibilities and power. President Jimmy Carter was the first modern president to rely on his vice president—Walter Mondale—as a major adviser. Under President George W. Bush, Dick Cheney became the most powerful vice president in history. Cheney was able to place his supporters throughout the bureaucracy and exert influence on a wide range of issues. He could exercise this degree of power, however, only because he had the support of the president. In contrast, Vice President Biden's relationship to President Obama was more conventional.

Vice presidents sometimes have become elected presidents in their own right. John Adams and Thomas Jefferson were the first to do so. Richard Nixon was elected president in 1968 after he had served as Dwight D. Eisenhower's vice president from 1953 to 1961. In 1988, George H. W. Bush was elected to the presidency after eight years as Ronald Reagan's vice president.

Presidential Succession

Eight vice presidents have become president because of the death of the president. John Tyler, the first to do so, took over William Henry Harrison's position in 1841, after Harrison had served only one month. No one knew whether Tyler should simply be a caretaker until a new president could be elected three and a half years later or whether he actually should be president. Tyler assumed that he was supposed to be the chief executive, and he acted as such—although he was commonly referred to as "His Accidency." Since then, vice presidents taking over the position of the presidency because of the incumbent's death or resignation have assumed the presidential powers.

But what should a vice president do if a president becomes incapable of carrying out necessary duties while in office? This question was not addressed in the original Constitution. Article II, Section 1, says only that "[i]n Case of the Removal of the President from Office, or of his Death, Resignation, or Inability to discharge the Powers and Duties of the said Office, the same shall devolve on [the same powers shall be exercised by] the Vice President." In October 1919, President Woodrow Wilson was incapacitated by a stroke. He had seventeen months left in his term of office. No one was willing to take responsibility for certifying that Wilson was unable "to discharge the powers and duties" of the presidency. In fact, most of his duties were assumed by cabinet members and even by the First Lady.

When Dwight Eisenhower became ill a second time in 1958, he entered into a pact with Richard Nixon specifying that the vice president could determine whether the president was incapable of carrying out his duties if the president could not communicate.

John F. Kennedy and Lyndon Johnson entered into similar agreements with their vice presidents. Finally, in 1967, the **Twenty-fifth Amendment** was passed, establishing procedures in the event of presidential incapacity, death, or resignation.

When the President Becomes Incapacitated.

According to the Twenty-fifth Amendment, when a president believes that he or she is incapable of performing the duties of office, the president must inform Congress in writing. Then the vice president serves as acting president until the president can resume normal duties. When the president is unable to communicate, a majority of the cabinet, including the vice president, can declare that fact to Congress. Then the vice president serves as acting president until the president resumes normal duties. If a dispute arises over the return of the president's ability, a two-thirds vote of Congress is required to allow the vice president to remain acting president. Otherwise, the president resumes normal duties.

When the Vice Presidency Becomes Vacant.

The Twenty-fifth Amendment also addresses the issue of how the president should fill a vacant vice presidency. Section 2 of the amendment states, "Whenever there is a vacancy in the office of the Vice President, the President shall nominate a Vice President who shall take office upon confirmation by a majority vote of both Houses of Congress." This is exactly what occurred when Richard Nixon's first vice president, Spiro Agnew, resigned in 1973 because of his alleged corruption while serving as governor of Maryland. Nixon turned to Gerald Ford as his choice for vice president, and Congress confirmed the appointment.

Then, when Nixon resigned on August 9, 1974, Ford automatically became president and nominated as his vice president Nelson Rockefeller. Congress confirmed Ford's choice. For the first time in the history of the country, neither the president nor the vice president had been elected to their positions.

Image 12–14 Only eight presidents have died in office, after which their vice presidents became president. When John F. Kennedy was assassinated in November 1963, Vice President Lyndon B. Johnson was sworn in as president by a federal judge. Standing alongside Johnson (1963–1969) was Kennedy's widow, Jacqueline Kennedy. *Who becomes president if both the president and the vice president are killed?*

Twenty-fifth Amendment

A 1967 amendment to the Constitution that establishes procedures for filling presidential and vice-presidential vacancies and makes provisions for presidential incapacity.

The Succession Act of 1947.

The question of who shall be president if both the president and the vice president die is answered by the Presidential Succession Act of 1947. If the president and vice president die, resign, or are disabled, the Speaker of the House will become president, after resigning from Congress. Next in line is the president pro tem of the Senate, followed by the cabinet officers in the order of the creation of their departments (see Table 12–3).

Table 12–3 Line of Succession to the Presidency of the United States

How might the public react if the Speaker of the House became president—and was of a different political party than the deceased president?

1. Vice President
2. Speaker of the House of Representatives
3. Senate President Pro Tempore
4. Secretary of State
5. Secretary of the Treasury
6. Secretary of Defense
7. Attorney General (head of the Justice Department)
8. Secretary of the Interior
9. Secretary of Agriculture
10. Secretary of Commerce
11. Secretary of Labor
12. Secretary of Health and Human Services
13. Secretary of Housing and Urban Development
14. Secretary of Transportation
15. Secretary of Energy
16. Secretary of Education
17. Secretary of Veterans Affairs
18. Secretary of Homeland Security

How you can make a difference

The most traditional form of communication with the White House is, of course, by letter.

- Letters to the president should be addressed to

  The President of the United States
  The White House
  1600 Pennsylvania Avenue N.W.
  Washington, DC 20500

- Letters may be sent to the First Lady at the same address.

- Will you get an answer? Almost certainly. The White House mail room is staffed by volunteers and paid employees who sort the mail for the president and tally the public's concerns. You may receive a standard response to your comments or a more personal, detailed response.

- It is possible to call the White House on the telephone and leave a message for the president or First Lady.

In most circumstances, the best choice is the round-the-clock comment line, which you can reach at 202-456-1111. When you call that number, an operator will take down your comments and forward them to the president's office.

- You can also send your comments and ideas to the White House using e-mail. Send comments to the president at

  comments@whitehouse.gov

- Address e-mail to the vice president at

  vice_president@whitehouse.gov

KEY TERMS

advice and consent **327**
appointment power **324**
cabinet **338**
chief diplomat **327**
chief executive **324**
chief legislator **329**
chief of staff **340**
civil service **324**
commander in chief **326**
constitutional power **334**
diplomatic recognition **328**

emergency power **334**
executive agreement **328**
Executive Office of the
  President (EOP) **339**
executive privilege **336**
expressed power **334**
Federal Register **335**
head of state **323**
impeachment **337**
inherent power **334**
kitchen cabinet **338**

National Security
  Council (NSC) **341**
Office of Management and
  Budget (OMB) **341**
pardon **325**
patronage **332**
pocket veto **330**
reprieve **325**
signing statement **337**
State of the Union
  message **329**

statutory power **334**
Twelfth Amendment **323**
Twenty-fifth
  Amendment **343**
veto message **330**
War Powers
  Resolution **326**
White House Office **340**

CHAPTER SUMMARY

Learning Outcome 1 The office of the presidency in the United States, combining as it does the functions of chief of state and chief executive, was unique at the time of its creation. The framers of the Constitution were divided over whether the president should be a weak or a strong executive.

Learning Outcome 2 The requirements for the office of the presidency are outlined in Article II, Section 1, of the Constitution. The president's roles include both formal and informal duties. The constitutional roles of the president include head of state, chief executive, commander in chief,

chief diplomat, and chief legislator. The president also acts as party chief.

As head of state, the president is ceremonial leader of the government. As chief executive, the president is bound to enforce the acts of Congress, the judgments of the federal courts, and treaties. The chief executive has the power of appointment and the power to grant reprieves and pardons.

As commander in chief, the president is the ultimate decision maker in military matters. As chief diplomat, the president recognizes foreign governments, negotiates treaties, signs agreements, and nominates and receives ambassadors.

The role of chief legislator includes recommending legislation to Congress, lobbying for the legislation, approving laws, and exercising the veto power. Presidents are also leaders of their political parties. Presidents rely on their personal popularity to help them fulfill these functions.

Learning Outcome 3 In addition to constitutional and inherent powers, the president has statutory powers written into law by Congress. Presidents also have a variety of special powers not available to the other branches of the government. These include emergency powers and the power to issue executive orders, to invoke executive privilege, and to issue signing statements.

Abuses of executive power are dealt with by Articles I and II of the Constitution, which authorize the House and Senate to impeach and remove the president, vice president, or other officers of the federal government for committing "Treason, Bribery, or other high Crimes and Misdemeanors."

Learning Outcome 4 The president receives assistance from the cabinet and from the Executive Office of the President (including the White House Office).

Learning Outcome 5 The vice president is the constitutional officer assigned to preside over the Senate and to assume the presidency in the event of the death, resignation, removal, or disability of the president. The Twenty-fifth Amendment, passed in 1967, established procedures to be followed in case of presidential incapacity, death, or resignation and when filling a vacant vice presidency.

ADDITIONAL RESOURCES

The president has a website at **whitehouse.gov** that is designed both to entertain and to provide information about the president's programs. One of the most entertaining parts of the site is "We the People," accessible from the White House home page. We the People lets you create and sign petitions addressed to the government. At any time, there may be up to one hundred open petitions on topics ranging from student loans to the protection of African elephants. Visit We the People and locate a petition you can support. You should have no trouble finding one.

Online Resources

- Inaugural addresses of American presidents from George Washington to Barack Obama are available at **www.bartleby.com/124**.

- In no field is the president more powerful, relative to the rest of the government, than in foreign policy. If you have an interest in that topic, consider following the Foreign Policy website at **www.foreignpolicy.com**.

Books

Barron, David J. *Waging War: The Clash between Presidents and Congress, 1776 to ISIS.* New York: Simon & Schuster, 2016. The employment of the U.S. armed forces has long been a source of conflict between the president and Congress, as Barron explains. He is a federal appeals court judge.

Bruff, Harold H. *Untrodden Ground: How Presidents Interpret the Constitution.* Chicago: University of Chicago Press, 2015. Bruff, a law professor at the University of Colorado, shows how presidential decisions have shaped the basic law of our nation.

Clinton, Hillary Rodham. *Hard Choices.* New York: Simon & Schuster, 2014. Clinton's account of her years as secretary of state under President Obama, together with an explanation of how those experiences drive her view of the future.

Video

American Experience: The Presidents—A box set, released in 2012, that contains eleven presidential biographies produced by PBS. All presidents are from the twentieth century, and they range from Theodore Roosevelt to Bill Clinton. The collection provides one of the most detailed and enjoyable accounts available of U.S. history as seen through the lives of its presidents.

The American President—A 1995 romantic comedy with plenty of ideas about both romance and government. Michael Douglas is the widower president who falls for a lobbyist, played by Annette Bening. Douglas's comedic performance has been called his best.

Quiz

Multiple Choice and Fill-Ins

Learning Outcome 1 Identify the types of people who typically undertake serious campaigns for the presidency.

1. If no presidential candidate has a majority in the electoral college, the question of who should become president is decided by:
   a. the U.S. House.
   b. the U.S. Senate.
   c. the United States Supreme Court.

2. To date, only one president has been a Roman Catholic, and that person was _____ __ _____.

Learning Outcome 2 Distinguish among the major roles of the president, including head of state, chief executive, commander in chief, chief diplomat, chief legislator, party chief, and politician.

3. Our president is both head of state and chief executive, which means that the president:
   a. engages in ceremonial activities both at home and abroad, as well as faithfully ensuring that the acts of Congress are enforced.
   b. designates the vice president to represent the United States in public ceremonies abroad.
   c. makes sure that treaties are upheld but delegates other actions to the cabinet.

4. When the president issues an executive order, such action represents the president's _____ _____.

Learning Outcome 3 Describe some of the special powers of the president, and tell how a president can be removed from office.

5. Upon impeachment by the House of Representatives, the president:
   a. must leave office immediately.
   b. cannot run for reelection.
   c. is tried by the Senate.

6. A president who disagrees with a part of legislation that he or she has signed into law can make a written declaration regarding the law's enforcement. This declaration is called a _____ _____.

Learning Outcome 4 Explain the organization of the executive branch and, in particular, the executive office of the president.

7. The White House chief of staff, the ambassador to the United Nations, and the head of the Environmental Protection Agency:
   a. have at different times been named members of the president's cabinet.
   b. are all part of the Executive Office of the President (EOP).
   c. are not subject to presidential appointment.

8. The president, vice president, secretaries of state and defense, and national security adviser are part of the

   _____ _____ _____.

Learning Outcome 5 Evaluate the role of the vice president, and describe what happens if the presidency becomes vacant.

9. If the president dies, the vice president takes over. If the vice president is also unavailable, then the following officer becomes president:
   a. the president pro tempore of the Senate.
   b. the Speaker of the House.
   c. the secretary of state.

10. The only formal duty imposed on the vice president by the Constitution is to preside over the _____.

Essay Questions

1. What characteristics do you think voters look for when choosing a president? Might these characteristics change as a result of changes in the political environment and the specific problems facing the nation? If you believe voters almost always look for the same characteristics when selecting a president, do you believe they do so? If voters seek somewhat different people as president depending on circumstances, which circumstances favor which kinds of leaders?

2. Many presidents have been lawyers, though George W. Bush was a businessman, Ronald Reagan was an actor, and Jimmy Carter was a naval officer and peanut entrepreneur. What advantages might these three presidents have gained from their career backgrounds? In particular, what benefits might Ronald Reagan have derived from his experience as an actor?

Answers to multiple-choice and fill-in questions: 1. a, 2. John F. Kennedy, 3. a, 4. legislative power, 5. c, 6. signing statement, 7. a, 8. National Security Council, 9. b, 10. Senate.

THE BUREAUCRACY

A national park ranger holds a cake honoring the 125th anniversary of Yosemite National Park as a young honorary ranger cuts a piece. *How popular are the government workers who manage our national parks?*
Fresno Bee/Getty Images

These five **LEARNING OUTCOMES** *below are designed to help improve your understanding of this chapter:*

1: Discuss the nature of the federal bureaucracy, and identify the largest federal spending programs.

2: Describe the various types of agencies and organizations that make up the federal executive branch.

3: Explain how government employees are hired and how the civil service is administered.

4: Evaluate different methods that have been put into place to reform bureaucracies and make them more efficient.

5: Discuss how federal agencies make rules and the role of Congress in this process.

What if...

We Simplified the Income Tax System?

Background

In 1913, the Sixteenth Amendment to the Constitution let Congress levy an income tax. In that year, not even 1 percent of Americans paid this tax. Today, the top rate is 39.6 percent. The Tax Code runs about 75,000 pages. Filing consumes vast amounts of time and money. As a result, every few years someone proposes simplifying our tax system.

What If We Had a Simpler Tax System?

Some conservatives have proposed a flat tax in which everyone pays the same rate, say 20 percent. A large standard deduction benefits low earners. Such a plan is a political nonstarter. A flat tax would inevitably result in large tax-rate cuts for the wealthy. To collect enough revenue, it would require equally large increases for the middle class.

Why Is the Tax System Complicated?

Different income tax rates are not really what makes the system complicated. After all, a table that fully defines the various tax brackets can easily fit on a postcard. A major cause of complication is the vast collection of rules on what "income" even means. Such rules rarely trouble people whose income consists of wages or salaries—they are an issue, rather, for investors and businesspeople. For the middle class, complications are typically due to the huge number of possible tax deductions and credits. The deductions and credits available to businesses are even more numerous, and are responsible for most of the length of the Tax Code. Of course, every type of business has its favorite clauses in the Code.

Who Might Win— and Who Might Lose?

Relatively low-income people usually don't have enough possible deductions to bother itemizing on their returns. Rather, they take the standard deduction, which is larger than what they could gain by itemizing. Tax simplification could affect homeowners, small businesspeople, and others with large deductions. Reform could reduce their overall tax rate, but at the price of abolishing many deductions. Consider some possible changes that reformers have suggested:

- We could curb the deductibility of charitable contributions. Yet funding for the entire nonprofit sector is based on soliciting tax-deductible contributions from the middle class and the wealthy. Would people continue to donate if they couldn't get a tax deduction? Charities, churches, and colleges do not want to find out.

- Deductions for interest on home loans (mortgages) could be limited. This step would reduce the incentive to borrow to buy a house. Real estate agents, mortgage lenders, and potential home buyers would oppose such a change.

- Current law provides a vast number of education incentives. We could collapse all of them into just one. This change would make the system easier to understand, so more people might claim the incentive. Total support for education could fall, however.

- Currently, elderly persons can deduct uninsured medical expenses that exceed 7.5 percent of income. We could repeal that. Yet repeal would damage the finances of many people confined to nursing homes, who can now deduct most of what the nursing homes charge.

For Critical Analysis

▶ **What could the government do to help groups such as charities that might be damaged by the loss of tax deductions?**

▶ **Why might both Republicans and Democrats oppose a simpler tax system?**

Image 13–1 Advertising a tax preparation service shortly before the April income tax deadline. *Why do some people wait until the last minute to file?*

Bloomberg/Getty Images

Faceless bureaucrats—this image provokes a negative reaction from many, if not most, Americans. Polls consistently report that the majority of Americans support "less government." The same polls, however, report that the majority of Americans support almost every specific program that the government undertakes. The conflict between the desire for small government and the desire for the benefits that only a large government can provide has been a constant feature of American politics. For example, the goal of preserving endangered species has widespread support. At the same time, many people believe that restrictions imposed under the Endangered Species Act violate the rights of landowners. Helping the elderly pay their medical bills is a popular objective, but hardly anyone enjoys paying the Medicare tax that supports this effort. (Indeed, politicians and citizens have frequently called for tax reform, as explained in the chapter-opening *What If . . .* feature.)

In this chapter, we describe the size, organization, and staffing of the federal bureaucracy. We review modern attempts at bureaucratic reform and the process by which Congress exerts ultimate control over the bureaucracy. We also discuss the bureaucracy's role in making rules and setting policy.

bureaucracy
An organization that is structured hierarchically to carry out specific functions.

Weberian model
A model of bureaucracy developed by the German sociologist Max Weber, who viewed bureaucracies as rational, hierarchical organizations in which decisions are based on logical reasoning.

The Nature and Scope of the Federal Bureaucracy

Bureaucracy is the name given to an organization that is structured hierarchically to carry out specific functions. Generally, bureaucracies are characterized by an organizational chart. The units of the organization are divided according to the specialization and expertise of the employees.

Learning Outcome **1:**

Discuss the nature of the federal bureaucracy, and identify the largest federal spending programs.

Public and Private Bureaucracies

We should not think of bureaucracy as unique to government. Any large corporation or university can be considered a bureaucratic organization, even though the term *bureaucracy* is most often applied to government agencies. The fact is that the handling of complex problems requires a division of labor. Individuals must concentrate their skills on specific, well-defined aspects of a problem and depend on others to solve the rest of it.

Public, or government, bureaucracies differ from private organizations in some important ways, however. A private corporation has a single leader—its chief executive officer (CEO). Public bureaucracies do not have a single leader. Although the president is the chief administrator of the federal system, all agencies are subject to the dictates of Congress for their funding, staffing, and, indeed, their continued existence. Public bureaucracies supposedly serve all citizens, while private ones serve private interests.

One other important difference between private corporations and government bureaucracies is that government bureaucracies are not organized to make a profit. Rather, they are supposed to perform their functions as efficiently as possible to conserve taxpayers' dollars.

Models of Bureaucracy

Several theories have been offered to help us better understand the ways in which bureaucracies function. Each of these theories focuses on specific features of bureaucracies.

Weberian Model. The classic model, or **Weberian model,** of the modern bureaucracy was proposed by the German sociologist Max Weber.[1] He argued that the increasingly

---

1. Max Weber, *Theory of Social and Economic Organization*, ed. Talcott Parsons (1947; repr., Eastford, Conn.: Martino Fine Books, 2012).

complex nature of modern life, coupled with the steadily growing demands placed on governments by their citizens, made the formation of bureaucracies inevitable. According to Weber, most bureaucracies—whether in the public or private sector—are organized hierarchically and governed by formal procedures. The power in a bureaucracy flows from the top downward. Decision-making processes in bureaucracies are shaped by detailed technical rules that promote similar decisions in similar situations.

Bureaucrats are specialists who attempt to resolve problems through logical reasoning and data analysis instead of "gut feelings" and guesswork. Individual advancement in bureaucracies is supposed to be based on merit rather than on political connections. Indeed, the modern bureaucracy, according to Weber, should be an apolitical organization.

Acquisitive Model. Other theorists do not view bureaucracies in terms as benign as Weber's. Some believe that bureaucracies are acquisitive in nature. Proponents of the **acquisitive model** argue that top-level bureaucrats will always try to expand, or at least to avoid any reductions in, the size of their budgets. Although government bureaucracies are not-for-profit enterprises, bureaucrats want to maximize the size of their budgets and staffs, which are the most visible trappings of power in the public sector. These efforts are also prompted by the desire of bureaucrats to "sell" their products—such as national defense, public housing, or agricultural subsidies—to both Congress and the public.

Monopolistic Model. Because government bureaucracies seldom have competitors, some theorists have suggested that these bureaucratic organizations may be explained best by a **monopolistic model.** The analysis is similar to that used by economists to examine the behavior of monopolistic firms. Monopolistic bureaucracies—like monopolistic firms—essentially have no competitors and act accordingly. Because monopolistic bureaucracies usually are not penalized for chronic inefficiency, they have little reason to adopt cost-saving measures or to make more productive use of their resources.

The Size of the Bureaucracy

In 1789, the new government's bureaucracy was tiny. There were three departments—State (with nine employees), War (with two employees), and Treasury (with thirty-nine employees)—and the Office of the Attorney General (which later became the Department of Justice). The bureaucracy was still small in 1798. At that time, the secretary of state had seven clerks and spent a total of $500 (about $10,100 in 2017 dollars) on stationery and printing. In that same year, an appropriations act allocated $1.4 million (or $28.4 million in 2017 dollars) to the War Department.[2]

Government Employment Today. Times have changed, as we can see in Figure 13–1, which shows various federal agencies and the number of civilian employees in each. Excluding 1.3 million military service members but including employees of the legislative and judicial branches and the U.S. Postal Service, the federal bureaucracy includes approximately 2.6 million employees. That number has remained relatively stable for the past several decades. It is somewhat deceiving, however, because many other individuals work directly or indirectly for the federal government as subcontractors or consultants.

Conventionally, attempts to measure the size of the federal bureaucracy also leave out the men and women of the Army, Navy, Air Force, and Marines. In 2016, these personnel numbered 1,301,000. Despite their service ethos, it cannot be denied that the armed forces are gigantic bureaucracies with all the characteristics of bureaucracies everywhere.

The figures for federal government employment are only part of the story. Figure 13–2 shows the growth in government employment at the federal, state, and local levels. Since

Image 13–2 German sociologist Max Weber (1864–1920) created the classic model of the modern bureaucracy. *Does the power in the classic bureaucracy flow upward, downward, or horizontally?*

acquisitive model

A model of bureaucracy that views top-level bureaucrats as seeking to expand the size of their budgets and staffs to gain greater power.

monopolistic model

A model of bureaucracy that compares bureaucracies to monopolistic business firms. Lack of competition in either circumstance leads to inefficient and costly operations.

2. Leonard D. White, *The Federalists: A Study in Administrative History, 1789–1801,* 6th ed. (New York: Macmillan, 1967).

Figure 13–1 Federal Agencies and Their Respective Numbers of Civilian Employees

Why does the Department of Defense need so many civilian employees?

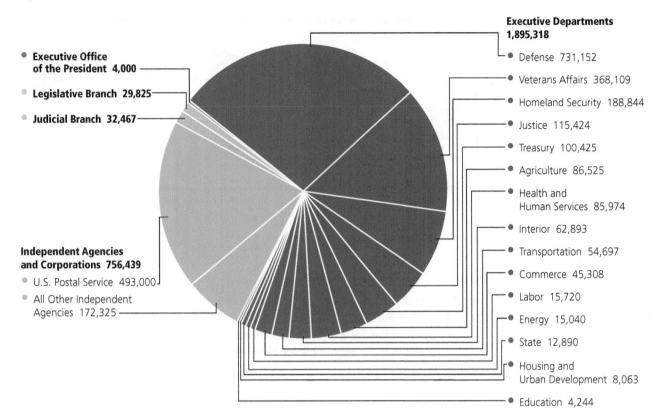

Executive Departments 1,895,318
- Defense 731,152
- Veterans Affairs 368,109
- Homeland Security 188,844
- Justice 115,424
- Treasury 100,425
- Agriculture 86,525
- Health and Human Services 85,974
- Interior 62,893
- Transportation 54,697
- Commerce 45,308
- Labor 15,720
- Energy 15,040
- State 12,890
- Housing and Urban Development 8,063
- Education 4,244

Executive Office of the President 4,000

Legislative Branch 29,825

Judicial Branch 32,467

Independent Agencies and Corporations 756,439
- U.S. Postal Service 493,000
- All Other Independent Agencies 172,325

Sources: U.S. Office of Personnel Management, March 2016; and the Office of Management and Budget.

1959, this growth was mainly at the state and local levels. If all government employees are included, about 16 percent of all civilian nonfarm employment is accounted for by government.

The Impact of Ronald Reagan. Notice in Figure 13–2 that government employment as a share of the total U.S. population grew rapidly until 1980. In that year, Republican Ronald Reagan was elected president. Under Reagan, government employment actually fell, in large part because of the elimination of revenue sharing, a program through which the federal government transferred large sums to state and local governments. While government employment picked up later in Reagan's administration, it never resumed the constant upward course characteristic of the 1960s and 1970s. In short, Reagan's "conservative revolution" had a genuine impact on the trajectory of government.

The Great Recession and its aftermath also had a major impact on government spending and employment. In 2009, the number of state and local government workers began to fall, because these governments could not collect enough revenue to fund their previous levels of activity. From August 2008 to the beginning of 2013, state and local government employment fell by about 730,000.

Federal Employment and Federal Spending. While Figure 13–1 provides a good overview of the number of federal employees, it does not accurately depict federal spending. For example, employees of the U.S. Postal Service (USPS) make up about a quarter

Figure 13–2 Government Employment 1959–2016

What kinds of workers might local governments have laid off after 2009?

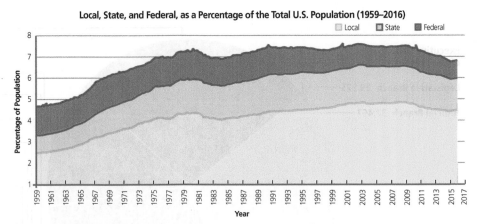

Local, State, and Federal, as a Percentage of the Total U.S. Population (1959–2016)

Sources: U.S. Census Bureau and Bureau of Labor Statistics.

of the pie chart. Yet for decades the postal service has been entirely self-supporting and has drawn no funds from the government at all. (Recent financial troubles have raised the question of whether the USPS can remain self-supporting in the future, however.) In contrast, the employees of the Social Security Administration make up only 3 percent of the federal workforce, but they are responsible for 25 percent of what the federal government spends.

The Federal Budget

In 1929, spending by all levels of government was equivalent to only about 11 percent of the nation's gross domestic product (GDP). For fiscal year 2017, it was about 36 percent.

Image 13–3 Even at $0.47 for the one-ounce first-class rate, postage in the United States is a bargain by international standards. First-class rates are $0.77 in Japan, $0.88 in France, and $0.84 in Britain. *Why has the U.S. Postal Service experienced financial difficulties?*

Social Spending. Studies repeatedly show that most Americans have a very inaccurate idea of how the federal budget is spent. Figure 13–3 can help. This pie chart demonstrates that about 40 percent of all federal spending goes to two programs that benefit older Americans—Social Security and Medicare. Additional social programs, many aimed at low-income individuals and families, push the total amount of social spending past the 60 percent mark. Because of these additional social programs, the federal government spends much more on the poor than many people realize. Medicaid, a joint federal-state program that provides health-care services, is the largest of these programs. (CHIP, which is combined with Medicaid in the figure, is the Children's Health Insurance Program.) In contrast, traditional cash welfare—Temporary Assistance for Needy Families (TANF)—accounts for only 0.4 percent of the budget ($17 billion) and is buried in the "Miscellaneous low-income and disability support" slice.

Defense and the Rest. Military defense and veterans' benefits are about a fifth of the whole. Interest payments on the national debt are about 7 percent. "Everything else," which includes education and transportation, amounts to only 12 percent of the budget. Foreign aid, which is included in the "everything else" slice, is 1.4 percent, or $56 billion. This is a substantial sum, but it is much smaller than many people imagine. Frequently, politicians will claim that they can balance the federal budget by making large cuts to this 12 percent slice of federal spending. A quick look at Figure 13–3 reveals that such claims are not based on reality. Where does the federal government get the funds that support its spending? We answer that question in this chapter's *Consider the Source* feature.

cabinet department
One of the fifteen major departments of the executive branch.

line organization
In the federal government, an administrative unit that is directly accountable to the president.

The Organization of the Federal Bureaucracy

Within the federal bureaucracy are a number of different types of government agencies and organizations. Figure 13–5 outlines the several bodies within the executive branch, as well as the separate organizations that provide services to Congress, to the courts, and directly to the president.

The executive branch, which employs most of the government's staff, has four major types of structures. They are (1) cabinet departments, (2) independent executive agencies, (3) independent regulatory agencies, and (4) government corporations. Each has a distinctive relationship to the president, and some have unusual internal structures, overall goals, and grants of power.

Learning Outcome **2:**

Describe the various types of agencies and organizations that make up the federal executive branch.

Cabinet Departments

The fifteen **cabinet departments** are the major service organizations of the federal government. They can also be described in management terms as **line organizations.** This means

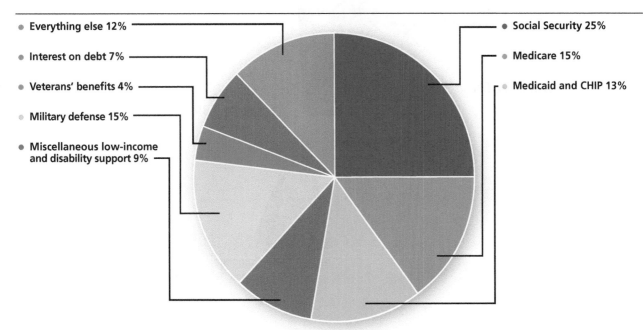

Figure 13–3 Federal Government Spending, Fiscal Year 2017

Do you find some of these percentages surprising? If so, which ones?

- Everything else 12%
- Interest on debt 7%
- Veterans' benefits 4%
- Military defense 15%
- Miscellaneous low-income and disability support 9%

- Social Security 25%
- Medicare 15%
- Medicaid and CHIP 13%

Source: usgovernmentspending.com.

Consider the source

Federal Government Revenues

Where does the federal government get the funds that support its spending? Figure 13–4 can help answer that question. As you might expect, the personal income tax provides the largest share of federal revenues, about 43 percent. About 12 percent is borrowed—this pie slice represents the sale of new U.S. debt obligations, such as bonds. While borrowing is down substantially compared to what it was in the depths of the Great Recession, it is still large enough to concern many people.

The Source

The ultimate source for the data in Figure 13–4—and also Figure 13–3—is the federal budget prepared by the Office of Management and Budget (OMB). You can find the budget at www.whitehouse.gov, the president's website. At the bottom of the page, click on "Office of Management and Budget." On the OMB page, click on "Historical Tables." You'll find data on budget receipts, outlays, deficits, and the federal debt for the current period, for past years, and projected into the future.

An alternative source is a series of websites run by Christopher Chantrill, a conservative activist. These include www.usgovernmentspending.com and www.usgovernmentrevenue.com. Most of Chantrill's data come from the OMB, but his sites are often easier to follow than the material supplied by the OMB itself. Figure 13–4 is based on www.usgovernmentrevenue.com. You might try visiting one of these websites. Using provided controls, try checking out spending or taxes as a percent of the gross domestic product (GDP—a measurement of the total economy).

For Critical Analysis

▶ **Why would many economists find "percent of GDP" a better way to measure taxes and spending than sums reported in current dollars?**

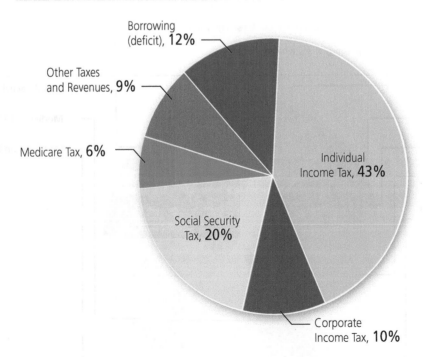

Figure 13–4 Federal Revenue Sources

Borrowing (deficit), 12%

Other Taxes and Revenues, 9%

Medicare Tax, 6%

Social Security Tax, 20%

Individual Income Tax, 43%

Corporate Income Tax, 10%

that they are directly accountable to the president and are responsible for performing government functions, such as printing money and training troops. These cabinet departments were created by Congress when the need for each department arose. The first department to be created was State, and the most recent one was Homeland Security, established in 2003. A president might ask that a new department be created or an old one abolished, but the president has no power to do so without legislative approval from Congress.

Figure 13–5 Organizational Chart of the Federal Government

Consider a few of the independent agencies listed at the bottom of the chart. *Why might each of these agencies have been made independent?*

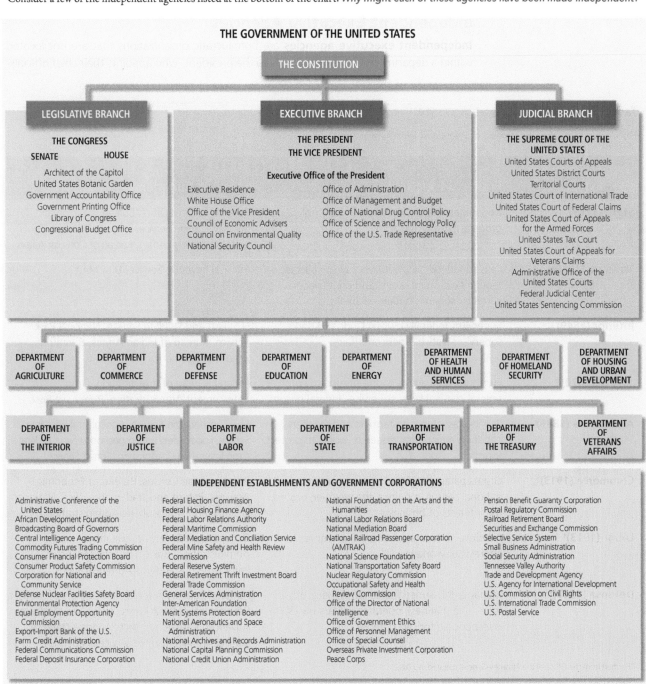

independent executive agency
A federal agency that is not part of a cabinet department but reports directly to the president.

Each department is headed by a secretary (except for the Justice Department, which is headed by the attorney general). Each department also has several levels of undersecretaries, assistant secretaries, and other personnel.

Presidents theoretically have considerable control over the cabinet departments, because presidents are able to appoint or fire all of the top officials. Even cabinet departments do not always respond to the president's wishes, though. One reason why presidents are frequently unhappy with their departments is that the entire bureaucratic structure below the top political levels is staffed by permanent employees. Many of these employees are committed to established programs or procedures and resist change. Table 13–1 shows each cabinet department. The table also describes some of the functions of each of the departments.

Independent Executive Agencies

Independent executive agencies are bureaucratic organizations that are not located within a department but report directly to the president, who appoints their chief officials.

Table 13–1 Cabinet Departments

Why do you think the Department of Homeland Security was created?

Department and Year Established	Principal Functions	Selected Subagencies
State (1789)	Negotiates treaties, develops foreign policy, protects citizens abroad.	Passport Services Office, Bureau of Diplomatic Security, Foreign Service, Bureau of Human Rights and Humanitarian Affairs, Bureau of Consular Affairs.
Treasury (1789)	Pays all federal bills, borrows funds, collects federal taxes, mints coins and prints paper currency, supervises national banks.	Internal Revenue Service, U.S. Mint.
Interior (1849)	Supervises federally owned lands and parks, supervises Native American affairs.	U.S. Fish and Wildlife Service, National Park Service, Bureau of Indian Affairs, Bureau of Land Management.
Justice (1870)*	Furnishes legal advice to the president, enforces federal criminal laws, supervises federal prisons.	Federal Bureau of Investigation, Drug Enforcement Administration, Bureau of Prisons.
Agriculture (1889)	Provides assistance to farmers and ranchers, conducts agricultural research, works to protect forests.	Soil Conservation Service, Agricultural Research Service, Food Safety and Inspection Service, Federal Crop Insurance Corporation, Forest Service.
Commerce (1913)†	Grants patents and trademarks, conducts a national census, monitors the weather, protects the interests of businesses.	Bureau of the Census, Bureau of Economic Analysis, Patent and Trademark Office, National Oceanic and Atmospheric Administration.
Labor (1913)†	Administers federal labor laws, promotes the interests of workers.	Occupational Safety and Health Administration, Bureau of Labor Statistics, Employment Standards Administration.
Defense (1947)‡	Manages the armed forces (army, navy, air force, and marines), operates military bases, is responsible for civil defense.	National Security Agency; Joint Chiefs of Staff; Departments of the Air Force, Navy, Army; Defense Advanced Research Projects Agency; Defense Intelligence Agency; the service academies.

*Formed from the Office of the Attorney General (created in 1789).

†Formed from the Department of Commerce and Labor (created in 1903).

‡Formed from the Department of War (created in 1789) and the Department of the Navy (created in 1798).

When a new federal agency is created—the Environmental Protection Agency, for example—Congress decides where it will be located in the bureaucracy. In recent decades, presidents often have asked that a new organization be kept separate or independent rather than added to an existing department, particularly if a department may be hostile to the agency's creation. Table 13–2 describes the functions of selected independent executive agencies.

independent regulatory agency
An agency outside the major executive departments that is charged with making and implementing rules and regulations within a specific area.

Independent Regulatory Agencies

Typically, an **independent regulatory agency** is responsible for a specific type of public policy. Its function is to make and implement rules and regulations in a particular sphere of action to protect the public interest. The earliest such agency was the Interstate Commerce Commission (ICC), which was established in 1887 when Americans began to seek some form of government control over the rapidly growing business and industrial sector. This new form of organization, the independent regulatory agency, was supposed to

Table 13–1 Cabinet Departments *(continued)*

Department and Year Established	Principal Functions	Selected Subagencies
Housing and Urban Development (1965)	Deals with the nation's housing needs, develops and rehabilitates urban communities, oversees resale of mortgages.	Government National Mortgage Association, Office of Community Planning and Development, Office of Fair Housing and Equal Opportunity.
Transportation (1967)	Finances improvements in mass transit; develops and administers programs for highways, railroads, and aviation.	Federal Aviation Administration, Federal Highway Administration, National Highway Traffic Safety Administration, Federal Transit Administration.
Energy (1977)	Promotes the conservation of energy and resources, conducts research and development.	Federal Energy Regulatory Commission, National Nuclear Security Administration.
Health and Human Services (1979)§	Promotes public health, administers Medicare and Medicaid, enforces pure food and drug laws, conducts and sponsors health-related research.	Food and Drug Administration, Centers for Disease Control and Prevention, National Institutes of Health, Centers for Medicare and Medicaid Services.
Education (1979)§	Coordinates federal programs and policies for education, administers aid to education, promotes educational research.	Office of Elementary and Secondary Education, Office of Postsecondary Education, Office of Vocational and Adult Education, Office of Federal Student Aid.
Veterans Affairs (1988)	Promotes the welfare of veterans of the U.S. armed forces.	Veterans Health Administration, Veterans Benefits Administration, National Cemetery Systems.
Homeland Security (2003)	Attempts to prevent terrorist attacks within the United States, control America's borders, and minimize the damage from natural disasters.	U.S. Customs and Border Protection, U.S. Coast Guard, Secret Service, Federal Emergency Management Agency, U.S. Citizenship and Immigration Services, U.S. Immigration Customs Enforcement.

§Formed from the Department of Health, Education, and Welfare (created in 1953).

Table 13–2 Selected Independent Executive Agencies

Why might the Small Business Administration have been kept separate from the Commerce Department?

Name	Date Formed	Principal Functions
The Smithsonian Institution (4,678 employees)	1846	Runs the government's museums and the National Zoo.
Central Intelligence Agency (CIA) (number of employees is classified; NSA leaks give the number as 21,575)	1947	Gathers and analyzes political and military information about foreign countries, conducts covert operations outside the United States.
General Services Administration (GSA) (11,219 employees)	1949	Purchases and manages property of the federal government, oversees federal government spending projects, discovers overcharges in government programs.
National Science Foundation (NSF) (1,456 employees)	1950	Promotes scientific research, provides grants to schools for instructional programs in the sciences.
Small Business Administration (SBA) (4,006 employees)	1953	Protects the interests of small businesses, provides low-cost loans and management information to small businesses.
National Aeronautics and Space Administration (NASA) (17,128 employees)	1958	Is responsible for the U.S. space program, including the building, testing, and operating of space vehicles.
Environmental Protection Agency (EPA) (15,553 employees)	1970	Undertakes programs aimed at reducing air and water pollution, helps fight environmental hazards.
Social Security Administration (SSA)* (64,264 employees)	1995	Manages the government's Social Security programs, including Retirement and Survivors Insurance, Disability Insurance, and Supplemental Security Income.

*Separated from the Department of Health and Human Services (created in 1979).

make technical, nonpolitical decisions about rates, profits, and rules that would be for the benefit of all and that did not require congressional legislation. In the years that followed the creation of the ICC, other agencies were formed to regulate such areas as communication (the Federal Communications Commission) and nuclear power (the Nuclear Regulatory Commission). (The ICC was abolished in 1995.)

The Purpose and Nature of Regulatory Agencies. In practice, regulatory agencies are administered independently of all three branches of government. They were set up because Congress felt it was unable to handle the complexities and technicalities required to carry out specific laws. Regulatory agencies and commissions combine some functions of all three branches of government—legislative, executive, and judicial. They are legislative in that they make rules that have the force of law. They are executive in that they provide for the enforcement of those rules. They are judicial in that they decide disputes involving the rules they have made.

Heads of regulatory agencies and members of agency boards or commissions are appointed by the president with the consent of the Senate, although they do not report to the president. When an agency is headed by a board, rather than an individual, the members of the board cannot, by law, all be from the same political party. Presidents can influence regulatory agency behavior by appointing people of their own parties or individuals who share their political views when vacancies occur, in particular when the chair is vacant.

Table 13–3 Selected Independent Regulatory Agencies

Some members of Congress were opposed to the creation of the Consumer Financial Protection Bureau.
What might have been the reasons for the opposition?

Name	Date Formed	Principal Functions
Federal Reserve System Board of Governors (Fed) (1,526 federal employees; employment in the entire Fed is 20,544)	1913	Determines policy on interest rates, credit availability, and the money supply.
Federal Trade Commission (FTC) (1,171 employees)	1914	Combats unfair trade practices, seeks to prevent monopolies in the business sector, protects consumer rights.
Securities and Exchange Commission (SEC) (4,665 employees)	1934	Regulates the nation's stock exchanges, in which shares of stock are bought and sold; requires full disclosure of the financial profiles of companies that sell stocks and bonds.
Federal Communications Commission (FCC) (1,631 employees)	1934	Regulates communications by radio, television, wire, satellite, and cable.
National Labor Relations Board (NLRB) (1,596 employees)	1935	Protects employees' rights to join unions and bargain collectively with employers, attempts to prevent unfair labor practices by both employers and unions.
Equal Employment Opportunity Commission (EEOC) (2,241 employees)	1964	Works to eliminate discrimination based on religion, gender, race, color, national origin, age, or disability; examines claims of discrimination.
Nuclear Regulatory Commission (NRC) (3,661 employees)	1974	Ensures that nuclear reactors in the United States are built and operated safely, inspects such reactors.
Consumer Financial Protection Bureau (1,623 employees)	2010	Protects consumers in the financial sector; has jurisdiction over banks, securities firms, payday lenders, mortgage-servicing operations, debt collectors, and others.

Members may be removed by the president only for causes specified in the law creating the agency. Table 13–3 describes the functions of selected independent regulatory agencies.

Agency Capture. Over the last several decades, some observers have concluded that regulatory agencies, although nominally independent, may in fact not always be so. They contend that many agencies have been captured by the very industries and firms that they were supposed to regulate, and therefore make decisions based on the interests of the industry, not the general public. The results of **agency capture** have been less competition rather than more competition, higher prices rather than lower prices, and fewer choices rather than more choices for consumers.

Deregulation and Reregulation. During the presidency of Jimmy Carter (1977–1981), significant deregulation (the removal of regulatory restraints—the opposite of regulation) was initiated. For example, Carter appointed a chairperson of the Civil Aeronautics Board (CAB) who gradually eliminated regulation of airline fares and routes. Deregulation continued under President Ronald Reagan (1981–1989). During the administration of George H. W. Bush (1989–1993), however, calls for reregulation of many businesses increased and several new regulatory acts were passed.

agency capture
The act by which an industry being regulated by a government agency gains direct or indirect control over agency personnel and decision makers.

Under President Bill Clinton (1993–2001), the Interstate Commerce Commission was eliminated, and the banking and telecommunications industries, along with many other sectors of the economy, were deregulated. At the same time, there was extensive regulation to protect the environment, a trend somewhat attenuated by the George W. Bush administration.

Regulation Today. After the financial crisis of September 2008, many people saw inadequate regulation of the financial industry as a major cause of the nation's economic difficulties. During President Obama's administration, therefore, reregulation of that industry became a major objective. After intense debate, Congress passed a comprehensive financial industry regulation plan in 2010.

Americans have had conflicting views about the amount of regulation that is appropriate for various industries ever since the government began to undertake serious regulatory activities. Many people find regulation to be contrary to the spirit of free enterprise and the American tradition of individualism. Yet in cases such as BP's Deepwater Horizon oil spill disaster in the Gulf of Mexico in 2010, citizens of all political stripes were outraged to learn that the relevant regulatory agency at the time, the Minerals Management Service, had failed to do its job.

Image 13–4 National Transportation Safety Board workers inspect the wreckage of a UPS cargo plane that crashed in a field near Birmingham, Alabama. The pilot and co-pilot died, but no other injuries were reported. *Why might people prefer that such investigations be undertaken by the government?*

Handout/Getty Images

Government and Government-controlled Corporations

Another form of bureaucratic organization in the United States is the **government corporation.** Although the concept is borrowed from the world of business, there are important differences between public and private corporations.

A private corporation has shareholders (stockholders) who elect a board of directors, who in turn choose the corporate officers, such as the CEO. When a private corporation makes a profit, it must pay taxes (unless it avoids them through various legal loopholes). It distributes the after-tax profits to shareholders as dividends or plows the profits back into the corporation to make new investments, or both.

A government corporation has a board of directors and managers, but it does not usually have any stockholders. The public cannot buy shares of stock in a typical government corporation, and if the entity makes a profit, it does not distribute the profit as dividends. Nor does it have to pay taxes on profits—the profits remain in the corporation or are passed on to the U.S. Treasury. Table 13–4 describes the functions of selected government corporations.

Bankruptcy. The federal government can also take effective control of a private corporation in a number of different circumstances. One is bankruptcy. When a company files for bankruptcy, it asks a federal judge for relief from its creditors. The judge, operating under bankruptcy laws established by Congress (as specified in the Constitution), is ultimately responsible for the fate of the enterprise. When a bank fails, the government has a special interest in protecting customers who have deposited funds with the bank. For that reason, the failing institution is taken over by the Federal Deposit Insurance Corporation (FDIC), which ensures continuity of service to bank customers.

government corporation

An agency of government that administers a quasi-business enterprise. These corporations are used when government activities are primarily commercial.

Table 13–4 Selected Government Corporations

Would it be a good idea for the Postal Service to add new services in an attempt to earn more revenue? Why or why not?

Name	Date Formed	Principal Functions
Tennessee Valley Authority (TVA) (10,900 employees)	1933	Operates a Tennessee River control system and generates power for a seven-state region, promotes the economic development of the region, controls floods and promotes the navigability of the Tennessee River.
Federal Deposit Insurance Corporation (FDIC) (6,460 employees)	1933	Insures individuals' bank deposits up to $250,000, oversees the business activities of banks.
Export-Import Bank of the United States (Ex-Im Bank) (423 employees)	1933	Promotes the sale of American-made goods abroad, grants loans to foreign purchasers of American products.
National Railroad Passenger Corporation (AMTRAK) (20,000 employees)	1970	Provides a national and intercity rail passenger service, controls more than 21,000 miles of track and serves 500 communities.
U.S. Postal Service (USPS)* (493,000 employees)	1971	Delivers mail throughout the United States and its territories, is the largest government corporation.

*Formed from the Post Office Department (an executive department).

Government Ownership of Private Enterprises. The federal government can also obtain partial or complete ownership of a private corporation by purchasing its stock. Before 2008, such takeovers were rare, although they occasionally happened. When Continental Illinois, then the nation's seventh-largest bank, failed in 1984, the FDIC wound up in control of the institution for ten years before it could find a buyer.

The Bank Bailout. The Continental Illinois rescue provided a blueprint for the massive bank bailout initiated under President George W. Bush in October 2008. The government made investments in more than eight hundred businesses, including banks, automobile companies, and the giant insurance company AIG. The bailout program was tremendously unpopular. Still, in time, the government recovered its investments and even turned a small profit.

Government-Sponsored Enterprises. An additional type of corporation is the government-sponsored enterprise, a business created by the federal government itself, which then sells part or all of the corporation's stock to private investors. Until 2008, the leading examples of this kind of company were the Federal Home Loan Mortgage Corporation, known as Freddie Mac, and the Federal National Mortgage Association, commonly known as Fannie Mae. Both of these firms buy mortgages from banks and bundle them into securities that can be sold to investors. When the housing market collapsed during the Great Recession, so—eventually—did Freddie Mac and Fannie Mae.

Investors had always assumed that the federal government backed the obligations of the two enterprises, even though the government had never issued an explicit guarantee. In September 2008, the implicit guarantee became real when the government seized the two companies in what was effectively a bankruptcy. Freddie Mac and Fannie Mae became government-owned corporations. Eventually, they returned to profitability, and today all profits go to the U.S. Treasury.

Staffing the Bureaucracy

There are two categories of bureaucrats: political appointees and civil servants. As noted earlier, the president can make political appointments to most of the top jobs in the federal bureaucracy. The president also can appoint ambassadors to foreign posts. All of the jobs that are considered "political plums" and that usually go to the politically well connected are listed in *Policy and Supporting Positions,* a book published by the Government Printing Office after each presidential election. Informally (and appropriately), this has been called the "Plum Book." The rest of the national government's employees belong to the civil service and obtain their jobs through a much more formal process.

Political Appointees

To fill the positions listed in the "Plum Book," the president and the president's advisers solicit suggestions from politicians, businesspersons, and other prominent individuals. Appointments to these positions offer the president a way to pay off outstanding political debts. Presidents often use ambassadorships to reward individuals for their campaign contributions. But the president must also take into consideration such things as the candidate's ability to actually do the job.

The Aristocracy of the Federal Government. Political appointees are in some sense the aristocracy of the federal government. But their powers, although they appear formidable on paper, are often exaggerated. Like the president, a political appointee will occupy her or his position for a comparatively brief time. Political appointees often leave office before the president's term ends. In fact, the average term of service for political

Image 13–5 Students lobby against a near-doubling of the interest rates on federally subsidized Stafford loans. The loans are available through the Department of Education. In August 2013, Congress repealed most of the increase. *Is a college degree worth incurring large debts?*

Mark Wilson/Getty Images

appointees is less than two years. As a result, most appointees have little background for their positions and may be mere figureheads. Often, they only respond to the paperwork that flows up from below. Additionally, the professional civil servants who make up the permanent civil service may not feel compelled to carry out their current chief's directives quickly, because they know that he or she will not be around for very long.

The Difficulty in Firing Civil Servants. This inertia is compounded by the fact that it is very difficult to discharge civil servants. In recent years, fewer than 0.1 percent of federal employees have been fired for incompetence. Because discharged employees may appeal their dismissals, many months or even years can pass before the issue is resolved conclusively. This occupational rigidity helps to ensure that most political appointees, no matter how competent or driven, will not be able to exert much meaningful influence over their subordinates, let alone implement dramatic changes in the bureaucracy itself.

History of the Federal Civil Service

When the federal government was formed in 1789, it had no career public servants but rather consisted of amateurs who were almost all Federalists. When Thomas Jefferson took over as president, few federal administrative jobs were held by members of his party, so he fired more than one hundred officials and replaced them with his own supporters. Then, for the next twenty-five years, a growing body of federal administrators gained experience and expertise, becoming in the process professional public servants. These administrators stayed in office regardless of who was elected president. The bureaucracy had become a self-maintaining, long-term element within government.

To the Victors Belong the Spoils. When Andrew Jackson took over the White House in 1828, he could not believe how many appointed officials (appointed before he became president, that is) were overtly hostile toward him and his Democratic Party. Because the bureaucracy was reluctant to carry out his programs, Jackson did the obvious: he fired federal officials—more than had been fired by all his predecessors combined. The **spoils system**—an application of the principle that to the victors belong the spoils—became the standard method of filling federal positions. Whenever a new president was elected from a party different from the party of the previous president, there would be an almost complete turnover in the staffing of the federal government.

The Civil Service Reform Act of 1883. Jackson's spoils system survived for a number of years, but it became increasingly corrupt. In addition, the size of the bureaucracy increased by 300 percent between 1851 and 1881. As the bureaucracy grew larger, the cry for civil service reform became louder. Reformers began to look to the example of several European countries—in particular, Germany. That country had established a professional civil service that operated under a **merit system**, in which job appointments were based on competitive examinations. The German system was the inspiration for Max Weber, mentioned earlier in this chapter.

In 1883, the **Pendleton Act**—or **Civil Service Reform Act**—was passed, placing the first limits on the spoils system.

spoils system
The awarding of government jobs to political supporters and friends.

merit system
The selection, retention, and promotion of government employees on the basis of competitive examinations.

Pendleton Act (Civil Service Reform Act)
An act that established the principle of employment on the basis of merit and created the Civil Service Commission to administer the personnel service.

Image 13–6 Federal Communications Commission chairman Tom Wheeler at a meeting of the commissioners in 2014. At the meeting, commissioners voted in favor of a proposal to regulate Internet broadband providers. *What kinds of regulations are appropriate for the Internet?*

KAREN BLEIER/Getty Images

Library of Congress Prints and Photographs Division

The act established the principle of employment on the basis of open, competitive examinations and created the **Civil Service Commission** to administer the personnel service. Only 10 percent of federal employees were covered by the merit system initially. Later laws, amendments, and executive orders, however, increased the coverage to more than 90 percent of federal employees. The effects of these reforms were felt at all levels of government.

The Supreme Court strengthened the civil service system in 1976 and in 1980.[3] In those two cases, the Court used the First Amendment to forbid government officials from discharging or threatening to discharge public employees solely for not being supporters of the political party in power unless party affiliation is an appropriate requirement for the position. A 1990 ruling added further enhancements to the civil service system.[4] The Court's ruling in that year effectively prevented the use of partisan political considerations as the basis for hiring, promoting, or transferring most public employees. An exception was permitted, however, for senior policymaking positions, which usually go to officials who will support the programs of the elected leaders.

Image 13–7 President James A. Garfield was assassinated in 1881 by a disappointed office seeker. One result of this crime was the passage of the Pendleton Act in 1883, which created a career civil service. *What kinds of problems would result today if we relied, even in part, on the spoils system?*

The Civil Service Reform Act of 1978. In 1978, the Civil Service Reform Act abolished the Civil Service Commission and created two new federal agencies to perform its duties. To administer the civil service laws, rules, and regulations, the act created the Office of Personnel Management (OPM). The OPM is empowered to recruit, interview, and test potential government workers and determine who should be hired. The OPM makes recommendations to the individual agencies as to which persons meet the standards (typically, the top three applicants for a position), and the agencies then decide whom to hire. To oversee promotions, employees' rights, and other employment matters, the act created the Merit Systems Protection Board (MSPB). The MSPB evaluates charges of wrongdoing, hears employee appeals of agency decisions, and can order corrective action against agencies and employees.

Federal Employees and Political Campaigns. In 1933, when President Franklin D. Roosevelt set up his New Deal, a veritable army of civil servants was hired to staff the many new agencies that were created. Because the individuals who worked in these agencies owed their jobs to the Democratic Party, it seemed natural for them to campaign for Democratic candidates. The Democrats who controlled Congress in the mid-1930s did not object. But in 1938, a coalition of conservative Democrats and Republicans took control of Congress and forced through the Hatch Act—or Political Activities Act—of 1939. The act prohibited federal employees from actively participating in the political management of campaigns. It also forbade the use of federal authority to influence nominations and elections, and it outlawed the use of bureaucratic rank to pressure federal employees to make political contributions.

Hatch Act Controversies. The Hatch Act created a controversy that lasted for decades. Many contended that the act deprived federal employees of their First Amendment freedoms of speech and association. In 1972, a federal district court declared the act unconstitutional. The United States Supreme Court, however, reaffirmed the

Civil Service Commission
The initial central personnel agency of the national government; created in 1883.

3. *Elrod v. Burns*, 427 U.S. 347 (1976); and *Branti v. Finkel*, 445 U.S. 507 (1980).

4. *Rutan v. Republican Party of Illinois*, 497 U.S. 62 (1990).

challenged portion of the act in 1973, stating that the government's interest in preserving a nonpartisan civil service was so great that the prohibitions should remain.[5]

Twenty years later, Congress addressed the criticisms of the Hatch Act by passing the Federal Employees Political Activities Act of 1993. This act, which amended the Hatch Act, lessened the harshness of the 1939 act in several ways. Among other things, the 1993 act allowed federal employees to run for office in nonpartisan elections, participate in voter-registration drives, make campaign contributions to political organizations, and campaign for candidates in partisan elections.

Modern Attempts at Bureaucratic Reform

Learning Outcome **4:**

Evaluate different methods that have been put into place to reform bureaucracies and make them more efficient.

As long as the federal bureaucracy exists, attempts to make it more open, efficient, and responsive to the needs of U.S. citizens will continue. The most important actual and proposed reforms in the last several decades include sunshine laws, privatization, and more protection for so-called whistleblowers.

Sunshine Laws before and after 9/11

In 1976, Congress enacted the **Government in the Sunshine Act.** It required for the first time that all multiheaded federal agencies—agencies headed by a committee instead of an individual—hold their meetings regularly in public session. The bill defined meetings as almost any gathering, formal or informal, of agency members, including a conference telephone call. The only exceptions to this rule of openness are discussions of matters such as court proceedings or personnel problems, and these exceptions are specifically listed in the bill. Sunshine laws now exist at all levels of government.

Information Disclosure. In 1966, the federal government passed the Freedom of Information Act (FOIA), which required federal government agencies, with certain exceptions, to disclose to individuals information contained in government files. FOIA requests are helpful not just to individuals. Indeed, the major beneficiaries of the act have been news organizations, which have used it to uncover government waste, scandals, and incompetence.

As one example, in 2014 the Associated Press obtained records that revealed police efforts to restrict airspace to keep away news helicopters during violent street protests in Ferguson, Missouri. In recent years, however, news organizations have found it more difficult to use the FOIA. In particular, the Obama administration set new records for censoring government files, denying access to information, and failing to address FOIA requests in a timely fashion.

Curbs on Information Disclosure. Since the terrorist attacks of September 11, 2001, the trend toward open government has been reversed at both the federal and the state levels. Within weeks after September 11, 2001, federal agencies removed hundreds, if not thousands, of documents from Internet sites, public libraries, and the reading rooms found in various federal government departments. Information contained in some of the documents included diagrams of power plants and pipelines, structural details on dams, and safety plans for chemical plants. The military also immediately began restricting information about its current and planned activities, as did the Federal Bureau of Investigation. These agencies were concerned that terrorists could make use of this information to plan attacks.

Government in the Sunshine Act
A law that requires all committee-directed federal agencies to conduct their business regularly in public session.

5. *United States Civil Service Commission v. National Association of Letter Carriers,* 413 U.S. 548 (1973).

Image 13–8 National Guard members build a sandbag levy against flooding by the North Platte River in Wyoming. *Is the National Guard part of the federal bureaucracy?*

Privatization, or Contracting Out

Another approach to bureaucratic reform is **privatization,** which occurs when government services are replaced by services from the private sector. For example, the government has contracted with private firms to operate prisons. Supporters of privatization argue that some services can be provided more efficiently by the private sector. A similar scheme involves furnishing vouchers to government "clients" in lieu of services. For example, instead of supplying housing, the government could offer vouchers that recipients could use to "pay" for housing in privately owned buildings.

The privatization, or contracting-out, strategy has been most successful on the local level. Some municipalities have contracted with private companies for such services as trash collection. This approach is not a cure-all, however, because many functions, particularly on the national level, cannot be contracted out in any meaningful way.

The increase in the amount of government work being contracted out to the private sector has led to significant controversy in recent years. Some have criticized the lack of competitive bidding for many contracts that the government has awarded. Another concern is the perceived lack of government oversight of the work done by private contractors.

Saving Costs through E-Government

Many contend that the communications revolution brought about by the Internet has not only improved the efficiency with which government agencies deliver services to the public but also helped to reduce the cost of government. Agencies can now communicate with members of the public, as well as other agencies, via e-mail. Additionally, every federal agency now has a website to which citizens can go to find information about agency services instead of calling or appearing in person at a regional agency office.

Although data-rich high-tech systems have provided new, efficient ways of accomplishing the government's work, privacy concerns have become an issue when the government collects data on individuals. As one example, the American public has never accepted the concept of a national ID card, even though many other nations require their citizens to obtain such ID. Still, it is difficult to live a normal life without a Social Security number and a state-issued ID such as a driver's license.

Helping Out the Whistleblowers

A **whistleblower** is someone who blows the whistle on (brings to public attention) a gross governmental inefficiency or an illegal action. Whistleblowers may be clerical workers, managers, or even specialists, such as scientists.

Laws Protecting Whistleblowers. The 1978 Civil Service Reform Act prohibits reprisals against whistleblowers by their superiors, and it set up the Merit Systems Protection Board as part of this protection. Many federal agencies also have toll-free hotlines

privatization

The replacement of government services with services provided by private firms.

whistleblower

Someone who brings to public attention gross governmental inefficiency or an illegal action.

that employees can use anonymously to report bureaucratic waste and inappropriate behavior. About 35 percent of all calls result in agency action or follow-up.

Further protection for whistleblowers was provided in 1989, when Congress passed the Whistleblower Protection Act. That act established an independent agency, the Office of Special Counsel (OSC), to investigate complaints brought by government employees who have been demoted, fired, or otherwise punished for reporting government fraud or waste.

Some state and federal laws encourage employees to blow the whistle on their employers' wrongful actions by providing monetary incentives to the whistleblowers. At the federal level, the False Claims Act of 1986 allows a whistleblower who has disclosed information about a fraud against the U.S. government to receive a monetary award. If the government chooses to prosecute the case and wins, the whistleblower receives between 15 and 25 percent of the proceeds. If the government declines to intervene, the whistleblower can bring a suit on behalf of the government and, if the suit is successful, will receive between 25 and 30 percent of the proceeds.

The Problem Continues. Despite these efforts to help whistleblowers, there is little evidence that they truly receive much protection. More than 41 percent of the employees who turned to the OSC for assistance in a recent three-year period stated that they were no longer employees of the government agencies on which they had blown the whistle.

Additionally, in 2006 the United States Supreme Court placed restrictions on lawsuits brought by public workers.[6] The case involved an assistant district attorney, Richard Ceballos, who wrote a memo asking if a county sheriff's deputy had lied in a search warrant affidavit. Ceballos claimed that he was subsequently demoted and denied a promotion. The outcome of the case turned on whether an employee has a First Amendment right to criticize an employment-related action. The Court deemed that when he wrote his memo, Ceballos was speaking as an employee, not a citizen, and was thus subject to his employer's disciplinary actions. The ruling affects millions of governmental employees.

Whistleblowers under Obama. During his 2008 campaign, Obama promised to protect whistleblowers. Many observers believe, however, that in fact the Obama administration's record on whistleblowers is one of the worst ever. This conclusion is based, in large part, on the administration's use of the Espionage Act of 1917 to prosecute persons who leaked national security information to the press. By 2013, the administration had launched seven such prosecutions. The Espionage Act has been used regularly against persons spying for foreign governments. Not since 1984, however, had the government initiated such a case based on leaks to the press.

The most recent—and most dramatic—case involved Edward Snowden, a National Security Agency (NSA) contractor. Snowden delivered a

Frank Cotham/The New Yorker Collection/Cartoon Bank.Com

Image 13–9 *"It's always cozy in here. We're insulated by layers of bureaucracy."*

6. *Garcetti v. Ceballos*, 547 U.S. 410 (2006).

Mark Wilson/Getty Images

enabling legislation

A statute enacted by Congress that authorizes the creation of an administrative agency and specifies the name, purpose, composition, functions, and powers of the agency being created.

Image 13–10 In 2013, Army Private First Class Bradley Manning was sentenced to thirty-five years in prison for giving classified U.S. government information to the anti-secrecy web site called WikiLeaks. In 2014, Manning sought a name change from Bradley Edward to Chelsea Elizabeth with the intention of living thereafter as a woman. *Is Manning a criminal, a hero—or both?*

vast collection of information on NSA data surveillance to journalists Glenn Greenwald and Laura Poitras. Stories based on the material appeared in the *Guardian* of Britain, in the *Washington Post* and the *New York Times*, and in a variety of other newspapers around the world. Was NSA surveillance of Americans proper? We examine that question in this chapter's *Which Side Are You On?* feature.

Snowden was aware of how the government had treated Private First Class Chelsea (formerly Bradley) Manning, an earlier leaker. Manning had been held in solitary confinement in ways that some critics saw as abusive. Snowden therefore relocated to Hong Kong, hoping that the Chinese government would grant him asylum. On learning that asylum would not be granted, Snowden then fled to Russia. Both Greenwald and Poitras also now live outside the United States.

Bureaucrats as Politicians and Policymakers

Learning Outcome **5:**

Discuss how federal agencies make rules and the role of Congress in this process.

Because Congress is unable to oversee the day-to-day administration of its programs, it must delegate certain powers to administrative agencies. Congress delegates power to agencies through **enabling legislation.** For example, the Federal Trade Commission was created by the Federal Trade Commission Act of 1914, the Equal Employment Opportunity Commission was created by the Civil Rights Act of 1964, and the Occupational Safety and Health Administration was created by the Occupational Safety and Health Act of 1970. The enabling legislation generally specifies the name, purpose, composition, functions, and powers of the agency.

Which side are you on?

Do the Benefits of NSA Snooping Outweigh the Harms?

How would you like it if the federal government accessed all of your tweets, Facebook posts, blogs, anything you put on Instagram or Pinterest, plus your phone calls, text messages, purchases, and Internet searches? You might feel outraged, or at least annoyed. In fact, the National Security Agency (NSA) is not only capable of snooping on everything just mentioned, but in many cases it is collecting such data. In 2013, former NSA contractor Edward Snowden revealed that the NSA has engaged in broad surveillance of American citizens, a practice that raises questions about our rights to be free from unreasonable searches. Snowden proclaimed, "I do not want to live in a world where everything I do and say is recorded." Do you?

Yes, the Benefits Outweigh the Harms

The NSA's defenders argue that it must continue its surveillance programs because the benefits are great. Of course the NSA collects a lot of data. That's what an intelligence agency does. The NSA's job is to collect information so as to learn of potential threats to the United States. The more information it has, the better it can protect us against terrorist actions. The NSA has a specific mission. It is not sifting through every possible piece of data. Rather, it is looking for evidence of high-profile threats to national security. The average American's phone calls, messaging, and Facebook postings do not raise red flags because the NSA isn't concerned with petty wrongdoing. It is looking for behavior that threatens national security.

Opponents of the NSA claim that its actions violate Fourth Amendment protections against unreasonable searches. But these opponents don't get to define what is or is not constitutional. Courts do that, and they have ruled that what the NSA does is legal. You may consider that unfair, but the NSA is hardly the only organization collecting data on Americans. Our credit card companies, online shopping services, and even grocery stores are collecting vast amounts of information as well. It's easy to tell a story about a runaway intelligence agency, but the truth is a lot less interesting.

Domestic Spying Is Unconstitutional and Wrong

NSA opponents don't agree that the agency's actions must be legal because a court has approved them. Judges make mistakes, and they are more likely to make them when they are allowed to hear only one side of the story. This is exactly what happens when the secret Foreign Intelligence Surveillance Court hears cases. No group can be trusted to police itself, but that is what we now do with our intelligence agencies.

The authors of the Bill of Rights believed that it is better to let some criminals go free than to suffer from a system that ignores due process of law. If the police could violate our constitutional rights, they would surely catch more criminals. But we would be less free. Our leaders appear to believe that stopping terrorist attacks is the only goal that the government needs to consider. But liberty also matters, and liberty is more fragile than security. We can recover quickly from a terrorist attack, but once liberty is lost, it is very hard to get it back.

The chances of an American being killed by a terrorist in a given year have been calculated variously as one in 3.5 million and one in 20 million. How much do we need to spend—and how much liberty should we give up—to make us safer than that? After a certain point, the costs swamp the benefits. If we want to live in a free society, we should demand that the NSA stop spying on us.

For Critical Analysis

⊙ The NSA also spies on our allies. What effect could this have on U.S. foreign relations?

In theory, the agencies should put into effect laws passed by Congress. Laws are often drafted in such vague and general terms, however, that they provide limited guidance to agency administrators as to how they should be implemented. This means that the agencies themselves must decide how best to carry out the wishes of Congress.

The discretion given to administrative agencies is not accidental. Congress has long realized that it lacks the technical expertise and the resources to monitor the implementation of its laws. Hence, administrative agencies are created to fill the gaps. This gap-filling role requires an agency to formulate administrative rules (regulations) to put flesh on the bones of the law. But it also forces the agency itself to become an unelected policymaker.

The Rulemaking Environment

Rulemaking does not occur in a vacuum. Suppose that Congress passes a new air-pollution law. The Environmental Protection Agency (EPA) might decide to implement the new law through a technical regulation on power-plant emissions. This proposed regulation would be published in the *Federal Register,* a daily government publication, so that interested parties would have an opportunity to comment on it. Individuals and companies that opposed parts or all of the rule might then try to convince the EPA to revise or redraft the regulation. Some parties might try to persuade the agency to withdraw the proposed regulation altogether. In any event, the EPA would consider these comments in drafting the final version of the regulation.

Waiting Periods and Court Challenges. Once the final regulation has been published in the *Federal Register,* there is a sixty-day waiting period before the rule can be enforced. During that period, businesses, individuals, and state and local governments can ask Congress to overturn the regulation. After the sixty-day period has lapsed, the regulation can still be challenged in court by a party having a direct interest in the rule, such as a company that expects to incur significant costs in complying with it. The company could argue that the rule misinterprets the applicable law or goes beyond the agency's legal authority. An allegation by the company that the EPA made a mistake in judgment probably would not be enough to convince the court to throw out the rule. The company instead would have to demonstrate that the rule itself was "arbitrary and capricious."

Rick Loomis/Getty Images

Image 13–11 A worker looks out over 300 tons of trash piled up near the mouth of the Los Angeles River in Long Beach, California, after two days of heavy rain flushed the river. *How might the government protect the environment from large-scale littering?*

Controversies. How agencies implement, administer, and enforce legislation has resulted in controversy. For example, decisions made by agencies charged with administering the Endangered Species Act have led to protests from farmers, ranchers, and others whose economic interests have been harmed.

At times, a controversy may arise when an agency *refuses* to issue regulations to implement a particular law. During the George W. Bush administration, the EPA refused to issue regulations designed to curb the emission of carbon dioxide and other greenhouse gases. State and local governments, as well as a number of environmental groups, then sued the agency. Those bringing the suit claimed that the EPA was not fulfilling its obligation to implement the provisions of the Clean Air Act. Ultimately, the Supreme Court held that the EPA had the authority to—and should—regulate such gases.[7]

Negotiated Rulemaking

Since the end of World War II in 1945, companies, environmentalists, and other special interest groups have challenged government regulations in court. In the 1980s, however, the sheer wastefulness of attempting to regulate through litigation became increasingly apparent. Today, a growing number of federal agencies encourage businesses and public-interest groups to become directly involved in drafting regulations. Agencies hope that such participation may help to prevent later courtroom battles over the regulations.

Congress formally approved such a process, which is called *negotiated rulemaking*, in the Negotiated Rulemaking Act of 1990. The act authorizes agencies to allow those who will be affected by a new rule to participate in the rule-drafting process. If an agency chooses to engage in negotiated rulemaking, it must publish in the *Federal Register* the subject and scope of the rule to be developed, the names of parties that will be affected significantly by the rule, and other information. Representatives of the affected groups and other interested parties then may apply to be members of the negotiating committee. The agency is represented on the committee, but a neutral third party (not the agency) presides over the proceedings. Once the committee members have reached agreement on the terms of the proposed rule, a notice is published in the *Federal Register,* followed by a period for comments by any person or organization interested in the proposed rule. Negotiated rulemaking often is conducted under the condition that the participants promise not to challenge in court the outcome of any agreement to which they were a party.

Bureaucrats as Policymakers

Theories of public administration once assumed that bureaucrats do not make policy decisions but only implement the laws and policies promulgated by the president and legislative bodies. A more realistic view is that the agencies and departments of government play important roles in policymaking. As we have seen, many government rules, regulations, and programs are in fact initiated by the bureaucracy, based on its expertise and scientific studies. How a law passed by Congress eventually is translated into action—from the forms to be filled out to decisions about who gets the benefits—usually is determined within each agency or department. Even the evaluation of whether a policy has achieved its purpose usually is based on studies that are commissioned and interpreted by the agency administering the program.

The bureaucracy's policymaking role has often been depicted as an *iron triangle*. Recently, many political scientists have come to see the concept of an *issue network* as a more accurate description of the typical policymaking process.

---

7. *Massachusetts v. EPA,* 549 U.S. 497 (2007).

Image 13–12 These farmers—father and son—raise beef cattle on an Iowa farm. *To which part of the iron triangle in agriculture do they belong?*

Iron Triangles. In the past, scholars often described the bureaucracy's role in the policy-making process by using the concept of an **iron triangle**—a three-way alliance among legislators in Congress, bureaucrats, and interest groups. Consider as an example the development of agricultural policy. Congress, as one component of the triangle, includes two major committees concerned with agricultural policy, the House Committee on Agriculture and the Senate Committee on Agriculture, Nutrition, and Forestry. The Department of Agriculture, the second component of the triangle, has more than 85,000 employees, plus thousands of contractors and consultants. Agricultural interest groups, the third component of the triangle, include many large and powerful associations, such as the American Farm Bureau Federation, the National Cattlemen's Beef Association, and the National Corn Growers Association. These three components of the iron triangle work together, formally or informally, to create policy.

For example, the various agricultural interest groups lobby Congress to develop policies that benefit their groups' economic welfare. Members of Congress cannot afford to ignore the wishes of interest groups because those groups are potential sources of voter support and campaign contributions. The legislators in Congress also work closely with the Department of Agriculture, which, in implementing a policy, can develop rules that benefit—or at least do not hurt—certain industries or groups. The Department of Agriculture, in turn, supports policies that enhance the department's budget and powers. In this way, according to theory, agricultural policy is created that benefits all three components of the iron triangle.

iron triangle

The three-way alliance among legislators, bureaucrats, and interest groups to make or preserve policies that benefit their respective interests.

Issue Networks. With the growth in the complexity of government, policymaking also has become more complicated. The bureaucracy is larger, Congress has more committees and subcommittees, and interest groups are more powerful than ever. Although iron triangles still exist, often they are inadequate as descriptions of how policy is made today. Frequently, different interest groups concerned about a certain area of policy have conflicting demands, making agency decisions difficult. Additionally, during periods of divided government, departments are pressured by the president to take one approach and by Congress to take another.

Many scholars now use the term *issue network* to describe the policymaking process. An **issue network** consists of individuals or organizations that support a particular policy position on the environment, taxation, consumer safety, or some other issue. Typically, an issue network includes legislators and/or their staff members, interest group leaders, bureaucrats, scholars and other experts, and representatives from the media. Members of a particular issue network work together to influence the president, members of Congress, administrative agencies, and the courts to affect public policy on a specific issue. Each policy issue may involve conflicting positions taken by two or more issue networks.

issue network

A group of individuals or organizations— which may consist of legislators and legislative staff members, interest group leaders, bureaucrats, scholars and other experts, and media representatives—that supports a particular policy position on a given issue.

Congressional Control of the Bureaucracy

Many political pundits doubt whether Congress can meaningfully control the federal bureaucracy. These commentators forget that Congress specifies in an agency's "enabling legislation" the powers of the agency and the parameters within which it can operate.

Additionally, Congress has the power of the purse and theoretically could refuse to authorize or appropriate funds for a particular agency. Whether Congress would actually take such a drastic measure would depend on the circumstances. It is clear, however, that Congress does have the legal authority to decide whether or not to fund administrative agencies.

Congress can also exercise oversight over agencies. Congressional committees conduct investigations and hold hearings to oversee an agency's actions, reviewing them to ensure compliance with congressional intentions. The agency's officers and employees can be ordered

Why should you care about **THE BUREAUCRACY?**

The federal government collects billions of pieces of information on Americans every year. Verifying the information that the government has on you can be important. On several occasions, the records of two people with similar names have become confused. Sometimes innocent persons have had the criminal records of other persons erroneously inserted in their files. Such disasters are not always caused by bureaucratic error. One of the most common crimes in today's world is "identity theft," in which one person makes use of another person's personal identifiers (such as a Social Security number) to commit fraud. In some instances, identity thieves have been arrested and even jailed under someone else's name.

to testify before a committee about the details of various actions. Through the questions and comments of members of the House or the Senate during the hearings, Congress indicates its positions on specific programs and issues. The views expressed in any investigations and hearings are taken seriously by agency officials, who often act on them.

How you can make a difference

The 1966 Freedom of Information Act (FOIA) requires that the federal government release, at your request, any identifiable information it has about you or about any other subject. Some categories of material are exempted, however.

- To request material, write directly to the Freedom of Information Act officer at the agency in question. You must have a relatively specific idea about the document or information you want to obtain.

- A second law, the Privacy Act of 1974, gives you access specifically to information the government may have collected about you. This law allows you to review records on file with federal agencies and to check those records for possible inaccuracies.

- If you want to look at any records or find out if an agency has a record on you, write to the agency head or Privacy Act officer, and address your letter to the specific agency. State that "under the provisions of the Privacy Act of 1974, 5 U.S.C. 522a, I hereby request a copy of (or access to) _____." Then describe the record that you wish to investigate.

- The General Services Administration (GSA) has published a citizen's guide, *Your Right to Federal Records.* You can locate this manual by entering its name into your favorite search engine.

KEY TERMS

acquisitive model 350	government corporation 360	issue network 373	spoils system 363
agency capture 359	Government in the Sunshine Act 365	line organization 353	Weberian model 349
bureaucracy 349		merit system 363	whistleblower 366
cabinet department 353	independent executive agency 356	monopolistic model 350	
Civil Service Commission 364	independent regulatory agency 357	Pendleton Act (Civil Service Reform Act) 363	
enabling legislation 368	iron triangle 372	privatization 366	

CHAPTER SUMMARY

Learning Outcome 1 Bureaucracies are hierarchical organizations characterized by a division of labor and extensive procedural rules. In addition to governments, major corporations and universities have bureaucratic organizations.

Several theories have been offered to describe bureaucracies. The Weberian model posits that bureaucracies are rational, hierarchical organizations in which decisions are based on logical reasoning. The acquisitive model views top-level bureaucrats as pressing for ever-larger budgets and staffs to augment their power. The monopolistic model focuses on the environment in which most government bureaucracies operate, stating that bureaucracies are inefficient and excessively costly to operate because they have no competitors.

Since the founding of the United States, the federal bureaucracy has grown from 50 to about 2.6 million employees (including the U.S. Postal Service, but excluding the military). Federal, state, and local employees together make up about 16 percent of the nation's civilian labor force. Social Security, Medicare, Medicaid, and military defense are the largest components of federal spending. Major sources of federal revenue include individual and corporate income taxes, Social Security and Medicare payroll taxes, and borrowing.

Learning Outcome 2 The federal bureaucracy consists of fifteen cabinet departments, as well as a large number of independent executive agencies, independent regulatory agencies, and government corporations.

Learning Outcome 3 A federal bureaucracy of career civil servants was formed during Thomas Jefferson's presidency. Andrew Jackson implemented a spoils system through which he appointed his own political supporters. A civil service based on professionalism and merit was the goal of the Civil Service Reform Act of 1883. Concerns that the civil service be freed from the pressures of politics prompted the passage of the Hatch Act in 1939. The Civil Service Reform Act of 1978 made significant changes in the administration of the civil service by creating the Office of Personnel Management and the Merit Systems Protection Board.

Learning Outcome 4 There have been many attempts to make the federal bureaucracy more open, efficient, and responsive to the needs of U.S. citizens. The most important reforms have included sunshine laws, privatization, and protection for whistleblowers.

Learning Outcome 5 Congress delegates much of its authority to federal agencies when it creates new laws. The bureaucrats who run these agencies may become important policymakers because Congress has neither the time nor the technical expertise to oversee the administration of its laws. In the agency rulemaking process, a proposed regulation is published. A comment period follows, during which interested parties may offer suggestions for changes.

Congress exerts ultimate control over all federal agencies because it controls the federal government's purse strings. The appropriations process provides a way to send messages of approval or disapproval to particular agencies, as do congressional hearings and investigations of agency actions.

ADDITIONAL RESOURCES

Online Resources

- Numerous links to federal agencies and information on the federal government can be found at the U.S. government's official website at **www.usa.gov**.

- One of the best sites sponsored by a federal agency is that of the Centers for Disease Control. For hilarious advice on what to do in a natural disaster, see the comic book *Preparedness 101: Zombie Pandemic* at **www.cdc.gov/phpr/documents/Zombie_GN_Final.pdf**.

Books

Chopra, Aneesh. *Innovative State: How New Technologies Can Transform Government*. New York: Grove Press, 2016. Chopra, the nation's first chief technology officer under President Obama, shows how government can work better by adopting new approaches to technology.

Goodsell, Charles T. *The New Case for Bureaucracy*. Washington, D.C.: CQ Press, 2014. Goodsell takes on critics of the U.S. federal bureaucracy, arguing that it is one of the best in the world. With Congress largely deadlocked, responsibility falls on the various federal agencies to keep the machinery of government running smoothly. Goodsell is a professor of public administration at Virginia Tech.

Grisinger, Joanna L. *The Unwieldy American State: Administrative Politics since the New Deal*. New York: Cambridge University Press, 2014. Grisinger details the evolution of the U.S. federal bureaucracy in the decades that followed the New Deal of the 1930s. This historical work describes the controversies that resulted in the bureaucracy that exists today. Grisinger is currently on the faculty at Northwestern University.

Video

FBI Takedown—A 2010 documentary by *National Geographic* that provides a straightforward examination of what the FBI really does, without glorification or condemnation. The National Geographic team was granted extraordinary access to make this film.

When the Levees Broke: A Requiem in Four Acts—A strong treatment of Hurricane Katrina's impact on New Orleans by renowned African American director Spike Lee. We learn about the appalling performance of authorities at every level and the suffering that could have been avoided. Lee's anger at what he sees adds spice to this 2006 production.

Quiz

Multiple Choice and Fill-Ins

Learning Outcome 1 Discuss the nature of the federal bureaucracy, and identify the largest federal spending programs.

1. In terms of federal dollars spent, the most important programs are:
   a. social programs, including Social Security and Medicare.
   b. the military and subsidies for corporations.
   c. foreign aid.

2. There are many models of bureaucratic behavior. One argues that top-level bureaucrats always want to expand their bureaucracies. This is called the _____ model.

Learning Outcome 2 Describe the various types of agencies and organizations that make up the federal executive branch.

3. The heads of federal regulatory agencies and members of agency boards and commissions are appointed by:
   a. the president acting alone.
   b. the president with the consent of the Senate.
   c. the Supreme Court.

4. When a federal agency's function is to make and implement rules and regulations to protect the public interest, it is called a(n) _____ _____ _____.

Learning Outcome 3 Explain how government employees are hired and how the civil service is administered.

5. The first significant legislation aimed at making the federal civil service nonpartisan and independent was:
   a. the Civil Service Act of 1978.
   b. the Hatch Act.
   c. the Pendleton Act of 1883.

6. In the early days of this country, when one party won the presidency, government employees were often fired and replaced with those who supported the incoming president's party. This was called the _____ _____.

Learning Outcome 4 Evaluate different methods that have been put into place to reform bureaucracies and make them more efficient.

7. Privatization means that:
   a. the government must provide individuals with the information it has on them.
   b. private companies replace members of the civil service in providing a government service.
   c. bonuses are awarded for efficient work.

8. Under the Obama administration, _____ faced criminal charges with unprecedented frequency.

Learning Outcome 5 Discuss how federal agencies make rules and the role of Congress in this process.

9. An issue network consists of individuals or organizations that support a particular policy position. A typical issue network includes:
   a. Congress, the president's cabinet, and the Supreme Court.
   b. federal judges, congressional staff, and the heads of certain private corporations.
   c. legislators (or their staff), interest group leaders, bureaucrats, scholars and other experts, and the media.

10. Because Congress cannot oversee the daily administration of its many programs, it delegates power to agencies through _____ _____.

Essay Questions

1. The U.S. attorney general, head of the Justice Department, is appointed by the president and is frequently the president's close political ally. Should the attorney general and other U.S. attorneys be appointed on a partisan basis? Why or why not?

2. If Congress tried to make civil servants easier to fire, what political forces might stand in the way?

Answers to multiple-choice and fill-in questions: 1. a, 2. acquisitive, 3. b, 4. independent regulatory agency, 5. c, 6. spoils system, 7. b, 8. whistleblowers, 9. c, 10. enabling legislation.

THE COURTS

United States Supreme Court justices attend President Obama's final State of the Union address in January 2016. In the front row, from the left: Chief Justice John Roberts, and then Justices Anthony Kennedy, Ruth Bader Ginsburg, Stephen Breyer, and Sonia Sotomayor. *Why might some justices choose to skip this event?*
Chip Somodevilla/Getty Images

These five **LEARNING OUTCOMES** *below are designed to help improve your understanding of this chapter:*

1: Explain the main sources of American law, including constitutions, statutes and regulations, and the common law tradition.

2: Describe the structure of the federal court system and such basic judicial requirements as jurisdiction and standing to sue.

3: Discuss the procedures used by the United States Supreme Court and the various types of opinions it hands down.

4: Evaluate the manner in which federal judges are selected.

5: Consider the ways in which the Supreme Court makes policy, and explain the forces that limit the activism of the courts.

What if...

Arguments before the Supreme Court Were Televised?

Background

Since 1955, the United States Supreme Court has allowed audio recordings of oral arguments before the Court. Also, during every session of the Supreme Court, a court reporter transcribes every word that is spoken, even with indications when there is laughter. You can find written transcripts and audio recordings of each oral argument by going to www.supremecourt.gov. Today, many states have gone one step further—they allow appellate court sessions to be televised. The federal appellate courts and the Supreme Court have resisted televising their proceedings, however.

What If Arguments before the Supreme Court Were Televised?

Presumably, coverage of Supreme Court proceedings would be undertaken in the same way that sessions in the Senate and the House of Representatives are televised by C-SPAN. The C-SPAN coverage includes no commentaries about the proceedings in the chambers of Congress. The television coverage is straightforward, word for word, and often quite boring.

In the Supreme Court, similar television coverage would consist of one or two cameras and their operators discreetly positioned in the courtroom where the nine justices hear oral arguments and question the attorneys. Another C-SPAN channel might have to be created to televise Supreme Court proceedings. A low-cost alternative would be Internet video streaming. Available anywhere in the world, Internet video streaming would allow the rest of the world to better understand the American judicial system.

The Supreme Court could follow the states, which have already developed a wide variety of rules governing television coverage of court proceedings.[a] Most states' rules allow the presiding judge to limit or prohibit coverage. Most states also allow the parties to object to television coverage, and some require the parties' consent.

If Supreme Court proceedings were televised, we could expect a media "mini-industry" to follow, particularly on the Internet. There might be new websites with portions of Supreme Court proceedings shown in video along with commentary by legal and political experts.

Grandstanding— A Possibility?

Certain sitting judges and others have argued against televising Supreme Court sessions because of the possibility of "grandstanding." In other words, they are worried that justices might ask questions and make comments during the proceedings in the hopes that such comments would become sound bites on the evening news. Justice Anthony M. Kennedy has said that televising proceedings would "change our collegial dynamic." Grandstanding by lawyers presenting oral arguments is also a possible danger.

In contrast, Judge Diarmuid O'Scannlain of the U.S. Court of Appeals for the Ninth Circuit believes that the concerns about grandstanding and politicking in the courtroom are "overstated." He argues that televising appellate court proceedings depoliticizes them and improves the public's perception of the legal process.

For Critical Analysis

▷ How wide an audience do you believe the television proceedings of the Supreme Court would have?

▷ Do you think that televised proceedings of the Supreme Court would significantly increase public awareness of Supreme Court decisions? Why or why not?

Image 14–1 The scales of justice. *Why is the woman representing justice blindfolded?*

Paul Matthew Photography/Shutterstock.com

---

a. See the information provided by the Radio Television Digital News Association by visiting www.rtdna.org/content/cameras_in_court.

s Alexis de Tocqueville, a French commentator on American society in the 1800s, noted, "scarcely any political question arises in the United States that is not resolved, sooner or later, into a judicial question."[1] Our judiciary forms part of our political process. The instant that judges interpret the law, they become actors in the political arena—policymakers working within a political institution.

The most important political force within our judiciary is the United States Supreme Court. The justices of the Supreme Court are not elected but are appointed by the president and confirmed by the Senate. The same is true for all other federal court judges. Because Supreme Court justices are so important in our governmental system, it has been suggested that arguments before the Court should be televised, as this chapter's opening *What If . . .* feature discussed.

How do courts make policy? Why do the federal courts play such an important role in American government? The answers to these questions lie, in part, in our colonial heritage. Most of American law is based on the English system, particularly the English *common law tradition.* In that tradition, the decisions made by judges constitute an important source of law. We open this chapter with an examination of this tradition and of the various other sources of American law. We then look at the federal court system— how it is organized, how its judges are selected, how these judges affect policy, and how they are restrained by our system of checks and balances.

Sources of American Law

The body of American law includes the federal and state constitutions, statutes passed by legislative bodies, administrative law, and case law—the legal principles expressed in court decisions. Case law is based in part on the common law tradition, which dates to the earliest English settlements in North America.

The Common Law Tradition

In 1066, the Normans conquered England, and William the Conqueror and his successors began the process of unifying the country under their rule. One of the ways in which they did this was to establish king's courts. Before the conquest, disputes had been settled according to local custom. The king's courts sought to establish a common, or uniform, set of rules for the whole country. As the number of courts and cases increased, portions of the most important decisions of each year were gathered together and recorded in *Year Books.* Judges who were settling disputes similar to ones that had been decided before used the *Year Books* as the basis for their decisions. If a case was unique, judges had to create new rules, but they based their decisions on the general principles suggested by earlier cases. The body of judge-made law that developed under this system is still used today and is known as the **common law.**

Stare Decisis. The practice of deciding new cases with reference to former decisions— that is, according to **precedent**—became a cornerstone of the English and American judicial systems. It is embodied in the doctrine of ***stare decisis*** (pronounced *ster-*ay dih-*si*-ses), a Latin phrase that means "to stand on decided cases." The doctrine of *stare decisis* obligates judges to follow the precedents set previously by their own courts or by higher courts that have authority over them.

Examples of Precedents. For example, a lower state court in California would be obligated to follow a precedent set by the California Supreme Court. That lower court,

Learning Outcome **1:**

Explain the main sources of American law, including constitutions, statutes and regulations, and the common law tradition.

common law
The body of law developed from judicial decisions in English and U.S. courts, not attributable to a legislature.

precedent
A court ruling bearing on subsequent legal decisions in similar cases. Judges rely on precedents in deciding cases.

stare decisis
To stand on decided cases; the judicial policy of following precedents established by past decisions.

---

1. Alexis de Tocqueville, *Democracy in America,* trans. George Lawrence (New York: Harper & Row, 1966), p. 248.

case law

Judicial interpretations of common law principles and doctrines, as well as interpretations of constitutional law, statutory law, and administrative law.

however, would not be obligated to follow a precedent set by the supreme court of another state, because each state court system is independent. Of course, when the United States Supreme Court decides an issue, all of the nation's other courts are obligated to abide by the Court's decision—because the Supreme Court is the highest court in the land.

Constitutions

The constitutions of the federal government and the states set forth the general organization, powers, and limits of government. The U.S. Constitution is the supreme law of the land. A law in violation of the Constitution, no matter what its source, may be declared unconstitutional and thereafter cannot be enforced. Similarly, the state constitutions are supreme within their respective borders (unless they conflict with the U.S. Constitution or federal laws and treaties made in accordance with it). The Constitution thus defines the political playing field on which state and federal powers are reconciled.

Statutes and Administrative Regulations

Although the English common law provides the basis for both our civil and our criminal legal systems, statutes (laws enacted by legislatures) have become increasingly important in defining the rights and obligations of individuals. Federal statutes may relate to any subject that is a concern of the federal government and may apply to areas ranging from hazardous waste to federal taxation. State statutes include criminal codes, commercial laws, and laws covering a variety of other matters. Cities, counties, and other local political bodies also pass statutes, which are called *ordinances*. These ordinances may deal with such issues as real estate zoning and public safety.

Rules and regulations issued by administrative agencies are another source of law. Today, much of the work of the courts consists of interpreting these laws and regulations and applying them to the specific circumstances of the cases that come before the courts.

Case Law

Because we have a common law tradition, in which the doctrine of *stare decisis* plays an important role, the decisions rendered by the courts also form an important body of law, collectively referred to as **case law.** Case law includes judicial interpretations of common law principles and doctrines, as well as interpretations of constitutional provisions, statutes, and administrative agency regulations. As you learned in previous chapters, it is up to the courts—ultimately, if necessary, the Supreme Court—to decide what a constitutional provision or a statutory phrase means. In doing so, the courts, in effect, establish law.

Courts in many of the nations formerly governed or settled by Britain—Australia, Canada, Ireland, the United States, and others—exhibit some broad similarities. All make use of the common law, as well as statutes and administrative regulations. All share the basic judicial requirements that you will learn about shortly. In some lands formerly ruled by Britain, such as India, Nigeria, and Pakistan, the common law is supplemented by local traditional law.

Image 14-2 A law student looks up cases in a law library. *Would it be easier to find cases online? Why or why not?*

VStock LLC/Tanya Constantine/Getty Images

Beyond our borders

Gay Rights around the World

Few laws show greater international variation than the ones governing lesbian, gay, bisexual, and transgender (LGBT) individuals. Nations can be divided into three classes. In one group, same-sex unions are wholly or partially recognized. Such nations include Germany, which allows civil unions, and Mexico, where recognition varies by state. A second group does not recognize same-sex unions, but also does not criminalize same-sex behavior. For example, China has a "three nos" policy: "no approval, no disapproval, no promotion." In about seventy countries, however, same-sex intimacy is illegal. (In thirty of these, lesbianism is not outlawed.) In Iran, Saudi Arabia, and a few other nations, same-sex relations are punishable by death.

The French Revolution

Traditional societies have rarely seen same-sex intimacy as a topic for the law to address. In the West, however, following the establishment of Christianity as the official religion, "sodomy laws" outlawed gay relations. Hostile to the church, leaders of the French Revolution (1789–1799) adopted a new legal code that repealed religiously inspired laws—including those against sodomy. French conquests extended the new code to Belgium and the Netherlands.

In the nineteenth century, newly independent Latin American nations adopted the French code, and many of them repealed sodomy laws. Brazil legalized homosexuality in 1830, fifty-eight years before it abolished slavery. When France, Belgium, and the Netherlands established colonial empires, they did not introduce sodomy laws into these traditional societies. The British, in contrast, imposed such laws on their empire. Today, sodomy laws are common in Muslim lands—and former British colonies. Of course, in many places where gay relations are not officially illegal, LGBT individuals must still fear discrimination and violence.

Same-Sex Marriage Takes the Stage

In the second half of the twentieth century, country by country, same-sex relations were decriminalized across Europe and almost all of the Americas. The most conservative U.S. states were among the last to decriminalize, in 2003. By the twenty-first century, same-sex marriage was on the agenda in Europe and the Americas. Denmark established "registered partnerships" in 1989. The Netherlands was the first jurisdiction to legalize same-sex marriage in 2001. Belgium, Quebec, and Massachusetts followed in 2003. Today, most nations in the Western world recognize either same-sex marriage or civil unions.

For Critical Analysis

▶ **Especially in the United States, the courts have taken the lead in establishing same-sex marriage. Why might that be so?**

Nations that do not share the common law tradition typically rely on a statutory code alone, in what is called the civil law system. Judges under the civil law system are not bound by precedent in the way that judges are under the common law system. Differing legal traditions and social customs around the world can have a substantial impact on how various nations address important issues, as you can see in this chapter's *Beyond Our Borders* feature.

The Federal Court System

The United States has a dual court system, with state courts and federal courts. Each of the fifty states, as well as the District of Columbia, has its own independent system of courts. This means that there are fifty-two court systems in total. Here we focus on the federal courts.

Basic Judicial Requirements

Certain requirements must be met before a case can be brought in any court system, state or federal. Two important requirements are *jurisdiction* and *standing to sue.*

Learning Outcome **2:**
Describe the structure of the federal court system and such basic judicial requirements as jurisdiction and standing to sue.

Jurisdiction. A state court can exercise **jurisdiction** (the authority of the court to hear and decide a case) over the residents of a particular geographic area, such as a county or district. A state's highest court, or supreme court, has jurisdictional authority over all residents within the state.

Because the Constitution established a federal government with limited powers, federal jurisdiction is also limited. Article III, Section 1, of the U.S. Constitution limits the jurisdiction of the federal courts to cases that involve either a federal question or diversity of citizenship. A **federal question** arises when a case is based, at least in part, on the U.S. Constitution, a treaty, or a federal law. A person who claims that her or his rights under the Constitution, such as the right to free speech, have been violated could bring a case in a federal court. **Diversity of citizenship** exists when the parties to a lawsuit are from different states or (more rarely) when the suit involves a U.S. citizen and a government or citizen of a foreign country. The amount in controversy must be at least $75,000 before a federal court can take jurisdiction in a diversity case, however.

Given the significant limits on federal jurisdiction, most lawsuits and criminal cases are heard in state, rather than federal, courts. A defendant or a party to a dispute handled by a state court may file an appeal with a state appeals court, or even the state's supreme court. Appeals cannot be taken to a federal court, however, unless there is a federal question at stake.

Standing to Sue. Another basic judicial requirement is standing to sue, or a sufficient "stake" in a matter to justify bringing suit. The party bringing a lawsuit must have suffered a harm, or have been threatened by a harm, as a result of the action that led to the dispute in question. Standing to sue also requires that the controversy at issue be a justiciable (pronounced jus-*tish*-a-bul) controversy. A **justiciable controversy** is a controversy that is real and substantial, as opposed to hypothetical or academic. In other words, a court will not give advisory opinions on hypothetical questions.

Parties to Lawsuits

In most lawsuits, the parties are the plaintiff (the person or organization that initiates the lawsuit) and the defendant (the person or organization against whom the lawsuit is brought). There may be a number of plaintiffs and defendants in a single lawsuit. In the past several decades, many lawsuits have been brought by interest groups. Interest groups play an important role in our judicial system, because they **litigate**—bring to trial—or assist in litigating most cases of racial or gender-based discrimination, almost all civil liberties cases, and more than one-third of the cases involving business matters. Interest groups also file **amicus curiae** (pronounced ah-*mee*-kous *kur*-ee-eye) **briefs,** or "friend of the court" briefs, in more than 50 percent of these kinds of cases.

Sometimes, interest groups or other plaintiffs will bring a **class-action suit,** in which whatever the court decides will affect all members of a class similarly situated (such as users of a particular product manufactured by the defendant in the lawsuit). The strategy of class-action lawsuits was pioneered by such groups as the National Association for the Advancement of Colored People (NAACP), the Legal Defense Fund, and the Sierra Club.

Procedural Rules

Both the federal and the state courts have established procedural rules that shape the litigation process. These rules are designed to protect the rights and interests of the parties and to ensure that the litigation proceeds in a fair and orderly manner. The rules also serve to identify the issues that must be decided by the court—thus saving court time and costs. Court decisions may also apply to trial procedures. For example, the Supreme Court

---

jurisdiction

The authority of a court to decide certain cases. Not all courts have the authority to decide all cases. Where a case arises and what its subject matter is are two jurisdictional issues.

federal question

A question that has to do with the U.S. Constitution, acts of Congress, or treaties. A federal question provides a basis for federal jurisdiction.

diversity of citizenship

The condition that exists when the parties to a lawsuit are citizens of different states or when the parties are citizens of a U.S. state and citizens or the government of a foreign country. Diversity of citizenship can provide a basis for federal jurisdiction.

justiciable controversy

A controversy that is real and substantial, as opposed to hypothetical or academic.

litigate

To engage in a legal proceeding or seek relief in a court of law; to carry on a lawsuit.

amicus curiae brief

A brief (a document containing a legal argument supporting a desired outcome in a particular case) filed by a third party, or *amicus curiae* (Latin for "friend of the court"), who is not directly involved in the litigation but who has an interest in the outcome of the case.

class-action suit

A lawsuit filed by an individual seeking damages for "all persons similarly situated."

has held that the parties' attorneys cannot discriminate against prospective jurors on the basis of race or gender. Some lower courts have also held that people cannot be excluded from juries because of their sexual orientation or religion.

The parties must comply with procedural rules and with any orders given by the judge during the course of the litigation. When a party does not follow a court's order, the court can cite him or her for contempt. A party who commits *civil* contempt (failing to comply with a court's order for the benefit of another party to the proceeding) can be taken into custody, fined, or both, until that party complies with the court's order. A party who commits *criminal* contempt (obstructing the administration of justice or disrespecting the rules of the court) also can be taken into custody and fined but cannot avoid punishment by complying with a previous order.

Types of Federal Courts

As you can see in Figure 14–1, the federal court system is basically a three-tiered model consisting of (1) U.S. district courts and various specialized courts of limited jurisdiction (not all of the latter are shown in the figure), (2) intermediate U.S. courts of appeals, and (3) the United States Supreme Court.

U.S. District Courts. The U.S. district courts are trial courts. A **trial court** is what the name implies—a court in which trials are held and testimony is taken. The U.S. district courts are courts of **general jurisdiction,** meaning that they can hear cases involving a broad array of issues. Federal cases involving most matters typically are heard in district courts. The other courts on the lower tier of the model shown in Figure 14–1 are courts of **limited jurisdiction,** meaning that they try cases involving only certain types of claims, such as tax claims or bankruptcy petitions.

There is at least one federal district court in every state. The number of judicial districts has varied historically owing to population changes and corresponding caseloads, but no entirely new district has been created since California was redivided in 1966. Today, there

trial court
The court in which most cases begin.

general jurisdiction
A court's authority to hear cases without significant restriction. A court of general jurisdiction normally can hear a broad range of cases.

limited jurisdiction
A court's authority to hear cases that is restricted to certain types of claims, such as tax claims or bankruptcy petitions.

Figure 14–1   The Federal Court System

Why do you think Congress created courts of limited jurisdiction?

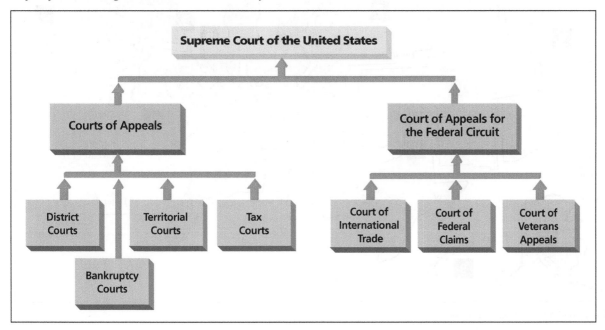

appellate court

A court having jurisdiction to review cases and issues that were originally tried in lower courts.

are 94 federal judicial districts and 678 authorized district court judgeships. The Southern District of New York has the largest number of judges—28. The Central District of California is second with 27.

A party who is dissatisfied with the decision of a district court can appeal the case to the appropriate U.S. court of appeals, or federal **appellate court.** Figure 14–2 shows the jurisdictional boundaries of the district courts (which are state boundaries, unless otherwise indicated by dotted lines within a state) and of the U.S. courts of appeals.

Many federal administrative agencies and most executive departments also employ administrative law judges who resolve disputes arising under the rules governing their agencies. For example, the Social Security Administration might hold a hearing to determine whether a specific class of individuals is entitled to collect a particular benefit. If all internal Social Security appeals processes have been exhausted, a party may have a right to file an appeal in a federal district court. Appeals from the decisions of other agencies may be heard by the district courts, the U.S. courts of appeals, or even a specialized federal court, depending on the agency.

U.S. Courts of Appeals. There are thirteen U.S. courts of appeals—also referred to as U.S. circuit courts of appeals. Twelve of these courts, including the U.S. Court of Appeals for the District of Columbia, hear appeals from the federal district courts located within their respective judicial circuits (geographic areas over which they exercise jurisdiction).

Figure 14–2 Geographic Boundaries of Federal District Courts and U.S. Courts of Appeals

Why might Congress add more judges to a district instead of creating new districts?

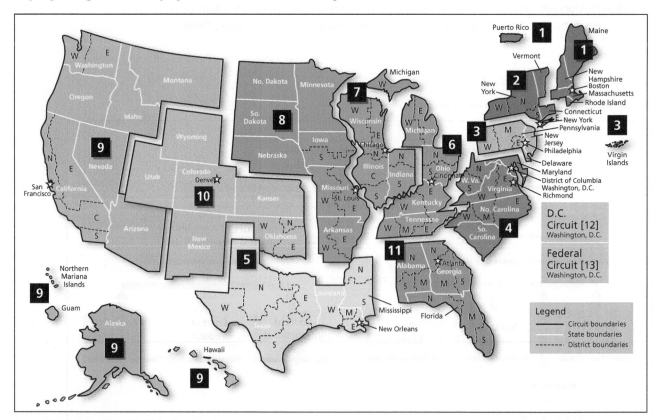

Source: Administrative Office of the United States Courts.

The Court of Appeals for the Thirteenth Circuit, called the Federal Circuit, has national appellate jurisdiction over certain types of cases, such as cases involving patent law and those in which the U.S. government is a defendant.

Note that when an appellate court reviews a case decided in a district court, the appellate court does not conduct another trial. Rather, a panel of three or more judges reviews the record of the case on appeal, which includes a transcript of the trial proceedings. The panel determines whether the trial court committed an error. Usually, appellate courts do not look at questions of *fact* (such as whether a party did, in fact, commit a certain action, such as burning a flag). Instead, they look at questions of *law* (such as whether the act of burning a flag is a form of speech protected by the First Amendment to the Constitution). An appellate court will challenge a trial court's finding of fact only when the finding is clearly contrary to the evidence presented at trial or when there is no evidence to support the finding.

A party can petition the United States Supreme Court to review an appellate court's decision. The likelihood that the Supreme Court will grant the petition is slim, however, because the Court reviews only a small percentage of the cases decided by the appellate courts. This means that decisions made by appellate courts usually are final.

The United States Supreme Court. The highest level of the three-tiered model of the federal court system is the United States Supreme Court. When the Supreme Court came into existence in 1789, it had six justices. In the following years, more justices were added. Since 1869, there have been nine positions on the Court.

According to the language of Article III of the U.S. Constitution, there is only one national Supreme Court. All other courts in the federal system are considered "inferior." Congress is empowered to create other inferior courts as it deems necessary. The inferior courts that Congress has created include the district courts, the federal courts of appeals, and the federal courts of limited jurisdiction.

Although the Supreme Court can exercise original jurisdiction (that is, act as a trial court) in certain cases, such as those affecting foreign diplomats and those in which a state is a party, most of its work is as an appellate court. The Court hears appeals not only from the federal appellate courts but also from the highest state courts. Note, though, that the United States Supreme Court can review a state supreme court decision only if a federal question is involved. Because of its importance in the federal court system, we look more closely at the Supreme Court later in this chapter.

Federal Courts and the War on Terrorism

As noted, the federal court system includes a variety of trial courts of limited jurisdiction, dealing with matters such as tax claims or international trade. The government's attempts to combat terrorism have drawn attention to certain specialized courts that meet in secret. We look next at these courts, as well as at the role of the federal courts with respect to the detainees accused of terrorism.

The FISA Court. The federal government created the first secret court in 1978. In that year, Congress passed the Foreign Intelligence Surveillance Act (FISA), which established a court to hear requests for warrants for the surveillance of suspected spies. Officials can request a

Image 14–3 Chief Justice John Roberts. *What topics might a justice avoid when speaking publicly?*

warrant without having to reveal to the suspect or to the public the information used to justify the warrant or even that the warrant exists. The FISA court has approved almost all of the thousands of requests for warrants that officials have submitted. There is no public access to the court's proceedings or records. Hence, when the court authorizes surveillance, suspects normally do not even know that they are under scrutiny. All FISA court judges are appointed by the chief justice of the Supreme Court without review by any other authority.

In the aftermath of the terrorist attacks on September 11, 2001, the George W. Bush administration expanded the powers of the FISA court. Previously, FISA had allowed secret domestic surveillance only if the "purpose" was to combat intelligence gathering by foreign powers. Amendments to FISA enacted after 9/11 changed this wording to "a significant purpose"—meaning that warrants may now be requested to obtain evidence that can be used in criminal trials.

The FISA Court and the National Security Agency. Some of the National Security Agency (NSA) material that Edward Snowden leaked to the press in 2013 dealt with the FISA court. One of the first stories described a FISA court order that required Verizon to provide a daily, ongoing feed of all landline *metadata* (data about data) to the NSA. That included metadata on domestic calls. Metadata, in this case, include information about calls, such as time, who called, and who was called. They do not include the content of actual conversations. It soon came out that the FISA court had effectively granted the NSA the right to collect metadata on all phone calls, regardless of carrier.

The FISA court apparently justified the massive data collection through a "special needs" exception to the Fourth Amendment's requirement of a warrant for searches and seizures. It would seem that under this exception the Fourth Amendment does not apply to national security surveillance. These revelations touched off a massive debate between advocates of civil liberties and those concerned about national security.

DECISIONS, DECISIONS, DECISIONS

Alien "Removal Courts." In 1996, Congress passed the Anti-Terrorism and Effective Death Penalty Act. The new law was a response to the bombing of a federal building in 1995 in Oklahoma City, which killed 168 people. Even though the perpetrators of this crime were white U.S. citizens whose motives were entirely domestic, the new law focused on noncitizens. For example, the act created an alien "removal court" to hear evidence against suspected "alien terrorists." The judges in this court rule on whether there is probable cause for deportation. If so, a public deportation proceeding is held in a U.S. district court. The prosecution does not need to follow procedures that normally apply in criminal cases. In addition, the defendant cannot see the evidence that the prosecution used to secure the hearing.

The Federal Courts and Suspected Terrorists. After the 9/11 attacks, the U.S. military took custody of hundreds of suspected terrorists seized in Afghanistan and elsewhere and held them at Guantánamo Bay, Cuba. According to the Bush administration, they could be held indefinitely. The handling of

Image 14–4

the prisoners at Guantánamo has been a source of ongoing controversy. The Supreme Court held, first in 2004 and then in 2006, that the Bush administration's treatment of these detainees violated the U.S. Constitution.[2]

In response to the Court's 2006 decision, Congress passed an act that eliminated federal court jurisdiction over challenges by detainees based on *habeas corpus*. (This term refers to the right of a detained person to challenge the legality of his or her detention before a judge.) In 2008, in *Boumediene v. Bush*, the Court ruled that the provisions restricting the federal courts' jurisdictional authority over detainees' *habeas corpus* challenges were illegal.[3] The decision gave Guantánamo detainees the right to challenge their detention in federal civil courts. In 2010, however, a federal appeals court ruled that the administration had the right to detain prisoners indefinitely at Bagram Air Base in Afghanistan because the prison is located on foreign soil and within a war zone.[4]

The Supreme Court at Work

The Supreme Court begins its regular annual term on the first Monday in October and usually adjourns in late June or early July of the next year. Special sessions may be held after the regular term ends, but only a few cases are decided in this way. More commonly, cases are carried over until the next regular session.

Of the total number of cases that are decided each year in U.S. courts, those reviewed by the Supreme Court represent less than one in four thousand. Included in these, however, are decisions that profoundly affect our lives. In recent years, the United States Supreme Court has decided issues involving the right to bear arms, health-care reform, and campaign finance. Other cases have involved affirmative action programs, religious freedom, abortion, and many other matters with significant consequences for the nation.

Because the Supreme Court exercises a great deal of discretion over the types of cases it hears, it can influence the nation's policies by issuing decisions in some types of cases and refusing to hear appeals in others, thereby allowing lower court decisions to stand. Indeed, the fact that George W. Bush assumed the presidency in 2001 instead of Al Gore, his Democratic opponent, was largely due to a Supreme Court decision to review a Florida court's ruling. In *Bush v. Gore*, the Supreme Court reversed the Florida court's order to recount manually the votes in selected Florida counties—a decision that effectively handed the presidency to Bush.[5]

Which Cases Reach the Supreme Court?

Many people are surprised to learn that in a typical case, there is no absolute right of appeal to the Supreme Court. The Court's appellate jurisdiction is almost entirely discretionary—the Court chooses which cases it will decide. The justices never explain

Learning Outcome **3:**

Discuss the procedures used by the United States Supreme Court and the various types of opinions it hands down.

Image 14–5 United States Supreme Court Justice Clarence Thomas stands in his chambers with three of his clerks. *Why is a Supreme Court clerkship a desirable position for a young attorney?*

---

2. *Hamdi v. Rumsfeld*, 542 U.S. 507 (2004); *Hamdan v. Rumsfeld*, 548 U.S. 557 (2006).

3. 553 U.S. 723 (2008).

4. *Maqaleh v. Gates*, 605 F.3d 84 (D.C.Cir. 2010).

5. 531 U.S. 98 (2000).

their reasons for hearing certain cases and not others, so it is difficult to predict which case or type of case the Court might select.

Factors That Bear on the Decision. A number of factors bear on the decision to accept a case. If a legal question has been decided differently by various lower courts, it may need resolution by the highest court. A ruling may be necessary if a lower court's decision conflicts with an existing Supreme Court ruling. In general, the Court considers whether the issue could have significance beyond the parties to the dispute.

Another factor is whether the solicitor general is asking the Court to take a case. The solicitor general, a high-ranking presidential appointee within the Justice Department, represents the national government before the Supreme Court and promotes presidential policies in the federal courts. He or she decides what cases the government should ask the Supreme Court to review and what position the government should take in cases before the Court.

Granting Petitions for Review. If the Court decides to grant a petition for review, it issues a **writ of *certiorari*** (pronounced sur-shee-uh-*rah*-ree). The writ orders a lower court to send the Supreme Court a record of the case for review. The vast majority of the petitions for review are denied. A denial is not a decision on the merits of a case, nor does it indicate agreement with the lower court's opinion. (The judgment of the lower court remains in force, however.) Therefore, denial of the writ has no value as a precedent. The Court will not issue a writ unless at least four justices approve of it. This is called the **rule of four.**[6]

Court Procedures

Once the Supreme Court grants *certiorari* in a particular case, the justices do extensive research on the legal issues and facts involved in the case. (Of course, some preliminary research is necessary before deciding to grant the petition for review.) Each justice is entitled to four law clerks, who undertake much of the research and preliminary drafting necessary for the justice to form an opinion.

The Court normally does not hear any evidence, as is true with all appeals courts. The Court's consideration of a case is based on the abstracts, the record, and the briefs. The attorneys are permitted to present **oral arguments.** Unlike the practice in most courts, lawyers addressing the Supreme Court can be (and often are) questioned by the justices at any time during oral arguments. All statements and the justices' questions during oral arguments are recorded.

The justices meet to discuss and vote on cases in conferences held throughout the term. In these conferences, in addition to deciding cases already before the Court, the justices determine which new petitions for *certiorari* to grant. These conferences are strictly private—no stenographers, audio recorders, or video cameras are allowed.

Decisions and Opinions

When the Court has reached a decision, its opinion is written. The **opinion** contains the Court's ruling on the issue or issues presented, the reasons for its decision, the rules of law that apply, and other information. In many cases, the decision of the lower court is **affirmed,** resulting in the enforcement of that court's judgment or decree. If the Supreme Court believes that the lower court made the wrong decision, however, the decision will be **reversed.** Sometimes the case will be **remanded** (sent back to the court that originally heard the case) for a new trial or other proceeding. For instance, a lower court might have

---

writ of *certiorari*

An order issued by a higher court to a lower court to send up the record of a case for review.

rule of four

A United States Supreme Court procedure by which four justices must vote to grant a petition for review if a case is to come before the full court.

oral arguments

The arguments presented in person by attorneys to an appellate court. Each attorney presents to the court reasons why the court should rule in her or his client's favor.

opinion

A statement by a judge or a court of the decision reached in a case. An opinion sets forth the applicable law and details the reasoning on which the ruling was based.

affirm

To declare that a court ruling is valid and must stand.

reverse

To annul, or make void, a court ruling on account of some error or irregularity.

remand

To send a case back to the court that originally heard it.

---

6. The "rule of four" is modified when seven or fewer justices participate, which occurs from time to time. When that happens, as few as three justices can grant *certiorari*.

held that a party was not entitled to bring a lawsuit under a particular law. If the Supreme Court holds to the contrary, it will remand (send back) the case to the trial court with instructions that the trial go forward.

The Court's written opinion sometimes is unsigned; this is called an opinion *per curiam* ("by the court"). Typically, the Court's opinion is signed by all the justices who agree with it. When in the majority, the chief justice decides who writes the opinion and may choose to write it personally. When the chief justice is in the minority, the senior justice on the majority side assigns the opinion.

Types of Opinions.

When all justices unanimously agree on an opinion, the opinion is written for the entire Court (all the justices) and can be deemed a **unanimous opinion**. When there is not a unanimous opinion, a **majority opinion** is written, outlining the views of the majority of the justices involved in the case. Often, one or more justices who feel strongly about making or emphasizing a particular point that is not made or emphasized in the majority written opinion will write a **concurring opinion**. That means the justice writing the concurring opinion agrees (concurs) with the conclusion given in the majority written opinion but wants to make or clarify a particular point or to voice disapproval of the grounds on which the decision was made.

Note that it is also possible for a group of justices to issue a **plurality opinion**. Such an opinion does not represent a majority of the Court, but it will still decide the case because one or more concurring opinions agrees with its verdict.

Finally, in other than unanimous opinions, one or more **dissenting opinions** are usually written by those justices who do not agree with the majority. The dissenting opinion is important because it often forms the basis of the arguments used years later if the Court reverses the previous decision and establishes a new precedent.

Publishing Opinions.

Shortly after the opinion is written, the Supreme Court announces its decision from the bench. The clerk of the Court also releases the opinion for online publication. Ultimately, the opinion is published in the *United States Reports*, which is the official printed record of the Court's decisions.

The Court's Dwindling Caseload.

Some have complained that the Court reviews too few cases each term, thus giving the lower courts insufficient guidance on important issues. Indeed, the number of signed opinions issued by the Court has dwindled notably since the 1980s. For example, in its 1982–1983 term, the Court issued signed opinions in 151 cases. By the early 2000s, this number had dropped to between 70 and 80 per term. In the term ending in June 2016, the number was 81.

The Selection of Federal Judges

All federal judges are appointed. The Constitution, in Article II, Section 2, states that the president is to appoint the justices of the Supreme Court with the advice and consent of the Senate. Congress has established the same procedure for staffing other federal courts. This means that the Senate and the president jointly decide who shall fill every vacant judicial position, no matter what the level.

There are currently 874 federal judicial posts at all levels, although at any given time many of these positions are vacant. Once appointed to a federal judgeship, a person holds that job for life. Judges serve until they resign, retire voluntarily, or die. Federal judges who engage in blatantly illegal conduct may be removed through impeachment, although such action is rare.

---

unanimous opinion
A Court opinion or determination on which all judges agree.

majority opinion
A court opinion reflecting the views of the majority of the judges.

concurring opinion
A separate opinion prepared by a judge who supports the decision of the majority of the court but who wants to make or clarify a particular point or to voice disapproval of the grounds on which the decision was made.

plurality opinion
An opinion by a minority of the Court that decides a case because it is supported by one or more concurring opinions.

dissenting opinion
A separate opinion in which a judge dissents from (disagrees with) the conclusion reached by the majority of the court and expounds his or her own views about the case.

Learning Outcome **4:**

Evaluate the manner in which federal judges are selected.

Image 14–6 Sonia Sotomayor is the first Latina justice on the Supreme Court. Oddly, even though about half of all Americans are Protestant, as of 2016 every member of the Court was either Catholic or Jewish. *How might the justices' personal backgrounds affect their decisions?*

In contrast to federal judges, many state judges—including the judges who sit on state supreme courts—are chosen by the voters in elections. Inevitably, judicial candidates must raise campaign funds. What arguments favor the election of judges? What problems can such a system create? We examine such questions in this chapter's *Which Side Are You On?* feature.

Judicial Appointments

Candidates for federal judgeships are suggested to the president by the Department of Justice, senators, other judges, the candidates themselves, and lawyers' associations and other interest groups. In selecting a candidate to nominate for a judgeship, the president considers not only the person's competence but also other factors, including the person's political philosophy (as will be discussed shortly), ethnicity, and gender.

The nomination process—no matter how the nominees are obtained—always works the same way. The president makes the actual nomination, submitting the name to the Senate. To reach a conclusion, the Senate Judiciary Committee (operating through subcommittees) invites testimony, both written and oral, at its various hearings. The Senate then either confirms or rejects the nomination.

Federal District Court Judgeship Nominations.
Although the president officially nominates federal judges, in the past the nomination of federal district court judges actually originated with a senator or senators of the president's party from the state in which there was a vacancy (if such a senator existed). In effect, judicial appointments were a form of political patronage. President Jimmy Carter (1977–1981) ended this tradition by establishing independent commissions to oversee the initial nomination process. President Ronald Reagan (1981–1989) abolished Carter's nominating commissions and established complete presidential control of nominations.

A practice used in the Senate, called **senatorial courtesy,** is a constraint on the president's freedom to appoint federal district judges. Senatorial courtesy allows a senator of the president's political party to veto a judicial appointment in her or his state. During much of American history, senators from the "opposition" party (the party to which the president does not belong) have also enjoyed the right of senatorial courtesy, although their veto power has varied over time.

In 2000, Orrin Hatch, Republican chair of the Senate Judiciary Committee, announced that the opposition party (at that point, the Democrats) would no longer be allowed to invoke senatorial courtesy. When the Democrats took over the Senate following the elections of 2006, a Democrat, Patrick J. Leahy, became chair of the Judiciary Committee. Leahy let it be known that the old bipartisan system of senatorial courtesy would return.

Federal Courts of Appeals Appointments.
There are many fewer appointments to the federal courts of appeals than federal district court appointments, but they are more important. Federal appellate judges handle more important matters, and therefore presidents take a keener interest in the nomination process for such judgeships. Also, the U.S. courts of appeals have become "stepping-stones" to the Supreme Court.

senatorial courtesy

In federal district court judgeship nominations, a tradition allowing a senator to veto a judicial appointment in his or her state.

Steve Petteway/Collection of the Supreme Court of the United States

Which side are you on?

Should State Judges Be Elected?

The nation's founders sought to insulate the courts from popular passions. As a result, all of the judges and justices in the federal court system are appointed by the president and confirmed by the Senate. Federal judges and justices are appointed for life. In thirty-nine states, in contrast, some or all state judges must face election and reelection.

The question of whether state judges should be elected or whether they should be appointed has proved to be very divisive. Many in the legal community agreed with a former Oregon Supreme Court justice, Hans A. Linde, when he pointed out that "to the rest of the world, American adherence to judicial elections is as incomprehensible as our rejection of the metric system." Public opinion polls, however, regularly show strong public support for electing judges.

The People's Will Should Prevail

Those who advocate the election of state judges see the issue as a simple matter of democracy. Judges cannot be insulated from politics. Governors who appoint judges are highly political creatures and are likely to appoint members of their own party. If politics is going to play a role, the people ought to have their say directly. In addition, researchers at the University of Chicago School of Law found that elected judges wrote more opinions than appointed judges.

We let ordinary people participate in the legal process through the jury system, and they ought to be able to choose judges as well. That way, the people can be confi-dent that judges will respond to popular concerns, such as the fear of crime. Without elections, judges living in safe, upscale neighborhoods may fail to appreciate what it is like to fear for your safety on an everyday basis.

Electing Judges Leads to Corruption

Former United States Supreme Court justice Sandra Day O'Connor condemned the practice of electing judges: "No other nation in the world does that because they realize you are not going to get fair and impartial judges that way." Opponents of judicial elections observe that most voters do not have enough information to make sensible choices when they vote for judicial candidates.

Judicial candidates raise considerable funds from the lawyers who will appear before them if they win. Additional campaign funds are raised by special interest groups. People who want to elect judges think that the candidates they vote for will, for example, be "tough on crime." Often, they are. But those who oppose judicial elections contend that elected judges will also tilt toward the wealthy groups that put them in office, and away from the interests of ordinary people.

For Critical Analysis

◗ In some states, judicial candidates are nominated by political parties. What consequences can follow from such explicit partisan identification?

Supreme Court Appointments. As we have mentioned, the president nominates Supreme Court justices. Table 14–1 summarizes the background of all Supreme Court justices through 2016. As you can see, the most common occupational background of the justices at the time of their appointment has been private legal practice or state or federal judgeship. Those nine justices who were in federal executive posts at the time of their appointment held the high offices of secretary of state, comptroller of the treasury, secretary of the navy, postmaster general, secretary of the interior, chairman of the Securities and Exchange Commission, and secretary of labor. In the "Other" category under "Occupational Position before Appointment" in Table 14–1 are two justices who were professors of law (including William H. Taft, a former president) and one justice who was a North Carolina state employee with responsibility for organizing and revising the state's statutes.

Table 14–1 Background of United States Supreme Court Justices through 2016

The practice of nominating sitting judges to the Supreme Court has become increasingly common. **Why might that be so?**

	Number of Justices (112 = Total)
Occupational Position before Appointment	
Federal judgeship	31
Private legal practice	25
State judgeship	21
Federal executive post	9
U.S. attorney general	7
U.S. senator	6
State governor	3
Deputy or assistant U.S. attorney general	2
U.S. solicitor general	3
U.S. representative	2
Other	3
Religious Background	
Protestant	83
Roman Catholic	14
Unitarian	7
Jewish	7
No religious affiliation	1
Age on Appointment	
Under 40	5
41–50	33
51–60	60
61–70	14
Political Party Affiliation	
Democrat	46
Republican	44
Federalist (to 1835)	13
Jeffersonian Republican (to 1828)	7
Whig (to 1861)	1
Independent	1
Educational Background	
College graduate	96
Not a college graduate	16
Gender	
Male	108
Female	4
Race	
Non-Hispanic White	109
African American	2
Hispanic	1

Sources: Congressional Quarterly, *Congressional Quarterly's Guide to the U.S. Supreme Court* (Washington, D.C.: Congressional Quarterly Press, 1996); and authors' updates.

The Special Role of the Chief Justice. The chief justice is not only the head of a group of nine justices who interpret the law. In essence, he or she is also the chief executive officer of a large bureaucracy that includes more than one thousand judges with lifetime tenure, hundreds of magistrates and bankruptcy judges with limited tenure, and a staff of about thirty thousand.

The chief justice is the chair of the Judicial Conference of the United States, a policymaking body that sets priorities for the federal judiciary. This position means that the chief justice indirectly oversees the $7 billion budget of the federal judiciary.

Finally, the chief justice appoints the director of the Administrative Office of the United States Courts. The chief justice and the director select judges who sit on judicial committees that examine international judicial relations, technology, and a variety of other topics.

Partisanship and Judicial Appointments. In most circumstances, the president appoints judges or justices who belong to the president's own political party. Presidents see their federal judiciary appointments as the one sure way to institutionalize their political views long after they have left office. By 1993, for example, Presidents Ronald Reagan and George H. W. Bush together had appointed nearly three-quarters of all federal court judges. This preponderance of Republican-appointed federal judges strengthened the legal moorings of the conservative social agenda on a variety of issues, ranging from abortion to civil rights. President Bill Clinton, a Democrat, had the opportunity to appoint 371 federal district and appeals court judges, thereby shifting the ideological makeup of the federal judiciary. George W. Bush appointed 322 federal district and appeals court judges, again ensuring a majority of Republican-appointed judges in the federal courts.

Supreme Court Appointments by Bush. President George W. Bush also had the opportunity to fill two Supreme Court vacancies—those left by the death of Chief Justice William Rehnquist and by the retirement of Justice Sandra Day O'Connor. Bush appointed two conservatives to these positions—John G. Roberts, Jr., who became chief justice, and Samuel Alito, Jr., who replaced O'Connor. The appointment of Alito, in particular, strengthened the rightward movement of the Court that had begun years before with the appointment of Rehnquist as chief justice. This was because Alito was a reliable member of the Court's conservative wing, whereas O'Connor had been a "swing voter."

Supreme Court Appointments by Obama. President Barack Obama had two opportunities to fill Supreme Court vacancies in the first two years of his term. The vacancies resulted from the retirement of Justices David Souter and John Paul Stevens. Both had been members of the Court's so-called liberal wing, so Obama's appointments did not change the ideological balance of the Court. Obama chose two women: Sonia Sotomayor, who had been an appeals court judge and was the Court's first Hispanic member, and Elena Kagan, who had been Obama's solicitor general.

The Senate's Role. Ideology also plays a large role in the Senate's confirmation hearings, and presidential nominees to the Supreme Court have not always been confirmed. In fact, almost 20 percent of presidential nominations to the Supreme Court have either been rejected or not acted on by the Senate. There have been many acrimonious battles over Supreme Court appointments when the Senate and the president have not seen eye to eye about political matters.

Controversial Supreme Court Appointments. One of the most memorable of these rejections was the Senate's refusal to confirm Robert Bork—an unusually conservative nominee—in 1987. Many observers saw the Bork confirmation battle as a turning point after which confirmations became much more partisan. Another controversial appointment was that of Clarence Thomas, who underwent an extremely volatile confirmation hearing, replete with charges against him of sexual harassment. He was ultimately confirmed by the Senate, however.

President Clinton had little trouble gaining approval for both of his nominees to the Supreme Court: Ruth Bader Ginsburg and Stephen G. Breyer. President George W. Bush's nominees faced hostile grilling in their confirmation hearings, however, and Bush was forced to withdraw the nomination of White House counsel Harriet Miers when it became clear she would not be confirmed.

Image 14–7 U.S. Court of Appeals Judge Merrick Garland was nominated by President Obama to replace the late Supreme Court Justice Antonin Scalia. The Republican-controlled Senate said that it would not hold confirmation hearings on him in 2016. *Do you think that decision was politically motivated?*

The Controversy Following the Death of Justice Scalia. In February 2016, Justice Antonin Scalia died unexpectedly. Scalia had been the lion of the Court's conservative wing, always ready to issue scathing assessments of liberal opinions. (It is a sign of the Court's collegiality that Scalia was also a close personal friend of liberal Justice Ruth Ginsburg.) President Obama then nominated as Scalia's replacement Merrick Garland, the chief judge of the court of appeals for the District of Columbia circuit. Garland was as moderate a judge as Obama could be expected to name. By replacing Scalia, however, Garland would inevitably swing the Court significantly to the left.

The nomination was issued in the middle of the 2016 presidential primaries. Republicans in the Senate recognized that if they could postpone action on Scalia's replacement until 2017, there was a chance that a new Republican president might make the nomination. Senate Republicans therefore announced that they would not even hold hearings on Garland's nomination. While not entirely unprecedented, this was a relatively unusual step. Donald Trump's victory in 2016 proved that the Republican plan was politically astute. Trump had promised to nominate a justice as conservative as Scalia.

Lower Court Appointment Battles. Presidents have often had great trouble with appointments to district and appeals courts. For an extended period during the presidency of Bill Clinton, the Republican majority in Congress adopted a strategy of trying to block almost every action taken by the administration—including judicial appointments.

Image 14–8 The late Justice Antonin Scalia addresses a conference of the Legal Services Corporation. This government-sponsored corporation provides civil legal assistance to low-income Americans. *Why has filling Scalia's seat on the Court been so contentious?*

The modern understanding that sixty votes are required before the Senate will consider a major measure has given the minority party significant power as well. After 2000, the Democratic minority in the Senate was able to hold up many of George W. Bush's more controversial judicial appointments. Frustrated Republican senators threatened to use the "nuclear option," under which Senate rules would be revised to disallow filibusters against judicial nominees. In the end, a bipartisan group engineered a compromise to preserve the filibuster.

President Obama also had considerable difficulty in getting his judicial candidates approved by the Senate. This was especially true after the 2010 elections, when a number of newly elected Republicans replaced Democratic senators. Democratic frustration with Republican blocking tactics came to a head in 2013. In that year, Democrats exercised the "nuclear option," abolishing filibusters against executive branch nominees and all judicial nominees other than to the Supreme Court. Some observers doubt that use of the filibuster against Supreme Court nominees would survive a heated nomination contest.

Learning Outcome 5:

Consider the ways in which the Supreme Court makes policy, and explain the forces that limit the activism of the courts.

Policymaking and the Courts

The partisan battles over judicial appointments reflect an important reality in today's American government: the importance of the judiciary in national politics. Because appointments to the federal bench are for life, the ideology of judicial appointees can affect national policy for years to come. Although the primary function of judges in our system of government is to interpret and apply the laws, inevitably judges make policy when carrying out this task. One of the major policymaking tools of the federal courts is their power of judicial review.

Judicial Review

Remember from earlier in this text that the power of the courts to determine whether a law or action by the other branches of government is constitutional is known as the power of *judicial review.* This power enables the judicial branch to act as a check on the other two branches of government, in line with the system of checks and balances established by the U.S. Constitution.

The power of judicial review is not mentioned in the Constitution, however. Rather, it was established by the United States Supreme Court's decision in *Marbury v. Madison.*[7] In that case, in which the Court declared that a law passed by Congress violated the Constitution, the Court claimed such a power for the judiciary:

> *It is emphatically the province and duty of the Judicial Department to say what the law is. Those who apply the rule to a particular case must of necessity expound and interpret that rule. If two laws conflict with each other, the courts must decide on the operation of each.*

---

7. 5 U.S. 137 (1803).

If a federal court declares that a federal or state law or policy is unconstitutional, the court's decision affects the application of the law or policy only within that court's jurisdiction. For this reason, the higher the level of the court, the greater the impact of the decision on society. Because of the Supreme Court's national jurisdiction, its decisions have the greatest impact. For instance, when the Supreme Court held that an Arkansas state constitutional amendment limiting the terms of congresspersons was unconstitutional, laws establishing term limits in twenty-three other states were also invalidated.[8]

Judicial Activism and Judicial Restraint

Judicial scholars like to characterize different judges and justices as being either "activist" or "restraintist."

Judicial Activism. The doctrine of **judicial activism** rests on the conviction that the federal judiciary should take an active role by using its powers to check the activities of Congress, state legislatures, and administrative agencies when those governmental bodies exceed their authority. One of the Supreme Court's most activist eras was the period from 1953 to 1969, when the Court was headed by Chief Justice Earl Warren. The Warren Court propelled the civil rights movement forward by holding, among other things, that laws permitting racial segregation violated the equal protection clause.

Judicial Restraint. In contrast, the doctrine of **judicial restraint** rests on the assumption that the courts should defer to the decisions made by the legislative and executive branches, because members of Congress and the president are elected by the people, whereas members of the federal judiciary are not. Because administrative agency personnel normally have more expertise than the courts do in the areas regulated by the agencies, the courts likewise should defer to agency rules and decisions. In other words, under the doctrine of judicial restraint, the courts should not thwart the implementation of legislative acts and agency rules unless they are clearly unconstitutional.

Political Implications. In the past, judicial activism was often linked with liberalism, and judicial restraint with conservatism. In fact, though, a conservative judge can be activist, just as a liberal judge can be restraintist. In the 1950s and 1960s, the Supreme Court was activist and liberal. Some observers believe that the Roberts Court, with its conservative majority, has become increasingly activist over time.

The *Citizens United v. Federal Election Commission* decision, in which the Court struck down long-standing campaign finance laws, lends credence to this view. Some believed that the Court was stepping back from conservative judicial activism when it upheld most of Obama's health-care reform legislation in June 2012. Others, however, note that the Court also blocked the attempt by Congress to force states to expand the Medicaid program. This step was an innovation in limiting the power of Congress.

Strict versus Broad Construction

Other terms that are often used to describe a justice's philosophy are *strict construction* and *broad construction*. Justices who believe in **strict construction** look to the "letter of the law" when they attempt to interpret the Constitution or a particular statute. Those who favor **broad construction** try to determine the context and purpose of the law.

As with the doctrines of judicial restraint and judicial activism, strict construction is often associated with conservative political views, whereas broad construction is often linked with liberalism. These traditional political associations sometimes appear to be

judicial activism
A doctrine holding that the federal judiciary should take an active role by using its powers to check the activities of governmental bodies when those bodies exceed their authority.

judicial restraint
A doctrine holding that the courts should defer to the decisions made by the elected representatives of the people in the legislative and executive branches when possible.

strict construction
A judicial philosophy that looks to the "letter of the law" when interpreting the Constitution or a particular statute.

broad construction
A judicial philosophy that looks to the context and purpose of a law when making an interpretation.

---

8. *U.S. Term Limits v. Thornton*, 514 U.S. 779 (1995).

Image 14–9 When Elena Kagan was confirmed as a justice of the United States Supreme Court, she became only the fourth woman to hold this position. *Why has it taken so long for women to win appointment as Supreme Court justices?*

reversed, however. Consider the Eleventh Amendment to the Constitution, which rules out lawsuits in federal courts "against one of the United States by Citizens of another State, or by Citizens or Subjects of any Foreign State." Nothing is said about citizens suing their own states, and strict construction would therefore find such suits to be constitutional. Conservative justices, however, have construed this amendment broadly to deny citizens the constitutional right to sue their own states in most circumstances. John T. Noonan, Jr., a federal appellate court judge who was appointed by a Republican president, has described these rulings as "adventurous."[9]

Broad construction is often associated with the concept of a "living constitution." The late Supreme Court justice Antonin Scalia, in contrast, said that "the Constitution is not a living organism, it is a legal document. It says something and doesn't say other things." Scalia believed that jurists should stick to the plain text of the Constitution "as it was originally written and intended."

The Roberts Court

John Roberts became chief justice in 2005, following the death of Chief Justice William H. Rehnquist. Replacing one conservative chief justice with another did not immediately change the Court's ideological balance. The real change came in January 2006, when Samuel Alito replaced Sandra Day O'Connor. Unlike O'Connor, Alito was firmly in the conservative camp. This fact had consequences. In a 2007 case, for example, the Court upheld a 2003 federal law banning partial birth abortion, by a close (five-to-four) vote.[10]

The Nature of the Court's Conservatism. The Supreme Court's conservative drift continued in the following years. In 2010, for example, the Court issued two major opinions, both of which were major victories for the political right. In *Citizens United v. Federal Election Commission*, as noted earlier, the Court struck down long-standing campaign finance laws.[11] A second major ruling was *McDonald v. Chicago*, in which the Court held that all state and local governments are bound to recognize the right to bear arms as an individual right.[12] In these and other key cases, Justice Kennedy cast the deciding vote.

Although the Roberts Court is widely characterized as conservative, its philosophy is not identical with the conservatism of the Republicans in Congress or the broader conservative movement. True, justices such as Scalia and Thomas could rightly be characterized as in full agreement with the conservative movement. Justice Kennedy and even Chief Justice Roberts, however, clearly "march to their own drummer." As one example, the Court has shown a degree of sympathy for the rights of gay men and lesbians that cannot be found in the Republican Party platform. It was Justice Kennedy, after all, who in 2003 wrote the opinion in *Lawrence v. Texas* striking down laws that ban gay sex nationwide.[13] Chief Justice Roberts demonstrated his independence in 2012 by authoring the opinion that affirmed the constitutionality of Obamacare.[14]

9. John T. Noonan, Jr., *Narrowing the Nation's Power: The Supreme Court Sides with the States* (Berkeley: University of California Press, 2002).
10. *Gonzales v. Carhart,* 550 U.S. 124 (2007).
11. 558 U.S. 50 (2010).
12. 561 U.S. 3025 (2010).
13. 539 U.S. 558 (2003).
14. *National Federation of Independent Business v. Sebelius,* 567 U.S. ___ (2012).

Figure 14–3 The Roberts Court

The members of the United States Supreme Court as of 2016. *What consequences can follow when the Court has only eight members?*

The Supreme Court of the United States

Recent Supreme Court Rulings. The Court provided more examples of its brand of conservatism in 2013. The Court continued to take a favorable approach to gay rights. In *United States v. Windsor,* it ruled that the federal government could not refuse to recognize same-sex marriages authorized by the states.[15] In contrast, to the satisfaction of conservatives, the Court struck down part of the Voting Rights Act of 1965.[16]

Many of the most important rulings in 2014 also gave heart to conservatives. In June, the Court ruled that a thirty-five-foot buffer zone in Massachusetts that limited the access of antiabortion protestors to abortion clinics was too large.[17] Also in that month,

15. 133 S.Ct. 2675 (2013).
16. *Shelby County v. Holder,* 570 U.S. ___ (2013).
17. *McCullen v. Coakley,* 573 U.S. ___ (2014).

the Court decided that closely held corporations had the right to deny their employees birth control benefits in insurance plans that conformed to the Affordable Care Act.[18] This ruling, *Burwell v. Hobby Lobby*, was applauded by religious conservatives and denounced by feminist groups.

In the term ending in 2015, several important rulings confirmed the limits of the Court's conservatism. In *King v. Burwell,* the Court once again turned back a challenge to the Affordable Care Act.[19] *Obergefell v. Hodges* established a nationwide constitutional right to same-sex marriage.[20]

Will We Again Have a Liberal Court? Many observers thought that the term ending in 2016 would mark a return to a more robust conservatism. The cases that the Court chose for that term suggested as much. In February, however, Justice Scalia died unexpectedly, and the Senate indicated that it would not fill his seat until 2017. The Court, therefore, no longer had a conservative majority, but was split four-to-four.

2016: A Divided Court. When the Supreme Court is equally divided on an opinion, the ruling of the lower court is upheld, but the "decision" does not constitute a precedent. If two appeals courts issue conflicting rulings, an evenly divided Court cannot determine which appeals court is correct, and different regions of the country may therefore have different laws. Chief Justice Roberts tried hard to prevent such outcomes in 2016, but he was not entirely successful.

Why should you care about **THE COURTS?**

Legislative bodies may make laws and ordinances, but legislation is given its practical form by court rulings. Therefore, if you care about the effects of a particular law, pay attention to how the courts are interpreting it. For example, do you believe that sentences handed down for certain crimes are too lenient—or too strict? Legislative bodies can attempt to establish sentences for various offenses, but the courts inevitably retain considerable flexibility in determining what happens in any particular case.

True, in two cases, the Court stopped attempts by President Obama to use his executive powers to set policy. The first case temporarily blocked actions by the Environmental Protection Agency to regulate carbon dioxide emissions from power plants.[21] The second, a four-to-four decision, blocked for at least a year Obama's attempt to prevent the deportation of up to 5 million unauthorized immigrants.[22] Another four-to-four split had a more liberal result: in effect, it allowed California public employee unions to continue collecting fees from nonmembers.[23] An abortion ruling was more decisive: the Court struck down parts of a restrictive Texas antiabortion law.[24]

The Court and the Elections. To an extent unprecedented in U.S. history, the future of the Supreme Court in 2016 depended on the outcome of the November elections. A Republican president would probably enjoy a Republican Senate, and would be able to name a highly conservative replacement for Scalia. If this happened, the Roberts Court would regain its conservatism and keep it for the indefinite future. A Democratic president with a Democratic Senate would push the Court in a decidedly liberal direction. A Democratic president and a Republican Senate, however, would probably produce one of the most highly contested nomination battles ever.

---

18. 134 S.Ct. 2751 (2014).
19. 576 U.S. ___ (2015).
20. 135 S.Ct. 2584 (2015).
21. The Court did this through an injunction that blocked an appellate court ruling. The actual Supreme Court case, *West Virginia v. EPA,* was not decided until the 2016–2017 term.
22. *United States v. Texas,* 579 U.S. ___ (2016).
23. *Friedrichs v. California Teachers Association,* 578 U.S. ___ (2016).
24. *Whole Woman's Health v. Hellerstedt,* 579 U.S. ___ (2016).

What Checks Our Courts?

Our judicial system is one of the most independent in the world. But the courts do not have absolute independence, for they are part of the political process. Political checks limit the extent to which courts can exercise judicial review and engage in an activist policy. These checks are exercised by the executive branch, the legislature, the public, and, finally, the judiciary itself.

Executive Checks. President Andrew Jackson was once supposed to have said, after Chief Justice John Marshall made an unpopular decision, "John Marshall has made his decision; now let him enforce it."[25] This purported remark goes to the heart of **judicial implementation**—the enforcement of judicial decisions in such a way that those decisions are translated into policy. The Supreme Court simply does not have any enforcement powers, and whether a decision will be implemented depends on the cooperation of the other two branches of government. Rarely, though, will a president refuse to enforce a Supreme Court decision, as President Jackson did. To take such an action could mean a significant loss of public support and could even lead to impeachment hearings in the House. More commonly, presidents exercise influence over the judiciary by appointing new judges and justices as federal judicial seats become vacant.

Executives at the state level may also refuse to implement court decisions with which they disagree. A notable example of such a refusal occurred in Arkansas after the Supreme Court ordered schools to desegregate "with all deliberate speed" in 1955.[26] Arkansas governor Orval Faubus refused to cooperate with the decision and used the state's National Guard to block the integration of Central High School in Little Rock. Ultimately, President Dwight Eisenhower had to federalize the Arkansas National Guard to force it to stand down and then send regular Army troops to Little Rock to quell the violence that had erupted.

Legislative Checks. Courts may make rulings, but often the legislatures at local, state, and federal levels are required to appropriate funds to carry out the courts' rulings. A court, for example, may decide that prison conditions must be improved, but it is up to the legislature to authorize the funds necessary to carry out the ruling. When such funds are not appropriated, the court that made the ruling, in effect, has been checked.

Constitutional Amendments. Courts' rulings can be overturned by constitutional amendments at both the federal and the state levels. For example, the Sixteenth Amendment to the U.S. Constitution, ratified in 1913, overturned a United States Supreme Court ruling that found the income tax to be unconstitutional. Proposed constitutional amendments to reverse court decisions on school prayer, abortion, and same-sex marriage have failed.

Rewriting Laws. Finally, Congress or a state legislature can rewrite (amend) old laws or enact new ones to overturn a court's rulings if the legislature concludes that the court is interpreting laws or legislative intentions erroneously. For example, in 2009 Congress passed (and President Obama signed) the Lilly Ledbetter Fair Pay Act, which resets the statute of limitations for filing an equal-pay lawsuit each time an employer issues a discriminatory paycheck. The law was a direct answer to *Ledbetter v. Goodyear,* in which the Supreme Court held that the statute of limitations begins on the date the pay was agreed upon, not on the date of the most recent paycheck.[27] The new legislation made it much easier for employees to win pay-discrimination lawsuits.

---

25. The decision that Jackson was referring to was *Cherokee Nation v. Georgia,* 30 U.S. 1 (1831).
26. *Brown v. Board of Education,* 349 U.S. 294 (1955)—the second *Brown* decision.
27. 550 U.S. 618 (2007).

judicial implementation
The way in which court decisions are translated into policy.

Image 14-10 A criminal defense lawyer representing a murder suspect makes a point in a California state court. *Why are most criminal cases held in state courts?*

The states can also negate or alter the effects of Supreme Court rulings, when such decisions allow it. A good case in point is *Kelo v. City of New London*.[28] In that case, the Supreme Court allowed a city to take private property for redevelopment by private businesses. Since that case was decided, a majority of states have passed legislation limiting or prohibiting such actions.

Public Opinion. Public opinion plays a significant role in shaping government policy, and certainly the judiciary is not excepted from this rule. One problem is that persons affected by a Supreme Court decision that is contrary to their views may simply ignore it. Officially sponsored prayers were banned in public schools in 1962, yet it was widely known that the ban was (and still is) ignored in many southern and rural districts. What can the courts do in this situation? Unless someone complains about the prayers and initiates a lawsuit, the courts can do nothing.

Additionally, the courts themselves necessarily are influenced by public opinion to some extent. After all, judges are not "islands" in our society. Their attitudes are influenced by social trends, just as the attitudes and beliefs of all persons are. Courts generally tend to avoid issuing decisions that they know will be noticeably at odds with public opinion. In part, this is because the judiciary, as a branch of the government, prefers to avoid creating divisiveness among members of the public. Also, a court—particularly the Supreme Court—may lose stature if it decides a case in a way that markedly diverges from public opinion.

Naturally, liberal and conservative justices may look to different strands of public opinion. With conservative majorities, the Rehnquist and Roberts courts tended to reflect conservative opinion. Two cases on states' rights illustrate this tendency. In 1995, the Court held, for the first time in sixty years, that Congress had overreached its powers under the commerce clause when it attempted to regulate the possession of guns in school zones. According to the Court, the possession of guns in school zones had nothing to do with the commerce clause.[29] Yet in a 2005 case, the Court ruled that Congress's power to regulate commerce allowed it to ban marijuana use even when a state's law permitted such use and the growing and use of the drug were strictly local in nature.[30] What these two rulings had in common was that they supported policies generally considered to be conservative—the right to possess firearms on the one hand, and strict laws against marijuana on the other.

Judicial Traditions and Doctrines. Supreme Court justices (and other federal judges) typically exercise self-restraint in fashioning their decisions. In part, this restraint stems from their knowledge that the other two branches of government and the public can exercise checks on the judiciary, as previously discussed. To a large extent, however, this restraint is mandated by various judicially established traditions and doctrines. For example, in exercising its discretion to hear appeals, the Supreme Court will not hear a meritless appeal just so it can rule on the issue.

Also, when reviewing a case, the Supreme Court frequently narrows its focus to just one issue or one aspect of an issue involved in the case. In the past, the Court has rarely made broad, sweeping decisions on issues. Furthermore, the doctrine of *stare*

---

28. 545 U.S. 469 (2005).
29. *United States v. Lopez*, 514 U.S. 549 (1995).
30. *Gonzales v. Raich*, 545 U.S. 1 (2005).

Al Seib/Getty Images

decisis acts as a restraint because it obligates the courts, including the Supreme Court, to follow established precedents when deciding cases. Only rarely will courts overrule a precedent.

Hypothetical and Political Questions. Other judicial doctrines and practices also act as restraints. As already mentioned, the courts will hear only what are called justiciable disputes—disputes that arise out of actual cases. In other words, a court will not hear a case that involves a merely hypothetical issue.

Additionally, if a political question is involved, the Supreme Court often will exercise judicial restraint and refuse to rule on the matter. A **political question** is one that the Supreme Court declares should be decided by the elected branches of government— the executive branch, the legislative branch, or those two branches acting together. For example, the Supreme Court has refused to rule on whether women in the military should be allowed to serve in combat units, preferring instead to defer to the executive branch's decisions on the matter. (In January 2013, the Department of Defense lifted the ban on women serving in combat units.) Generally, though, fewer questions are deemed political questions by the Supreme Court today than in the past.

The Impact of the Lower Courts. Higher courts can reverse the decisions of lower courts. Lower courts can act as a check on higher courts, too. Lower courts can ignore— and have ignored—Supreme Court decisions. Usually, they do so indirectly. A lower court might conclude, for example, that the precedent set by the Supreme Court does not apply to the exact circumstances in the case before the court. Alternatively, the lower court may decide that the Supreme Court's decision was ambiguous with respect to the issue before the lower court. The fact that the Supreme Court rarely makes broad and clear-cut statements on any issue makes it easier for lower courts to interpret the Supreme Court's decisions in different ways.

political question

An issue that a court believes should be decided by the executive or legislative branch—or these two branches acting together.

Image 14–11 News media interns carry Supreme Court decisions across the plaza of the Supreme Court building. The Court had just legalized same-sex marriage nationwide. *Why are the interns in such a hurry?*

How you can make a difference

Public opinion can have an effect on judicial policies. Whichever cause may interest you, there is probably an organization that pursues lawsuits to benefit that cause and could use your support. A prime example is the modern women's movement, which undertook a long series of lawsuits to change the way women are treated in American life. The courts only rule on cases that are brought before them, and the women's movement changed American law by filing—and winning—case after case.

- In 1965, a federal circuit court opened a wide range of jobs for women by overturning laws that kept women out of work that was "too hard" for them.

- In 1974, the Court ruled that employers could not use the "going market rate" to justify lower wages for women.

- In 1978, an Oregon court became the first of many to find that a man could be prosecuted for raping his wife.

Today, groups such as the National Organization for Women continue to support lawsuits to advance women's rights.

KEY TERMS

affirm **388**	diversity of citizenship **382**	litigate **382**	rule of four **388**
amicus curiae brief **382**	federal question **382**	majority opinion **389**	senatorial courtesy **390**
appellate court **384**	general jurisdiction **383**	opinion **388**	*stare decisis* **379**
broad construction **395**	judicial activism **395**	oral arguments **388**	strict construction **395**
case law **380**	judicial implementation **399**	plurality opinion **389**	trial court **383**
class-action suit **382**	judicial restraint **395**	political question **401**	unanimous opinion **389**
common law **379**	jurisdiction **382**	precedent **379**	writ of *certiorari* **388**
concurring opinion **389**	justiciable controversy **382**	remand **388**	
dissenting opinion **389**	limited jurisdiction **383**	reverse **388**	

CHAPTER SUMMARY

Learning Outcome 1 American law is rooted in the common law tradition. The common law doctrine of *stare decisis* (which means "to stand on decided cases") obligates judges to follow precedents established previously by their own courts or by higher courts that have authority over them. Precedents established by the United States Supreme Court, the highest court in the land, are binding on all lower courts. Fundamental sources of American law include the U.S. Constitution and state constitutions, statutes enacted by legislative bodies, regulations issued by administrative agencies, and case law.

Learning Outcome 2 Article III, Section 1, of the U.S. Constitution limits the jurisdiction of the federal courts to cases involving (a) a federal question, which is a question based, at least in part, on the U.S. Constitution, a treaty, or a federal law, or (b) diversity of citizenship—which arises when parties to a lawsuit are from different states or when the lawsuit involves a foreign citizen or foreign government. The federal court system is a three-tiered model consisting of (a) U.S. district (trial) courts and various lower courts of limited jurisdiction, (b) intermediate U.S. courts of appeals, and (c) the United States Supreme Court. Cases may be appealed from the district courts to the appellate courts. In most cases, the decisions of the federal appellate courts are final because the Supreme Court hears relatively few cases.

Learning Outcome 3 The Supreme Court's decision to review a case is influenced by many factors, including the significance of the issues involved and whether the solicitor general is asking the Court to take the case. After a case is accepted, the justices (with the help of their law clerks) undertake research on the issues involved in the case, hear oral arguments from the parties, meet in conference to discuss and vote on the issues, and announce the opinion, which is then released for publication. Types of opinions include unanimous, majority, plurality, concurring, and dissenting opinions.

Learning Outcome 4 Federal judges are nominated by the president and confirmed by the Senate. Once appointed, they hold office for life, barring gross misconduct. The nomination and confirmation process, particularly for Supreme Court justices, is often extremely politicized. Democrats and Republicans alike realize that justices may occupy seats on the Court for decades and naturally want to have persons appointed who share their basic views. Nearly 20 percent of all presidential nominations to the Supreme Court either have been rejected or have not been acted on by the Senate.

Learning Outcome 5 In interpreting and applying the law, judges inevitably become policymakers. The most important policymaking tool of the federal courts is the power of judicial review. This power was not mentioned specifically in the Constitution, but the Supreme Court claimed the power for the federal courts in its 1803 decision in *Marbury v. Madison*.

Judges who take an active role in checking the activities of the other branches of government sometimes are characterized as "activist" judges, and judges who defer to the decisions of the other branches are sometimes regarded as "restraintist" judges. The Warren Court of the 1950s and 1960s was activist in a liberal direction, whereas the Roberts Court has become increasingly activist in a conservative direction.

Checks on the powers of the federal courts include executive checks, legislative checks, public opinion, and judicial traditions and doctrines.

ADDITIONAL RESOURCES

Online Resources

- To access the Supreme Court's official website, where Supreme Court decisions are made available within hours of their release, go to **www.supremecourt.gov**.

- You can find information on the justices of the Supreme Court, as well as their decisions, at the Oyez Project of the Chicago-Kent College of Law, Illinois Institute of Technology. Visit **www.oyez.org**.

Books

Caplan, Lincoln. *American Justice 2016: The Political Supreme Court*. Philadelphia: University of Pennsylvania Press, 2016. A member of the editorial board of the *New York Times,* Caplan contemplates the promise and perils of a politicized judiciary.

Coyle, Marcia. *The Roberts Court: The Struggle for the Constitution*. New York: Simon & Schuster (paperback), 2014. This work offers a ringside seat to the struggle to lay down the law of the land. Acclaimed reporter Marcia Coyle is the chief Washington correspondent for the *National Law Journal.* She has covered the Supreme Court for twenty years and regularly appears on PBS's *NewsHour.*

Ginsburg, Ruth Bader. *My Own Words*. With Mary Hartnett and Wendy W. Williams. New York: Simon & Schuster, 2016. Supreme Court Justice Ruth Ginsburg has become something of a popular cult figure as "the notorious RBG." Here, she tells the story of her life with the help of two law professors.

Video

Gideon's Trumpet—A 1980 film, starring Henry Fonda as the small-time criminal James Earl Gideon. The film shows the path a case must take to reach the Supreme Court and the importance of cases decided there.

The Supreme Court—A four-part PBS series that won a 2008 Parents' Choice Gold Award. It follows the history of the Supreme Court from the Chief Justice Marshall to the earliest days of the Roberts Court. Some of the many topics discussed are the Court's dismal performance in the Civil War era, its conflicts with President Franklin Roosevelt, its role in banning African American segregation, and its place in the abortion controversy.

Quiz

Multiple Choice and Fill-Ins

Learning Outcome 1 Explain the main sources of American law, including constitutions, statutes and regulations, and the common law tradition.

1. One important source of American law is:
   a. the rights and duties of workers as expressed in employment agreements.
   b. case law based in part on the common law tradition.
   c. case law based in part on the federal tradition.

2. The supreme law of the land in the United States is the
   _____ _____ _____.

Learning Outcome 2 *Describe the structure of the federal court system and such basic judicial requirements as jurisdiction and standing to sue.*

3. The distinction between federal district courts and federal appellate courts can be summarized by the following statement:
   a. federal district courts are trial courts that hear evidence, but federal appellate courts do not hear evidence.
   b. federal district courts only hear appeals from federal appellate courts.
   c. federal appellate courts only accept cases involving state constitutions.

4. To bring a lawsuit, a party must show that he or she suffered an actual harm or is threatened by an actual harm as a result of the action that led to the dispute. If so, then that party has
   _____ ___ _____.

Learning Outcome 3 Discuss the procedures used by the United States Supreme Court and the various types of opinions it hands down.

5. "I'll take it all the way to the Supreme Court." A lawyer cannot truthfully promise this because:
   a. the Supreme Court may be too far away from the state in which the controversy occurred.
   b. the Supreme Court only hears a limited number of cases in which a federal question is involved.
   c. the Supreme Court is not in session for a full twelve months each year.

6. When the U.S. Supreme Court issues an opinion that has the support of the entire Court, it is called a unanimous opinion. Otherwise, the Court issues a majority opinion. Those justices in the minority who do not agree with the majority opinion often write a _____ _____.

Learning Outcome 4 Evaluate the manner in which federal judges are selected.

7. The most common occupational position held by a Supreme Court justice before appointment has been:
   a. U.S. senator.
   b. state governor.
   c. federal judgeship.

8. The tradition of _____ _____ gives U.S. senators considerable power over federal judicial appointments in each senator's own state.

Learning Outcome 5 Consider the ways in which the Supreme Court makes policy, and explain the forces that limit the activism of the courts.

9. When a federal court declares that a federal or state law or policy is unconstitutional, that court is engaging in:
   a. judicial review.
   b. congressional condemnation.
   c. administrative oversight.

10. The doctrine of _____ _____ rests on the conviction that the federal judiciary should actively use its powers to check the laws passed by Congress and state legislatures.

Essay Questions

1. What are the benefits of having lifetime appointments to the United States Supreme Court? What problems might such appointments cause? What would be the likely result if Supreme Court justices faced term limits?

2. In the section "What Checks Our Courts," under "Public Opinion," we described how the Supreme Court ruled in favor of states' rights in a gun-control case and against states' rights in a marijuana case. Why do you think the justices might have come to different conclusions in these two cases?

DOMESTIC AND ECONOMIC POLICY

Demonstrators march down Middle Street in Portland, Maine, to protest budget cuts at the University of Southern Maine. *Why have many states cut their support for higher education?*
Portland Press Herald/Getty Images

These six **LEARNING OUTCOMES** *below are designed to help improve your understanding of this chapter:*

1: Describe the five steps of the policymaking process, using the health-care reform legislation as an example.

2: Explain why illegal immigration is seen as a problem, and cite some of the steps that have been taken in response to it.

3: Discuss recent developments in crime rates and incarceration.

4: Evaluate the federal government's responses to past high oil prices and the controversy over climate change.

5: Define *unemployment, inflation, fiscal policy, public debt,* and *monetary policy.*

6: Describe the various taxes that Americans pay, and discuss some of the controversies surrounding taxation.

What if...

We Returned to the Gold Standard?

Background

If you look at a dollar bill, you won't find much information about what is "backing" the bill. In fact, the only thing that backs the dollar is your certainty that everyone will accept it in payment for goods, services, and debts. Until 1964, however, the U.S. government issued dollar bills with the statement: "This certifies that there is on deposit in the treasury of the United States of America one dollar in silver payable to the bearer on demand." Apparently, the dollar was backed by silver.

In reality, it was backed by a law that set the value of the currency in terms of a specified quantity of gold. This was the gold standard. Until the 1930s, much of the world was on a gold standard. Nations agreed to redeem their currencies for a fixed amount of gold at the request of any holder of that currency. The heyday of the gold standard was from 1870 to 1914, although Britain had been on a gold standard since the 1820s.

For decades, most economists have assumed that the gold standard was history. In recent years, however, some Republicans have argued for a return to the gold standard. In a recent public opinion poll, 44 percent of those questioned favored the idea of a return to gold.

What If We Returned to the Gold Standard?

The first thing that the federal government would have to do is decide on the free convertibility of dollars for gold. If it used current gold prices, you would be able to exchange, say, $1,350 for an ounce of gold. Obviously, if the government declared an exchange rate that was equal to the world price of gold, you would have little incentive to ask a bank to give you gold for your dollars. If you really wanted gold, you would simply buy it on the open market.

Inflation and Deflation

Those in favor of a gold standard often argue that only "hard money" can prevent inflation, or a sustained rise in average prices and a loss in value of the currency. Indeed, from 1971, when President Richard Nixon eliminated the last vestiges of the gold standard, to 2017, average prices rose by about six times. In 1971, gold was worth $35 per ounce. If the price of gold had gone up at the same rate as everything else, it would now cost about $200 per ounce. In fact, the price of an ounce today is, as noted, close to $1,350.

If we had remained on the gold standard after 1971, therefore, the dollar might have more than six times its 1971 value. That means average prices would have fallen to less than one-sixth of their previous levels. Instead of inflation, there would have been a massive *deflation*, in which the value of the dollar would have increased hugely while the prices of everything else collapsed.

A gold standard, therefore, does not guarantee price stability. Consider also what would happen if we were suddenly able to mine vast quantities of new gold. This has happened. In the years after 1900, when new South African gold flooded the market, inflation reached 10 percent.

More typically, however, a gold standard threatens to cause deflation, and most economists consider deflation a much more dangerous condition than inflation. Deflation has been associated with severe depressions. In the Great Depression, for example, average prices fell by about 25 percent from 1929 to 1933. It's a good bet, therefore, that if we ever did return to the gold standard, we would probably leave it again soon.

For Critical Analysis

▶ **If the government creates "fiat money" (money not backed by any commodity), as it now does, how can it avoid inflation or deflation?**

▶ **Why does gold hold more fascination as the basis of a monetary system than, say, copper, steel, wheat, corn, or other commodities?**

Image 15–1 *Why would a gold standard make it hard to control the value of the dollar?*

Misunseo/Shutterstock.com

Part of the public-policy debate in our nation involves domestic problems. **Domestic policy** can be defined as all laws, government planning, and government actions that concern internal issues of national importance. Consequently, the span of such policies is enormous. Domestic policies range from relatively simple issues, such as what the speed limit should be on interstate highways, to more complex ones, such as how best to protect our environment or how we should manage the nation's money supply, as discussed in this chapter's opening *What If . . .* feature. Many of our domestic policies are formulated and implemented by the federal government, but a number of others are the result of the combined efforts of federal, state, and local governments.

We can define several types of domestic policy. *Regulatory policy* seeks to define what is and is not legal. Setting speed limits is obviously regulatory policy. *Redistributive policy* transfers income from certain individuals or groups to others, often based on the belief that these transfers enhance fairness. Social Security is an example. *Promotional policy* seeks to foster or discourage various economic or social activities, typically through subsidies and tax breaks. A tax credit for buying a fuel-efficient car would qualify as promotional. Typically, whenever a policy decision is made, some groups will be better off and some groups will be hurt. All policymaking generally involves such a dilemma.

In this chapter, we look at domestic policy issues involving health care, immigration, crime, and energy and the environment. We also examine national economic policies undertaken by the federal government.

The Policymaking Process: Health Care as an Example

Learning Outcome **1:**

How does any issue get resolved? First, of course, the issue must be identified as a problem. Often, policymakers have only to open their local newspapers or letters from their constituents to discover that a problem is brewing. On rare occasions, a crisis—such as that brought about by the terrorist attacks of September 11, 2001—creates the need to formulate policy. Like most Americans, however, policymakers receive much of their information from the national media. Finally, various lobbying groups provide information to members of Congress.

No matter how simple or how complex the problem, those who make policy follow a number of steps. We can divide the process of policymaking into five steps: (1) agenda building, (2) policy formulation, (3) policy adoption, (4) policy implementation, and (5) policy evaluation. The health-care legislation passed in 2010 can be used to illustrate this process. Although this legislation passed several years ago, it remains a major political issue to this day.

In March 2010, President Barack Obama signed into law the **Affordable Care Act,** a massive overhaul of the nation's health-care funding system. A few days later, Obama signed the Health Care and Education Reconciliation Act, a series of adjustments to the main legislative package. These two measures constituted the most important legislative package since 2010. They have become known by the nickname *Obamacare*.

Describe the five steps of the policymaking process, using the health-care reform legislation as an example.

Health Care: Agenda Building

First of all, an issue must get on the agenda. In other words, Congress must become aware that a problem requires congressional action. Agenda building may occur as the result of a crisis, technological change, or mass media campaign, as well as through the efforts of strong political personalities and effective lobbying groups. To understand how health care came to be an important issue, and how health-care reform became part of the national agenda, we need to examine the background of the issue.

domestic policy

All laws, government planning, and government actions that concern internal issues of national importance, such as poverty, crime, and the environment.

Affordable Care Act

A law passed in 2010 that seeks, among other things, to ensure health-care insurance for American citizens. The act is supplemented by the Health Care and Education Reconciliation Act and nicknamed "Obamacare."

gross domestic product (GDP)
The dollar value of all final goods and services produced in a one-year period.

Medicare
A federal health-insurance program that covers U.S. residents over the age of sixty-five. The costs are met by a tax on wages and salaries.

Medicaid
A joint state-federal program that provides medical care to the poor (including indigent elderly persons in nursing homes). The program is funded out of general government revenues.

entitlement program
A government program that entitles a defined class of people to obtain benefits. Entitlements operate under open-ended budget authorizations that do not limit how much can be spent.

Health Care's Role in the American Economy. As of 2015, health care was estimated to account for 17 percent of the total U.S. economy. In 1965, about 6 percent of our national income was spent on health care, but that percentage has risen since, as you can see in Figure 15–1. Per capita spending on health care is greater in the United States than almost anywhere else in the world. Measured by the percentage of the **gross domestic product (GDP)** devoted to health care, America spends about half again more than France or Germany. (See Figure 15–2.)

As of 2010, before the reform legislation was implemented, government spending on health care constituted about 50 percent of total health-care spending. Private insurance accounted for more than 30 percent of payments for health care. The remainder— less than 20 percent—was paid directly by individuals or by charities. The government programs **Medicare** and **Medicaid** have been the main sources of hospital and other medical benefits for about 100 million Americans—one-third of the nation's population. Many of these people are elderly.

Entitlement Programs. Like Social Security, Medicare and Medicaid are **entitlement programs.** Anyone who meets specific requirements is *entitled* to benefits under such programs. The federal government can estimate how much it will have to pay out in entitlements but cannot set an exact figure in advance. Congress does not reauthorize entitlement programs on a regular basis, as it does with *discretionary spending*. Rather, once established, an entitlement program continues indefinitely until Congress specifically alters it. (That does not mean that discretionary spending programs are unimportant—our armed forces are funded through discretionary spending.) Entitlement programs can be politically controversial, as we explain in this chapter's *Which Side Are You On?* feature.

Medicare. The Medicare program, which was created in 1965 under President Lyndon Johnson, pays hospital and physician bills for U.S. residents over the age of sixty-five. Since

Figure 15–1 Percentage of Total National Income Spent on Health Care in the United States

The portion of total national income spent on health care has risen since 1965. *What might people spend more on if health care were less expensive?*

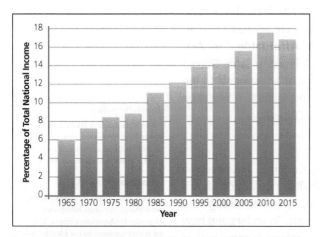

Sources: U.S. Department of Commerce; U.S. Department of Health and Human Services; Deloitte and Touche LLP; VHA, Inc.; Centers for Medicare and Medicaid Services, Organization for Economic Cooperation and Development.

Figure 15–2 Cost of Health Care in Economically Advanced Nations

Cost is given as a percentage of total gross domestic product (GDP). Figures are for 2014 and 2015. *Is it a problem or an advantage that U.S. physicians are among the world's best paid?*

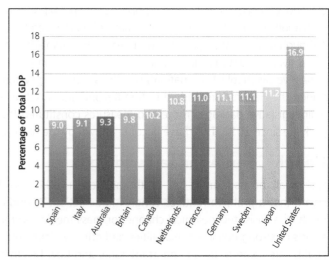

Source: Excerpted and adapted from the Organization for Economic Cooperation and Development, *OECD Health Data*, 2016.

Which side are you on?

Does Entitlement Spending Corrupt Us?

Certain federal benefits are called entitlements because you are entitled to receive them if you meet specific requirements. If you meet certain age and previous earnings requirements, you can receive a monthly Social Security check. If you lose your job, you may be entitled to unemployment benefits for a certain number of weeks. If your family income is below a certain level, you are typically entitled to benefits from the Supplemental Nutrition Assistance Program (SNAP, formerly called food stamps).

In recent years, federal entitlement spending has ballooned. Indeed, big government has gotten bigger in large part because Americans are receiving more entitlement payments every year. At all levels combined, government spending now has a value equivalent to about 36 percent of GDP. Some have argued that large-scale entitlement spending is corrupting us.

The More You Give People, the Less They'll Work

Conservatives point out that entitlement transfers—adjusted for rising prices and population growth—are now more than seven times what they were in 1960. (In part, this is because major programs such as Medicare and Medicaid were created in the 1960s.) Currently, almost half of Americans live in a household that receives at least one government benefit. If you count tax deductions, almost every household receives benefits.

Consider SNAP benefits. In 2007, 26 million Americans received them. By 2016, about 46 million Americans received them. The same story applies to Social Security disability payments. Four million people received disability checks in 1988. Today, disability checks are distributed to almost 11 million people. Fewer people are now in the labor force, and those who are work fewer hours per year. Since 2000, the labor force participation rate has fallen continuously, even during boom times. Many believe that increased entitlement benefits have reduced people's desire to join the labor force. In other words, entitlements corrupt.

Entitlements Are a Needed Part of the Social Contract

While the statistics just presented are accurate, political progressives do not accept the conclusions drawn. With an aging society, we should expect to pay more for Social Security. The same is true for government-financed health care. Health-care expenses are driven up not only by larger numbers of the elderly, but also by increasingly expensive (and effective) medical procedures.

Contrary to what some have argued, Americans are not divided between "makers" and "takers." At various times in our lives, we are all takers, and almost all of us are makers. As President Obama said in his second inaugural address, "The commitments we make to each other—through Medicare, and Medicaid, and Social Security—these things do not sap our initiative; they strengthen us. . . . they free us to take the risks that make this country great."

Americans believe in hard work as much as they always have. The Pew Economic Mobility Project sampled Americans on what is essential for getting ahead. More than 90 percent responded "hard work," and almost 90 percent answered "ambition." That doesn't sound like corruption.

For Critical Analysis

▶ Who ultimately pays for entitlement programs?

2006, Medicare has also paid for at least part of the prescription drug expenses of the elderly. In return for paying a tax on their earnings (currently set at 2.9 percent of wages and salaries for most people), retirees are assured that the majority of their hospital and physician bills will be paid for with public funds.

Medicaid. In recent decades, the joint federal-state taxpayer-funded Medicaid program for the "working poor" has generated a major expansion of government entitlements. In 1990, total Medicaid spending was around $40 billion. By fiscal year 2017,

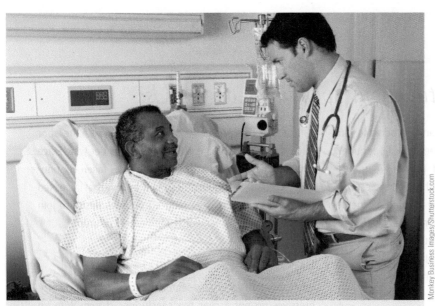

Image 15–2 A physician visits with a patient in a hospital ward. *How might this patient pay for hospitalization services?*

the total cost of Medicaid and the Children's Health Insurance Program (CHIP) was about $611 billion. At the end of the twentieth century, 34 million people were enrolled in the programs. As of 2016, there were more than 70 million enrolled.

Currently, the federal government pays more than 85 percent of Medicaid's total cost. The states pay the rest. Wealthy states must pick up a greater share of the tab than poor ones. As you will learn later in this section, the new health-care reform legislation adopted in 2010 has expanded considerably the share of the population that is eligible for Medicaid.

The Problem of the Uninsured. In 2013, before Obamacare was fully implemented, about 42 million Americans—more than 18 percent of the population—did not have health insurance. The uninsured population has been relatively young, in part due to Medicare, which covers almost everyone over the age of sixty-five. Also, younger workers are more likely to be employed in entry-level jobs without health-insurance benefits.

The traditional system of health care in the United States was based on the assumption that employers would provide health insurance to working-age persons. Many small businesses, however, simply have not been able to afford to offer their workers health insurance. In 2015, employer-provided health insurance cost an average of $6,251 for single coverage and $17,545 for family coverage, according to the Kaiser Family Foundation.

The Problem of High Costs. High medical costs are a problem not only for individuals with inadequate or nonexistent insurance coverage. They are also a problem for the system as a whole. Over the past four decades, per capita spending on health care in the United States grew at an average rate of 4.9 percent per year, even when corrected for inflation. A main driver of the growth in health-care spending was new medical technologies and services.

In addition, people over the age of sixty-five run up health-care bills that are far larger than those incurred by the rest of the population. As a federal problem, therefore, health-care spending growth remains chiefly a Medicare issue, even after the implementation of the new health-care measures. In 2016, the government's Medicare trustees reported that by 2028 the Medicare trust fund was projected to run out of funds necessary to pay for all of its obligations.

Health Care: Policy Formulation

During the next step in the policymaking process, various policy proposals are discussed among government officials and the public. Such discussions may take place in the printed media, on television, and in the halls of Congress. Congress holds hearings, the president voices the administration's views, and the topic may even become a campaign issue.

For more than half a century, liberals had sought to establish a universal health-insurance system in this country. All attempts, however, went nowhere. After the 2008 elections, though, the Democrats were in complete control of Congress and the presidency. Universal health insurance now appeared to be politically possible.

Under Democratic plans, universal coverage would result from a mandate that all citizens must obtain health insurance from some source—an employer, Medicare or Medicaid, or a plan from a private-sector insurance company through a market sponsored by the federal government or a state government. Low-income families would receive a subsidy to help them pay their insurance premiums.

Health Care: Policy Adoption

The third step in the policymaking process involves choosing a specific policy from among the proposals that have been discussed.

President Obama largely delegated the drafting of a health-care plan to Congress. In contrast, recent presidents had often sought to push presidential proposals through the legislative process without significant alteration. Obama's tactics made it easier to bring Congress on board, but the political cost was high. Much of the political maneuvering required for passage was highly unpopular with the public.

One key element of the proposed legislation was the *individual mandate,* a requirement to buy insurance. Congressional Democrats adopted the individual mandate because without it, there was no way that the numbers would add up: universal coverage was impossible unless everyone—healthy and sick alike—chipped in. Unfortunately for the Democrats, the individual mandate allowed the Republicans to accuse the Democrats of "forcing" people to do something, never a popular position in America.

Funding the legislation required additional taxes. Democrats in the House called for heavier taxes on the rich, while the Senate proposed taxes on drug and insurance companies. In the end, the two chambers compromised on some of each.

Initially, popular support for health-care reform, as reported by opinion polls, was relatively high. Support eroded quickly, however, as Congress took up the actual legislation.

Passage. The House and Senate passed different versions of the legislation in late 2009. Passing the reform legislation became more complicated in January 2010, after a Republican won a Massachusetts special election to fill a vacant U.S. Senate seat. The election meant that the Senate Democrats lost their sixtieth vote, which was necessary to end filibusters. If the House and Senate versions of the bill were reconciled in a conference committee—the normal procedure—Senate Democrats would not be able to pass the resulting compromise.

Democrats, however, assembled enough support in the House to pass the Senate bill unaltered, thus eliminating the need for a conference committee. Obamacare was the law of the land. The new legislation did not receive the vote of a single Republican.

Details of the Legislation. Most of the major provisions of the new legislation did not go into effect until 2014. Some provisions took effect quickly, however. Young adults were allowed to stay on their parents' health plans until they turned twenty-six, and insurance companies could not drop people when they became sick.

In 2014, most of the program kicked in, including the following:

- A ban on excluding people with preexisting conditions from insurance plans.

- State health-insurance exchanges where individuals and small businesses can buy policies from commercial insurance companies.

- Subsidies to help persons with incomes up to four times the federal poverty level purchase coverage on the exchanges.

- Medicaid coverage for individuals with incomes up to 133 percent of the poverty level (but only in participating states).

Health Care: Policy Implementation

The fourth step in the policymaking process involves the implementation of the policy alternative chosen by Congress. Government action must be implemented by bureaucrats, the courts, police, and individual citizens.

Congressional Opposition. Implementation would not occur, of course, if Obamacare could be abolished. Complete repeal of the legislation, however, was hard. Repeal would have to pass both chambers of Congress and survive a presidential veto. Also, much of the reform took the form of an entitlement program. Therefore, even if Republicans in Congress were able to "defund" certain aspects of the reforms, most of the new policies would survive.

Opposition in the Courts and in the States. Many conservative state officials challenged the constitutionality of the Affordable Care Act in court. In 2012, however, the Supreme Court ruled that most of the act was constitutional. The one exception: the Court threw out the mechanism by which the federal government could force states to expand their Medicaid programs.

Medicaid expansion was fully funded by the federal government for the first six years and funded at 90 percent thereafter. Still, a large number of conservative state governments exercised their option to refuse expansion. As a result, several million low-income persons were not immediately eligible for coverage.

Setting Up the Exchanges. On October 1, 2013, the state and federal exchanges were scheduled to open. Many of the state exchange websites experienced only a moderate number of initial problems. Some were so badly built that they had to be scrapped.

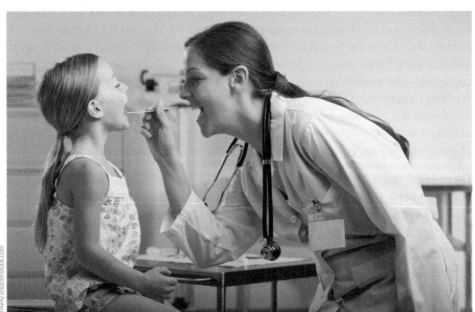

Image 15–3 A young girl receives a checkup from a pediatrician. The Affordable Care Act contains special provisions to reduce the cost of preventive health care. *Why might that be so?*

The federal exchanges, set up in states that refused to establish their own, had tremendous difficulties for several months. By January 2014, however, the federal exchanges were functioning adequately.

Health Care: Policy Evaluation

After a policy has been implemented, it is evaluated. When a policy has been in place for a given period of time, groups inside and outside the government conduct studies to determine how the program has actually worked. Based on this feedback and the perceived success or failure of the policy, a new round of policymaking initiatives may be undertaken to improve on the effort.

A majority of the public has had a negative opinion of Obamacare since it was passed, although a majority also supports changing rather than abolishing it. Democrats had assumed that after full implementation, the reforms would gain broad public support. But most people continue to get their insurance through an employer, Medicare, or some other preexisting system. These people have no actual experience with the reforms and therefore often judge them based on their own partisan preferences. The 2016 elections gave Republicans complete control of the government. There was now a chance that the reform would be abolished. Yet that would mean taking health-care insurance away from millions.

Despite the claims of many conservatives, by 2016 the reforms were, for the most part, meeting anticipated goals. With more people insured, the nation's total health-care bill is larger than in the past in absolute terms, though not as a percentage of GDP. Surprisingly, the rate of increase in total costs has fallen. For example, annual Medicare costs per person are about $1,000 below the sums projected earlier. One reason is that the Affordable Care Act contains a variety of measures that pressure physicians and hospitals to curb expenses. Many believed that these measures would have no effect. This judgment may have been too pessimistic.

According to Gallup, the share of uninsured adults dropped from 18 percent in 2013 to 11 percent in 2016. Clearly, although millions have gained insurance, Obamacare is not truly universal. Low-income persons in states that did not expand Medicaid have lost out. Some people have refused to participate. (The income tax penalties for nonparticipation are low.) Finally, illegal immigrants are simply not allowed to participate in the programs.

Immigration

In recent years, immigration rates in the United States have been among the highest since their peak in the early twentieth century. Every year, more than 1 million people immigrate to this country legally, a figure that does not include the large number of unauthorized immigrants. Those born on foreign soil now constitute about 13 percent of the U.S. population—more than twice the percentage of thirty years ago.

Since 1977, four out of five immigrants have come from Latin America or Asia. Hispanics have overtaken African Americans as the nation's largest minority. If current immigration rates continue, by 2050 minority groups collectively will constitute the majority of Americans. If such groups were to form coalitions, they could increase their political power dramatically. The white plurality would no longer control American politics, though it would remain the largest single group.

Some regard the high rate of immigration as a plus for America because it offsets a low birthrate and aging population. Immigrants expand the workforce and help to support, through their taxes, government programs that benefit older Americans, such as Medicare and Social Security. In contrast, nations that do not have high immigration rates, such as Japan, are experiencing serious challenges due to their aging populations.

Learning Outcome **2:**

Explain why illegal immigration is seen as a problem, and cite some of the steps that have been taken in response to it.

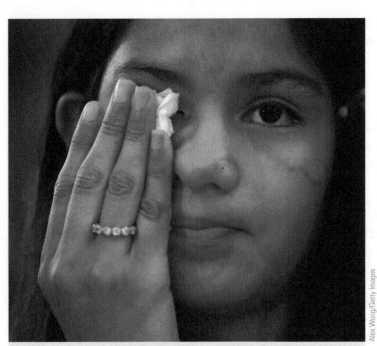

Image 15–4 A twelve-year-old unauthorized immigrant wipes tears as she tells her story of escaping from violence in her home country of Honduras. She is testifying before the Congressional Progressive Caucus. *Should young people fleeing from violence be granted asylum in the United States? Why or why not?*

A significant number of U.S. citizens, however, believe that immigration—both legal and illegal—negatively affects America. They argue, among other things, that the large number of immigrants seeking work results in lower wages for Americans, especially those with few skills. They also worry about the cost of providing immigrants with services such as education and medical care.

The Issue of Unauthorized Immigration

Illegal or unauthorized immigration is a major national issue. The largest number of unauthorized immigrants are from Latin America, especially Mexico. A current estimate is that there are about 11 million such people. Almost all illegal immigrants come to work, and hiring them was not illegal until 1986. Today, laws designed to prevent the employment of undocumented workers are enforced more strictly than in the past.

In polls by Gallup and other organizations, Americans express opinions about illegal immigration (the term used in the questions) that are highly contradictory. A majority of respondents express sympathy toward the immigrants and believe that a way should be found to normalize their status. Less than a fifth favor immediate, permanent deportation. In the very same polls, however, two-thirds agree that states should be able to set their own immigration laws and that police officers should be able to question anyone about their immigration status. Half believe that illegal immigration to seek work should be a crime.

While a majority of Americans believe that the illegal immigration problem is serious, most do not consider it a priority issue for the government. Those who do consider it a priority, however, have very strong feelings on the topic—and in American politics, a minority with strong feelings can often outweigh a largely indifferent majority.

The Immigration Debate

The split in the public's attitudes has been reflected in differences among the nation's leaders over how to handle the issue of illegal immigration. Most Republicans in Congress have favored a harder line toward illegal immigrants than have most Democrats. There have been exceptions. Republican president George W. Bush was a strong—if unsuccessful—advocate of immigration reform. By Obama's first term, however, Republicans in Congress were substantially united against reform.

State Immigration Laws. In April 2010, Arizona's governor signed the nation's toughest-ever bill on illegal immigration. The law criminalized the failure to carry immigration documents, and it required police to stop and question anyone suspected of being in the country illegally. The law also penalized anyone transporting, sheltering, or assisting illegal aliens. Opponents contended that the act would lead to harassment of Latinos regardless of their citizenship status. Arizona had earlier passed the nation's toughest law penalizing employers who hired undocumented workers.

In June 2012, the United States Supreme Court ruled that Arizona could not make an immigrant's failure to register under federal law a state crime, could not make it a felony for illegal immigrants to work, and could not arrest people without warrants if they might be deportable under federal law. The Court did not block police from investigating the immigration status of anyone they stop. It left the door open, however, to future challenges to this law based on equal protection principles.[1]

In 2011, Alabama adopted a new law aimed at illegal immigration that was in many respects even tougher than the Arizona legislation. Much of the law is currently blocked as a result of federal court rulings, however, and several provisions were invalidated by the Supreme Court's Arizona ruling. Georgia, Indiana, South Carolina, and Utah have also passed laws that attempt to reduce illegal immigration.

Immigration and the Obama Administration. During his first presidential campaign, Barack Obama supported reforms that would give illegal immigrants a path toward citizenship. Reform was put off to allow Congress to concentrate on health-care issues, however. Obama focused instead on border security and rounding up deportable persons. In fact, in Obama's first term, his administration deported 1.5 million illegal immigrants, an all-time record.

The resulting Latino dissatisfaction with the administration raised the question of whether Hispanics would turn out to vote for Democratic candidates in forthcoming elections. The 2012 Republican presidential candidates, however, took a hard line against illegal immigration. Also, in June 2012, Obama announced a new policy under which immigration authorities would suspend deportations of unauthorized immigrants who were brought into the country as children and who were not otherwise in trouble with the law. In the end, Latinos and Asian Americans turned out for the Democrats in large numbers during the 2012 elections.

Current Disputes. Following the 2012 elections, some Republicans announced that they were open to changing their positions on immigration. By 2014, however, that party was again blocking new legislation. One reason was opposition to an executive order issued by President Obama in 2014. Under the order, more than 4 million unauthorized immigrants were protected from deportation and allowed to obtain work permits. In 2015, a district court judge stayed (suspended) the order. The Supreme Court confirmed the stay in 2016, but on a four-to-four vote that did not set a precedent.

Crime in the Twenty-First Century

Learning Outcome **3:**

Discuss recent developments in crime rates and incarceration.

Almost all polls taken in the United States in the past several decades have shown that crime remains one of the major concerns of the public. A related issue that has been on the domestic policy agenda for decades is the status of the nation's prisons.

Crime in American History

In every period in the history of this nation, people have voiced apprehension about crime. During the Civil War, mob violence and riots erupted in several cities. After the Civil War, people in San Francisco were told that "no decent man is in safety to walk the streets after dark; while at all hours, both night and day, his property is jeopardized by incendiarism [arson] and burglary."[2]

In fact, studies by historians have shown that preindustrial agricultural communities had very high levels of interpersonal violence, and that crime rates in the United States and other Western countries fell steadily from the second quarter of the nineteenth century into the twentieth century. Some historians suggest that this century-long decline came

---

1. *Arizona v. United States,* 567 U.S. ___ (2012).

2. President's Commission on Law Enforcement and Administration of Justice, *Challenge of Crime in a Free Society* (Washington, D.C.: Government Printing Office, 1967), p. 19.

Image 15–5 Prisoners at the Deuel Vocational Institution in Tracy, California. This prison is a reception center for new prisoners of the California Department of Corrections and Rehabilitation (CDCR). The prisoners are from northern California county jails. The facility also houses a number of low-security inmates. *Do overcrowded prisons violate prisoners' rights?*

about because industrialization, urbanization, and the growth of bureaucratic institutions such as factories and schools socialized the lower classes into patterns of conformity and rule observance.

The United States then experienced a substantial crime wave in the 1920s and the first half of the 1930s. This was the period of Prohibition, when the production and sale of alcoholic beverages was illegal. Criminals such as the famous Al Capone organized gangs to provide illicit alcohol to the public. After the end of Prohibition, crime rates dropped until after World War II (1939–1945).

An explosive growth in violent crime began in the 1960s. The murder rate per 100,000 people in 1964 was 4.9, whereas in 1994 it was estimated at 9.3, an increase of almost 100 percent. Since 1995, however, violent crime rates have declined. Some argue that this decline is due to the growing economy the United States has generally enjoyed since about 1993. Others claim that the billions in additional funds that the federal and state governments allotted to curbing crime in the past few years has led to less crime. Still others claim that an increase in the number of persons who are jailed or imprisoned is responsible for the reduction. Some have even argued that a reduction in environmental lead levels—lead is a powerful neurotoxin—has reduced the number of persons susceptible to criminal behavior. You can see changes in the rates of homicides, violent crimes, and thefts in Figures 15–3, 15–4, and 15–5, respectively.

Homicide rates may have risen in several major cities in 2015, although rates were stable or in decline elsewhere. The rises have been attributed to a decline in police-community relations following incidents in which unarmed African Americans died due to police shootings or while in police custody. The rise in homicides

Figure 15–3   Homicide Rates

Homicide rates recently declined to levels last seen in the 1960s. (The 2001 rate does not include deaths attributed to the 9/11 terrorist attacks.) *How might advances in medical care affect these numbers?*

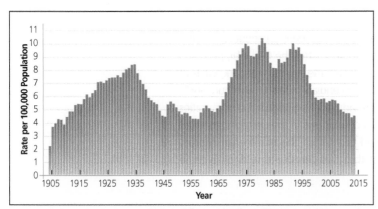

Sources: U.S. Department of Justice; and National Center for Health Statistics, *Vital Statistics.*

has been dubbed the *Ferguson effect*, after a Missouri city that experienced one such fatal incident, followed by demonstrations and civil unrest. Still, even in cities that may have experienced such an effect—for example, Baltimore—homicide rates are far below what they were several years ago.

The Prison Population Bomb

Many Americans believe that the best solution to the nation's crime problem is to impose stiff prison sentences on offenders. Such sentences, in fact, have become national policy. By 2014, U.S. prisons and jails held 2.3 million people. About two-thirds of the incarcerated population were in state or federal prisons, with the remainder held in local jails. About 70 percent of the persons held in local jails were awaiting court action. The other 30 percent were serving sentences.

The number of incarcerated persons has grown rapidly in recent years. In 1990, for example, the total number of persons held in U.S. jails or prisons was still only 1.1 million. From 1995 to 2002, the incarcerated population grew at an average of 3.8 percent annually. The rate of growth slowed after 2002, however, and the number of prisoners has fallen since 2011.

The Incarceration Rate. Some groups of people are much more likely to find themselves behind bars than others. Men are more than ten times more likely to be incarcerated than women. Prisoners are also disproportionately African American. To measure how frequently members of particular groups are imprisoned, the standard statistic is the **incarceration rate.** This rate is the number of people incarcerated for every 100,000 persons in a particular population group. To put it another way, an incarceration rate of 1,000 means that 1 percent of a particular group is in custody. Using this statistic, we can say that U.S. men had an incarceration rate of 1,398 in 2009, compared with a rate of 131 for U.S. women.

The numbers we have, close to an all-time high, mean that more than 1 male out of every 100 was in jail or prison in this country. Figure 15–6 shows selected incarceration rates by gender, race, and age. Note the very high incarceration rate for African Americans between the ages of thirty and thirty-four—at any given time, almost 11 percent of this group was in jail or prison. The government has not updated these detailed statistics since 2009. Instead of the incarceration rate—an international standard—the government now releases *imprisonment rates,* that is, the rates *only* for persons convicted of a crime. Given that hundreds of thousands of Americans are locked up at any given time but have not been convicted of an offense, this change results in substantially lower rates. It is hard to avoid the conclusion that the change was a deliberate policy decision.

Figure 15–4 Violent Crime Rates

Violent crime rates began a steep decline in 1995. The crimes included in this chart are rape, robbery, aggravated and simple assault, and domestic violence. *Do you think people today are more or less likely to report crimes than in the past? Why?*

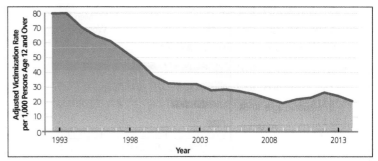

Source: U.S. Department of Justice; rape, robbery, domestic violence, and assault data are from the *National Crime Victimization Survey.*

Figure 15–5 Theft Rates

Theft rates have declined significantly since the 1970s. Theft is defined as completed or attempted theft of property or cash without personal contact. *Have you personally taken steps to avoid becoming a theft victim? If so, what were they?*

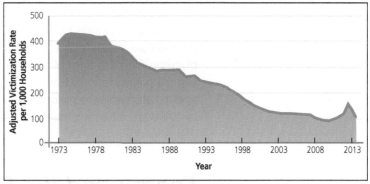

Source: U.S. Department of Justice, *National Crime Victimization Survey.*

incarceration rate

The number of persons held in jail or prison for every 100,000 persons in a particular population group.

Why do you think the government may have stopped updating incarceration statistics?

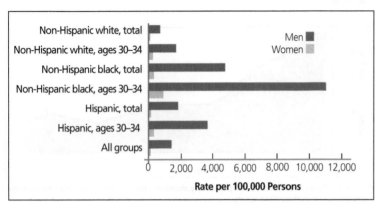

Source: "Prison Inmates at Midyear 2009," *Bureau of Justice Statistics Bulletin*, U.S. Department of Justice (2010).

How do American incarceration rates compare with those of other countries? We answer that question in this chapter's *Consider the Source* feature.

Prison Construction and Conditions. To house a growing number of inmates, prison construction and management have become sizable industries in the United States. Ten years ago, prison overcrowding was a major issue. In 1994, for example, state prisons had a rated capacity of about 500,000 inmates but actually held 900,000 people. The prisons were therefore operating at 80 percent above capacity. Today, after a major prison construction program, many state prisons are operating within their capacity, but some state systems are still at 20 percent above capacity or more. The federal prison system is still 37 percent above capacity. In 1923, there were only 61 prisons in the entire United States. Today, there are 1,821.

Effects of Incarceration. When imprisonment keeps truly violent felons behind bars longer, it prevents them from committing additional crimes. The average predatory street criminal commits fifteen or more crimes each year when not behind bars. But most prisoners are in for a relatively short time and are released on parole early, often because of prison overcrowding. Many then find themselves back in prison because they have violated parole, typically by using illegal drugs. Indeed, of the 1.5 million people who are arrested each year, the majority are arrested for drug offenses. Given that from 20 million to 40 million Americans violate one or more drug laws each year, the potential "supply" of prisoners seems almost limitless.

Energy and the Environment

Learning Outcome **4:**

Evaluate the federal government's responses to past high oil prices and the controversy over climate change.

A major part of President Obama's agenda was directed at energy and environmental issues. Energy policy addresses two major problems: (1) America's reliance on foreign oil, much of which is produced by unfriendly regimes, and (2) climate change (or global warming) purportedly caused by increased emissions of carbon dioxide (CO_2) and other greenhouse gases.

Energy Independence—A Strategic Issue

As of 2015, the United States imported about 24 percent of the petroleum it consumed. Almost half of U.S. imports come from two friendly neighbors, Canada and Mexico, and less than one-third from Middle Eastern countries, primarily Saudi Arabia. The world's largest oil exporters include a number of nations that are not friends of the United States. Russia is the world's second-largest oil exporter, after Saudi Arabia. Other major exporters include Venezuela and Iran. Both are openly hostile to American interests, and Venezuela is a major source of U.S. oil imports.

While the United States has not yet attained the goal of energy independence, the nation has taken significant steps in that direction. American reliance on foreign oil is

NEWS Consider the source

How Many People Do Other Countries Send to Prison?

The United States has more people in jail or prison than any other country in the world. That fact is not necessarily surprising, because the United States also has one of the world's largest total populations. More to the point, the United States has almost the highest reported incarceration *rate* of any country on earth. North Korea almost certainly has a higher incarceration rate than the United States, but that nation does not report its incarceration statistics. (One human rights organization estimates the North Korean rate as 825 prisoners for every 100,000 inhabitants.) Many small island nations have unusually high incarceration rates, and one—the Seychelles—manages to beat the United States with a rate of 799. The absolute number of persons locked up in these tiny countries, however, is quite small. Figure 15–7 compares the U.S. incarceration rate, measured by the number of prisoners per 100,000 residents, with incarceration rates in other major countries.

The Source

The data for Figure 15–7 come from the Institute for Criminal Policy Research (ICPR), a British group. It collects figures from national authorities around the world, but it does not do so uncritically. For example, the incarceration rate reported here for China comes from an estimate by a human rights group, not the Chinese government. (The ICPR reports the official figure as well.)

Figure 15–7 Incarceration Rates around the World

Incarceration rates of major nations, measured by the number of prisoners per 100,000 residents. *Why do you think other advanced nations are so much less likely to send people to prison?*

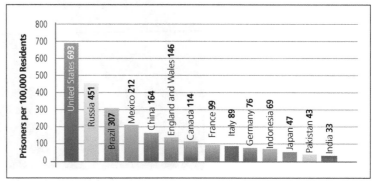

Source: Institute for Criminal Policy Research.

For Critical Analysis

○ To find incarceration rates for all nations, go to www.prisonstudies.org/highest-to-lowest/prison_population_rate and click on "apply." Why might large, poor nations such as India and Pakistan have low rates?

---

down dramatically from what it was only a few years ago. In 2006, almost 60 percent of our oil came from abroad, compared to the current 24 percent. What changes were responsible for this turnaround?

High Prices and New Production. If the price of a commodity goes up, producers of that commodity have an incentive to produce more of it. The price of gasoline has certainly risen in recent years. In the summer of 2008, the price of gasoline exceeded $4 for the first time. Clearly, petroleum producers had an incentive to extract more crude oil, if possible. The question was, could they?

Some experts doubted that enough new oil could be extracted to keep prices from rising indefinitely. They underestimated the impact of increased applications of technology in the form of hydraulic fracturing, or **fracking.** This process involves injecting water, sand, and chemicals under high pressure into hydrocarbon-bearing rocks, releasing oil or natural gas. The high price of oil made fracking profitable.

fracking

Short for *hydraulic fracturing,* the injection of a high-pressure solution of water, sand, and chemicals into hydrocarbon-bearing rocks, releasing oil or natural gas.

Image 15–6 A Texas worker unloads a mixture of oil, sediment, and water generated during hydraulic fracturing (fracking). Components of the mixture will be separated and either recycled or eliminated. *Why is fracking controversial?*

Fracking has had an even greater impact on the supply of natural gas. A few years ago, it seemed likely that the United States would need to import natural gas. Imports would be expensive, because gas cannot be transported by ship efficiently unless it is converted to liquefied natural gas (LNG). By 2012, however, so much natural gas was available domestically that the nation had run out of storage space. Plans were under way to export LNG from terminals built to import it. Low natural gas prices plus new air-pollution regulations made coal uncompetitive as a source of electricity. As a result, plans for 168 new coal-based power plants were abandoned, and about 100 existing plants were scheduled for retirement. Despite concerns that fracking might harm drinking-water supplies or otherwise damage the environment, use of the process grew rapidly.

In the summer of 2014, a barrel of crude oil cost more than $100. By the end of the year, the price was cut in half and seemed set to remain between $40 and $50 for years to come. The cause was clear—fracking had done its work. The United States, not Saudi Arabia, was now the "swing producer" that would determine the price of oil. By mid-2016, gasoline was about $2.15 per gallon in most of the country.

The Politics of Expensive Oil. The price of gasoline is a political issue, and some politicians have claimed that, if elected, they would bring it down. Crude oil prices are set worldwide, however, and the ability of the federal government to affect these prices is very limited. Still, the government has taken some steps to encourage increased supplies of gasoline.

President Obama issued higher fuel-efficiency standards for vehicles in 2009 and 2012. By 2016, new cars were to average 39 miles per gallon and light trucks 30. By 2025, the nation's combined fleet of new cars and light trucks must have an average fuel efficiency of 54.5 miles per gallon.

The federal government also subsidizes the development of alternative fuels. Subsidies to encourage the production of ethanol from corn are controversial. Critics charge that ethanol production is an inefficient method of producing energy. Ethanol also makes food more expensive by driving up the cost of corn. Subsidies for renewable energy sources, such as windmills and solar power panels, have attracted criticisms, too. A problem with wind and especially solar power has been high costs. Prices have fallen rapidly, however, and use of these technologies has risen quickly. Still, they are a small fraction of the nation's power supply.

Disasters in the Energy Industry. For some years, opening new areas for oil and gas drilling has been a major plank in the Republican Party platform. Democrats have been more reluctant, but in March 2010, President Obama announced that major new offshore tracts in the Atlantic would be open to deep-sea drilling. Less than one month later, the BP *Deepwater Horizon* oil spill disaster in the Gulf of Mexico began. The spill, the largest in American history, resulted in a temporary moratorium on new offshore drilling.

Unlike many Democrats, Obama also favored building new energy plants that would use nuclear power. Electric utilities planned several new nuclear plants, but these plans were shelved almost immediately. The major problem was that nuclear power could not compete on cost with natural gas. A second problem was safety. In March 2011, a giant tsunami struck northeast Japan and severely damaged four nuclear reactors located on the coast. The resulting radiation leaks convinced many people that new nuclear power plants would be dangerous.

Climate Change

In the 1990s, many scientists working on climate issues began to conclude that average world temperatures would rise significantly during the twenty-first century. Gases released by human activity, principally carbon dioxide (CO_2), may be producing a "greenhouse effect," trapping the sun's heat and slowing its release into outer space.

The Climate Change Debate. Most scientists who perform research on the world's climate believe that climate change will be significant, but there is considerable disagreement as to how much warming will actually occur. It is generally accepted that world temperatures have already increased by about 0.74 degrees Celsius over the past century. The United Nations' Intergovernmental Panel on Climate Change predicts increases ranging from 1.0 to 4.8 degrees Celsius by 2100. This range of estimates is rather wide and reflects the uncertainties involved in predicting the world's climate.

Climate change has become a major political football to be kicked back and forth by conservatives and liberals. Environmental groups and others have been pressing the federal government to take action now to avert a planet-threatening crisis. Their efforts are complicated by the fact that a major share of the American electorate does not believe that global warming is happening or, if it is happening, that it is caused by human activities. Disbelief in man-made climate change is a partisan phenomenon. According to one poll, skepticism about climate change among Republicans rose by 11 percentage points from 2008 to 2009, and a majority of Republicans now believe that global warming does not exist. The opinions of Democrats have not changed—about four-fifths of them accept that climate change is a problem. If there were no global warming, of course, there would be no reason to limit emissions of CO_2 and other greenhouse gases. By 2014, in the wake of superstorms and droughts, skepticism about climate change among Republicans and independents had eased somewhat—but opposition to CO_2 restrictions remained strong.

Addressing the Issue. In 2009, Democrats made an initial attempt to legislate on CO_2 emissions. The bill sank without a trace in the Senate. With Republicans in control of the House beginning in 2011, no further legislation was possible. Despite the lack of government action, by 2011 CO_2 emissions in the United States were down substantially from 2008. The most important cause was new power plants using natural gas instead of coal. (Gas does release some CO_2, but less than half as much as coal.) More fuel-efficient cars also contributed to the reduction.

Obama and the Environmental Protection Agency. It was also possible that the Environmental Protection Agency (EPA) might act without new legislation. In 2007, the Supreme Court found that the EPA had the authority to regulate the emission of CO_2 and other greenhouse gases under the Clean Air Act.[3] This decision opened up the possibility that the Obama administration might take action against greenhouse gas emissions by electrical power plants without new authority from Congress.

In 2009, the EPA issued a finding that greenhouse gases did in fact threaten the public health and welfare. In 2013, it issued rules covering new power plants. Coal-based power plants were already suffering serious price competition from natural gas, and the EPA's rules made the construction of new coal-based plants almost impossible.

In June 2014, President Obama announced proposed EPA rules covering existing power plants. The rules sought to cut emissions from such plants 30 percent by 2030. States were given a wide menu of options to meet the standards and would not necessarily have to close coal-based plants immediately. The long-term survival of coal-based electricity under the rules, however, appeared bleak. In 2014, a group of states sued the EPA in an attempt to overturn the rules. As we observed earlier in this text, in 2016 the Supreme Court blocked implementation pending a final ruling. With Trump as president, the proposed EPA plan will surely be abolished.

An additional controversy centered on the proposed Keystone XL pipeline. This project would carry petroleum from the Alberta oil sands (and North Dakota) to refineries on the Gulf Coast. Opponents of the pipeline claimed that the oil sands were one of the world's most pollution-intense sources of oil. Proponents argued for the economic benefits of greater supply. Republicans in Congress tried to force President Obama to approve the project. In 2015, however, Obama canceled the pipeline on environmental grounds.

The Politics of Economic Decision Making

Learning Outcome **5:**

Define *unemployment, inflation, fiscal policy, public debt,* and *monetary policy.*

Nowhere are the principles of public policymaking more obvious than in the economic decisions made by the federal government. The president and Congress are constantly faced with questions of economic policy. Such issues become especially important when the nation enters a recession.

Good Times, Bad Times

recession

Two or more successive quarters in which the economy shrinks instead of grows.

unemployment

The inability of those who are in the labor force to find a job; also, the number of those in the labor force actively looking for a job, but unable to find one.

inflation

A sustained rise in the general price level of goods and services.

Like any economy that is fundamentally capitalist, the U.S. economy experiences ups and downs. Good times—booms—are followed by lean years. If a slowdown is severe enough, it is called a **recession.** Recessions are characterized by increased **unemployment,** the inability of those who are in the labor force to find a job. The government tries to moderate the effects of such downturns. In contrast, booms are historically associated with another economic problem that the government must address—rising prices, or **inflation.**

---

3. *Massachusetts v. EPA,* 549 U.S. 497 (2007).

Unemployment. Some psychologists say that unemployment is one of the most traumatizing events in a person's life. Certainly, unemployment imposes costs on the entire economy, not just on the unemployed individuals. Since the Great Depression of the 1930s, fighting unemployment has been a major goal of the federal government. The federal government also provides unemployment insurance. Not all unemployed workers are eligible, however. In fact, only about one-third of the unemployed receive benefits. Benefits are not available to employees who quit their jobs voluntarily or are fired for cause (for example, constantly showing up late for work). They are also not paid to workers who are entering the labor force for the first time but cannot find a job.

Measuring Unemployment. Estimates of the number of unemployed are prepared by the U.S. Department of Labor. The Bureau of the Census also generates estimates using survey research data. Critics of the published unemployment rate calculated by the federal government

Image 15–7 A job seeker, center, shakes hands with a recruiter during an aerospace, maritime, and manufacturing job fair in Seattle. *Is unemployment still a major problem? Why or why not?*

believe that it fails to reflect the true numbers of discouraged workers and "hidden unemployed." There is no exact way to measure discouraged workers, however. The Department of Labor defines them as people who have dropped out of the labor force and are no longer looking for a job because they believe that the job market has little to offer them. As a result, some economists believe that a better way to look at the unemployment issue is to calculate the share of the population that is actually working.

Inflation. Rising prices, or inflation, can also be a serious economic and political problem. Inflation is a sustained upward movement in the average level of prices. Another way of defining inflation is as a decline in the purchasing power of money over time. The government measures inflation using the *consumer price index,* or CPI. The Bureau of Labor Statistics identifies a market basket of goods and services purchased by the typical consumer, and regularly checks the price of that basket. Over a period of many years, inflation can add up. For example, today's dollar is worth (very roughly) about a twentieth of what a dollar was worth a century ago. In effect, today's dollar is a 1917 nickel.

The Business Cycle. Economists refer to the regular succession of economic expansions and contractions as the *business cycle.* An extremely severe recession is called a *depression,* as in the example of the Great Depression of the 1930s. By 1933, actual output was 35 percent below the nation's productive capacity. Unemployment reached 25 percent. Compared with this catastrophe, recessions since 1945 have usually been mild. Nevertheless, the United States has experienced recessions with some regularity. Recession years since 1960 have included 1970, 1974, 1980, 1982, 1990, 2001, and, of course, 2008 and 2009.

To try to control the ups and downs of the national economy, the government has several policy options. One is to change the level of taxes or government spending. Another possibility involves influencing interest rates and the money side of the economy. We will examine taxing and spending, or **fiscal policy,** first.

fiscal policy

The federal government's use of taxation and spending policies to affect overall business activity.

Image 15–8 English economist John Maynard Keynes (1883–1946). *What inspired Keynes's theories?*

Walter Stoneman/Getty Images

Fiscal Policy

Fiscal policy is the domain of Congress. A fiscal policy approach to stabilizing the economy is often associated with the twentieth-century British economist John Maynard Keynes (1883–1946). Keynes originated the school of thought that today is called **Keynesian economics,** which supports the use of government spending and taxing to help stabilize the economy. (*Keynesian* is pronounced *kayn*-zee-un.) Keynes believed that there was a need for government intervention in the economy, in part because after falling into a recession or depression, a modern economy may become trapped in an ongoing state of less than full employment.

Government Spending and Borrowing. Keynes developed his fiscal policy theories during the Great Depression of the 1930s. He believed that the forces of supply and demand operated too slowly on their own in such a serious recession. Unemployment meant people had less to spend, and because they could not buy things, more businesses failed, creating additional unemployment. It was a vicious cycle. Keynes's idea was simple: in such circumstances, the *government* should step in and engineer the spending that is needed to return the economy to a more normal state.[4]

The spending promoted by the government could take either of two forms. The government could increase its own spending, or it could cut taxes, allowing the taxpayer to undertake the spending instead. To have the effect Keynes wanted, however, it was essential that the spending be financed by borrowing. In other words, the government should run a **budget deficit**—it should spend more than it receives.

Discretionary Fiscal Policy. Keynes originally developed his fiscal theories as a way of lifting an economy out of a major disaster such as the Great Depression. Beginning with the presidency of John F. Kennedy (1961–1963), however, policymakers have attempted to use Keynesian methods to "fine-tune" the economy. This is discretionary fiscal policy— *discretionary* meaning left to the judgment or discretion of a policymaker.

The Timing Problem. Attempts to fine-tune the economy face a timing problem. It takes a while to collect and assimilate economic data. Therefore, time may go by before an economic problem can be identified. After an economic problem is recognized, a solution must be formulated. There will be an action time lag between the recognition of a problem and the implementation of policy to solve it. Getting Congress to act can easily take a year or two. Finally, after fiscal policy is enacted, it takes time for the policy to affect the economy. Because fiscal policy time lags are long and variable, a policy designed to combat a recession may not produce results until the economy is already out of the recession.

Because of the timing problem, attempts by the government to employ fiscal policy in the past fifty years have typically taken the form of tax cuts or increases. Tax changes can take effect more quickly than government spending. In 2009, therefore, the Obama administration was employing an exceptional approach when it secured from Congress a roughly $900 billion package consisting largely of economic stimulus spending.

Criticisms of Keynes. Following World War II (1939–1945), Keynes's theories were integrated into the mainstream of economic thinking. There have always been economic schools of thought that consider Keynesian economics to be fatally flawed, however. These schools argue that either fiscal policy has no effect or it has negative side effects that outweigh any benefits. Some opponents of fiscal policy believe that the federal

Keynesian economics

A school of economic thought that favors active federal government policymaking to stabilize economy-wide fluctuations, including the use of discretionary fiscal policy.

budget deficit

Government expenditures that exceed receipts.

4. Robert Skidelsky, *Keynes: The Return of the Master* (New York: Public Affairs, 2010).

government should limit itself to monetary policy, which we will discuss shortly. Others believe that it is best for the government to do nothing at all.

It is worth noting that most voters have neither understood nor accepted Keynesian economics. Despite popular attitudes, politicians of both parties accepted Keynesian ideas for many years. Republican president Richard Nixon (1969–1974) is alleged to have said, "We are all Keynesians now." George W. Bush justified many of his policies using Keynesian language. During the first years of Obama's presidency, however, such thinking among Republicans in Congress vanished almost completely. Instead, Republicans rejected "countercyclical" policies, reflecting the popular belief that during a recession the government should "tighten its belt."

It did not help the Keynesian cause that Obama's 2009 economic stimulus package failed to end high rates of unemployment—Keynesian economists argued that the stimulus was less than half of what was needed to accomplish such a goal. When Obama, in his 2010 State of the Union address, employed the belt-tightening metaphor, Keynesians realized that they had lost control of the political discourse.

The Eclipse of Fiscal Policy. In 2011 and 2012, anti-Keynesian economic proposals dominated the political debate. Both Obama and the Republicans in the House issued competing federal budget plans based on long-term spending cuts. The Republicans also called for immediate cuts in federal and state spending. Yet the unemployment rate remained close to 9 percent, a figure that traditionally would have ruled out short-term efforts to reduce the deficit.

One consequence of the debate was that federal and state spending was, in fact, curbed. Keynesians argued that such steps were prolonging the nation's economic troubles. Conservatives, however, contended that other factors were at work in prolonging unemployment, such as structural changes in the economy and uncertainty resulting from Obama's policies. By the time of the 2016 elections, the size of the federal budget deficit was no longer a top political issue, in part because economic recovery had reduced the size of the deficit substantially. As a result, legislators from both major parties were more receptive to proposals that might have the side effect of increasing the deficit.

Deficit Spending and the Public Debt

The federal government typically borrows by selling U.S. Treasury bills, notes, and bonds, known collectively as *Treasury securities* and informally as **treasuries.** The sale of these federal obligations to corporations, private individuals, pension plans, foreign governments, foreign businesses, and foreign individuals adds to this nation's **public debt,** or **national debt.** In the past few years, foreign governments, especially those of China and Japan, have come to own about 50 percent of the net U.S. public debt. Thirty years ago, the share of the U.S. public debt held by foreigners was only 15 percent.

The Public Debt. There are two types of public debt—gross and net. The **gross public debt** includes all federal government interagency borrowings, which really do not matter. This is similar to your taking an IOU ("I owe you") out of your left pocket and putting it into your right pocket. Today, federal interagency borrowings account for about $5.2 trillion of the gross public debt. What is important is the **net public debt**—the public debt that does not include interagency borrowing. The best way to examine the relative importance of the public debt is to compare it with the *gross domestic product (GDP),* as is done in Figure 15–8. (Remember from earlier in this chapter that the gross domestic product is the dollar value of all final goods and services produced in a one-year period.) In the figure, you see that the public debt reached its peak during World War II and fell until 1975. From about 1960 to 2008, the net public debt as a percentage of GDP ranged between 25 and 50 percent.

treasuries

U.S. Treasury securities—bills, notes, and bonds; debt issued by the federal government.

public debt, or national debt

The total amount of debt carried by the federal government.

gross public debt

The net public debt plus interagency borrowings within the government.

net public debt

The accumulation of all past federal government deficits; the total amount owed by the federal government to individuals, businesses, and foreigners.

Figure 15–8 Net Public Debt as a Percentage of Gross Domestic Product

During World War II, the net public debt as a percentage of GDP grew dramatically. It fell thereafter but rose again from 1980 to 1992, under Republicans Reagan and G. H. W. Bush. The percentage fell under Democrat Clinton. **Why has it risen recently?**

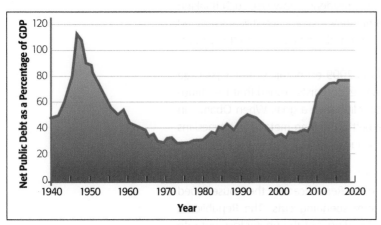

Source: Office of Management and Budget.

Note that the net public debt as a percentage of GDP can fall even when the federal government is still running a budget deficit. If the economy is growing faster than the debt, then the debt as a share of the economy will fall even if the debt itself is still rising slowly. For example, the government never actually paid off the sums it borrowed to finance World War II. Rather, the economy grew fast enough that, over time, the wartime debt ceased to be important.

The Public Debt in Perspective. From 1960 until the last few years of the twentieth century, the federal government spent more than it received in all but two years. Some observers considered those ongoing budget deficits to be the negative result of Keynesian policies. Others argued that the deficits actually resulted from the abuse of Keynesianism. Politicians have been more than happy to run budget deficits in recessions. They have sometimes refused to implement the other side of Keynes's recommendations—to run a *budget surplus* during boom times, or at least to keep the percentage growth of the debt well below the growth of GDP.

In 1993, however, President Bill Clinton (1993–2001) obtained a tax increase as the nation emerged from a mild recession. Between the tax increase and the "dot-com boom," the United States had a budget surplus each year from 1998 to 2002. Some commentators predicted that we would be running federal government surpluses for years to come.

Back to Deficit Spending. All of those projections went by the wayside because of several events. One event was the "dot-com bust" followed by the 2001–2002 recession, which lowered the rate of growth of not only the economy but also the federal government's tax receipts. Another event was a series of large tax cuts passed by Congress in 2001 and 2003 at the urging of President George W. Bush.

A third event took place on September 11, 2001. As a result of the terrorist attacks, the federal government spent much more than it had planned to spend on security against terrorism. Also, the government had to pay for the war in Iraq in 2003 and the occupation of that country thereafter. Finally, Congress authorized major increases in spending on discretionary programs.

The Great Recession dramatically increased the budget deficit and the level of public debt. Tax revenues collapsed, and spending on such items as unemployment compensation rose automatically. In addition, immediately upon taking office, President Obama obtained legislation from Congress that helped push the public debt to levels not seen since World War II. As noted, such high levels of debt became a major public issue. By 2013, however, due to spending curbs and increased tax collections, the annual federal deficit was falling. From a peak of $1.41 trillion in 2009, the deficit was down to $0.50 trillion in 2017. (As a share of GDP, the drop was from 9.8 percent to 2.6 percent.)

The Future of Deficit Spending. Can high levels of deficit spending go on forever? Certainly, they can go on for quite a long time for the U.S. government. After all, as long as individuals, businesses, and foreigners (especially foreign governments) are willing to purchase Treasury securities, the government can continue to engage in deficit spending. Still, before the onset of the Great Recession, most economists feared that if high levels of deficit spending went on long enough, the rest of the world—which owns about 50 percent of all Treasury securities—might lose faith in our government. Consequently, U.S. government borrowing might become more expensive. A vicious cycle might occur—more deficit spending could lead to higher interest rate costs on the U.S. debt, leading in turn to even larger deficits.

So far, however, there has been little sign that such a problem is imminent. On the contrary, following the financial crisis that struck on September 15, 2008, panicked investors piled into treasuries in the belief that these were the safest instruments in existence. The interest that the U.S. government must pay on its borrowing is also very low. In July 2016, the average interest rate on four-week Treasury bills—the shortest-term Treasury obligations—was 0.27 percent—an interest rate scarcely above zero. Correcting for inflation, anyone buying short-term treasuries was paying the U.S. government for the privilege of making loans to it. These developments have convinced some economists that as long as the dollar remains the world's dominant currency, "runs" on the dollar are not actually possible.

Monetary Policy

Controlling the rate of growth of the money supply is called **monetary policy.** This policy is the domain of the **Federal Reserve System,** also known simply as the **Fed.** The Fed is the most important regulatory agency in the U.S. monetary system.

The Fed performs a number of important functions. Perhaps the Fed's most important task is regulating the amount of money in circulation, which can be defined loosely as checking account balances and currency. The Fed also provides a system for transferring checks from one bank to another. In addition, it holds reserves deposited by most of the nation's banks, savings and loan associations, savings banks, and credit unions. Finally, it plays a role in supervising the banking industry.

Organization of the Federal Reserve System.
A board of governors manages the Fed. This board consists of seven full-time members appointed by the president with the approval of the Senate. There are twelve Federal Reserve district banks. The most important unit within the Fed is the **Federal Open Market Committee.** This is the body that actually determines the future growth of the money supply and other important economy-wide financial variables. This committee is composed of the members of the Board of Governors, the president of the New York Federal Reserve Bank, and presidents of four other Federal Reserve banks, rotated periodically.

The Board of Governors of the Federal Reserve System is independent. The president can attempt to influence the board, and Congress can threaten to merge the Fed into the Treasury Department, but as long as the Fed retains its independence, its chairperson and governors can do what they please. Hence, any talk about "the president's monetary policy" or "Congress's monetary policy" is inaccurate. The Fed remains an independent entity.

Loose and Tight Monetary Policies.
The Federal Reserve System seeks to stabilize nationwide economic activity by controlling the amount of money in circulation. Credit, like any good or service, has a cost. The cost of

Image 15–9 Federal Reserve chair Janet Yellen testifies at a congressional Joint Economic Committee hearing in December 2015. Shortly thereafter, the Fed raised its key interest rate by 0.25 percent. *Why did the Fed back off from further rate increases in 2016?*

monetary policy
The use of changes in the amount of money in circulation to alter credit markets, employment, and the rate of inflation.

Federal Reserve System (the Fed)
The agency created by Congress in 1913 to serve as the nation's central banking organization.

Federal Open Market Committee
The most important body within the Federal Reserve System. The Federal Open Market Committee decides how monetary policy should be carried out.

borrowing—the interest rate—is similar to the cost of any other aspect of doing business. When the cost of borrowing falls, businesspersons undertake more investment projects. When it rises, businesspersons undertake fewer projects. Consumers also react to interest rates when deciding whether to borrow funds to buy houses, cars, or other "big-ticket" items.

If the Fed implements a **loose monetary policy** (often called an "expansionary" policy), the supply of credit increases and its cost falls. If the Fed implements a **tight monetary policy** (often called a "contractionary" policy), the supply of credit falls (or fails to grow) and its cost increases. A loose money policy is often implemented to encourage economic growth. You may be wondering why any nation would want a tight money policy. The answer is to control inflation.

Time Lags for Monetary Policy.
You learned earlier that policymakers who implement fiscal policy—the manipulation of budget deficits and the tax system—experience problems with time lags. The Fed faces similar problems when it implements monetary policy.

Sometimes, accurate information about the economy is not available for months. Once the state of the economy is known, time may elapse before any policy can be put into effect. Still, the time lag in implementing monetary policy is usually much shorter than the lag in implementing fiscal policy. The Federal Open Market Committee meets eight times a year and can put a policy into effect relatively quickly. A change in the money supply may not have an effect for several months, however.

Monetary Policy during Recessions.
A tight monetary policy is effective as a way of taming inflation. (Some would argue that it is the *only* way that inflation can be stopped.) If interest rates go high enough, people *will* stop borrowing. How effective, though, is a loose monetary policy at ending a recession? Under normal conditions, it is very effective. A loose monetary policy will spur an expansion in economic activity.

To combat the Great Recession, however, the Fed reduced its interest rate effectively to zero. It could not go any lower. Yet when consumers had credit, they were still reluctant to make major purchases. Many businesses found that they had little need to borrow to invest in new activities—and no need to hire new staff. Overall demand for goods and services was so low that companies could produce all they needed with their existing capacity and workforce. Monetary policy had run out of steam—using it was like "pushing on a string." The government has little power to force banks to lend, and it certainly has no power to make people borrow and spend. As a result, the Obama administration placed its bets on fiscal policy.

Quantitative Easing and Forward Guidance.
During 2008 and 2009, the Fed developed a new way to respond to the failure of banks to lend. Relying on its ability to create money, it began to make loans itself, without turning to Congress for appropriations. The Fed bought debt issued by corporations. It bought securities that were based on student loans and credit-card debt. By 2009, the Fed had loaned out close to $2 trillion in fresh credit. In 2010 and 2011, the Fed implemented yet another new policy, called *quantitative easing,* in an attempt to make monetary policy more effective. Quantitative easing essentially means buying quantities of long-term treasuries and mortgage-backed securities to hold down long-term interest rates.

In 2013, the Fed began a policy of *tapering*. Under this plan, the Fed slowly reduced the size of its quantitative easing purchases. The quantitative easing program was ended in October 2014. The Fed also developed a program of *forward guidance*. Under this policy, the Fed made it clear that interest rates would remain low for a long time to come.

loose monetary policy
Monetary policy that makes credit inexpensive and abundant, possibly leading to inflation.

tight monetary policy
Monetary policy that makes credit expensive in an effort to slow inflation.

In 2015, however, for the first time since the onset of the Great Recession, the Fed began to contemplate the possibility of raising interest rates. In December of that year, it raised its key rate by 0.25 percent. Further increases planned for 2016, however, were postponed due to economic uncertainty.

loophole

A legal method by which individuals and businesses are allowed to reduce the tax liabilities owed to the government.

The Politics of Taxes

Learning Outcome **6:**

Federal taxes are enacted by Congress. Today, the Internal Revenue Code, which is the federal tax code, encompasses thousands of pages, thousands of sections, and thousands of subsections—our tax system is not very simple.

Americans pay a variety of taxes. At the federal level, the income tax is levied on most sources of income. Social Security and Medicare taxes are assessed on wages and salaries. There is an income tax for corporations, which has an indirect effect on many individuals. The estate tax is collected from property left behind by those who have died. State and local governments also assess taxes on income, sales, and land. Altogether, the value of all taxes collected by the federal government and by state and local governments is about 26 percent of GDP. This is a substantial sum, but it is less than what many other countries collect, as you can see in Figure 15–9.

Describe the various taxes that Americans pay, and discuss some of the controversies surrounding taxation.

Federal Income Tax Rates

Individuals and businesses pay income taxes based on tax rates. Not all of your income is taxed at the same rate. The first few dollars of income that you earn are not taxed at all. The highest rate is imposed on the "last" dollar you make. This highest rate is the *marginal* tax rate. Table 15–1 shows the 2017 marginal tax rates for individuals and married couples (which applied to income earned in the previous year, 2016). The higher the tax rate—the action on the part of the government—the greater the public's reaction to that tax rate. If the highest tax rate you pay on the income you make is 15 percent, then any method you can use to reduce your taxable income by one dollar saves you fifteen cents in tax liabilities that you owe to the federal government.

Individuals paying a 15 percent rate have a relatively small incentive to avoid paying taxes, but consider the individuals who faced a marginal tax rate of 94 percent in the 1940s, during and after World War II. They had a tremendous incentive to find legal ways to reduce their taxable incomes. For every dollar of income that was somehow deemed nontaxable, these taxpayers would reduce tax liabilities by ninety-four cents.

Loopholes and Lowered Taxes

Individuals and corporations facing high tax rates will adjust their earning and spending behavior to reduce their taxes. They will also make concerted attempts to get Congress to add **loopholes** to the tax law that allow them to reduce their taxable incomes. When Congress imposed very high tax rates on high

Figure 15–9 Total Amount of Taxes Collected as a Percentage of Gross Domestic Product (GDP) in Major Industrialized Nations

Why might the United States collect less in taxes than many other advanced nations?

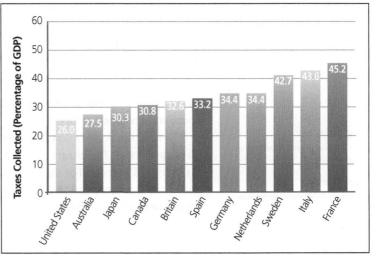

Source: Organization for Economic Cooperation and Development.

Table 15–1 Marginal Tax Rates for Single Persons and Married Couples (2016)

How likely is it that people in the 10 percent bracket will actually have to pay income taxes?

Marginal Tax Bracket	Single Persons	Married Filing Jointly
10%	Up to $9,275	Up to $18,550
15%	$9,276 to $37,650	$18,551 to $75,300
25%	$37,651 to $91,150	$75,301 to $151,900
28%	$91,151 to $190,150	$151,901 to $231,450
33%	$190,151 to $413,350	$231,451 to $413,350
35%	$413,351 to $415,050	$413,351 to $466,950
39.6%	$415,051 or more	$466,951 or more

incomes, it also provided for more loopholes than it does today. For example, special provisions enabled investors in oil and gas wells to reduce their taxable incomes.

Progressive and Regressive Taxation. As Table 15–1 shows, the greater your taxable income, the higher the marginal tax rate. Persons with large incomes pay a larger share of their income in income tax. A tax system in which rates go up with income is called a **progressive tax** system. The federal income tax is clearly progressive.

The income tax is not the only tax you must pay. For example, the federal Social Security tax is levied on all wage and salary income at a flat rate of 6.2 percent. (Employers pay another 6.2 percent, making the total effective rate 12.4 percent.) In 2016, however, there was no Social Security tax on wages and salaries in excess of $118,500. (This "cap" changes from year to year.) Persons with very high salaries, therefore, pay no Social Security tax on much of their wages. In addition, the tax is not levied on investment income (including capital gains, rents, royalties, interest, dividends, and profits from a business). The wealthy receive a much greater share of their income from these sources than others do. As a result, the wealthy pay a much smaller portion of their income in Social Security taxes than do the working poor. The Social Security tax is therefore a **regressive tax.**

To fund Medicare, a combined employer/employee 2.9 percent tax is also assessed on all wage income. The income of individuals that exceeds $200,000, however, is subject to a rate of 3.8 percent. For married couples filing jointly, the threshold is $250,000. Note that three-quarters of all taxpayers owe more in payroll taxes, such as Social Security and Medicare taxes, than they do in income taxes.

Why should you care about **DOMESTIC POLICY?**

What happens to entitlement programs will affect your life in two major ways. Entitlement spending will largely determine how much you pay in taxes throughout your working lifetime. Entitlement policy will also determine how much support you receive from the federal government when you grow old. Also, because entitlements make up such a large share of the federal budget, it is not possible to address the issue of budget deficits without considering entitlement spending. However these programs are changed, you will feel the financial effects throughout your life.

progressive tax
A tax that rises in percentage terms as incomes rise.

regressive tax
A tax that falls in percentage terms as incomes rise.

Image 15–10 Residents stand in line to file their federal income tax returns on the last legal day. *What kinds of taxpayers may find it difficult to finish their tax returns?*

Who Pays? The question of whether the tax system should be progressive—and if so, to what degree—is subject to vigorous political debate. Democrats in general and liberals in particular favor a tax system that is significantly progressive. Republicans and conservatives are more likely to prefer a tax system that is proportional or even regressive.

Overall, what kind of tax system do we have? The various taxes Americans pay pull in different directions. The federal estate tax is extremely progressive, because it is not imposed at all on smaller estates. Sales taxes are regressive because the wealthy spend a relatively smaller portion of their income on items subject to the sales tax. Table 15–2 lists the characteristics of major taxes. Add everything up, and the tax system as a whole is slightly progressive.

Table 15–2 Progressive versus Regressive Taxes

Progressive Taxes	Regressive Taxes
Federal income tax	Social Security tax
State income taxes	State sales taxes
Federal corporate income tax	Local real estate taxes
Estate tax	
Medicare tax	

How you can make a difference

Should Medicare and Social Security benefits be high, with the understanding that taxes must therefore go up? Should these programs be cut back in the hope of avoiding deficits and tax increases? Do entitlements mean that the old are fleecing the young—or is that argument irrelevant because we will all grow old someday? Progressives and conservatives disagree strongly about these questions. You can develop your own opinions by learning more about entitlement reform.

The following organizations take a conservative position on entitlements:

- National Center for Policy Analysis. Find its webpage on entitlement reform at www.ncpa.org/retirement.

- The Heritage Foundation. See what it has to say at www.heritage.org/issues/retirement-security.

The following organizations take a liberal stand on entitlements:

- National Committee to Preserve Social Security and Medicare presents its views at www.ncpssm.org.

- AARP (formerly the American Association of Retired Persons) defends retirement benefits at www.aarp.org/work/social-security.

KEY TERMS

Affordable Care Act **407**

budget deficit **424**

domestic policy **407**

entitlement program **408**

Federal Open Market Committee **427**

Federal Reserve System (the Fed) **427**

fiscal policy **423**

fracking **419**

gross domestic product (GDP) **408**

gross public debt **425**

incarceration rate **417**

inflation **422**

Keynesian economics **424**

loophole **429**

loose monetary policy **428**

Medicaid **408**

Medicare **408**

monetary policy **427**

net public debt **425**

progressive tax **430**

public debt, or national debt **425**

recession **422**

regressive tax **430**

tight monetary policy **428**

treasuries **425**

unemployment **422**

CHAPTER SUMMARY

Learning Outcome 1 Domestic policy consists of all laws, government planning, and government actions that concern internal issues of national importance. The policymaking process is initiated when policymakers become aware—through the media or from their constituents—of a problem that needs to be addressed. The process of policymaking includes agenda building, policy formulation, policy adoption, policy implementation, and policy evaluation.

Health-care spending accounts for about 17 percent of the U.S. economy. A major source of funding is Medicare, the federal program that pays health-care expenses of U.S. residents over the age of sixty-five.

Much of the population has lacked health insurance—a major political issue. In the past, individual health-insurance policies (not obtained through an employer) were expensive and often unobtainable at any price. In 2010, Congress passed a health-care reform package—the Affordable Care Act, nicknamed *Obamacare*—that provides near-universal coverage in the United States. It requires residents not already covered to purchase coverage, which is subsidized for low-income persons.

Learning Outcome 2 Today, more than 1 million immigrants enter the United States each year, and about 13 percent of the U.S. population consists of foreign-born persons. Illegal immigrants may number about 11 million. The status of these unauthorized immigrants (the Department of Homeland Security term) is a major political issue. Some people wish to give such persons a legally recognized status and allow them to become citizens someday. Others call for tougher laws against illegal immigration and against hiring illegal entrants.

Learning Outcome 3 There is widespread concern in this country about violent crime. The overall rate of violent crime has declined since 1995, however. In response to crime concerns, the United States has incarcerated an unusually large number of persons compared to other countries.

Learning Outcome 4 Issues concerning energy and the environment are on the nation's agenda. One problem is our reliance on petroleum imports, given that many petroleum exporters are hostile to American interests. In recent years, however, new production techniques such as fracking have increased the domestic supply of crude oil and especially of natural gas (thereby lowering their cost). Climate change, caused by the emission of CO_2 and other greenhouse gases, is a second major problem, although some dispute how serious it is.

Learning Outcome 5 Fiscal policy is the use of taxes and spending to affect the overall economy. Lower taxes or higher spending can increase the budget deficit, which some believe can stimulate the economy.

The federal government has run a deficit in most years since 1960. The deficit is met by U.S. Treasury borrowing. This adds to the public debt of the U.S. government. Although the budget was temporarily in surplus from 1998 to 2002, large deficits now seem likely for many years to come.

Monetary policy is controlled by the Federal Reserve System, or the Fed. Monetary policy consists of changing the rate of growth of the money supply in an attempt to either stimulate or cool the economy. A loose monetary policy, in which more money is created, encourages economic growth. A tight monetary policy, in which less money is created, may be the only effective way of ending an inflationary spiral.

Learning Outcome 6 U.S. taxes are about 26 percent of the gross domestic product. Individuals and corporations that pay taxes at the highest rates will try to pressure Congress into creating exemptions and tax loopholes. Loopholes allow high-income earners to reduce their taxable incomes. The federal income tax is progressive—tax rates increase as income increases. Some other taxes, such as the Social Security tax and state sales taxes, are regressive—they take a larger share of the income of poorer people.

ADDITIONAL RESOURCES

Online Resources

- Matthew Yglesias offers interesting commentary on economics and society from a liberal, free-market point of view. Follow him at **www.vox.com/authors/matthew-yglesias**.

- Harvard economics professor Greg Mankiw reviews economic events from a moderate conservative perspective. Find him at **gregmankiw.blogspot.com**.

Books

Graham, John D. *Obama on the Home Front: Domestic Policy Triumphs and Setbacks*. Bloomington: Indiana University Press, 2016. Graham is dean of the Indiana University School of Public and Environmental Affairs. Here, he considers the Obama presidency and how presidents can best implement their agendas when Congress is often hostile.

Miller, David. *Strangers in Our Midst: The Political Philosophy of Immigration*. Cambridge, Mass.: Harvard University Press, 2016. Reasoning from first principles, Miller advocates a "weak cosmopolitanism"

that is morally compatible with special consideration for our compatriots. He is a professor of political theory at Oxford University.

Piketty, Thomas. *Capital in the Twenty-First Century* (Arthur Goldhammer, translator). Cambridge, Mass.: Belknap Press, 2014. This book, a controversial economics blockbuster, contains vast amounts of data. The basic argument, though, is simple: without high taxes on the rich, our capitalist system naturally produces growing inequality. Piketty is a professor at the Paris School of Economics.

Video

An Inconvenient Truth—A 2006 Paramount Classics production of former vice president Al Gore's Oscar-winning documentary on climate change and actions that can be taken in response to this challenge.

The Other Side of Immigration—Based on more than seven hundred interviews, this documentary by Roy Germano asks why so many Mexicans come to the United States, and what happens to the families and communities they leave behind.

Quiz

Multiple Choice and Fill-Ins

Learning Outcome 1 Describe the five steps of the policymaking process, using the health-care reform legislation as an example.

1. The policymaking process includes, but is not limited to:
   a. agenda building, policy formulation, and policy adoption.
   b. agenda building, policy formulation, and judicial approval.
   c. agenda building, policy formulation, and state referendums.

2. The last two phases of the policymaking process involve policy _____ and policy _____.

Learning Outcome 2 Explain why illegal immigration is seen as a problem, and cite some of the steps that have been taken in response to it.

3. Within U.S. borders, illegal immigrants number as many as:
   a. 3 million.
   b. 11 million.
   c. 23 million.

4. Latino citizens have tended to vote for the _____ Party.

Learning Outcome 3 Discuss recent developments in crime rates and incarceration.

5. The incarceration rate is defined as:
   a. the number of people in prison or jail for every 1,000 persons.
   b. the number of people in prison or jail for every 100,000 persons.
   c. the number of people in prison or jail for every 1,000,000 persons.

6. Over the last twenty years, homicide and violent crime rates in America have _____.

Learning Outcome 4 Evaluate the federal government's responses to high oil prices and the controversy over climate change.

7. A major new source of increased energy supplies within the United States comes from:
   a. running existing wells at a faster pace.
   b. nuclear power.
   c. fracking (hydraulic fracturing).

8. Emissions of carbon dioxide (CO_2) have fallen since 2008 in part because of the increased use of _____ _____ in power plants.

Learning Outcome 5 Define *unemployment, inflation, fiscal policy, public debt,* and *monetary policy.*

9. Fiscal policy involves:
   a. government spending and changes in the money supply in circulation.
   b. government taxation and the changes in the money supply in circulation.
   c. government taxing and spending policies.

10. When an economic slowdown is severe enough, it is officially called a _____, which is characterized by increased _____.

Learning Outcome 6 Describe the various taxes that Americans pay, and discuss some of the controversies surrounding taxation.

11. The federal personal income tax system can be called:
    a. a progressive tax.
    b. a regressive tax.
    c. a degressive tax.

12. Americans who work for a salary typically pay federal income taxes, as well as payroll taxes that fund _____ and _____.

Essay Questions

1. Just how serious an offense should illegal immigration be? Construct arguments in favor of considering it a felony and arguments for viewing it as a mere civil infraction.

2. Until recently, Congress always opposed the establishment of a universal health-insurance system for the United States. What could the reasons for this stance have been? Are the reasons compelling? What political interests might oppose a universal system, and why?

FOREIGN POLICY

U.S. troops parachuting near Torun, Poland, in June 2016 as part of the NATO Anaconda-16 military exercise. Anaconda-16 was the largest-ever exercise involving NATO partners. It took place amid the West's worst standoff with Russia since the end of the Cold War. *Why is the United States committed to the defense of our NATO allies?*

JANEK SKARZYNSKI/Getty Images

These five **LEARNING OUTCOMES** *below are designed to help improve your understanding of this chapter:*

1: Define *foreign policy,* and discuss moral idealism versus political realism in foreign policy.

2: Describe recent foreign policy challenges that involve the use of force.

3: Discuss the use of diplomacy in addressing such issues as nuclear proliferation, the rise of China, and the confrontation between Israel and the Palestinians.

4: Explain the role of the president, executive agencies, and Congress in making U.S. foreign policy.

5: Cite the main themes in the history of U.S. foreign policy.

What if...

We Brought Back the Draft?

Background

Young people today have no direct memory of the draft—forced military service—because participation in the military became voluntary in 1973. From 1948 to 1973, however, all American males were subject to the draft. Required military service provided large forces to confront the Soviet Union during the Cold War (a period you will read about in this chapter). The draft was used during the war in Vietnam (1965–1975), when it became a heated issue. A few years ago, the idea of bringing back the draft reappeared in public debate. In 2006 and 2007, members of Congress and of George W. Bush's administration suggested that the draft be reinstated. After 2008, because of high unemployment and the drawdown of forces in Iraq and Afghanistan, the military had no difficulty in filling its enlistment quotas. As a result, there has been less talk of a draft. More recently, however, unemployment has fallen—and the number of potential conflicts has gone up.

What If We Brought Back the Draft?

If the draft were reinstated, the U.S. Selective Service would once again be a powerful bureaucratic organization. At the height of the Vietnam War, many young men over the age of eighteen focused much of their attention on avoiding the draft. The same might be true if we brought the draft back today.

Today, the pool of draft-eligible men (and women, if they are included) is much larger than required by the U.S. military. Even though the military has recently been stretched thin, "boots on the ground" are becoming less important as the military continues to evolve toward technological warfare. At the peak of the Vietnam War, there were more than 500,000 U.S. troops in Southeast Asia. At the 2010 peak, the United States fielded 112,000 troops in Iraq and 57,000 in Afghanistan, for a total of 169,000. Consequently, the Selective Service might have to create more draft deferments than were available during the Vietnam War.

Benefits of a Draft

At various times during the Iraq and Afghanistan wars, the Department of Defense was forced to extend tours of duty for units that were about to be brought home. A draft would prevent these kinds of troop shortages. In particular, a draft would eliminate the unfairness involved in stationing National Guard troops abroad for long periods of time.

If we brought back the draft, the U.S. military would include children of wealthy families, unlike the situation today. In principle, therefore, service to one's country would become more evenly distributed across social and economic classes. Some argue that a draft would cause Congress and the president to think differently about military operations. If the children of senators and representatives were drafted and sent to dangerous regions, those leaders might be more cautious about going to war.

The Draft as a Tax on the Young

Typically, draftees are paid nominal amounts—less than they could earn in the civilian sector. It is not necessary to pay draftees the relatively high salaries and benefits required to induce young Americans to volunteer for military service. As a result, with a draft, federal expenditures for military pay could decline. The financial burden of staging military actions abroad might fall in part on the draftees themselves. They would effectively be paying a tax consisting of the difference between what they could earn outside the U.S. military and what they were paid by the military.

For Critical Analysis

▶ Some argue that the volunteer nature of our U.S. military is responsible for the relatively small size of the antiwar movement in this country today. Why might that be so?

▶ What alternatives to military service might be possible?

Image 16–1 A drill instructor puts recruits through an upper body exercise at the Marine Corps Recruit Depot on Parris Island, South Carolina. *What effect might the volunteer armed forces have on the quality of recruits?*

Robert Nickelsberg/Getty Images

On September 11, 2001, Americans were forced to change their view of national security and of their relations with the rest of the world—literally overnight. No longer could citizens of the United States believe that national security issues involved only threats overseas or that the American homeland could not be attacked.

Within a few days, it became known that the 9/11 attacks on the World Trade Center and on the Pentagon had been planned and carried out by a terrorist network named al Qaeda that was directed by the radical Islamist leader Osama bin Laden. The network was closely linked to the Taliban government of Afghanistan, which had ruled that nation since 1996.

Americans were shocked by the success of the attacks. They wondered how our airport security systems could have failed so drastically. Shouldn't our intelligence community have known about and defended against this terrorist network? How could our foreign policy have been so blind to the anger of Islamist groups throughout the world?

In this chapter, we examine the tools of foreign policy and national security policy in light of the many challenges facing the United States today. One such challenge for U.S. foreign policymakers is how best to respond to the threat of terrorism. A question raised by the resulting U.S. military commitments is whether we need to bring back the draft, as we discussed in the chapter-opening *What If . . .* feature. We also review the history of American foreign policy.

Facing the World: Foreign and Defense Policies

The United States is only one nation in a world with almost two hundred independent countries, many located in regions where armed conflict is ongoing. What tools does our nation have to deal with the many challenges to its peace and prosperity? One tool is **foreign policy.** By this term, we mean both the goals the government wants to achieve in the world and the techniques and strategies used to achieve them. These techniques and strategies include **diplomacy, economic aid, technical assistance,** and military intervention. Sometimes foreign policies are restricted to statements of goals or ideas, such as the goal of helping to end world poverty. At other times, foreign policies involve comprehensive efforts to achieve particular objectives, such as preventing Iran from obtaining nuclear weapons.

As you will read later in this chapter, in the United States the *foreign policy process* usually originates with the president and those agencies that provide advice on foreign policy matters. Congressional action and national public debate often affect foreign policy formulation as well.

National Security and Defense Policies

As one aspect of overall foreign policy, **national security policy** is designed primarily to protect the independence and the political integrity of the United States. It concerns itself with the defense of the United States against actual or potential future enemies.

U.S. national security policy is based on determinations made by the Department of Defense, the Department of State, and a number of other federal agencies, including the National Security Council (NSC). The NSC acts as an advisory body to the president, but it has often been a rival of the State Department in influencing the foreign policy process.

Defense policy is a subset of national security policy. Generally, defense policy refers to the set of policies that direct the nature and activities of the U.S. armed forces. Defense policy also considers the types of armed forces units we need to have, such as rapid

---

Learning Outcome **1:**

Define *foreign policy,* and discuss moral idealism versus political realism in foreign policy.

foreign policy
A nation's external goals and the techniques and strategies used to achieve them.

diplomacy
The process by which nations carry on political relations with one another and resolve conflicts by peaceful means.

economic aid
Assistance to other nations in the form of grants, loans, or credits to buy the assisting nation's products.

technical assistance
The practice of sending experts in such areas as agriculture, engineering, or business to aid other nations.

national security policy
Foreign and domestic policy designed to protect the nation's independence and political integrity; policy that is concerned with the safety and defense of the nation.

defense policy
A subset of national security policy having to do with the U.S. armed forces.

response forces or Marine expeditionary forces. It also considers the types of weaponry that should be developed and maintained for the nation's security. Defense policies are proposed by the leaders of the nation's military forces and the secretary of defense, and these policies are greatly influenced by congressional decision makers.

Diplomacy

Diplomacy is another aspect of foreign policy. Diplomacy includes all of a nation's external relationships, from routine diplomatic communications to summit meetings among heads of state. More specifically, diplomacy refers to the settling of disputes and conflicts among nations by peaceful methods. Diplomacy is also the set of negotiating techniques by which a nation attempts to carry out its foreign policy. Of course, diplomacy can be successful only if the parties are willing to negotiate.

Idealism versus Realism in Foreign Policy

Since the earliest years of the republic, Americans have felt that their nation has a special destiny. The American experiment in political and economic liberty, it was thought, would provide the best possible life for its citizens and be a model for other nations. As the United States became a power in world politics, Americans came to believe that the nation's actions in the world should be guided by American political and moral principles.

Moral Idealism. This view of America's mission has led to the adoption of many foreign policy initiatives that are rooted in **moral idealism.** This philosophy views the world as fundamentally benign and assumes that most nations can be persuaded to take moral considerations into account when setting their policies.[1] In this perspective, nations should come together and agree to keep the peace, as President Woodrow Wilson (1913–1921) proposed for the League of Nations. Many foreign policy initiatives taken by the United States have been based on this idealistic view of the world. These include humanitarian relief efforts.

An example is U.S. assistance to West Africa in response to an outbreak of the Ebola virus first detected in December 2013. The disease infected about 30,000 people, and more than 11,000 died. Guinea, Liberia, and Sierra Leone were the most affected nations. The U.S. military established a major medical operation centered in Liberia. The region was proclaimed Ebola-free in June 2016. Of course, the United States had strategic as well as altruistic reasons for helping—if the disease were not stopped, it could spread and threaten Americans.

Political Realism. In opposition to the moral perspective is **political realism.** Realists see the world as a dangerous place in which each nation strives for its own survival and interests, regardless of moral considerations. The United States must therefore base its foreign policy decisions on cold calculations without regard to morality. Realists believe that other nations are, by definition, dangerous. A strong defense will show the world that the United States is willing to protect its interests. The practice of political realism in foreign policy allows the United States to sell weapons to military dictators who will support its policies, to support American business around the globe, and to repel terrorism through the use of force.

American Foreign Policy—A Mixture of Both. It is important to note that the United States has never been guided by only one of these principles. Instead, both moral idealism and political realism affect foreign policymaking. At times, idealism and realism

moral idealism

A philosophy that sees nations as normally willing to cooperate and agree on moral standards for conduct.

political realism

A philosophy that sees each nation acting principally in its own interests.

1. Eugene R. Wittkopf, Charles W. Kegley, and James M. Scott, *American Foreign Policy,* 7th ed. (Belmont, Calif.: Wadsworth Publishing, 2007).

can pull in different directions, making it difficult to establish a coherent policy. The so-called Arab Spring of 2011 serves as an example of such crosscurrents in American foreign policy.

Acting on the basis of political realism, the United States had built long-standing relationships with various dictators in the Arab world, including Hosni Mubarak of Egypt. Given such alliances, the United States had to determine whether to support existing governments when they came under attack by popular rebellions. President Barack Obama and Secretary of State Hillary Clinton, however, did not believe that realism and idealism were necessarily in conflict. The United States could support democratic movements and remain true to its values.

Initially, this strategy appeared to be workable because in Egypt and Tunisia, at least, the democratic rebels were winning. In 2013, however, the military seized power in Egypt, ending its experiment with democracy. In 2014, speaking at the graduation ceremony for the U.S. Military Academy, Obama was blunt: American relations with Egypt were again based on political realism.

In the end, Tunisia was the only nation in which the Arab Spring rebellions were a success. In Libya, rebels were initially successful in taking power only in the eastern region. The United States and its European allies then intervened with air strikes to assist the rebels. The Libyan dictator, Muammar Gaddafi, was overthrown and killed. Libya was unable to establish a coherent national government in subsequent years, however, and the country wound up divided between rival regimes. Critics accused idealists of supporting an irresponsible intervention.

Anjo Kan/Shutterstock.com

Image 16–2 Refugees from Syria, Afghanistan, and Africa disembark on the Greek island of Lesbos. They arrived from Turkey in a dinghy boat. *What, if anything, should the United States do about the fighting in Syria?*

Terrorism and Warfare

Learning Outcome **2:**

Describe recent foreign policy challenges that involve the use of force.

The foreign policy of the United States—whether idealist, realist, or both—must be formulated to deal with world conditions. In some instances, these policies have involved the use of force.

The Emergence of Terrorism

Terrorism is a systematic attempt to inspire fear to gain political ends. Typically, terrorism involves the indiscriminate use of violence against noncombatants. We often think of terrorists as nongovernmental agents. The term was first coined, however, to refer to the actions of the radicals who were in control of the government at the height of the French Revolution (1789–1799).

In the past, terrorism was a strategy generally employed by radicals who wanted to change the status of a particular nation or province. For example, over many years the Irish Republican Army undertook terrorist attacks in the British province of Northern Ireland with the aim of driving out the British and uniting the province with the Republic of Ireland. In Spain, the ETA organization employed terrorism with the goal of creating an independent Basque state in Spain's Basque region. In the twenty-first century, however,

terrorism

A systematic attempt to inspire fear to gain political ends, typically involving the indiscriminate use of violence against noncombatants.

the United States has confronted a new form of terrorism that is not associated with such clear-cut aims.

September 11. In 2001, terrorism came home to the United States in ways that few Americans could have imagined. In a well-coordinated attack, nineteen terrorists hijacked four airplanes and crashed three of them into buildings—two into the World Trade Center towers in New York City and one into the Pentagon in Washington, D.C. The fourth airplane crashed in a field in Pennsylvania, after the passengers fought the hijackers.

Why did the al Qaeda network plan and launch attacks on the United States? One reason was that the leaders of the network, including Osama bin Laden, were angered by the presence of U.S. troops on the soil of Saudi Arabia, which they regard as sacred. They also saw the United States as the primary defender of Israel against the Palestinians. The attacks were intended to frighten and demoralize America so that it would withdraw troops from the Middle East.

Image 16–3 FBI officers gather in front of the Pulse nightclub in June 2016 on the morning after a mass shooting that killed forty-nine people and wounded many others. The attacker, who claimed allegiance to ISIS, targeted Latin Night at the Pulse, a club popular with LGBT people. *Was this an act of terrorism, a hate crime, or both? Why?*

Al Qaeda's Ultimate Aims. Al Qaeda's ultimate goals, however, were not limited to forcing the United States to withdraw from the Middle East. Al Qaeda envisioned worldwide revolutionary change, with all nations brought under the theocratic rule of an Islamicist empire. Governments have successfully negotiated with terrorists who profess limited aims—today, radicals associated with the Irish Republican Army are part of a coalition government in Northern Ireland. In contrast, there is no way to negotiate with an organization such as al Qaeda.

Domestic Terrorism in the United States. Al Qaeda is not the only group ever to launch a terrorist attack on U.S. soil. Radicals opposed to the U.S. war in Vietnam set off bombs in the 1960s and 1970s (usually without fatalities). Right-wing terrorists were an issue in the 1990s—notably, a bomb set at a federal office building in Oklahoma City killed 168 people.

In more recent years, however, attacks by domestic Islamists have been the major concern. Such individuals are typically "self-radicalized" through the Internet and are not controlled by a foreign organization. As one example, in 2009 a Muslim U.S. Army psychiatrist fatally shot thirteen people at Fort Hood in Texas. A bombing at the Boston Marathon in 2013 killed three people and cost fourteen victims at least one of their legs. The alleged perpetrators were two self-radicalized Muslim brothers, one of them a U.S. citizen. A husband-and-wife team killed fourteen people in San Bernardino, California, in December 2015. A lone gunman managed to murder forty-nine people at a nightclub in Orlando, Florida, in June 2016. Other nations have experienced even more devastating attacks. Terrorists have launched multiple attacks in France, most notably in Paris in November 2015, when 130 victims died. In July 2016, 86 people died in an attack in Nice, France.

The War on Terrorism. After 9/11, President George W. Bush implemented stronger security measures to help ensure homeland security and protect U.S. facilities and personnel abroad. The president sought and received congressional support for heightened airport security, new laws allowing greater domestic surveillance of potential terrorists, and increased funding for the military. In addition, Bush launched two military efforts abroad. The first was to attack Al Qaeda's bases in Afghanistan, as well as the Taliban government of that country, which was allied with the terrorists. The second, which began in 2003, was a war against the dictatorial regime in Iraq.

Wars in Iraq

In 1990, the Persian Gulf became the setting for a major challenge to the international system set up after World War II (1939–1945). President Saddam Hussein of Iraq sent troops into the neighboring oil sheikdom of Kuwait, occupying that country. This was the most clear-cut case of aggression against an independent nation in half a century. In January 1991, U.S.-led coalition forces retook Kuwait, and the First Gulf War ended.

As part of the cease-fire that ended the First Gulf War, Iraq agreed to allow United Nations (UN) weapons inspectors to oversee the destruction of its missiles and all chemical and nuclear weapons development. In 1999, though, Iraq placed so many obstacles in the path of the UN inspectors that they withdrew from the country.

The Second Gulf War—The Iraq War. In 2002 and early 2003, President George W. Bush began assembling an international coalition that might support further military action in Iraq. Bush was unable to convince the UN Security Council that military force was necessary in Iraq, so the United States took the initiative. In March 2003, U.S. and British forces invaded Iraq and within a month had toppled Hussein's dictatorship. The process of establishing order in Iraq turned out to be very difficult, however.

Occupied Iraq. The people of Iraq are divided into three principal ethnic groups. The Kurdish-speaking people of the north were overjoyed by the invasion. The Arabs adhering to the Shiite branch of Islam live principally in the south and constitute a majority of the population. They were deeply skeptical of U.S. intentions. The Arabs belonging to the Sunni branch of Islam live mainly to the west of Baghdad. Many Sunnis considered the occupation to be a disaster.

In short order, a Sunni guerrilla insurgency arose and launched attacks against the coalition forces. A newly organized al Qaeda in Iraq sponsored suicide bombings and other attacks against coalition troops and the forces of the new Iraqi government. Al Qaeda also attacked Iraqi Shiites. The major bloodletting in the country now took place between Sunnis and Shiites. By late 2006, polls indicated that about two-thirds of Americans wanted to see an end to the Iraq War—a sentiment expressed in the 2006 elections.

Iraqi Endgame? In January 2007, President Bush announced a major increase, or "surge," in U.S. troop strength. Skeptics doubted that the new troop levels would have much effect on the outcome. In April 2007, however, Sunni tribal leaders rose up against al Qaeda and called in U.S. troops to help them. Al Qaeda, it seems, had badly overplayed its hand by terrorizing the Sunni population.

Image 16–4 A Syrian rebel loads his weapon during a battle with government forces in the city of Aleppo. The rebels are largely Sunni Arabs, while many regime supporters are Alawites, members of a minority group. *Why might many Syrian Christians support the government?*

AFP/Getty Images

During subsequent months, the Iraqi government gained substantial control over its own territory. Still, American attitudes toward the war remained negative. In 2008, President Bush and Iraqi prime minister Nouri al-Maliki negotiated a deadline for withdrawing U.S. troops. In fact, U.S. combat forces left Iraq in August 2010. The rest of the American troops were out by the end of 2011.

Afghanistan

The Iraq War was not the only military effort launched by the Bush administration as part of the war on terrorism. The first military effort was directed against al Qaeda camps in Afghanistan and the Taliban regime, which had ruled most of Afghanistan since 1996. In late 2001, after building a coalition of international allies and anti-Taliban rebels within Afghanistan, the United States began an air campaign against the Taliban regime. The anti-Taliban rebels, known as the Northern Alliance, were able to take Kabul, the capital, and oust the Taliban from power.

Image 16-5 A U.S. soldier investigates the scene of a suicide attack by three Taliban fighters at the Afghan-Pakistan border. *Why have so many Americans favored pulling our troops out of Afghanistan?*

The Return of the Taliban. The Taliban were defeated, but not destroyed. U.S. forces were unable to locate Osama bin Laden and other top al Qaeda leaders. The Taliban and al Qaeda both retreated to the rugged mountains between Afghanistan and Pakistan, where they were able to establish bases on the Pakistani side of the border. In 2003, the Taliban began to launch attacks against Afghan soldiers, foreign aid workers, and American troops. Through 2008 and 2009, the Taliban were able to take over a number of Pakistani districts, even as the United States began attacking suspected Taliban and al Qaeda targets in Pakistan using small unmanned aircraft.

Obama and Afghanistan. During 2009 and 2010, President Obama almost doubled the number of U.S. troops stationed in Afghanistan. At the same time, he announced that he would begin making troop withdrawals in 2011. The initial drawdown in forces was trivial, but more soldiers were brought home in subsequent years. By the end of 2014, the number of troops was down to about 10,000. Obama planned to withdraw these last troops by the end of 2016, but by October 2015 it was clear that such a withdrawal would be a mistake. U.S. troop levels therefore remained at about 10,000 into 2017 and possibly beyond.

The Death of bin Laden. The CIA and other U.S. intelligence forces were unable to develop information on Osama bin Laden's whereabouts until 2010. In that year and in 2011, the intelligence agencies obtained evidence that bin Laden might be living in a highly secure residential compound in Abbottabad, Pakistan, possibly under the protection of members of Pakistan's military.

On May 1, 2011, U.S. Navy SEALs launched a helicopter raid on the compound. In a brief firefight, the SEALs killed bin Laden and four others. Americans responded to President Obama's announcement of the operation with relief and satisfaction. Reactions in Pakistan itself were mostly negative—the raid was generally seen as a violation of Pakistan's sovereignty.

The death of bin Laden marked the eclipse of al Qaeda as a force in the Afghanistan-Pakistan region. It by no means marked the end of radical Islamic movements—often called *jihadist* movements—elsewhere in the world or even in Afghanistan and Pakistan.[2] The Islamic State in Iraq and Syria is the best known of these jihadist movements, but other major groups are fighting in Libya, Mali, Nigeria, Somalia, Yemen, and elsewhere.

The Civil War in Syria and the Rise of ISIS

The Arab Spring movement had an effect on Syria. After authorities in that country tortured and murdered young protestors in 2011, citizens rebelled against the dictator, Bashar al-Assad. The rebellion soon turned into a stalemate. Assad's forces inflicted horrifying casualties on the civilian population. By 2016, the death toll was well over 400,000, and almost half the country's people had been driven from their homes. The rebels were also fighting among themselves and increasingly dominated by radical Islamists who held beliefs similar to those of al Qaeda. With few attractive forces that America could back, political realism left the Obama administration reluctant to intervene.

The Rise of ISIS. The most hard-line Islamic group in Syria was the Islamic State in Iraq and Greater Syria (ISIS), also known as the Islamic State in Iraq and the Levant (ISIL) and as *Daesh,* an Arabic acronym. This group was a reorganized version of al Qaeda in Iraq, but in 2014, the international al Qaeda movement expelled ISIS due to its "brutal" attacks on other Muslims.

As its name implies, ISIS was active in both Syria and Iraq. In June 2014, ISIS launched a major offensive in Iraq that soon left it in control of Mosul, Iraq's second largest city, and of territory reaching within a few miles of Baghdad. Many Iraqi army units fled without fighting. ISIS was aided in its advance by an alliance with various Sunni groups that had grievances against the Shiite-led government of Iraq. At the end of June, ISIS changed its name to simply the "Islamic State" (IS). It announced that it sought to rule not only the Middle East, but the entire world.

The Islamic State in Iraq. IS soon began expelling, killing, and even enslaving religious minorities in the lands it controlled. These included Christians and members of the small Yazidi faith. IS also clashed with the Peshmerga, the militia of Iraq's autonomous Kurdish region.

By August 2014, it was clear that IS's plans for the Kurdish-speaking Yazidi amounted to genocide. President Obama therefore authorized air strikes to support Iraqi forces that were fighting IS. Support was initially limited to the Kurdish Peshmerga militia. After a reorganization of the Iraqi government to push out anti-Sunni leaders, the United States began to provide air support to the Iraqi government as well. In 2015, Iraqi forces began to retake ground from IS. In June 2016, the Sunni city of Fallujah fell to the government, and plans were under way to retake Mosul. By August 2016, United States forces in Iraq numbered about 5,500.

The Ongoing Catastrophe in Syria. By 2015, the civil war in Syria had developed into a three-way conflict among the government, IS, and more moderate rebel factions. Syrian Kurds located along the Turkish border constituted a fourth element. IS conquests in Iraq resulted in U.S. intervention in Syria for the first time. This included the bombing of IS targets and also support for the small number of Syrian rebels who were not Islamic radicals. President Obama was opposed to any additional U.S. involvement, arguing that such a step would not have positive results. Many foreign policy experts disagreed with that calculation, however.

In September, at the request of the Syrian government, the Russian air force began air strikes against both IS and the more moderate rebels. Russia claimed to be attacking IS,

---

2. *Jihad* is Arabic for "struggle." It frequently refers to the fight against perceived enemies of Islam.

but the majority of its strikes actually hit moderate targets. It appeared that the Syrian civil war was developing into an international war by proxy. Iran and Russia were in support of the government, while the United States and Saudi Arabia supported various rebel factions. Turkey's position was ambiguous, though it is nominally a U.S. NATO ally. In 2015, more than a million Syrian refugees poured into Europe through Turkey, precipitating a crisis in that continent.

U.S. Diplomatic Efforts

The United States has dealt with many international problems through diplomacy, rather than the use of armed force. Some of these issues include the proliferation of nuclear weapons, the growing power of China, and the confrontation between Israel and the Palestinians. Economic concerns can also be addressed through diplomacy.

Nuclear Weapons

In 1945, the United States was the only nation to possess nuclear weapons. Several nations quickly joined the "nuclear club," however, including the Soviet Union in 1949, Britain in 1952, France in 1960, and China in 1964. Few nations have made public their nuclear weapons programs since China's successful test of nuclear weapons in 1964. India and Pakistan, however, detonated nuclear devices within a few weeks of each other in 1998, and North Korea conducted an underground nuclear explosive test in October 2006. Several other nations, Israel in particular, are believed to possess nuclear weapons or the capability to produce them in a short time. Israel is known to possess more than one hundred nuclear warheads.

With nuclear weapons, materials, and technology available worldwide, it is conceivable that terrorists could obtain a nuclear device and use it in a terrorist act. In fact, a U.S. federal indictment filed in 1998 charged Osama bin Laden and his associates with trying to buy components for making a nuclear bomb "at various times" since 1992.

Nuclear Stockpiles. More than twenty-two thousand nuclear warheads are known to be stockpiled worldwide, although the exact number is uncertain. The United States and Russia dismantled many of their nuclear weapons systems after the end of the **Cold War** and the breakup of the Soviet Union in 1991 (discussed later in this chapter). Still, both retain sizable nuclear arsenals.

Nuclear Proliferation: Iran. For years, the United States, the European Union (EU), and the United Nations have tried to prevent Iran from becoming a nuclear power. In spite of these efforts, many observers believed that Iran was in the process of developing nuclear weapons—although Iran maintained that it was interested in developing nuclear power only for peaceful purposes. The group of nations talking with Iran included Britain, China, France, Germany, Russia, and the United States.

By 2009, the UN Security Council had voted three rounds of penalties called *sanctions* against Iran in reaction to its nuclear program. By 2012, it was clear that the sanctions were beginning to damage Iran's economy. Of special importance was the U.S. campaign to persuade other nations to stop importing Iranian oil, which enjoyed increasing success. The United States was also successful in cutting Iran off from the international banking system.

Some of the U.S. actions against Iran went well beyond sanctions. It was discovered in 2012 that the United States had deployed a computer worm that took down about one thousand of Iran's five thousand uranium enrichment centrifuges, destroying many

Cold War

The ideological, political, and economic confrontation between the United States and the Soviet Union following World War II.

of them completely. This covert operation may have delayed Iran's nuclear program by as much as a year. Perhaps even more alarming to Iran was a series of threats that Israel or the United States might bomb Iran's nuclear sites.

Negotiations with Iran. Before 2013, talks between Iran and the six nations just mentioned went nowhere. In 2013, however, Iran elected a new president, Hassan Rouhani, who initiated a "charm offensive" directed at the West. It appeared that for the first time, Iran was prepared to negotiate seriously. Under an interim deal signed in January 2014, Iran agreed to limit various nuclear activities during the following six months, and in return the six-country team would provide Iran with some sanctions relief.

Reaching a Deal. In July 2015, Iran reached a final deal with the six world powers and the European Union. The agreement lifted most sanctions in exchange for substantial restrictions on Iran's nuclear program. Iran agreed to give up its stockpile of medium-enriched uranium, cut its stockpile of low-enriched uranium by 98 percent, and reduce by about two-thirds the number of its gas centrifuges. For the next fifteen years, Iran may produce only limited amounts of low-enriched uranium. The International Atomic Energy Agency will be able to inspect all Iranian nuclear facilities.

Advocates of the deal contend that even if Iran were to drop out of it, the country would still be at least a year away from building a usable nuclear bomb. In that time, other nations would be able to impose pressure on Iran to change course. Critics of the deal included U.S. Republicans in Congress plus the government of Israel. In early 2015, Republican leaders invited Israel's prime minister, Benjamin Netanyahu, to address Congress on the Iran negotiations, without consulting the White House. This step raised the question of whether the Republicans and Netanyahu were trying to turn U.S.-Israeli relations into a partisan issue.

Nuclear Proliferation: North Korea. North Korea tested a nuclear device in 2006. An agreement reached in February 2007 provided that North Korea would start disabling its nuclear facilities and allow UN inspectors into the country. In return, China, Japan, Russia, South Korea, and the United States—the other members of the six-party negotiations—would provide aid to North Korea. North Korea, however, was allowed to keep its nuclear arsenal, which American intelligence officials believe may include as many as six nuclear bombs or the fuel to make them. In July 2007, North Korea dismantled one of its nuclear reactors and admitted UN inspectors into the country. In October 2008, the United States removed North Korea from its list of states that sponsor terrorism.

By 2009, however, North Korea was pulling back from its treaty obligations. In April, the country tested a long-range missile capable of delivering a nuclear warhead, in violation of a UN Security Council demand that it halt such tests. After the Security Council issued a statement condemning the test, North Korea ordered UN inspectors out of the country, broke off negotiations with the other members of the six-party talks, and conducted a second nuclear test. The United States and other parties have sought to persuade China to take the lead in bringing North Korea back to the negotiating table—China is the one nation that has significant economic leverage over North Korea.

KCNA KCNA/Reuters

Image 16–6 North Korean leader Kim Jong-un and his wife Ri Sol-ju attend the opening ceremony of the Rungna People's Pleasure Ground in Pyongyang. *Why is it so difficult to negotiate with North Korea?*

normal trade relations (NTR) status

A status granted through an international treaty by which each member nation must treat other members as well as it treats the country that receives its most favorable treatment. This status was formerly known as *most-favored-nation status*.

Chemical Weapons in Syria. Most nations have signed treaties banning the use of chemical weapons. In 2013, however, Bashar al-Assad's regime in Syria used nerve gas against districts under rebel control, with massive fatalities. President Obama proposed to respond to this act by launching air strikes and asked Congress for approval. Russia then announced that Syria would sign a treaty banning chemical weapons and give up its weapons.

To the surprise of many, the Assad regime cooperated with international inspectors. The weapons were moved to a U.S. ship equipped with decontamination systems. In 2014, President Obama announced that the destruction of the weapons was complete. That same year, however, Assad allegedly used chlorine gas against rebels. Chlorine is not a controlled substance, but its use as a weapon is banned.

The New Power: China

American policy has been to engage the Chinese gradually in diplomatic and economic relationships in the hope of turning the nation in a more pro-Western direction. An important factor in U.S.-Chinese relations has been the large and growing trade ties between the two countries. In 1980, China was granted *most-favored-nation status* for tariffs and trade policy on a year-to-year basis. To prevent confusion, in 1998 the status was renamed **normal trade relations (NTR) status.** In 2000, over objections from organized labor and human rights groups, Congress approved a permanent grant of NTR status to China. In 2001, Congress endorsed China's application to join the World Trade Organization (WTO), thereby effectively guaranteeing China's admission to that body.

While officially Communist, China today permits a striking degree of free enterprise. China has become substantially integrated into the world economic system, and it exports considerably more goods and services to the United States than it imports. As a result, its central bank has built up a huge reserve of U.S. federal government treasuries and other American obligations. Ultimately, the books must balance, but instead of importing U.S. goods and services, the Chinese have imported U.S. securities. The resulting economic imbalances are good for Chinese exporters, but create financial problems in both countries.

The United States has repeatedly asked China to address these imbalances by allowing its currency to rise in value relative to the American dollar. Recently, Chinese authorities have allowed some movement. They have also sought to rebalance their economy toward greater domestic consumption. China's own people are to consume more of the goods and services it produces. As a result, China's *current account surplus* (the most comprehensive measurement of excess exports) has fallen since 2011.

China's Explosive Economic Growth. The growth of the Chinese economy during the last thirty-five years is one of the most important developments in world history. For the past several decades, the Chinese economy has grown at a rate of about 10 percent annually, a long-term growth rate previously unknown in human history. Never have so many escaped poverty so quickly.

China now produces more steel than America and Japan combined. It generates more than 40 percent

Image 16–7 A worker in the Chinese city of Hangzhou checks a high-tech electronic toilet seat. Such devices are hugely popular in Japan, but are only now gaining a foothold in the United States. *Why do we import so many goods from China?*

of the world's output of cement. The new electrical generating capacity that China has been adding each year exceeds the entire installed capacity of Britain. (The new plants, which are usually coal fired, may promote global warming and also generate some of the world's worst air pollution.) Skyscrapers fill the skyline of every major Chinese city.

In 2007, for the first time, China manufactured more passenger automobiles than did the United States. China is building a limited-access highway system that, when complete, will be longer than the U.S. interstate highway system. The economy of China may already be larger than that of the United States. China, in short, is becoming the world's second superpower.

The Issue of Taiwan. Inevitably, economic power translates into military potential. Is this a problem? It could be if China had territorial ambitions. At this time, China does not appear to have an appetite for non-Chinese territory. China's leaders, however, appear to have a rather expansive concept of what is meant by "Chinese territory." For example, China has always considered the island of Taiwan to be Chinese territory. In principle, Taiwan agrees. Taiwan calls itself the "Republic of China" and officially considers its government to be the legitimate ruler of the entire country—that is, of both Taiwan and mainland China. This diplomatic fiction has remained in effect since 1949, when the Chinese Communist Party won a civil war and drove the anti-Communist forces off the mainland.

China's position is that, sooner or later, Taiwan must rejoin the rest of China. The position of the United States is that this reunification must not come about by force. Is peaceful reunification possible? China holds up Hong Kong as an example. Hong Kong came under Chinese sovereignty peacefully in 1997. The people of Taiwan, however, are far from considering Hong Kong to be an acceptable precedent.

Chinese Nationalism. Growing public expressions of Chinese nationalism have raised concern in some of China's neighbors. The Chinese government has sometimes appeared to support nationalist agitation because it benefits politically. When nationalism has seemed to be getting out of hand, however, the government has cracked down.

China has recently engaged in disputes with Japan, Vietnam, the Philippines, and other Asian nations over the ownership of dozens of uninhabited islands in the East China and South China Seas. In November 2011, President Obama visited Australia and promised to establish a new U.S. force of 2,500 marines at Darwin, on Australia's north coast. This development was widely perceived as an attempt to reassure nations in the area that were concerned about potential Chinese pressure. In one arena—cyberspace—Chinese-American relations were already quite heated. In 2013 and 2014, the United States accused the Chinese military of sponsoring cyberattacks on U.S. computer networks. We discuss Chinese nationalism in more depth in this chapter's *Which Side Are You On?* feature.

Israel and the Palestinians

As a longtime supporter of the state of Israel, the United States has undertaken to persuade the Israelis to negotiate with the Palestinian Arabs who live in the territories occupied by Israel. The conflict between Israel and the Palestinians, which began in 1948, has been extremely hard to resolve. The internationally recognized solution is for Israel to yield the West Bank and the Gaza Strip to the Palestinians in return for effective security commitments and abandonment by the Palestinians of any right of return to Israel proper.

The Palestinians, however, have been unwilling to stop terrorist attacks on Israel, and Israel has been unwilling to dismantle its settlements in the occupied territories. Further, the two parties have been unable to come to an agreement on how much of the West Bank should go to the Palestinians and what compensation (if any) the Palestinians should receive for abandoning all claims to settlement in Israel proper. Although it is clear that

Which side are you on?

Is China's Nationalism a Threat to World Peace?

China is the world's third largest country by land area. It is at least the second largest economy in the world. It is the world's largest international trading power. It also has, with 2.3 million active troops, the largest standing military force in the world.

The only permitted political leadership group in the country—the Chinese Communist Party—has long claimed that their country endured a century of humiliation by foreign powers. This "victim nation" narrative goes along with the contention that China is "finally standing up for itself." Recently, China's economic growth has slowed somewhat. It may not be a coincidence that China's leaders have begun placing a much greater emphasis on *nationalism*—an emotional attachment to a nation and its interests. Some people believe that China's nationalism is becoming a threat to world peace.

China Will No Longer Settle for Negotiation

A common tactic in authoritarian countries is to divert attention from domestic difficulties through foreign adventures. Witness the behavior of Russia's authoritarian leader Vladimir Putin. Putin has annexed Ukraine's Crimea Province in the name of protecting ethnic Russians. China appears to be headed down a similar road. Reportedly, the Chinese leadership sees the Great Recession and subsequent sluggish growth as evidence that America is in decline. They seem to have decided that they can now be more assertive. China is laying claim to almost the entire South China Sea. Tensions with neighboring countries such as Vietnam and the Philippines have led to actual clashes. China has also challenged Japan's control of uninhabited islands in the East China Sea.

In July 2016, a UN tribunal ruled against China and for the Philippines in a territorial dispute. Specifically, the tribunal found that China has no historical rights based on its "nine-dash line" map. China has used that map to claim rights over the entire South China Sea. China's response to the ruling was vitriolic.

China's Nationalism Is Exaggerated

There are those who do not believe China's nationalism is as great as reported in the Western press, or as fierce as you might expect from reading Chinese bloggers. Australian analyst Andrew Chubb finds that the average citizen in China would like to see the government compromise on the South China Sea territorial disputes. Those disputes were less important than issues such as corruption, income inequality, and food and drug safety. Chubb suggests that China's leaders are exaggerating popular nationalism in an attempt to bluff foreign governments into backing down. And if the Chinese leaders are bluffing, they are unlikely to pursue disputes to the point of war.

Within China, much of the most damaging nationalism takes the form of discrimination against ethnic groups. These include China's Muslim Uighurs and the people of Tibet. Large numbers of China's majority people (the Han Chinese) are moving into Uighur and Tibetan lands. Uighurs and Tibetans are becoming minorities in their own countries. Such developments, while disturbing, have nothing to do with world peace.

For Critical Analysis

▶ Considering Chinese nationalism, does it matter that China is a nuclear power? Why or why not?

any peace deal would require that Palestinians give up the right of return to Israel, the Palestinians have not yet abandoned that claim.

In 1991, under pressure from the United States, the Israelis opened talks with the Palestine Liberation Organization (PLO). In 1993, the PLO and Israel agreed to set up Palestinian self-government in the West Bank and the Gaza Strip in 1994.

The Collapse of the Israeli-Palestinian Peace Process. Negotiations between the Israelis and the Palestinians resulted in more agreements, but the agreements were rejected by Palestinian radicals, who began a campaign of suicide bombings in Israeli cities. In 2002, the Israeli government moved tanks and troops into Palestinian towns to kill or capture the terrorists. One result of the Israeli reoccupation was an almost complete—if temporary—collapse of the Palestinian Authority. In February 2004, Israeli prime minister Ariel Sharon announced a plan under which Israel would withdraw from the Gaza Strip regardless of whether a deal could be reached with the Palestinians.

The Rise of Hamas. In January 2006, the militant group Hamas won a majority of the seats in the Palestinian legislature. American and European politicians refused to talk to Hamas until it agreed to rescind its avowed desire to destroy Israel. In 2007, after fighting the PLO, Hamas wound up in complete control of the Gaza Strip, and the PLO retained exclusive power in the West Bank.

Israel sought to pressure the Hamas regime in the Gaza Strip to relinquish power through an economic blockade. Hamas retaliated by firing a series of rockets into Israel. In January 2009, Israel temporarily reoccupied the Gaza Strip.

Image 16–8 President Obama and Israel's Prime Minister Netanyahu are shown outside the Oval Office of the White House. Obama has attempted to push Netanyahu to accept a diplomatic solution to the Palestinian problem. *Why would a U.S. president seek to influence the head of the Israeli government?*

Israel and the Obama Administration. In February 2009, Israelis elected a new, more conservative government under Prime Minister Benjamin Netanyahu. The tough positions advocated by the new government threatened to create fresh obstacles to the peace process. In particular, the new government accelerated the growth of Israeli settlements on the West Bank, even though the Obama administration opposed such settlements. In 2013, the United States attempted to restart negotiations between Israel and the Palestinians. Secretary of State John Kerry took the lead in this effort. By 2014, however, the talks had collapsed again.

Again, Gaza. In June 2014, fighting broke out between Israel and the Hamas regime in the Gaza Strip. Hostilities were triggered by the abduction and murder of three Israeli youths in the West Bank. Israel blamed Hamas and arrested several hundred of its members. Hamas began firing rockets into Israel, and Israel bombed Hamas targets in response. A ceasefire was finally established in August. By that time, Gaza had suffered massive destruction and almost two thousand fatalities. Israel's casualties were much lighter. Israel's actions were condemned by many other nations. The United States, however, continued to give Israel strong support.

Still, by 2015, relations between the Israeli and U.S. governments were cooler than at any point in the last half century. By this time, the Obama administration had effectively given up on the peace process. Instead, the issue was Netanyahu's vehement rejection of negotiations with Iran, described earlier in this chapter.

Europe's Economic Troubles

U.S. foreign relations are not just a matter of waging wars or trying to prevent them. International economic coordination is another major field of action. One such issue—discussed in a previous section—is our trade relations with China. Beginning in 2010, however, the world's economic balance was threatened by some of our closest international friends, the nations of Europe. For other ways in which international economic

Beyond our borders

The Impact of Population Growth on America's Future Role in the World

After World War II, the United States faced an adversary—the Union of Soviet Socialist Republics (USSR)—which was alleged to have the second-largest economy in the world. Its military was definitely much larger than ours. Many believed that the Soviet army had defeated Hitler during World War II by the sheer force of numbers. By 1990, the Soviet population was 289 million, compared with America's 256 million. A year later, when the Soviet Union disintegrated, Russia was down to fewer than 149 million people.

For a time, Russia's economy didn't even appear on lists of the world's ten largest. The United States was now the world's third most populous nation, with U.S. military spending approaching that of all other nations combined.

Population Changes and World Power Relationships

By 2050, both India and China will have around 1.5 billion residents each, compared with 400 million Americans. Populations in Arab and South Asian Muslim nations are growing. Pakistan's population, for example, will increase from 144 million to 300 million by 2050. China's population is stabilizing. Not so the population of Africa. The continent's population was only 224 million in 1950, reached 821 million in 2000, and by 2050 will be more than 2 billion. Africa's

economy is growing, albeit slowly. We can predict, therefore, that over time African nations should become more important in world affairs. Russia is another story, as is Japan. By 2050, these two nations won't even be among the top ten nations of the world in population.

And What About the United States?

Currently, the United States is the only major power that is experiencing significant population growth. By 2050, the United States will have an estimated 4.12 percent of the world's population, down somewhat from 4.65 percent in 2000. In contrast, Russia's population is dwindling, sometimes at a shocking rate, because of poor diet, poor health care, and alcoholism.

Many Western European countries are predicted to lose population as well. Russia's importance may decline, and Western Europe and Japan could lose clout. The United States should remain one of the world's superpowers for a long time to come, but it is likely to be joined by China and, later on, India as well.

For Critical Analysis

○ Does it really matter whether the United States remains a superpower? Why or why not?

developments may affect the United States, see this chapter's *Beyond Our Borders* feature.

The European Union. Many Europeans consider the European Union (EU) to be one of their most important achievements. The EU, which grew out of the earlier European Economic Community, was seen as guaranteeing a permanent peace in Europe. Given that Europe was home to World Wars I and II—arguably the two greatest disasters in human history—such a peace is of the utmost importance to the United States and the world. In 2000, a majority of EU members sought to deepen their union through a common currency, the euro.

The Debt Crisis. The eighteen nations that share a common currency—the euro—were hit hard by the worldwide financial panic of 2008. In particular, the nations of the so-called Eurozone periphery faced a debt crisis. In Greece and, to a lesser extent, Portugal, the governments themselves had borrowed irresponsibly. In Ireland and Spain, many real estate loans went sour, threatening the survival of the banks that had made the loans. Ireland and Spain found themselves in danger when their governments assumed the debts of the threatened banks.

The nations of the euro periphery began running out of funds to service their debts, and they faced ruinous interest rates if they attempted to borrow in the financial markets. If a nation such as Britain, Japan, or the United States faced such a crisis, it could rely on its central bank—in America, the Fed—to serve as *lender of last resort* and simply "print" the necessary money. But the "Eurozone" nations did not control their own money supplies, and the European Central Bank (ECB) was barred from acting as lender of last resort. Investors began pulling funds out of the troubled nations, reducing their money supplies further. The panic threatened to spread to Italy. Eventually, Eurozone nations did come up with bailout loans for Greece, Ireland, Portugal, and Spain.

The German Question.

The response of the ECB to the crisis was to demand that troubled governments follow policies of fiscal austerity, in which they would meet their debts by major reductions in spending and increases in taxes. Such a policy directly contradicted the advice of Keynesian economics. Keynesians argued that austerity could push these nations further into recession, thus making the debt crisis even harder to resolve. Leaders of key nations such as Germany, however, were profoundly hostile to Keynesianism.

Why should you care about **FOREIGN POLICY?**

One foreign policy issue worth caring about is human rights. In many countries throughout the world, human rights are not protected. In some nations, people are imprisoned, tortured, or killed because they oppose the current regime. In other nations, certain ethnic or racial groups are oppressed by the majority population. The strongest reason for involving yourself with human rights issues in other countries is simple moral altruism—unselfish regard for the welfare of others. The defense of human rights is unlikely to put a single dollar in your pocket.

An additional problem has been Germany's tremendous trade surplus. In 2011, Germany's current account surplus passed that of China to become the largest in the world. Some economists argue that Germany should encourage its own citizens to consume more, through lower taxes or more spending on infrastructure. The result would be a more balanced German economy and greater economic growth throughout Europe and the world.

President Obama was among a number of world leaders calling for a German change of course. Obama's calculation was that a European austerity policy would plunge the continent back into recession, thus damaging the U.S. economy and slowing its recovery. European leaders, however, showed no signs that they were willing to retreat from the austerity program.

Greece at the Breaking Point.

The impact of the German-led austerity program was greater on Greece than any other country. In 2015, having experienced average wage cuts of 25 percent plus 30 percent unemployment, the Greek electorate rebelled against austerity. Voters threw out a multiparty coalition and gave Syriza—a seriously left-wing party—control of the government. Although Syriza promised that Greece would pay its debts, many economists believed that would be impossible. Greece's lenders finally agreed to a new repayment program, so default was forestalled, at least for a few years. Syriza initially attempted to resist the program, which imposed severe austerity measures on the Greek government. Its main lenders forced it to cave in.

Brexit.

A major concern during the Greek crisis was that Greece might be forced to exit from the Eurozone—or even from the EU as a whole. "Grexit" never happened. In 2013, however, British prime minister David Cameron promised a referendum on U.K. membership in the EU if his Conservative Party were to win the 2015 elections. Cameron's promise was aimed at unifying his own party and fending off defectors to the U.K. Independence Party, a minor anti-EU group. In 2015, the Conservatives won, and the referendum was duly held in June 2016. The United States, almost every other world power, and all major U.K. institutions backed "remain," but the "leave" campaign won by a narrow margin. Cameron was forced to resign.

The number-one issue for those endorsing "Brexit"—Britain's exit from the EU—was immigration. The vote was held in the wake of massive refugee flows into continental Europe from Syria and other troubled nations. Britain faced little pressure to accept Syrian refugees. Under EU law, however, all members are required to accept "three freedoms"— the free movement not only of goods and services, but also of investment capital and of labor. By 2016, thousands of Eastern Europeans had entered Britain seeking work.

The problem Britain faced after the Brexit vote was that other European nations were unwilling to separate the three freedoms. A new agreement between Britain and the EU could allow the U.K. to close its borders to European labor—but only if Britain left the "single market" in goods and services as well. The economic consequences of such a complete break appeared ominous. In late 2016, the new Conservative prime minister, Theresa May, began talks with her continental counterparts. The talks were shadowed by the possibility that the entire European project might be in danger of unraveling.

<table>
<tr><td>

Learning Outcome **4:**

Explain the role of the president, executive agencies, and Congress in making U.S. foreign policy.

</td><td>

Who Makes Foreign Policy?

Given the vast array of challenges in the world, developing a comprehensive U.S. foreign policy is a demanding task. Does this responsibility fall to the president, to Congress, or to both acting jointly? There is no easy answer to this question because, as constitutional authority Edwin S. Corwin once observed, the U.S. Constitution created between the president and Congress an "invitation to struggle" for control over the foreign policy process. Let us look first at the powers given to the president by the Constitution.

</td></tr>
</table>

Image 16–9 Henry Kissinger, left, was Nixon's chief foreign policy advisor not only while he was secretary of state, but also earlier, when he was national security advisor. Nixon had developed a strong reputation as an anti-communist. *How might that reputation have actually made it easier for Nixon and Kissinger to open up U.S.-Chinese relations?*

Constitutional Powers of the President

The Constitution confers on the president broad powers that are either explicit or implied in key constitutional provisions. Article II vests the executive power of the government in the president. The presidential oath of office given in Article II, Section 1, requires that the president "solemnly swear" to "preserve, protect and defend the Constitution of the United States."

War Powers. In addition, and perhaps more important, Article II, Section 2, designates the president as "Commander in Chief of the Army and Navy of the United States." Starting with Abraham Lincoln, all presidents have interpreted this authority dynamically and broadly. Indeed, since George Washington's administration, the United States has been involved in at least 125 undeclared wars that were conducted under presidential authority. For example, in 1950 Harry Truman ordered U.S. armed forces in the Pacific to counter North Korea's invasion of South Korea. Bill Clinton sent troops to Haiti and Bosnia. George W. Bush initiated wars in Afghanistan and Iraq, and Barack Obama undertook air strikes to support rebels in Libya.

AP Images

Treaties and Executive Agreements.
Article II, Section 2, of the Constitution also gives the president the power to make treaties, provided that the Senate concurs. Presidents usually have been successful in getting treaties through the Senate. In addition to this formal treaty-making power, the president makes use of executive agreements. Since World War II, executive agreements have accounted for almost 95 percent of the understandings reached between the United States and other nations.

Other Constitutional Powers.
An additional power conferred on the president in Article II, Section 2, is the right to appoint ambassadors, other public ministers, and consuls. In Section 3 of that article, the president is given the power to recognize foreign governments by receiving their ambassadors.

Other Sources of Foreign Policymaking

There are at least four foreign policymaking sources within the executive branch in addition to the president. These are the (1) Department of State, (2) National Security Council, (3) intelligence community, and (4) Department of Defense.

The Department of State.
In principle, the State Department is the executive agency that has primary authority over foreign affairs. It supervises U.S. relations with the nearly two hundred independent nations around the world and with the United Nations and other multinational groups. It staffs embassies and consulates throughout the world. It does this with one of the smallest budgets of the cabinet departments.

Image 16–10 President George W. Bush, fourth from the right, with his National Security Council (NSC) the day after the terrorist attacks on September 11, 2001. Secretary of State Colin Powell is to the left of the president. Vice President Dick Cheney is to the right. National Security Adviser Condoleezza Rice is at the far end of the table. *How important is the NSC's role in determining U.S. foreign policy?*

Doug Mills/AP Images

Newly elected presidents usually tell the American public that the new secretary of state is the nation's chief foreign policy adviser. In the Obama administration, this statement was a true description of the role of Secretaries of State Hillary Clinton and John Kerry. Under most presidents since World War II, however, the preeminence of the State Department in foreign policy has been limited. The State Department's image within the White House Executive Office and Congress (and even with foreign governments) has been poor—it has often been seen as a slow, plodding, bureaucratic maze of inefficient, indecisive individuals.

The National Security Council.
The job of the National Security Council (NSC), created by the National Security Act of 1947, is to advise the president on the integration of "domestic, foreign, and military policies relating to the national security." As it has turned out, the NSC—consisting of the president, the vice president, the secretaries of state and defense, the director of emergency planning, and often the chairperson of the

joint chiefs of staff and the director of the CIA—is used in just about any way the president wants to use it.

The role of national security adviser to the president seems to adjust to fit the player. Some advisers have come into conflict with heads of the State Department. Henry A. Kissinger, President Richard Nixon's flamboyant and aggressive national security adviser, rapidly gained ascendancy over William Rogers, the secretary of state.

Under President Obama, however, the national security adviser ceased to be the most important foreign policy adviser. Obama's national security advisers were minor figures, and in contrast to previous administrations, they were not part of the president's cabinet.

The Intelligence Community. The **intelligence community** consists of the forty or more government agencies and bureaus that are involved in intelligence activities. The CIA, created as part of the National Security Act of 1947, is the key official member of the intelligence community.

Covert Actions. Intelligence activities consist mostly of overt information gathering, but covert actions also are undertaken. Covert actions, as the name implies, are carried out in secret, and the American public rarely finds out about them. The CIA covertly aided in the overthrow of the Mossadegh regime in Iran in 1953 and was instrumental in destabilizing the Allende government in Chile from 1970 to 1973.

During the mid-1970s, the "dark side" of the CIA was partly uncovered when the Senate undertook an investigation of its activities. One of the major findings of the Senate Select Committee on Intelligence was that the CIA had routinely spied on American citizens domestically, supposedly a prohibited activity. Consequently, the CIA came under the scrutiny of oversight committees within Congress.

By 2001, the agency had come under fire again. Problems included the discovery that one of its agents had been spying on behalf of a foreign power, the inability of the agency to detect the nuclear arsenals of India and Pakistan, and, above all, its failure to obtain advance knowledge about the 9/11 terrorist attacks.

The Intelligence Community and the War on Terrorism. With the rise of terrorism as a threat, the intelligence agencies have received more funding and enhanced surveillance powers, but these moves have also provoked fears of civil liberties violations. Legislation enacted in 2004 established the Office of the Director of National Intelligence to oversee the intelligence community.

A simmering controversy that came to a boil in 2009 concerned the CIA's use of a technique called *waterboarding* while interrogating several prisoners in the years immediately following 9/11. Before 9/11, the government had defined waterboarding as a form of torture, but former vice president Dick Cheney, a public advocate of the practice, denied that it was. One concern was whether Bush administration officials would face legal action as a result of the practice. In May 2009, President Obama, even as he denounced waterboarding, assured CIA employees that no member of the agency would be penalized for following Justice Department rulings that had legitimized harsh interrogation methods.

The Department of Defense. The Department of Defense (DOD) was created in 1947 to bring all of the various activities of the American military establishment under the jurisdiction of a single department headed by a civilian secretary of defense. At the same time, the joint chiefs of staff, consisting of the commanders of the various military branches and a chairperson, was created to formulate a unified military strategy.

Although the Department of Defense is larger than any other federal department, it declined in size after the fall of the Soviet Union in 1991. In the subsequent ten years,

intelligence community
The government agencies that gather information about the capabilities and intentions of foreign governments or that engage in covert actions.

the total number of civilian employees was reduced by about 400,000, to approximately 665,000. After 9/11, the war on terrorism and combat in Afghanistan and Iraq drove the defense budget up again.

Congress Balances the Presidency

A new interest in the balance of power between Congress and the president on foreign policy questions developed during the Vietnam War (1965–1975). Sensitive to public frustration over the long and costly war and angry at Richard Nixon for some of his other actions as president, Congress attempted to establish limits on the power of the president in setting foreign and defense policy.

The War Powers Resolution. In 1973, Congress passed the War Powers Resolution over President Nixon's veto. The act limited the president's use of troops in military action without congressional consultation and approval. Most presidents, however, have not interpreted the consultation provisions of the act as meaning that Congress should be consulted before military action is taken. Instead, Presidents Ford, Carter, Reagan, George H. W. Bush, and Clinton ordered troop movements and then informed congressional leaders.

The War Powers Resolution was in the news again in 2011, when President Obama failed to seek congressional support for air strikes to support the rebels in Libya. The House passed a resolution rebuking the president, but the Senate refused to consider it.

Everett Historical/Shutterstock.com

Image 16–11 An F-18 Hornet fighter flies over the Pentagon, the massive building that houses the U.S. Department of Defense. *What does it say about American self-confidence that its military headquarters is so obvious from the air?*

The Power of the Purse. One of Congress's most significant constitutional powers is the so-called power of the purse. The president may order that a certain action be taken, but that order cannot be executed unless Congress funds it. When the Democrats took control of Congress in January 2007, many asked whether the new Congress would use its power of the purse to bring an end to the Iraq War, in view of strong public opposition to the war. Congress's decision was to add conditions to a war-funding request submitted by the president. The conditions required the president to establish timelines for the redeployment of American troops in Iraq. Bush immediately threatened to veto any bill that imposed conditions on the funding. His threat carried the day.

In this circumstance, the power of Congress was limited by political considerations. Congress did not even consider the option of refusing to fund the war altogether. For one thing, there was not enough support in Congress for such an approach. For another, the Democrats did not want to be accused of placing the troops in Iraq in danger. Additionally, the threat of a presidential veto significantly limited Congress's power. The Democrats simply did not have a large enough majority to override a veto.

The Major Foreign Policy Themes

Learning Outcome **5:**

Cite the main themes in the history of U.S. foreign policy.

The long view of American diplomatic ventures reveals some major themes underlying foreign policy. In the early years of the nation, presidents and the people generally agreed that the United States should avoid foreign entanglements and concentrate instead on its own development. From the beginning of the twentieth century until the present, however, a major theme has been increasing global involvement. The theme of the post–World War II years was the containment of communism. The theme for at least the first part of the twenty-first century is countering terrorism, as we discussed earlier in this chapter.

The Formative Years: Avoiding Entanglements

The founders of the United States had a basic mistrust of European governments. This was a logical position at a time when the United States was so weak militarily that it could not influence European developments directly. Moreover, being protected by oceans that took weeks to cross certainly allowed the nation to avoid foreign entanglements. During the 1800s, therefore, the United States generally stayed out of European conflicts and politics. In the Western Hemisphere, however, the United States pursued an active expansionist policy. The nation purchased Louisiana in 1803, annexed Texas in 1845, gained substantial territory from Mexico in 1848, purchased Alaska in 1867, and annexed Hawaii in 1898.

Image 16–12 James Monroe, the fifth president. *With what foreign policy doctrine is he most commonly associated?*

The Monroe Doctrine. President James Monroe, in a message to Congress in 1823, set out three principles: (1) European nations should not establish new colonies in the Western Hemisphere, (2) European nations should not intervene in the affairs of independent nations of the Western Hemisphere, and (3) the United States would not interfere in the affairs of European nations. The **Monroe Doctrine** was the underpinning of the U.S. **isolationist foreign policy** toward Europe, which continued throughout the 1800s.

The Spanish-American War and World War I. The end of the isolationist policy started with the Spanish-American War in 1898. Winning the war gave the United States possession of Guam, Puerto Rico, and the Philippines (which gained independence in 1946). On the heels of that war came World War I (1914–1918). The United States declared war on Germany in April 1917, because that country refused to give up its campaign of sinking all ships headed for Britain, including passenger ships from America. (Large passenger ships of that time commonly held over a thousand people, so the sinking of such a ship was a disaster comparable to the attack on the World Trade Center.)

In the 1920s, the United States went "back to normalcy," as President Warren G. Harding urged it to do. U.S. military forces were largely disbanded, defense spending dropped to about 1 percent of the total annual national income, and the nation returned to a period of isolationism.

The Era of Internationalism

Isolationism was permanently shattered by the bombing of the U.S. naval base at Pearl Harbor, Hawaii, on December 7, 1941. The surprise attack by the Japanese caused the deaths of 2,403 American servicemen. President Franklin Roosevelt asked Congress to declare war on Japan immediately, and the United States entered World War II. Germany then declared war on the United States.

At the conclusion of the war, the United States was the only major participating country to emerge with its economy intact, and even strengthened. The United States was also the only country to have control over operational nuclear weapons. President Harry Truman had made the decision to use two atomic bombs in August 1945 to end the war

Monroe Doctrine

A policy statement by President James Monroe in 1823. The United States would not accept any new European intervention in the Western Hemisphere. In return, the United States would not meddle in European affairs.

isolationist foreign policy

A policy of abstaining from an active role in international affairs or alliances, which characterized U.S. foreign policy toward Europe during most of the 1800s.

with Japan. (Historians still argue over the necessity of this action, which ultimately killed more than 100,000 Japanese and left an equal number permanently injured.) The United States truly had become the world's superpower.

The Cold War. The United States had become an uncomfortable ally of the Soviet Union after Adolf Hitler's invasion of that country. Soon after World War II ended, relations between the Soviet Union and the West deteriorated. The Soviet Union wanted a weakened Germany, and to achieve this, it insisted that Germany be divided in two, with East Germany becoming a buffer against the West. Little by little, the Soviet Union helped to install Communist governments in Eastern European countries, which began to be referred to collectively as the **Soviet bloc.** In response, the United States encouraged the rearming of Western Europe. The Cold War had begun.[3]

Containment Policy. In 1947, a remarkable article was published in *Foreign Affairs* magazine, signed by "X." The actual author was George F. Kennan, chief of the policy-planning staff for the State Department. The doctrine of **containment** set forth in the article became—according to many—the bible of Western foreign policy. "X" argued that whenever and wherever the Soviet Union could successfully challenge the West, it would do so. He recommended that our policy toward the Soviet Union be "firm and vigilant containment of Russian expansive tendencies."[4]

---

3. See John Lewis Gaddis, *The United Nations and the Origins of the Cold War* (New York: Columbia University Press, 1972).

4. X, "The Sources of Soviet Conduct," *Foreign Affairs*, July 1947, p. 575.

Soviet bloc

The Soviet Union and the Eastern European countries that installed Communist regimes after World War II and were dominated by the Soviet Union.

containment

A U.S. diplomatic policy adopted by the Truman administration to contain Communist power within its existing boundaries.

Library of Congress Prints and Photographs Division

Image 16–13 In a famous meeting in Yalta in February 1945, British prime minister Winston Churchill (left), U.S. president Franklin Roosevelt (center), and Soviet leader Joseph Stalin (right) decided on the fate of several nations in Europe, including Germany. *What happened to Germany immediately after World War II?*

Truman Doctrine

The policy adopted by President Harry Truman in 1947 to halt Communist expansion.

The containment theory was expressed clearly in the **Truman Doctrine,** which was enunciated by President Harry Truman in 1947. Truman held that the United States must help countries in which a Communist takeover seemed likely. Later that year, he backed the Marshall Plan, an economic assistance plan for Europe that was intended to prevent the expansion of Communist influence there. In 1949, the United States entered into a military alliance with a number of European nations called the North Atlantic Treaty Organization, or NATO, to offer a credible response to any Soviet military attack. Figure 16–1 shows the face-off between the U.S.-led NATO alliance and the Soviet-led Warsaw Pact—an agreement formed by Soviet-bloc nations to counter the NATO alliance.

Superpower Relations

During the Cold War, there was never any direct military conflict between the United States and the Soviet Union. Only on occasion did the United States enter a conflict with any Communist-led country. Two such occasions were in Korea and in Vietnam.

The Korean War. After the end of World War II, northern Korea was occupied by the Soviet Union, and southern Korea was occupied by the United States. The result was two rival Korean governments. In 1950, North Korea invaded South Korea. Under UN authority, the United States entered the war, which prevented an almost certain South Korean defeat. When U.S. forces were on the brink of conquering North Korea, however, China joined the

Figure 16–1 Europe during the Cold War

This map shows the face-off between NATO (led by the United States) and the Soviet bloc (the Warsaw Pact). Note that West Germany did not join NATO until 1955, and Albania suspended participation in the Warsaw Pact in 1960. France was out of NATO from 1966 to 1996, and Spain did not join until 1982. *Why might West Germany have been late to join NATO?*

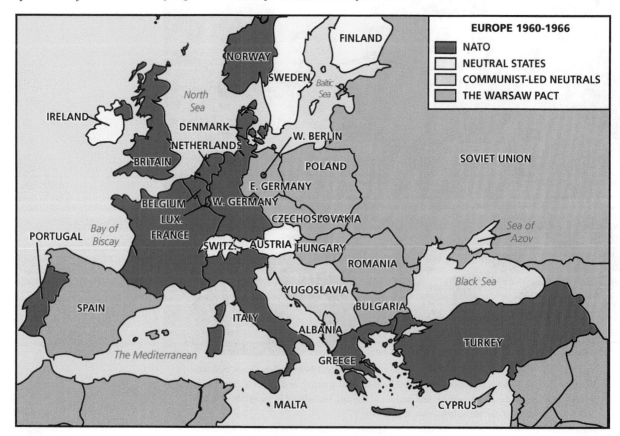

war on the side of the North, resulting in a stalemate. An armistice signed in 1953 led to the two Koreas that exist today. U.S. forces have remained in South Korea since that time.

The Vietnam War. The Vietnam War (1965–1975) also involved the United States in a civil war between a Communist north and pro-Western south. When the French army in Indochina was defeated by the Communist forces of Ho Chi Minh in 1954, two Vietnams were created. The United States assumed the role of supporting the South Vietnamese government against North Vietnam. American forces in Vietnam at the height of the U.S. involvement totaled more than 500,000 troops. More than 58,000 Americans were killed in the conflict. A peace agreement in 1973 allowed U.S. troops to leave the country, and in 1975 North Vietnam easily occupied Saigon (the South Vietnamese capital) and unified the nation.

Over the course of the Vietnam War, the debate over U.S. involvement became extremely heated and, as mentioned previously, spurred congressional efforts to limit the ability of the president to commit forces to armed combat. The military draft was also a major source of contention during the Vietnam War.

The Cuban Missile Crisis. Perhaps the closest the two superpowers came to a nuclear confrontation was the Cuban missile crisis in 1962. The Soviets placed missiles in Cuba, ninety miles off the U.S. coast, in response to Cuban fears of an American invasion and to try to balance an American nuclear advantage. President John F. Kennedy and his advisers rejected the option of invading Cuba, setting up a naval blockade around the island instead.

In October, the Soviet Union announced the withdrawal of its missile operations from Cuba. In exchange, the United States agreed not to invade Cuba in the future. Still, the United States maintained a comprehensive economic embargo of Cuba following this crisis. The relationship between the United States and Cuba did not substantially improve until 2015, when President Obama announced plans to establish diplomatic relations with the Cuban government.

A Period of Détente. The French word **détente** means a relaxation of tensions. By the end of the 1960s, it was clear that some efforts had to be made to reduce the threat of nuclear war between the United States and the Soviet Union. The Soviet Union gradually had begun to catch up in the building of bombers and missiles, thus balancing the nuclear scales between the two countries. Each nation had acquired the military capacity to destroy the other with nuclear weapons.

As the result of lengthy negotiations under Secretary of State Henry Kissinger and President Richard Nixon, the United States and the Soviet Union signed the **Strategic Arms Limitation Treaty (SALT I)** in May 1972. That treaty limited the number of offensive missiles each country could deploy.

The policy of détente was not limited to the U.S. relationship with the Soviet Union. Seeing an opportunity to capitalize on increasing friction between the Soviet Union and the People's Republic of China,

détente
A French word meaning a relaxation of tensions. The term characterized U.S.-Soviet relations as they developed under President Richard Nixon and Secretary of State Henry Kissinger.

Strategic Arms Limitation Treaty (SALT I)
A treaty between the United States and the Soviet Union to stabilize the nuclear arms competition between the two countries. The treaty was signed in May 1972.

Gary Hershorn/Files GMHSV/Reuters

Image 16–14 Soviet leader Mikhail Gorbachev (left) stands with U.S. president Ronald Reagan in 1987, shortly after the two men finished negotiations on a major arms-control treaty. *What happened to the Soviet Union in 1991?*

Kissinger secretly began negotiations to establish a new relationship with China. President Nixon eventually visited that nation in 1972. The visit set the stage for the formal diplomatic recognition of that country, which occurred during the Carter administration (1977–1981).

Nuclear Arms Agreements with the Soviet Union and Russia. In subsequent years, several American presidents negotiated and signed arms control agreements with the Soviet Union (and later, with Russia). These presidents included Republicans Ronald Reagan (1981–1989) and George H. W. Bush (1989–1993). The most recent such treaty, New START, was signed in 2010 by President Obama and Dmitry Medvedev, who was then president of Russia. New START reduced the number of permitted warheads to 1,550 for each side, a drop of about 30 percent from previous agreements. After some delays, the Senate ratified the treaty.

The Dissolution of the Soviet Union. In 1989, the fall of the Berlin Wall that had divided that city into eastern and western sectors marked the first step in the reunification of Germany. By then, it was clear that the Soviet Union had relinquished much of its political and military control over the states of Eastern Europe that formerly had been part of the Soviet bloc. No one expected the Soviet Union to dissolve into separate states as quickly as it did, however. Demands for political, ethnic, and religious autonomy grew. On the day after Christmas in 1991, the Soviet Union was officially dissolved. Figure 16–2 shows the situation in Europe today.

Figure 16–2 Europe after the Fall of the Soviet Union

This map shows the growth in European unity as marked by participation in transnational organizations. The United States continues to lead NATO (and would be orange if it were on the map). Note the reunification of Germany and the creation of new states from the former Yugoslavia and the former Soviet Union. Finally, Britain is currently planning to leave the EU. *Why would a nation such as Poland want to join NATO?*

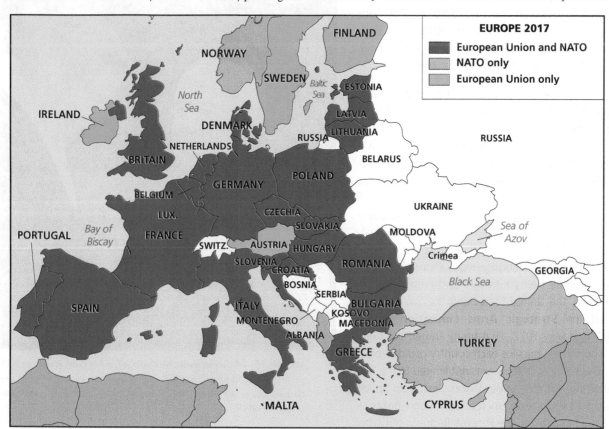

Russia under Putin. Vladimir Putin became Russia's second president in 2000, following Boris Yeltsin. Putin chipped away at Russia's democratic institutions, slowly turning the country into what was, in essence, an elected autocracy. When Putin's second term as president came to an end in 2008, he could not immediately run for reelection. He therefore engineered the election of one of his supporters, Dmitry Medvedev, as president. Medvedev promptly appointed Putin as prime minister. It was clear that Putin retained real power in Russia, and in 2012 Putin again took the presidency.

In recent years, the United States has become concerned over Russia's aggressive attitude toward its neighbors. For example, in 2008, Russian troops entered Georgia to prevent that nation from retaking an autonomous region that was under Russian protection. On several occasions since 2005, Russia has cut off the transmission of natural gas to Europe as a result of disputes. Russia also reacted angrily to U.S. plans for antimissile defenses in Eastern Europe, aimed at protecting Europe from a possible future Iranian attack. Russia appeared to believe that the defenses were directed against it.

Crisis in Ukraine. In November 2013, Ukraine's pro-Russian president Viktor Yanukovych abruptly broke off economic talks with the European Union, apparently under pressure from Putin. The resulting tumult was so intense that Yanukovych fled the country in February 2014. Parliament assumed power and began steering the country back toward Europe.

Putin denounced the new government as "fascist." Claiming the right to protect Russian-speaking populations in Ukraine, Putin annexed the Crimean Peninsula, which has an ethnic-Russian majority. Pro-Russian militias, with Russian support, forcibly took control of parts of two eastern provinces.

President Obama responded with a series of sanctions and was able to persuade European countries to follow suit. A greater blow to Russia was inflicted by the international financial community, which began withdrawing investments from the country. Attempts to obtain a cease-fire in eastern Ukraine had mixed results. The annexation of Crimea, however, appeared to be irreversible.

The Russian Challenge. As the former head of the Soviet Union's secret police, Vladimir Putin was clearly never an advocate of democracy. Almost all journalists who have opposed him have either fled Russia or are dead. Putin has called the collapse of the Soviet Union "a major geopolitical catastrophe of the century." His actions suggest that he wants to reverse it.

Putin has threatened all of the small Baltic countries—Estonia, Latvia, and Lithuania. Russia's air force has begun flying nuclear-armed bombers around the world on an ongoing basis. Russian jets have constantly violated the airspace of the Scandinavian and Baltic nations. Some of his government officials have casually mentioned in off-the-record discussions that Russia was prepared to use its nuclear weapons.

Unfortunately, the problem with Russia is not just Putin. Most Russians do not accept that their country should be one nation among many, playing by universal rules. They believe Russia is a great power that deserves special respect. In particular, neighboring countries cannot be allowed to pursue policies that conflict with Russian interests.

One consequence of Russian attitudes has been a move by NATO to bolster the defenses of the Baltic nations and Poland. Unfortunately, Putin has found Western supporters on the nationalist right. In France, the National Front has borrowed funds from Russia for use in upcoming elections. In the United States, Donald Trump has shown himself to be remarkably friendly to Putin, praising him as "a better leader than Obama." Trump not only questioned whether the United States should defend the Baltic states—NATO allies—but even raised the possibility of leaving the alliance altogether. Europeans found such statements by a presidential candidate to be profoundly unsettling.

How you can make a difference

What can you do to work for the improvement of human rights in other nations? One way is to join an organization that attempts to keep watch over human rights violations. By publicizing human rights violations, such organizations try to pressure nations into changing their practices. Sometimes, they are able to apply enough pressure and cause enough embarrassment that victims may be freed from prison or allowed to emigrate.

If you want to receive general information about the position of the United States on human rights violations, you can contact the State Department's Bureau of Democracy, Human Rights, and Labor at www.state.gov/j/drl/hr.

The following organizations are well known for their watchdog efforts in countries that violate human rights for political reasons:

- Amnesty International U.S.A. www.amnestyusa.org
- American Friends Service Committee afsc.org

KEY TERMS

Cold War **444**
containment **457**
defense policy **437**
détente **459**
diplomacy **437**
economic aid **437**

foreign policy **437**
intelligence community **454**
isolationist foreign policy **456**
Monroe Doctrine **456**

moral idealism **438**
national security policy **437**
normal trade relations (NTR) status **446**
political realism **438**

Soviet bloc **457**
Strategic Arms Limitation Treaty (SALT I) **459**
technical assistance **437**
terrorism **439**
Truman Doctrine **458**

CHAPTER SUMMARY

Learning Outcome 1 Foreign policy includes the nation's external goals and the techniques and strategies used to achieve them. Diplomacy involves the nation's external relationships and is an attempt to resolve conflict without resort to arms. U.S. foreign policy is based on both moral idealism and political realism.

Learning Outcome 2 Terrorism is the attempt to create fear to gain political ends by violence against noncombatants. It has become a major challenge facing the United States and other nations. The United States waged war on terrorism after the attacks of September 11, 2001.

In 1991 and again in 2003, the United States sent combat troops to Iraq. The second war in Iraq, begun in 2003, succeeded in toppling that nation's decades-long dictatorship

but led to a long, grinding conflict with insurgent forces. The campaign in Afghanistan, which grew out of the war on terrorism, has proven to be equally difficult. Currently, the United States is concerned with defeating IS (the "Islamic State") in Iraq and Syria.

Learning Outcome 3 Recent diplomatic efforts by the United States include containing the nuclear ambitions of Iran and North Korea. The rise of China as a world power and eventually a superpower introduces issues such as trade relations. American efforts to promote the peace process between Israel and the Palestinians have had limited success. World economic issues, such as the European economic crisis, demand U.S. attention.

Learning Outcome 4 The U.S. Constitution designates the president as commander in chief of the armed forces. Presidents have interpreted this authority broadly. They also have the power to make treaties and executive agreements. The State Department is the executive agency with primary authority over foreign affairs. The National Security Council also plays a major role. The intelligence community engages in activities from information gathering to covert operations. In response to the Vietnam War, Congress attempted to establish some limits on the power of the president through the War Powers Resolution of 1973.

Learning Outcome 5 In the early years of the nation, isolationism was the foreign policy strategy. With the start of the twentieth century, isolationism gave way to global involvement.

The end of the policy of isolationism toward Europe started with the Spanish-American War of 1898. U.S. involvement in Europe became more extensive when the United States entered World War I. The United States was the only major country to emerge from World War II with its economy intact and with operating nuclear weapons.

After World War II, the Cold War began. A policy of containment of the Soviet Union was enunciated in the Truman Doctrine. The United States signed nuclear arms control agreements with the Soviet Union under several presidents. After the fall of the Soviet Union, Russia emerged as a less threatening state. Under President Vladimir Putin, however, Russia has moved away from democracy and posed a military threat to its neighbors.

ADDITIONAL RESOURCES

Online Resources

- In addition to materials on international crises, the United Nations website contains a treasure trove of international statistics. To see these, go to **www.un.org/en**.

- *Foreign Policy* magazine reviews a wide variety of foreign policy topics. Visit it at **www.foreignpolicy.com**.

Books

Chollet, Derek. *The Long Game: How Obama Defied Washington and Redefined America's Role in the World.* New York: PublicAffairs, 2016. Chollet provides a detailed inside account of the ideas and strategy underlying Barack Obama's foreign policies. He spent six years serving the Obama administration in a variety of senior foreign policy positions.

Manuel, Anja. *This Brave New World: India, China, and the United States.* New York: Simon & Schuster, 2016. Manuel, cofounder of a major strategic consulting firm, believes that it is possible for the world's three most populous nations to be partners in shaping the future.

Worth, Robert F. *A Rage for Order: The Middle East in Turmoil, from Tahrir Square to ISIS.* New York: Farrar, Straus and Giroux, 2016. Worth provides insight into the Middle East through stories of individuals who have participated in recent events. He is a former Beirut bureau chief for the *New York Times.*

Video

The Russian Soul—A 2014 film by Andrew Hamilton. The Russian Federation is a highly advanced nation in many ways, but its government is corrupt and autocratic. This documentary asks why it is that Russians put up with such a system.

United 93—A 2006 documentary about the fourth airplane hijacked on 9/11. When they learned the fate of the other three planes through their cell phones, the passengers decided to fight back, with the result that the plane crashed in a Pennsylvania field, far from its intended target. United 93 takes place in real time and is almost unbearably moving. Several critics named it the best film of the year.

Quiz

Multiple Choice and Fill-Ins

Learning Outcome 1 Define *foreign policy,* and discuss moral idealism versus political realism in foreign policy.

1. As part of foreign policy, national security policy is designed to:
   a. provide economic assistance to other nations.
   b. ensure that all other countries respect each other's borders.
   c. protect the independence and political integrity of the United States.

2. U.S. support for foreign dictators is sometimes an example of _____ _____ in foreign policy.

Learning Outcome 2 Describe recent foreign policy challenges that involve the use of force.

3. Acts of terrorism are:
   a. the result of small-country governments' attempts to gain new territory.
   b. systematic attempts to inspire fear to gain political ends.
   c. due to large-country governments that failed in diplomacy.

4. The three major groups in Iraq are the _____ _____, the _____ _____, and the _____ .

Learning Outcome 3 Discuss the use of diplomacy in addressing such issues as nuclear proliferation, the rise of China, and the confrontation between Israel and the Palestinians.

5. The two countries that today represent the most serious problems with nuclear proliferation are:
   a. Iran and North Korea.
   b. Japan and Germany.
   c. China and Brazil.

6. The Palestinian territories are made up of the _____ _____ and the _____ _____.

Learning Outcome 4 Explain the roles of the president, executive agencies, and Congress in making U.S. foreign policy.

7. The intelligence community is involved in foreign policy and consists of:
   a. the CIA and the Department of Defense.
   b. more than forty government agencies and bureaus involved in intelligence activities.
   c. the CIA and the National Security Council.

8. As part of foreign policy, the Constitution gives the president the power to make _____ provided that the _____ concurs.

Learning Outcome 5 Cite the main themes in the history of U.S. foreign policy.

9. The Cold War refers to a period during which:
   a. the Soviet Union and the United States faced off throughout the world.
   b. the United States reverted back to isolationist policies.
   c. the United States engaged in economic conflict with many Asian countries.

10. Just after World War II, President Harry Truman vowed that the United States must help countries in which a Communist takeover seemed likely. This became known as the

   _____ _____.

Essay Questions

1. Some people believe that if no U.S. military personnel were stationed abroad, terrorists would have less desire to harm Americans or the United States. Do you agree? Why or why not?

2. Why do you think that North Korea and Iran might want to possess nuclear weapons, even though they can never hope to match the nuclear arsenals of the original nuclear powers?

Answers to multiple-choice and fill-in questions: 1. c, 2. political realism, 3. b, 4. Shiite Arabs/Sunni Arabs/Kurds, 5. a, 6. West Bank/Gaza Strip, 7. b, 8. treaties/ Senate, 9. a, 10. Truman Doctrine.

APPENDIX A

The Declaration of Independence

In Congress, July 4, 1776

A Declaration by the Representatives of the United States of America, in General Congress assembled. When in the Course of human Events, it becomes necessary for one People to dissolve the Political Bands which have connected them with another, and to assume among the Powers of the Earth, the separate and equal Station to which the Laws of Nature and of Nature's God entitle them, a decent Respect to the Opinions of Mankind requires that they should declare the causes which impel them to the Separation.

We hold these Truths to be self-evident, that all Men are created equal, that they are endowed by their Creator with certain unalienable Rights, that among these are Life, Liberty, and the Pursuit of Happiness—That to secure these Rights, Governments are instituted among Men, deriving their just Powers from the Consent of the Governed, that whenever any Form of Government becomes destructive of these Ends, it is the Right of the People to alter or to abolish it, and to institute new Government, laying its Foundation on such Principles, and organizing its Powers in such Forms, as to them shall seem most likely to effect their Safety and Happiness. Prudence, indeed, will dictate that Governments long established should not be changed for light and transient Causes; and accordingly all Experience hath shewn, that Mankind are more disposed to suffer, while Evils are sufferable, than to right themselves by abolishing the Forms to which they are accustomed. But when a long Train of Abuses and Usurpations, pursuing invariably the same Object, evinces a Design to reduce them under absolute Despotism, it is their Right, it is their Duty, to throw off such Government, and to provide new Guards for their future Security. Such has been the patient Sufferance of these Colonies; and such is now the Necessity which constrains them to alter their former Systems of Government. The History of the present King of Great-Britain is a History of repeated Injuries and Usurpations, all having in direct Object the Establishment of an absolute Tyranny over these States. To prove this, let Facts be submitted to a candid World.

He has refused his Assent to Laws, the most wholesome and necessary for the public Good.

He has forbidden his Governors to pass Laws of immediate and pressing Importance, unless suspended in their Operation till his Assent should be obtained; and when so suspended, he has utterly neglected to attend to them.

He has refused to pass other Laws for the Accommodation of large Districts of People, unless those People would relinquish the Right of Representation in the Legislature, a Right inestimable to them, and formidable to Tyrants only.

He has called together Legislative Bodies at Places unusual, uncomfortable, and distant from the Depository of their Public Records, for the sole Purpose of fatiguing them into Compliance with his Measures.

He has dissolved Representative Houses repeatedly, for opposing with manly Firmness his Invasions on the Rights of the People.

He has refused for a long Time, after such Dissolutions, to cause others to be elected; whereby the Legislative Powers, incapable of Annihilation, have returned to the People at large for their exercise; the State remaining in the mean time exposed to all the Dangers of Invasion from without, and Convulsions within.

He has endeavoured to prevent the Population of these States; for that Purpose obstructing the Laws for Naturalization of Foreigners; refusing to pass others to encourage their Migrations hither, and raising the Conditions of new Appropriations of Lands.

He has obstructed the Administration of Justice, by refusing his Assent to Laws for establishing Judiciary Powers.

He has made Judges dependent on his Will alone, for the Tenure of their offices, and the Amount and payment of their Salaries.

He has erected a Multitude of new Offices, and sent hither Swarms of Officers to harass our People, and eat out their Substance.

He has kept among us, in Times of Peace, Standing Armies, without the consent of our Legislatures.

He has affected to render the Military independent of, and superior to the Civil Power.

He has combined with others to subject us to a Jurisdiction foreign to our Constitution, and unacknowledged by our Laws; giving his Assent to their Acts of pretended Legislation:

For quartering large Bodies of Armed Troops among us:

For protecting them, by a mock Trial, from Punishment for any Murders which they should commit on the Inhabitants of these States:

For cutting off our Trade with all Parts of the World:

For imposing Taxes on us without our Consent:

For depriving us, in many cases, of the Benefits of Trial by Jury:

For transporting us beyond Seas to be tried for pretended Offences:

For abolishing the free System of English Laws in a neighbouring Province, establishing therein an arbitrary Government, and enlarging its Boundaries, so as to render it at once an Example and fit Instrument for introducing the same absolute Rule into these Colonies:

For taking away our Charters, abolishing our most valuable Laws, and altering fundamentally the Forms of our Governments:

For suspending our own Legislatures, and declaring themselves invested with Power to legislate for us in all Cases whatsoever.

He has abdicated Government here, by declaring us out of his Protection and waging War against us.

He has plundered our Seas, ravaged our Coasts, burnt our towns, and destroyed the Lives of our People.

He is, at this Time, transporting large Armies of foreign Mercenaries to compleat the works of Death, Desolation, and Tyranny, already begun with circumstances of Cruelty and Perfidy, scarcely paralleled in the most barbarous Ages, and totally unworthy the Head of a civilized Nation.

He has constrained our fellow Citizens taken Captive on the high Seas to bear Arms against their Country, to become the Executioners of their Friends and Brethren, or to fall themselves by their Hands.

He has excited domestic Insurrections amongst us, and has endeavoured to bring on the Inhabitants of our Frontiers, the merciless Indian Savages, whose known Rule of Warfare, is an undistinguished Destruction, of all Ages, Sexes and Conditions.

In every state of these Oppressions we have Petitioned for Redress in the most humble Terms: Our repeated Petitions have been answered only by repeated Injury. A Prince, whose Character is thus marked by every act which may define a Tyrant, is unfit to be the Ruler of a free People.

Nor have we been wanting in Attentions to our British Brethren. We have warned them from Time to Time of Attempts by their Legislature to extend an unwarrantable Jurisdiction over us. We have reminded them of the Circumstances of our Emigration and Settlement here. We have appealed to their native Justice and Magnanimity, and we have conjured them by the Ties of our common Kindred to disavow these Usurpations, which, would inevitably interrupt our Connections and Correspondence. They too have been deaf to the Voice of Justice and of Consanguinity. We must, therefore, acquiesce in the Necessity, which denounces our Separation, and hold them, as we hold the rest of Mankind, Enemies in War, in Peace, Friends.

We, therefore, the Representatives of the UNITED STATES OF AMERICA, in General Congress Assembled, appealing to the Supreme Judge of the World for the Rectitude of our Intentions, do, in the Name, and by the Authority of the good People of these Colonies, solemnly Publish and Declare, That these United Colonies are, and of Right ought to be, Free and Independent States; that they are absolved from all Allegiance to the British Crown, and that all political Connection between them and the State of Great-Britain, is and ought to be totally dissolved; and that as Free and Independent States, they have full Power to levy War, conclude Peace, contract Alliances, establish Commerce, and to do all other Acts and Things which Independent States may of right do. And for the support of this declaration, with a firm Reliance on the Protection of divine Providence, we mutually pledge to each other our lives, our Fortunes, and our sacred Honor.

APPENDIX B

The Constitution of the United States*

The Preamble

We the People of the United States, in Order to form a more perfect Union, establish Justice, insure domestic Tranquility, provide for the common defence, promote the general Welfare, and secure the Blessings of Liberty to ourselves and our Posterity, do ordain and establish this Constitution for the United States of America.

The Preamble declares that "We the People" are the authority for the Constitution (unlike the Articles of Confederation, which derived their authority from the states). The Preamble also sets out the purposes of the Constitution.

ARTICLE I. (Legislative Branch)

The first part of the Constitution, Article I, deals with the organization and powers of the lawmaking branch of the national government, the Congress.

Section 1. Legislative Powers

All legislative Powers herein granted shall be vested in a Congress of the United States, which shall consist of a Senate and House of Representatives.

Section 2. House of Representatives

Clause 1: Composition and Election of Members. The House of Representatives shall be composed of Members chosen every second Year by the People of the several States, and the Electors in each State shall have the Qualifications requisite for Electors of the most numerous Branch of the State Legislature.

Each state has the power to decide who may vote for members of Congress. Within each state, those who may vote for state legislators may also vote for members of the House of Representatives (and, under the Seventeenth Amendment, for U.S. senators). When the Constitution was written, nearly all states limited voting rights to white male property owners or taxpayers at least twenty-one years old. Subsequent amendments granted voting power to African American men, all women, and everyone at least eighteen years old.

Clause 2: Qualifications. No Person shall be a Representative who shall not have attained to the Age of twenty five Years, and been seven Years a Citizen of the United States, and who shall not, when elected, be an Inhabitant of that State in which he shall be chosen.

Each member of the House must be at least twenty-five years old, a citizen of the United States for at least seven years, and a resident of the state in which she or he is elected.

Clause 3: Apportionment of Representatives and Direct Taxes. Representatives [and direct Taxes][1] shall be apportioned among the several States which may be included within this Union, according to their respective Numbers [which shall be determined by adding to the whole Number of free Persons, including those bound to Service for a Term of Years, and excluding Indians not taxed, three fifths of all other Persons].[2] The actual Enumeration shall be made within three Years after the first Meeting of the Congress of the United States, and within every subsequent Term of ten Years, in such Manner as they shall by Law direct. The Number of Representatives shall not exceed one for every thirty Thousand, but each State shall have at Least one Representative; and until such enumeration shall be made, the State of New Hampshire shall be entitled to chuse three, Massachusetts eight, Rhode Island and Providence Plantations one, Connecticut five, New York six, New Jersey four, Pennsylvania eight, Delaware one, Maryland six, Virginia ten, North Carolina five, South Carolina five, and Georgia three.

A state's representation in the House is based on the size of its population. Population is counted in each decade's census, after which Congress reapportions House seats. Since early in the twentieth century, the number of seats has been limited to 435.

Clause 4: Vacancies. When vacancies happen in the Representation from any State, the Executive Authority thereof shall issue Writs of Election to fill such Vacancies.

The "Executive Authority" is the state's governor. When a vacancy occurs in the House, the governor calls a special election to fill it.

Clause 5: Officers and Impeachment. The House of Representatives shall chuse their Speaker and other Officers; and shall have the sole Power of Impeachment.

The power to impeach is the power to accuse. In this case, it is the power to accuse members of the executive or judicial branch of wrongdoing or abuse of power. Once a bill of impeachment is issued, the Senate holds the trial.

---

*The spelling, capitalization, and punctuation of the original have been retained here. Brackets indicate passages that have been altered by amendments to the Constitution. We have added article titles (in parentheses), section titles, and clause designations. We have also inserted annotations in blue italic type.

---

1. Modified by the Sixteenth Amendment.
2. Modified by the Fourteenth Amendment.

Section 3. The Senate

Clause 1: Term and Number of Members. The Senate of the United States shall be composed of two Senators from each State [chosen by the Legislature thereof],[3] for six Years; and each Senator shall have one Vote.

Every state has two senators, each of whom serves for six years and has one vote in the upper chamber. Since the Seventeenth Amendment was passed in 1913, all senators have been elected directly by voters of the state during the regular election.

Clause 2: Classification of Senators. Immediately after they shall be assembled in Consequence of the first Election, they shall be divided as equally as may be into three Classes. The Seats of the Senators of the first Class shall be vacated at the Expiration of the second Year, of the second Class at the Expiration of the fourth Year, and of the third Class at the Expiration of the sixth Year, so that one third may be chosen every second Year; [and if Vacancies happen by Resignation, or otherwise, during the Recess of the Legislature of any State, the Executive thereof may make temporary Appointments until the next Meeting of the Legislature, which shall then fill such Vacancies].[4]

One-third of the Senate's seats are open to election every two years (in contrast, all members of the House are elected simultaneously).

Clause 3: Qualifications. No Person shall be a Senator who shall not have attained to the Age of thirty Years, and been nine Years a Citizen of the United States, and who shall not, when elected, be an Inhabitant of that State for which he shall be chosen.

Every senator must be at least thirty years old, a citizen of the United States for a minimum of nine years, and a resident of the state in which he or she is elected.

Clause 4: The Role of the Vice President. The Vice President of the United States shall be President of the Senate, but shall have no Vote, unless they be equally divided.

The vice president presides over meetings of the Senate but cannot vote unless there is a tie. The Constitution gives no other official duties to the vice president.

Clause 5: Other Officers. The Senate shall chuse their other Officers, and also a President pro tempore, in the Absence of the Vice President, or when he shall exercise the Office of President of the United States.

The Senate votes for one of its members to preside when the vice president is absent. This person is usually called the president pro tempore because of the temporary nature of the position.

Clause 6: Impeachment Trials. The Senate shall have the sole Power to try all Impeachments. When sitting for that Purpose, they shall be on Oath or Affirmation. When the President of the United States is tried, the Chief Justice shall preside: And no Person shall be convicted without the Concurrence of two thirds of the Members present.

The Senate conducts trials of officials that the House impeaches. The Senate sits as a jury, with the vice president presiding if the president is not on trial.

Clause 7: Penalties for Conviction. Judgment in Cases of Impeachment shall not extend further than to removal from Office, and disqualification to hold and enjoy any Office of honor, Trust, or Profit under the United States: but the Party convicted shall nevertheless be liable and subject to Indictment, Trial, Judgment, and Punishment, according to Law.

On conviction of impeachment charges, the Senate can only force an official to leave office and prevent him or her from holding another office in the federal government. The individual, however, can still be tried in a regular court.

Section 4. Congressional Elections: Times, Manner, and Places

Clause 1: Elections. The Times, Places and Manner of holding Elections for Senators and Representatives, shall be prescribed in each State by the Legislature thereof; but the Congress may at any time by Law make or alter such Regulations, except as to the Places of chusing Senators.

Congress set the Tuesday after the first Monday in November in even-numbered years as the date for congressional elections. In states with more than one seat in the House, Congress requires that representatives be elected from districts within each state. Under the Seventeenth Amendment, senators are elected at the same places as other officials.

Clause 2: Sessions of Congress. [The Congress shall assemble at least once in every Year, and such Meeting shall be on the first Monday in December, unless they shall by Law appoint a different Day.][5]

Congress has to meet every year at least once. The regular session now begins at noon on January 3 of each year, subsequent to the Twentieth Amendment, unless Congress passes a law to fix a different date. Congress stays in session until its members vote to adjourn. Additionally, the president may call a special session.

Section 5. Powers and Duties of the Houses

Clause 1: Admitting Members and Quorum. Each House shall be the Judge of the Elections, Returns, and Qualifications of its own Members, and a Majority of each shall constitute a Quorum to do Business; but a smaller Number may adjourn from day to day, and may be authorized to compel the Attendance of absent Members, in such Manner, and under such Penalties as each House may provide.

Each chamber may exclude or refuse to seat a member-elect.
  The quorum rule requires that 218 members of the House and 51 members of the Senate be present to conduct business. This rule normally is not enforced in the handling of routine matters.

---

3. Repealed by the Seventeenth Amendment.
4. Modified by the Seventeenth Amendment.

5. Changed by the Twentieth Amendment.

Clause 2: Rules and Discipline of Members. Each House may determine the Rules of its Proceedings, punish its Members for disorderly Behaviour, and, with the Concurrence of two thirds, expel a Member.

The House and the Senate may adopt their own rules to guide their proceedings. Each may also discipline its members for conduct that is deemed unacceptable. No member may be expelled without a two-thirds majority vote in favor of expulsion.

Clause 3: Keeping a Record. Each House shall keep a Journal of its Proceedings, and from time to time publish the same, excepting such Parts as may in their Judgment require Secrecy; and the Yeas and Nays of the Members of either House on any question shall, at the Desire of one fifth of those Present, be entered on the Journal.

The journals of the two chambers are published at the end of each session of Congress.

Clause 4: Adjournment. Neither House, during the Session of Congress, shall, without the Consent of the other, adjourn for more than three days, nor to any other Place than that in which the two Houses shall be sitting.

Congress has the power to determine when and where to meet, provided, however, that both chambers meet in the same city. Neither chamber may recess for more than three days without the consent of the other.

Section 6. Rights of Members
Clause 1: Compensation and Privileges. The Senators and Representatives shall receive a Compensation for their services, to be ascertained by Law, and paid out of the Treasury of the United States. They shall in all Cases, except Treason, Felony and Breach of the Peace, be privileged from Arrest during their Attendance at the Session of their respective Houses, and in going to and returning from the same; and for any Speech or Debate in either House, they shall not be questioned in any other Place.

Congressional salaries are to be paid by the U.S. Treasury rather than by the members' respective states. The original salaries were $6 per day; in 1857 they were $3,000 per year. Both representatives and senators were paid a base salary of $174,000 in 2014.
    Treason is defined in Article III, Section 3. A felony is any serious crime. A breach of the peace is any indictable offense less than treason or a felony. Members cannot be arrested for things they say during speeches and debates in Congress. This immunity applies to the Capitol Building itself and not to their private lives.

Clause 2: Restrictions. No Senator or Representative shall, during the Time for which he was elected, be appointed to any civil Office under the Authority of the United States, which shall have been created, or the Emoluments whereof shall have been encreased during such time; and no Person holding any Office under the United States, shall be a Member of either House during his Continuance in Office.

During the term for which a member was elected, he or she cannot concurrently accept another federal government position.

Section 7. Legislative Powers: Bills and Resolutions
Clause 1: Revenue Bills. All Bills for raising Revenue shall originate in the House of Representatives; but the Senate may propose or concur with Amendments as on other Bills.

All tax and appropriation bills for raising money have to originate in the House of Representatives. The Senate, though, often amends such bills and may even substitute an entirely different bill.

Clause 2: The Presidential Veto. Every Bill which shall have passed the House of Representatives and the Senate, shall, before it becomes a Law, be presented to the President of the United States; If he approve he shall sign it, but if not he shall return it, with his Objections to the House in which it shall have originated, who shall enter the Objections at large on their Journal, and proceed to reconsider it. If after such Reconsideration two thirds of that House shall agree to pass the Bill, it shall be sent together with the Objections, to the other House, by which it shall likewise be reconsidered, and if approved by two thirds of that House, it shall become a Law. But in all such Cases the Votes of both Houses shall be determined by Yeas and Nays, and the Names of the Persons voting for and against the Bill shall be entered on the Journal of each House respectively. If any Bill shall not be returned by the President within ten Days (Sundays excepted) after it shall have been presented to him, the Same shall be a Law, in like Manner as if he had signed it, unless the Congress by their Adjournment prevent its Return in which Case it shall not be a Law.

When Congress sends the president a bill, he or she can sign it (in which case it becomes law) or send it back to the chamber in which it originated. If it is sent back, a two-thirds majority of each chamber must pass it again for it to become law. If the president neither signs it nor sends it back within ten days, it becomes law anyway, unless Congress adjourns in the meantime.

Clause 3: Actions on Other Matters. Every Order, Resolution, or Vote to which the Concurrence of the Senate and House of Representatives may be necessary (except on a question of Adjournment) shall be presented to the President of the United States; and before the Same shall take Effect, shall be approved by him, or being disapproved by him, shall be repassed by two thirds of the Senate and House of Representatives, according to the Rules and Limitations prescribed in the Case of a Bill.

The president must have the opportunity to either sign or veto everything that Congress passes, except votes to adjourn and resolutions not having the force of law.

Section 8. The Powers of Congress
Clause 1: Taxing. The Congress shall have Power to lay and collect Taxes, Duties, Imposts and Excises, to pay the Debts and provide for the common Defence and general Welfare of the United States; but all Duties, Imposts and Excises shall be uniform throughout the United States;

Duties *are taxes on imports and exports.* Impost *is a generic term for tax.* Excises *are taxes on the manufacture, sale, or use of goods.*

Clause 2: Borrowing. To borrow Money on the credit of the United States;

Congress has the power to borrow money, which is normally carried out through the sale of U.S. Treasury bonds on which interest is paid. Note that the Constitution places no limit on the amount of government borrowing.

Clause 3: Regulation of Commerce. To regulate Commerce with foreign Nations, and among the several States, and with the Indian Tribes;

This is the commerce clause, *which gives to Congress the power to regulate interstate and foreign trade. Much of the activity of Congress is based on this clause.*

Clause 4: Naturalization and Bankruptcy. To establish an uniform Rule of Naturalization, and uniform Laws on the subject of Bankruptcies throughout the United States;

Only Congress may determine how aliens can become citizens of the United States. Congress may make laws with respect to bankruptcy.

Clause 5: Money and Standards. To coin Money, regulate the Value thereof, and of foreign Coin, and fix the Standard of Weights and Measures;

Congress mints coins and prints and circulates paper money. Congress can establish uniform measures of time, distance, weight, and the like. In 1838, Congress adopted the English system of weights and measurements as our national standard.

Clause 6: Punishing Counterfeiters. To provide for the Punishment of counterfeiting the Securities and current Coin of the United States;

Congress has the power to punish those who copy American currency and pass it off as real. Currently, the penalty may be imprisonment for up to fifteen years plus fines.

Clause 7: Roads and Post Offices. To establish Post Offices and post Roads;

Post roads include all routes over which mail is carried—highways, railways, waterways, and airways.

Clause 8: Patents and Copyrights. To promote the Progress of Science and useful Arts, by securing for limited Times to Authors and Inventors the exclusive Right to their respective Writings and Discoveries;

Authors' and composers' works are protected by copyrights established by copyright law, which currently is the Copyright Act of 1976, as amended. Copyrights are valid for the life of the author or composer plus seventy years. Inventors' works are protected by patents, which vary in length of protection from fourteen to twenty years. A patent gives a person the exclusive right to control the manufacture or sale of her or his invention.

Clause 9: Lower Courts. To constitute Tribunals inferior to the supreme Court;

Congress has the authority to set up all federal courts, except the Supreme Court, and to decide what cases those courts will hear.

Clause 10: Punishment for Piracy. To define and punish Piracies and Felonies committed on the high Seas, and Offences against the Law of Nations;

Congress has the authority to prohibit the commission of certain acts outside U.S. territory and to punish certain violations of international law.

Clause 11: Declaration of War. To declare War, grant Letters of Marque and Reprisal, and make Rules concerning Captures on Land and Water;

Only Congress can declare war, although the president, as commander in chief, can make war without Congress's formal declaration. Letters of marque and reprisal authorized private parties to capture and destroy enemy ships in wartime. Since the middle of the nineteenth century, international law has prohibited letters of marque and reprisal, and the United States has honored the ban.

Clause 12: The Army. To raise and support Armies, but no Appropriation of Money to that Use shall be for a longer Term than two Years;

Congress has the power to create an army; the funds used to pay for it must be appropriated for no more than two-year intervals. This latter restriction gives ultimate control of the army to civilians.

Clause 13: Creation of a Navy. To provide and maintain a Navy;

This clause allows for the maintenance of a navy. In 1947, Congress created the U.S. Air Force.

Clause 14: Regulation of the Armed Forces. To make Rules for the Government and Regulation of the land and naval Forces;

Congress sets the rules for the military mainly by way of the Uniform Code of Military Justice, which was enacted in 1950 by Congress.

Clause 15: The Militia. To provide for calling forth the Militia to execute the Laws of the Union, suppress Insurrections and repel Invasions;

The militia is known today as the National Guard. *Both Congress and the president have the authority to call the National Guard into federal service.*

Clause 16: How the Militia Is Organized. To provide for organizing, arming, and disciplining the Militia, and for governing such Part of them as may be employed in the Service of the United States, reserving to the States respectively, the Appointment of the Officers, and the Authority of training the Militia according to the discipline prescribed by Congress;

This clause gives Congress the power to "federalize" state militia (National Guard). When called into such service, the National Guard is subject to the same rules that Congress has set forth for the regular armed services.

Clause 17: Creation of the District of Columbia. To exercise exclusive Legislation in all Cases whatsoever, over such District (not exceeding ten Miles square) as may, by Cession of particular States, and the Acceptance of Congress, become the Seat of the Government of the United States, and to exercise like Authority over all Places purchased by the Consent of the Legislature of the State in which the Same shall be, for the Erection of Forts, Magazines, Arsenals, dock-Yards, and other needful Buildings;—And

Congress established the District of Columbia as the national capital in 1791. Virginia and Maryland had granted land for the District, but Virginia's grant was returned because it was believed it would not be needed. Today, the District covers sixty-nine square miles.

Clause 18: The Elastic Clause. To make all Laws which shall be necessary and proper for carrying into Execution the foregoing Powers, and all other Powers vested by this Constitution in the Government of the United States, or in any Department or Officer thereof.

This clause—the necessary and proper clause, *or the* elastic clause—*grants no specific powers, and thus it can be stretched to fit different circumstances. It has allowed Congress to adapt the government to changing needs and times.*

Section 9. The Powers Denied to Congress
Clause 1: Question of Slavery. The Migration or Importation of such Persons as any of the States now existing shall think proper to admit, shall not be prohibited by the Congress prior to the Year one thousand eight hundred and eight, but a Tax or duty may be imposed on such Importation, not exceeding ten dollars for each Person.

"Persons" referred to slaves. Congress outlawed the slave trade in 1808.

Clause 2: Habeas Corpus. The privilege of the Writ of Habeas Corpus shall not be suspended, unless when in Cases of Rebellion or Invasion the public Safety may require it.

A writ of habeas corpus is a court order directing a sheriff or other public officer who is detaining another person to "produce the body" of the detainee so the court can assess the legality of the detention.

Clause 3: Special Bills. No Bill of Attainder or ex post facto Law shall be passed.

A bill of attainder is a law that inflicts punishment without a trial. An ex post facto law is a law that inflicts punishment for an act that was not illegal when it was committed.

Clause 4: Direct Taxes. [No Capitation, or other direct, Tax shall be laid, unless in Proportion to the Census or Enumeration herein before directed to be taken.][6]

A capitation is a tax on a person. A direct tax is a tax paid directly to the government, such as a property tax. This clause was intended to prevent Congress from levying a tax on slaves per person and thereby taxing slavery out of existence.

Clause 5: Export Taxes. No Tax or Duty shall be laid on Articles exported from any State.

Congress may not tax any goods sold from one state to another or from one state to a foreign country. (Congress does have the power to tax goods that are bought from other countries, however.)

Clause 6: Interstate Commerce. No Preference shall be given by any Regulation of Commerce or Revenue to the Ports of one State over those of another: nor shall Vessels bound to, or from, one State, be obliged to enter, clear, or pay Duties in another.

Congress may not treat different ports within the United States differently in terms of taxing and commerce powers. Congress may not give one state's port a legal advantage over the ports of another state.

Clause 7: Treasury Withdrawals. No Money shall be drawn from the Treasury, but in Consequence of Appropriations made by Law; and a regular Statement and Account of the Receipts and Expenditures of all public Money shall be published from time to time.

Federal funds can be spent only as Congress authorizes. This is a significant check on the president's power.

Clause 8: Titles of Nobility. No Title of Nobility shall be granted by the United States: And no Person holding any Office of Profit or Trust under them, shall, without the Consent of the Congress, accept of any present, Emolument, Office, or Title, of any kind whatever, from any King, Prince, or foreign State.

No person in the United States may hold a title of nobility, such as duke or duchess. This clause also discourages bribery of American officials by foreign governments.

Section 10. Those Powers Denied to the States
Clause 1: Treaties and Coinage. No State shall enter into any Treaty, Alliance, or Confederation; grant Letters of Marque and Reprisal; coin Money; emit Bills of Credit; make any Thing but gold and silver Coin a Tender in Payment of Debts; pass any Bill of Attainder, ex post facto Law, or Law impairing the Obligation of Contracts, or grant any Title of Nobility.

Prohibiting state laws "impairing the Obligation of Contracts" was intended to protect creditors. (Shays' Rebellion—an attempt to prevent courts from giving effect to creditors' legal actions against debtors—occurred only one year before the Constitution was written.)

---

6. Modified by the Sixteenth Amendment.

Clause 2: Duties and Imposts. No State shall, without the Consent of the Congress, lay any Imposts or Duties on Imports or Exports, except what may be absolutely necessary for executing its inspection Laws; and the net Produce of all Duties and Imposts, laid by any State on Imports or Exports, shall be for the Use of the Treasury of the United States; and all such Laws shall be subject to the Revision and Controul of the Congress.

Only Congress can tax imports. Further, the states cannot tax exports.

Clause 3: War. No State shall, without the Consent of Congress, lay any Duty of Tonnage, keep Troops, or Ships of War in time of Peace, enter into any Agreement or Compact with another State, or with a foreign Power or engage in War, unless actually invaded, or in such imminent Danger as will not admit of delay.

A duty of tonnage is a tax on ships according to their cargo capacity. No states may tax ships according to their cargo unless Congress agrees. Additionally, this clause forbids any state to keep troops or warships during peacetime or to make a compact with another state or foreign nation unless Congress so agrees. A state, in contrast, can maintain a militia, but its use has to be limited to disorders that occur within the state—unless, of course, the militia is called into federal service.

ARTICLE II. (Executive Branch)

Section 1. The Nature and Scope of Presidential Power

Clause 1: Four-Year Term. The executive Power shall be vested in a President of the United States of America. He shall hold his Office during the Term of four Years, and, together with the Vice President, chosen for the same Term, be elected, as follows.

The president has the power to carry out laws made by Congress, called the executive power. *He or she serves in office for a four-year term after election. The Twenty-second Amendment limits the number of times a person may be elected president.*

Clause 2: Choosing Electors from Each State. Each State shall appoint, in such Manner as the Legislature thereof may direct, a Number of Electors, equal to the whole Number of Senators and Representatives to which the State may be entitled in the Congress; but no Senator or Representative, or Person holding an Office of Trust or Profit under the United States, shall be appointed an Elector.

The "Electors" are known more commonly as the "electoral college." The president is elected by electors—that is, representatives chosen by the people—rather than by the people directly.

Clause 3: The Former System of Elections. [The Electors shall meet in their respective States, and vote by Ballot for two Persons, of whom one at least shall not be an Inhabitant of the same State with themselves. And they shall make a List of all the Persons voted for, and of the Number of Votes for each; which List they shall sign and certify, and transmit sealed to the Seat of the Government of the United States, directed to the President of the Senate. The President of the Senate shall, in the Presence of the Senate and House of Representatives, open all the Certificates, and the Votes shall then be counted. The Person having the greatest Number of Votes shall be the President, if such Number be a Majority of the whole Number of Electors appointed; and if there be more than one who have such Majority, and have an equal Number of Votes, then the House of Representatives shall immediately chuse by Ballot one of them for President; and if no Person have a Majority, then from the five highest on the List the said House shall in like Manner chuse the President. But in chusing the President, the Votes shall be taken by States, the Representation from each State having one Vote; A quorum for this Purpose shall consist of a Member or Members from two thirds of the States, and a Majority of all the States shall be necessary to a Choice. In every Case, after the Choice of the President, the Person having the greater Number of Votes of the Electors shall be the Vice President. But if there should remain two or more who have equal Votes, the Senate shall chuse from them by Ballot the Vice President.][7]

The original method of selecting the president and vice president was replaced by the Twelfth Amendment. Apparently, the framers did not anticipate the rise of political parties and the development of primaries and conventions.

Clause 4: The Time of Elections. The Congress may determine the Time of chusing the Electors, and the Day on which they shall give their Votes; which Day shall be the same throughout the United States.

Congress set the Tuesday after the first Monday in November every fourth year as the date for choosing electors. The electors cast their votes on the Monday after the second Wednesday in December of that year.

Clause 5: Qualifications for President. No person except a natural born Citizen, or a Citizen of the United States, at the time of the Adoption of this Constitution, shall be eligible to the Office of President; neither shall any Person be eligible to that Office who shall not have attained to the Age of thirty five Years, and been fourteen Years a Resident within the United States.

The president must be a natural-born citizen, be at least thirty-five years of age when taking office, and have been a resident within the United States for at least fourteen years.

Clause 6: Succession of the Vice President. [In Case of the Removal of the President from Office, or of his Death, Resignation or Inability to discharge the Powers and Duties of the said Office, the same shall devolve on the Vice President, and the Congress may by Law provide for the Case of Removal, Death, Resignation or Inability, both of the President and Vice President, declaring what Officer shall then act as President, and such Officer shall act accordingly, until the Disability be removed, or a President shall be elected.][8]

---

7. Changed by the Twelfth Amendment.
8. Modified by the Twenty-fifth Amendment.

This section provided for the method by which the vice president was to succeed to the presidency, but its wording is ambiguous. It was replaced by the Twenty-fifth Amendment.

Clause 7: The President's Salary. The President shall, at stated Times, receive for his Services, a Compensation, which shall neither be encreased nor diminished during the Period for which he shall have been elected, and he shall not receive within that Period any other Emolument from the United States, or any of them.

The president maintains the same salary during each four-year term. Moreover, she or he may not receive additional cash payments from the government. Originally set at $25,000 per year, the salary is currently $400,000 a year plus $169,000 in various expense accounts.

Clause 8: The Oath of Office. Before he enter on the Execution of his Office, he shall take the following Oath or Affirmation: "I do solemnly swear (or affirm) that I will faithfully execute the Office of President of the United States, and will to the best of my Ability, preserve, protect and defend the Constitution of the United States."

The president is "sworn in" prior to beginning the duties of the office. The taking of the oath of office occurs on January 20, following the November election. The ceremony is called the inauguration. *The oath of office is administered by the chief justice of the United States Supreme Court.*

Section 2. Powers of the President
Clause 1: Commander in Chief. The President shall be Commander in Chief of the Army and Navy of the United States, and of the Militia of the several States, when called into the actual Service of the United States; he may require the Opinion, in writing, of the principal Officer in each of the executive Departments, upon any Subject relating to the Duties of their respective Offices, and he shall have Power to grant Reprieves and Pardons for Offences against the United States, except in Cases of Impeachment.

The armed forces are placed under civilian control because the president is a civilian but still commander in chief of the military. The president may ask for the help of the head of each of the executive departments (thereby creating the cabinet). The cabinet members are chosen by the president with the consent of the Senate, but they can be removed without Senate approval.

The president's clemency powers extend only to federal cases. In those cases, he or she may grant a full or conditional pardon, or reduce a prison term or fine.

Clause 2: Treaties and Appointment. He shall have Power, by and with the Advice and Consent of the Senate, to make Treaties, provided two thirds of the Senators present concur; and he shall nominate, and by and with the Advice and Consent of the Senate, shall appoint Ambassadors, other public Ministers and Consuls, Judges of the supreme Court, and all other Officers of the United States, whose Appointments are not herein otherwise provided for, and which shall be established by Law; but the Congress may by Law vest the Appointment of such inferior Officers, as they think proper, in the President alone, in the Courts of Law, or in the Heads of Departments.

Many of the major powers of the president are identified in this clause, including the power to make treaties with foreign governments (with the approval of the Senate by a two-thirds vote) and the power to appoint ambassadors, Supreme Court justices, and other government officials. Most such appointments require Senate approval.

Clause 3: Vacancies. The President shall have Power to fill up all Vacancies that may happen during the Recess of the Senate, by granting Commissions which shall expire at the end of their next Session.

The president has the power to appoint temporary officials to fill vacant federal offices without Senate approval if the Congress is not in session. Such appointments expire automatically at the end of Congress's next term.

Section 3. Duties of the President
He shall from time to time give to the Congress Information of the State of the Union, and recommend to their Consideration such Measures as he shall judge necessary and expedient; he may, on extraordinary Occasions, convene both Houses, or either of them, and in Case of Disagreement between them, with Respect to the Time of Adjournment, he may adjourn them to such Time as he shall think proper; he shall receive Ambassadors and other public Ministers; he shall take Care that the Laws be faithfully executed, and shall Commission all the Officers of the United States.

Annually, the president reports on the state of the union to Congress, recommends legislative measures, and proposes a federal budget. The State of the Union speech is a statement not only to Congress but also to the American people. After it is given, the president proposes a federal budget and presents an economic report. At any time, the president may send special messages to Congress while it is in session. The president has the power to call special sessions, to adjourn Congress when its two chambers do not agree on when to adjourn, to receive diplomatic representatives of other governments, and to ensure the proper execution of all federal laws. The president further has the ability to empower federal officers to hold their positions and to perform their duties.

Section 4. Impeachment
The President, Vice President and all civil Officers of the United States, shall be removed from Office on Impeachment for, and Conviction of, Treason, Bribery, or other high Crimes and Misdemeanors.

Treason *denotes giving aid to the nation's enemies. The phrase* high crimes and misdemeanors *is usually considered to mean serious abuses of political power. In either case, the president or vice president may be accused by the House (called an* impeachment) *and then removed from office if convicted by the Senate. (Note that impeachment does not mean removal but rather refers to an accusation of treason or high crimes and misdemeanors.)*

ARTICLE III. (Judicial Branch)

Section 1. Judicial Powers, Courts, and Judges

The judicial Power of the United States, shall be vested in one supreme Court, and in such inferior Courts as the Congress may from time to time ordain and establish. The Judges, both of the supreme and inferior Courts, shall hold their Offices during good Behaviour, and shall, at stated Times, receive for their Services a Compensation, which shall not be diminished during their Continuance in Office.

The Supreme Court is vested with judicial power, as are the lower federal courts that Congress creates. Federal judges serve in their offices for life unless they are impeached and convicted by Congress. The payment of federal judges may not be reduced during their time in office.

Section 2. Jurisdiction

Clause 1: Cases under Federal Jurisdiction. The judicial Power shall extend to all Cases, in Law and Equity, arising under this Constitution, the Laws of the United States, and Treaties made, or which shall be made, under their Authority;—to all Cases affecting Ambassadors, other public Ministers and Consuls;—to all Cases of admiralty and maritime Jurisdiction;—to Controversies to which the United States shall be a Party;—to Controversies between two or more States; [—between a State and Citizens of another State;—][9] between Citizens of different States;—between Citizens of the same State claiming Lands under Grants of different States, [and between a State, or the Citizens thereof, and foreign States, Citizens or Subjects.][10]

The federal courts take on cases that concern the meaning of the U.S. Constitution, all federal laws, and treaties. They also can take on cases involving citizens of different states and citizens of foreign nations.

Clause 2: Cases for the Supreme Court. In all Cases affecting Ambassadors, other public Ministers and Consuls, and those in which a State shall be a Party, the supreme Court shall have original Jurisdiction. In all the other Cases before mentioned, the supreme Court shall have appellate Jurisdiction, both as to Law and Fact, with such Exceptions, and under such Regulations as the Congress shall make.

In a limited number of situations, the Supreme Court acts as a trial court and has original jurisdiction. These cases involve a representative from another country or involve a state. In all other situations, the cases must first be tried in the lower courts and then can be appealed to the Supreme Court. Congress may, however, make exceptions. Today, the Supreme Court acts as a trial court of first instance on rare occasions.

Clause 3: The Conduct of Trials. The Trial of all Crimes, except in Cases of Impeachment, shall be by Jury; and such Trial shall be held in the State where the said Crimes shall have been committed; but when not committed within any State, the Trial shall be at such Place or Places as the Congress may by Law have directed.

Any person accused of a federal crime is granted the right to a trial by jury in a federal court in that state in which the crime was committed. Trials of impeachment are an exception.

Section 3. Treason

Clause 1: The Definition of Treason. Treason against the United States, shall consist only in levying War against them, or, in adhering to their Enemies, giving them Aid and Comfort. No Person shall be convicted of Treason unless on the Testimony of two Witnesses to the same overt Act, or on Confession in open Court.

Treason is the making of war against the United States or giving aid to its enemies.

Clause 2: Punishment. The Congress shall have Power to declare the Punishment of Treason, but no Attainder of Treason shall work Corruption of Blood, or Forfeiture except during the Life of the Person attainted.

Congress has provided that the punishment for treason ranges from a minimum of five years in prison and/or a $10,000 fine to a maximum of death. "No Attainder of Treason shall work Corruption of Blood" prohibits punishment of the traitor's heirs.

ARTICLE IV. (Relations among the States)

Section 1. Full Faith and Credit

Full Faith and Credit shall be given in each State to the public Acts, Records, and judicial Proceedings of every other State. And the Congress may by general Laws prescribe the Manner in which such Acts, Records and Proceedings shall be proved, and the Effect thereof.

All states are required to respect one another's laws, records, and lawful decisions. There are exceptions, however. A state does not have to enforce another state's criminal code. Nor does it have to recognize another state's grant of a divorce if the person obtaining the divorce did not establish legal residence in the state in which it was given.

Section 2. Treatment of Citizens

Clause 1: Privileges and Immunities. The Citizens of each State shall be entitled to all Privileges and Immunities of Citizens in the several States.

A citizen of a state has the same rights and privileges as the citizens of another state in which he or she happens to be.

Clause 2: Extradition. A Person charged in any State with Treason, Felony, or other Crime, who shall flee from Justice, and be found in another State, shall on Demand of the executive Authority of the State from which he fled, be delivered up, to be removed to the State having Jurisdiction of the Crime.

Any person accused of a crime who flees to another state must be returned to the state in which the crime occurred.

---

9. Modified by the Eleventh Amendment.
10. Modified by the Eleventh Amendment.

Clause 3: Fugitive Slaves. [No Person held to Service or Labour in one State, under the Laws thereof, escaping into another, shall, in Consequence of any Law or Regulation therein, be discharged from such Service or Labour, but shall be delivered up on Claim of the Party to whom such Service or Labour may be due.][11]

This clause was struck down by the Thirteenth Amendment, which abolished slavery in 1865.

Section 3. Admission of States

Clause 1: The Process. New States may be admitted by the Congress into this Union; but no new State shall be formed or erected within the Jurisdiction of any other State; nor any State be formed by the Junction of two or more States, or Parts of States, without the Consent of the Legislatures of the States concerned as well as of the Congress.

Only Congress has the power to admit new states to the Union. No state may be created by taking territory from an existing state unless the state's legislature so consents.

Clause 2: Public Land. The Congress shall have Power to dispose of and make all needful Rules and Regulations respecting the Territory or other Property belonging to the United States; and nothing in this Constitution shall be so construed as to Prejudice any Claims of the United States, or of any particular State.

The federal government has the exclusive right to administer federal government public lands.

Section 4. Republican Form of Government

The United States shall guarantee to every State in this Union a Republican Form of Government, and shall protect each of them against Invasion; and on Application of the Legislature, or of the Executive (when the Legislature cannot be convened) against domestic Violence.

Each state is promised a republican form of government—that is, one in which the people elect their representatives. The federal government is bound to protect states against any attack by foreigners or during times of trouble within a state.

ARTICLE V. (Methods of Amendment)

The Congress, whenever two thirds of both Houses shall deem it necessary, shall propose Amendments to this Constitution, or on the Application of the Legislatures of two thirds of the several States, shall call a Convention for proposing Amendments, which, in either Case, shall be valid to all Intents and Purposes, as Part of this Constitution, when ratified by the Legislatures of three fourths of the several States, or by Conventions in three fourths thereof, as the one or the other Mode of Ratification may be proposed by the Congress; Provided that no Amendment which may be made prior to the Year One thousand eight hundred and eight shall in any Manner affect the first and fourth Clauses in the Ninth Section of the First Article; and that no State, without its Consent, shall be deprived of its equal Suffrage in the Senate.

Amendments may be proposed in either of two ways: by a two-thirds vote of each chamber (Congress) or at the request of two-thirds of the states. Ratification of amendments may be carried out in two ways: by the legislatures of three-fourths of the states or by the voters in three-fourths of the states. No state may be denied equal representation in the Senate.

ARTICLE VI. (National Supremacy)

Clause 1: Existing Obligations. All Debts contracted and Engagements entered into, before the Adoption of this Constitution shall be as valid against the United States under this Constitution, as under the Confederation.

During the Revolutionary War and the years of the Confederation, Congress borrowed large sums. This clause pledged that the new federal government would assume those financial obligations.

Clause 2: Supreme Law of the Land. This Constitution, and the Laws of the United States which shall be made in Pursuance thereof; and all Treaties made, or which shall be made, under the Authority of the United States, shall be the supreme Law of the Land; and the Judges in every State shall be bound thereby, any Thing in the Constitution or Laws of any State to the Contrary notwithstanding.

This is typically called the supremacy clause; *it declares that federal law takes precedence over all forms of state law. No government at the local or state level may make or enforce any law that conflicts with any provision of the Constitution, acts of Congress, treaties, or other rules and regulations issued by the president and his or her subordinates in the executive branch of the federal government.*

Clause 3: Oath of Office. The Senators and Representatives before mentioned, and the Members of the several State Legislatures, and all executive and judicial Officers, both of the United States and of the several States, shall be bound by Oath or Affirmation, to support this Constitution; but no religious Test shall ever be required as a Qualification to any Office or public Trust under the United States.

Every federal and state official must take an oath of office promising to support the U.S. Constitution. Religion may not be used as a qualification to serve in any federal office.

ARTICLE VII. (Ratification)

The Ratification of the Conventions of nine States shall be sufficient for the Establishment of this Constitution between the States so ratifying the Same.

Nine states were required to ratify the Constitution. Delaware was the first and New Hampshire the ninth.

---

11. Repealed by the Thirteenth Amendment.

Done in Convention by the Unanimous Consent of the States present the Seventeenth Day of September in the Year of our Lord one thousand seven hundred and Eighty seven and of the Independence of the United States of America the Twelfth. In witness whereof we have hereunto subscribed our Names,

Go. WASHINGTON
Presid't.
and deputy from Virginia

Attest William Jackson Secretary

DELAWARE
- Geo. Read
- Gunning Bedford jun
- John Dickinson
- Richard Bassett
- Jaco. Broom

MARYLAND
- James McHenry
- Dan of St. Thos. Jenifer
- Danl. Carroll

VIRGINIA
- John Blair
- James Madison Jr.

NORTH CAROLINA
- Wm. Blount
- Richd. Dobbs Spaight
- Hu. Williamson

SOUTH CAROLINA
- J. Rutledge
- Charles Cotesworth Pinckney
- Charles Pinckney
- Pierce Butler

GEORGIA
- William Few
- Abr. Baldwin

NEW HAMPSHIRE
- John Langdon
- Nicholas Gilman

MASSACHUSETTS
- Nathaniel Gorham
- Rufus King

CONNECTICUT
- Wm. Saml. Johnson
- Roger Sherman

NEW YORK
- Alexander Hamilton

NEW JERSEY
- Wh. Livingston
- David Brearley
- Wm. Paterson
- Jona. Dayton

PENNSYLVANIA
- B. Franklin
- Thomas Mifflin
- Robt. Morris
- Geo. Clymer
- Thos. FitzSimons
- Jared Ingersoll
- James Wilson
- Gouv. Morris

AMENDMENTS TO THE CONSTITUTION OF THE UNITED STATES[12]

AMENDMENT I.
(Religion, Speech, Assembly, and Petition)

Congress shall make no law respecting an establishment of religion, or prohibiting the free exercise thereof; or abridging the freedom of speech, or of the press; or the right of the people peaceably to assemble, and to petition the Government for a redress of grievances.

Congress may not create an official church or enact laws limiting the freedom of religion, speech, the press, assembly, and petition. These guarantees, like the others in the Bill of Rights (the first ten amendments), are not absolute—each may be exercised only with regard to the rights of other persons.

AMENDMENT II.
(Militia and the Right to Bear Arms)

A well regulated Militia, being necessary to the security of a free State, the right of the people to keep and bear Arms, shall not be infringed.

To protect itself, each state has the right to maintain a volunteer armed force. States and the federal government may regulate but not completely ban the possession and use of firearms by individuals.

AMENDMENT III.
(The Quartering of Soldiers)

No Soldier shall, in time of peace be quartered in any house, without the consent of the Owner, nor in time of war, but in a manner to be prescribed by law.

Before the Revolutionary War, it had been common British practice to quarter soldiers in colonists' homes. Military troops do not have the power to take over private houses during peacetime.

AMENDMENT IV.
(Searches and Seizures)

The right of the people to be secure in their persons, houses, papers, and effects, against unreasonable searches and seizures, shall not be violated, and no Warrants shall issue, but upon probable cause, supported by Oath or affirmation, and particularly describing the place to be searched, and the persons or things to be seized.

Here the word warrant means "justification" and refers to a document issued by a magistrate or judge indicating the name, address, and possible offense committed. Anyone asking for the warrant, such as a police officer, must be able to convince the magistrate or judge that an offense probably has been committed.

AMENDMENT V.
(Grand Juries, Self-Incrimination, Double Jeopardy, Due Process, and Eminent Domain)

No person shall be held to answer for a capital, or otherwise infamous crime, unless on a presentment or indictment of a Grand Jury, except in cases arising in the land or naval forces, or in the Militia, when in actual service in time of War or public danger; nor shall any person be subject for the same offence to be twice put in jeopardy of life or limb; nor shall be compelled in any criminal case to be a witness against himself, nor be deprived of life, liberty, or property, without due process of law; nor shall private property be taken for public use, without just compensation.

There are two types of juries. A grand jury considers physical evidence and the testimony of witnesses and decides whether there is sufficient reason to bring a case to trial. A petit jury hears the case at trial and decides it. "For the same offence to be twice put in jeopardy of life or limb" means to be tried twice for the same crime. A person may not be tried for the same crime twice or forced to give evidence against herself or himself. No person's right to life, liberty, or property may be taken away except by lawful means, called the due process of law. Private property taken for public use must be paid for by the government.

AMENDMENT VI.
(Criminal Court Procedures)

In all criminal prosecutions, the accused shall enjoy the right to a speedy and public trial, by an impartial jury of the State and district wherein the crime shall have been committed, which district shall have been previously ascertained by law, and to be informed of the nature and cause of the accusation; to be confronted with the witnesses against him; to have compulsory process for obtaining witnesses in his favor, and to have the Assistance of Counsel for his defence.

Any person accused of a crime has the right to a fair and public trial by a jury in the state in which the crime took place. The charges against that person must be indicated. Any accused person has the right to a lawyer to defend him or her and to question those who testify against him or her, as well as the right to call people to speak in his or her favor at trial.

AMENDMENT VII.
(Trial by Jury in Civil Cases)

In Suits at common law, where the value in controversy shall exceed twenty dollars, the right of trial by jury shall be preserved, and no fact tried by jury, shall be otherwise re-examined in any Court of the United States, than according to the rules of the common law.

A jury trial may be requested by either party in a dispute in any case involving more than $20. If both parties agree to a trial by a judge without a jury, the right to a jury trial may be put aside.

---

12. On September 25, 1789, Congress transmitted to the state legislatures twelve proposed amendments, two of which, having to do with congressional representation and congressional pay, were not adopted. The remaining ten amendments became the Bill of Rights. In 1992, the amendment concerning congressional pay was adopted as the Twenty-seventh Amendment.

AMENDMENT VIII.
(Bail, Cruel and Unusual Punishment)

Excessive bail shall not be required, nor excessive fines imposed, nor cruel and unusual punishments inflicted.

Bail is an amount of money that a person accused of a crime may be required to deposit with the court as a guaranty that she or he will appear in court when requested. The amount of bail required or the fine imposed as punishment for a crime must be reasonable compared with the seriousness of the crime involved. Any punishment judged to be too harsh or too severe for a crime is prohibited.

AMENDMENT IX.
(The Rights Retained by the People)

The enumeration in the Constitution, of certain rights, shall not be construed to deny or disparage others retained by the people.

Many civil rights that are not explicitly enumerated in the Constitution are still held by the people.

AMENDMENT X.
(Reserved Powers of the States)

The powers not delegated to the United States by the Constitution, nor prohibited by it to the States, are reserved to the States respectively, or to the people.

Those powers not delegated by the Constitution to the federal government or expressly denied to the states belong to the states and to the people. This amendment in essence allows the states to pass laws under their "police powers."

AMENDMENT XI.
(Ratified on February 7, 1795—
Suits against States)

The Judicial power of the United States shall not be construed to extend to any suit in law or equity, commenced or prosecuted against one of the United States by Citizens of another State, or by Citizens or Subjects of any Foreign State.

This amendment has been interpreted to mean that a state cannot be sued in federal court by one of its own citizens, by a citizen of another state, or by a foreign country.

AMENDMENT XII.
(Ratified on June 15, 1804—
Election of the President)

The Electors shall meet in their respective states, and vote by ballot for President and Vice-President, one of whom, at least, shall not be an inhabitant of the same State with themselves; they shall name in their ballots the person voted for as President, and in distinct ballots the person voted for as Vice-President, and they shall make distinct lists of all persons voted for as President, and of all persons voted for as Vice-President, and of the number of votes for each, which lists they shall sign and certify, and transmit sealed to the seat of the government of the United States, directed to the President of the Senate;—The President of the Senate shall, in the presence of the Senate and House of Representatives, open all the certificates and the votes shall then be counted;—The person having the greatest number of votes for President, shall be the President, if such number be a majority of the whole number of Electors appointed; and if no person have such majority, then from the persons having the highest numbers not exceeding three on the list of those voted for as President, the House of Representatives shall choose immediately, by ballot, the President. But in choosing the President, the votes shall be taken by States, the representation from each State having one vote; a quorum for this purpose shall consist of a member or members from two-thirds of the States, and a majority of all States shall be necessary to a choice. [And if the House of Representatives shall not choose a President whenever the right of choice shall devolve upon them, before the fourth day of March next following, then the Vice-President shall act as President, as in the case of the death or other constitutional disability of the President.][13]—The person having the greatest number of votes as Vice-President, shall be the Vice-President, if such number be a majority of the whole number of Electors appointed, and if no person have a majority, then from the two highest numbers on the list, the Senate shall choose the Vice-President; a quorum for the purpose shall consist of two-thirds of the whole number of Senators, and a majority of the whole number shall be necessary to a choice. But no person constitutionally ineligible to the office of President shall be eligible to that of Vice-President of the United States.

The original procedure set out for the election of president and vice president in Article II, Section 1, resulted in a tie in 1800 between Thomas Jefferson and Aaron Burr. It was not until the next year that the House of Representatives chose Jefferson to be president. This amendment changed the procedure by providing for separate ballots for president and vice president.

AMENDMENT XIII.
(Ratified on December 6, 1865—
Prohibition of Slavery)

Section 1.

Neither slavery nor involuntary servitude, except as a punishment for crime whereof the party shall have been duly convicted, shall exist within the United States, or any place subject to their jurisdiction.

Some slaves had been freed during the Civil War. This amendment freed the others and abolished slavery.

Section 2.

Congress shall have power to enforce this article by appropriate legislation.

---

13. Changed by the Twentieth Amendment.

AMENDMENT XIV.
(Ratified on July 9, 1868—
Citizenship, Due Process, and
Equal Protection of the Laws)

Section 1.
All persons born or naturalized in the United States, and subject to the jurisdiction thereof, are citizens of the United States and of the State wherein they reside. No State shall make or enforce any law which shall abridge the privileges or immunities of citizens of the United States; nor shall any State deprive any person of life, liberty, or property, without due process of law; nor deny to any person within its jurisdiction the equal protection of the laws.

Under this provision, states cannot make or enforce laws that take away rights given to all citizens by the federal government. States cannot act unfairly or arbitrarily toward, or discriminate against, any person.

Section 2.
Representatives shall be apportioned among the several States according to their respective numbers, counting the whole number of persons in each State, excluding Indians not taxed. But when the right to vote at any election for the choice of electors for President and Vice President of the United States, Representatives in Congress, the Executive and Judicial officers of a State, or the members of the Legislature thereof, is denied to any of the male inhabitants of such State, being [twenty-one][14] years of age, and citizens of the United States, or in any way abridged, except for participation in rebellion, or other crime, the basis of representation therein shall be reduced in the proportion which the number of such male citizens shall bear to the whole number of male citizens twenty-one years of age in such State.

Section 3.
No person shall be a Senator or Representative in Congress, or elector of President and Vice President, or hold any office, civil or military, under the United States, or under any State, who having previously taken an oath, as a member of Congress, or as an officer of the United States, or as a member of any State legislature, or as an executive or judicial officer of any State, to support the Constitution of the United States, shall have engaged in insurrection or rebellion against the same, or given aid or comfort to the enemies thereof. But Congress may by a vote of two-thirds of each House, remove such disability.

This provision forbade former state or federal government officials who had acted in support of the Confederacy during the Civil War to hold office again. It limited the president's power to pardon those persons. Congress removed this "disability" in 1898.

Section 4.
The validity of the public debt of the United States, authorized by law, including debts incurred for payment of pensions and bounties for services in suppressing insurrection or rebellion, shall not be questioned. But neither the United States nor any State shall assume or pay any debt or obligation incurred in aid of insurrection or rebellion against the United States, or any claim for the loss or emancipation of any slave, but all such debts, obligations and claims shall be held illegal and void.

Section 5.
The Congress shall have power to enforce, by appropriate legislation, the provisions of this article.

AMENDMENT XV.
(Ratified on February 3, 1870—
The Right to Vote)

Section 1.
The right of citizens of the United States to vote shall not be denied or abridged by the United States or by any State on account of race, color, or previous condition of servitude.

No citizen can be refused the right to vote simply because of race or color or because that person was once a slave.

Section 2.
The Congress shall have power to enforce this article by appropriate legislation.

AMENDMENT XVI.
(Ratified on February 3, 1913—Income Taxes)

The Congress shall have power to lay and collect taxes on incomes, from whatever source derived, without apportionment among the several States, and without regard to any census or enumeration.

This amendment allows Congress to tax income without sharing the revenue so obtained with the states according to their population.

AMENDMENT XVII.
(Ratified on April 8, 1913—
The Popular Election of Senators)

Section 1.
The Senate of the United States shall be composed of two Senators from each State, elected by the people thereof, for six years; and each Senator shall have one vote. The electors in each State shall have the qualifications requisite for electors of the most numerous branch of the State legislatures.

Section 2.
When vacancies happen in the representation of any State in the Senate, the executive authority of such State shall issue writs of election to fill such vacancies: *Provided,* That the legislature of any State may empower the executive thereof to make temporary appointments until the people fill the vacancies by election as the legislature may direct.

Section 3.
This amendment shall not be so construed as to affect the election or term of any Senator chosen before it becomes valid as part of the Constitution.

---

14. Changed by the Twenty-sixth Amendment.

This amendment modified portions of Article I, Section 3, that related to election of senators. Senators are now elected by the voters in each state directly. When a vacancy occurs, either the state may fill the vacancy by a special election, or the governor of the state involved may appoint someone to fill the seat until the next election.

AMENDMENT XVIII.
(Ratified on January 16, 1919—Prohibition)

Section 1.
After one year from the ratification of this article the manufacture, sale, or transportation of intoxicating liquors within, the importation thereof into, or the exportation thereof from the United States and all territory subject to the jurisdiction thereof for beverage purposes is hereby prohibited.

Section 2.
The Congress and the several States shall have concurrent power to enforce this article by appropriate legislation.

Section 3.
This article shall be inoperative unless it shall have been ratified as an amendment to the Constitution by the legislatures of the several States, as provided in the Constitution, within seven years from the date of the submission hereof to the States by the Congress.[15]

This amendment made it illegal to manufacture, sell, and transport alcoholic beverages in the United States. It was repealed by the Twenty-first Amendment.

AMENDMENT XIX.
(Ratified on August 18, 1920—Women's Right to Vote)

Section 1.
The right of citizens of the United States to vote shall not be denied or abridged by the United States or by any State on account of sex.

Section 2.
Congress shall have power to enforce this article by appropriate legislation.

Women were given the right to vote by this amendment, and Congress was given the power to enforce this right.

AMENDMENT XX.
(Ratified on January 23, 1933— The Lame Duck Amendment)

Section 1.
The terms of the President and Vice President shall end at noon on the 20th day of January, and the terms of Senators and Representatives at noon on the 3d day of January, of the years in which such terms would have ended if this article had not been ratified; and the terms of their successors shall then begin.

This amendment modified Article I, Section 4, Clause 2, and other provisions relating to the president in the Twelfth Amendment. The taking of the oath of office was moved from March 4 to January 20.

Section 2.
The Congress shall assemble at least once in every year, and such meeting shall begin at noon on the 3d day of January, unless they shall by law appoint a different day.

Congress changed the beginning of its term to January 3. The reason the Twentieth Amendment is called the Lame Duck Amendment is that it shortens the time between when a member of Congress is defeated for reelection and when he or she leaves office.

Section 3.
If, at the time fixed for the beginning of the term of the President, the President elect shall have died, the Vice President elect shall become President. If a President shall not have been chosen before the time fixed for the beginning of his term, or if the President elect shall have failed to qualify, then the Vice President elect shall act as President until a President shall have qualified; and the Congress may by law provide for the case wherein neither a President elect nor a Vice President elect shall have qualified, declaring who shall then act as President, or the manner in which one who is to act shall be selected, and such person shall act accordingly until a President or Vice President shall have qualified.

This part of the amendment deals with problem areas left ambiguous by Article II and the Twelfth Amendment. If the president dies before January 20 or fails to qualify for office, the presidency is to be filled as described in this section.

Section 4.
The Congress may by law provide for the case of the death of any of the persons from whom the House of Representatives may choose a President whenever the right of choice shall have devolved upon them, and for the case of the death of any of the persons from whom the Senate may choose a Vice President whenever the right of choice shall have devolved upon them.

Congress has never created legislation pursuant to this section.

Section 5.
Sections 1 and 2 shall take effect on the 15th day of October following the ratification of this article.

Section 6.
This article shall be inoperative unless it shall have been ratified as an amendment to the Constitution by the legislatures of three-fourths of the several States within seven years from the date of its submission.

AMENDMENT XXI.
(Ratified on December 5, 1933— The Repeal of Prohibition)

Section 1.
The eighteenth article of amendment to the Constitution of the United States is hereby repealed.

---

15. The Eighteenth Amendment was repealed by the Twenty-first Amendment.

Section 2.
The transportation or importation into any State, Territory, or possession of the United States for delivery or use therein of intoxicating liquors, in violation of the laws thereof, is hereby prohibited.

Section 3.
This article shall be inoperative unless it shall have been ratified as an amendment to the Constitution by conventions in the several States, as provided in the Constitution, within seven years from the date of the submission hereof to the States by the Congress.

The amendment repealed the Eighteenth Amendment but did not make alcoholic beverages legal everywhere. Rather, they remained illegal in any state that so designated them. Many such "dry" states existed for a number of years after 1933. Today, there are still "dry" counties within the United States, in which the sale of alcoholic beverages is illegal.

AMENDMENT XXII.
(Ratified on February 27, 1951— Limitation of Presidential Terms)

Section 1.
No person shall be elected to the office of the President more than twice, and no person who has held the office of President, or acted as President, for more than two years of a term to which some other person was elected President shall be elected to the office of President more than once. But this Article shall not apply to any person holding the office of President when this Article was proposed by the Congress, and shall not prevent any person who may be holding the office of President, or acting as President, during the term within which this Article becomes operative from holding the office of President or acting as President during the remainder of such term.

Section 2.
This article shall be inoperative unless it shall have been ratified as an amendment to the Constitution by the legislatures of three-fourths of the several States within seven years from the date of its submission to the States by the Congress.

No president may serve more than two elected terms. If, however, a president has succeeded to the office after the halfway point of a term in which another president was originally elected, then that president may serve for more than eight years, but not to exceed ten years.

AMENDMENT XXIII.
(Ratified on March 29, 1961— Presidential Electors for the District of Columbia)

Section 1.
The District constituting the seat of Government of the United States shall appoint in such manner as the Congress may direct:

A number of electors of President and Vice President equal to the whole number of Senators and Representatives in Congress to which the District would be entitled if it were a State, but in no event more than the least populous State; they shall be in addition to those appointed by the States, but they shall be considered, for the purposes of the election of President and Vice President, to be electors appointed by a State; and they shall meet in the District and perform such duties as provided by the twelfth article of amendment.

Section 2.
The Congress shall have power to enforce this article by appropriate legislation.

Citizens living in the District of Columbia have the right to vote in elections for president and vice president. The District of Columbia has three presidential electors, whereas before this amendment it had none.

AMENDMENT XXIV.
(Ratified on January 23, 1964— The Anti–Poll Tax Amendment)

Section 1.
The right of citizens of the United States to vote in any primary or other election for President or Vice President, for electors for President or Vice President, or for Senator or Representative in Congress, shall not be denied or abridged by the United States, or any State by reason of failure to pay any poll tax or other tax.

Section 2.
The Congress shall have power to enforce this article by appropriate legislation.

No government shall require a person to pay a poll tax to vote in any federal election.

AMENDMENT XXV.
(Ratified on February 10, 1967—Presidential Disability and Vice-Presidential Vacancies)

Section 1.
In case of the removal of the President from office or of his death or resignation, the Vice President shall become President.

Whenever a president dies or resigns from office, the vice president becomes president.

Section 2.
Whenever there is a vacancy in the office of the Vice President, the President shall nominate a Vice President who shall take office upon confirmation by a majority vote of both Houses of Congress.

Whenever the office of the vice presidency becomes vacant, the president may appoint someone to fill this office, provided Congress consents.

Section 3.
Whenever the President transmits to the President pro tempore of the Senate and the Speaker of the House of Representatives his written declaration that he is unable to discharge the powers and duties of his office, and until he transmits to them a written

declaration to the contrary, such powers and duties shall be discharged by the Vice President as Acting President.

Whenever the president believes she or he is unable to carry out the duties of the office, she or he shall so indicate to Congress in writing. The vice president then acts as president until the president declares that she or he is again able to carry out the duties of the office.

Section 4.

Whenever the Vice President and a majority of either the principal officers of the executive departments or of such other body as Congress may by law provide, transmit to the President pro tempore of the Senate and the Speaker of the House of Representatives their written declaration that the President is unable to discharge the powers and duties of his office, the Vice President shall immediately assume the powers and duties of the office as Acting President.

Thereafter, when the President transmits to the President pro tempore of the Senate and the Speaker of the House of Representatives his written declaration that no inability exists, he shall resume the powers and duties of his office unless the Vice President and a majority of either the principal officers of the executive department or of such other body as Congress may by law provide, transmit within four days to the President pro tempore of the Senate and the Speaker of the House of Representatives their written declaration that the President is unable to discharge the powers and duties of his office. Thereupon Congress shall decide the issue, assembling within forty-eight hours for that purpose if not in session. If the Congress, within twenty-one days after receipt of the latter written declaration, or, if Congress is not in session, within twenty-one days after Congress is required to assemble, determines by two-thirds vote of both Houses that the President is unable to discharge the powers and duties of his office, the Vice President shall continue to discharge the same as Acting President; otherwise, the President shall resume the powers and duties of his office.

Whenever the vice president and a majority of the members of the cabinet believe that the president cannot carry out her or his duties, they shall so indicate in writing to Congress. The vice president shall then act as president. When the president believes that she or he is able to carry out her or his duties again, she or he shall so indicate to the Congress. However, if the vice president and a majority of the cabinet do not agree, Congress must decide by a two-thirds vote within three weeks who shall act as president.

AMENDMENT XXVI.
(Ratified on July 1, 1971—
The Eighteen-Year-Old Vote)

Section 1.

The right of citizens of the United States, who are eighteen years of age or older, to vote shall not be denied or abridged by the United States or by any State on account of age.

No one over eighteen years of age can be denied the right to vote in federal or state elections by virtue of age.

Section 2.

The Congress shall have power to enforce this article by appropriate legislation.

AMENDMENT XXVII.
(Ratified on May 7, 1992—Congressional Pay)

No law, varying the compensation for the services of the Senators and Representatives, shall take effect, until an election of representatives shall have intervened.

This amendment allows the voters to have some control over increases in salaries for congressional members. Originally submitted to the states for ratification in 1789, it was not ratified until 203 years later, in 1992.

APPENDIX C

Federalist Papers, Nos. 10, 51, & 78

In 1787, after the newly drafted U.S. Constitution was submitted to the thirteen states for ratification, a major political debate ensued between the Federalists (who favored ratification) and the Anti-Federalists (who opposed ratification). Anti-Federalists in New York were particularly critical of the Constitution, and in response to their objections, Federalists Alexander Hamilton, James Madison, and John Jay wrote a series of eighty-five essays in defense of the Constitution. The essays were published in New York newspapers and reprinted in other newspapers throughout the country.

For students of American government, the essays, collectively known as the Federalist Papers, are particularly important because they provide a glimpse of the founders' political philosophy and intentions in designing the Constitution—and, consequently, in shaping the American philosophy of government.

We have included in this appendix three of these essays: Federalist Papers Nos. 10, 51, and 78. Each essay has been annotated by the authors to indicate its importance in American political thought and to clarify the meaning of particular passages.

Federalist Paper No. 10

Federalist Paper No. 10, penned by James Madison, has often been singled out as a key document in American political thought. In this essay, Madison attacks the Anti-Federalists' fear that a republican form of government will inevitably give rise to "factions"—small political parties or groups united by a common interest—that will control the government. Factions will be harmful to the country because they will implement policies beneficial to their own interests but adverse to other people's rights and to the public good. In this essay, Madison attempts to lay to rest this fear by explaining how, in a large republic such as the United States, there will be so many different factions, held together by regional or local interests, that no single one of them will dominate national politics.

Madison opens his essay with a paragraph discussing how important it is to devise a plan of government that can control the "instability, injustice, and confusion" brought about by factions.

Among the numerous advantages promised by a well-constructed Union, none deserves to be more accurately developed than its tendency to break and control the violence of faction. The friend of popular governments never finds himself so much alarmed for their character and fate as when he contemplates their propensity to this dangerous vice. He will not fail, therefore, to set a due value on any plan which, without violating the principles to which he is attached, provides a proper cure for it. The instability, injustice, and confusion introduced into the public councils have, in truth, been the mortal diseases under which popular governments have everywhere perished, as they continue to be the favorite and fruitful topics from which the adversaries to liberty derive their most specious declamations. The valuable improvements made by the American constitutions on the popular models, both ancient and modern, cannot certainly be too much admired; but it would be an unwarrantable partiality to contend that they have as effectually obviated the danger on this side, as was wished and expected. Complaints are everywhere heard from our most considerate and virtuous citizens, equally the friends of public and private faith and of public and personal liberty, that our governments are too unstable, that the public good is disregarded in the conflicts of rival parties, and that measures are too often decided, not according to the rules of justice and the rights of the minor party, but by the superior force of an interested and overbearing majority. However anxiously we may wish that these complaints had no foundation, the evidence of known facts will not permit us to deny that they are in some degree true. It will be found, indeed, on a candid review of our situation, that some of the distresses under which we labor have been erroneously charged on the operation of our governments; but it will be found, at the same time, that other causes will not alone account for many of our heaviest misfortunes; and, particularly, for that prevailing and increasing distrust of public engagements and alarm for private rights which are echoed from one end of the continent to the other. These must be chiefly, if not wholly, effects of the unsteadiness and injustice with which a factious spirit has tainted our public administration.

Madison now defines what he means by the term faction.

By a faction I understand a number of citizens, whether amounting to a majority or minority of the whole, who are united and actuated by some common impulse of passion, or of interest, adverse to the rights of other citizens, or the permanent and aggregate interests of the community.

Madison next contends that there are two methods by which the "mischiefs of faction" can be cured: by removing the causes of faction or by controlling their effects. In the following paragraphs, Madison explains how liberty itself nourishes factions. Therefore, to abolish factions would involve abolishing liberty—a cure "worse than the disease."

There are two methods of curing the mischiefs of faction: the one, by removing its causes; the other, by controlling its effects.

There are again two methods of removing the causes of faction: the one, by destroying the liberty which is essential to its existence; the other, by giving to every citizen the same opinions, the same passions, and the same interests.

It could never be more truly said than of the first remedy that it was worse than the disease. Liberty is to faction what air is to fire, an aliment without which it instantly expires. But it could not be a less folly to abolish liberty, which is essential to political life, because it nourishes faction than it would be to wish the annihilation of air, which is essential to animal life, because it imparts to fire its destructive agency.

The second expedient is as impracticable as the first would be unwise. As long as the reason of man continues fallible, and he is at liberty to exercise it, different opinions will be formed. As long as the connection subsists between his reason and his self-love, his opinions and his passions will have a reciprocal influence on each other; and the former will be objects to which the latter will attach themselves. The diversity in the faculties of men, from which the rights of property originate, is not less an insuperable obstacle to a uniformity of interests. The protection of these faculties is the first object of government. From the protection of different and unequal faculties of acquiring property, the possession of different degrees and kinds of property immediately results; and from the influence of these on the sentiments and views of the respective proprietors ensues a division of the society into different interests and parties.

The latent causes of faction are thus sown in the nature of man; and we see them everywhere brought into different degrees of activity, according to the different circumstances of civil society. A zeal for different opinions concerning religion, concerning government, and many other points, as well of speculation as of practice; an attachment to different leaders ambitiously contending for pre-eminence and power; or to persons of other descriptions whose fortunes have been interesting to the human passions, have, in turn, divided mankind into parties, inflamed them with mutual animosity, and rendered them much more disposed to vex and oppress each other than to co-operate for their common good. So strong is this propensity of mankind to fall into mutual animosities that where no substantial occasion presents itself the most frivolous and fanciful distinctions have been sufficient to kindle their unfriendly passions and excite their most violent conflicts. But the most common and durable source of factions has been the various and unequal distribution of property. Those who hold and those who are without property have ever formed distinct interests in society. Those who are creditors, and those who are debtors, fall under a like discrimination. A landed interest, a manufacturing interest, a mercantile interest, a moneyed interest, with many lesser interests, grow up of necessity in civilized nations, and divide them into different classes, actuated by different sentiments and views. The regulation of these various and interfering interests forms the principal task of modern legislation and involves the spirit of party and faction in the necessary and ordinary operations of government.

No man is allowed to be a judge in his own cause, because his interest would certainly bias his judgment, and, not improbably, corrupt his integrity. With equal, nay with greater reason, a body of men are unfit to be both judges and parties at the same time; yet what are many of the most important acts of legislation but so many judicial determinations, not indeed concerning the rights of single persons, but concerning the rights of large bodies of citizens? And what are the different classes of legislators but advocates and parties to the causes which they determine? Is a law proposed concerning private debts? It is a question to which the creditors are parties on one side and the debtors on the other. Justice ought to hold the balance between them. Yet the parties are, and must be, themselves the judges; and the most numerous party, or in other words, the most powerful faction must be expected to prevail. Shall domestic manufacturers be encouraged, and in what degree, by restrictions on foreign manufacturers? [These] are questions which would be differently decided by the landed and the manufacturing classes, and probably by neither with a sole regard to justice and the public good. The apportionment of taxes on the various descriptions of property is an act which seems to require the most exact impartiality; yet there is, perhaps, no legislative act in which greater opportunity and temptation are given to a predominant party to trample on the rules of justice. Every shilling with which they overburden the inferior number is a shilling saved to their own pockets.

It is in vain to say that enlightened statesmen will be able to adjust these clashing interests and render them all subservient to the public good. Enlightened statesmen will not always be at the helm. Nor, in many cases, can such an adjustment be made at all without taking into view indirect and remote considerations, which will rarely prevail over the immediate interest which one party may find in disregarding the rights of another or the good of the whole.

The inference to which we are brought is that the causes of faction cannot be removed and that relief is only to be sought in the means of controlling its effects.

Having concluded that "the causes of faction cannot be removed," Madison now looks in some detail at the other method by which factions can be cured—by controlling their effects. This is the heart of his essay. He begins by positing a significant question: How can you have self-government without risking the possibility that a ruling faction, particularly a majority faction, might tyrannize over the rights of others?

If a faction consists of less than a majority, relief is supplied by the republican principle, which enables the majority to defeat its sinister views by regular vote. It may clog the administration, it may convulse the society; but it will be unable to execute and mask its violence under the forms of the Constitution. When a majority is included in a faction, the form of popular government, on the other hand, enables it to sacrifice to its ruling passion or interest both the public good and the rights of other citizens. To secure the public good and private rights against the danger of such a faction, and at the same time to preserve the spirit and the form of popular government, is then the great object to which our inquiries are directed. Let me add that it is the great desideratum by which alone this form of government can be rescued from the opprobrium under which it has so long labored and be recommended to the esteem and adoption of mankind.

Madison now sets forth the idea that one way to control the effects of factions is to ensure that the majority is rendered incapable of acting in concert in order to "carry into effect schemes of oppression." He goes on to state that in a democracy, in which all citizens participate personally in government decision making, there is no way to prevent the majority from communicating with each other and, as a result, acting in concert.

By what means is this object attainable? Evidently by one of two only. Either the existence of the same passion or interest in a majority at the same time must be prevented, or the majority, having such coexistent passion or interest, must be rendered, by their number and local situation, unable to concert and carry into effect schemes of oppression. If the impulse and the opportunity be suffered to coincide, we well know that neither moral nor religious motives can be relied on as an adequate control. They are not found to be such on the injustice and violence of individuals, and lose their efficacy in proportion to the number combined together, that is, in proportion as their efficacy becomes needful.

From this view of the subject it may be concluded that a pure democracy, by which I mean a society consisting of a small number of citizens, who assemble and administer the government in person, can admit of no cure for the mischiefs of faction. A common passion or interest will, in almost every case, be felt by a majority of the whole; a communication and concert results from the form of government itself; and there is nothing to check the inducements to sacrifice the weaker party or an obnoxious individual. Hence it is that such democracies have ever been spectacles of turbulence and contention; have ever been found incompatible with personal security or the rights of property; and have in general been as short in their lives as they have been violent in their deaths. Theoretic politicians, who have patronized this species of government, have erroneously supposed that by reducing mankind to a perfect equality in their political rights, they would at the same time be perfectly equalized and assimilated in their possessions, their opinions, and their passions.

Madison now moves on to discuss the benefits of a republic with respect to controlling the effects of factions. He begins by defining a republic and then pointing out the "two great points of difference" between a republic and a democracy: a republic is governed by a small body of elected representatives, not by the people directly; and a republic can extend over a much larger territory and embrace more citizens than a democracy can.

A republic, by which I mean a government in which the scheme of representation takes place, opens a different prospect and promises the cure for which we are seeking. Let us examine the points in which it varies from pure democracy, and we shall comprehend both the nature of the cure and the efficacy which it must derive from the Union.

The two great points of difference between a democracy and a republic are: first, the delegation of the government, in the latter, to a small number of citizens elected by the rest; secondly, the greater number of citizens and greater sphere of country over which the latter may be extended.

In the following four paragraphs, Madison explains how in a republic, particularly a large republic, the delegation of authority to elected representatives will increase the likelihood that those who govern will be "fit" for their positions and that a proper balance will be achieved between local (factional) interests and national interests. Note how he stresses that the new federal Constitution, by dividing powers between state governments and the national government, provides a "happy combination in this respect."

The effect of the first difference is, on the one hand, to refine and enlarge the public views by passing them through the medium of a chosen body of citizens, whose wisdom may best discern the true interest of their country and whose patriotism and love of justice will be least likely to sacrifice it to temporary or partial considerations. Under such a regulation it may well happen that the public voice, pronounced by the representatives of the people, will be more consonant to the public good than if pronounced by the people themselves, convened for the purpose. On the other hand, the effect may be inverted. Men of factious tempers, of local prejudices, or of sinister designs, may, by intrigue, by corruption, or by other means, first obtain the suffrages, and then betray the interests of the people. The question resulting is, whether small or extensive republics are most favorable to the election of proper guardians of the public weal; and it is clearly decided in favor of the latter by two obvious considerations.

In the first place, it is to be remarked that however small the republic may be the representatives must be raised to a certain number in order to guard against the cabals of a few; and that however large it may be, they must be limited to a certain number in order to guard against the confusion of a multitude. Hence, the number of representatives in the two cases not being in proportion to that of the constituents, and being proportionally greater in the small republic, it follows that if the proportion of fit characters be not less in the large than in the small republic, the former will present a greater option, and consequently a greater probability of a fit choice.

In the next place, as each representative will be chosen by a greater number of citizens in the large than in the small republic, it will be more difficult for unworthy candidates to practice with success the vicious arts by which elections are too often carried; and the suffrages of the people being more free, will be more likely to center on men who possess the most attractive merit and the most diffusive and established characters.

It must be confessed that in this, as in most other cases, there is a mean, on both sides of which inconveniencies will be found to lie. By enlarging too much the number of electors, you render the representative too little acquainted with all their local circumstances and lesser interests; as by reducing it too much, you render him unduly attached to these, and too little fit to comprehend and pursue great and national objects. The federal Constitution forms a happy combination in this respect; the great and aggregate interests being referred to the national, the local and particular to the State legislatures.

Madison now looks more closely at the other difference between a republic and a democracy—namely, that a republic can encompass a larger territory and more citizens than a democracy can. In the remaining paragraphs of his essay, Madison concludes that in a large republic, it will be difficult for factions to act in concert. Although a factious group—religious, political, economic, or otherwise—may control a local or regional government, it will have little chance of gathering a national following. This is because in a large republic, there will be numerous factions whose work will offset the work of any one particular faction ("sect"). As Madison phrases it, these numerous factions will "secure the national councils against any danger from that source."

The other point of difference is the greater number of citizens and extent of territory which may be brought within the compass of republican than of democratic government; and it is this circumstance principally which renders factious combinations less to be dreaded in the former than in the latter. The smaller the society, the fewer probably will be the distinct parties and interests composing it; the fewer the distinct parties and interests, the more frequently will a majority be found of the same party; and the smaller the number of individuals composing a majority, and the smaller the compass within which they are placed, the more easily will they concert and execute their plans of oppression. Extend the sphere and you take in a greater variety of parties and interests; you make it less probable that a majority of the whole will have a common motive to invade the rights of other citizens; or if such a common motive exists, it will be more difficult for all who feel it to discover their own strength and to act in unison with each other. Besides other impediments, it may be remarked that, where there is a consciousness of unjust or dishonorable purposes, communication is always checked by distrust in proportion to the number whose concurrence is necessary.

Hence, it clearly appears that the same advantage which a republic has over a democracy in controlling the effects of faction is enjoyed by a large over a small republic—is enjoyed by the Union over the States composing it. Does this advantage consist in the substitution of representatives whose enlightened views and virtuous sentiments render them superior to local prejudices and to schemes of injustice? It will not be denied that the representation of the Union will be most likely to possess these requisite endowments. Does it consist in the greater security afforded by a greater variety of parties, against the event of any one party being able to outnumber and oppress the rest? In an equal degree does the increased variety of parties comprised within the Union increase this security. Does it, in fine, consist in the greater obstacles opposed to the concert and accomplishment of the secret wishes of an unjust and interested majority? Here again the extent of the Union gives it the most palpable advantage.

The influence of factious leaders may kindle a flame within their particular States but will be unable to spread a general conflagration through the other States. A religious sect may degenerate into a political faction in a part of the Confederacy; but the variety of sects dispersed over the entire face of it must secure the national councils against any danger from that source. A rage for paper money, for an abolition of debts, for an equal division of property, or for any other improper or wicked project, will be

less apt to pervade the whole body of the Union than a particular member of it, in the same proportion as such a malady is more likely to taint a particular county or district than an entire State.

In the extent and proper structure of the Union, therefore, we behold a republican remedy for the diseases most incident to republican government. And according to the degree of pleasure and pride we feel in being republicans ought to be our zeal in cherishing the spirit and supporting the character of federalists.

Publius

(James Madison)

Federalist Paper No. 51

Federalist Paper No. 51, also authored by James Madison, is another classic in American political theory. Although the Federalists wanted a strong national government, they had not abandoned the traditional American view, particularly notable during the revolutionary era, that those holding powerful government positions could not be trusted to put national interests and the common good above their own personal interests. In this essay, Madison explains why the separation of the national government's powers into three branches—executive, legislative, and judicial—and a federal structure of government offer the best protection against tyranny.

To what expedient, then, shall we finally resort, for maintaining in practice the necessary partition of power among the several departments as laid down in the Constitution? The only answer that can be given is that as all these exterior provisions are found to be inadequate the defect must be supplied, by so contriving the interior structure of the government as that its several constituent parts may, by their mutual relations, be the means of keeping each other in their proper places. Without presuming to undertake a full development of this important idea I will hazard a few general observations which may perhaps place it in a clearer light, and enable us to form a more correct judgment of the principles and structure of the government planned by the convention.

In the next two paragraphs, Madison stresses that for the powers of the different branches (departments) of government to be truly separated, the personnel in one branch should not be dependent on another branch for their appointment or for the "emoluments" (compensation) attached to their offices.

In order to lay a due foundation for that separate and distinct exercise of the different powers of government, which to a certain extent is admitted on all hands to be essential to the preservation of liberty, it is evident that each department should have a will of its own; and consequently should be so constituted that the members of each should have as little agency as possible in the appointment of the members of the others. Were this principle rigorously adhered to, it would require that all the appointments for the supreme executive, legislative, and judiciary magistracies should be drawn from the same fountain of authority, the people, through channels having no communication whatever with one another. Perhaps such a plan of constructing the several departments would be less difficult in practice than it may in contemplation appear. Some difficulties, however, and some additional expense would attend the execution of it. Some deviations, therefore, from the principle must be admitted. In the constitution of the judiciary department in particular, it might be inexpedient to insist rigorously on the principle: first, because peculiar qualifications being essential in the members, the primary consideration ought to be to select that mode of choice which best secures these qualifications; second, because the permanent tenure by which the appointments are held in that department must soon destroy all sense of dependence on the authority conferring them.

It is equally evident that the members of each department should be as little dependent as possible on those of the others for the emoluments annexed to their offices. Were the executive magistrate, or the judges, not independent of the legislature in this particular, their independence in every other would be merely nominal.

In the following passages, which are among the most widely quoted of Madison's writings, he explains how the separation of the powers of government into three branches helps to counter the effects of personal ambition on government. The separation of powers allows personal motives to be linked to the constitutional rights of a branch of government. In effect, competing personal interests in each branch will help to keep the powers of the three government branches separate and, in so doing, will help to guard the public interest.

But the great security against a gradual concentration of the several powers in the same department consists in giving to those who administer each department the necessary constitutional means and personal motives to resist encroachments of the others. The provision for defense must in this, as in all other cases, be made commensurate to the danger of attack. Ambition must be made to counteract ambition. The interest of the man must be connected with the constitutional rights of the place. It may be a reflection on human nature that such devices should be necessary to control the abuses of government. But what is government itself but the greatest of all reflections on human nature? If men were angels, no government would be necessary. If angels were to govern men, neither external nor internal controls on government would be necessary. In framing a government which is to be administered by men over men, the great difficulty lies in this: you must first enable the government to control the governed; and in the next place oblige it to control itself. A dependence on the people is, no doubt, the primary control on the government; but experience has taught mankind the necessity of auxiliary precautions.

This policy of supplying, by opposite and rival interests, the defect of better motives, might be traced through the whole system of human affairs, private as well as public. We see it particularly displayed in all the subordinate distributions of power, where the constant aim is to divide and arrange the several offices in such a manner as that each may be a check on the other—that the private interest of every individual may be a sentinel over the public rights. These inventions of prudence cannot be less requisite in the distribution of the supreme powers of the State.

Madison now addresses the issue of equality between the branches of government. The legislature will necessarily predominate, but if the executive is given an "absolute negative" (absolute veto power) over legislative actions, this also could lead to an abuse of power. Madison concludes that the division of the legislature into two "branches" (parts, or chambers) will act as a check on the legislature's powers.

But it is not possible to give to each department an equal power of self-defense. In republican government, the legislative authority necessarily predominates. The remedy for this inconveniency is to divide the legislature into different branches; and to render them, by different modes of election and different principles of action, as little connected with each other as the nature of their common functions and their common dependence on the society will admit. It may even be necessary to guard against dangerous encroachments by still further precautions. As the weight of the legislative authority requires that it should be thus divided, the weakness of the executive may require, on the other hand, that it should be fortified. An absolute negative on the legislature appears, at first view, to be the natural defense with which the executive magistrate should be armed. But perhaps it would be neither altogether safe nor alone sufficient. On ordinary occasions it might not be exerted with the requisite firmness, and on extraordinary occasions it might be perfidiously abused. May not this defect of an absolute negative be supplied by some qualified connection between this weaker department and the weaker branch of the stronger department, by which the latter may be led to support the constitutional rights of the former, without being too much detached from the rights of its own department?

If the principles on which these observations are founded be just, as I persuade myself they are, and they be applied as a criterion to the several State constitutions, and to the federal Constitution, it will be found that if the latter does not perfectly correspond with them, the former are infinitely less able to bear such a test.

In the remainder of the essay, Madison discusses how a federal system of government, in which powers are divided between the states and the national government, offers "double security" against tyranny.

There are, moreover, two considerations particularly applicable to the federal system of America, which place that system in a very interesting point of view.

First. In a single republic, all the power surrendered by the people is submitted to the administration of a single government; and the usurpations are guarded against by a division of the government into distinct and separate departments. In the compound republic of America, the power surrendered by the people is first divided between two distinct governments, and then the portion allotted to each subdivided among distinct and separate departments. Hence a double security arises to the rights of the people. The different governments will control each other, at the same time that each will be controlled by itself.

Second. It is of great importance in a republic not only to guard the society against the oppression of its rulers, but to guard one part of the society against the injustice of the other part. Different interests necessarily exist in different classes of citizens. If a majority be united by a common interest, the rights of the minority will be insecure. There are but two methods of providing against this evil: the one by creating a will in the community independent of the majority—that is, of the society itself; the other, by comprehending in the society so many separate descriptions of citizens as will render an unjust combination of a majority of the whole very improbable, if not impracticable. The first method prevails in all governments possessing an hereditary or self-appointed authority. This, at best, is but a precarious security; because a power independent of the society may as well espouse the unjust views of the major as the rightful interests of the minor party, and may possibly be turned against both parties. The second method will be exemplified in the federal republic of the United States. Whilst all authority in it will be derived from and dependent on the society, the society itself will be broken into so many parts, interests and classes of citizens, that the rights of individuals, or of the minority, will be in little danger from interested combinations of the majority.

In a free government the security for civil rights must be the same as that for religious rights. It consists in the one case in the multiplicity of interests, and in the other in the multiplicity of sects. The degree of security in both cases will depend on the number of interests and sects; and this may be presumed to depend on the extent of country and number of people comprehended under the same government. This view of the subject must particularly recommend a proper federal system to all the sincere and considerate friends of republican government, since it shows that in exact proportion as the territory of the Union may be formed into more circumscribed Confederacies, or States, oppressive combinations of a majority will be facilitated; the best security, under the republican forms, for the rights of every class of citizen, will be diminished; and consequently the stability and independence of some member of the government, the only other security, must be proportionally increased. Justice is the end of government. It is the end of civil society. It ever has been and ever will be pursued until it be obtained, or until liberty be lost in the pursuit. In a society under the forms of which the stronger faction can readily unite and oppress the weaker, anarchy may as truly be said to reign as in a state of nature, where the weaker individual is not secured against the violence of the stronger; and as, in the latter state, even the stronger individuals are prompted, by the uncertainty of their condition, to submit to a government which may protect the weak as well as themselves; so, in the former state, will the more powerful factions or parties be gradually induced, by a like motive, to wish for a government which will protect all parties, the weaker as well as the more powerful.

It can be little doubted that if the State of Rhode Island was separated from the Confederacy and left to itself, the insecurity of rights under the popular form of government within such narrow limits would be displayed by such reiterated oppressions of factious majorities that some power altogether independent of the people would soon be called for by the voice of the very factions whose misrule had proved the necessity of it. In the extended republic of the United States, and among the great variety of interests, parties, and sects which it embraces, a coalition of a majority of the whole society could seldom take place on any other principles than those of justice and the general good; whilst there being thus less danger to a minor from the will of a major party, there must be less pretext, also, to provide for the security of the former, by introducing into the government a will not dependent on the latter, or, in other words, a will independent of the society itself. It is no less certain than it is important, notwithstanding the contrary opinions which have been entertained, that the larger the society, provided it lie within a practicable sphere, the more duly capable it will be of self-government. And happily for the republican cause, the practicable sphere may be carried to a very great extent by a judicious modification and mixture of the *federal principle.*

Publius
(James Madison)

Federalist Paper No. 78

In this essay, Alexander Hamilton looks at the role of the judicial branch (the courts) in the new government fashioned by the Constitution's framers. The essay is historically significant because, among other things, it provides a basis for the courts' power of judicial review, which was not explicitly set forth in the Constitution (see Chapters 2 and 13).

After some brief introductory remarks, Hamilton explains why the founders decided that federal judges should be appointed and given lifetime tenure. Note how he describes the judiciary as the "weakest" and "least dangerous" branch of government. Because of this, claims Hamilton, "all possible care" is required to enable the judiciary to defend itself against attacks by the other two branches of government. Above all, the independence of the judicial branch should be secured, because if judicial powers were combined with legislative or executive powers, there would be no liberty.

We proceed now to an examination of the judiciary department of the proposed government.

In unfolding the defects of the existing Confederation, the utility and necessity of a federal judicature have been clearly pointed out. It is the less necessary to recapitulate the considerations there urged, as the propriety of the institution in the abstract is not disputed; the only questions which have been raised being relative to the manner of constituting it, and to its extent. To these points, therefore, our observations shall be confined.

The manner of constituting it seems to embrace these several objects: 1st. The mode of appointing the judges. 2d. The tenure by which they are to hold their places. 3d. The partition of the judiciary authority between different courts, and their relations to each other.

First. As to the mode of appointing the judges; this is the same with that of appointing the officers of the Union in general, and has been so fully discussed in the last two numbers, that nothing can be said here which would not be useless repetition.

Second. As to the tenure by which the judges are to hold their places; this chiefly concerns their duration in office; the provisions for their support; the precautions for their responsibility.

According to the plan of the convention, all judges who may be appointed by the United States are to hold their offices during good behavior; which is conformable to the most approved of the State constitutions and among the rest, to that of this State. Its propriety having been drawn into question by the adversaries of that plan, is no light symptom of the rage for objection, which disorders their imaginations and judgments. The standard of good behavior for the continuance in office of the judicial magistracy, is certainly one of the most valuable of the modern improvements in the practice of government. In a monarchy it is an excellent barrier to the despotism of the prince; in a republic it is a no less excellent barrier to the encroachments and oppressions of the representative body. And it is the best expedient which can be devised in any government, to secure a steady, upright, and impartial administration of the laws.

Whoever attentively considers the different departments of power must perceive, that, in a government in which they are separated from each other, the judiciary, from the nature of its functions, will always be the least dangerous to the political rights of the Constitution; because it will be least in a capacity to annoy or injure them. The Executive not only dispenses the honors, but holds the sword of the community. The legislature not only commands the purse, but prescribes the rules by which the duties and rights of every citizen are to be regulated. The judiciary, on the contrary, has no influence over either the sword or the purse; no direction either of the strength or of the wealth of the society; and can take no active resolution whatever. It may truly be said to have neither force nor will, but merely judgment; and must ultimately depend upon the aid of the executive arm even for the efficacy of its judgments.

This simple view of the matter suggests several important consequences. It proves incontestably, that the judiciary is beyond comparison the weakest of the three departments of power; that it can never attack with success either of the other two; and that all possible care is requisite to enable it to defend itself against their attacks. It equally proves, that though individual oppression may now and then proceed from the courts of justice, the general liberty of the people can never be endangered from that quarter; I mean so long as the judiciary remains truly distinct from both the legislature and the Executive. For I agree, that "there is no liberty, if the power of judging is not separated from the legislative and executive powers." And it proves, in the last place, that as liberty can have nothing to fear from the judiciary alone, but would have everything to fear from its union with either of the other departments; that as all the effects of such a union must ensue from a dependence of the former on the latter, notwithstanding a nominal and apparent separation; that as, from the natural feebleness of the judiciary, it is in continual jeopardy of being overpowered, awed, or influenced by its co-ordinate branches; and that as nothing can contribute so much to its firmness and independence as permanency in office, this quality may therefore be justly regarded as an indispensable ingredient in its constitution, and, in a great measure, as the citadel of the public justice and the public security.

Hamilton now stresses that the "complete independence of the courts" is essential in a limited government, because it is up to the courts to interpret the laws. Just as a federal court can decide which of two conflicting statutes should take priority, so can that court decide whether a statute conflicts with the Constitution. Essentially, Hamilton sets forth here the theory of judicial review—the power of the courts to decide whether actions of the other branches of government are (or are not) consistent with the Constitution. Hamilton points out that this "exercise of judicial discretion, in determining between two contradictory laws," does not mean that the judicial branch is superior to the legislative branch. Rather, it "supposes" that the power of the people (as declared in the Constitution) is superior to both the judiciary and the legislature.

The complete independence of the courts of justice is peculiarly essential in a limited Constitution. By a limited Constitution, I understand one which contains certain specified exceptions to the legislative authority; such, for instance, as that it shall pass no bills of attainder, no ex-post-facto laws, and the like. Limitations of this kind can be preserved in practice no other way than through the medium of courts of justice, whose duty it must be to declare all acts contrary to the manifest tenor of the Constitution void. Without this, all the reservations of particular rights or privileges would amount to nothing. Some perplexity respecting the rights of the courts to pronounce legislative acts void, because contrary to the Constitution, has arisen from an imagination that the doctrine would imply a superiority of the judiciary to the legislative power. It is urged that the authority which can declare the acts of another void, must necessarily be superior to the one whose acts may be declared void. As this doctrine is of great importance in all the American constitutions, a brief discussion of the ground on which it rests cannot be unacceptable.

There is no position which depends on clearer principles, than that every act of a delegated authority, contrary to the tenor of the commission under which it is exercised, is void. No legislative act, therefore, contrary to the Constitution, can be valid. To deny this, would be to affirm, that the deputy is greater than his principal; that the servant is above his master; that the representatives of the people are superior to the people themselves; that men acting by virtue of powers, may do not only what their powers do not authorize, but what they forbid.

If it be said that the legislative body are themselves the constitutional judges of their own powers, and that the construction they put upon them is conclusive upon the other departments, it may be answered, that this cannot be the natural presumption, where it is not to be collected from any particular provisions in the Constitution. It is not otherwise to be supposed, that the Constitution could intend to enable the representatives of the people to substitute their will to that of their constituents. It is far more rational to suppose, that the courts were designed to be an intermediate body between the people and the legislature, in order, among other things, to keep the latter within the limits assigned to their authority. The interpretation of the laws is the proper and peculiar province of the courts. A constitution is, in fact, and must be regarded by the judges, as a fundamental law. It therefore belongs to them to ascertain its meaning, as well as the meaning of any particular act proceeding from the legislative body. If there should happen to be an irreconcilable variance between the two, that which has the superior obligation and validity ought, of course, to be preferred; or, in other words, the Constitution ought to be preferred to the statute, the intention of the people to the intention of their agents.

Nor does this conclusion by any means suppose a superiority of the judicial to the legislative power. It only supposes that the power of the people is superior to both; and that where the will of the legislature, declared in its statutes, stands in opposition to that of the people, declared in the Constitution, the judges ought to be governed by the latter rather than the former. They ought to regulate their decisions by the fundamental laws, rather than by those which are not fundamental.

This exercise of judicial discretion, in determining between two contradictory laws, is exemplified in a familiar instance. It not uncommonly happens, that there are two statutes existing at one time, clashing in whole or in part with each other, and neither of them containing any repealing clause or expression. In such a case, it is the province of the courts to liquidate and fix their meaning and operation. So far as they can, by any fair construction, be reconciled to each other, reason and law conspire to dictate that this should be done; where this is impracticable, it becomes a matter of necessity to give effect to one, in exclusion of the other. The rule which has obtained in the courts for determining their relative validity is, that the last in order of time shall be preferred to the first. But this is a mere rule of construction, not derived from any positive law, but from the nature and reason of the thing. It is a rule not enjoined upon the courts by legislative provision, but adopted by themselves, as consonant to truth the propriety, for the direction of their conduct as interpreters of the law. They thought it reasonable, that between the interfering acts of an equal authority, that which was the last indication of its will should have the preference.

But in regard to the interfering acts of a superior and subordinate authority, of an original and derivative power, the nature and reason of the thing indicate the converse of that rule as proper to be followed. They teach us that the prior act of a superior ought to be preferred to the subsequent act of an inferior and subordinate authority; and that accordingly, whenever a particular statute contravenes the Constitution, it will be the duty of the judicial tribunals to adhere to the latter and disregard the former.

It can be of no weight to say that the courts, on the pretense of a repugnancy, may substitute their own pleasure to the constitutional intentions of the legislature. This might as well happen in the case of two contradictory statutes; or it might as well happen in every adjudication upon any single statute. The courts must declare the sense of the law; and if they should be disposed to exercise will instead of judgment, the consequence would equally be the substitution of their pleasure to that of the legislative body. The observation, if it prove anything, would prove that there ought to be no judges distinct from that body.

If, then, the courts of justice are to be considered as the bulwarks of a limited Constitution against legislative encroachments, this consideration will afford a strong argument for the permanent tenure of judicial offices, since nothing will contribute so much as this to that independent spirit in the judges which must be essential to the faithful performance of so arduous a duty.

The independence of the judges is equally requisite to guard the Constitution and the rights of individuals from the effects of those ill humors, which the arts of designing men, or the influence of particular conjunctures, sometimes disseminate among the people themselves, and which, though they speedily give place to better information, and more deliberate reflection, have a tendency, in the meantime, to occasion dangerous innovations in the government, and serious oppressions of the minor party in the community. Though I trust the friends of the proposed Constitution will never concur with its enemies, in questioning that fundamental principle of republican government, which admits the right of the people to alter or abolish the established Constitution, whenever they find it inconsistent with their happiness, yet it is not to be inferred from this principle, that the representatives of the people, whenever a momentary inclination happens to lay hold of a majority of their constituents, incompatible with the provisions of the existing Constitution, would, on that account, be justifiable in a violation of those provisions; or that the courts would be under a greater obligation to connive at infractions in this shape, than when they had proceeded wholly from the cabals of the representative body. Until the people have, by some solemn and authoritative act, annulled or changed the established form, it is binding upon themselves collectively, as well as individually; and no presumption, or even knowledge, of their sentiments, can warrant their representatives in a departure from it, prior to such an act. But it is easy to see, that it would require an uncommon portion of fortitude in the judges to do their duty as faithful guardians of the Constitution, where legislative invasions of it had been instigated by the major voice of the community.

But it is not with a view to infractions of the Constitution only, that the independence of the judges may be an essential safeguard against the effects of occasional ill humors in the society. These sometimes extend no farther than to the injury of the private rights of particular classes of citizens, by unjust and partial laws. Here also the firmness of the judicial magistracy is of vast importance in mitigating the severity and confining the operation of such laws. It not only serves to moderate the immediate mischiefs of those which may have been passed, but it operates as a check upon the legislative body in passing them; who, perceiving that obstacles to the success of iniquitous intention are to be expected from the scruples of the courts, are in a manner compelled, by the very motives of the injustice they meditate, to qualify their attempts. This is a circumstance calculated to have more influence upon the character of our governments, than but few may be aware of. The benefits of the integrity and moderation of the judiciary have already been felt in more States than one; and though they may have displeased those whose sinister expectations they may have disappointed, they must have commanded the esteem and applause of all the virtuous and disinterested. Considerate men, of every description, ought to prize whatever will tend to beget or fortify that temper in the courts; as no man can be sure that he may not be tomorrow the victim of a spirit of injustice, by which he may be a gainer today. And every man must now feel, that the inevitable tendency of such a spirit is to sap the foundations of public and private confidence, and to introduce in its stead universal distrust and distress.

That inflexible and uniform adherence to the rights of the Constitution, and of individuals, which we perceive to be indispensable in the courts of justice, can certainly not be expected from judges who hold their offices by a temporary commission. Periodical appointments, however regulated, or by whomsoever made, would, in some way or other, be fatal to their necessary independence. If the power of making them was committed either to the Executive or legislature, there would be danger of an improper complaisance to the branch which possessed it; if to both, there would be an unwillingness to hazard the displeasure of either; if to the people, or to persons chosen by them for the special purpose, there would be too great a disposition to consult popularity, to justify a reliance that nothing would be consulted but the Constitution and the laws.

Hamilton points to yet another reason why lifetime tenure for federal judges will benefit the public: effective judgments rest on a knowledge of judicial precedents and the law, and such knowledge can only be obtained through experience on the bench. A "temporary duration of office," according to Hamilton, would "discourage individuals [of 'fit character'] from quitting a lucrative practice to serve on the bench" and ultimately would "throw the administration of justice into the hands of the less able, and less well qualified."

There is yet a further and a weightier reason for the permanency of the judicial offices, which is deducible from the nature of the qualifications they require. It has been frequently remarked, with great propriety, that a voluminous code of laws is one of the inconveniences necessarily connected with the advantages of a free government. To avoid an arbitrary discretion in the courts, it is indispensable that they should be bound down by strict rules and precedents, which serve to define and point out their duty in every particular case that comes before them; and it will readily be conceived from the variety of controversies which grow out of the folly and wickedness of mankind, that the records of those precedents must unavoidably swell to a very considerable bulk, and must demand long and laborious study to acquire a competent knowledge of them. Hence it is, that there can be but few men in the society who will have sufficient skill in the laws to qualify them for the stations of judges. And making the proper deductions for the ordinary depravity of human nature, the number must be still smaller of those who unite the requisite integrity with the requisite knowledge. These considerations apprise us, that the government can have no great option between fit character; and that a temporary duration in office, which would naturally discourage such characters from quitting a lucrative line of practice to accept a seat on the bench, would have a tendency to throw the administration of justice into hands less able, and less well qualified, to conduct it with utility and dignity. In the present circumstances of this country, and in those in which it is likely to be for a long time to come, the disadvantages on this score would be greater than they may at first sight appear; but it must be confessed, that they are far inferior to those which present themselves under other aspects of the subject.

Upon the whole, there can be no room to doubt that the convention acted wisely in copying from the models of those constitutions which have established good behavior as the tenure of their judicial offices, in point of duration; and that so far from being blamable on this account, their plan would have been inexcusably defective, if it had wanted this important feature of good government. The experience of Great Britain affords an illustrious comment on the excellence of the institution.

Publius
(Alexander Hamilton)

APPENDIX D

Justices of the United States Supreme Court since 1900

Chief Justices

Name	Years of Service	State App't from	Appointing President	Age at App't	Political Affiliation	Educational Background*
Fuller, Melville Weston	1888–1910	Illinois	Cleveland	55	Democrat	Bowdoin College; studied at Harvard Law School
White, Edward Douglass	1910–1921	Louisiana	Taft	65	Democrat	Mount St. Mary's College; Georgetown College (now University)
Taft, William Howard	1921–1930	Connecticut	Harding	64	Republican	Yale; Cincinnati Law School
Hughes, Charles Evans	1930–1941	New York	Hoover	68	Republican	Colgate University; Brown; Columbia Law School
Stone, Harlan Fiske	1941–1946	New York	Roosevelt, F.	69	Republican	Amherst College; Columbia
Vinson, Frederick Moore	1946–1953	Kentucky	Truman	56	Democrat	Centre College
Warren, Earl	1953–1969	California	Eisenhower	62	Republican	University of California, Berkeley
Burger, Warren Earl	1969–1986	Virginia	Nixon	62	Republican	University of Minnesota; St. Paul College of Law (Mitchell College)
Rehnquist, William Hubbs	1986–2005	Virginia	Reagan	62	Republican	Stanford; Harvard; Stanford University Law School
Roberts, John G., Jr.	2005–present	District of Columbia	Bush, G. W.	50	Republican	Harvard; Harvard Law School

Associate Justices

Name	Years of Service	State App't from	Appointing President	Age at App't	Political Affiliation	Educational Background*
Harlan, John Marshall	1877–1911	Kentucky	Hayes	61	Republican	Centre College; studied law at Transylvania University
Gray, Horace	1882–1902	Massachusetts	Arthur	54	Republican	Harvard College; Harvard Law School
Brewer, David Josiah	1890–1910	Kansas	Harrison	53	Republican	Wesleyan University; Yale; Albany Law School
Brown, Henry Billings	1891–1906	Michigan	Harrison	55	Republican	Yale; studied at Yale Law School and Harvard Law School
Shiras, George, Jr.	1892–1903	Pennsylvania	Harrison	61	Republican	Ohio University; Yale; studied law at Yale and privately
White, Edward Douglass	1894–1910	Louisiana	Cleveland	49	Democrat	Mount St. Mary's College; Georgetown College (now University)
Peckham, Rufus Wheeler	1896–1909	New York	Cleveland	58	Democrat	Read law in father's firm
McKenna, Joseph	1898–1925	California	McKinley	55	Republican	Benica Collegiate Institute, Law Department
Holmes, Oliver Wendell, Jr.	1902–1932	Massachusetts	Roosevelt, T.	61	Republican	Harvard College; studied law at Harvard Law School

*Sources: Educational background information derived from Elder Witt, *Guide to the U.S. Supreme Court,* 2d ed. (Washington, D.C.: Congressional Quarterly Press, Inc., 1990). Reprinted with the permission of the publisher. Plus authors' update.

(continued)

Associate Justices (continued)

Name	Years of Service	State App't from	Appointing President	Age at App't	Political Affiliation	Educational Background
Day, William Rufus	1903–1922	Ohio	Roosevelt, T.	54	Republican	University of Michigan; University of Michigan Law School
Moody, William Henry	1906–1910	Massachusetts	Roosevelt, T.	53	Republican	Harvard; Harvard Law School
Lurton, Horace Harmon	1910–1914	Tennessee	Taft	66	Democrat	University of Chicago; Cumberland Law School
Hughes, Charles Evans	1910–1916	New York	Taft	48	Republican	Colgate University; Brown University; Columbia Law School
Van Devanter, Willis	1911–1937	Wyoming	Taft	52	Republican	Indiana Asbury University; University of Cincinnati Law School
Lamar, Joseph Rucker	1911–1916	Georgia	Taft	54	Democrat	University of Georgia; Bethany College; Washington and Lee University
Pitney, Mahlon	1912–1922	New Jersey	Taft	54	Republican	College of New Jersey (Princeton); read law under father
McReynolds, James Clark	1914–1941	Tennessee	Wilson	52	Democrat	Vanderbilt University; University of Virginia
Brandeis, Louis Dembitz	1916–1939	Massachusetts	Wilson	60	Democrat	Harvard Law School
Clarke, John Hessin	1916–1922	Ohio	Wilson	59	Democrat	Western Reserve University; read law under father
Sutherland, George	1922–1938	Utah	Harding	60	Republican	Brigham Young Academy; one year at University of Michigan Law School
Butler, Pierce	1923–1939	Minnesota	Harding	57	Democrat	Carleton College
Sanford, Edward Terry	1923–1930	Tennessee	Harding	58	Republican	University of Tennessee; Harvard; Harvard Law School
Stone, Harlan Fiske	1925–1941	New York	Coolidge	53	Republican	Amherst College; Columbia University Law School
Roberts, Owen Josephus	1930–1945	Pennsylvania	Hoover	55	Republican	University of Pennsylvania; University of Pennsylvania Law School
Cardozo, Benjamin Nathan	1932–1938	New York	Hoover	62	Democrat	Columbia University; two years at Columbia Law School
Black, Hugo Lafayette	1937–1971	Alabama	Roosevelt, F.	51	Democrat	Birmingham Medical College; University of Alabama Law School
Reed, Stanley Forman	1938–1957	Kentucky	Roosevelt, F.	54	Democrat	Kentucky Wesleyan University; Foreman Yale; studied law at University of Virginia and Columbia University; University of Paris
Frankfurter, Felix	1939–1962	Massachusetts	Roosevelt, F.	57	Independent	College of the City of New York; Harvard Law School
Douglas, William Orville	1939–1975	Connecticut	Roosevelt, F.	41	Democrat	Whitman College; Columbia University Law School
Murphy, Frank	1940–1949	Michigan	Roosevelt, F.	50	Democrat	University of Michigan; Lincoln's Inn, London; Trinity College
Byrnes, James Francis	1941–1942	South Carolina	Roosevelt, F.	62	Democrat	Read law privately
Jackson, Robert Houghwout	1941–1954	New York	Roosevelt, F.	49	Democrat	Albany Law School
Rutledge, Wiley Blount	1943–1949	Iowa	Roosevelt, F.	49	Democrat	University of Wisconsin; University of Colorado

Associate Justices (continued)

Name	Years of Service	State App't from	Appointing President	Age at App't	Political Affiliation	Educational Background
Burton, Harold Hitz	1945–1958	Ohio	Truman	57	Republican	Bowdoin College; Harvard Law School
Clark, Thomas Campbell	1949–1967	Texas	Truman	50	Democrat	University of Texas
Minton, Sherman	1949–1956	Indiana	Truman	59	Democrat	Indiana University College of Law; Yale Law School
Harlan, John Marshall	1955–1971	New York	Eisenhower	56	Republican	Princeton; Oxford University; New York Law School
Brennan, William J., Jr.	1956–1990	New Jersey	Eisenhower	50	Democrat	University of Pennsylvania; Harvard Law School
Whittaker, Charles Evans	1957–1962	Missouri	Eisenhower	56	Republican	University of Kansas City Law School
Stewart, Potter	1958–1981	Ohio	Eisenhower	43	Republican	Yale; Yale Law School
White, Byron Raymond	1962–1993	Colorado	Kennedy	45	Democrat	University of Colorado; Oxford University; Yale Law School
Goldberg, Arthur Joseph	1962–1965	Illinois	Kennedy	54	Democrat	Northwestern University
Fortas, Abe	1965–1969	Tennessee	Johnson, L.	55	Democrat	Southwestern College; Yale Law School
Marshall, Thurgood	1967–1991	New York	Johnson, L.	59	Democrat	Lincoln University; Howard University Law School
Blackmun, Harry A.	1970–1994	Minnesota	Nixon	62	Republican	Harvard; Harvard Law School
Powell, Lewis F., Jr.	1972–1987	Virginia	Nixon	65	Democrat	Washington and Lee University; Washington and Lee University Law School; Harvard Law School
Rehnquist, William H.	1972–1986	Arizona	Nixon	48	Republican	Stanford; Harvard; Stanford University Law School
Stevens, John Paul	1975–2010	Illinois	Ford	55	Republican	University of Colorado; Northwestern University Law School
O'Connor, Sandra Day	1981–2006	Arizona	Reagan	51	Republican	Stanford; Stanford University Law School
Scalia, Antonin	1986–2016	Virginia	Reagan	50	Republican	Georgetown University; Harvard Law School
Kennedy, Anthony M.	1988–present	California	Reagan	52	Republican	Stanford; London School of Economics; Harvard Law School
Souter, David Hackett	1990–2009	New Hampshire	Bush, G. H. W.	51	Republican	Harvard; Oxford University
Thomas, Clarence	1991–present	District of Columbia	Bush, G. H. W.	43	Republican	Holy Cross College; Yale Law School
Ginsburg, Ruth Bader	1993–present	District of Columbia	Clinton	60	Democrat	Cornell University; Columbia Law School
Breyer, Stephen G.	1994–present	Massachusetts	Clinton	55	Democrat	Stanford University; Oxford University; Harvard Law School
Alito, Samuel Anthony, Jr.	2006–present	New Jersey	G. W. Bush	55	Republican	Princeton University; Yale Law School
Sotomayor, Sonia Marie	2009–present	New York	Obama	55	Democrat	Princeton University; Yale Law School
Kagan, Elena	2010–present	District of Columbia	Obama	50	Democrat	Princeton and Oxford Universities; Harvard Law School

APPENDIX E

Party Control of Congress since 1904

Congress	Years	President	Majority Party in House	Majority Party in Senate
59th	1905–1907	T. Roosevelt	Republican	Republican
60th	1907–1909	T. Roosevelt	Republican	Republican
61st	1909–1911	Taft	Republican	Republican
62d	1911–1913	Taft	Democratic	Republican
63d	1913–1915	Wilson	Democratic	Democratic
64th	1915–1917	Wilson	Democratic	Democratic
65th	1917–1919	Wilson	Democratic	Democratic
66th	1919–1921	Wilson	Republican	Republican
67th	1921–1923	Harding	Republican	Republican
68th	1923–1925	Harding/Coolidge	Republican	Republican
69th	1925–1927	Coolidge	Republican	Republican
70th	1927–1929	Coolidge	Republican	Republican
71st	1929–1931	Hoover	Republican	Republican
72d	1931–1933	Hoover	Democratic	Republican
73d	1933–1935	F. Roosevelt	Democratic	Democratic
74th	1935–1937	F. Roosevelt	Democratic	Democratic
75th	1937–1939	F. Roosevelt	Democratic	Democratic
76th	1939–1941	F. Roosevelt	Democratic	Democratic
77th	1941–1943	F. Roosevelt	Democratic	Democratic
78th	1943–1945	F. Roosevelt	Democratic	Democratic
79th	1945–1947	F. Roosevelt/Truman	Democratic	Democratic
80th	1947–1949	Truman	Republican	Democratic
81st	1949–1951	Truman	Democratic	Democratic
82d	1951–1953	Truman	Democratic	Democratic
83d	1953–1955	Eisenhower	Republican	Republican
84th	1955–1957	Eisenhower	Democratic	Democratic
85th	1957–1959	Eisenhower	Democratic	Democratic
86th	1959–1961	Eisenhower	Democratic	Democratic
87th	1961–1963	Kennedy	Democratic	Democratic
88th	1963–1965	Kennedy/Johnson	Democratic	Democratic
89th	1965–1967	Johnson	Democratic	Democratic
90th	1967–1969	Johnson	Democratic	Democratic
91st	1969–1971	Nixon	Democratic	Democratic
92d	1971–1973	Nixon	Democratic	Democratic
93d	1973–1975	Nixon/Ford	Democratic	Democratic
94th	1975–1977	Ford	Democratic	Democratic
95th	1977–1979	Carter	Democratic	Democratic
96th	1979–1981	Carter	Democratic	Democratic
97th	1981–1983	Reagan	Democratic	Republican
98th	1983–1985	Reagan	Democratic	Republican
99th	1985–1987	Reagan	Democratic	Republican
100th	1987–1989	Reagan	Democratic	Democratic
101st	1989–1991	G. H. W. Bush	Democratic	Democratic
102d	1991–1993	G. H. W. Bush	Democratic	Democratic
103d	1993–1995	Clinton	Democratic	Democratic
104th	1995–1997	Clinton	Republican	Republican
105th	1997–1999	Clinton	Republican	Republican
106th	1999–2001	Clinton	Republican	Republican
107th	2001–2003	G. W. Bush	Republican	Democratic
108th	2003–2005	G. W. Bush	Republican	Republican
109th	2005–2007	G. W. Bush	Republican	Republican
110th	2007–2009	G. W. Bush	Democratic	Democratic
111th	2009–2011	Obama	Democratic	Democratic
112th	2011–2013	Obama	Republican	Democratic
113th	2013–2015	Obama	Republican	Democratic
114th	2015–2017	Obama	Republican	Republican
115th	2017–2019	Trump	Republican	Republican

APPENDIX F

Presidents of the United States

	Term of Service	Age at Inauguration	Political Party	College or University	Occupation or Profession
1. George Washington	1789–1797	57	None		Planter
2. John Adams	1797–1801	61	Federalist	Harvard	Lawyer
3. Thomas Jefferson	1801–1809	57	Jeffersonian Republican	William and Mary	Planter, Lawyer
4. James Madison	1809–1817	57	Jeffersonian Republican	Princeton	Lawyer
5. James Monroe	1817–1825	58	Jeffersonian Republican	William and Mary	Lawyer
6. John Quincy Adams	1825–1829	57	Jeffersonian Republican	Harvard	Lawyer
7. Andrew Jackson	1829–1837	61	Democrat		Lawyer
8. Martin Van Buren	1837–1841	54	Democrat		Lawyer
9. William H. Harrison	1841	68	Whig	Hampden-Sydney	Soldier
10. John Tyler	1841–1845	51	Whig	William and Mary	Lawyer
11. James K. Polk	1845–1849	49	Democrat	U. of N. Carolina	Lawyer
12. Zachary Taylor	1849–1850	64	Whig		Soldier
13. Millard Fillmore	1850–1853	50	Whig		Lawyer
14. Franklin Pierce	1853–1857	48	Democrat	Bowdoin	Lawyer
15. James Buchanan	1857–1861	65	Democrat	Dickinson	Lawyer
16. Abraham Lincoln	1861–1865	52	Republican		Lawyer
17. Andrew Johnson	1865–1869	56	National Union†		Tailor
18. Ulysses S. Grant	1869–1877	46	Republican	U.S. Mil. Academy	Soldier
19. Rutherford B. Hayes	1877–1881	54	Republican	Kenyon	Lawyer
20. James A. Garfield	1881	49	Republican	Williams	Lawyer
21. Chester A. Arthur	1881–1885	51	Republican	Union	Lawyer
22. Grover Cleveland	1885–1889	47	Democrat		Lawyer
23. Benjamin Harrison	1889–1893	55	Republican	Miami	Lawyer
24. Grover Cleveland	1893–1897	55	Democrat		Lawyer
25. William McKinley	1897–1901	54	Republican	Allegheny College	Lawyer
26. Theodore Roosevelt	1901–1909	42	Republican	Harvard	Author
27. William H. Taft	1909–1913	51	Republican	Yale	Lawyer
28. Woodrow Wilson	1913–1921	56	Democrat	Princeton	Educator
29. Warren G. Harding	1921–1923	55	Republican		Editor
30. Calvin Coolidge	1923–1929	51	Republican	Amherst	Lawyer
31. Herbert C. Hoover	1929–1933	54	Republican	Stanford	Engineer
32. Franklin D. Roosevelt	1933–1945	51	Democrat	Harvard	Lawyer
33. Harry S. Truman	1945–1953	60	Democrat		Businessman
34. Dwight D. Eisenhower	1953–1961	62	Republican	U.S. Mil. Academy	Soldier
35. John F. Kennedy	1961–1963	43	Democrat	Harvard	Author
36. Lyndon B. Johnson	1963–1969	55	Democrat	Southwest Texas State	Teacher
37. Richard M. Nixon	1969–1974	56	Republican	Whittier	Lawyer
38. Gerald R. Ford‡	1974–1977	61	Republican	Michigan	Lawyer
39. James E. Carter, Jr.	1977–1981	52	Democrat	U.S. Naval Academy	Businessman
40. Ronald W. Reagan	1981–1989	69	Republican	Eureka College	Actor
41. George H. W. Bush	1989–1993	64	Republican	Yale	Businessman
42. Bill Clinton	1993–2001	46	Democrat	Georgetown	Lawyer
43. George W. Bush	2001–2009	54	Republican	Yale	Businessman
44. Barack Obama	2009–2017	47	Democrat	Columbia	Lawyer
45. Donald Trump	2017–	70	Republican	Fordham	Real estate developer

*Church preference; never joined any church.
†The National Union Party consisted of Republicans and War Democrats. Johnson was a Democrat.
**Inaugurated Dec. 6, 1973, to replace Agnew, who resigned Oct. 10, 1973.

	Religion	Born	Died	Age at Death	Vice President	
1.	Episcopalian	Feb. 22, 1732	Dec. 14, 1799	67	John Adams	(1789–1797)
2.	Unitarian	Oct. 30, 1735	July 4, 1826	90	Thomas Jefferson	(1797–1801)
3.	Unitarian*	Apr. 13, 1743	July 4, 1826	83	Aaron Burr	(1801–1805)
					George Clinton	(1805–1809)
4.	Episcopalian	Mar. 16, 1751	June 28, 1836	85	George Clinton	(1809–1812)
					Elbridge Gerry	(1813–1814)
5.	Episcopalian	Apr. 28, 1758	July 4, 1831	73	Daniel D. Tompkins	(1817–1825)
6.	Unitarian	July 11, 1767	Feb. 23, 1848	80	John C. Calhoun	(1825–1829)
7.	Presbyterian	Mar. 15, 1767	June 8, 1845	78	John C. Calhoun	(1829–1832)
					Martin Van Buren	(1833–1837)
8.	Dutch Reformed	Dec. 5, 1782	July 24, 1862	79	Richard M. Johnson	(1837–1841)
9.	Episcopalian	Feb. 9, 1773	Apr. 4, 1841	68	John Tyler	(1841)
10.	Episcopalian	Mar. 29, 1790	Jan. 18, 1862	71		
11.	Methodist	Nov. 2, 1795	June 15, 1849	53	George M. Dallas	(1845–1849)
12.	Episcopalian	Nov. 24, 1784	July 9, 1850	65	Millard Fillmore	(1849–1850)
13.	Unitarian	Jan. 7, 1800	Mar. 8, 1874	74		
14.	Episcopalian	Nov. 23, 1804	Oct. 8, 1869	64	William R. King	(1853)
15.	Presbyterian	Apr. 23, 1791	June 1, 1868	77	John C. Breckinridge	(1857–1861)
16.	Presbyterian*	Feb. 12, 1809	Apr. 15, 1865	56	Hannibal Hamlin	(1861–1865)
					Andrew Johnson	(1865)
17.	Methodist*	Dec. 29, 1808	July 31, 1875	66		
18.	Methodist	Apr. 27, 1822	July 23, 1885	63	Schuyler Colfax	(1869–1873)
					Henry Wilson	(1873–1875)
19.	Methodist*	Oct. 4, 1822	Jan. 17, 1893	70	William A. Wheeler	(1877–1881)
20.	Disciples of Christ	Nov. 19, 1831	Sept. 19, 1881	49	Chester A. Arthur	(1881)
21.	Episcopalian	Oct. 5, 1829	Nov. 18, 1886	57		
22.	Presbyterian	Mar. 18, 1837	June 24, 1908	71	Thomas A. Hendricks	(1885)
23.	Presbyterian	Aug. 20, 1833	Mar. 13, 1901	67	Levi P. Morton	(1889–1893)
24.	Presbyterian	Mar. 18, 1837	June 24, 1908	71	Adlai E. Stevenson	(1893–1897)
25.	Methodist	Jan. 29, 1843	Sept. 14, 1901	58	Garret A. Hobart	(1897–1899)
					Theodore Roosevelt	(1901)
26.	Dutch Reformed	Oct. 27, 1858	Jan. 6, 1919	60	Charles W. Fairbanks	(1905–1909)
27.	Unitarian	Sept. 15, 1857	Mar. 8, 1930	72	James S. Sherman	(1909–1912)
28.	Presbyterian	Dec. 29, 1856	Feb. 3, 1924	67	Thomas R. Marshall	(1913–1921)
29.	Baptist	Nov. 2, 1865	Aug. 2, 1923	57	Calvin Coolidge	(1921–1923)
30.	Congregationalist	July 4, 1872	Jan. 5, 1933	60	Charles G. Dawes	(1925–1929)
31.	Friend (Quaker)	Aug. 10, 1874	Oct. 20, 1964	90	Charles Curtis	(1929–1933)
32.	Episcopalian	Jan. 30, 1882	Apr. 12, 1945	63	John N. Garner	(1933–1941)
					Henry A. Wallace	(1941–1945)
					Harry S. Truman	(1945)
33.	Baptist	May 8, 1884	Dec. 26, 1972	88	Alben W. Barkley	(1949–1953)
34.	Presbyterian	Oct. 14, 1890	Mar. 28, 1969	78	Richard M. Nixon	(1953–1961)
35.	Roman Catholic	May 29, 1917	Nov. 22, 1963	46	Lyndon B. Johnson	(1961–1963)
36.	Disciples of Christ	Aug. 27, 1908	Jan. 22, 1973	64	Hubert H. Humphrey	(1965–1969)
37.	Friend (Quaker)	Jan. 9, 1913	Apr. 22, 1994	81	Spiro T. Agnew	(1969–1973)
					Gerald R. Ford**	(1973–1974)
38.	Episcopalian	July 14, 1913	Dec. 26, 2006	93	Nelson A. Rockefeller§	(1974–1977)
39.	Baptist	Oct. 1, 1924			Walter F. Mondale	(1977–1981)
40.	Disciples of Christ	Feb. 6, 1911	June 5, 2004	93	George H. W. Bush	(1981–1989)
41.	Episcopalian	June 12, 1924			J. Danforth Quayle	(1989–1993)
42.	Baptist	Aug. 19, 1946			Albert A. Gore	(1993–2001)
43.	Methodist	July 6, 1946			Dick Cheney	(2001–2009)
44.	United Church of Christ	Aug. 4, 1961			Joe Biden	(2009–2017)
45.	Presbyterian	June 14, 1946			Michael Pence	(2017–)

‡Inaugurated Aug. 9, 1974, to replace Nixon, who resigned that same day.
§Inaugurated Dec. 19, 1974, to replace Ford, who became president Aug. 9, 1974.

GLOSSARY

A

acquisitive model   A model of bureaucracy that views top-level bureaucrats as seeking to expand the size of their budgets and staffs to gain greater power.

actual malice   Either knowledge of a defamatory statement's falsity or a reckless disregard for the truth.

advice and consent   Terms in the Constitution describing the U.S. Senate's power to review and approve treaties and presidential appointments.

affirm   To declare that a court ruling is valid and must stand.

affirmative action   A policy in educational admissions and job hiring that gives special attention or compensatory treatment to traditionally disadvantaged groups in an effort to overcome present effects of past discrimination.

Affordable Care Act   A law passed in 2010 that seeks, among other things, to ensure health-care insurance for American citizens. The act is supplemented by the Health Care and Education Reconciliation Act and nicknamed "Obamacare."

agency capture   The act by which an industry being regulated by a government agency gains direct or indirect control over agency personnel and decision makers.

agenda setting   Determining which public-policy questions will be debated or considered.

aggregator   A website that provides search and aggregation services, but creates little or no original content.

amicus curiae brief   A brief (a document containing a legal argument supporting a desired outcome in a particular case) filed by a third party, or *amicus curiae* (Latin for "friend of the court"), who is not directly involved in the litigation but who has an interest in the outcome of the case.

Anti-Federalist   An individual who opposed the ratification of the new Constitution in 1787. The anti-federalists were opposed to a strong central government.

appellate court   A court having jurisdiction to review cases and issues that were originally tried in lower courts.

appointment power   The authority vested in the president to fill a government office or position. Positions filled by presidential appointment include those in the executive branch and the federal judiciary, commissioned officers in the armed forces, and members of the independent regulatory commissions.

appropriation   The passage, by Congress, of a spending bill specifying the amount of authorized funds that actually will be allocated for an agency's use.

arraignment   The first act in a criminal proceeding, in which the defendant is brought before a court to hear the charges against him or her and enter a plea of guilty or not guilty.

Australian ballot   A secret ballot prepared, distributed, and tabulated by government officials at public expense. Since 1888, all states have used the Australian ballot rather than an open, public ballot.

authoritarianism   A type of regime in which only the government itself is fully controlled by the ruler. Social and economic institutions exist that are not under the government's control.

authority   The right and power of a government or other entity to enforce its decisions.

authorization   A formal declaration by a legislative committee that a certain amount of funding may be available to an agency. Some authorizations terminate in a year; others are renewable automatically without further congressional action.

B

bias   An inclination or preference that interferes with impartial judgment.

bicameral legislature   A legislature made up of two parts, called chambers. The U.S. Congress, composed of the House of Representatives and the Senate, is a bicameral legislature.

bicameralism   The division of a legislature into two separate assemblies.

bill of attainder   A law that inflicts punishment without a trial.

Bill of Rights   The first ten amendments to the U.S. Constitution.

block grant   A federal grant that provides funds to a state or local government for a general functional area, such as criminal justice or mental-health programs.

blog   From *Web log*. A website where an individual or group posts regular updates on their ideas or experiences.

boycott   A form of pressure or protest—an organized refusal to purchase a particular product or deal with a particular business.

broad construction   A judicial philosophy that looks to the context and purpose of a law when making an interpretation.

budget deficit   Government expenditures that exceed receipts.

bureaucracy   An organization that is structured hierarchically to carry out specific functions.

C

cabinet   An advisory group selected by the president to aid in making decisions. The cabinet includes the heads of fifteen executive departments and others named by the president.

cabinet department   One of the fifteen major departments of the executive branch.

capitalism   An economic system characterized by the private ownership of wealth-creating assets, free markets, and freedom of contract.

case law   Judicial interpretations of common law principles and doctrines, as well as interpretations of constitutional law, statutory law, and administrative law.

casework   Personal work for constituents by members of Congress.

categorical grant   A federal grant to a state or local government for a specific program or project.

caucus   A meeting of party members to select candidates and propose policies.

checks and balances   A major principle of the American system of government whereby each branch of the government can check the actions of the others.

chief diplomat   The role of the president in recognizing foreign governments, making treaties, and effecting executive agreements.

chief executive   The role of the president as head of the executive branch of the government.

chief legislator   The role of the president in influencing the making of laws.

chief of staff   The person who is named to direct the White House Office and advise the president.

civil disobedience   A nonviolent, public refusal to obey allegedly unjust laws.

civil law   The law regulating conduct between private persons over noncriminal matters, including contracts, domestic relations, and business interactions.

civil liberties   Those personal freedoms, including freedom of religion and freedom of speech, that are protected for all individuals. Civil liberties restrain the government from taking certain actions against individuals.

civil rights   Generally, all rights rooted in the Fourteenth Amendment's guarantee of equal protection under the law.

civil service   A collective term for the body of employees working for the government. Generally, "civil service" is understood to apply to all those who gain government employment through a merit system.

Civil Service Commission   The initial central personnel agency of the national government; created in 1883.

class-action suit   A lawsuit filed by an individual seeking damages for "all persons similarly situated."

climate control   The use of public relations techniques to create favorable public opinion toward an interest group, industry, or corporation.

closed primary   A type of primary in which the voter is limited to choosing candidates of the party of which he or she is a member.

coattail effect   The influence of a popular candidate on the success of other candidates on the same party ticket.

Cold War   The ideological, political, and economic confrontation between the United States and the Soviet Union following World War II.

commander in chief   The role of the president as supreme commander of the military forces of the United States and of the state National Guard units when they are called into federal service.

commerce clause   The section of the Constitution in which Congress is given the power to regulate trade among the states and with foreign countries.

commercial speech   Advertising statements, which increasingly have been given First Amendment protection.

common law   Judge-made law that originated in England from decisions shaped according to prevailing customs. Decisions were applied to similar situations and thus gradually became common to the nation.

concurrent powers   Powers held jointly by the national and state governments.

concurring opinion   A separate opinion prepared by a judge who supports the decision of the majority of the court but who wants to make or clarify a particular point or to voice disapproval of the grounds on which the decision was made.

confederal system   A system consisting of a league of independent states, in which the central government created by the league has only limited powers over the states.

confederation   A political system in which states or regional governments retain ultimate authority except for those powers they expressly delegate to a central government; a voluntary association of independent states, in which the member states agree to limited restraints on their freedom of action.

conference committee   A special joint committee appointed to reconcile differences when bills pass the two chambers of Congress in different forms.

consensus   General agreement among the citizenry on an issue.

conservatism   A set of beliefs that includes a limited role for the national government in helping individuals, support for traditional ideals and life choices, and a cautious response to change.

conservative movement   An American movement in the 1950s that provided a comprehensive ideological framework for conservative politics.

constituent   A person represented by a legislator or other elected or appointed official.

constitutional power   A power vested in the president by Article II of the Constitution.

containment   A U.S. diplomatic policy adopted by the Truman administration to contain Communist power within its existing boundaries.

content provider   On the Internet, an individual or organization that generates original content.

continuing resolution   A temporary funding law that Congress passes when an appropriations bill has not been decided by the beginning of the new fiscal year on October 1.

cooperative federalism   A model of federalism in which the states and the national government cooperate in solving problems.

cracking   In gerrymandering, splitting the opposing party's voters into many different districts.

credentials committee   A committee used by political parties at their national conventions to determine which delegates may participate. The committee inspects the claim of each prospective delegate to be seated as a legitimate representative of his or her state.

criminal law   The law that defines crimes and provides punishment for violations. In criminal cases, the government is the prosecutor.

D

de facto **segregation**   Racial segregation that occurs because of past social and economic conditions and residential racial patterns.

de jure **segregation**   Racial segregation that occurs because of laws or administrative decisions by public agencies.

dealignment   A decline in party loyalties that reduces long-term party commitment.

defamation of character   Wrongfully hurting a person's good reputation. The law imposes a general duty on all persons to refrain from making false, defamatory statements about others.

defense policy   A subset of national security policy having to do with the U.S. armed forces.

democracy   A system of government in which political authority is vested in the people. The term is derived from the Greek words *demos* ("the people") and *kratos* ("authority").

Democratic Party   One of the two major American political parties evolving out of the Republican Party of Thomas Jefferson.

democratic republic   A republic in which representatives elected by the people make and enforce laws and policies.

détente   A French word meaning a relaxation of tensions. The term characterized U.S.-Soviet relations as they developed under President Richard Nixon and Secretary of State Henry Kissinger.

devolution   The transfer of powers from a national or central government to a state or local government.

diplomacy   The process by which nations carry on political relations with one another and resolve conflicts by peaceful means.

diplomatic recognition   The formal acknowledgment of a foreign government as legitimate.

direct democracy   A system of government in which political decisions are made by the people directly, rather than by their elected representatives; probably attained most easily in small political communities.

direct primary   A primary election in which voters decide party nominations by voting directly for candidates.

direct technique   An interest group activity that involves personal interaction with government officials to further the group's goals.

discharge petition   A procedure by which a bill in the House of Representatives can be forced (discharged) out of a committee that has refused to report it for consideration by the House. The petition must be signed by an absolute majority (218) of representatives and is used only on rare occasions.

dissenting opinion   A separate opinion in which a judge dissents from (disagrees with) the conclusion reached by the majority of the court and expounds his or her own views about the case.

diversity of citizenship   The condition that exists when the parties to a lawsuit are citizens of different states or when the parties are citizens of a U.S. state and citizens or the government of a foreign country. Diversity of citizenship can provide a basis for federal jurisdiction.

divided government   A situation in which one major political party controls the presidency and the other controls one or more chambers of Congress, or in which one party controls a state governorship and the other controls part or all of the state legislature.

divided opinion   Public opinion that is polarized between two quite different positions.

domestic policy   All laws, government planning, and government actions that concern internal issues of national importance, such as poverty, crime, and the environment.

dual federalism   A model of federalism in which the states and the national government each remain supreme within their own spheres. The doctrine looks on nation and state as co-equal sovereign powers. Neither the state government nor the national government should interfere in the other's sphere.

E

earmarks   Special provisions in legislation to set aside funds for projects that have not passed an impartial evaluation by agencies of the executive branch. Also known as *pork*.

economic aid   Assistance to other nations in the form of grants, loans, or credits to buy the assisting nation's products.

elastic clause, or necessary and proper clause   The clause in Article I, Section 8, that grants Congress the power to do whatever is necessary to execute its specifically delegated powers.

elector   A member of the electoral college, which selects the president and vice president. Each state's electors are chosen in each presidential election year according to state laws.

electoral college   A group of persons called electors selected by the voters in each state and the District of Columbia (D.C.). This group officially elects the president and vice president of the United States.

elite theory   A perspective holding that society is ruled by a small number of people who hold the ultimate power to further their self-interests.

emergency power   An inherent power exercised by the president during a period of national crisis.

enabling legislation   A statute enacted by Congress that authorizes the creation of an administrative agency and specifies the name, purpose, composition, functions, and powers of the agency being created.

entitlement program   A government program that entitles a defined class of people to obtain benefits. Entitlements operate under open-ended budget authorizations that do not limit how much can be spent.

enumerated power   A power specifically granted to the national government by the Constitution. The first seventeen clauses of Article I, Section 8, specify most of the enumerated powers of Congress.

equality   As a political value, the idea that all people are of equal worth.

establishment clause   The part of the First Amendment prohibiting the establishment of a church officially supported by the national government. It determines the legality of giving state and local government aid to religious organizations and schools, allowing or requiring school prayers, and teaching evolution versus creationism.

***ex post facto* law**   A law that inflicts punishment for an act that was not illegal at the time it was committed.

exclusionary rule   A judicial policy prohibiting the admission at trial of illegally obtained evidence.

executive agreement   An international agreement made by the president, without senatorial ratification, with the head of a foreign state.

executive budget   The budget prepared and submitted by the president to Congress.

Executive Office of the President (EOP)   An organization established by President Franklin Roosevelt to assist the president in carrying out major duties.

executive privilege   The right of executive officials to withhold information from or to refuse to appear before a legislative committee.

expressed power   A power of the president that is expressly written into the Constitution or into statutory law.

F

Fairness Doctrine   A Federal Communications Commission rule enforced between 1949 and 1987 that required radio and television to present controversial issues in a manner that was (in the commission's view) honest, equitable, and balanced.

fall review   The annual process in which the OMB, after receiving formal federal agency requests for funding for the next fiscal year, reviews the requests, makes changes, and submits its recommendations to the president.

Federal Election Commission (FEC)   The federal regulatory agency with the task of enforcing federal campaign laws. As a practical matter, the FEC's role is largely limited to collecting data on campaign contributions.

federal mandate   A requirement in federal legislation that forces states and municipalities to comply with certain rules.

Federal Open Market Committee   The most important body within the Federal Reserve System. The Federal Open Market Committee decides how monetary policy should be carried out.

federal question   A question that has to do with the U.S. Constitution, acts of Congress, or treaties. A federal question provides a basis for federal jurisdiction.

Federal Register   A publication of the U.S. government that prints executive orders, rules, and regulations.

Federal Reserve System (the Fed)   The agency created by Congress in 1913 to serve as the nation's central banking organization.

federal system   A system of government in which power is divided between a central government and regional, or subdivisional, governments. Each level must have some domain in which its policies are dominant and some genuine political or constitutional guarantee of its authority.

Federalist   The name given to one who was in favor of the adoption of the U.S. Constitution and the creation of a federal union with a strong central government.

felony   A serious crime punishable in most jurisdictions by a prison sentence longer than one year.

feminism   The movement that supports political, economic, and social equality for women.

filibuster   The use of the Senate's tradition of unlimited debate as a delaying tactic to block a bill.

first budget resolution   A resolution passed by Congress in each May that sets overall revenue and spending goals for the following fiscal year.

fiscal   Having to do with government revenues and expenditures.

fiscal federalism   A process by which funds raised through taxation or borrowing by one level of government (usually the national government) are spent by another level (typically state or local governments).

fiscal policy   The federal government's use of taxation and spending policies to affect overall business activity.

fiscal year (FY)   A twelve-month period that is used for bookkeeping, or accounting, purposes. Usually, the fiscal year does not coincide with the calendar year. For example, the federal government's fiscal year runs from October 1 through September 30.

focus group   A small group of individuals who are led in discussion by a professional consultant in order to gather opinions on and responses to candidates and issues.

foreign policy   A nation's external goals and the techniques and strategies used to achieve them.

fracking   Short for *hydraulic fracturing*, the injection of a high-pressure solution of water, sand, and chemicals into hydrocarbon-bearing rocks, releasing oil or natural gas.

framing   Establishing the context of a polling question or a media report. Framing can mean fitting events into a familiar story or activating preconceived beliefs.

free exercise clause   The provision of the First Amendment guaranteeing the free exercise of religion. The provision constrains the national government from prohibiting individuals from practicing the religion of their choice.

free rider problem   The difficulty interest groups face in recruiting members when the benefits they achieve can be gained without joining the group.

front-loading   The practice of moving presidential primary elections to the early part of the campaign to maximize the impact of these primaries on the nomination.

front-runner   The presidential candidate who appears to be ahead at a given time in the primary season.

G

gender discrimination   Any practice, policy, or procedure that denies equality of treatment to an individual or to a group because of gender.

gender gap   The difference between the percentage of women who vote for a particular candidate and the percentage of men who vote for the candidate.

general election   An election open to all eligible voters, normally held on the first Tuesday in November, that determines who will fill various elected positions.

general jurisdiction   A court's authority to hear cases without significant restriction. A court of general jurisdiction normally can hear a broad range of cases.

generational effect   The long-lasting effect of the events of a particular time on the political opinions of those who came of political age at that time.

gerrymandering   The drawing of legislative district boundary lines for the purpose of obtaining partisan advantage. A district is said to be gerrymandered when its shape is manipulated to determine which party will win it.

GOP   A nickname for the Republican Party; stands for "grand old party."

government   The institution that has the ultimate authority for making decisions that resolve conflicts and allocate benefits and privileges within a society.

government corporation   An agency of government that administers a quasi-business enterprise. These corporations are used when government activities are primarily commercial.

Government in the Sunshine Act   A law that requires all committee-directed federal agencies to conduct their business regularly in public session.

grandfather clause   A device used by southern states to disenfranchise African Americans. It restricted voting to those whose ancestors had voted before 1867.

Great Compromise   The compromise between the New Jersey and Virginia Plans that created one chamber of the Congress based on population and one chamber representing each state equally; also called the Connecticut Compromise.

gross domestic product (GDP)   The dollar value of all final goods and services produced in a one-year period.

gross public debt   The net public debt plus interagency borrowings within the government.

H

Hastert rule   A rule adopted by Republicans in the U.S. House, under which a Republican Speaker will not bring a measure to the floor for a vote unless it has the support of a majority of the Republican members.

Hatch Act   An act passed in 1939 that restricted the political activities of government employees. It also prohibited a political group from spending more than $3 million in any campaign and limited individual contributions to a campaign committee to $5,000.

head of state   The role of the president as ceremonial head of the government.

Hispanic   A term used by the federal government to describe someone who can claim a heritage from a Spanish-speaking country.

house effect   In public opinion polling, an effect in which one polling organization's results consistently differ from those reported by other poll takers.

I

ideology   A comprehensive set of beliefs about the nature of people and about the role of an institution or government.

imminent lawless action test   The current standard established by the Supreme Court for evaluating the legality of advocacy speech. Such speech can be forbidden only when it is "directed to inciting . . . imminent lawless action."

impeachment   An action by the House of Representatives to accuse the president, vice president, or other civil officers of the United States of committing "Treason, Bribery, or other high Crimes and Misdemeanors."

incarceration rate   The number of persons held in jail or prison for every 100,000 persons in a particular population group.

incorporation theory   The view that the protections of the Bill of Rights apply to state governments through the Fourteenth Amendment's due process clause.

independent   A voter or candidate who does not identify with a political party.

independent executive agency   A federal agency that is not part of a cabinet department but reports directly to the president.

independent expenditures   Nonregulated contributions from PACs, organizations, and individuals. The funds may be spent on advertising or other campaign activities, so long as those expenditures are not coordinated with those of a candidate.

independent regulatory agency   An agency outside the major executive departments that is charged with making and implementing rules and regulations within a specific area.

indirect primary   A primary election in which voters choose convention delegates, and the delegates determine the party's candidate in the general election.

indirect technique   A strategy employed by interest groups that uses third parties to influence government officials.

inflation   A sustained rise in the general price level of goods and services.

inherent power   A power of the president derived from the statements in the Constitution that "the executive Power shall be vested in a President" and that the president should "take Care that the Laws be faithfully executed"; defined through practice rather than through law.

initiative   A procedure by which voters can petition to vote on a law or a constitutional amendment.

institution   An ongoing organization that performs certain functions for society.

instructed delegate   A legislator who is an agent of the voters who elected him or her and who votes according to the views of constituents regardless of personal beliefs.

intelligence community   The government agencies that gather information about the capabilities and intentions of foreign governments or that engage in covert actions.

interest group   An organized group of individuals sharing common objectives who actively attempt to influence policymakers.

intermediate, or exacting, scrutiny   The standard used by the courts to determine whether a law or government action improperly discriminates against women.

Internet service provider (ISP)   A company or organization that provides Internet connectivity to end users or to servers.

interstate compact   An agreement between two or more states. Agreements on minor matters are made without congressional consent, but any compact that tends to increase the power of the contracting states relative to other states or relative to the national government generally requires the consent of Congress.

invisible primary   The pre-primary campaign to win supporters among elected officials, fund-raisers, interest groups, and opinion leaders.

iron triangle   The three-way alliance among legislators, bureaucrats, and interest groups to make or preserve policies that benefit their respective interests.

isolationist foreign policy   A policy of abstaining from an active role in international affairs or alliances, which characterized U.S. foreign policy toward Europe during most of the 1800s.

issue advocacy   Advertising paid for by interest groups that support or oppose a candidate's position on an issue without mentioning voting or elections.

issue network   A group of individuals or organizations—which may consist of legislators and legislative staff members, interest group leaders, bureaucrats, scholars and other experts, and media representatives—that supports a particular policy position on a given issue.

J

joint committee   A legislative committee composed of members from both chambers of Congress.

judicial activism   A doctrine holding that the federal judiciary should take an active role by using its powers to check the activities of governmental bodies when those bodies exceed their authority.

judicial implementation   The way in which court decisions are translated into policy.

judicial restraint   A doctrine holding that the courts should defer to the decisions made by the elected representatives of the people in the legislative and executive branches when possible.

judicial review   The power of the Supreme Court and other courts to examine and possibly declare unconstitutional federal or state laws and other acts of government.

jurisdiction   The authority of a court to decide certain cases. Not all courts have the authority to decide all cases. Where a case arises and what its subject matter is are two jurisdictional issues.

justiciable controversy   A controversy that is real and substantial, as opposed to hypothetical or academic.

K

Keynesian economics   A school of economic thought that favors active federal government policy-making to stabilize economy-wide fluctuations, including the use of discretionary fiscal policy.

kitchen cabinet   The informal advisers to the president.

L

labor movement   The economic and political expression of working-class interests.

latent interests   Public-policy interests that are not recognized or addressed by a group at a particular time.

Latino   An alternate word for *Hispanic*. The feminine is *Latina*.

lawmaking   The process of establishing the legal rules that govern society.

legislature   A governmental body primarily responsible for the making of laws.

legitimacy   Popular acceptance of the right and power of a government or other entity to exercise authority.

libel   A written defamation of a person's character, reputation, business, or property rights.

liberalism   A set of beliefs that includes the advocacy of positive government action to improve the welfare of individuals, support for civil rights, and tolerance for political and social change.

libertarianism   A political ideology based on skepticism or opposition toward most government activities.

liberty   The greatest freedom of the individual that is consistent with the freedom of other individuals in the society.

limited government   A government with powers that are limited either through a written document or through widely shared beliefs.

limited jurisdiction   A court's authority to hear cases that is restricted to certain types of claims, such as tax claims or bankruptcy petitions.

line organization   In the federal government, an administrative unit that is directly accountable to the president.

literacy test   A test administered as a precondition for voting, often used to prevent African Americans from exercising their right to vote.

litigate   To engage in a legal proceeding or seek relief in a court of law; to carry on a lawsuit.

lobbyist   An organization or individual who is employed to influence legislation and the administrative decisions of government.

loophole   A legal method by which individuals and businesses are allowed to reduce the tax liabilities owed to the government.

loose monetary policy   Monetary policy that makes credit inexpensive and abundant, possibly leading to inflation.

M

Madisonian model   A structure of government proposed by James Madison in which the powers of the government are separated into three branches: executive, legislative, and judicial.

majoritarianism   A political theory holding that, in a democracy, the government ought to do what the majority of the people want.

majority   The age at which a person is entitled by law to the right to manage her or his own affairs.

majority leader of the House   The party leader elected by the majority party in the House of Representatives.

majority opinion   A court opinion reflecting the views of the majority of the judges.

majority rule   A basic principle of democracy asserting that the greatest number of citizens in any political unit should select officials and determine policies.

material incentive   A reason or motive based on the desire to enjoy certain economic benefits or opportunities.

media   The channels of mass communication.

Medicaid   A joint state-federal program that provides medical care to the poor (including indigent elderly persons in nursing homes). The program is funded out of general government revenues.

Medicare   A federal health-insurance program that covers U.S. residents over the age of sixty-five. The costs are met by a tax on wages and salaries.

merit system   The selection, retention, and promotion of government employees on the basis of competitive examinations.

midterm elections   National elections in which candidates for president are not on the ballot. In midterm elections, voters choose all members of the U.S. House of Representatives and one-third of the members of the U.S. Senate.

minority leader of the House   The party leader elected by the minority party in the House.

monetary policy   The use of changes in the amount of money in circulation to alter credit markets, employment, and the rate of inflation.

monopolistic model   A model of bureaucracy that compares bureaucracies to monopolistic business firms. Lack of competition in either circumstance leads to inefficient and costly operations.

Monroe Doctrine   A policy statement by President James Monroe in 1823. The United States would not accept any new European intervention in the Western Hemisphere. In return, the United States would not meddle in European affairs.

moral idealism   A philosophy that sees nations as normally willing to cooperate and agree on moral standards for conduct.

motivated reasoning   The process of beginning with the conclusion you want, and only then assembling data and arguments to back up your conclusions.

N

national committee   A standing committee of a national political party established to direct and coordinate party activities between national party conventions.

national convention   The meeting held every four years by each major party to select presidential and vice-presidential candidates, write a platform, choose a national committee, and conduct party business.

National Security Council (NSC)   An agency in the Executive Office of the President that advises the president on national security.

national security policy   Foreign and domestic policy designed to protect the nation's independence and political integrity; policy that is concerned with the safety and defense of the nation.

natural rights   Rights held to be inherent in natural law, not dependent on governments. John Locke stated that natural law, being superior to human law, specifies certain rights of "life, liberty, and property."

net public debt   The accumulation of all past federal government deficits; the total amount owed by the federal government to individuals, businesses, and foreigners.

network neutrality   The principle that an ISP should treat all Internet traffic equally.

normal trade relations (NTR) status   A status granted through an international treaty by which each member nation must treat other members as well as it treats the country that receives its most favorable treatment. This status was formerly known as *most-favored-nation status.*

O

Office of Management and Budget (OMB)   A division of the Executive Office of the President. The OMB assists the president in preparing the annual budget, clearing and coordinating departmental agency budgets, and supervising the administration of the federal budget.

office-block, or Massachusetts, ballot   A form of general election ballot in which candidates for elective office are grouped together under the title of each office. It emphasizes voting for the office and the individual candidate, rather than for the party.

ombudsperson   A person who hears and investigates complaints by private individuals against public officials or agencies. (From the Swedish word *ombudsman*, meaning "representative.")

open primary   A primary in which any registered voter can vote (but must vote for candidates of only one party).

opinion   A statement by a judge or a court of the decision reached in a case. An opinion sets forth the applicable law and details the reasoning on which the ruling was based.

opinion leader   One who is able to influence the opinions of others because of position, expertise, or personality.

opinion poll   A method of systematically questioning a small, selected sample of respondents who are deemed representative of the total population.

oral arguments   The arguments presented in person by attorneys to an appellate court. Each attorney presents to the court reasons why the court should rule in her or his client's favor.

order   A state of peace and security. Maintaining order by protecting members of society from violence and criminal activity is one of the oldest purposes of government.

oversight   The process by which Congress follows up on laws it has enacted to ensure that they are being enforced and administered in the way Congress intended.

P

packing   In gerrymandering, packing as many voters as possible of the opposing party into a single district.

pardon   A release from the punishment for, or legal consequences of, a crime. A pardon can be granted by the president before or after a conviction.

party identification   Linking oneself to a particular political party.

party organization   The formal structure and leadership of a political party, including election committees; local, state, and national executives; and paid professional staff.

party platform   A document drawn up at each national convention, outlining the policies, positions, and principles of the party.

party-column, or Indiana, ballot   A form of general election ballot in which all of a party's candidates for elective office are arranged in one column under the party's label and symbol. It emphasizes voting for the party, rather than for the office or individual.

party-in-government   All of the elected and appointed officials who identify with a particular political party.

party-in-the-electorate   Those members of the general public who identify with a political party or who express a preference for one party over another.

patronage   The rewarding of faithful party workers and followers with government employment or contracts.

peer group   A group whose members share common social characteristics. These groups play an important part in the socialization process, helping to shape attitudes and beliefs.

Pendleton Act (Civil Service Reform Act)   An act that established the principle of employment on the basis of merit and created the Civil Service Commission to administer the personnel service.

pluralism   A theory that views politics as a conflict among interest groups. Political decision making is characterized by compromise and accommodation.

plurality   A number of votes cast for a candidate that is greater than the number of votes for any other candidate but not necessarily a majority.

plurality opinion   An opinion by a minority of the Court that decides a case because it is supported by one or more concurring opinions.

pocket veto   A special veto exercised by the chief executive after a legislative body has adjourned. Bills not signed by the chief executive die after a specified period of time. If Congress wishes to reconsider such a bill, it must be reintroduced in the following session of Congress.

podcasting   A method of distributing multimedia files, such as audio or video files, for downloading onto mobile devices or personal computers.

police power   The authority to legislate for the protection of the health, morals, safety, and welfare of the people. In the United States, most police power is reserved to the states.

policy demanders   Individuals or interest group members who participate in political parties with the intent to see that certain policies are adopted or specific groups favored.

political action committee (PAC)   A committee set up by and representing a corporation, labor union, or special-interest group. PACs raise and give campaign donations.

political consultant   A paid professional hired to devise a campaign strategy and manage a campaign.

political culture   A patterned set of ideas, values, and ways of thinking about government and politics that characterize a people.

political party   A group of political activists who organize to win elections, operate the government, and determine public policy.

political question   An issue that a court believes should be decided by the executive or legislative branch—or these two branches acting together.

political realism   A philosophy that sees each nation acting principally in its own interests.

political socialization   The process by which people acquire political beliefs and values.

political trust   The degree to which individuals express trust in the government and political institutions, usually measured through a specific series of survey questions.

politics   The struggle over power or influence within organizations or informal groups that can grant benefits or privileges.

poll tax   A special tax that had to be paid as a qualification for voting. In 1964, the Twenty-fourth Amendment to the Constitution outlawed the poll tax in national elections, and in 1966 the Supreme Court declared it unconstitutional in state elections as well.

popular sovereignty   The concept that ultimate political authority is based on the will of the people.

precedent   A court ruling bearing on subsequent legal decisions in similar cases. Judges rely on precedents in deciding cases.

president pro tempore   The temporary presiding officer of the Senate in the absence of the vice president.

presidential primary   A statewide primary election of delegates to a political party's national convention, held to determine a party's presidential nominee.

primary election   An election in which political parties choose their candidates for the general election.

priming   A way in which the media can alter public perceptions of an issue—by choosing which facts they include in the reporting.

prior restraint   Restraining an activity before it has actually occurred. When expression is involved, this means censorship.

privatization   The replacement of government services with services provided by private firms.

progressive   A popular alternative to the term *liberal*.

progressive tax   A tax that rises in percentage terms as incomes rise.

property   Anything that is or may be subject to ownership. As conceived by the political philosopher John Locke, the right to property is a natural right superior to human law (laws made by government).

public agenda   Issues that are perceived by the political community as meriting public attention and governmental action.

public debt, or national debt   The total amount of debt carried by the federal government.

public figure   A public official or any other person, such as a movie star, known to the public because of his or her position or activities.

public interest   The best interests of the overall community; the national good, rather than the narrow interests of a particular group.

public opinion   The aggregate of individual attitudes or beliefs shared by some portion of the adult population.

purposive incentive   A reason for supporting or participating in the activities of a group that is based on agreement with the goals of the group. For example, someone with a strong interest in human rights might have a purposive incentive to join Amnesty International.

R

ratification   Formal approval.

rational basis review   The standard used by the courts to determine the constitutionality of a law or government action if neither strict scrutiny nor intermediate scrutiny applies.

realignment   A process in which a substantial group of voters switches party allegiance, producing a long-term change in the political landscape.

reapportionment   The allocation of seats in the House of Representatives to each state after a census.

recall   A procedure allowing the people to vote to dismiss an elected official from state office before his or her term has expired.

recession   Two or more successive quarters in which the economy shrinks instead of grows.

reconciliation   A special rule that can be applied to budget bills sent from the House of Representatives to the Senate. Reconciliation measures cannot be filibustered.

redistricting   The redrawing of the boundaries of the congressional districts within each state.

referendum   An electoral device whereby legislative or constitutional measures are referred by the legislature to the voters for approval or disapproval.

registration   The entry of a person's name onto the list of registered voters for elections. To register, a person must meet certain legal requirements of age, citizenship, and residency.

regressive tax   A tax that falls in percentage terms as incomes rise.

remand   To send a case back to the court that originally heard it.

representation   The function of members of Congress as elected officials representing the views of their constituents as well as larger national interests.

representative assembly   A legislature composed of individuals who represent the population.

representative democracy   A form of government in which representatives elected by the people make and enforce laws and policies; may retain the monarchy in a ceremonial role.

reprieve   A formal postponement of the execution of a sentence imposed by a court of law.

republic   A form of government in which sovereign power rests with the people, rather than with a king or a monarch.

Republican Party   One of the two major American political parties. It emerged in the 1850s as an antislavery party and consisted of former northern Whigs and antislavery Democrats.

reverse   To annul, or make void, a court ruling on account of some error or irregularity.

reverse discrimination   The situation in which an affirmative action program discriminates against those who do not have minority status.

rule of four   A United States Supreme Court procedure by which four justices must vote to grant a petition for review if a case is to come before the full court.

Rules Committee   A standing committee of the House of Representatives that provides special rules under which specific bills can be debated, amended, and considered by the House.

S

sampling error   The difference between a sample's results and the true result if the entire population had been interviewed.

second budget resolution   A resolution passed by Congress in each September that sets "binding" limits on taxes and spending for the following fiscal year.

select committee   A temporary legislative committee established for a limited time period and for a special purpose.

Senate majority leader   The chief spokesperson of the majority party in the Senate, who directs the legislative program and party strategy.

Senate minority leader   The party officer in the Senate who commands the minority party's opposition to the policies of the majority party and directs the legislative program and strategy of his or her party.

senatorial courtesy   In federal district court judgeship nominations, a tradition allowing a senator to veto a judicial appointment in his or her state.

seniority system   A custom followed in both chambers of Congress specifying that the member of the majority party with the longest term of continuous service will be given preference when a committee chairperson (or a holder of some other significant post) is selected.

separate-but-equal doctrine   The doctrine holding that separate-but-equal facilities do not violate the equal protection clause of the Fourteenth Amendment to the U.S. Constitution.

separation of powers   The principle of dividing governmental powers among different branches of government.

service sector   The sector of the economy that provides services—such as health care, banking, and education—in contrast to the sector that produces goods.

sexual harassment   Unwanted physical or verbal conduct or abuse of a sexual nature that interferes with a recipient's job performance, creates a hostile work environment, or carries with it an implicit or explicit threat of adverse employment consequences.

signing statement   A written declaration that a president may make when signing a bill into law. Such statements may point out sections of the law that the president deems unconstitutional.

slander The public uttering of a false statement that harms the good reputation of another. The statement must be made to, or within the hearing of, a person other than the defamed party.

social contract A voluntary agreement among individuals to secure their rights and welfare by creating a government and abiding by its rules.

social movement A movement that represents the demands of a large segment of the public for political, economic, or social change.

socialism A political ideology based on strong support for economic and social equality. Socialists traditionally envisioned a society in which major businesses were taken over by the government or by employee cooperatives.

socioeconomic status The value assigned to a person due to occupation or income. An upper-class person, for example, has high socioeconomic status.

soft money Campaign contributions unregulated by federal or state law, usually given to parties and party committees to help fund general party activities.

solidary incentive A reason or motive that follows from the desire to associate with others and to share with others a particular interest or hobby.

sound bite A brief, memorable comment that easily fits into news broadcasts.

Soviet bloc The Soviet Union and the Eastern European countries that installed Communist regimes after World War II and were dominated by the Soviet Union.

Speaker of the House The presiding officer in the House of Representatives. The Speaker is always a member of the majority party and is the most powerful and influential member of the House.

spin An interpretation of campaign events or election results that is favorable to the candidate's campaign strategy.

spin doctor A political campaign adviser who tries to convince journalists of the truth of a particular interpretation of events.

splinter party A new party formed by a dissident faction within a major political party. Often, splinter parties have emerged when a particular personality was at odds with the major party.

split-ticket voting Voting for candidates of two or more parties for different offices, such as voting for a Republican presidential candidate and a Democratic congressional candidate.

spoils system The awarding of government jobs to political supporters and friends.

spring review The annual process in which the Office of Management and Budget (OMB) requires federal agencies to review their programs, activities, and goals and submit their requests for funding for the next fiscal year.

standing committee A permanent committee in the House or Senate that considers bills within a certain subject area.

stare decisis To stand on decided cases; the judicial policy of following precedents established by past decisions.

state A group of people occupying a specific area and organized under one government. It may either be a nation or a subunit of a nation.

state central committee The principal organized structure of each political party within each state. This committee is responsible for carrying out policy decisions of the party's state convention.

State of the Union message An annual message to Congress in which the president proposes a legislative program. The message is addressed not only to Congress but also to the American people and to the world.

statutory power A power created for the president through laws enacted by Congress.

straight-ticket voting Voting exclusively for the candidates of one party.

Strategic Arms Limitation Treaty (SALT I) A treaty between the United States and the Soviet Union to stabilize the nuclear arms competition between the two countries. The treaty was signed in May 1972.

strict construction A judicial philosophy that looks to the "letter of the law" when interpreting the Constitution or a particular statute.

strict scrutiny A judicial standard for assessing the constitutionality of a law or government action when the law or action threatens to interfere with a fundamental right or potentially discriminates against members of a suspect classification.

suffrage The right to vote; the franchise.

super PAC A political organization that aggregates unlimited contributions by individuals and organizations to be spent independently of candidate committees.

superdelegate   A party leader or elected official who is given the right to vote at the party's national convention. Superdelegates are not selected at the state level.

supremacy clause   The constitutional provision that makes the Constitution and federal laws superior to all conflicting state and local laws.

supremacy doctrine   A doctrine that asserts the priority of national law over state laws. This principle is stated in Article VI of the Constitution, which provides that the Constitution, the laws passed by the national government under its constitutional powers, and all treaties constitute the supreme law of the land.

suspect classification   A classification, such as race, religion, or national origin, that triggers strict scrutiny by the courts when a law or government action potentially discriminates against members of the class.

swing voters   Voters who frequently swing their support from one party to another.

symbolic speech   Expression made through articles of clothing, gestures, movements, and other forms of nonverbal conduct. Symbolic speech is given substantial protection by the courts.

T

technical assistance   The practice of sending experts in such areas as agriculture, engineering, or business to aid other nations.

terrorism   A systematic attempt to inspire fear to gain political ends, typically involving the indiscriminate use of violence against noncombatants.

third party   A political party other than the two major political parties (Republican and Democratic).

tight monetary policy   Monetary policy that makes credit expensive in an effort to slow inflation.

tipping   A phenomenon that occurs when a group that is becoming more numerous over time grows large enough to change the political balance in a district, state, or country.

total fertility rate   A statistic that measures the average number of children that women in a given group are expected to have over the course of a lifetime.

totalitarian regime   A form of government that controls all aspects of the political, social, and economic life of a nation.

transgender persons   Persons who experience a mismatch between their gender identity and the gender assigned to them at birth.

treasuries   U.S. Treasury securities—bills, notes, and bonds; debt issued by the federal government.

trial court   The court in which most cases begin.

Truman Doctrine   The policy adopted by President Harry Truman in 1947 to halt Communist expansion.

trustee   A legislator who acts according to her or his conscience and the broad interests of the entire society.

Twelfth Amendment   An amendment to the Constitution, adopted in 1804, that requires the separate election of the president and the vice president by the electoral college.

Twenty-fifth Amendment   A 1967 amendment to the Constitution that establishes procedures for filling presidential and vice-presidential vacancies and makes provisions for presidential incapacity.

two-party system   A political system in which only two parties have a reasonable chance of winning.

U

unanimous opinion   A Court opinion or determination on which all judges agree.

unemployment   The inability of those who are in the labor force to find a job; also, the number of those in the labor force actively looking for a job, but unable to find one.

unicameral legislature   A legislature with only one legislative chamber, as opposed to a bicameral (two-chamber) legislature, such as the U.S. Congress. Today, Nebraska is the only state in the Union with a unicameral legislature.

unitary system   A centralized governmental system in which ultimate governmental authority rests in the hands of the national, or central, government.

universal suffrage   The right of all adults to vote for their government representatives.

V

veto message   The president's formal explanation of a veto when legislation is returned to Congress.

vote-eligible population   The number of people who, at a given time, enjoy the right to vote in national elections.

voter turnout   The percentage of citizens taking part in the election process; the number of eligible voters that actually "turn out" on election day to cast their ballots.

voting-age population   The number of people of voting age living in the country at a given time, regardless of whether they have the right to vote.

W

War Powers Resolution   A law passed in 1973 spelling out the conditions under which the president can commit troops without congressional approval.

wave election   An election in which voters display dissatisfaction with one of the major parties through a "wave" of support for the other. In contrast to a realigning election, the results of a wave election are not permanent.

Weberian model   A model of bureaucracy developed by the German sociologist Max Weber, who viewed bureaucracies as rational, hierarchical organizations in which decisions are based on logical reasoning.

Whig Party   A major party in the United States during the first half of the nineteenth century, formally established in 1836. The Whig Party was anti-Jackson and represented a variety of regional interests.

whip   A member of Congress who aids the majority or minority leader of the House or the Senate.

whistleblower   Someone who brings to public attention gross governmental inefficiency or an illegal action.

White House Office   The personal office of the president, which tends to presidential political needs and manages the media.

white primary   A state primary election that restricted voting to whites only. It was outlawed by the Supreme Court in 1944.

working class   Traditionally, individuals or families in which the head of household was employed in manual or unskilled labor. Currently, often defined as those with no more than a high school diploma.

writ of *certiorari*   An order issued by a higher court to a lower court to send up the record of a case for review.

writ of *habeas corpus*   *Habeas corpus* means, literally, "you have the body." A writ of *habeas corpus* is an order that requires jailers to bring a prisoner before a court or judge and explain why the person is being held.

INDEX